D1064106

The CASSELL

DICTIONARY OF

Folklore

The CASSELL

DICTIONARY OF

Folklore

David Pickering

CASSELL

This edition first published in the UK 1999 by
Cassell
Wellington House
125 Strand
London WC2R 0BB

British Library Cataloguing-in-Publication Data
A catalogue record for this book is available from the British Library

ISBN 0-304-34786-8

Designed and typeset by Geoff Green

Printed and bound in Great Britain by Mackays of Chatham

To Jan, Edward and Charles

Introduction

The word folklore was coined in 1846 by the English antiquary William John Thoms, to express the concept of folk culture, the study of which was first accepted as a legitimate form of academic inquiry around the beginning of the 19th century as a result of the efforts of the Brothers Grimm and other scholars. Its definition has never been precise, but the term is now generally understood to encompass a wide range of beliefs, customs, dances, games, rituals, superstitions, songs, legends, myths, taboos, tales, proverbs and sayings descended from the oral tradition, as relayed through succeeding generations by singers, storytellers and – later – chroniclers and folklorists.

The boundaries between folklore and the related fields of mythology and religion are often obscure. For the purposes of this book anything that is primarily historical, mythological or sacred in nature has been excluded. A few entries, inevitably, defy such attempts at categorization and thus the reader will find, for instance, articles on the Holy Grail and on St George and other saints with long-standing folkloric reputations, as well as accounts of such semi-historical figures as Charlemagne, King Arthur and Robin Hood.

Every culture in the world boasts its own proud folkloric tradition, reflecting a universal desire to keep alive the legends and lore of earlier times. The preservation of such traditions strengthens national and ethnic identities and value systems as well as consolidating relationships within social groups. Many nations, indeed, trace their very origins back to myth – in Britain's case to Brutus and his companions from Troy who are supposed to have founded what they called Troia Nova on British shores. The Irish, meanwhile, have been known to trace the first human inhabitants of their country back via the kings of Spain, Greece and Egypt to the biblical Noah and Celtic legend is rich in details of the giants, fairies and other supernatural inhabitants of the country before the first humans arrived. It is also folklore's role to pass on lessons of life learned by preceding generations: even today many fables and legends retain an educative aspect, as evidenced by modern 'urban legends' emphasizing the potential dangers of such technological innovations as the motor car, food processor and microwave oven.

The folkloric tradition has played a role in virtually every sphere of human activity, proving a fount of inspiration in religion, art, science, history and literature among much else. As well as contributing to the mythic consciousness of the world's cultures and adding a human dimension to everyday existence, its extraordinary diversity feeds the imagination and remains a testament to human inventiveness. Conversely, the recurring similarities between features of the folkloric traditions of otherwise apparently unrelated cultures, from otherworlds and water spirits to hags and sleeping kings, has been a source of much debate over the years. Folklorists have expended much energy upon the question of whether the world's cultures have a single shared origin, or whether such parallels are the result of coincidences made inevitable by each society going through a similar evolutionary process. Although some traditions have relatively clear historical roots, others are shrouded in obscurity and would seem to have been passed down from before the dawn of recorded history. Because of this, the debate about how the folkloric traditions of the world have evolved seems likely to remain open. Often legends, customs and beliefs are reworked as they are absorbed by subsequent cultures, the gods of one people being identified as the legendary heroes, fairies or demons of another, but perhaps retaining the attributes bestowed in an earlier age. In Britain, the advent of Christianity had a particularly marked effect upon existing folklore and many of our most cherished traditions combine elements of both heritages.

This book makes only modest claims to be comprehensive, but does aim to cover most of the central themes and traditions in world folklore, as well as a large body of more eclectic material. Where a tale, character or myth is specific to a particular culture this is indicated. If not thus specified it should be assumed that the article in question applies fairly broadly across the English-speaking world and that to be more precise would be speculative and possibly misleading. Although the bulk of the text concentrates upon the folkloric traditions of Europe and the USA the reader will also find selective coverage of legends and lore from other parts of the globe, from Africa and India to South America and the Far East.

The text includes articles on folk tales, festivals, customs, legendary heroes, old wives' tales, fabulous creatures, folk remedies and other items of folkloric interest from many cultural traditions. Entries are arranged alphabetically to assist in the location of specific material. Headwords are generally given in the form in which they are most familiar to the modern reader, although variant spellings are sometimes also given, and cross-references to related articles are clearly indicated. Sources consulted have included a large number of reference books on the subject (too numerous to mention individually), to which the author readily admits a debt.

It should be noted, incidentally, that many of the folk remedies described herein are not supported by modern scientific understanding and that some ingredients (such as ragwort and rue) may actually have hallucinogenic or even poisonous properties and can be very dangerous.

Finally, the author would like to extend his thanks to Cassell.

David Pickering
Buckingham, May 1999

THE DICTIONARY

A

abandoned children The theme of abandoned children is a central motif of folk tales and legends in many of the world's cultures. In European tradition it is familiar today from such fairytales as 'Babes in the Wood' and 'Hansel and Gretel' and from the stories surrounding such legendary characters as HAVELOCK THE DANE and TALIESIN. Often the children concerned are no more than babies, set adrift on rivers, deserted deep in the forest or otherwise left to the devices of fate, typically because their birth threatens disaster to someone else (often one of the parents). Frequently the child is found and reared by kind-hearted peasants or by sympathetic animals until it is of an age to return to its home and claim its birthright, often taking revenge upon the parent who disowned it or upon the witch or sorcerer who caused its abandonment in the first place. Sometimes (especially in Celtic and Norse legend) the child becomes a celebrated knight or warrior and kills the guilty parent before its real identity is known.

Variants upon the theme include tales in which wives or aged parents are similarly abandoned to their fate. A rather brutal Eurasian story-telling genre relates how an adulterous woman has her hands cut off and is cast out by her family in some desolate spot. After a variety of adventures she is reunited with her husband after drinking from a fountain of youth and by this means having her hands restored.

Authorities have suggested that the motif was intended originally as an allegory meant to illustrate the time in each child's life when it must fend for itself.

Abbot of Misrule *See* LORD OF MISRULE.

Abbots Bromley horn dance *See* HORN DANCE.

abiku In West African folklore, a species of night demon that preys solely upon young children. Sometimes identified as a demon of the forest, the abiku may seek to possess the body of a young child, rather than simply feed on it (although, having no stomach, they have an insatiable appetite). In order to drive such spirits away a child's elder relatives might ring bells loudly in its vicinity, fit the child with jewellery made of IRON or else scratch the child's face so that it becomes less attractive as a host for such demons.

abominable snowman *See* YETI.

abracadabra Magical invocation that is chiefly associated today with stage conjurors and pantomime witches, but which has in fact a much longer history as a cabbalistic charm. First mentioned in the writings of the Gnostic physician Quintus Serenus Scammonicus in the 2nd century AD, abracadabra comprises the abbreviated forms of the Hebrew words *Ab* ('Father'), *Ben* ('Son') and *Ruach A Cadsch* ('Holy Spirit'), although an alternative derivation relates the word to Abraxas, a god with snakes for feet who

I

was worshipped in Alexandria in pre-Christian times.

The charm was said to have special powers against fevers, toothache and other ailments, as well as providing protection against bad luck. Sufferers from such conditions were advised to wear metal AMULETS or pieces of parchment inscribed with the word repeated several times, with the first and last letter removed each time until the last line read just 'A'. According to the thinking behind the charm, the evil force generating the illness would decrease as the word grew shorter. Once the charm had proved effective (after a period of nine days), the wearer was instructed to remove the parchment and to throw it backwards over their shoulder into an eastwards-flowing stream before sunrise.

Such charms were, according to Daniel Defoe in his *Journal of the Plague Year* (1722), widely worn in London in the 17th century as protection against the plague. Simply saying the word out loud is also said to summon up strong supernatural forces, hence its use by contemporary stage performers and entertainers.

acheri In Indian folklore, the ghost of a young girl, who spreads sickness among human children. The dreaded acheri is supposed to live in the mountains and to descend from time to time to roam through human settlements, looking for victims. As protection against her influence, many children are made to wear a bright red thread around the neck.

acorn The fruit of the OAK, which has been associated with a variety of folkloric beliefs since the earliest times. The oak was venerated by the Druids, and was similarly revered by many ancient civilizations, including that of Greece (the goddess Artemis was often depicted wearing a string of acorns).

Acorns are considered lucky, and were once habitually carried about the person to safeguard both luck and health. The Norse legend that THOR sheltered from a thunderstorm under an oak tree, for instance, has led to the belief that keeping an acorn on a windowsill will prevent a house from being struck by LIGHTNING.

In the UK, one old tradition has it that if a woman carries an acorn on her person it will delay the ageing process and keep her forever young (a reference to the longevity of the oak tree itself). Young lovers, meanwhile, may place two acorns, representing themselves and the objects of their affection, in a bowl of water in order to predict whether they have a future together: if the acorns drift towards each other they are certain to marry. In the 17th century, a juice extracted from acorns was administered to habitual drunkards to cure them of their condition or else to give them the strength to resist another bout of drinking.

act of truth Motif of legends and folk tales from all around the world, in which a solemn declaration is followed by some event (usually of a supernatural nature) that either proves or disproves what has been claimed. Similar in operation to the medieval concept of trial by ordeal, the act of truth motif can take many forms, including tests of courage, chivalry and chastity. Examples of the device include the sword in the stone of Arthurian romance, which only a true king can extract, and those oaths in which the person concerned asks to be struck down dead (or otherwise punished) if what he claims is untrue.

Adam Bell Legendary English outlaw who is usually depicted in company with his fellow outlaws CLYM OF THE CLOUGH and WILLIAM OF CLOUDESLY. Famed for his skill as an archer, he and Clym managed to rescue William of Cloudesly when he was taken prisoner and was about to be hanged. Subsequently all three became royal favourites after winning the pardon of the king for their various misdeeds. He is sometimes identified as Adam Cupid, an English incarnation of the classical Cupid, whose arrows inspired love in his targets. Shakespeare refers to 'Young Adam Cupid, he that shot so trim' in *Romeo and Juliet*.

adlet In Inuit folklore, a species of dog people which is said to have resulted from a BEAST MARRIAGE between an Inuit woman and a dog. According to legend, the union produced five monsters and five dog people. The five dogs were set adrift on a raft but survived to create the other human races, while the five monsters became the founders of a terrifying race of cannibals. Other Native American groups share similar legends about dog people, sometimes identified as the erqigdlit.

Aedh In Irish mythology, a prince of Leinster who was kidnapped by the FAIRIES while still a child. After spending three years in the land of the fairies he managed to escape, and was restored to a fully human form by St Patrick before returning to his father's court.

Aegir The Norse god of the ocean. Married to Ran, he sired nine daughters, known as 'the billows', who always wore white robes and veils.

Aesir The gods of Norse mythology, who inhabit ASGARD. Chief among them are ODIN, THOR, BALDUR, and LOKI. Among the lesser gods are Aegir, Tiu, Brag, Vidar, Hoder, Hermoder, Hoenir, Odnir and Vali. Their wives include FREYA, FRIGGA, Iduna, Nanna, Ran and Sif. According to legend they have ruled in heaven since the dawn of time, meeting every day at the foot of the great world tree YGGDRASIL to discuss the affairs of the world. Their reign is fated to end at RAGNAROK, when Asgard will be attacked by the FROST GIANTS.

Aesop's fables A series of animal fables popularly supposed to have been written by Aesop, a deformed Phrygian slave, in the 6th century BC. In fact, it seems that Aesop's celebrated tales, each of which illustrates a particular moral truth, are much older, and earlier versions have been found in Egyptian papyri dating from nearly 1,000 years before Aesop's time. Socrates rendered many of Aesop's tales in verse while in prison, and later collections of importance included that of Babrius in the 3rd century AD, which was rediscovered in a monastery on Mount Athos in 1844. Legend has it that Aesop's stories so delighted his second master, Iadmon, that he was eventually granted his freedom and went on to become adviser to King Croesus of Lydia.

Among the most famous of the tales are those of the tortoise and the hare (in which the slow but steady pace of the tortoise outstrips the faster speed of the hare), and the fox and the cat (in which the cat's simple ruse of climbing a tree saves it from a dog, while the much cleverer fox, who cannot climb, is killed).

aes sidhe *See* SIDHE.

afreet (or **afrit**) A class of JINNI that is considered the second most powerful species of demon in Islamic tradition. These greatly feared demons were typically depicted as huge giants with cruel, vicious natures.

afterbirth The placenta, expelled after CHILDBIRTH, is traditionally held to have various magical properties, and to retain a magical link with the baby even after the child is safely delivered. In many cultures the afterbirth must be treated with reverence and may be given ceremonial burial. A tree may then be planted over the spot, and henceforth the health of the tree will be closely linked with that of the child through sympathetic magic. It is thought to be particularly ominous if the afterbirth is eaten by some animal, as the child in question will thus inherit the animal qualities of the creature concerned.

Until relatively recent times it was claimed that the number of lumps in the placenta, or else the number of 'pops' that it made as it burned, would reveal how many children a woman was fated to have. Another old belief links the time the placenta takes to burn to the newly delivered baby's life expectancy (although it should be noted that some authorities insist that burning the placenta invites great misfortune).

afterworld *See* OTHERWORLD.

Agravaine In Arthurian legend, one of the knights of the ROUND TABLE. He is identified as the son of King Lot of Orkney and Morgause, the sister of MOR-GAN LE FAY, and as one of the brothers of Sir GAWAIN. He plotted with MORDRED to unmask the adulterous liaison between GUINEVERE and LANCELOT, but was killed by the latter when he attempted to accost the queen directly.

ahuizotl In Aztec mythology, a monkey-like water-dwelling monster reputed to drown mortals venturing near its pool. It was depicted in carvings as a cross between a monkey and a dog, with a hand fixed to the end of its long tail. It was said to strip its victims' bodies of eyes, nails and teeth. The only consolation for the dead was that their souls would go to heaven, as the ahuizotl was commonly believed to be a servant of the rain god.

Ailill mac Matach Legendary Irish king of Connacht, who was the husband of Queen MEDB. It was his ownership of the great bull Finnbennach ('White Horn') that led the jealous Medb to yearn for possession of the Great Dun Bull of Ulster, thus provoking bitter violence between the two kingdoms (*see* TAIN BO CUAILNCE). Ailill was clearly dominated by his wife and seems to have been unable to prevent her taking many lovers, although he did engineer the death of one of them, FERGUS MAC ROICH. He was in his turn killed by Conall Cernach on the orders of Medb after she surprised her husband enjoying female company on May Day.

Aillen mac Midhna In Irish mythology, a malevolent musician who served the court of the TUATHA DE DANANN. The music Aillen mac Midhna made on his tambourine had the power to send all listeners into an entranced sleep, and each year, during the festival of SAMHAIN, he would visit the royal palace at TARA and destroy it with fire from his nostrils after lulling the court to sleep with his tunes. After 23 such visits he was finally overcome and beheaded by FIONN MAC CUMHAILL, who managed to rouse himself from sleep by inhaling the fumes given off by the point of his famous poisonous spear.

Aine In Irish mythology, a SWAN MAIDEN and goddess of SOVEREIGNTY who is variously identified as the wife or daughter of MANANNAN MAC LIR. Medieval legend relates how Aine was discovered bathing in a river and raped by Gearoid Iarla (Earl Gerald of Desmond), who stole the cloak she needed to revert to her swan form and forced her into marriage with him. She bore him a son, Earl Fitzgerald, but the child vanished beneath the surface of Lough Gur after his father broke a TABOO laid on him when he shouted in surprise at his offspring's supernatural powers. Aine herself escaped to Knock Aine, on the shore of the same lough. The earl was himself a noted sorcerer, who is reputed to have departed this earth in the form of a goose.

airi In Indian folklore, a species of mountain spectre that is said to roam desolate mountain regions with a pack of ghost hounds. Few mortals, it is claimed, can set eyes upon the terrifying airi without dying of fright, but those who survive the encounter may be rewarded by being shown caves full of treasure.

Airlie drum of death *See* DRUM.

Aladdin One of the most famous of the tales in the collection known as the ARA-BIAN NIGHTS. Although it was included in the original manuscripts only as a supplementary tale, it has become one of the most familiar of all fairy tales, inspiring numerous storybook, pantomime, film, and cartoon versions.

The tale begins with Aladdin, the penniless and lazy son of a poor Chinese widow, being recruited by an African sorcerer (sometimes identified by the name Abanazar) to enter a magical cave and retrieve from it an old oil lamp. Aladdin helps himself to some of the treasure he finds in the cave but, suspicious of the sorcerer's motives, insists upon being helped out of the cave before he will hand over the lamp. The sorcerer flies into a fury and shuts the lad up in the cave. Trapped in the dark, Aladdin distractedly rubs the magic signet ring the sorcerer has lent him for protection while he is in the cave and is startled to find a JINNI appear. The jinni releases Aladdin from the cave and he returns home with the treasure and the mysterious lamp.

Some time later Aladdin's mother, now living in some luxury with her son, decides to clean the lamp and thus conjures up the jinni of the lamp, who places his services at Aladdin's disposal. Aladdin subsequently sets out to win the hand of the emperor's daughter, using the jinni's magic to fulfil various seemingly impossible challenges set by the emperor. On his wedding night he takes his new bride to a magnificent palace of jewels that he has built for them to live in, but the sorcerer now turns up, disguised, and persuades Aladdin's wife to exchange the old magic lamp for an ordinary new one. Once in possession of the lamp the sorcerer exiles Aladdin's wife, along with her palace, to the deserts of Africa. Aladdin, however, employs the jinni of the ring to retrieve the lamp and thus brings his wife back. The tale ends with Aladdin defeating and killing the sorcerer and succeeding his father-in-law as emperor of China.

The tale exists in numerous variant forms, and would appear to have absorbed many features of the wider folk-telling tradition, including such details as the underground treasure cave, the magic lamp, and the theme of the penniless wastrel making good through cunning rather than any innate good quality. Variants of the tale in other cultures often have the hero being aided not by jinni but by some sympathetic animal for which he has previously performed some service. In Bohemia he is aided by a dog, cat and snake, whose lives he has saved. In Albania he gains possession of a wishing stone rather than a ring or lamp, while elsewhere he is given a magic watch, which ends up being dropped in the sea (from which it is rescued by a friendly fish).

albatross Large seabird, capable of long-sustained flight, which has been considered a symbol of ominous portent in SAILORS' LORE since time immemorial. The appearance of an albatross, said to be the incarnation of a drowned seafarer's soul, is widely thought to herald a coming storm. Killing an albatross is especially foolhardy and will bring permanent misfortune to both ship and crew, a tradition that was much promoted by Samuel Taylor Coleridge in his 'Rime of the Ancient Mariner'.

Anxiety about the reputation of the albatross has survived into modern times: Scottish seamen have been known to object to the use of Swan Vesta matches because the swan on the matchbox resembles an albatross, while in 1959 the crew of the cargo ship *Calpean Star*, which was carrying an albatross to a German zoo, blamed the bird for a series of mishaps that befell them during the voyage (when the bird died on the ship 50 of the crew demanded immediate release from their work).

Running somewhat against this tradition in former times was the sailors' custom of killing such birds in order to make tobacco pouches out of their large webbed feet. In Japan, meanwhile, the bird is thought to be a servant of the sea god, and its appearance is thus welcomed. The albatross' gliding flight, incidentally, has given rise to the popular idea that the bird can actually sleep aloft.

Alberich In Norse legend, the king of the DWARFS. Tradition has it that Alberich holds court in a huge underground palace, where he guards the hoard of the Nibelungs. According to the NIBELUNG-ENLIED, it was Alberich who presented Siegfried with the magic sword BAL-MUNG and a cloak of INVISIBILITY (just two examples of the marvellous objects fashioned by his dwarf subjects). In Wagner's account of the Nibelung legend, however, Alberich is an ugly dwarf who steals the gold of the Rhine Maidens but is subsequently seized by the gods and forced to give up everything he has in exchange for his freedom.

Albion Ancient poetical name for Great Britain, usually applied to the country before the arrival of BRUT and his Trojan companions. It is thought to have come from the Latin *albus* ('white'), a reference to the white cliffs of Dover, or alternatively from the Celtic *alp*. Legend has it, however, that the name may refer to Neptune's son, a GIANT called Albion, who discovered the country and ruled it for 44 years, or else to Albia, the eldest of the 50 daughters of the King of Syria who were all married on the same day and subsequently exiled to Britain after murdering their husbands on their wedding night. Yet another derivation of the name suggests it refers to St Alban, the first Christian martyr in Britain.

alchemy The pseudo-scientific quest to find a means of transmuting base metals into GOLD and SILVER that obsessed European and Arabic culture during the late medieval period (although it had previously also been a preoccupation of thinkers in ancient Greece and Egypt). The other chief aim of alchemy was the discovery of an ELIXIR VITAE.

Combining basic chemistry with a range of folkloric and occult concepts, alchemy was often thought of as a philo-sophical pursuit, despite its very practical aims. The underlying theory shared by most alchemists was that all substances were composed of one fundamental form of matter. By removing all impurities this essential material – often referred to as the PHILOSOPHER'S STONE - might then be combined with carefully selected ingredients to produce a desired end product (which might include magic potions and medicines as well as various precious metals).

The quest to find a means of making gold and silver from other metals proved futile, but this did not prevent many imposters claiming success. Tricks employed to dupe others included the use of crucibles with false bottoms in which a little gold was concealed, kept in place by a wax plug that melted when the crucible was heated.

alectryomancy Method of DIVINA-TION, in which a white COCK is placed in a circle divided into 26 segments, each containing a grain of wheat. The order in which the cock eats the grains as a magic incantation is delivered will spell out the answer to any question previously posed, be it an unknown lover's name or the identity of the next ruler. A cock thus employed is said to have predicted the coming to power of the Roman emperor Theodorus, and the practice has been resurrected for various purposes in many countries ever since.

alfar In Norse mythology, a race of dwarflike spirits that were the predecessors of the ELF and FAIRY peoples. They fell into two broad categories - the liosalfar or light elves, who lived in ALFHELM under the sun god Frey, and the svartalfar or dark elves, who lived in the underground realm ruled over by WAYLAND THE SMITH.

Alfhelm In Norse mythology, the home of the light elves (*see* ALFAR) in ASGARD. It is usually described as an airborne kingdom midway between heaven and earth.

Ali Baba The central character in the story of 'Ali Baba and the Forty Thieves', which constitutes one of the most famous episodes in the collection of tales known as the ARABIAN NIGHTS. It appears, however, to have been a fairly late addition to the collection, added as recently as the 18th century.

The story relates how Ali Baba, a poor woodgatherer, watches as a 40-strong robber band conceal a hoard of stolen gold in a cave, opening and closing the entrance through the use of magic incantations – 'Open Sesame' to open it and 'Close Sesame' to close it. When the robbers have gone he tries the magic formula himself, and then loads some of the riches onto his donkeys and carries it home. Realizing that he must keep his good luck secret, Ali Baba tells no one of his new-found wealth, but soon arouses the suspicions of his brother Kasim and his wife. When Ali Baba borrows some scales from Kasim's wife she hides some wax in the bottom of the bowl ,and when Ali Baba returns the scales he fails to notice that a gold piece is stuck there. Kasim forces Ali Baba to reveal his secret and at once sets out to help himself to some of the robbers' hoard. Unfortunately, having entered the cave, he forgets the form of words he needs in order to get out again, and when the robbers return they find him still there and kill him. His corpse is quartered and hung on the inside of the cave door as a warning to others, and here Ali Baba finds it.

Ali Baba takes the parts of Kasim's body away with him and persuades a local cobbler to stitch the body back together for burial, blindfolding the man so that he does not know in which house he is working. It is not long, however, before the robbers, hearing the cobbler talking about his mysterious job, realize someone else knows about their hiding place. Their initial attempts to get the cobbler to show them the culprit's house by blindfolding him and making him retrace his steps are twice foiled by Ali Baba's servant girl Morgiana, who duplicates the mark the cobbler makes upon their door on the doors of all the neighbouring houses. On the third attempt, however, they succeed in locating Ali Baba's house.

Having disguised himself as an oil merchant the leader of the robbers enters Ali Baba's home. The rest of the robbers are concealed in large oil jars with orders not to show themselves until the signal is given to emerge and kill Ali Baba. The jars are brought into the house, but Morgiana hears a voice from one of them asking her if it is time to come out yet. Pretending to be the oil merchant, she tells the robbers to stay where they are and then boils up some oil from the one filled jar. She then pours some of the scalding liquid into each jar, thus killing all the robbers in turn. The vengeful robber leader returns to the house disguised as a cloth merchant, but Morgiana realizes who he is and kills him also. Ali Baba is duly grateful to Morgiana and as a reward promises her his son in marriage.

The story would appear to have absorbed elements of folk-telling traditions from India, Arabia, Africa, Estonia, and Finland, including the magic password, the treasure cave, and the borrowed scales. There is even a Welsh equivalent of the tale, in which a band of warriors hide in leather sacks in order to ambush BRAN when he tries to rescue BRANWEN from Ireland. In a Cypriot version an ogre seeks to fool the hero by hiding his men in bales.

Allen-a-Dale See ROBIN HOOD.

All Hallows' Eve See HALLOWE'EN.

almond The almond tree and its fruit have considerable significance in the folklore of many cultures. According to Greek myth, the almond had its origins in a story of doomed love. Briefly, Phyllis was transformed into such a tree after she committed suicide when her betrothed, Demophon, failed to appear on the day set for their marriage (he was in fact merely delayed). The Roman writer Pliny alleged that eating five almonds was a cure for drunkenness, while later authorities had it that almonds would prevent cancer if taken on a daily basis, but would prove fatal if eaten by foxes. In Christian folklore the almond, a symbol of promise and wariness, is closely associated with the Virgin Mary, and it was Aaron's rod of almond that sprang into blossom as a proof of the divine favour he enjoyed (a tradition later absorbed into the legend of TANNHÄUSER). In China the almond represents patience and long-suffering.

Amadan In Irish folklore, a sprite whose touch is reputed to cause strokes. Although he may strike at random, he is said to concentrate on visiting such afflictions on criminals and trespassers on fairy ground, and is allegedly particularly active in the month of June. Only by calling on God can a victim hope for protection from his attentions.

Amadis of Gaul Legendary French hero whose life inspired a celebrated prose romance of the same title. The oldest surviving account of his story is a Spanish version written in 1508, but it would appear that this was based upon earlier Portuguese or Spanish versions originating in the 14th century. In many respects the tale borrows from earlier Arthurian myth.

Amadis of Gaul was the result of an illicit liaison between Perion, king of Wales, and Elizena, princess of Brittany. Because of his illegitimacy he was abandoned as a baby, becoming known as the Child of the Sun, but he nonetheless grew up to become a great knight, variously known as the Lion Knight (after the device on his shield), Beltenebros (meaning 'darkly beautiful'), the Lovely Obscure, the Knight of the Green Sword, and the Knight of the Dwarf, among other titles. Acclaimed for his chivalry, he had many adventures before winning the hand of the English princess Oriana. He was also admired as a poet, musician and linguist.

amber Translucent yellowish fossilized resin, which has long been a focus of folkloric interest.

According to the legends of the ancient world, amber originated as the tears of the sisters of the dead Greek hero Meleager, and pieces of amber have been worn in AMULET form since classical times in the belief that they bestow various medicinal benefits (particularly in the case of children) and also offer protection against witchcraft and nightmares. In fact, evidence suggests that amber was widely traded across prehistoric Europe long before classical times.

Over the centuries amber has been especially valued as a preventive against the plague, and was also worn as jewellery in the belief that it made a woman smell more desirable to her lover - hence the tradition of mothers giving their daughters a necklace of amber beads as a wedding gift. Even in relatively modern times amber has been credited with curing such ailments as whooping cough and asthma.

Amfortas *See* FISHER KING.

Amis and Amiles Old French romance dating from the late 12th century, in which two knights (otherwise identified as Amys and Amylion) at the court of CHARLEMAGNE memorably demonstrate their loyalty to one another. The ultimate test of their friendship comes after Amiles replaces Amis at a trial by combat and is consequently punished with leprosy. Amis learns in a dream that the only way to save his friend is to sacrifice his own two children. He gladly slays his offspring and Amiles is healed. The two children are then restored to life.

The basic plot of the tale was probably borrowed from an Oriental original, and by the 12th century it was among the best-known tales included in the Charlemagne cycles.

Amleth Legendary Danish prince, who was the model for Shakespeare's Hamlet. According to the original legend, Amleth

8

was the son of Horvendil, king of Jutland. After Horvendil was murdered by his brother Feng, Amleth feigned madness in order to escape a similar fate. Feng went on to marry Horvendil's widow and subsequently sent Amleth to England and Scotland, plotting to have him killed on his arrival. Amleth outwitted him on both occasions and ultimately returned to Denmark to do battle, making his own army look much bigger by propping up dead bodies as though they were alive. He defeated Feng and took the throne alongside his two wives, one an English princess and the other a queen of Scotland. He ultimately met his own death in battle.

amulet A CHARM that is worn as a necklace, bracelet or other decoration about the person in order to benefit from its magical properties. The word itself comes from the Arabic *hamala*, meaning 'to carry'; hamala is also the name of the neck cord from which the faithful suspend their Koran. Usually made from a gemstone, bone or other natural material, the amulet has a long history and is known to virtually all cultures. Among the most familiar amulets are rabbit's feet, horseshoes, four-leaf clovers, dice, garlic, teeth, birthstones, coral and medallions bearing the images of the saints (notably St Christopher), as well as lucky coins, rings, stones, photographs and sundry other items. Ancient Egyptians laid great store in amulets bearing such sacred symbols as the ankh (a t-shaped cross surmounted by a loop) and the eye of Horus (a stylized eye pattern representing the all-seeing eye of the sun god Horus), while early Christians believed themselves safe if they wore Saint John's Gospel around the neck, carried relics of the 'true cross' or else inserted a slip of paper bearing the Lord's Prayer into one of their shoes.

More recent manifestations have included the charm bracelet, to which are attached miniature metal likenesses of such lucky symbols as boots and horseshoes (a custom of late-Victorian origin),

and a short-lived fad for wearing a violin's D string around the waist in the hope that the wearer would benefit from its harmonious associations. Charms peculiar to specific regions include the red pepper, which is revered for its luck-giving qualities in Italy. The wearing of such amulets is said to bestow general protection against the EVIL EYE and against bad luck, witchcraft, and disease rather than against one threat in particular (more accurately the role of the TALISMAN).

It has been suggested that all modern jewellery has its roots in the wearing of amulets, although it is rare today for jewellery to be worn for purposes other than mere adornment.

See also ABRACADABRA; TATTOO.

Amys and Amylion *See* AMIS AND AMILES.

ancestor worship The veneration of dead ancestors is a feature of many cultures past and present. Prayers and offerings are made by descendants in many societies even today in the hope that the dead will exercise some benevolent influence upon the lives of their surviving relatives. Sometimes this worship is formalized and exists on a national basis, as seen in the mass commemorations of deceased national leaders and other notables that are observed in virtually every modern society today.

In earlier times ancestor worship could extend to human sacrifice and the presentation of gifts of great value, from goods, weapons and jewellery to icons of the deceased depicting them on their journey to the afterlife. The seriousness with which the business of laying the dead to rest is still conducted today may be in part a relic of such veneration.

See also BURIAL CUSTOMS.

Andersen, Hans Christian Danish author and folklorist, who ranks among the most celebrated of all collectors and writers of fairy tales. Born in 1805, he was the son of an impoverished shoemaker and after failing to find work in the theatre in Copenhagen took up a career as a writer (despite his lack of education). He wrote 138 fairy tales between 1835 and 1872, intending them to be read by children and adults alike. Among the most famous are *The Little Mermaid*, *The Snow Queen*, *The Tinder Box* and *The Ugly Duckling*. The popularity of Andersen's versions of the stories, most of which he adapted from the oral tradition, had greatly revived public interest in fairytales by the time the author died in 1872.

Angus mac Og (or **Aengus, Oengus**) In Irish mythology, the god of youth. The son of DAGDA and BOANN, he was raised by Midhir, the king of the SIDHE, and fell passionately in love with the beautiful SWAN MAIDEN Caer Ibormeith after she visited him in his dreams. With help from BODB he eventually found her at Loch Bel Bracon during the festival of Samhain and joined her in the form of a swan. They returned to his underworld palace at Bruig na Boinne (identified today with New Grange, County Meath). He subsequently became the foster-father of DIARMUID.

animals Animals of all kinds feature in rituals, legends and folk tales throughout world culture, reflecting the curiosity humans have always had about other species with which they share the earth. Variously motivated by fear, admiration or the desire to share the remarkable powers of other species, people have long worshipped animals and associated them with gods and the supernatural, often identifying them as the reincarnated souls of dead ancestors. Participants in important rituals often impersonate animals that are deemed to have particular sacred significance. Boars, bulls, dogs, horses, pigs, rams and stags figure prominently in the folklore of the Celts, while lions, crocodiles, elephants, hippos and vultures are among the most magically potent creatures of African myth, and bears, coyotes, eagles and wolves are included among the supernatural characters of Native American lore. Other animals particularly noted for their mystical attributes around the world include cats, donkeys, foxes, lizards, snakes and spiders.

The ritual importance of certain animals is reflected in the TABOOS that abound concerning the eating of their flesh. In various parts of the modern world the consumption of the meat of such animals as cows and pigs may still be considered taboo in certain communities, often for religious reasons. Where animals are hunted for their flesh it may be considered important to observe rituals asking for the forgiveness of the prey so that its soul is not offended and does not return seeking revenge.

Frequently the animal characters of fable and legend are endowed with the power of speech and other human attributes. Often they are believed to possess great wisdom, although they may also be represented as stubborn or stupid and variously suspected of avarice, jealousy, and hatred of humans. Many animal stories have clear allegorical points to make about human existence, and numerous tribal societies claimed descent from animals or birds' eggs. Often the world itself is said to rest on an animal's back, typically a turtle or elephant, and earthquakes are explained as this creature shifting under the weight.

The notion that certain animals can change their shape into that of human beings at will is shared by many cultures, with a wide variety of tales concerning SELKIES, SWAN MAIDENS and similar fanciful beings. Human imagination has also furnished folklore with a menagerie of fabulous creatures, as detailed in medieval BESTIARIES. Some of these inventions, such as DRAGONS, MERMAIDS and WORMS, feature prominently in legends throughout the world.

The relationship between humankind and the animal world is a central theme of countless tales and legends. Folklore is replete with stories of BEAST MARRIAGES, of animal nurses who rear great heroes after they have been abandoned as infants, and of beasts that lend supernatural aid to humans. Another genre of animal fable celebrates the ingenuity of various animal tricksters, whose ranks include such greatly loved characters as Reynard the Fox and Brer Rabbit.

Animals of various kinds are feared as omens of misfortune or death (see SEVEN WHISTLERS), and may be suspected of being witches' FAMILIARS or the DEVIL in disguise, while others by way of contrast are welcomed as harbingers of good fortune or as protectors against evil. Observation of animal behaviour, meanwhile, may furnish the knowledgeable with advance warning of changes in the weather or even of important events in human affairs, such as the imminence of war (see DIVINATION).

In medieval times animals might be blamed for all manner of misfortune, and were on occasion actually put on trial in formal courts. Such trials not only involved domestic animals, but also such creatures as rats, caterpillars, ants, beetles and leeches. The proceedings usually culminated in a sentence of death despite the efforts of the defending lawyers; however, in the case of some leeches tried in Lausanne in 1451 the accused were allowed to live but sternly warned to leave the district within three days. The last such animal trial is said to have taken place in England in 1777, when a dog was brought before a court in Chichester. Other measures against offending animals over the centuries have included exorcism and the use of various charms.

Many folk beliefs concerning animals have their origin in the folklore of rural communities and are closely connected to the welfare of those involved in animal husbandry or other work on the land. Thus, fruit trees should always be planted with a dead animal of some kind beneath their roots, in order to guarantee a good crop, and farmers will never make any compliment about the condition of an animal entered in a competition for fear of tempting fate.

In folk medicine, most really effective potions and spells include animal ingredients, from the belief that the patient will benefit by sharing in the animal's magical properties. Thus, in former times, the impotent might be fed parts of a rabbit, famed for its procreative abilities, while those suffering from whooping cough might be fed hairs taken from a donkey, which makes a similar braying noise.

See also entries for individual animals; BIRDS; FISH; INSECTS.

Ankou *See* CHURCHYARD WATCHER.

anniversary The marking of past events in private or public life through some celebration on the relevant date is a feature of the social life of virtually all modern societies. Anniversaries such as BIRTHDAYS and wedding anniversaries rank among the minor rites of passage in most people's lives. In the case of wedding anniversaries each one has unique significance, with special celebrations being reserved for 25th, 40th, 50th, and 60th wedding anniversaries in particular. Other wedding anniversaries are generally celebrated privately, and may be ignored altogether. Some people exchange gifts on their wedding anniversary according to a traditional list that dictates the best materials for gifts for given anniversaries. This list may vary, but a typical modern version runs as follows: 1st, cotton; 2nd, paper; 3rd, leather; 4th, fruit or flowers; 5th, wood; 6th, sugar or iron; 7th, wool; 8th, bronze; 9th, copper or pottery; 10th, tin; 15th, crystal; 20th, china; 25th, silver; 30th, pearl; 35th, coral; 40th, ruby; 45th, sapphire; 50th, gold; 55th, emerald; 60th, diamond; 70th, platinum.

Annwn According to Welsh legend, the underworld paradise where souls of the dead go. Ruled over by ARAWN, it is usually described as lying underground, although in some accounts it is depicted as a floating castle or island. It was visited from time to time by mortals: an early Welsh poem describing a mission to

Annwn to steal a magic cauldron is thought to have been a model for the Grail story of later Arthurian myth. Annwn was also identified as the home of the WILD HUNT.

ant The humble but hardworking ant has long exercised fascination, and has consequently inspired numerous folk beliefs. Some Native American peoples even consider the ant to have been the origin of humanity itself. Elsewhere ants are identified as messengers of the gods, or as the reincarnation of children who have died unbaptized. In Cornwall, ants are called muryans and are supposed to be fairies in the last phase of their life on earth – or alternatively to be the transmuted souls of ancient Druids punished for refusing to accept Christianity. It is said in that part of the world, incidentally, that a piece of tin left in an ants' nest at a certain period in the moon's cycle will be magically transformed into silver.

The discovery of ants in the house is sure to be followed by the master of the house falling ill (although, in contrast, considerable prosperity is at hand if ants build a nest close to the door). Treading on ants will trigger a shower of rain, and bad weather can be expected if a colony of ants is observed to be unusually active or if the ants are busy carrying their eggs to a new location. It is contended that ants never sleep, and that eating ants' eggs with honey is a sure treatment for those suffering from unrequited love.

Ants' eggs were once much used in potions for treating various illnesses, and the bodies of crushed ants were particularly valued for their efficacy in curing warts when made into a paste with vinegar (the mixture being completed with the addition of a snail). The bite of an ant is also often claimed to have healing properties. In Scotland, deafness was sometimes treated by pouring a potion of ants' eggs and onion juice into the affected ear.

antler dance *See* HORN DANCE.

apple The apple tree and its fruit are associated with a host of folkloric traditions, many inspired by its central role in the story of the biblical Eden (although the fateful fruit eaten by Adam and Eve is not actually identified as an apple in the original account).

Apple trees that produced blossom and fruit simultaneously were one of the features of the Celtic paradise, and the apple is ever-present in the mythology of the Greeks and Romans as well as in Norse legend, which depicts the gods feasting on the apples of perpetual youth that grow in ASGARD. The otherworldly paradise AVALON, to which the mortally wounded King ARTHUR was called, probably took its name from the Welsh *afal*, meaning apple. Later on, in medieval times, a farmer could lay claim to a piece of common land by enclosing it and planting an apple tree on it.

Apple orchards have been regarded as hallowed places since Roman times, and in many parts of the world the destruction of an apple orchard was an act to be dreaded by all concerned (in the 7th century AD an offender who cut down an apple tree was obliged under English law to pay the fine of one cow). In various parts of England, notably the West Country, the custom of apple-howling or WASSAILING is still observed, usually on Twelfth Night, to drive away evil spirits and thus guarantee a good crop. In the USA, a glimpse of the sun on Christmas morning is an encouraging sign that the apple trees will prosper, particularly if the trees are subsequently blessed by rain on St Swithin's Day (before which the fruit should never be picked and eaten). The appearance of blossom on an apple tree in the autumn, however, is an omen of death, and in some societies an apple may be placed in the hands of a child who has died, as a symbol of innocence.

When it comes to harvesting the fruit, it is considered most unwise to leave one apple on the tree after the rest have been picked, and if the apple remains there till the following spring a death is sure to occur. Conversely, however, in some areas an apple is always left on the tree to appease unseen spirits. A German tradition claims that an apple tree will prosper for many years if the first fruit of the season is eaten by a woman who has had many children.

The apple has always been associated with love and marriage. To reveal a future spouse's identity, for instance, a boy or girl should name a few apple pips after intended partners and place them on his or her cheek, the most likely prospect being represented by the last pip to fall. If a solution is still unforthcoming, placing a single apple pip representing a potential partner in a fire, intoning 'If you love me, bounce and fly, if you hate me, lie and die', and then observing what happens might produce the required answer. In Austria, a girl may cut an apple open on Saint Thomas's Night (3 July) to examine the pips: if there is an even number she will marry soon, but if one of the pips is cut then trouble can be expected and she may never find a husband.

Having tried the pips without success, there remains the stalk. Young girls, desiring to know the initial of their true love's first name, may twist the stalk once for each letter of the alphabet: the stalk will snap at the right letter. To establish the first initial of his surname the same procedure is followed while tapping the apple with the severed stalk until it pierces the skin. There is also the peel, which may be tossed over the shoulder and then inspected to learn from its shape the first letter of a future partner's name.

The most potent time for such rituals is identified as HALLOWE'EN, when such magic is at its most powerful. Children in the English-speaking world still 'duck' for apples floating in water, apparently a relic of an ancient druidic divination ritual.

A poultice of rotten apples was once recommended for curing rheumatic eyes, and potions employing both the blossom and the fruit were widely used in beauty treatments. Apple blossom, incidentally, should never be brought into the home,

for illness will shortly follow it in. When it comes to eating the fruit, the old proverb 'An apple a day keeps the doctor away' has some support from modern scientific thinking. There is also a superstition that the fruit must be wiped clean first, or the Devil will appear. Finally, ancient wisdom has it that no bad or immoral woman can make good apple sauce.

See also APPLE-TREE MAN; JOHNNY APPLESEED.

Apple-Tree Man In the folklore of southwest England, a spirit of apple orchards. He is usually identified as the oldest tree in the orchard, which in former times was honoured with various rites and offerings to ensure the future of the crop.

See also WASSAILING.

April Fool's Day The first day of April, on which special licence is traditionally given to the playing of practical jokes. Possibly descended from an ancient Roman festival, the custom took hold in France after 1564, when the date of the NEW YEAR was changed from 25 March to 1 January on the adoption of the Gregorian calendar. Festivities marking the start of the New Year had been for centuries celebrated on the first day of April, postponed till then because 25 March often fell in Holy Week. With the change in the date, many French peasants played the trick of arriving unexpectedly at their neighbours on 1 April to fool them into thinking it was still the first day of the New Year. The date subsequently became enshrined in many parts of the world as a day to test the humour of friends and neighbours, the most popular tricks including sending people on pointless errands. The tradition has been enlarged in scope in modern times by the sometimes very plausible hoax stories perpetrated by national newspapers and television and radio companies.

Tradition has it that licence for such jokes expires at 12 noon, and that any jokes attempted after that time will bring bad luck to the originator of them. Anyone who fails to respond to jokes played on them in the proper spirit of tolerance and amusement will also suffer bad luck.

Equivalents of April Fool's Day in other cultures include the Huli festival of India, which incorporates a similar tradition of playing practical jokes.

Arabian Nights Influential collection of Middle Eastern fables and folk tales that is probably descended ultimately from Persian legend. Titled in full *The Arabian Nights' Entertainment*, but also known as *The Thousand and One Nights*, the collection as we now have it was based on an Egyptian text written around the 15th century. The earliest known version is an Arabic translation of the 8th century. It would appear that the original Arabic title, *Alf Laylah Wa Laylah*, was intended to suggest an infinite number of stories rather than 1,001 or any other precise number. The tales themselves include stories drawn from a wide range of cultures apart from the Persian, among them the Egyptian, Indian and Jewish folkloric traditions.

The tales were supposedly related by Scheherazade, the bride of the Sultan Schahriah, in order to delay her execution. The sultan had been betrayed by his first wife, and after executing her had consequently vowed to complete his revenge by taking a new wife each night and having her strangled in the morning. In the end only the two daughters of the vizier, Scheherazade and her sister, were left. Scheherazade bravely volunteered to become the next bride, and each night told the sultan an absorbing tale, leaving the ending of the tale to the next evening so that the sultan had no option but to spare her for one more day in order to find out what happened. Ultimately, the sultan was won over by Scheherazade's stories and changed his mind about executing her. He had also fallen in love with her, and she in the meantime had borne three children by him.

The stories were introduced to Europe through a French translation by Antoine Galland in the early 18th century, working from a Syrian text. English translations followed shortly afterwards. The most famous tales include those of SIN-BAD the sailor, ALADDIN and ALI BABA. The sensational success of the tales contributed greatly to the contemporary passion for all things Oriental in the early 19th century.

Arawn In Welsh folklore, the king of the underworld (*see* ANNWN). Usually depicted as a huntsman in pursuit of a white stag with his pack of hounds, he is best known from the story of his meeting with PWYLL, Lord of Dyfed, while out hunting. Because Pwyll had insulted Arawn by disrupting his hunting, the latter insisted upon Pwyll killing Hafgar, his rival for the kingship of the underworld. The two lords accordingly exchanged places, with Arawn assuming the rule of Dyfed for a year. The conflict between Arawn and Hafgar is commonly interpreted in terms of an allegory of the rivalry between summer and winter.

Arianrhod In Welsh mythology, the beautiful mistress of Caer Sidi, the tower of initiation in the underworld. According to the MABINOGION, it is at her tower that poets receive divine wisdom and the dead find shelter between incarnations. Arianrhod is identified as the daughter of the mother-goddess Don either by King Math or by her own brother GWYDION, and legend tells of her attempt to succeed to the prestigious post of Math's footholder when it became vacant. In order to be accepted she had to pass a test of virginity, which required stepping over Math's wand. As she stepped over the wand she gave birth to two children, one of whom was immediately taken into protection by Gwydion. In her fury at this humiliation Arianrhod laid a GEIS upon the remaining baby, LLEU LLAW GYFFES, depriving him of a name, arms and a human wife. With Gwydion's help Lleu eventually overcame all these debilitating restrictions.

Armstrong, Johnny Scottish folk hero whose unhappy fate was told in traditional Border ballads. He was a rebel during the reign of James V (1513–42), but was offered the chance to meet the king in peace and ask for a pardon. Suitably impressed by the gesture, Armstrong came to the royal court and presented himself – only for his plea for pardon to be rejected and for him to be condemned to death. Armstrong and his companions tried to fight their way out of the trap but all were killed, with the exception of one man, who survived to tell the tale of Johnny Armstrong's sad deception and murder.

Arthur Legendary British king who ranks among the most celebrated figures in the folkloric tradition of the whole English-speaking world. Numerous tales are told of his adventures and of the chivalric exploits of his knights (the knights of the ROUND TABLE), and the Arthurian canon of stories has long been central to the mythology and literature of the British Isles.

The son of IGRAINE, the wife of the duke of Tintagel, and UTHER PENDRAGON, king of all England, Arthur was raised in the care of ECTOR OF THE FOREST SAUVAGE on the advice of the sorcerer MERLIN, and was kept ignorant of his royal parentage. While still a young man he claimed the throne after successfully pulling out the sword in the stone (a sword immovably sunk into a large rock, from which only a rightful king could dislodge it), after many other famous knights had failed.

As king, Arthur established his court at CAMELOT, where his knights were encouraged to aim for the highest ideals of chivalry. As well as sending out knights to perform heroic deeds and to fight evil wherever they might encounter it, Arthur also presided over the quest for the HOLY GRAIL – the supreme challenge in which the one flawless knight, GALAHAD, even-

tually succeeded. Arthur himself established an enduring reputation for his wisdom and for his noble nature, and for many years his kingdom was apparently both stable and law-abiding. In early versions of Arthurian legend the king embarks on many adventures himself, but later it is more usually his knights who venture out in his name.

This did not mean, however, that Arthur's reign was untroubled, for both he and his knights were fallible and prey to human temptation and weakness. After the successful search for the Holy Grail was concluded, the Round Table slowly disintegrated under the weight of quarrels and acts of betrayal. The adulterous affair between Arthur's queen, GUINEVERE, and the noblest of his knights, LANCELOT, was a fatal blow to Arthur's court. Arthur was alerted to the liaison by his evil son (or nephew) MORDRED, setting in train a sequence of events that culminated in the disastrous Battle of CAMLAN, during which many of the knights were killed. Arthur managed to kill Mordred but himself suffered a mortal wound. At his request his magic sword EXCALIBUR was returned by Sir BEDIVERE to the LADY OF THE LAKE, and he set sail attended by three otherworldly queens to AVALON, where he would be healed ready for the day when he would return once more.

Legend has it that Arthur lies sleeping with his knights deep underground awaiting the day when he will rise again to save his country in its hour of need (replacing BRAN THE BLESSED in this role). The site of his underground chamber is variously said to be located at Alderly Edge in Cheshire, Richmond Castle in Yorkshire and Sewingshields near Hadrian's Wall, among other places. There is also a strong local tradition that he was buried at Glastonbury Abbey in southwest England, and monks during the reign of Henry II (1154–89) claimed to have found his grave there, which is still marked today.

It is likely that the legendary Arthur

was based on a real historical figure, a Romano-British king of the 6th or 7th century AD who led the resistance against the invading Saxons. There are, however, virtually no mentions of him in contemporary Celtic folklore and it seems likely that the Arthur we know now was largely a later literary invention. Many details of Arthurian legend were grafted on centuries after the historical Arthur lived. The presence of Merlin, for instance, appears to date from Geoffrey of Monmouth's *Historia Regum Britanniae*, written in the 12th century. The Round Table, meanwhile, was introduced by Robert Wace in his Anglo-French *Geste des Bretons*, written around 1154, and the theme of chivalry came with the 12th-century English priest Layamon's translation of Wace's work. The characters as we now know them owe much to Sir Thomas Malory's *Morte d'Arthur*, written in the middle of the 15th century.

Asgard In Norse mythology, the home of the gods and the resting place of slain Viking heroes. The name was derived from the Norse *as* ('god') and *gard* ('enclosure' or 'yard'). Legend has it that Asgard is divided into 12 realms, each of which is ruled by one of the gods. These realms include VALHALLA, the great mead-hall presided over by ODIN himself, Gladsheim, and Thrudheim, which is ruled by THOR. Situated at the very heart of the universe and separated from earth by a vast gulf, Asgard can only be reached by means of the rainbow bridge BIFROST.

ash The ash has always been of special importance among the trees and plants valued for their magical properties, and to damage an ash in any way has long been considered a perilous act. The ash played a crucial role in the mythologies of the Greeks, Romans and the Nordic peoples. Norse folklore gave the ash tree pride of place as the world tree YGGDRASIL, which connects heaven with hell. An uprooted ash was also identified in Norse mythology as the source of the material from which the first man, Askr, was made. The ash was similarly revered in pre-Christian Britain.

The ash is widely reputed to repel evil. Herdsmen and shepherds in the British Isles traditionally favour sticks or crooks made of ash, as they believe these provide protection for their livestock against evil (most walking sticks are made of ash to this day), and diviners use forked ash twigs to detect the presence of underground copper mines. Scottish midwives once fed newborn babies a drop or two of ash sap as their very first drink in order to give them lifelong protection against witchcraft. Other peoples maintain that the ash is fatal to snakes, which detest even its shadow and would rather risk fire than crawl over one of its twigs. In the USA, wearing a sprig of ash in the hat is considered a reliable safeguard against snakebite.

In terms of weather prediction, it is widely believed that if the oak comes into leaf before the ash a good summer is to be expected, as explained in a traditional English rhyme: 'If the ash tree appears before the oak, then there'll be a very great soak; / But if the oak comes before the ash, then expect a very small splash.'

One of the more ominous folk beliefs connected with the tree runs to the effect that if the winged seeds of the ash fail to appear then a member of the royal family or some other prominent person is sure to die. It is said that no ash tree in England produced seeds in the season preceding the execution of Charles I in 1649.

The ash also has its uses in DIVINATION. In England a young girl may find out who her future husband will be by placing an even-leaved sprig of ash in her left shoe or glove, or else in her bosom: she will then marry the first man she meets. An alternative suggests she sleep with the sprig beneath her pillow so as to see her true love in her dreams.

The annals of folk medicine recommend the ash for the treatment of various bodily complaints. Passing a child with rickets three times through a newly created cleft in an ash tree at sunrise, for instance, was formerly widely recognized as an infallible cure for the ailment (although it will return subsequently if the tree dies). Chips of ash may also be used to treat other conditions, such as warts and whooping cough, and back in 1688 a two-day nosebleed suffered by James II was reportedly staunched by stuffing bits of ash up the royal nose.

ashes The ashes of a spent FIRE have particular significance in the folklore of many cultures. The ashes of ritual bonfires were particularly valued in many early societies as they could be sprinkled on the fields mixed with the seeds to promote the fertility of the coming crop. The ashes of the dead have great symbolic significance throughout the world even today and are much revered in some regions for their magical properties. In Africa, there are numerous records of the ashes of a deceased person being mixed with food and eaten by relatives in the belief that they will thus inherit some of the dead person's attributes. In ancient Egypt, ashes taken from the funeral pyres of people with red hair were considered particularly conducive to bountiful harvests. Ashes might also be mixed into the food given to livestock to promote their health.

In Britain and the USA, ashes provide some protection against WITCHCRAFT, and in Wales ashes from fires lit during the BELTANE festival were formerly placed in shoes to safeguard the wearer from the threat of coming sorrow. According to French tradition, ashes will preserve a household from storm damage if scattered over it, while in South America and elsewhere ashes tossed in the air play an important role in rain-making rituals.

Ashes were formerly much used for the purposes of DIVINATION. In Yorkshire, ashes spread over the hearth on either New Year's Eve or Saint Mark's Eve (24 April) may give a hint as to what the coming 12 months have in store: footprints discovered in them the following morning prophesy a death if they lead towards the door, but anticipate a new member of the household if going in some other direction. Many reports exist of people identifying the shape of coffins or wedding rings in the ashes of their fires, giving unmistakable clues about coming events.

aspen Also called the shiver tree, the aspen is best known for its trembling leaves, which stir in the slightest of winds. Folklore explains that the aspen shivers in shame and horror because its wood was used for Christ's cross, or else because it failed to bow its head when Christ passed by.

The aspen is prized for its efficacy in treating a range of medical ailments, particularly fever (in which the patient shivers like the tree). The sufferer pins a lock of his or her hair to the nearest aspen with the accompanying rhyme: 'Aspen tree, aspen tree, I prithee to shake and shiver instead of me.' The sufferer then has to return home without uttering a word, or the charm will not work.

An alternative method is to cut a small hole in the tree at midnight and to place nail parings from the sufferer into it before closing the hole up and thus trapping the fever permanently. In Cheshire, locals similarly recommend rubbing warts with bacon and then hiding the bacon in a slit cut into an aspen tree: as the bacon decays the warts will fade from the sufferer's skin and be transferred to the tree's bark.

ass The humble ass, or donkey, upon which Christ is said to have ridden into Jerusalem, inevitably has an exalted place among the animals in folklore. Its magical significance is not confined to the Christian world, however: in the ancient world, for instance, the ass was linked with the sun-god Ra in Egyptian mythology, and with Dionysus by the Greeks. Often, though, the creature is identified as stubborn and slow-witted, and this is generally how it appears in folk tales and legends around the world.

In Christian countries the dark lines across the shoulders of the ass are often associated with the cross upon which Christ was crucified. As a consequence of this biblical connection, it was formerly believed that the DEVIL was unable to assume the disguise of the creature. Another tradition links the lines on the animal's back to the Old Testament story of Balaam, who struck his ass and was henceforth reminded of his cruelty by the cross that remained.

Whatever the origins of the markings, it used to be believed that three hairs plucked from the shoulders of an ass could cure measles or whooping cough if worn in a black silk or muslin bag around the neck. The link with whooping cough may have originated in the harsh cough of sufferers, which sounds not unlike the braying of an ass. Alternatively, a patient might be passed three times over and under an ass to effect a cure, or, in southern England, be fed the three hairs, finely chopped, in bread and butter. Irish sages formerly treated scarlet fever by forcing hairs removed from the sufferer down the throat of an ass.

Ancient advice suggests that scorpion stings, snakebites and toothache can be treated by simply sitting on an ass, facing its tail, or else by applying the lung of an ass to the wound. One way to get even with an enemy is to rub his head with the hoof clippings of an ass, upon which his own head will turn into that of an ass.

In many societies, the ass (which is often believed, incidentally, to be deaf to music) is widely regarded as a lucky animal, and it is thought particularly beneficial for a pregnant woman to see an ass, for it will ensure her unborn child grows up to be wise and well behaved. By the same token, farmers often keep asses among their cows to preserve the luck of the herd and to help to prevent the loss of calves through premature labour. Tradition dictates that no one ever sees a dead ass because the animal can sense its coming demise and will hide itself away. Finding the body of a deceased ass is consequently particularly lucky, and some people will insist on jumping over it for luck. Lastly, rain can be expected if an ass brays and twitches its ears.

Assipattle In the folklore of the Orkney Islands, an idle young man whose battle with a terrifying sea monster became the subject of Scottish legend. Tradition has it that Assipattle got his name (originally 'Ash-pate') from his habit of lounging in the ashes in front of the fire, and had a reputation for boasting of doing great deeds without ever seeming to do anything at all. When the dreadful Stoorworm ravaged the country and seized Princess Gemdelovely, however, Assipattle revealed his cunning by setting sail in a small boat equipped with a knife and a pail of burning peats. When the Stoorworm swallowed the boat he used the knife to cut open its liver and poured the burning peats into the hole. The monster spewed him out in its agony and died. Assipattle was hailed as a hero and was duly rewarded with the princess's hand in marriage.

Astolat, Maid of *See* ELAINE DE ASTOLAT.

astrology The tradition of 'reading' the stars and planets and predicting from their relative positions what the future holds. Broadly speaking, the year is divided into a ZODIAC of 12 houses, each with its own symbol and set characteristics, which determine a person's emotional capabilities and ambitions depending on the house they were born in. Astrology, with its accompanying horoscopes published in daily newspapers and so forth, is generally dismissed by the scientific establishment, but retains a fascination for millions of people, who not only know their own star sign but are also versed in their alleged strengths and weaknesses, as dictated by professional astrologers.

The study of the stars has ranked among the intellectual preoccupations of all the world's major civilizations, being first developed by the ancient Babylonians, and it continues today as a respectable science in the form of astronomy. Astrology, which first fell foul of scientific thinking in the 16th century, offers some kind of logic behind the apparently random happenings of daily life. Critics claim that it is ludicrous to suggest that one twelfth of the world's population will all experience 'a pleasant financial surprise' or a 'falling out with a close friend' on the same day, but this over-simplifies the system, which depends not just on the alignment of the planets on the day of birth but on the precise hour.

In defiance of all the logical arguments against them, the predictions of the astrologers do (perhaps inevitably due to the law of averages) sometimes impress. Examples that have been cited in support of the 'science' of astrology have included the warnings that were signalled by the positions of the planets in November 1963 just prior to the assassination of President John F. Kennedy. The same stars failed, however, to give any notice of the outbreak of World War II in 1939, although repeated predictions of Allied victory during the course of the war played a big part in boosting morale – to the extent that some members of Parliament in Britain demanded the silencing of the astrologers because their optimism threatened to undermine the willingness of the public to make the necessary sacrifices to the war effort. On the German side, Adolf Hitler was notorious for his reliance upon what his astrologers concluded – as indeed were many other military leaders before him. In more recent times Nancy Reagan consulted her astrologer on behalf of her husband, US President Ronald Reagan.

The positions of the planets, the sun and the moon, have long had an occult relevance and are of primary importance in the preparation of innumerable potions and spells. Many plants and other materials only retain their magical properties at given times of the planetary cycles. Back in the 15th and 16th centuries astrological information was considered particularly useful in medicine, the planets governing the welfare of the internal organs and the zodiac influencing the surface anatomy. Treatments thus depended largely upon analysing the planets' effect upon the four bodily humours, blood, black bile, yellow bile and phlegm.

Atlantis Legendary continent that is supposed to have disappeared into the Atlantic Ocean as punishment for the sacrilegious behaviour of its priests. The legend of Atlantis, commonly depicted as an earthly paradise, is the best known example of the stories of DROWNED LANDS that are a feature of many folkloric traditions. Plato described it as a vast territory larger than Asia Minor. The legend of Atlantis may have been inspired by the actual loss of towns and villages to the sea at various low-lying points on the western European seaboard. Various attempts have been made to attach the Atlantis legend to particular places, the most plausible including the Aegean island of Santoríni (Thera), which was largely destroyed by a volcanic eruption around 1550 BC. Another theory locates it in the central Atlantic, thus supposedly explaining the similarities between the cultures of ancient civilizations on the two sides of the ocean. British tradition claims that survivors of the inundation of Atlantis resettled in parts of Britain, providing the island with its first priesthood.

Auld Lang Syne *See* BURNS NIGHT.

aurora The dancing lights, sometimes coloured, that appear from time to time in the night sky as a result of charged solar particles being attracted towards the earth's magnetic poles. They are most often seen at northerly latitudes in the northern hemisphere, and at southerly latitudes in the southern hemisphere. The aurora in the northern hemisphere is variously called the Aurora Borealis, the Northern Lights, the Burning Spears or the Merry Dancers. That in the southern hemisphere is called the Aurora Australis. The phenomenon is particularly revered by the Inuit peoples, who interpret these lights in the sky as the spirits of the blessed dead sporting in the heavens. According to ancient Norse mythology, however, the aurora was light reflected by the shields of the VALKYRIES.

Other peoples have seen in such displays more ominous portents, and in lands where they only make occasional appearances they have been considered a precursor of war or of other national misfortune – a tradition strengthened when the lights were seen as far south as London in 1939, and at Cleveland, Ohio, just before the Japanese attacked Pearl Harbor in December 1941. In northern England the lights are sometimes called Lord Derwentwater's Lights in memory of the bright display of 24 February 1716 when James, Earl of Derwentwater was executed for his part in the failed Jacobite rebellion of the previous year.

Avalon In Arthurian legend, the otherworld to which King ARTHUR goes to be healed after receiving a mortal wound at the Battle of CAMLAN. Sometimes referred to as Apple Island (after the Welsh *afal*, apple), it is usually described in terms of a lush paradise where the inhabitants live in good health to an old age. Ruled over by the enchantress MORGAN LE FAY, it was here that Arthur's magic sword EXCALIBUR was forged. Tradition locates Avalon at Glastonbury in Somerset, where the grave of Arthur and Guinevere was allegedly discovered by monks in the late 12th century.

See also ISLANDS OF THE BLEST.

axe The axe, one of the earliest tools to be invented, has considerable significance in the folklore of many cultures. Made of stone and later iron, itself considered a magical metal, the axe came to play a prominent role in the rituals of pre-Christian religions, and its image is to be found at many sacred sites, including Stonehenge. Axes frequently figure among the grave goods found at Neolithic burial sites. Many deities and other spirits were conventionally depicted wielding an axe as a symbol of their power.

Witches were alleged to 'milk' axes, thereby stealing milk from all the cows in the area, although axes were also reputed to repel witches and other evil-doers. An upturned axe could also be used in the detection of thieves, the suspects being obliged to dance in a circle around it until the axe fell over, the haft pointing towards the culprit.

In some European countries it is said that cattle persuaded to step over an axe on their way to the fields in the spring will be impervious to curses and other evil influences. In the USA, meanwhile, it is considered unlucky to carry an axe into the home, as this will bring about the death of a member of the family, and bad luck is also to be expected in the wake of any dream in which an axe appears.

See also AXIOMANCY.

axiomancy Method of DIVINATION that involves the use of an AXE. There were various ways in which an axe could be used to reveal knowledge of the future or the answers to particular queries. One of these was to balance a piece of agate or some other semiprecious stone on a red-hot axe blade and then observe how it responded when a question was asked. If it fell off and bounced three times then it might indicate the presence of buried treasure nearby.

Aymon, four sons of The heroes of a medieval French CHANSON DE GESTE entitled *Doon de Mayence*, written around the early 13th century. The four sons of Aymon of Dordone were Alard, Guichard, Renauld and Richard, who became famous for their deeds of valour fighting against the armies of the Emperor CHARLEMAGNE. They were also famed for their legendary horse BAYARD, which could extend its back to seat all four sons together. Variants of the legend may be found in many other cultural traditions, including those of the Netherlands, Italy, and Spain.

B

Baba Yaga Legendary Russian ogress who was reputed to feed on young children. She was said to live deep in the forest, in a house that could move around on long chicken-like legs. She herself could fly through the air in an iron cauldron, sweeping away all trace of her passing with her broom. She guarded a fountain of youth, which few people managed to reach safely. She closely resembles the German goddess BERCHTA.

Babes in the Wood English folk tale relating the story of two children who are abandoned in a deep forest by order of their wicked uncle. Based on an old English ballad registered in 1595, the story is usually presented now in the form of a pantomime, though it has also inspired operas and melodramas.

On the death of their father, two young children (whose names change from one version to another) come under the guardianship of their uncle. The uncle, however, is eager to inherit the fortune left to the children and persuades two 'ruffians strong' to murder the infants in a deep wood. One of the murderers relents at the last moment and instead kills his companion before abandoning the children to their fate. In the original ballad, 'The Children in the Wood; or, the Norfolk Gentleman's Last Will and Testament', the children die and their bodies are covered with leaves by a sympathetic robin redbreast. The wicked uncle subsequently finds that everything goes wrong for him: his own sons perish, he loses all his livestock and money, and he finally dies in prison, racked with remorse. The surviving murderer is arrested for highway robbery and confesses to his guilt. Later versions of the story as adapted in Victorian times have a more optimistic ending: the children survive by feeding on blackberries before being rescued by ROBIN HOOD, and the treachery of the wicked uncle (sometimes identified as the Sheriff of Nottingham) is finally exposed.

Similar tales about abandoned children are common to several cultures, and it has been suggested that the English ballad may itself have been derived from an earlier Italian model.

See also ABANDONED CHILDREN.

Babe the Blue Ox *See* PAUL BUNYAN.

Badb In Irish mythology, the goddess of war, one of the three aspects of MORRIGAN. Usually depicted as a raven or hooded crow, she was reputed to provoke armies to battle, to select those who would fall in the field and to interfere so that conflict always ended as she wished. In her guise as the WASHER AT THE FORD, she appeared both to King CORMAC and to CUCHULAINN as a harbinger of death, and consequently came to be associated with the BANSHEE.

badger The badger is noted in the folklore of many countries both for its courage and for its persistence. The animal is also associated in Native North

American folklore with childbirth, while the Japanese believe that the creature has the ability to change its shape at will. An ancient rustic belief from Yorkshire claims that the badger has longer legs at the back and shorter legs on one side in order to help it to run across and up slopes. Elsewhere in Europe, badgers' teeth are particularly prized by gamblers, who claim they guarantee success in any wager.

bakemono In Japanese folklore, a class of malevolent demons including a variety of GHOSTS and GOBLINS. They are often depicted as repulsive long-haired spirits lacking feet.

bakru In South American folklore, a race of 'little people' who were supposedly created by evil sorcerers out of flesh and wood. They were said to manifest in couples and to be distinguishable from other spirits by virtue of their large heads and child-sized bodies. Anyone who tried to harness the magic of bakrus for their own ends was warned that they would inevitably be punished for this temerity.

Balan See BALIN.

Baldur In Norse mythology, the god of light. The son of ODIN and FRIGGA, he was invulnerable to all weapons except MISTLETOE, and ultimately met his death at the hands of his own brother, the blind Hodur, who was tricked by LOKI into throwing a spear of mistletoe at his sibling. Odin ordered Hermod, the messenger of the gods, to fetch Baldur back from the underworld, but he failed in his attempt.

Balin In Arthurian legend, the knight who delivered the DOLOROUS BLOW. The brother of Balan, he was imprisoned after killing the nephew of King ARTHUR, and subsequently incurred the wrath of King Pelles after killing the latter's evil brother Garlon. Balin then accidentally wounded Pelles in both thighs with his

spear, thus bringing about the WASTE-LAND (*see also* WOUNDED KING). Legend recalls how Balin and Balan eventually killed each other after donning borrowed armour and thus failing to recognize each other. They were buried by MERLIN in a single grave.

ballad Narrative folk song of chiefly European tradition, typically relating semi-historical or fabulous adventures in love and war. The genre was well established by the end of the medieval period, when such songs often formed the basis of the repertory of itinerant professional singers, although many of the tales recounted dated back many centuries earlier. The music accompanying such narratives varied widely in nature, including plaintive solo laments as well as lively dance music.

The most famous ballads in the British tradition include several based on the life of ROBIN HOOD, the so-called 'Border ballads' associated with the Scottish Borders, and such tales of tragic love as the celebrated 'Barbara Allen'. Countless others tell of similar doomed love affairs, as well as fights against dragons and encounters with demons, ghosts and witches as well as other non-supernatural subjects ranging from battles to murders and executions of celebrated criminals among other newsworthy events. Equivalents of the genre in other European cultures include the Spanish *romancero* and the Russian *byliny*.

Important ballad collections were first made in the 19th century, and these subsequently had a profound effect alongside other folk music upon contemporary music forms. Early collectors made a distinction between 'traditional' or 'folk' ballads that typically described a celebrated legend or historical event and 'street' ballads that were generally about contemporary events and preoccupations and often took the form of parodies of well-known poems or already extant folk tunes. Examples of the latter genre were frequently sold in the streets in huge numbers in the form of crudely printed 'broadsheets' and these are now sometimes viewed as early incarnations of the modern newspaper.

In the 19th century the term ballad was redefined through its association with the sentimental 'drawing-room' ballads that were played on parlour pianos in middle-class households throughout Victorian England. Generally written by professional songwriters, these were often modelled upon popular opera and in their turn paved the way for the popular songs of the 20th century, in which the word 'ballad' came to be applied to any song of a lyrical, reflective nature. Drawing-room ballads sometimes recounted stories similar to those related in earlier ballad tradition, but the majority expressed heartfelt romantic or religious sentiments and have long since become unfashionable.

Balmung In Norse mythology, the magical SWORD offered by ODIN to the warrior who could pull it free from the tree that he had thrust the blade into. Also called Gram, it was the work of WAYLAND THE SMITH, and was reputed to guarantee its master victory in battle. After nine princes had failed to withdraw the sword, SIGMUND, the Völsung hero, managed to dislodge it and claim it as his own. Odin subsequently destroyed the sword in battle, but it was later repaired and used by SIGURD to kill FAFNIR after he took the form of a terrifying dragon.

Balor In Irish mythology, the evil king of the FOMORIANS. He was a formidable foe who could kill an opponent with a mere glance from his single eye, which had been imbued with deadly power after he spied on the magic-making of some druids. It was said that in battle Balor would order four men to lift his great eyelid so that the power of his eye could be directed against his enemies.

Because it had been prophesied that Balor would meet his death at the hands of his own grandson, he kept his daughter

Ethniu in isolation on an island to prevent her taking lovers. There, however, she was visited by Cian, and subsequently she gave birth to his son LUGH. Ultimately, during the second battle of MAG TUIRED, Lugh used his sling to put out his grandfather's single death-dealing eye and thus killed him. Such was the force of the shot that the deadly eye was pushed right through the back of Balor's head, killing several of his followers who happened to be standing in the line of fire. His body was hung on a sacred hazel tree, from which it dripped poison. The dreadful Balor is thought to have been the model for the giant YSPADDADEN.

bannik In Russian folklore, a breed of household demon that is usually to be found in the bathhouse. The bannik has a mixed reputation, and is sometimes suspected of scalding bathers with hot water, and even of killing them. On other occasions it will place its hand on the bather's back: if the touch is soft this is deemed a good omen for the bather, but a sharp scratch is more ominous, warning of evil to come. To appease the bannik some bathers will leave a little water in the bathtub together with some soap.

See also DOMOVIK.

banshee In Celtic folklore, a supernatural spirit whose unearthly wailing is much feared in Ireland and western Scotland as an omen of approaching death. The banshee is usually heard at night, and is variously described as a young and beautiful woman, or else as an ugly old hag. Many clans and families claim their own banshee guardian spirit, whose supernatural ululations give notice of the imminent death of one of their number. Examples of famous banshees include the one linked to the baronial Rossmore family of County Monaghan, Ireland, whose wailing was first heard in 1801 and who has since allegedly heralded the death of each person to succeed to the barony (including that of the sixth baron in 1958). According to Scottish legend a banshee (or caoineag as it sometimes referred to in Scotland) was heard wailing on the eve of the massacre of Glencoe.

Some claim that the banshee wail is made by the fairies, who sense the coming of death and want to warn the family. The Gaelic *bean sidhe*, from which the term banshee originally came, in fact means 'fairy woman'. Alternatively, the banshee may be identified as a dead ancestor or perhaps as the vengeful spirit of a woman who has suffered some wrong at the family's hands. Sometimes the banshee is not heard as a human voice, but as a beating drum.

See also WASHER AT THE FORD.

barbegazi In Alpine folklore, a species of mountain spirit that inhabits the snowy peaks of the French and Swiss Alps. Called barbegazi after the French *barbe glacée* ('frozen beard'), they are depicted as dwarf-like beings who are generally shy of contact with humans, but who have been known to warn travellers of avalanches and other perils. They are said to have abnormally large feet, which they use to glide swiftly over the snow. However, they hibernate during the summer months as they are unable to withstand warm temperatures.

barguest *See* BLACK DOG.

Barlaam and Josaphat Indian romance that became well known in the folklore of medieval Europe. First translated into Greek around the 6th century, the story (which resembles tales surrounding the youth of the Buddha) tells how the monk Barlaam converted the Hindu prince Josaphat to Christianity. The story of the three caskets, of which only one contains anything of value, was borrowed by Shakespeare when he wrote *The Merchant of Venice*.

barren ground A patch of sterile ground where nothing will grow because of some curse or other evil event that has occurred there. Ominous sites of this kind

can be found all over the world, and there is usually some local legend to account for them. Among the best-known examples in the British Isles are the spot in the Scilly Isles where the drowned English admiral Sir Cloudesley Shovel was temporarily laid after his fleet was wrecked in 1707, with the loss of many lives, and the summit of Dragon Hill in Berkshire, where ST GEORGE is said to have killed the dragon, whose blood permanently poisoned the soil. Other localities boast graves where the grass never grows, notably that of William Davies in Montgomery churchyard, hanged in 1821 for a crime of which he protested his innocence to the last.

basil Widely used culinary herb that has been credited with a range of magical properties over the centuries. Basil was supposed in ancient times to be an antidote to the poison of the BASILISK, hence its name. According to the Greeks, it also represents hatred and bad luck, while Italians by contrast consider it a token of love. Hindus, meanwhile, believe a leaf of basil placed on a corpse will protect the spirit of the dead person from evil. Elsewhere, the plant is associated with the DEVIL, and is believed to give birth to scorpions.

basilisk Legendary monster described as a cross between a cock and a serpent. Also known as the cockatrice, the basilisk was described in classical times by Pliny, who alleged that the creature was born from a cock's egg hatched by a snake or toad. Identified as the king of the serpents, it was usually depicted with the head and feet of a cock, the tail of a serpent, and, occasionally, wings. It was believed that its breath and gaze were so deadly they could kill mortals instantly, but also that the creature could be overcome by tricking it into seeing its own reflection in a mirror, which would lead to its own immediate demise. It has been speculated that the legend of the basilisk may have had its roots in stories about the hooded cobra.

bat With their nocturnal flights and habit of roosting in secluded shadowy places such as ruins and caves, bats have long been associated with the darker side of folklore, being linked in many cultures with witchcraft and death. Even today it is thought to be very unlucky for a bat to enter the home as this is said to threaten the life of one of the occupants. Other ominous traditions claim that the DEVIL and his witches turn into bats in order to enter people's houses, as do VAMPIRES, and that the sight of bats flying vertically upwards and then dropping back to earth is a sign that evil spirits and ghosts are walking abroad.

The apparently erratic flight paths of bats led people in former times to believe that the creatures were blind, and this notion seems to have inspired the common misconception that they can easily get inextricably entangled in women's hair. The Earl of Cranbrook once tested this theory by placing bats in the hair of three female volunteers: all the bats freed themselves without difficulty.

In some countries, such as China and Poland, bats have significance as sacred creatures, and may be interpreted as symbols of long life and happiness. In Australian Aboriginal culture the bat also demands respect, and anyone who kills a bat risks the shortening of their own life. In Germany, gamblers were once reputed to attach a bat's heart to their arm with a red thread to bring them luck, while in Austria it was said that possession of a bat's right eye brought with it the gift of INVISIBILITY. Elsewhere, bats' blood is used in black magic, especially in VOODOO and in the celebration of black masses. Sundry other folk beliefs concerning bats include the notions that those who wash their face in bats' blood will be rewarded with the ability to see in the dark, and that those who slip a few drops of bats' blood into a lover's drink will promote passion in the drinker.

Other miscellaneous folk beliefs concerning bats include the tradition that the sight of bats flying early in the evening is a sign of good weather in the offing. Another belief, originally from the Isle of Man, suggests that it is good luck to have a bat fall on you.

bay In classical times the bay (or laurel) tree was sacred to the sun god Apollo and to Asclepius, the god of medicine, and was associated with victory, honour and general good luck. It has retained these associations in folklore over the centuries, and until relatively recent times boughs of bay were popular as a form of Christmas decoration, just as they were when the ancient Romans celebrated the New Year. Christians, meanwhile, saw in the bay's ability to revive after most other plants would have died a symbol of the Resurrection, and took to carrying bay at funerals.

Bay or laurel has long been considered an effective defence against evil spirits, ghosts and witchcraft, and a bay tree planted near the house was once said to safeguard the occupants from the plague and other ill luck. The trees are also said to be immune from lightning and thus to offer a safe retreat in a thunderstorm (the Roman emperor Tiberius always donned a crown of laurel in thundery weather). If a bay tree suddenly withers, however, then very bad luck is in the offing, particularly threatening the death of one of the family. If all the bay trees in the country wither together then a national catastrophe, such as the death of the king or the coming of plague, is to be expected.

The tree's medicinal properties continue to be revered, and bay leaves carried about the person are said to give protection against all manner of disease. Bay leaves can also be used in DIVINATION. Soothsayers burned bay leaves to study how they were consumed by the flames, or inhaled the smoke as the leaves burned in order to experience the narcotic effects. If bay leaves burn noisily when thrown onto a fire then good luck will ensue; if they burn without a sound then misfortune will surely follow. Pinned to the pillow on the eve of St Valentine's Day, bay leaves will also allow a dreamer visions of his or her future sweetheart.

Bayard The fabulous horse that was given by CHARLEMAGNE to the Four Sons of AYMON. According to legend the horse's back could extend to seat all four riders together. Although in all other aspects an apparently ordinary mount, it was capable of miraculous speed, and was apparently endowed with the gift of human speech. Bayard (which means 'bay-coloured' in French) was described in the works of Boiardo, Ariosto and Tasso, among other Renaissance writers.

beans Bean plants have had special magical associations since ancient times, being particularly linked with death and ghosts. Disciples of Pythagoras in ancient Greece observed a taboo against eating them, as did the ancient Egyptians, while the Romans offered gifts of beans to the dead on what was called the Bean Calends, and customarily ate them at funerals (beans still featured in British funeral ritual until the 19th century). Beans also have special significance in the folklore of Japan, and in that of various Indian and African peoples, and in the Far East bean flowers may be scattered around the house to ward off demons. Several Native American tribes have special bean festivals connected with ensuring a good crop in the future.

In European culture, the magical properties of beans are reflected in their role in several traditional tales, notably 'Jack and the Beanstalk'. They were also once used in some legal processes in deciding a suspect's guilt, the arraigned person being obliged to pick one of two beans from a bag: if the bean was black he was guilty of the crime, if white he was deemed innocent.

In the southwest counties of England local tradition insists that kidney beans must be planted on the third day of May if they are to prosper, while elsewhere gardeners are advised to plant their beans on the feast days of St David and St Chad (the first two days in March) or otherwise when the leaves of the elm are as big as a farthing.

As a means of DIVINATION, cooks in northern England sometimes concealed a single bean in a pea pod when preparing a meal: whoever got the bean would be the first to marry. On Midsummer's Eve, people were invited to hunt for three hidden beans, one peeled, one partly peeled and the third unpeeled: finding the peeled bean promised a lifetime of poverty, the half-peeled bean a relatively affluent existence and the unpeeled bean meant great wealth in store.

In folk medicine, rubbing the white inner lining of a bean pod on a wart is said to be an effective means of treatment, while the consumption of bean pods in wine and vinegar, or of the distilled water of the flowers, is said to promote beauty and improve the complexion (although it might also bring on nightmares).

The flower of the bean provokes foreboding in many societies, largely through the ancient idea that the souls of the departed lurk in the blooms. In some parts of the British Isles accidents are said to be more frequent when the bean plants are in blossom, and the appearance of a white-flowering bean plant in a bean patch is considered particularly ominous, prophesying imminent death. Superstition warns in particular against sleeping in a bean field, for this will either bring on nightmares or else rob the sleeper of his sanity. The strong perfume emitted by bean flowers will similarly make a person lightheaded or foolish.

bear Although long vanished from the wild in many parts of Europe, the bear features in many European legends and folk beliefs, and still plays an active part in the folklore of the USA and Canada and other parts of the world where it continues to thrive.

Bears were revered by many early societies, and were sometimes regarded as a species of ancestor spirit. They are frequently linked with the supernatural and the DEVIL, and many sorcerers have been credited with the power to assume the shape of a bear. English folklore also boasts several ghost bears, the most famous of which are alleged to manifest at Worcester Cathedral, at the Tower of London and in Cheyne Walk, Chelsea. Folk tales from several cultures talk of marriages contracted between bears and humans (although others depict the bear as rather slow in intellect and thus easily outwitted by the FOX and other cleverer animals). In Arthurian legend, meanwhile, the name Arthur itself was derived from the Old English *arth* ('bear').

Native Americans in the USA and Canada still revere the creature and traditionally give their apologies to any bear they have killed, laying out the different parts of its carcass according to ordained ritual. The Inuit (Eskimos) in particular follow a strict routine after killing a polar bear for fear of offending its spirit, while Lapp hunters who have killed a bear are considered unclean and are obliged to live apart from their fellows for the space of three days. White backwoodsmen once maintained that bears mated only once every seven years, when the commotion was such that cattle for miles around would lose their unborn calves. In both North America and in Scandinavia people may be reluctant to mention the word 'bear', preferring such euphemisms as 'the old man' and 'golden feet' in order not to invite attack.

Back in the times when bears were commonly seen at English fairs, dancing in chains or being tormented in bear-baiting booths, a number of curious beliefs sprang up based on erroneous conclusions about the creatures' behaviour. For example, it was believed that bears obtain sustenance by sucking on their own paws, and that they literally lick their newborn cubs into a bear shape when first delivered.

The animal also has significance in folk medicine, being widely considered a potent force in healing. Boiling some bear's fur in aquae vitae and then wrapping it round the feet is said to cure fits, while bear fat can be used to treat various aches and pains, and also to counter baldness. It was once said that a child with whooping cough would be cured if given a ride on a bear's back. Eating a bear's heart was reputed to endow great courage, while bears' teeth were valued as a charm against toothache (in the USA bears' teeth were commonly given to teething children). Sleeping on a bearskin, meanwhile, is said to be very beneficial for those suffering from backache.

See also GOLDILOCKS AND THE THREE BEARS.

beard The wearing of beards has long been considered a symbol of virility, authority, wisdom and strength. Gods of both pagan and Christian tradition were frequently depicted with beards, and cutting off a warrior's beard was thought an insult of the most potent kind. Muslims still swear by the beard of the Prophet, while Sikhs wear beards as a symbol of their faith. The beard's power of renewal led to the widespread notion that facial hair was a divine gift and should never be trimmed (if only because an enemy might obtain the clippings and thus secure magical influence over the wearer).

The beard has come and gone according to the dictates of fashion (taxes imposed on beards by Elizabeth I, for instance, led to their virtual disappearance for a period during her reign). In the late 19th century the fact that beards were sported by more than one member of the British royal family consolidated their association with royalty, encouraging many subjects to grow their own. Modern superstition has it, however, that men with beards are not to be trusted, and throughout Europe a man with a red beard is likely to be considered untrustworthy or hot-tempered (recalling the red beards of the Vikings perhaps). The same applies to a man whose beard or moustache is one colour and his hair another.

See also BLUEBEARD.

beast marriage The motif of the beast marriage is found in folk tales from all round the world. Such tales revolve around the marriage of humans to a variety of beasts that have the ability to take human form at will. In their human shape these shape-shifting animals often prove loyal spouses, and may even have children by their human partners.

Among the shape-changing creatures involved in such marriages are bears, bulls, foxes, seals and swans. Sometimes the beast involved has been trapped in human guise after it has been prevented from returning to its animal form through the theft of its skin. If, after years as a faithful partner, it manages to locate its skin at a later date it typically escapes in its original form, never to return. It may also revert to its animal form if its partner breaks a condition imposed at the time of the marriage, for instance through violence or angry words.

In other cases the beast is actually a human who has been transformed into a beast by magic and is subsequently redeemed through love and restored to his or her human shape.

See also ADLET; AINE; BEAUTY AND THE BEAST; DOLPHIN; FOX MAIDEN; SEAL MAIDEN; SELKIE; SWAN MAIDEN.

beating the bounds English folk ceremony that involves the ritual thrashing of boundary stones marking the extent of a particular parish. The ceremony takes place in a number of English villages, towns and cities on or around Ascension Day, and harks back to the reign of Elizabeth I, when the boundaries between parishes had much greater significance in the life of the community than they do today. In what is predominantly religious occasion, the participants typically go in procession from one stone to another, led by a church choir. The stones are beaten with willow switches (in former times a young boy might be thrashed at the stone or otherwise ducked in a nearby ditch or pool), thus fixing knowledge of these all-important boundaries in

everyone's mind. Prayers may also be said for the success of the coming harvest.

See also RIDING THE MARCHES.

Beauty and the Beast Enduring European fairy tale that concerns the story of a girl whose selfless love for an ugly monster restores him to his original shape as a handsome prince. The tale is common to several cultural traditions, although the modern form of the story in the English-speaking world can be traced back to versions written by Marie Leprince de Beaumont (1711-80), translated into English in 1757, and subsequently by Charles PERRAULT, whose 1697 version was translated into English in 1729. All variants of the story belong to an ancient tradition of legends concerning BEAST MARRIAGES that is shared by the Basque, German, Swiss, English, Italian, Portuguese, Lithuanian, Magyar and Indian peoples (among others). Variant details include the identification of the Beast as a serpent, wolf, pig or even a crocodile.

The story begins with a penniless merchant coming across an apparently deserted castle in a remote part of the forest. Here he helps himself to a beautiful rose as a gift for his lovely daughter. On picking the rose he is threatened by the hideous monster who lives in the castle, and he is only released after he promises to hand over his daughter to the Beast. The daughter, today usually identified by the name Beauty or Belle, dutifully presents herself at the Beast's castle, and he soon falls in love with her and her winning ways. When Beauty learns by gazing into a magic mirror that her father is ill, however, she begs to be allowed to visit him. The Beast warns her not to stay too long, as he will die if she is absent for more than a week. Forgetting her promise, Beauty lingers overlong with her father, and when she returns to the castle she finds the Beast is dying. Her grief at the Beast's fate breaks the spell that binds him, and he is magically restored to the handsome young prince he was before being transformed by a malevolent spell.

Bedivere In Arthurian legend, one of the knights of the ROUND TABLE. He was listed among the knights in the earliest Arthurian stories, but subsequently was somewhat overshadowed by LANCELOT. It was to Sir Bedivere (or Bedwyr) that EXCALIBUR was entrusted after King Arthur suffered his mortal wound.

bee The value traditionally placed on bees is reflected in the richness of the folklore associated with them. Bees have long been considered bearers of goodwill from the gods (or by some as the souls of the departed), and are usually interpreted as signifying wisdom and industry.

Reverence for bees predates Christianity, but Christians have also applied their own mythology to the creatures, claiming that the first bees were conceived in Paradise or, according to Breton legend, sprang from the tears of Christ on the cross. Christians also maintain that singing a psalm in front of the hive will give new heart to a swarm that is not doing well, and furthermore that at midnight on Christmas Eve the bees themselves hum the hundredth psalm in their hives. It is most unwise to kill one of these so-called 'servants of God', and they should be kept informed of all the most important events that take place in the owner's home, particularly news of deaths and marriages. If the bees resume their buzzing after hearing the tidings then they will not fly away.

The appearance of a swarm of bees in a garden is a sign of great prosperity in the offing. More ominous is the sight of bees swarming on a dead tree or hedge, or in the chimney, which all agree is a portent of death. Moving bees to a new hive must never be attempted without informing the swarm of the planned move first. Moreover, bees should only be moved on Good Friday, or they will surely die, and they must never be exchanged for cash but must instead be bartered for other goods (stolen bees will fail to prosper). In moving the hive, the bees must never be carried over running water, for this will cause them all to perish. Owners of bees are also warned that they must never allow their swarms to be disturbed by the sound of argument or swearing, which will offend them and may cause them to leave. If bees suddenly vacate their hive then death is at hand.

Dreaming of bees is lucky, and a bee flying into the house advises of the coming of a stranger. A bee alighting on a person's hand is a promise of coming wealth, and in Scotland the superstitious formerly caught the first bee of the season and kept it in their purse in the expectation that this would increase their riches. Another tradition, common to both US and English folklore, holds that bees will never sting a girl who passes through a swarm, as long as she is a virgin.

Beeswax candles have long been used in churches, especially in funeral services, and beeswax dissolved in water was believed in the Middle Ages to be a cure for the condition of erysipelas (it is also said that the ashes of burned bees sprinkled over the shoes will cure flat feet). The sting of a bee is traditionally considered beneficial in the treatment of arthritis, gout, neuritis and rheumatism (a notion partly backed by science).

beetle The ancient Egyptians revered the scarab beetle as a symbol of the sun god Ra, but relations between beetles and humans have rarely been so warm. Back in 1587, a case was even brought before the court in the town of St Julien, France in which local beetles were charged with causing damage in the vineyards of the area. In a later generation the havoc caused by the Colorado beetle was such that in the late 19th century some desperate US farmers even attempted to exorcize the creature from the country.

Most of the folk beliefs associated with beetles concern bad luck and prophecies of death. Perhaps the most widely observed tradition is the fear that death is in the offing if a beetle walks over a person's shoe. In Scotland, the appearance of a beetle in a room where the family are all seated is likewise believed to be an omen of terrible bad luck, which will be intensified if the creature is then killed, while elsewhere in Europe beetles similarly signify death, storms and other varieties of ill fortune.

Of the countless species of beetle, a few have been singled out for special attention. The stag beetle, with its ominous-looking jaws, has been linked with the DEVIL, while the burying beetle, said by Scottish legend to have betrayed the infant Jesus to his pursuers in Egypt, used to be routinely killed by children in Scotland. The same tradition claims that the dung beetle countered the treachery of the burying beetle by lying to Christ's pursuers to the effect that their quarry had passed by a year previously. Scottish children accordingly allow the dung beetle to live but may turn it onto its back for telling an untruth. Irish superstition has it that when a devil's coach-horse beetle arches its tail it is delivering a curse, while in England, the tapping of the death-watch beetle in the timbers of an old house is a warning of imminent death (the tapping is really made to attract a mate). Conversely, German superstition claims that it is good luck if a cockchafer beetle (linked with fertility in pre-Christian times) settles on a person's hand, and the cockchafer is similarly associated with good fortune in France, where it was formerly carried in public processions.

In parts of Africa, throwing beetles into a lake plays a part in some rainmaking ceremonies, and in many countries killing a beetle is said to bring on rain. Arab slave owners used to tie beetles to an ever-shortening length of thread attached to a nail to force runaway slaves to return against their will. Finally, according to East Anglian belief, allowing a dead beetle to rot on a thread round a child's neck will cure the infant of whooping cough.

See also LADYBIRD.

Befana In Italian folklore, a kindly FAIRY who fills stockings hung up by children with presents on Twelfth Night. An equivalent of FATHER CHRISTMAS, Befana is greeted with noisy street celebrations, and dolls representing Befana are placed in windows to indicate that the occupants are awaiting a visit from her. Naughty children may open their stockings to find only pebbles and lumps of charcoal. The name Befana is a corruption of the Latin *Epiphania*, Epiphany being another name for Twelfth Night, when the Magi visited the infant Jesus. Legend has it that Befana declined an invitation to accompany the Magi on their journey, explaining that she was too busy with her domestic chores and would meet them when they came back. The Magi went another way on their return journey, however, and she has since spent every Twelfth Night looking for them.

Befind In Irish Celtic legend, a FAIRY who is said to attend expectant mothers during CHILDBIRTH. It was once customary to lay out a table for the Befind as labour got under way, as she might be persuaded to make predictions about the child's future and to bestow various gifts of magic. She was sometimes identified as ETAIN, or as the sister of BOANN, queen of the fairies.

beheading game Motif of Celtic legend, in which a hero is challenged to trade a single blow with a GIANT or some other supernatural foe. The hero is allowed to take the first blow and cuts off his opponent's head, but instead of dying the latter replaces his head and demands the right to return the blow. The courage with which the hero accepts his fate is then presented as a test of his worth. The most famous examples of such beheading games include the tale of Sir GAWAIN and the Green Knight, and an episode in the life of the great Irish warrior CUCHULAINN.

The motif is thought to have been intended originally as an allegory of the changing seasons, the giant representing the old season and the hero the new season to whom he must give way.

See also BRICRIU'S FEAST

Behemoth Huge monster of Judaeo-Christian tradition, which is sometimes depicted as a terrifying demon. Described in the biblical Book of Job, Behemoth has a vast appetite but cannot reproduce as the earth would not provide sufficient sustenance for two such creatures. Legend has it that Behemoth will perish at the second coming of the Messiah, and its flesh will provide a huge feast for the righteous on that day. In Muslim legend Behemoth is portrayed as a huge fish, which supports in turn a massive bull, a ruby and the earth itself.

See also LEVIATHAN.

bell Bells have been employed in many of the world's religions and social rituals since the earliest times, and they have inevitably acquired an extensive mythology of their own over the centuries (despite attempts to limit their use by the Puritans). Hand bells were used in ancient Egypt during the festival of Isis, and both the Greeks and Romans rang bells to mark the passing of the hours and for other practical purposes. In the Christian world, church bells are sometimes 'baptized' in special ceremonies, given names and decorated with flowers or engraved with special inscriptions designed to ward off evil. This tendency to treat bells as living beings is extended in the belief that they will refuse to ring if they are insulted, and may even exact revenge on anyone who harms them or tries to steal them.

Bells are almost universally credited with the power of frightening off evil spirits, fairies and other supernatural entities, and in many parts of the world prized animals are fitted with small bells to protect them against the EVIL EYE as well as to alert the herdsman of his stock's whereabouts. The sound of bells is also said to cause witches riding on broomsticks to plummet to the ground, and to scare away snakes and mice. In the church itself, a 'passing bell' is rung on the death of a local person; this not only summons the congregation to prayer, but also drives away any evil spirits lured by the presence of death. Bells also play a crucial role in the ancient Catholic 'bell, book and candle' ritual of excommunication, the bell tolling for the 'dead' sinner. Ringing church bells at harvest time, meanwhile, is said to ensure a bumper crop, and the sound might also cause a storm to abate by distracting the malevolent spirit behind the wind and rain.

The image of the bell is widely associated with weddings, conveying good luck and protection from misfortune, and many modern good-luck charms come in the form of miniature bells. Nonetheless, if a bell is heard to toll before the end of a wedding ceremony, this may well be deemed a sign of bad luck, probably signifying the premature death of one of the happy couple. By way of contrast, a bell ringing during labour will ease the pains of childbirth. It is traditionally held that children born as the bell strikes the hour of three, six, nine or twelve will grow up with the gift of second sight, and will also have the ability to see ghosts.

On the darker side, a bell that tolls by itself when no one is pulling on the rope is widely feared as an omen of death. However, bells will also sound under their own volition if they detect the presence of a saint or in order to give warning of a crime committed nearby. Specially cast hand bells – containing mercury, lead, silver, gold, tin, copper and iron, and left to 'mature' for seven days buried in a cemetery – figure prominently in the rituals of necromancy, the black art of calling up the dead to divine the future.

Sailors are particularly sensitive to the sound of bells, and may interpret a bell tolling at the apparent touch of an unseen hand as an omen of shipwreck. Seafarers are similarly nervous of the ringing sound produced by glass tumblers, and will quickly silence the noise in the hope of averting disaster. A ship's bell, moreover, is supposed to embody the very soul of the vessel, and is consequently much respected. It is said that such a bell will never fail to ring, even if securely lashed, if the ship itself goes down.

Bells were traditionally considered to have considerable efficacy in folk medicine. It was formerly believed, for instance, that ringing church bells would protect the local community from plague, while in more recent times mothers in the USA have been known to give their children drinks from upturned bells to cure them of stuttering. In Scotland, back in the 18th century, a bell at the Chapter of St Fillan was much revered for its efficacy in curing the mad: the afflicted person was dipped in the so-called Saint's Pool, and the bell, which was about one foot in height, was carefully set on the head of the patient, who would immediately experience an improvement in his or her health. Grease taken from bells was recommended for the treatment of various skin problems, among several other conditions.

In British folklore, legends of drowned cities (see DROWNED LANDS) are rarely complete without the detail that the bells of submerged churches can still be heard striking far below the waves.

Belphegor In medieval folklore, a woman-hating demon who was sent to earth by the other demons after they had become alarmed at the marital bliss being enjoyed by humans. Belphegor married several mortal women in succession in order to find out the secrets of married life, but was so horrified by the nagging of his wives that he fled back to Hell where there were no women. His story is told in works by Machiavelli and Ben Jonson, among others.

The medieval Belphegor, who was sometimes associated with the sin of sloth, was in fact derived from a much more ancient mythological figure, a fairly obscure god of the Moabites identified by the same name.

Beltane One of the four major Celtic festivals of the year. Signalling the beginning of the summer, it was celebrated on 30 April, and has long since been absorbed into the MAY DAY festivities. Also called Beltaine or Beltene, and named after the Celtic god of light Belenus, it marked the time when livestock were taken out of winter pasture to feed on spring grass. The rituals usually included the lighting of a bonfire from which a brand was taken to rekindle domestic hearths, thus promoting the prosperity of the whole community. Suggestions that the festival was also celebrated in early times with human sacrifice remain unproven.

See also LUGHNASADH; OIMELC; SAMHAIN.

Beowulf Legendary dragon-slaying warrior-hero whose epic story is related in a celebrated Old English poem. Composed in the West Saxon dialect around AD 700, the poem recounts how Beowulf, leader of the Geats of southern Sweden, does battle with the fearsome monster Grendel, which has been ravaging the lands of Hrothgar, king of the Danes. Having ripped off Grendel's arm after a long struggle the hero is then obliged to do battle with Grendel's mother, who emerges from her lake seeking revenge for the injuries done to her offspring. After a bitter fight in the monster's underwater cave, Beowulf returns to Hrothgar's court carrying her head. In the third part of the poem Beowulf himself is finally killed fighting a huge dragon and is then given a ceremonial funeral befitting so celebrated a hero.

Much of the material of the poem would appear to have been borrowed from earlier sagas, although various details reflect the desire of later writers to put the tale in a Christian context (with the monsters, for instance, being identified as the descendants of Cain).

Berchta In German folklore, an ugly HAG with whom naughty children are sometimes threatened. Berchta (or Bertha), who has a single foot and an iron nose, is thought to be descended from an ancient pagan goddess of south German mythology whose worship declined after the introduction of Christianity. She is believed to punish slovenly housewives with nasty diseases, but is also fond of children who are well-behaved and likes to rock the cradle when the mother is away. Her feast day falls on Twelfth Night, when it is customary to leave out a little food for her. If this custom is neglected she may rip open the stomach of a mortal in order to help herself to the food inside; she will then sew up the wound using a ploughshare for a needle and iron chain as thread.

Bertha *See* BERCHTA.

bestiary Medieval compilation listing the actual and fabulous beasts believed to exist in the known world. Such publications were the subject of widespread fascination between the 11th and 14th centuries, and did much to promote belief in such fabulous creatures as the UNICORN. Many of them incorporated the stories and theories expressed in the anonymous 3rd-century AD *Physiologus*, which was much read in medieval Europe. The most celebrated examples included compilations by the scholars Philippe de Thaun, Guillaume le Clerc and Richard de Fournival.

Bhagavadgita *See* MAHABHARATA.

bhuta In Hindu folklore, a breed of malevolent demon that includes a variety of ghosts, goblins and other spirits. They are reputed to haunt such gloomy places as forests and cemeteries, feeding off the flesh of the living, and on occasion possessing the bodies of the recently dead. Because they cannot bear to touch the earth their attentions can be avoided by lying still on the ground.

bibliomancy The practice of consulting books for the purposes of DIVINATION, a procedure otherwise known as sortilege (although this term also embraces divination by the drawing of lots). Although records exist of works by Virgil, Homer and other classical authors being used in a similar way the practice is today chiefly associated with such sacred religious books as the Koran and the Bible.

Keeping the eyes closed, the reader – presumably confident that his hand is guided by God – stabs a passage at random with his finger, a pin or a silver knife, and then divines from the selected verse what lies in store in relation to a specific query. If performed before noon on New Year's Day the questioner may find out what will happen over the following 12 months. One derivative of the custom popular in the USA suggests that a lover may divine the true character of a partner by consulting the first chapter of the Book of Proverbs in this way and reading the numbered verse that corresponds to the other's age.

A variant of the custom involves the use of a Bible and a door key in the business of love divination. According to a time-honoured ritual a girl may assess the suitability of a suitor by firstly inserting her door key between the pages of the Song of Solomon, binding and suspending the Bible with her garter or stocking, asking two friends to place their middle fingers onto the protruding key ring and then chanting the 'Many waters cannot quench love' verse from the Song of Solomon. If the Bible moves at all during this ritual or falls to the ground then the proposed union is a good one; if nothing happens the girl will never marry. The same procedure can be followed to determine a lover's faithfulness (the Bible will 'turn' to the right if all is well) or else to find out a future partner's initials, the alphabet being chanted until the Bible turns. Virtually the same ritual (of which records exist from as early as the 14th century) was formerly employed in the detection of thieves, the names of the suspects being read out as passages from the Bible were recited until the Bible turned, indicating who was the guilty party. Alternatively, the key was spun on top of the Bible until it came to rest pointing towards the culprit.

Bicorn A mythical cow of medieval French folklore that was said to grow fat feeding on the flesh of good husbands. Its name (meaning 'two-horns') suggests it should be interpreted as a symbol of cuckoldry. Its counterpart was the chichevache, a half-starved cow said to feed only on good wives.

biersal In German folklore, a variety of KOBOLD that is said to live in beer cellars, cleaning the bottles and generally keeping the place tidy in exchange for a jug of beer every day. If neglected, the biersal is likely to take revenge by causing various acts of petty vandalism.

See also CLURICAUN.

Bifrost In Norse mythology, the rainbow bridge that links earth with ASGARD, the home of the gods. According to legend, the bridge consists of air, fire and water and is guarded by the god HEIMDAL. The thunder god THOR, being the largest of the gods, was forbidden to use the bridge in case it broke under his weight. Legend claimed that Bifrost was ultimately doomed to break under the feet of the attacking giants at RAGNAROK. The name Bifrost itself comes from the Icelandic *bifa* ('tremble') and *rost* ('path').

bigfoot Fabled creature of the remote forests of northwest North America, which in many respects resembles the ABOMINABLE SNOWMAN of the Himalayas. Called the sasquatch by Native Americans, the bigfoot is described as a tall gorilla-like humanoid covered with hair. It is usually reported walking upright, like a human, and as making a quick retreat if spotted. Photographs and film of such creatures have failed to provide conclusive proof of the existence of the bigfoot. Stories about such beings go back well before the 20th century, with reports of mysterious footprints being made as early as 1811. A specimen was allegedly caught and examined in 1884, but there is scant evidence to substantiate this claim.

birch Sacred to the Norse god THOR, the birch tree is associated with a host of folk beliefs, reflecting the wood's usefulness in a wealth of practical applications, ranging from maypoles and brushes to arrows and spoons.

The birch has always been respected for its protective powers, and many country people once wore sprigs of birch to keep them safe from the EVIL EYE and other misfortune. Boughs of birch were formerly placed over doorways to prevent evil spirits from coming in, and the tree was widely credited with warding off wicked fairies and demons, who disliked its magical properties. Madmen and naughty children were beaten with birch sticks in the belief that the evil spirits within them would thus be driven out, and in many areas at Eastertime young girls were lightly struck with bundles of birch twigs decorated with strips of ribbon and silk in the conviction that this would safeguard them from vermin, flies and back trouble over the coming year.

Putting birch sprigs in dung heaps and other places where witches are supposed to gather will allegedly oblige them to hold their covens elsewhere, while adorning livestock with birch will similarly protect them from baleful influences. Planting a birch tree beside the front door is also a good strategy, for any witch trying to enter must count every leaf on the tree before she can do so – a challenge all but the most determined witches are likely to decline. The tree must not be allowed to touch or overhang the house, however, as this will only bring sickness and bad luck to those within. In some areas the birch tree continues to be treated with healthy respect, and it is recommended that to be on the safe side any person walking beneath one should cross their fingers.

The birch also has many applications in folk medicine, being used in various preparations to heal wounds, treat infertility and cure such complaints as gout.

bird The apparently miraculous power of flight enjoyed by birds has inspired innumerable legends and folkloric beliefs over the centuries. The fact that birds seem literally to inhabit the heavens prompted many early religions to cast their gods in the form of birds of various kinds, and many species have retained particular folkloric significance to this day. Soothsayers in ancient Rome learned to predict the future through their analysis of bird flight and song, while other cultures credited birds with having their own language and links with the supernatural, the birds themselves often being interpreted as the reincarnation of dead souls. Dark-coloured birds that fly around trees without ever seeming to settle are said to be the souls of evil-doers, although another popular tradition (from France) maintains that when unbaptized children die they become birds for a time until accepted into heaven.

The appearance of certain birds (particularly those with black plumage, such as crows and ravens) may be regarded as an omen of death or some other coming misfortune and may be associated with the DEVIL and WITCHCRAFT. Other species, such as the robin and the wren, may be famous for doing acts of kindness on behalf of mortals, leading them out of danger, for instance, or bringing the gift of fire. On occasion they may even acquire the power of speech so as to pass on to humans truths communicated to them by the gods. Birds of prey are typically associated with courage and other martial qualities, hence their association with gods and heroes in numerous legends and folk tales. Less obviously aggressive species such as doves are typically linked with gentler qualities such as mercy, love and peace.

According to time-honoured superstition it is very ominous for a bird of any description to enter the home, as this constitutes a sure sign of the approaching death of someone in the household, as does a bird tapping on the windowpane or coming down the chimney. Many people refuse to allow any bird or its eggs into the home, and it is thought unlucky even to have bird-patterned wallpaper or crockery or other items with pictures of birds on them. Some birds of apparently supernatural origin have attached themselves to particular families or offices in much the same way as the BANSHEE, appearing when a family member or office-holder is dying. A famous example is the pair of white birds that appear when a bishop of Salisbury is dying, supposedly seen as recently as 1911.

See also ALBATROSS; CHICKEN; COCK; CROW; CUCKOO; DIVINATION; DOVE; EAGLE; HEN; KINGFISHER; LAPWING; LARK; MAGPIE; NIGHTINGALE; OWL; PEACOCK; RAVEN; ROBIN; SWALLOW; SWAN; WREN.

birth *See* CHILDBIRTH.

birthday The annual anniversary of a person's birth is celebrated with considerable enthusiasm in many cultures, being considered a rite of passage worthy of formal recognition. This is not a universal approach, however, as some other cultures (such as that of the Australian Aborigines) consider it unlucky to count the passing years and do not keep a record of a person's age. Features of modern birthday celebrations include the giving of cards and presents and the holding of birthday parties at which special cakes decorated with candles are eaten. The occasion is never complete without the singing of 'Happy Birthday to You', a simple celebratory song published by the US organist and composer Mildred J. Hill in 1893 (although it was not until 1935 that it appeared with the present words).

The holding of riotous birthday parties is thought to have had its roots in the belief that by making a lot of noise evil spirits will be frightened away, and so will not interfere with the celebrant at this vulnerable time. Echoing certain New Year traditions, the progress of events on a person's birthday is said by the superstitious to herald the pattern of fortune the person concerned will enjoy over the following 12 months. In particular, celebrants are advised not to cry on their birthday, as this means they will cry every day of the coming year. Lucky days to be born upon include the first day of a month, year, or cycle of the moon.

See also ASTROLOGY; BIRTHSTONE; ZODIAC.

birthmark Folklore offers a number of explanations for birthmarks on the skin of the newborn, usually blaming them on some shock or evil influence to which the mother has been exposed during pregnancy (a theory long since discredited by medical science). In some cultures birthmarks are considered lucky, the mark of God, while in others they are attributed to the influence of the DEVIL. Expectant mothers may be advised to sprinkle themselves with black pepper to ensure their babies are not thus disfigured. It is believed in some quarters that birthmarks will vanish if licked regularly by the mother in the baby's early weeks (a contention that is, extraordinarily enough, backed by science in certain limited circumstances). In the USA, babies born with a 'double' birthmark on the head are expected to travel widely and to divide their lives between two continents.

birthstone The tradition that each month of the year has its own particular precious or semiprecious gemstone (or gemstones) has persevered into modern times, fuelled by the vested interest of jewellers everywhere, while many other folk customs and beliefs have fallen into disuse. A person's birthstone depends on the month of their birth, and possession of the appropriate stone, with its associated qualities, is reputed to ensure the

owner's continuing good luck. Conversely, it is sometimes maintained (although not by jewellers) that it is unlucky to wear stones associated with other months – opal, in particular, will allegedly prove unlucky and even fatal if worn by anyone not born in October.

Authorities differ over the exact allocation of the stones to the months, but the following list represents perhaps the most widely agreed version:

January (garnet, representing truth and constancy);

February (amethyst, representing sincerity and sobriety);

March (bloodstone, representing courage and presence of mind);

April (diamond, representing innocence and light);

May (emerald, representing success in love);

June (agate, representing health and longevity, or pearl, representing purity and tears);

July (carnelian, representing contentment and friendship, or ruby, representing courage and purity);

August (sardonyx, representing marital happiness);

September (sapphire, representing love, or chrysolite, representing happiness);

October (opal, representing hope);

November (topaz, representing fidelity);

December (turquoise, representing prosperity).

Black Annis In English legend, a blue-faced HAG reputed to haunt the Dane Hills of Leicestershire. Described as having a single eye, long fangs and iron claws, this cave-dwelling monster is said to feed voraciously upon human beings, but can be repelled by various charms.

See also CAILLEACH BHEURE.

Black Bess *See* TURPIN, DICK.

black dog Spectral dog of ancient Celtic tradition, reputed to haunt places associated with death throughout the British Isles. Many churchyards and isolated graves claim a black dog (or barguest, as it is called in northern England), and sightings have also been reported at places where murders have been committed. Descriptions vary, some dogs apparently having huge eyes, while others lack heads altogether. Locals speak fearfully of the howling of black dogs, and many claim that the DEVIL himself can manifest in such a form. Sightings of spectral dogs are usually a cause of alarm, and may be interpreted as omens of impending disaster or death. In some parts of southwest England, however, their appearance may be welcomed, as such dogs are believed to come to the aid of lone travellers to keep them on the right track.

See also GYTRASH.

black magic *See* WITCHCRAFT.

blacksmith Because the blacksmith works with the mystical element of FIRE, as well as with the magically potent HORSE and also with IRON, he has always been regarded as a somewhat magical figure himself. Local legends occasionally describe how knights transformed by magic into standing stones stir from their petrified state to lead their horses to the smithy in the dead of night to be shod by the blacksmith, and the blacksmith has often been credited with more knowledge of the supernatural than other people. The blacksmith's anvil is a particular focus of magic, and it was once common for sick children to be taken to the blacksmith so that they might be held over the anvil and thus cured of their ailment. In some areas the patient was laid naked on the anvil, and the blacksmith tapped the child lightly with his hammer three times to effect a cure. Blacksmiths were also respected as 'blood-charmers', capable of staunching a haemorrhage through their special occult knowledge.

Blacksmiths are supposedly reluctant to work on Good Friday, claiming that the DEVIL will claim their soul if they hammer nails on such an inauspicious day. The blacksmiths of Gretna Green, a village just north of the Scottish border with England, are fondly remembered for the tradition that until relatively recent times they were allowed to marry eloping couples over the anvil there (although in fact it was not always the blacksmith himself who oversaw these ceremonies in which eloping couples from England took advantage of the less restrictive marriage laws of Scotland).

See also HORSESHOE.

Bladud Legendary king of Britain who is credited with the foundation of the Temple of Minerva at Bath. He was also reputed to have built himself a pair of wings and to have attempted to fly with these, only to crash to his death after leaping from the Temple of Apollo in Trinovantum. Legend identifies him as the father of LEAR.

Blarney Stone A Stone set in the wall of Blarney Castle near Cork in Ireland that is supposed to endow anyone who kisses it with great powers of eloquence. The legend goes that when a certain Cormac MacCarthy was faced with a difficult lawsuit in 1602 he had a dream in which the fairy queen Cliodna advised him to kiss the first stone he saw in the morning. Having done as she advised he discovered he suddenly enjoyed great eloquence. In order to avoid sharing this gift with everyone else he had the stone set high up in the walls of Blarney Castle, and as a result anyone who wishes to kiss the stone today has to be lowered over the parapet to reach it. An alternative version of the legend suggests the reputation of the stone originated in the eloquence with which Cormac MacCarthy managed to outwit the English official Lord Carew when the latter demanded the surrender of Blarney Castle: each day Carew expected MacCarthy to hand the castle over, but each day MacCarthy's weasel words left Carew still waiting, until ultimately he became a laughing stock throughout Ireland.

Blessed Islands *See* ISLANDS OF THE BLEST.

Blodeuwedd *See* LLEU LLAW GYFFES.

blood Long before scientists began to understand the composition of blood and its properties, the folklore of virtually all cultures had recognized its vital role. A common idea was that blood was the seat of the soul and the essence of life itself. Sorcerers regarded blood as one of the most potent ingredients in spells and used it to obtain control over others, to subdue demons, to draw magic circles, and to drink in certain initiation ceremonies. They also used it in charms to release the victims of possession, and in potions to ward off disease and bad luck.

Important pacts were often sealed with blood as proof of the seriousness of both parties. In many societies individuals also swore loyalty to one another by becoming 'blood brothers', cutting their skin in order to allow their blood to intermingle – a practice today usually associated with Native American peoples. Pacts between witches and Satan were always signed in blood, and it was believed by many that the power of witches actually resided in their blood, which they used to suckle their FAMILIARS. Thus the body of an executed witch had to be completely consumed by fire to prevent her powers being passed on to her familiars. 'Scoring' witches or werewolves 'above the breath' (in other words, ripping open the skin of the forehead, nose and mouth) was reputed to rob them of their supernatural powers. According to medieval authorities, witches might also be restrained by trapping samples of their blood, hair, nail trimmings or urine in a special 'witch bottle'.

The Aztecs were notorious for their extravagant sacrifices of human blood spilled in the hope of attracting divine favour. Masai warriors in East Africa, meanwhile, drink the blood of lions in the conviction that they will thus inherit the animals' courage, just as Norse hunters once drank the blood of bears in order to share their great strength. Hunters around the world share the ancient custom of smearing themselves with the blood of their prey in order to protect themselves from the dead animal's avenging soul, as in the 'blooding' ceremony in which new members of a fox hunt are thus daubed.

The outrage over the shedding of 'innocent' blood, combined with the difficulty entailed in removing dried bloodstains from fabrics and floorboards, has further added to the mythology of blood. Several historic sites boast magically ineradicable bloodstains. In Holyrood Palace in Edinburgh, for example, it is claimed that the blood of David Riccio, Mary, Queen of Scots' Italian secretary, is still visible on the floor where he was stabbed to death. Another example is found in the US state of Maine, where a patch of moss marking the scene of a massacre of Native Americans by white settlers turns blood-red once a year. There are also numerous sites where the grass will not grow after blood has been spilt there in the course of some act of violence perpetrated on the spot (*see* BARREN GROUND). Not unrelated is the notion that the body of a murdered person will bleed if touched or even if approached by the murderer.

Loss of blood was formerly deemed doubly serious, for it implied a loss of 'spirit' as well as a purely physical loss, and it was of paramount importance that the flow be stemmed as quickly as possible. For centuries people have laid great faith in the idea that nosebleeds and other haemorrhages can be staunched by muttering certain verses from the Bible (such as the Lord's Prayer and the sixth verse of the 16th chapter of Ezekiel). Other treatments include tying a key round the sufferer's neck; dressing the wound with ashes, cobwebs or snakeskins; applying a snail and a stone to the wound; and sprinkling on holy water. If all else fails, the patient can be brought to a 'blood-charmer', a person credited with the power of stemming haemorrhages (often the local BLACKSMITH).

An ancient German tradition claims that a drop of blood from the little finger of a man's left hand slipped into a woman's drink will cause her to fall in love with him. Variations on this spell found elsewhere in the world suggest the same result if a girl offers the object of her affections a drink to which she has added a drop of her menstrual blood.

Blood has been credited with a variety of healing powers. In medieval Britain, for instance, it was believed that lepers could be cured by washing them in the blood of children or virgins, or else by placing them under the gallows so that the blood of a hanged man dripped upon them. For their part, English doctors in the 17th century were much taken by the concept of 'sympathetic powder', a mysterious substance that could be applied to a sample of blood taken from the patient; once this was done, the condition of the sufferer would improve through the workings of sympathetic magic. Poor circulation, it was said, could be improved by eating walnut leaves picked before 24 June. The evil Hungarian Countess Elizabeth Báthory (1560–1614), meanwhile, believed that bathing in virgins' blood would preserve her beauty and accordingly was alleged to have immersed herself in the blood of scores of slaughtered servant girls. She was eventually arrested but escaped the death penalty through the influence of her powerful family and was walled up in her own bedchamber, dying in her tiny cell four years later.

See also MENSTRUATION; VAMPIRE.

Bluebeard Murderous blue-bearded tyrant whose evil deeds were related in a famous folk tale recorded by Charles Perrault in 1697 and later included in the collections made by the Brothers Grimm. The story has variant forms in many cultures, which makes attempts to identify the model for Bluebeard as the historical Gilles de Rais (1404–40), a French aristocrat who murdered scores of young children, or Henry VIII relatively futile. He has also been equated with the DEVIL, and with a variety of OGRES, TROLLS and other demons.

Bluebeard is a rich man who marries seven sisters in succession. Each bride dies in mysterious circumstances. Ultimately, Bluebeard's latest bride (the youngest sister) disobeys his instructions not to unlock a certain door in his castle and finds inside this secret room the bodies of her murdered sisters. Bluebeard subsequently discovers that his secret has been found out through the ineradicable bloodstain he finds on the key with which his wife has unlocked the door. He decides to dispose of her in the same way as his previous wives, but she escapes a bloody fate through the timely arrival of her brothers, who put Bluebeard to death. Alternatively, she manages to restore her sisters to life and lures Bluebeard into a trap in which he is similarly killed by the brothers.

The tale is often interpreted on a moralistic level as a warning to wives tempted to disobey their husbands, or more generally as a warning against giving in to curiosity.

Blunderbore English GIANT who ultimately falls victim to the cunning of JACK THE GIANT-KILLER. He is sometimes identified as the giant that Jack strangles after lowering a noose over his head (or heads) as he stands beneath the high tower in which Jack has been imprisoned. Alternatively, he is identified as the giant who tries to kill Jack as he lies sleeping, but who is subsequently deceived into cutting open his own stomach.

Boann In Irish mythology the queen of the TUATHA DE DANANN. She bore ANGUS MAC OG by DAGDA, who seduced her while her husband Elcmar was absent. She came to grief after arrogantly ignoring the taboo against looking into the magical well of Nechtan. After she looked into the well and walked three times around it in an anticlockwise direction the water gushed out of it and snatched one of her eyes, a hand and a thigh. Thus disfigured, Boann tried to hide herself in the sea, but before she could reach it she drowned in the river that is now named after her – the Boyne.

boar The wild boar occupied an important place in the mythology of many ancient cultures, notably those of the Celtic and Norse peoples. Renowned for its ferocity, the boar appears in many tales and legends, often as the formidable quarry of famed warrior-heroes. The most fearsome of these boars include the TWRCH TRWYTH, which pitted itself against King ARTHUR and his knights, and the boar that inflicted a mortal wound upon the Irish hero DIARMUID.

Supernatural boars figured prominently in Norse legend, and boar was the traditional dish eaten by the gods in Valhalla. The ancient Celtic population of the British Isles had several varieties of boar cult. Centuries later a boar's head remained a highlight of the Christmas menu in England (it is still eaten with great ceremony at Queen's College, Oxford, to the accompaniment of the famous 'Boar's Head Carol'). Superstitions surrounding the boar in the British Isles went largely out of currency after the creature (whose tusks were said to glow red-hot during the chase) became extinct throughout the country during the 17th century. Elsewhere in northern Europe, however, folklore still speaks of spectral boars as part of the ghostly WILD HUNT that careers across the winter sky. In Ireland, meanwhile, the wild boar is alleged to be one of the guises favoured by the DEVIL.

See also PIG.

bodach In Scottish folklore, a malevolent spirit that is said to emerge from the chimney to torment naughty children or else to warn of imminent death. The bodach (a term meaning 'old man') is usually depicted as a wizened old man

who lurks in the warmth of the smoke from the domestic hearth. He offers no threat to children that are good, and will not enter the room if the hearth is sprinkled with SALT.

See also BOGEY; CAILLEACH BHEURE.

Bodb In Irish mythology, a warrior-hero who became the king of the TUATHA DE DANANN. Identified as the son of DAGDA, he features in a number of celebrated legends, including one in which he helps to unite ANGUS MAC OG with his dream lover Caer Ibormeith.

bogey A class of HOBGOBLIN with which naughty children throughout the English-speaking world may be threatened. The term itself is not an old one, dating only from the 19th century, although belief in evil mischief-making demons who may punish the disobedient is ancient. In the popular imagination the bogey or bogie (or bogeyman) is an ill-defined figure, usually described as black in colour. He may be credited with the power to change his shape and is believed to lurk in dark, gloomy places, emerging only at night. He is sometimes equated with the DEVIL, occasionally called 'Old Bogey'.

See also BOGGART; BOGLE; BUGBEAR; BUGGANE; PUCK.

boggart In the folklore of northern England, a breed of mischief-making GOBLIN equivalent to the BOGEY. Unlike the bogey, the boggart is usually associated with a particular house or location and, like the BROWNIE or KOBOLD, may lend assistance with domestic chores but turn nasty if offended. If angered the boggart may indulge in acts of petty vandalism and POLTERGEIST activity.

bogle In Scottish folklore a breed of mischievous HOBGOBLIN analogous to the BOGGART or BOGEY. These roguish demons may be accused of all manner of acts of petty mischief, although they are reputed to reserve their most malicious deeds for the punishment of thieves and other miscreants.

bone Like BLOOD and other body parts, bone was once assumed to contain something of the essence of the soul and was thus to be treated with respect. Disturbing interred bones has long been thought to risk serious consequences, as the dead were supposed to be laid to rest with all their body parts so that they might rise entire on the Day of Judgement. Conversely, possession of human and animal bones has always been of considerable importance to the witch and sorcerer, for numerous spells and charms require bone as an ingredient. Bones were formerly much used in DIVINATION: for example, the shoulder-blades of sheep and goats were examined for information about future events, and smaller bones were tossed like dice, the pattern they made giving the answer to various queries. Bones could also be used in the delivering of CURSES (as practised by Australian Aborigines in a curious 'bone-pointing' ceremony). In various parts of the world, great store is placed on the power of musical instruments made of human bone, which are alleged to keep evil influences at bay (*see* SINGING BONE).

British tradition stresses that it is most unwise to throw bones from a meal into the fire, for any person who does so is sure to suffer from toothache, rheumatism or some other related malady. Children should also be dissuaded from falling asleep 'upon bones' – that is, upon the lap – in order to avoid bad luck.

Bone has many uses in folk medicine, being employed in the treatment of a range of physical ailments. Drinking powdered bone with red wine is said to be a certain cure for dysentery, while gout may be treated by applying a paste comprising a mixture of soil and grease scraped from shin bones found in a graveyard. Carrying a knuckle bone about the person is a traditional cure for cramp.

The carefully preserved bones of saints were in former times much revered on account of the many miraculous cures that were supposedly effected by their touch and in medieval times there was a flourishing trade in such relics (many, if not all, of which were clearly counterfeit).

Bonfire Night *See* GUY FAWKES NIGHT.

Book of the Dun Cow Early Irish manuscript in which are collected various legends and histories dating from the 8th and 9th centuries. It was probably written around the year 1100 by monks at Clonmacroise monastery, and is so called because it was allegedly first transcribed on the hide of a dun cow. It includes a version of the TAIN BO CUAILNGE among other celebrated episodes of Celtic myth.

bottle imp A spirit or demon that is confined in a bottle, usually by magic, in punishment for some misdeed. This popular motif features in folk tales from many parts of the world, although today it is most closely connected with the story of ALADDIN, who finds a JINNI thus imprisoned in a lamp, and with Irish folklore, in which it is usually a LEPRECHAUN that is thus restrained. In return for its release the imprisoned spirit typically agrees to grant its rescuer three wishes. Tradition sometimes warns that if a person dies while in possession of such a bottle imp he or she will be doomed to go to hell.

bracken In the folklore of many cultures bracken is an especially potent plant, commonly credited with the power to promote fertility or to ward off evil. Evil spirits dislike bracken, apparently because when a bracken stem is cut the pattern revealed within resembles the Greek letter *chi*, the first letter of Christ's name (recalling a tradition that the infant Christ was laid on bracken in his manger). An alternative English tradition claims that these markings depict the oak in which Charles II hid from his enemies, or else that they spell out the initials belonging to a future partner of the person who severed the stem.

Bracken spores are prized throughout Europe as they are supposed to bestow the gifts of INVISIBILITY and of power over all creatures. Gathering these spores is no easy task, however, for it must be done only in the hour before midnight on Midsummer's Eve and without touching the spores themselves with the hands. To add to the difficulty, demons will act to prevent the spores being successfully gathered, and few tales survive of anyone managing to obtain them.

See also FERN

Bran and Sceolan *See* DOG.

Bran mac Febal

In Irish legend, a warrior hero who travelled to the mythical land of women called TIR NAM BAN. He was informed of the existence of Tir Nam Ban by MANANNAN MAC LIR and received a warm welcome there, being invited to remain as an immortal. After what seemed but a short time he and his men decided to return to Ireland, however, only to discover that many years had passed since their departure and that they had themselves become no more than legend. One of their number, Nechtan, jumped from their ship and swam to the shore, but was instantly turned to dust as the years caught up with him. The rest of Bran's party sailed on, realizing that the same fate would befall them if they ever touched mortal land again.

Bran the Blessed

Legendary Irish hero who also occupies a prominent place in British mythology. According to Welsh legend Bran (or Bendigeid Vran) was a GIANT, born the son of LLYR.

The most celebrated episode in his life began when he handed over a life-restoring cauldron to the Irish on the marriage of his sister BRANWEN to the Irish king Matholwch. The gift was by way of compensation for insults delivered by his half-brother EFNISIEN. He subsequently waged war with the Irish to rescue Branwen from captivity, Bran himself wading across the Irish Sea to reach the far shore. Branwen's son Gwern was acclaimed king of Ireland in Matholwch's place, but Efnisien threw Gwern into the fire and fighting was resumed. The Irish made good their losses through the use of Bran's life-restoring cauldron, until Efnisien destroyed it. In the end there were just five pregnant women left on the Irish side and seven survivors of the British force. Bran himself sustained a mortal wound in the heel. At his own request his head was cut off and was preserved, still magically alive, by his followers for 87 years before being buried at the White Tower in London, where it was believed it would defend Britain from foreign invasion.

In many respects the legends of Bran the Blessed would appear to have developed from those associated with Cronos, the father of Zeus in Greek myth. According to later Arthurian myth King ARTHUR had Bran's head dug up, as he himself wished to become Britain's sole guardian. The tradition that Britain will never fall so long as ravens remain at the Tower of London clearly derives from the legend of Bran (whose name actually means 'raven').

Branwen

In Welsh legend, the sister of BRAN THE BLESSED, whose marriage to the Irish king Matholwch led to prolonged hostilities between the British and the Irish. The daughter of LLYR, she bore Matholwch's son Gwern, who was subsequently made king in his father's stead. She was obliged to work in Matholwch's kitchens as a result of the insults he had suffered from Branwen's half-brother EFNISIEN, but managed to get word of her plight to her brother Bran by taming a starling and sending it to Britain. Her son Gwern was acclaimed king but was then thrown into the fire by Efnisien, and in the ensuing renewal of hostilities many warriors on both sides were killed. Branwen herself died of grief and was buried in Anglesey. She is sometimes interpreted as representing the Celtic concept of SOVEREIGNTY.

Brendan (or **Brandon**) **the Navigator, St** Semi-historical Irish patron saint of seafarers, whose life became a favourite subject of Celtic legend. The historical Brendan was born at Tralee around 484 and is reputed to have founded the abbey of Clonfert among many other important religious houses. By the time of his death around 577 he is said to have presided over at least 3000 monks throughout Ireland.

According to the romance called *The Voyage of Brandon*, written in the 10th or 11th century, Brendan embarked on an epic seven-year voyage in a small skin-covered boat to seek out an earthly paradise located somewhere in the west (*see* ISLANDS OF THE BLEST). Legendary incidents that are supposed to have taken place during the journey included an attempted landfall on what turned out to be the back of a huge whale. On another occasion shoals of fish are said to have gathered around the boat to hear St Brendan saying mass.

The lands Brendan reached have been variously identified as the Hebrides, Iceland, the Canary Islands or even America. In many respects the legends attached to St Brendan's name resemble those associated with MAELDUINE. Various significant landmarks in Ireland still bear Brendan's name and he became the focus of a significant cult following throughout the Celtic world in the early medieval period.

Brer Rabbit *See* UNCLE REMUS.

Bres mac Elatha In Irish mythology, the son of the goddess ERIU and the mortal youth ELATHA, one of the FOMORIANS. He was made king on condition that he would surrender his sovereignty if he ever committed any wrong. He proved a harsh ruler who heaped insults upon his mother's people, the TUATHA DE DANANN, making them work for him in exchange for food. The Tuatha rose up in rebellion and Bran joined the Fomorians at the second battle of MAG TUIRED. During the battle, he engaged in magical combat with LUGH, and on losing was forced to drink 300 buckets of sour milk, upon which he died. A variant account states that his life was spared on condition that he advised the Tuatha in agriculture.

Bricriu's Feast One of the most celebrated episodes in the ULSTER CYCLE of stories relating the adventures of the warriors at the court of King CONCHOBAR. Surnamed Nemthenga or Poison-Tongue, Bricriu was a notorious mischief-maker, and while hosting a feast for Conchobar's court whipped up dissension between CUCHULAINN, Conall and Loegaire by assigning to each the 'hero's feast' (the champion's portion) usually reserved for the best warrior. The argument was eventually settled by the giant Cu Roi Mac Daire challenging the rivals to play a BEHEADING GAME. Only Cuchulainn was prepared to participate, and thus won recognition as the first among them.

Brigid *See* BRIGIT.

Brigit In Irish mythology, a daughter of DAGDA, identified as the patroness of poets, healers and smiths. She became the wife of BRES MAC ELATHA and bore his son RUADAN. When Ruadan was killed by Goibniu, smith to the TUATHA DE DANAAN, Brigit sang for him the first 'keening' heard in Ireland. In Scottish legend, she was identified as Brigid and was closely associated with spring, her arrival each year signalling the end of the winter reign of the CAILLEACH BHEURE.

In Christian folklore she became synonymous with the 5th-century St Brigid or St Bride of Kildare, founder of the first Christian nunnery in Ireland. Known as 'Mary of the Gael' and supposedly midwife to the Virgin Mary, she has long since been regarded as the second patron saint of Ireland (the first being St Patrick). Another legend tells how she cavorted about wearing a crown of candles in order to distract the attention of Herod's soldiers from discovering the infant Jesus.

Britannia Personification of Britain, representing the concept of SOVEREIGN-TY. Commonly depicted as a warrior woman equipped with helmet, shield and trident, she was identified as the patron goddess of Britain by the Romans and made her first appearance upon the country's coinage in the 2nd century AD. In terms of her appearance and weaponry she would appear to have been influenced by the Roman goddess Minerva.

brownie In Scottish folklore, a mischievous household spirit. Brownies are usually described as dwarf-like creatures dressed entirely in brown. They are reputed to help with the domestic chores in exchange for a bowl of milk, but are easily offended and will vacate the premises if offered any other kind of reward.

Brunhild *See* BRYNHILD.

Brut Legendary king of Britain, from whom the ancient Britons claimed descent. Called Brutus by the Romans, he was identified as the great-grandson of the Trojan Aeneas. He fled his native Rome for Greece after accidentally killing his own father and became a leader of the Trojans in their captivity following the fall of Troy. On the instructions of the goddess Diana he sailed to Britain to found a new Troy, establishing the city of Trinovantum on the banks of the Thames. He is reputed to have made landfall at Totnes in Devon, where his footprint may still be seen in a stone set into the town's main street. Having arrived safely in Britain he is said to have managed to defeat the race of giants who previously inhabited the country, making GOG AND MAGOG his slaves.

Brynhild (or Brunhild) Legendary heroine of Germanic and Norse folklore, sometimes identified as the leader of the VALKYRIES. According to various sagas, notably the NIBELUNGENLIED (later reworked by Richard Wagner in his celebrated Ring Cycle), Brynhild was punished by ODIN for rebelling against his rule and was sent into an enchanted sleep within an impassable circle of fire. She was eventually rescued by SIGURD (Siegfried in the *Nibelungenlied*), who claimed her for himself and presented her with a magic ring. Sigurd, however, forgot his love for Brynhild after drinking a magic potion and married GUDRUN instead. He subsequently covertly took the place of Gudrun's brother Gunnar to win for him Brynhild's hand by virtue of his great courage, in the process retrieving the magic ring. Brynhild duly married Gunnar, but was furious when she discovered how she had been deceived and in her anger brought about Sigurd's death. Unable to face life without Sigurd, however, she committed suicide and was laid alongside him on his funeral pyre.

bucca In Cornish folklore, a breed of HOBGOBLIN associated with seafaring and mining. Sailors formerly believed in the bucca's power to foretell shipwrecks, while miners claimed to have heard the tapping of the bucca in their tin mines. It was thought wise to appease the bucca with small gifts of food and ale, as (like many other equivalent sprites and demons) he could be easily offended.

bugbear In English folklore, a variety of HOBGOBLIN that was reputed to take the form of a bear. Like the BOGEY, the BOGGART, and other similar entities, it was often used in former times as a threat to naughty children.

buggane In the folklore of the Isle of Man, a malevolent breed of GOBLIN. Traditionally portrayed with huge heads and with long fangs and nails, they are credited with the ability to change their shape and to spend their time looking for opportunities to undo the work of human beings. They are often believed to reside in the vicinity of waterfalls and other bodies of water.

bull The great strength and virility of the bull made it a potent symbol in early folklore. Savage bulls feature in a number of ancient legends, and the beast was widely understood to exemplify the qualities of kingship and strength in battle. Many societies revered sacred bulls and had their own bull cults, which placed great importance upon the sacrifice of bulls. In later times witches sometimes claimed in their confessions that the DEVIL often appeared at their covens in the form of a bull.

Custom dictates that because of their divine nature bulls are immune from being struck by lightning (a bull-pen is thus deemed an excellent place to shelter during a thunderstorm). A bull's heart stuck with thorns or pins and kept in the fireplace, meanwhile, will ward off witches. Because the bull was famed for its virility, dishes of bulls' testicles were once considered among the most powerful of all aphrodisiac recipes.

See also COW; TAIN BO CUAILNGE.

bunyip In Australian Aboriginal folklore, a swamp-dwelling monster reputed to feed on the flesh of humans. This large and cumbersome creature, possibly inspired originally by sightings of seals, is supposedly able to cross both water and dry land to reach its prey, and today is still used as a threat to naughty children.

burial customs The business of interring the remains of the dead has always been taken very seriously, and the folklore of every culture is heavy with taboos and rituals that must be observed if the souls of the deceased are to prosper and the living are to be untroubled by their GHOSTS.

One of the most widespread traditional beliefs is that the body should be buried in as complete a state as possible. If a limb is missing, for instance, the deceased risks spending the whole of eternity without it, and in the past people often preserved lost teeth and so forth so that they might be buried in the grave with the rest of the body when they finally died. As a result of this belief cremation was considered undesirable in many parts of Europe until relatively recent times. In northern England, the dead person might be buried with his or her own Bible, hymn book and Sunday school class ticket. Elsewhere treasured personal belongings were often buried with the dead. Some people in the Christian world still balk, however, at the idea of a wife being buried with her wedding ring or with other pieces of jewellery on the grounds that such demonstrations of vanity will cause offence in Paradise.

When it comes to the actual interment yet more taboos and superstitions apply. In Christian Europe sites towards the eastern and southern boundaries of a graveyard are generally agreed to be the most desirable, the northern quarter (colder and less open to the sun) being reserved in former times for paupers and criminals. In former times suicides were commonly denied burial in hallowed ground and were usually interred at crossroads and other inauspicious sites. In the past, the opening of a new graveyard sometimes posed a significant challenge, for no one would volunteer one of their deceased relatives for the 'honour' of being the first to be interred, despite the free choice of location. The reason for this reluctance was the widespread belief that the DEVIL always claims the soul of the first corpse. The difficulty was usually overcome by burying an animal of some kind first. In France, the last person to be buried in the year becomes a symbol of death, and their image will be seen by those fated to die the following year.

Most curious of all is the ancient British practice of symbolic burial, which involves the faked burial of a living person (usually a sick child) in the belief that this will fool the evil spirits causing the malady and promote the patient's recovery. In Ireland, the custom is particularly linked with children born at Whitsun, who are otherwise fated to kill or be killed. Similarly, 'dipping' someone repeatedly into an open grave is said to be effective in the treatment of fever, whooping cough and rheumatism, among other ailments.

See also CHURCHYARD WATCHER; DEATH; FUNERAL RITES.

Burns Night Annual celebration enjoyed in Scottish communities throughout the world on 25 January, which is the birthday of the Scottish poet Robert Burns (1759–96). Traditional highlights of the occasion include a Burns Supper, which features the parading and eating of a haggis, as well as speeches, songs, recitations, and dancing. The haggis is often brought in to the accompaniment of bagpipe music, and then Burns' 'Address to a Haggis' is recited over it. Toasts are also drunk to the memory of the poet, to 'the lasses' and (often, but not always) to the Queen.

bwbachod In Welsh folklore, a breed of household spirit roughly equivalent to the BROWNIE. The bwbachod (or bwca) will lend assistance with domestic chores unless offended, in which case it will play practical jokes and generally make a nuisance of itself. It will become particularly incensed if in the vicinity of teetotallers or dissenting ministers of religion.

bwca *See* BWBACHOD.

byliny *See* BALLAD.

C

cabbalism Ancient philosophical system, originally of Jewish origin, which has exerted some influence on European folklore over the centuries. This body of secret lore, allegedly first revealed by God to Abraham, suggests that human existence is but the lowest of ten planes of being through which the spirit may progress, guided by an understanding of this highly complex and often mystifying system, which is passed down from one generation of wise men to the next.

Combining astrology with sophisticated concepts about the principles of unity and divinity, cabbalism offers practitioners a route to greater understanding of the mysterious workings of the universe and encompasses many magical processes, including the working of CHARMS, the science of ALCHEMY and communication with the dead.

Central to the rites of cabbalism are the use of various magical numbers and names. Certain names are alleged to have magical power in themselves, and these continue to be incorporated into the elaborate rituals of modern occultists. Examples of these include Hokhmah and Reshith (male gods of wisdom), Hesed (god of love and mercy), Netsah (god of endurance), Binah (goddess of understanding and intelligence), Din or Geburah (goddess of power), Hod (goddess of majesty) and Tifereth (goddess of beauty).

Cader Idris *See* IDRIS.

Caer *See* ANGUS MAC OG.

Cailleach Bheure In Scottish mythology, a blue-faced HAG associated with winter. According to ancient tradition, she reappeared each year at the festival of SAMHAIN, bringing with her the cold weather of the winter months. Her reign ended at the festival of BELTANE, when she was replaced by BRIGIT, who ushered in the spring. On this date the Cailleach Bheure was said to lay down her staff under a holly bush and to turn to stone. Her son was the god of youth, whom she pursued without rest.

The Cailleach Bheure is sometimes identified as the LOATHLY LADY of Celtic and Arthurian myth, and as the lover of several of the knights of the ROUND TABLE, although she tended to lose some of the more fearsome aspects of her character in later legend. She is also reputed to be a guardian of deer, wolves, and other wild creatures and is sometimes depicted as a corn spirit.

In Irish folklore she is known as the Cailleach Bheare, a mountain goddess reputed to live in southwest Ireland who enjoyed perpetual youth and thus outlived her many successive husbands. In Manx folklore she is called the caillagh ny groamagh. Various remarkable land formations around the British Isles are attributed to the Cailleach Bheure in her various guises, among them the islands of the Scottish Hebrides, which are said to have fallen into the sea when the strings of her apron broke.

Caledfwlch *See* EXCALIBUR.

Caliburn *See* EXCALIBUR.

calumet The 'pipe of peace' of Native American tradition. Named the calumet by French Canadians, from the Norman French *chalumeau* ('reed' or 'musical pipe'), the pipe of peace was smoked in company as a symbol of trust and friendship, the pipe being passed among all those present. By inhaling smoke from the pipe the celebrants were believed to be brought closer to the Great Spirit in the sky (to which the smoke then went). Promises made by celebrants when the pipe of peace was smoked were held to be doubly binding.

The smoking of the calumet had important social significance to many Native American peoples, and the occasion was often celebrated with great solemnity and ritual dancing. The pipe itself was adorned with all manner of decoration, often including feathers taken from the sacred eagle. The pipe itself was usually made from ash wood, the bowl often being constructed from the soft red stone called catlinite, from Dakota.

Camber In British legend, the second son of BRUT. He was entrusted with the rule of Wales, which was formerly known in medieval Latin as Cambria in his honour.

camel The camel features in numerous folk tales from North Africa and the Middle East, and is usually depicted as dim-witted, bad-tempered, clumsy and stubborn. It is often made fun of by other animals, although it was admired in the lore of various Christian cultures because of its reputation for sexual abstinence. In Islamic tradition, the favourite camel of the prophet Muhammad was called Al Kaswa, and this beast is still revered for its swiftness, having carried Muhammad all the way from Jerusalem to Mecca in just four strides and having thus earned its place in heaven.

Camelot In Arthurian legend, the court of King ARTHUR and the ROUND TABLE. Allegedly constructed by MERLIN in the space of one night, Camelot has been variously located at sites in southwest England, of which the most favoured include the hillfort of Cadbury in Somerset. Among other possible sites are Winchester (where an ancient copy of the Round Table is still on display today), Caerleon in south Wales and Camelford, near Tintagel in Cornwall.

Camlan In Arthurian legend, the last battle of King ARTHUR and the knights of the ROUND TABLE. In the course of the fighting against Arthur's nephew MORDRED most of the knights were killed. Arthur himself was mortally wounded by Mordred, who was also killed. The site of the battle has sometimes been located at Camelford, near Tintagel in Cornwall.

candle The widespread use of candles in occult and religious observance around the globe is a reminder of the great reverence with which FIRE of all kinds was regarded in many ancient religions. The pagan belief that fire could ward off evil was readily absorbed into Christian mythology, and many surviving folk beliefs relating to candles in the English-speaking world emphasize their protective power. In many cultures even today candles are lit as a matter of course when someone marries, when the corpses of the newly deceased are laid out, or (chiefly in Catholic countries) when prayers are said. It is widely believed that if a candle burns with a blue flame it reveals the presence of a ghost or other supernatural spirit in the vicinity, or otherwise warns of imminent calamity. A candle that gutters and creates a trail or 'winding sheet' of melted wax provides a similar warning. A sparking wick, on the other hand, foretells the arrival of a stranger or the delivery of a letter.

The tradition that it is unlucky to burn three candles together is probably descended from the ancient tradition that only a clergyman should be allowed to light three candles at the altar. It is also considered unlucky to light more than two candles with a single taper. Another tradition insists that candles should never be left burning in an empty room – unless it is Christmas Eve, in which case a large candle may be left to burn all through the night to ensure the prosperity of the household over the following 12 months (a relic of an old story in which candle-light led the infant Jesus through the darkness). In Wales it is said that an altar candle that goes out during the course of a church service is a sure omen of the imminent death of a clergyman.

Best known of all is the practice, derived originally from ancient Greek custom, of lighting candles on a birthday cake, usually one for each year so far lived. By blowing out every candle with a single breath the person celebrating his or her birthday is allowed to make a wish, which will come true as long as it is not divulged to anyone else.

Witches were formerly widely suspected of using candles in their spells, employing them to exert magical influence over their victims. The usual procedure was to identify a candle as a particular person, often by incorporating a sample of their blood or hair in the wax, and then to stick the candle with pins and set light to it, thus causing the victim excruciating agony and even death. In love magic, it was said that if a girl walked backwards downstairs while holding a candle and then turned suddenly on reaching the bottom she would come face to face with her future lover.

See also HAND OF GLORY.

Candlemas Christian festival celebrated on 2 February in honour of the Virgin Mary. Marking the anniversary of Christ's first visit to the Temple with his mother, Candlemas is celebrated in many Catholic countries with candlelit processions and special services. It also has wider folkloric significance, suggesting links with earlier pagan spring festivals when torchlit processions to the fields were staged to ensure the health of the coming crop. Witches considered Candlemas to be one of the four important dates upon which to hold their sabbaths. Even today in many countries candles blessed during the Christian festival are kept as protection against witchcraft, as well as against illness and thunderstorms.

Particular attention is paid to the state of the weather at Candlemas in different countries. In several regions of the British Isles, good weather at Candlemas may be interpreted as a warning of severe weather at a later date.

See also GROUNDHOG DAY; HEDGEHOG.

caoineag *See* BANSHEE.

cap of invisibility *See* INVISIBILITY.

cargo cult Belief system recorded among island populations of the Pacific Ocean. Associated primarily with the islands of Melanesia, cargo cults seem to have been inspired initially by the arrival of ships and aeroplanes whose cargoes were a source of wonder to the indigenous populations. Some island peoples developed the theory that by making various ritual preparations they might hasten the arrival of these vessels and the redemptive magic they represented. Thus, even in recent years isolated peoples have been reported building imitation airstrips and jetties in the hope of enticing a magical aeroplane or ship to their island. These rites may also include sexual abstinence and the construction of model vessels, invoking the influence of sympathetic magic.

carnival Riotous street celebration of a type still celebrated in many parts of the world. The roots of the modern carnival lie in medieval celebrations marking the return of spring, which themselves evoked the fertility rituals of much earlier pagan tradition. The exuberance of the typical carnival suggests the resurgence of life associated with the new season, while the great noise and colour of these events reflects the belief that this will frighten away any evil spirits and demons left over from the winter. The theme of fertility is embodied today in the parading of near-naked women, while the presence of fire eaters is a relic of ancient fire festivals connected with the purification of the earth and livestock.

Carnival traditions today include a wide range of festivities, from processions of performers dressed in fantastic costumes to lively dancing and the performance of folk dramas. Many carnivals take place in the period preceding Lent, marking a last outburst of exuberant excess before the traditional 40 days' fasting and abstinence. The most famous carnivals around the world include the Mardi Gras festival for which New Orleans is justly renowned, the carnivals of Rio de Janeiro and other Brazilian cities, the Venice carnival in which participants often wear fabulous masks and London's Notting Hill Carnival.

Caswallan In Welsh legend, a British king whose reign is described in the MABINOGION. Otherwise known as Cassivelaunus, Belgic king of the Catuvellauni, he was originally an historical figure who led British resistance to the Romans in 54 BC. In later legend he is said to have conquered Britain with the aid of a cloak of invisibility while BRAN was absent from the country.

cat The cat occupies an important place in folklore in many parts of the world, appearing in numerous tales and in the mythology of many cultures. To many early peoples, including the ancient Egyptians (who venerated the cat goddess Bastet), the cat had divine status and it was the greatest folly to kill one (a crime punishable by death in Egypt). Whole households went into official mourning if a cat died, and the corpse would be buried with much ceremony (thousands of mummified cats have been found over the years). Many aspects of these ancient beliefs have survived through succeeding centuries into modern times: it was from ancient Egyptian mythology, in fact, that the modern belief that a cat has nine lives was derived (apparently inspired by the creature's fabled ability to survive falls that would kill other animals).

Among the mythical cats of early European legend was a giant wildcat that terrorized mythical Britain until eventually overcome by King ARTHUR, with the help of Sir KAY. The cat was also revered as a totem of various Gaelic tribes, and Caithness in Scotland was apparently named after the Catti ('cat-people') clan. Scottish legend, meanwhile, bequeathed to posterity the cruel practice of the taghgairm, a method of DIVINATION that involved roasting a live cat over a fire until other cats appeared to rescue it by answering any questions that might then be put to them.

In later centuries the cat became closely identified throughout Europe and colonial North America with witchcraft, and even today no depiction of a witch is complete without her black cat. Such cats were, it was alleged, fed on the blood of their mistresses and carried out evil deeds on their behalf. Because of these ominous links it was once widely believed that kittens born in May, a month particularly associated with the dead and with the practice of witchcraft, should be drowned at once. Other people would show reluctance to discuss family matters if a cat was present, just in case it was really a witch's FAMILIAR or even a witch in disguise. In eastern Europe, cats were sometimes marked with a cross to prevent them turning into witches, while in France cats suspected of being witches might be caged and burned alive.

Most significant of all is a cat that is entirely black in colour, which is widely understood to bring luck when crossing someone's path. In some parts of the USA, Spain and Belgium, however, black cats are greatly feared and white and grey cats are preferred. White cats, by way of contrast, are widely distrusted throughout

Europe, while stray tortoiseshell cats are most unwelcome in the home for fear that they bring bad luck with them. Cats should never be bought with money, incidentally, for doing so means they will never be good mouse catchers.

Much may be learned from the way a cat behaves, according to superstition. A sneezing cat promises rain, while a cat that sits with its back to the fire knows that a storm or cold weather is on the way. A cat that scratches a table leg warns of an imminent change in the weather. Cats wash themselves or frolic with abandon when wet weather is in the offing, but if they choose the doorway for their ablutions this is taken as a sure sign in some parts of the USA that a clergyman is about to arrive.

Cats bestow good luck on newlyweds if they appear next to the bride, but in parts of Europe must be caught and killed if they jump over a coffin, as this is thought to put in peril the soul of the deceased. In other circumstances killing a cat is ill-advised, however, as the DEVIL may then have the right to claim the soul of the guilty party. Many people even today have reservations about allowing a cat to sleep with their children on the grounds that it may sleep on their faces and cause them to suffocate – an anxiety that in former times led to the belief that cats will maliciously 'suck' the breath of sleeping infants and kill them.

Miners avoid saying the word 'cat' while underground for fear that this will cause disaster, and in the past were known to refuse to enter a mine if a cat had been seen below. Seafarers, though, like to take a luck-giving black cat on their voyages and generally avoid showing it any cruelty, as this may lead to a severe storm being whipped up.

See also DICK WHITTINGTON; KING O' THE CATS; PUSS IN BOOTS.

caterpillar The cultures of several nations allow a small niche for the caterpillar. Central European tradition claims that the creature is a creation of witches or the DEVIL, while in parts of Africa the dead are reputed to be reborn as caterpillars. In some parts of England, tossing a furry caterpillar over the left shoulder is said to bring good luck, although handling such a caterpillar can in reality produce a very nasty skin rash. It was formerly believed that wearing a caterpillar in a bag about the neck until the creature died was effective as a cure for whooping cough or fever. Folk medicine also claims that chewing a caterpillar alleviates toothache, and further recommends the use of caterpillars in a salve to treat snakebite. Caterpillars themselves will allegedly die if approached by women who are menstruating.

cauff riddling An old Yorkshire folk custom, in which some chaff is scattered in a barn at midnight on New Year's Eve or on some other 'magical' date of the year for the purposes of divination. If nothing is seen, then all will go well in the coming year, but if a spectral coffin with two bearers is seen the person concerned is fated to die in the next 12 months.

caul The amniotic membrane that sometimes covers a newly-delivered baby's head. Cauls have great significance in folklore and have a special place in SAILORS' LORE. It is generally believed that anyone thus born or in ownership of a preserved caul will enjoy good luck, become an eloquent speaker and, most important of all, be protected from death by drowning. Such was the intensity of belief in this idea that cauls were regularly advertised in the press in the 18th and 19th centuries and have often changed hands for quite considerable sums of money even in relatively modern times. In the Netherlands and elsewhere people born with cauls are said to have special psychic powers and to enjoy the gift of second sight. The caul must be carefully looked after or the health of the person to which it belongs will suffer. It is maintained by some that a caul should be buried with its owner when he or she dies, or the ghost of the deceased will walk abroad in search of it.

cauldron The cauldron had special significance in early legend and pagan religion, and is also one of the indispensable objects associated with WITCHCRAFT and other magic making. In many cultures the cauldron represents the renewal of life, a notion presumably derived from the primary importance of cooking pots in everyday life.

The Norse and the Celts in particular gave the cauldron a special place in their mythology, with legends of magic cauldrons variously dispensing life, death, inspiration and wisdom. In Celtic mythology, DAGDA possessed a famous cauldron, which provided an inexhaustible supply of food, while BRAN THE BLESSED had a cauldron that could magically restore the dying to life.

A number of sacred cauldrons bearing religious symbols were given sacred burial in bogs and lakes around Europe. Cauldrons also feature prominently in the folklore of various African, Asian and Native American peoples.

See also HALLOWS.

ceasg In Scottish folklore, a species of MERMAID that will grant three wishes if captured. Combining the upper body of a woman with the tail of a salmon, a ceasg can be persuaded to perform various favours for mortals, even to the extent of taking a human husband, but is also said to lure young men into the sea, from which they never return. She is reputed to keep her soul hidden in some object or natural landscape feature.

See also SELKIE.

Ceridwen In Welsh mythology, a sorceress sometimes identified as the goddess of inspiration. Having given birth to Tegid Foel's beautiful daughter Creirwy and his ugly son Afagddu, she decided to compensate the latter for his unattractive looks by brewing for him a magic potion bestowing great knowledge.

Unfortunately, after a year's preparation, a young boy called Gwion Bach, who had been set to the task of stirring the potion, tasted the brew after it splashed onto his finger and thus benefited from the knowledge that Afagddu should have enjoyed. Ceridwen in her fury pursued the lad in many guises and eventually gobbled him up after he took the form of a grain of wheat and she turned into a hen. She subsequently gave birth to him nine months later and, unwilling to kill him, put him in a leather bag and set him adrift on a river (*see* TALIESIN).

Cernunnos In Celtic mythology, the horned god who in subsequent centuries became synonymous with the DEVIL.

Celtic folklore identified Cernunnos as the lord of the beasts and saw him as a personification of the earth's fertility. He was variously depicted with antlers, animal skin and cloven hoofs (evoking the hunt), or as a ram-headed serpent, with a chieftain's torc about his neck. The horns were a sign not only of his virility but also of divine power. Cernunnos apparently came with the Celts to the British Isles around 1000 years before Christ. Evidence of early veneration of him has been found far and wide: when, for instance, the altar at Notre Dame in Paris was repaired towards the end of the 18th century a much older altar was found within it, bearing a carving of this Celtic pagan deity.

Cernunnos had no place in Christian doctrine, however, and in due course he was transformed from a powerful fertility-promoting benefactor to a figure of evil, hence his identification with Satan, who inherited various aspects of his physical appearance, including his cloven hoofs and animal horns.

chalk hill figures Huge figures of men or animals carved on chalk hillsides by the early inhabitants of the British Isles. The age of many of these figures is a subject of some debate, as is what they represented to the people who made them.

The vast white horse carved on White Horse Hill near Uffington in south Oxfordshire is perhaps the most famous of several huge horse figures. It is sometimes explained as commemorating King Alfred's victory over the Danes nearby, but would also appear to evoke pre-Christian horse worship. Alternatively, it marks the site of the famous battle between St GEORGE and the Dragon.

The naked, club-wielding giant at Cerne Abbas in Dorset is almost as famous and may be a representation of Hercules carved by Roman soldiers in the 2nd century AD after Emperor Commodus (who believed he was a reincarnation of Hercules) revived worship of this mythical figure. If not Hercules, the giant may represent the god Helith. According to local legend a real giant was killed on the hill and the people of Cerne Abbas created the figure by tracing the outline of the giant's body in the turf. Alternatively, the figure is sometimes ascribed to monks from the nearby abbey, who cut it as a joke aimed at their abbot. Another more recent theory emphasizes the lack of written evidence for the figure before 1694 and claims that it may have been cut during the English Civil War by servants of Lord Holles who intended it as a lampoon of Oliver Cromwell. Locally the figure is considered a potent fertility symbol and until relatively recently a maypole was set up each year in the earth enclosure known as the 'Frying Pan' a little further up the hill, above the giant's left arm, for villagers to celebrate their May Day festivities.

This and the Long Man of Wilmington near Lewes are notable for their huge phalluses, and reports continue to be made of couples furtively making love within these figures in the belief that this will promote their fertility. Several such figures may mark Iron Age burial mounds.

Some figures are of relatively recent creation but others are clearly very ancient and feature in local legends of great antiquity. The periodic cleaning of the figures was formerly the occasion for much local rejoicing and the playing of folk games.

changeling The offspring of a FAIRY or some other supernatural entity that is secretly put in the place of a human child to be brought up by the unsuspecting parents. The idea that fairies and other malevolent spirits might steal human babies and replace them with their own young – who are typically described as deformed, sickly or evil in character – is very ancient and speaks to the darkest fears of new parents. Babies were deemed to be particularly vulnerable to such interference when not yet baptized, and the folklore of many cultures recommended a wide range of charms and amulets that might prevent their replacement with a changeling. Another tradition had it that if the worst happened and a changeling was introduced then the parents had to make the new baby laugh in order to break the spell, or else to abuse the changeling so cruelly that the fairies would rush back to retrieve their offspring. In former times any baby that was born with a deformity or abnormality, or which failed to prosper physically, might be explained away as a changeling.

chansons de geste A genre of medieval French epic poetry that flourished between the 11th and 15th centuries. Celebrating the *gestes* ('deeds') of legendary heroes, the most famous *chansons* ('songs') include the *Chanson de Roland*, one of the earliest of many such works depicting the adventures of knights at the court of CHARLEMAGNE. The stories recounted in the poems are generally set in the 8th and 9th centuries, and may well have been taken from oral tradition.

charivari French term for the widespread folk practice of signalling the disapproval of the community for some social or moral offence by hounding the culprits with rowdy demonstrations. Variously known in the British Isles as 'riding the stang', 'low-belling' or 'rough music', the custom is thought to have ancient roots and is common to many cultures.

Such action was usually directed against couples who had broken some sexual taboo, typically by setting up home without getting married or otherwise being involved in an adulterous relationship. Such behaviour, it was feared, would result in the whole community suffering through the failure of crops or disease among livestock, and it was thus considered important to make it clear to God or the spirits that the rest of the neighbourhood did not accept responsibility for the offence. The procedure usually involved a mob of locals banging pots and pans and generally making as much noise as possible in the vicinity of the culprits' house in the hope of driving away any evil demons (and perhaps the perpetrators themselves). Occasionally, effigies of the guilty parties were drawn through the streets in donkey carts or publicly burned. In France the practice became so uncontrolled that the church actually banned such victimization, although it never quite died out there and indeed was taken by French settlers to French Canada and Louisiana among other places.

The victims of such demonstrations rarely regained their reputations in the community, and in most cases were obliged to leave the neighbourhood before any more serious action was taken against them. Reports of such demonstrations continued in the British Isles as late as the end of the 19th century. The modern tradition of playing practical jokes on husbands-to-be (and in some places, brides-to-be) on their stag night may have evolved from this older custom.

Charlemagne The first Holy Roman emperor, whose reign inspired many legends. Born in AD 742, Charlemagne (also known as Charles the Great or Carolus Magnus) was the eldest son of Pepin (III) the Short, and in due course ruled over most of western Europe. He became king of the Franks in 771 and, having helped Pope Leo III quash a rebellion in Rome, was crowned emperor in 800. Revered for his wisdom, he proved a fine administrator, law-maker, educator and protector of the church, bringing Christianity to many neighbouring countries and waging war against the Moors in Spain. He was supposedly eight feet tall and so strong he could bend three horseshoes in his hands. He is said to have been married nine times. He died in 814 and was buried at Aix-la-Chapelle (Aachen), although ancient legend has it that he lies asleep, crowned and armed, in Oldenburg, Hesse, awaiting the day when he will be needed to do battle against the Antichrist. German legend claims that in years of good harvest he crosses the Rhine on a bridge of gold to bless the cornfields and vineyards.

The 12 knights (or paladins) who attended Charlemagne's court were celebrated for their chivalric idealism, and many tales were told of their great courage in battle.

See also CHANSON DE GESTE; OLIVER; ROLAND.

charm A chant, ritual or magical object that is believed to provide protection against some supernatural or other magical threat. Every culture has its lucky charms, often to be worn or carried about the person, as well as forms of words to be spoken in given circumstances – on retiring for the night, when ill or on undertaking some perilous activity, for example. Many charms invoke the names of Christian saints, as in the well-known 'White Paternoster': 'Matthew, Mark, Luke, and John, / Bless the bed that I lie on.' The church in former times took a dim view of such charms, warning that with very few exceptions only prayers in their standard Catholic form were permissible, and that the use of variations might result in the conjuring up of a demon. In pre-Reformation Scotland, indeed, anyone found guilty of employing charms could face death by burning.

At their least exotic, charms extend to the conventional 'Bless you' voiced when someone sneezes. This is supposed to prevent the person who has sneezed falling victim to interference by malevolent forces at a moment when he or she is vulnerable, for the soul might be accidentally expelled from the body in a sneeze, and saying 'Bless you' may assist in its return. Other charms offer protection from toothache, bleeding and other bodily ills, whether of supernatural origin or not.

An alternative to speaking a charm is to write it down and carry it on a string around the neck or inscribed on some form of amulet. In 1882 a charm was found scrawled on a piece of paper hidden in a crevice of a chimney joist in a cottage in Madeley, Shropshire. It was clearly intended to safeguard the household from all threat of evil, and read thus: 'I charge all witches and ghosts to depart from this house, in the great names of Jehovah, Alpha and Omega.'

See also AMULET; CURSE; HEX; SPELL; TALISMAN.

cheese rolling The English custom of rolling large cheeses down steep slopes as part of the celebrations marking the coming of the spring. Still staged each year on Cooper's Hill, near Brockworth in Gloucestershire, the event involves a mob of runners pursuing a large cheese down a steep slope, the winner being the person who catches up with the cheese before it gets to the bottom. In most cases the cheese outruns everybody and the winner is the first person to get to the foot of the slope.

Such ceremonies, which appear to date back to the 16th century, were originally observed in order to maintain sheep-grazing rights on common land in the surrounding area.

cherry Like many other trees, the cherry has its own special significance in world folklore. In the Far East the cherry represents female sexuality, and elsewhere it is similarly associated with the feminine sex. Growers of cherry trees in Switzerland, for instance, traditionally offer the first fruit of the tree to a woman who has recently given birth, for this will ensure the tree always fruits plentifully. Among the black slaves of the American South it was common for women suffering from excessive bleeding during MENSTRUATION or following childbirth to drink an infusion of cherry bark.

Cherry stones are the subject of a variety of widely observed folk customs. These include the practice of counting out the stones of consumed cherries one by one while chanting 'This year, next year, some time, never' to find out when one will be married. Others include the custom of flicking cherrystones towards the ceiling by squeezing them between the fingers: if the ceiling is reached at the first attempt then the marksman is destined to marry shortly.

chestnut Various beneficial properties are assigned by folklore to the horse chestnut tree, and more specifically to its nuts. Carrying two chestnuts about the person is said on both sides of the Atlantic to relieve the pain of arthritis, backache and rheumatism. If edible chestnuts, the fruit of the Spanish chestnut tree, are eaten boiled with honey and glycerine they are reputed to alleviate asthma. Superstition also recommends leaving an offering of a few chestnuts on the table at HALLOWE'EN as gifts for the dead.

Chichevache *See* BICORN.

childbirth The process of birth has always been recognized as being of prime importance as the first of the various rites of passage that every person goes through, and is consequently the focus of a vast body of folklore around the world. Early societies regarded the whole process as being strongly magical in nature, and even today the presence of expectant mothers may invoke strong reactions in different communities, ranging from reverence for their condition to revulsion and even fear, with the mother-to-be being kept in seclusion and forbidden to touch food or weapons in case she contaminates them.

The significant health risks involved in the process, which was altogether more hazardous in past centuries, means that much of the folklore on the subject addresses itself to the use of magic to protect both mother and baby at this perilous time. In remote parts of Europe people still open all the doors in the house and untie any knots in the mother-to-be's clothing to make delivery easier. Other measures to assist the mother in labour include placing a razor-sharp axe blade edge-up under the bed, spilling a little salt in her palm, placing silver coins taken from a church in her mattress, and bringing an empty hornets' nest into the room. In Kentucky, birthing assistants may tickle the mother's nose with a feather, while elsewhere in the USA she may be offered a drink partly drunk by another woman, or given a potion made from the powdered rattles of rattlesnakes.

Among the many birthing customs that have long since fallen into disuse are driving iron nails into the bed to keep away evil spirits; laying the mother on the bare earth floor (from which she might derive extra strength); hanging charms in the room to ward off witches; and ringing the church bells or, failing this, tying a piece of bell rope round the mother's waist to summon up divine assistance. Hanging a garment of clothing borrowed from a man whose wife is known to be unfaithful to him may also aid the process, according to the Irish. Once the baby is delivered, chicken feathers may be burnt under the bed to stop any bleeding.

Much can be predicted about a baby's future from the circumstances of its birth. A baby born in a wagon, by Caesarean section, or when the mother's head lies in a northerly direction is deemed especially lucky, as is a baby born with an extra finger or toe. If the baby is born in the breech position (feet first), according to one old English superstition, the child –

called a 'footling' – is fated to be lamed in an accident unless its legs are hastily rubbed with bay leaves. However, the child will also benefit from special healing powers – as will a baby whose mother dies in giving birth. If the father is already dead at the time of the baby's birth it may find consolation in the possession of special occult powers.

The timing of the birth is important, according to astrology, as the phase of the moon, the state of the tides, the date, the day of the week and the hour of the day all have an influence on the baby's character. Babies born under a new moon, for instance, are fated to a life of failure (or conversely will grow up very strong). According to the Sicilians a baby's sex is determined by the phase of the moon at the hour of its birth: it will be a girl if the moon is on the wane and a boy if it is waxing. Babies born when tides are on the ebb are allegedly doomed to die at a young age.

Babies born at Christmas or New Year can look forward to a lifetime of good luck. Unluckiest of all are the babies born on CHILDERMAS DAY (28 December) or on 21 March, which, according to US superstition, is a day of particularly bad omen. US superstition also suggests that babies born between 23 June and 23 July will be unlucky, and those born in May will never enjoy good health.

When it comes to the day of the week, a widely known European rhyme offers a summary of what may be expected: 'Monday's child is fair of face; / Tuesday's child is full of grace; / Wednesday's child is full of woe; / Thursday's child has far to go; / Friday's child is loving and giving; / Saturday's child works hard for a living; / But the child born on the Sabbath Day / Is blithe and bonny, good and gay.'

Babies arriving at midnight will be able to see ghosts, while a 'chime child' born at three, six, nine or twelve noon (the hours when church bells chime) may prove unlucky in life, but will be able to see things others cannot see, and will also be safe from witchcraft. Births that take place at sunrise bode well for the future, but babies born at sunset will be lazy in later life.

See also CAUL; CHURCHING; COUVADE.

Childermas Day Holy Innocents' Day, on which Christians remember the slaughter of the infants by Herod, as recounted in the Bible. Commemorated on 28 December, Childermas Day is widely held to be the unluckiest day of the year. Children born at Childermas are supposedly sentenced to ill-fated lives, and no new project should be embarked upon on that date, for it will surely end in failure; neither should new clothes be worn for the first time. Tradition warns that even such mundane domestic chores as washing and trimming fingernails should not be attempted on this day. Perhaps in reference to the origins of the festival, though, children's parties were in former times often held on Childermas Day in parts of northern England.

Childe Roland *See* ROLAND.

Christmas In the Christian calendar, the celebration of Christ's birth, which in its modern form incorporates many features descended from much older pagan winter festivals. In Britain and the American colonies, until 1752 Christmas was celebrated on what is now 6 January ('Old Christmas Day'), but since the change in the calendar that took place in that year it has been fixed at 25 December. The location of Christ's birthday at this time is thought to have reflected the early church's desire to absorb pagan midwinter festivities into its own calendar. Significantly, long before Christ this was the time when ancient Romans celebrated their Saturnalia (in honour of the god Saturn) and subsequently ceremonies venerating the sun god Mithras. The rituals marking the winter solstice, celebrated on 21 December in the Norse calendar, probably also had an impact. It was because of these pagan connections that the Puritans prohibited Christmas celebrations on both sides of the Atlantic during the 17th century. It was not, indeed, until the latter half of the 20th century that residents of Presbyterian Scotland began to celebrate Christmas with anything like the enthusiasm of people south of the Scottish border.

In former times the festivities got into earnest on Christmas Eve, when there was much feasting and jollity and the burning of the YULE LOG took place. Then, as now, homes were decorated with boughs of greenery, including MISTLETOE (a custom which has its roots in Norse mythology). Centrepiece of the Christmas decorations in virtually every home in the English-speaking world today is the Christmas tree, a symbol of Christmas that was imported from longstanding German tradition in the 19th century, although this practice would appear to have its roots ultimately in the tree worship of various pre-Christian societies, to whom evergreens represented fertility and good fortune.

Fairies are supposed to hold masses in Christ's honour at the bottom of mines at the hour of midnight on Christmas Eve, and farm animals are widely believed to kneel in homage at this hour and to be blessed with the power of speech – although it is fatal for a human to overhear what they say. The ghosts of dead ancestors are thought to return to their old homes at this time of year, and in some areas householders will leave food out for them in the hope that they will not be caused any offence. During the night St Nicholas, in his modern guise as FATHER CHRISTMAS or Santa Claus, will fill stockings hung on the chimney breast with presents. The giving of gifts at Christmas does not, as is popularly supposed, derive ultimately from the gifts that the Magi brought the infant Jesus shortly after his birth, but probably from a much older tradition of present-giving associated with the Roman Saturnalia.

The modern fixation on a 'white' Christmas with a generous fall of snow probably derives from an old notion that this signifies fewer deaths in the year to come. Whatever the weather, it is unlucky to attempt any but the most essential work, such as the feeding of animals, on Christmas Day.

Various superstitions surround the traditional Christmas Day menu, particularly the Christmas pudding. During its preparation this must have been stirred – in an east to west or sunrise direction – by every member of the household, even babies, if the luck of the household is to prosper. Those who stir the pudding are allowed to make a wish as they do so. Into the mixture may be placed such charms as a silver coin, which will bestow luck upon the finder, a ring, which will hasten a wedding in the family, and a thimble, for prosperity.

See also HOLLY; IVY; KRISS KRINGLE; NEW YEAR; TWELFTH NIGHT; WASSAILING.

churching In British folklore, the purification of a new mother after CHILD-BIRTH. In former times it was considered very important for a safely delivered mother to make her first trip out of the house after childbirth to the church, to give thanks for her survival and also to be spiritually cleansed. Until she did this, contact with her might be avoided by many people as this was deemed to be unlucky. A new mother, having so recently had such intimate contact with the powerful magic forces associated with birth, was also thought to be vulnerable to interference by evil spirits until she made her first visit to church after her confinement. If she chose to visit a female friend instead of going to church, tradition had it that the latter would bear her own child within the year.

Known in Scotland as 'kirking', the custom has its equivalents in many other cultures across Europe and elsewhere in the world.

churchyard watcher The spirit of the person most recently buried in a church-yard, whose duty (according to ancient British tradition) it is to watch over the other people buried there until the time comes to summon another living person to the grave and thus to be relieved. In former times in some rural areas there could be some controversy when a churchyard was closed, as the relatives of the last person buried there might complain that this meant the deceased was condemned to watch over the churchyard forever. Unseemly brawls would sometimes break out if two funeral parties met in the churchyard at the same time and each tried to ensure that their own friend or relative was not the last to be laid to rest.

The sound of the churchyard watcher's cart making its way down country lanes was much feared in many communities. Variants of the tradition elsewhere in the world include the Ankou figure of Breton folklore who is said to lay an unseen hand on those who are doomed to die or to scythe down anyone who comes within his reach.

churning The process by which milk is churned into butter is one of the mysterious everyday phenomena that much engaged the peasant mind in bygone centuries. Folklore consequently developed many theories to explain why milk sometimes failed to 'turn'. The blame for this might be placed upon the state of the tides (milk would not turn, it was claimed, if the tide was going out), or else to someone in the milking parlour being in love. More often than not, however, the problem was blamed on the malevolent interference of fairies or witches.

Whether witchcraft or some other agency was suspected, it was generally thought that reciting certain magical CHARMS as the churning was in progress would be of help. Other countermeasures included tossing a pinch of salt into the fire before commencing work, dropping a silver coin or three hairs from the tail of a black cat into the milk, and using a churn made of ROWAN wood, which has the power to repel witches. The Irish claimed that dipping the hand of a dead man in the mixture would prove equally effective (*see* DEAD HAND). If witchcraft was the cause, plunging a red-hot poker (or in New England a heated HORSESHOE) into the milk was supposed to give the culprit a nasty burn and so enable the churning to continue without further interference. In many places a horseshoe was nailed permanently to the bottom of the churn to ward off such threats.

It was generally agreed that if any stranger arrived in the parlour during butter-making he or she had to be persuaded to lend a hand in the churning, or the process would not work.

Cid, El Spanish knight whose heroic deeds in battle against the Moors inspired numerous legends. Otherwise known as Rodrigo Díaz de Vivar, El Cid (a title derived from the Arabic *seyyid*, meaning 'lord') was born around 1043 and subsequently fought on behalf of Alfonso VI of Castile and later as a mercenary before taking Valencia in 1093 and becoming its ruler. He died in 1099.

The exploits of El Cid were elaborated in medieval legend, and he became well established as a national hero and defender of Christianity – although as a soldier of fortune he fought for both Christians and Moors at different times. His feats formed the basis for many Spanish romances, chronicles and other literary works, among them the great 12th-century poetic epic *El cantar de mío Cid* ('The Song of the Cid') and Corneille's tragedy *Le Cid* (1636). Like other similar figures he was renowned for his great strength and courage.

Cinderella European fairy tale that also exists in numerous versions in other parts of the world. Some 500 variants of the tale have been identified in Europe alone, and few tales are as universally known. It is probable that the story was first told in the Orient, and the earliest known version is Chinese, tentatively dated to the 9th century AD. In this prototype the heroine,

Yang Ts Tsu, is abused by her stepmother until a mysterious stranger provides her with fine clothes and golden shoes and thus enables her to become the king's wife. The story may also have been influenced by the Greek legend of Rhodope, who loses one of her slippers when it is stolen by an eagle and taken to the king of Memphis, who falls in love with its delicate beauty and determines to seek out the wearer.

The modern version of the tale known throughout the English-speaking world may be traced back to the variant recorded by Charles Perrault in his *Tales of Mother Goose* (1697), with English translations of the story being published as early as 1721. It was probably Perrault who introduced the details of the glass slipper and the FAIRY GODMOTHER. The glass slipper may have been a deliberate elaboration of Perrault's, or may have crept in through a confusion of the French *verre* ('glass') and *vair* ('fur').

The story of Cinderella begins with her banishment to the kitchens on the orders of her wicked stepmother, aided and abetted by the two ugly sisters who have come with her. When an invitation arrives at the house for all eligible young women to attend a royal ball, where they will be introduced to the prince, Cinderella is automatically excluded by the rest of the family. On the night of the ball Cinderella weeps in despair until comforted by her fairy godmother, who promises to reward her for some previous kindness. The fairy godmother uses her magic to turn a pumpkin into a magnificent coach, complete with attendants and horses, and dresses Cinderella in a fine ball gown, with two tiny glass slippers. As she leaves for the ball Cinderella is warned that the magic will cease to work at midnight and that then she will return to her former state.

The prince duly falls in love with Cinderella when he sees her at the ball, but is broken-hearted when she flees from the palace as the clock strikes midnight and her beautiful dress is reduced to the rags she had before. The prince discovers, however, that she has left behind one of her glass slippers, and subsequently sets about finding the girl whose foot it fits. At length he arrives at Cinderella's home and, after rejecting the two ugly sisters, he is reunited with his true love. They marry and live happily ever after. In early versions of the tale the ugly sisters are punished by having their eyes pecked out by birds, or meet some other equally horrific end.

Details of the plot vary considerably from culture to culture. A Turkish version of the tale, for instance, has the heroine cooking an omelette that is then transformed into a magic carpet, which carries her off to the royal ball. In Hindu variants, Cinderella represents the dawn, while her wicked relatives are clouds, and the prince the life-renewing sun. In a Swedish equivalent she receives supernatural assistance not from a fairy godmother but from an ox. Alternative names for the heroine herself in other languages include the French Cendrillon and the Italian la Cenerentola.

Clootie Scottish name for the DEVIL. Otherwise called Auld Clootie, this euphemism refers to the Devil's *cloots* ('cloven hoofs'). In some rural areas Auld Clootie was appeased by leaving a small plot of land unfarmed and reserved for the Devil's own use.

clover Some authorities trace the mystical significance of clover back to biblical legend, identifying it as the plant that Eve stole when she was expelled from Paradise. Its reputation was further enhanced by the story that St Patrick used the three-leafed clover to demonstrate the nature of the Holy Trinity – hence its use as an Irish national symbol. Because of these religious associations the plant has always been considered an effective defence against witchcraft and valued as a charm against other forms of evil. It was also prized for its protective properties by the Druids.

Finding a four-leafed clover has always been thought lucky, and many people believe that a person who finds one will meet his or her future lover that same day. Superstition has it that the four-leafed clover will only grow where a mare has foaled, and that the four leaflets represent fame, wealth, a faithful lover and good health. It is further claimed that anyone who wears a four-leafed clover will be able to see fairies. Wearing a two-leafed clover in the right shoe is a ruse sometimes favoured by young girls: it is said that they will marry the first man they meet, or someone of the same name. Opinion is mixed about five-leafed clovers: they may guarantee great riches, or they may threaten illness unless given away at once.

Herbalists have long recommended potions incorporating clover for the treatment of various skin problems.

clown Ludicrous trickster-entertainer figure who is familiar throughout world folklore. Although the clown of the modern English-speaking world has been reduced to little more than a children's entertainer, he is a relic of a much more important tradition that formerly played a prominent role in the folk customs of many societies. The appearance and character of the modern clown owes much to medieval dramatic convention, notably to the Italian *commedia dell'arte* and English morality plays, but in ancient times the clown was widely considered to be a sacred figure.

Masked clowns were commonly supposed to enjoy direct communication with the spirit world, and in many parts of the world they inspired awe and fear as well as laughter with their frequently grotesque buffoonery. They were sometimes believed to possess a wide range of magic powers relating to all aspects of life, ranging from health and fertility to the state of the weather, and in many cases they were considered to be supernatural figures in much the same mould as sorcerers and witches.

The comic antics of clowns in former times were often obscene in nature, reflecting their ancient association with fertility and sex magic. Thus, it has always been accepted for clowns to indulge in female impersonation and, in past centuries, to wear large phalluses. Their antics were generally supposed to distract the attentions of evil spirits during important ritual celebrations, and clowns often banged drums or shook rattles for the same purpose. They were also allowed special licence in criticizing the ruling classes, a role that was later passed to the fools and jesters of medieval courts.

cluricaun In Irish folklore a breed of mischievous ELF sometimes regarded as synonymous with the LEPRECHAUN. These elves were commonly depicted as evil, wrinkled old men who worked as shoemakers to the fairies. They were supposed to possess knowledge of the whereabouts of hidden treasure, and were often said to lurk in dark wine cellars, sampling the bottles without compunction.

Clym of the Clough In British folklore, a legendary outlaw who is often depicted in company with ADAM BELL and WILLIAM OF CLOUDESLY. Like his companions, Clym of the Clough (pronounced 'cluff' and meaning 'Clement of the Cliff' was famed for his skill with bow and arrow. He was generally said to have lived long before ROBIN HOOD and to have resided in Englewood Forest near Carlisle. His adventures were recounted in the form of a ballad preserved in Percy's *Reliques* (1765).

cock The cock has considerable folkloric significance, bolstered in the Christian world by the biblical story of the cock that crowed three times on Peter's repudiation of Christ. It featured prominently in the folklore of many pre-Christian societies, being variously revered, observed and sacrificed to establish contact with the world of the spirits.

At the root of the cock's reputation in magic is its time-honoured association with the SUN, which rises each dawn to the sound of the cockerel's call. The crowing of the cock is widely believed to repel ghosts and demons of the night, and according to Norse tradition will turn TROLLS still roaming abroad to stone. Christian folklore claims the protective power of the cock's call can be traced back to the cock that crowed at the birth of Christ.

The depiction of cocks on weathervanes reflects the traditional belief that cocks are particularly sensitive to the state of the weather. A cock that crows more lustily than usual or while perched on a gate is widely understood to be giving notice of a change in the weather. If it crows in the early evening, rain can be expected. If it crows during the night, however, it warns of the coming of death, and the crowing of any cock at an inauspicious moment, such as the birth of a child or when someone is about to depart on a journey, is widely considered a very bad omen.

White cocks are regarded as especially lucky and are prized as guardians of the farmyard, but black cocks are traditionally associated with evil spirits in many parts of the world. Cocks that crow on Christmas Eve are commemorating the anniversary of Christ's birth, and both real cocks and the cocks on weathervanes on church towers are destined to crow on the Day of Judgement to awaken the dead.

Cocks feature as a prime ingredient in various spells. Epilepsy may be cured, according to Scottish tradition, by burying a cock beneath the sufferer's bed, while sanity may be restored by burying a cock at the point where two estates meet.

See also ALECTRYOMANCY.

Cockaigne, Land of Legendary land of idleness and luxury that featured in European legends of the medieval period. In the 13th-century Middle English poem *The Land of Cockaygne* it is described as a paradise for gluttons in which the houses are made of barley-sugar cakes, the streets are paved with pastry, and the shops give away their produce for nothing. Equivalents of Cockaigne in other cultures include the German Schlaraffenland. In some tales it is variously identified with the cities of London and Paris.

Cole, Old King Legendary British king who features in a famous English nursery rhyme, in which he is described as 'a merry old soul' who calls for his pipe, his glass, and his fiddlers three. He is usually identified as a 3rd-century king who gave his name to Colchester, although he has also been linked (perhaps fancifully) with the Irish Celtic hero FIONN MAC CUMHAILL. Another ancient theory claims he was the grandfather of the Emperor Constantine.

common riding See RIDING THE MARCHES.

Conchobar In Irish mythology, a famous warrior-hero and king of Ulster. The son of Nessa and the druid Cathbad, and the uncle of CUCHULAINN, Conchobar succeeded FERGUS MAC ROICH as king and presided over his court at Emain Macha near Armagh. He planned to marry DEIRDRE, whom he had brought up, but she eloped with NAOISE and he set off in long pursuit. At length he persuaded the guilty pair to return to Ulster, but broke his promise of immunity from punishment and had Naoise killed, claiming Deirdre as his wife. Legend has it that he suffered divine retribution by seeing all his own sons die before him. His own death is said to have come about when he heard of the crucifixion of Christ. In his rage a sling-shot that had been lodged in his brain as the result of an old injury was dislodged and he died.

Conla In Irish mythology, the son of CUCHULAINN and Aoife. His tragedy furnished a celebrated episode of Irish legend. He was brought up by Aoife alone, but was dispatched to join his father in Ireland as soon as he reached manhood. Unfortunately, Aoife also placed upon him a GEIS that prohibited him from revealing his identity to a lone warrior. She also made him promise never to refuse a challenge and never to give way to anyone. Thus, when Cuchulainn sent one messenger after another to find out who the stranger was he refused to tell them and each in turn challenged Conla to fight, provoked by this apparent snub. To confound matters, the heroic code of the knights of Ulster forbade two warriors meeting a lone stranger. Conla successfully killed one envoy after another until ultimately Cuchulainn himself arrived to fight. Having delivered a mortal blow, Cuchulainn belatedly realized the stranger's identity when he called out his mother's name as he died.

Cophetua Legendary African king whose tale is told in the English ballad 'King Cophetua and the Beggar-Maid'. This famous ballad tells how Cophetua is passionately opposed to women, but changes his mind on falling in love with the beggar-maid Penelophon and eventually marries her. The story was included among Percy's *Reliques* (1765) and was referred to by Shakespeare in his plays *Romeo and Juliet*, *Love's Labour's Lost* and *Richard III*.

coral The tradition that coral is highly effective in warding off evil dates back to Roman times if not earlier. Gifts of coral necklaces are still sometimes offered to infants at their christening to preserve them from harm. Coral is also supposed, when rubbed against the gums, to lessen the pain of teething, and also to prevent nightmares. Red coral in particular is said to deter evil and to protect ships and houses from storms. It is alleged that red coral worn about the person will turn pale if its owner falls ill, regaining its original colour as the patient recovers.

Cormac mac Airt In Irish mythology, a king of TARA who was celebrated for his great wisdom, and who was considered to be the Irish Solomon. Raised by a she-wolf, he restored Tara to its former greatness after becoming king. His daughter GRAINNE became the wife of the great hero FIONN MAC CUMHAILL, leader of the FIANNA. Cormac died after choking on a salmon bone. According to one legend, he converted to Christianity before his death and was buried upright, facing towards the east. He would appear to have been based upon a real historical ruler, who lived in the 3rd century AD.

Legend has it that Cormac was the possessor of a marvellous golden cup, which he received from the sea god Manannan mac Lir. This would shatter if three lies were told over it, but would become whole again if three truths were spoken over it. Cormac used the cup in administering justice, thus establishing his reputation as a wise adjudicator.

Cormoran Fearsome Cornish GIANT who is usually identified as the first victim of JACK THE GIANT-KILLER. He ravaged much of Cornwall until King ARTHUR invited a hero to come forward and kill him. Jack succeeded in the task by luring Cormoran into a deep pit and thus managing to chop off his head, which he then presented to the king as proof of his feat. Arthur rewarded the lad with a magnificent belt inscribed with the words 'This is the valiant Cornish man / That slew the giant Cormoran.'

corn dolly In English folk custom a small figure or other shape traditionally made by plaiting corn from the last sheaf of the year's harvest. In times gone by such corn dollies were carefully preserved through the winter to ensure the success of the next year's harvest.

Corn has been cultivated for some 7,000 years in western Europe (longer in the Near East), and pagan societies revered a host of corn gods and goddesses. These deities were kept symbolically alive in such dollies, which would be carefully preserved until the following summer

(in later times they were customarily hung up in the chimney-piece). The corn dollies commonly sold in craft shops today are usually bought as good-luck emblems, although they are rarely made from the last sheaf of corn as they once were.

See also HARVEST CUSTOMS.

corrigan In the folklore of Celtic Brittany, a breed of female FAIRY that is reputed to delight in causing mischief to Christians. Possibly based upon memories of an obscure druidess, their crimes range from relatively minor offences to stealing human babies and replacing them with CHANGELINGS.

couvade Widely recorded ritual custom connected with CHILDBIRTH, in which the father imitates the symptoms of pregnancy and labour, as though he is giving birth himself. In some societies, as the time of delivery approaches (or alternatively after it has taken place), the father takes to his bed and is treated as if he is the mother. This curious notion derives either from the prejudice that men, allegedly stronger and more intelligent than females, are better able to defend the unborn child's interests, or else from the idea that such actions will confuse any malevolent spirits.

cow The economic importance of cattle through the ages is reflected in the richness of the folklore surrounding them. Some early societies venerated the cow as a sacred animal, as it is still considered in Hindu India. Symbolizing fertility and health, it was widely associated with the MOON, and great care was taken to protect the animals with charms and other ritual procedures. In many cultures cattle were deemed to be protected by particular gods or goddesses, such as the Celtic BRIGIT. Further protection might be sought for the animals by such magical acts as driving them through the ashes of ritual fires, thus warding off the threat of disease and interference from evil spirits.

Hanging necklaces of leaves and plants round the necks of cattle and thrashing the beasts with sprigs of greenery was also supposed to keep the animals fertile.

Cows occupied a central position in the economy of early Britain and Ireland and were once actually used as a unit of currency. Ancient drovers' roads across the countryside can still be traced and are a focus of local legend. Many important dates in the folkloric calendar revolved around cattle. In Celtic ritual, for instance, the festival of BELTANE marked the time when cattle were taken to their summer pastures, while the festival of SAMHAIN involved the slaughter of cattle for the coming winter.

Cows feature in a number of well-known folk tales (such as JACK AND THE BEANSTALK) and in the legends of many cultures. In Norse mythology, for instance, the cosmic cow Audhumla created the first human by licking salt from the earth. The cow was also said to know the direct path to heaven (hence the now neglected tradition of a cow accompanying funeral processions in Germany and Scandinavia). In common with other farmyard animals, cattle are said to kneel in homage to Christ on Christmas Eve and to speak with human voices – although anyone who overhears what they say is doomed to instant death. This tradition recalls the folk belief that cows gathered round the manger in which the infant Jesus lay.

Safeguards that may be taken against interference from witches and other evil spirits include fixing boughs of rowan wood over the door to the cow shed and, in Ireland at least, sprinkling the floor of the stalls with primroses. The luck of each individual animal is believed to reside in the rope that is used to tether it, and cows were customarily sold complete with their tethers. The breath of a cow was once alleged to be most beneficial to the health, and those suffering from consumption were often recommended to sleep in the company of cattle: it is still claimed by some that farm hands never

contract tuberculosis. A little cattle dung may also be used as a poultice for wounds or, in Northumberland in times gone by, to cure headaches.

See also BULL.

coyote In Native American folklore the coyote has particular significance as a trickster hero in numerous folk tales and legends. Like the FOX and the WOLF the coyote is renowned for its great cunning, but is also deceitful, vicious and lustful. In some stories he is identified as the bringer of fire to earth. According to the Crow peoples the coyote was the creator of the earth and all the living creatures upon it. Many tribal groups perform coyote dances when a warrior dies.

crane The crane features prominently in the folkloric tradition of many cultures throughout the world. It is variously considered an emblem of long life (as it is in China), as a messenger from the gods (as in Japan), or as a crafty trickster who is the central character in many folk tales. It is also credited with great patience and magic power. Several characters in ancient Irish legend are transformed into cranes. The HALLOWS of Ireland were reputedly kept safe from the threat of evil in a bag made of crane skin.

cricket The folklore of many cultures identifies the cricket as a lucky creature, whose appearance in the home is especially welcome as an omen of good fortune. It is consequently bad luck to kill a cricket or for one to leave the home. White crickets, however, might excite apprehension in some parts of the world if they appear on the hearth, as they foretell a death in the household. The rasping sound produced when crickets rub their hind legs together is also feared by some people as a warning of death or else of severe weather, although the sound is much to be welcomed if heard on Christmas Eve as this is considered a promise of great good fortune.

crocodile African and Indian folklore places considerable mystic significance upon the crocodile, perhaps reflecting the creature's divine status among the ancient Egyptians, whose deities included the crocodile god Sobek. A symbol of treachery linked with the magic of the EVIL EYE, the crocodile is said to weep when it has eaten all but the head of its human victims, and these 'crocodile tears' turn magically to jewels to lure further human prey. The crocodile may also make pitiful groaning noises to beguile gullible victims. In parts of West Africa the crocodile is said to be the reincarnated form of a murdered man, who will seek out and kill his murderer. Elsewhere the animals are said to house the souls of dead ancestors. The creature inevitably appears in numerous folk tales, sometimes marrying mortal women.

Crocodile blood is prized in folk medicine for the treatment of snakebites and eye problems. Fried crocodile meat is used to dress wounds, while the skin is combined with oil and vinegar as an anaesthetic, and the fat also has powerful medicinal properties.

croquemitaine In French folklore, a species of HOBGOBLIN or sprite traditionally used as a threat by parents and nurses against unruly children.

See also BUGBEAR.

cross Central to Christian iconography, the cross has considerable significance in the folklore of the Christian world, being credited both with the power to ward off evil and with various healing properties. It does, however, also have magical potency in non-Christian cultures, appearing in such forms as the ankh of ancient Egypt, the swastika of eastern folklore, and the runic crosses put over the graves of kings and heroes in pagan Scandinavia.

The cross emerged as a symbol of Christianity around the 5th century AD, but it was not until the medieval period that it became widely accepted as the most evocative of all Christian emblems.

The actual cross upon which Christ was crucified is said to have been made of palm, cedar, olive or cypress wood among other types of timber. The beam of cedar that formed the upright of the cross was said to have been cut down originally by Solomon and buried beneath the pool of Bethesda, from which it emerged shortly before the date set for Christ's Crucifixion. Many legends were told of the cross and its fate after the Crucifixion, and numerous religious centres throughout Europe and beyond prize relics identified as splinters from the cross itself, claiming for them many miracles of healing.

Because of its sacred associations, the cross is widely reputed to repel evil spirits of all kinds, from VAMPIRES to the DEVIL himself. A simple cross of straw or sticks laid on the ground is reputed to be sufficient to repel witches, who are sure to stumble as they walk over it, and similar crosses may also be placed at doors and windows or over pig sties and bee hives to prevent interference from evil spirits (the French favour crossed bunches of flowers for this purpose). Making a cross by crossing one's fingers is common even today as a countermeasure against the threat of evil, and so too is crossing the legs, a favourite ploy of superstitious gamblers.

Splinters taken from crosses or even samples of moss growing on a cross are valued in folk medicine. Making the sign of the cross upon one's shoe will cure cramp and pins and needles in the foot, while stitches and other minor ailments may also be relieved in much the same way. Marking a foodstuff with the sign of the cross will similarly protect it from interference by witches or evil spirits (*see* HOT CROSS BUN).

crossing the line *See* SAILORS' LORE.

crow The death-black colouring of the crow, in combination with its intelligence, has led to the bird being regarded as one of the most ominous of all creatures in world folklore. Variously identified as a messenger of the gods or servant of the DEVIL, and later as a FAMILIAR of the traditional witch, the crow is widely viewed as a harbinger of warfare and death. It is particularly to be feared if it alights upon a house or taps at a windowpane. A crow settling in a churchyard is likewise deemed an omen that there will be a funeral in the near future.

Crows that leave a wood en masse are interpreted as a sign of coming famine, and crows that fly at one another are indicative of the outbreak of war. Crows that flock early in the day and fly towards the sun are a sign of good weather (as is a crow that croaks an even number of times), but bad weather is on the way if they are noisy and active around water in the dusk (or if a single crow croaks an odd number of times). In northern England children in former times would see a single crow off with the threat: 'Crow, crow, get out of my sight, / Or else I'll eat thy liver and thy lights.'

Cuchulainn In Irish legend, the greatest of the knights of Ulster known as the RED BRANCH, whose adventures form the basis of the ULSTER CYCLE. The son of the king's sister Dechtire and the sun god LUGH, Cuchulainn was described as immensely powerful and very handsome, despite the seven fingers he had on each hand and the seven toes he had on each foot (not to mention the seven pupils he had in each eye). He was originally named Setanta, but while still a child was renamed Cuchulainn (meaning 'Culainn's hound') after he killed the savage hound belonging to Culainn, the smith of King CONCHOBAR, and agreed to guard Culainn's forge himself until the latter found another guard dog. Cuchulainn subsequently trained as a knight with SCATHACH in Alba (Scotland), and became famous for his ability to make prodigious leaps and for his mastery in battle wielding his fatal spear, the celebrated GAE BULG.

Among the many feats performed by Cuchulainn were victory in battle over the club-carrying giant Cu Roi mac Daire (who had previously shaved Cuchulainn's head), defending Ulster single-handedly against the forces of Queen MEDB of Connacht (see TAIN BO CUAILNGE), and slaughtering many other formidable foes in single combat, including his old friend Ferdiad and his only son CONLA, whom he failed to recognize until it was too late. Descriptions of Cuchulainn in battle report how he worked himself up into a frenzy, his body distorting into strange shapes and blood gushing from his head. Ultimately he was overcome himself by Lugaid, son of Cu Roi mac Daire, whose magic tricked Cuchulainn into throwing aside the invincible Gae Bulg.

Cuchulainn also had a famous sword, called Cruaidin Cailidcheann ('hard-headed'), and two horses called Liath Macha and Dubh Sanglainn that pulled his chariot. He had many lovers, although he spurned the attentions of MORRIGAN, thus making an implacable enemy of her.

cuckoo The cuckoo is widely considered to be a herald of the spring and is consequently associated throughout Europe with good fortune, love and new life. Its habit of putting its eggs in the nests of other birds, however, means that it is also widely recognized as an emblem of the cuckold.

The majority of folk beliefs relating to the cuckoo concern its distinctive call, and many people today listen out for the 'first cuckoo of the spring'. Luckiest of all is the person who hears the first cuckoo on 28 April, of all dates the most propitious, according to Welsh tradition. Ill luck, however, will attend anyone who hears a cuckoo before 6 April or after Midsummer Day. Whatever condition a person is in when the first call is heard will remain unchanged for the next 12 months. It is consequently unlucky to hear the cuckoo when hungry or ill in bed, and some people will burst into a run on hearing the sound, reasoning that this will ensure they are busy all year long.

German tradition, meanwhile, recommends turning over any coins that happen to be in one's pocket when the cuckoo's call is heard as this guarantees continued prosperity over the ensuing 12 months or more.

According to a Scottish tradition, the number of times a cuckoo calls signifies the number of years a person has left to live, although the unmarried claim this refers in their case to the years that will pass before their wedding. The number of petitions that are made to the bird for information of this nature is said to be the real reason why the bird leaves its eggs in other birds' nests, having no time to build its own. Lastly, the disappearance of cuckoos in the winter is easily explained by one ancient but persistent tradition: they have all turned into hawks.

See also GOTHAM, WISE MEN OF.

Culhwch In Welsh mythology, a warrior hero identified as the nephew of King ARTHUR. His name (meaning 'pigsty') referred to the circumstances of his birth in a pigsty. After his mother Goleuddydd's death Culhwch's father remarried, and his new stepmother placed him under an obligation (*see* GEIS) to the effect that he should marry no one but OLWEN, the daughter of the terrifying 'chief giant' Yspaddaden, who lived in his fortress at Pencawr. Olwen's father, who knew that his own death would come with his daughter's marriage, demanded that Culhwch perform 39 seemingly impossible tasks before he would consent to his suit. With the aid of various knights of the ROUND TABLE, Culhwch completed the tasks, the most formidable of which included slaying the fearsome giant boar called the TWRCH TRWYTH and fetching some of the THIRTEEN TREASURES OF BRITAIN from the Underworld (a feat that Arthur himself undertook). When Yspaddaden demonstrated that he was still unwilling to allow Culhwch to marry Olwen, Culhwch attacked his castle, killed him and claimed her anyway.

curse The invocation of supernatural power usually via a verbal or written formula to inflict harm upon someone or something. Belief in the power of the curse, which may be either spoken or written, is both widespread and ancient. Numerous curses inscribed on tablets by ancient Romans have been found at archaeological sites throughout Europe, and even today the curses of gypsies or others credited with the power of the EVIL EYE may excite fear among the superstitious, especially in Southern Europe.

In some cases words alone are thought to be enough to have the desired result. In others the curse must be accompanied with some ritual action to make it effective. At one trial of witches in the 17th century just saying the words 'A pox take it' were deemed quite enough to cause harm to any person, animal or object. Some people maintain that a curse can be delivered silently, and that by simply 'ill-wishing' someone, a victim can be caused trouble. This ill wish is, however, usually accompanied by some gesture, such as spitting, pointing a finger or delivering a penetrating stare.

Belief in the power of the curse, or hex, in western European society in the 16th and 17th centuries was such that people would make considerable efforts to repair relations with any suspected witch whom they had offended, making good the damage done or retracting the insult that had led to the curse being made, often with some gift or other favour to ensure that the curse would be lifted. In some cultures, however, it was believed that no curse could be withdrawn once made.

There was once a flourishing trade in the buying and selling of curses, a practice that dates as far back as ancient Greece. Curses could be sold in the form of incantations or potions and might be directed at specific individuals or at whole families, exerting their baleful influence on succeeding generations through the centuries. Typical of this phenomenon was the cursing well of St Elian at

Llanelian-yn-Rhos near Colwyn Bay in Wales, where until at least the late 19th century people paid to toss down the well lead boxes containing curses against their enemies. Victims of such curses could, however, bribe the keeper of the well to retrieve the box containing the relevant curse if this was thought necessary. Other areas boasted 'cursing stones', where witches repaired to utter terrible curses against their enemies.

Even in the 20th century, a curse may cause many people to live their lives in a state of considerable trepidation – most famously in the case of the opening of the tomb of Tutankhamun in Egypt's Valley of the Kings in 1922. When several of those connected with the celebrated excavation died premature and mysterious deaths the rumour spread that this was in punishment for breaking into the grave, as warned in a curse (now mysteriously disappeared) that was reportedly inscribed over the entrance.

In some societies fear of the curse remains as strong as ever, and many cases have been documented of victims going into a permanent physical and mental decline, even to the point of death, upon learning that someone has cursed them. From time to time stories about curses surface in news reports: to cite just one of these, in 1953 a rancher in Arizona actually shot and killed a woman whom he and his neighbours believed had put a curse on his wife.

See also SPELL; TABOO.

Cymbeline Legendary king of Britain, who was apparently loosely based upon the historical early British king Cunobeline. Claiming descent from BRUT, he was supposedly brought up in the household of the Emperor Augustus, and had two sons, Guiderius and Arviragus. Shakespeare's play *Cymbeline* combines the legend with the story of Imogen from Boccaccio's *Decameron*.

D

daffodil As a harbinger of spring, the daffodil is generally considered a lucky flower and is widely associated with new life (hence the tradition of planting daffodils on graves). The flower features in many folk beliefs and superstitions across the British Isles. In Wales, for instance, where the daffodil is a national emblem, the person who finds the first daffodil of the year is said to enjoy considerable prosperity throughout the coming months, earning more gold than silver. If, however, the first daffodil hangs its head towards the finder he is fated to suffer an ill-omened year. Elsewhere it is claimed that a single daffodil should never be brought indoors, as this will bring bad luck – although a bunch of daffodils implies no such misfortune. Some say daffodils should never be allowed into the house before the first goslings or chicks have hatched.

Dagda (or Daghda) In Irish mythology, the leader of the TUATHA DE DANANN, and the son of Eladu. Dagda combined with LUGH and OGMA against the FOMORIANS, going into battle wielding a huge magical club (when reversed this club healed wounds and could restore the dead to life). His other possessions included an inexhaustible cauldron, two pigs (one of which roasted while the other renewed itself to be eaten again), and a magic harp, which summoned the seasons. Identified as a father god of the Tuatha, Dagda was depicted as a large, fat man whose short tunic left his buttocks bare (apparently a reference to his association with sexuality and fertility, and emphasizing his role as a symbol of abundance). As well as having a healthy sexual appetite he was also famed for his great hunger. It was said that when the Fomorians tried to overcome him by offering him an enormous amount of food he showed no signs of surfeit: although there was so much food that the cauldron that held it was sunk deep into the ground, Dagda went on ladling out the contents with a massive spoon capable of holding a man and a woman.

Legend has it that Dagda mated with MORRIGAN as she stood astride the River Unius, and also fathered Boann's son Oenghus. As well as being called Dagda (meaning 'Good God'), he was also known as Eochaid Ollathair ('All-Father') and Ruad Rofessa ('Lord of Great Knowledge'). He is supposed to have given up the leadership of the Tuatha after their defeat by the MILESIANS and their exile underground.

Dagonet In Arthurian legend, the jester at the court of King ARTHUR. A great favourite of the king's, he was granted a knighthood as a joke, but subsequently distinguished himself in tournaments. His lively wit was celebrated in Malory's *Morte d'Arthur*.

Daire Mac Fiachna In Irish mythology, the chief of Ulster whose quarrel with MEDB over the possession of his magnificent bull led to the TAIN BO

CUAILNGE. Legend has it that Daire changed his mind about lending the bull to Medb for a year when he learned that she would have taken it by force if he had refused. When Medb's messengers came to take the animal away he turned them back, thus making hostilities inevitable.

daisy The daisy is a cheerful little plant, and is suitably associated with innocence and loyalty. A touching tradition has it that daisy seeds are sown by the spirits of stillborn babies to console their sorrowing parents, although another explanation of their origin identifies them as having sprouted from the tears of the sorrowing Mary Magdalene.

Most people in the English-speaking world are familiar with the time-honoured custom of plucking the petals from a daisy one by one with the words 'He/she loves me, he/she loves me not' to establish the faithfulness of a lover (this should really be done at the hour of midday, facing towards the sun). Putting daisy roots under the pillow, meanwhile, will grant a dreamer visions of a future partner. Eating the first daisy of the season will ensure good luck for the rest of the year; failing this, it should be stepped on to prevent it growing on one's grave before the year is through. Drinking a potion made from daisies will cure madness and the plant may also be used in the treatment of a myriad of minor ailments, from the curing of warts to the restoring of hair colour.

The daisy's name comes from the Old English *daeges ege* ('day's eye') and refers to the opening of the plant's petals with each new day. When the petals of the daisy are open fully this is widely taken to be a sign of good weather in the offing.

Dame Durden In English folklore, the archetypal housewife, who sets about her daily tasks with proverbial cheerfulness. According to an old song lauding her character, she is assisted by five milkmaids and five serving men, and has her hands full sorting out the inevitable love affairs that develop between her charges.

dance Dancing has been a prominent feature of religious and folkloric celebrations all round the world since before the dawn of history. The folk dance tradition embraces a huge range of dance types and styles, many of which have their roots in ancient ritual dances used in religious worship and for such purposes as invoking the fertility of the land.

In their original form many dances celebrated the cycle of the seasons or the renewal of life, while others were intended as active appeals to the gods, as acts of appeasement to the spirits of animals killed in the hunt, or as invocations of the supernatural intended to ensure fertility or protection from some threat. Warriors in many cultures performed war dances to rouse their passions before going into battle (*see also* GHOST DANCE), and might dance again in celebration of their victory (an example being the 'Highland fling' of Scottish tradition) and to appease the ghosts of their dead enemies. In some societies people performed sun dances to persuade the sun to shine once more during an ECLIPSE, or rain-making dances in times of drought. Some of these dances are still performed today (for instance, the maypole and morris dances of MAY DAY), even though the original intent behind them may be forgotten.

Dancers may variously hold sticks, bells, rattles, animal horns and other objects as they perform. Some stick dances are thought to have developed originally as a means of making young warriors more familiar with their weapons, while others imitate the use of agricultural implements. Often these implements are banged upon the ground, apparently to stir the soil to life or else to drive out evil spirits that might threaten the coming harvest.

All round the world dancing has always been a prominent feature in the celebration of significant social events and RITES OF PASSAGE, such as initiations, weddings and funerals. Although continued today primarily for social reasons, such dancing was originally supposed to safeguard the initiate (whether a child, bride and groom or deceased person) from the threat posed by evil spirits. On a more fundamental level, such dancing serves to strengthen group identity and to emphasize the importance of the rituals themselves. Conversely, dance is notable by its absence from the rituals of Christianity: the medieval Church objected to the pagan associations of such activity and repeatedly condemned dancing as an un-Christian pastime. It does, however, play a prominent role in some other religious traditions: in India, for instance, the god Shiva is usually depicted dancing to keep the world in motion.

Some dances are reserved for men or for priests or shamans (*see* SHAMANISM), who may dance feverishly in order to enter trances and thus establish communication with the spirit world. Among those reserved for men are the Cossack dances of Russia and the Ukraine, which are typical in requiring performers to demonstrate their strength (and by association their virility) by performing a series of physically demanding steps. Other dances, such as the Spanish *filado*, imitate the action of domestic activities such as spinning and are danced by women alone. On other occasions men and women of all ranks dance indiscriminately together. Most modern dances, incidentally, have developed not from more obviously folkloric forms but from ancient courtship dances, in which male and females usually danced together in pairs. These dances often imitated the actions of courtship and were on occasion frankly obscene in nature. One of the most celebrated examples of the courtship dance is the Spanish flamenco, which is today widely recognized as having considerable artistic merit. Other dances are still known primarily from their context in folklore, among them the Italian tarantella, a frenzied dance supposedly performed to negate the effects of the bite of the tarantula spider.

Dancing is commonly identified as a favourite pastime of supernatural creatures. Mortals venturing into the underworld in a variety of legends frequently reported how they were invited to join in dancing with their supernatural hosts, while European folklore repeatedly warns of the dangers inherent in spying upon the fairies as they perform their magical fairy circle dances.

Dancing has also been long thought of as a feature of the traditional witches' sabbath. The earliest surviving records of witches dancing at their revels date back to at least the 13th century. In 1282, for instance, a Scottish priest from Inverkeithing was accused of being a sorcerer after he admitted leading young girls of the parish in an obscene phallic dance, probably of pagan origin, as part of the Easter celebrations. Perhaps the most notorious of the dances performed by witches at their covens was the 'hare and hounds' ritual dance in which the Devil or the leader of the coven, playing the role of the hound, furiously chased one of the female witches, impersonating the hare. At the climax of the dance, the hound caught the hare, wrestled her to the ground and had intercourse with her.

Other lively sabbath dances included 'follow-my-leader', and a range of circle dances, which were always performed in a 'widdershins' direction, that is, contrary to the course of the sun. Modern witches still incorporate dancing in their rituals. Best known of these dances is the 'Dance of the Wheel', a circular dance round a bonfire performed to mark the winter solstice. At the climax of the dance the high priest and priestess leap through the flames hand in hand, followed by the rest of the witches in couples.

See also DANSE MACABRE; FURRY DANCE; GHOST DANCE; HORN DANCE; MORRIS DANCE; NUTTER'S DANCE; SWORD DANCE.

dandelion Wild plant that has inspired assorted superstitions and folk beliefs. Perhaps the commonest tradition relating to the dandelion is that the number of puffs it takes to remove all the tufts from a dandelion 'clock' indicates the time of day. Alternatively, it denotes how many years a person must wait before their wedding day, or the number of children a girl may expect. Ancient traditions variously warn that anyone who picks a dandelion will wet their bed, that dandelions will remain closed in the morning if rain is due, and that the summer will be hot but wet if they bloom in April and July. Dandelion tea is highly recommended by herbalists for purifying the blood, for rheumatism and for liver complaints.

danse macabre Traditional allegorical depiction of DEATH, in which Death himself is symbolized as a skeleton who leads the living of all ranks away in his dance. Of medieval origin, it became a familiar theme of drama, literature and the arts throughout Europe in the wake of the Black Death, and is still a feature of carnival processions in Germany, Spain and other countries, with dancers following in the wake of a performer in a skeleton or clown costume.

Davy Jones In English SAILORS' LORE, an evil spirit of the sea who claims the souls of drowned seafarers. A shadowy figure apparently of 18th-century origin, he may have had his roots in the West Indian DUPPY, or else in the biblical Jonah. Another tradition identifies Davy Jones as a historical pirate. Sailors still talk of 'Davy Jones's locker' (meaning the bottom of the sea), in which drowned seafarers spend eternity.

days of the week Each of the seven days of the week has its own character and significance in folklore around the world. In the English-speaking world these notions are generally based upon traditional astrological attitudes.

Monday got its name from the Old English *Monandaeg* ('day of the moon'). It is not the luckiest of days, and is consequently not a good time to sign a contract, to expect favours, to do any mending, to give money, or to embark on a new project (though, conversely, the Irish actually prefer Mondays to begin new tasks). French tradition claims that couples who marry on a Monday will become insane, while in Ireland Monday is a bad time to dig a grave. The first Monday in April, the second Monday in August, and the last Monday in December are considered the unluckiest days in the year, marking respectively the anniversaries of Cain's birth, the destruction of Sodom and Gomorrah and the betrayal of Christ by Judas Iscariot.

Tuesday, ruled by Mars, was named after the Norse god Tiu, son of ODIN. It is a day for fighting or for the competitive pursuit of business. It is also a good day for weddings. It is not, however, a good day on which to undergo a medical operation, or even to trim the fingernails.

Wednesday, governed by Mercury, got its name from Woden's (or Odin's) day, and is a day of somewhat mixed potential. Recommended as a day to embark on courses of medical treatment, to write letters and to ask for favours, it is a bad time to get married, to buy anything expensive or (for obscure reasons) to wear gloves. Especially unlucky is a Wednesday that coincides with a new moon (although US tradition declares Wednesday to be the luckiest day of the week).

Thursday, influenced by Jupiter, was named after the Norse thunder god THOR. It is also a day of contrasting fortune. Lucky for weddings, making vital decisions and taking legal advice, it is less ideal for spinning yarn, beginning a new job, eating chicken, wearing rubies or sending the children for their first day at school. In Germany it is considered the unluckiest day of the week.

Friday, subject to Venus, was named after FREYA, the Norse goddess of love. It is widely held to be unlucky and a day when evil influences are at work – especially if it happens to be the 13th day of the month. It was on a Friday that Eve offered the apple to Adam in the Garden of Eden and that Christ was crucified. Friday is also a holy day in the Islamic week. Friday is also supposedly the day favoured for the holding of witches' covens, and was formerly the usual day for hangings. Accidents are said to be more frequent on Fridays, and clothes made on the day will not fit. Projects or trips begun on a Friday will not prosper, and any person who laughs on a Friday, says one old proverb, will cry on Sunday. It is also an inauspicious day for moving house or for weddings. Formerly, in some parts of the British Isles, those who courted their lovers on Friday were hounded by friends and neighbours banging noisily on pans and kettles. According to one old Shropshire folk belief, news received on a Friday makes a physical impression upon the hearer in the form of a new wrinkle for every tiding. Children born on Friday will prove unlucky, but will enjoy the gifts of second sight and healing.

Saturday, ruled by Saturn (after whom it was named), is sacred to Jews as the Sabbath and a day when no work can be allowed to take place. More widely it is considered a lucky day to set out on a journey. Dreams told to others on a Saturday are sure to come true, but the day is not recommended for starting new projects, for performing good deeds, or for leaving hospital. Scottish tradition states that persons born on a Saturday will be able to see ghosts. The weather always includes a fine spell on Saturdays, in remembrance of the fact that it was the day on which God created man.

Sunday, influenced by the sun (after which it was named) and the Sabbath in the Christian week, is the luckiest day of all. Children born on Sundays are especially blessed, and are immune from witchcraft; they may also have psychic powers. It is bad luck to work, to make the bed, to cut the hair or the fingernails, to cry, to sew, or to court someone on a Sunday, but the day is otherwise ideal for medical treatments, for setting out to sea and for the fulfilling of various generous acts towards others.

The significance of the day upon which a person is born is neatly summarized by a traditional English rhyme: 'Monday's child is fair of face; Tuesday's child is full of grace; Wednesday's child is full of woe; Thursday's child has far to go; Friday's child is loving and giving; Saturday's child works hard for its living; But the child that is born on the Sabbath day is blithe and bonny, and good and gay.' Another old English rhyme that has long ranked among the most familiar of children's playground chants interprets the chief events in the life of the fictional Solomon Grundy through reference to the different days of the week: 'Solomon Grundy, born on Monday, christened on Tuesday, married on Wednesday, took ill on Thursday, died on Saturday, buried on Sunday: this is the end of Solomon Grundy.'

dead hand The hand of a corpse, whose touch was once widely held to have considerable healing powers. This macabre notion applied particularly to the bodies of suicides and newly executed criminals, and in former times patients frequently petitioned executioners to be allowed to touch the body of a hanged man, usually paying a small fee for the privilege. The treatment was recommended especially for those suffering from cancer, scrofula, warts, sores and neck and throat problems, the dead man's hand being used to stroke the affected part shortly after death. Some women also put faith in the procedure as a cure for infertility. Rings taken from the hand of a dead man can similarly be used to alleviate various minor ailments.

See also HAND OF GLORY.

death The folklore of all the world's cultures pays particular attention to death, identifying it as perhaps the most significant of all the rites of passage. Even today death is surrounded by ritual and taboo, much of which has very ancient origins.

Death is inevitably the focus of a vast body of superstition. Every culture, for instance, boasts a code of omens that warn of imminent death, the most common including the appearance of black creatures such as crows, the inexplicable howling of dogs, and the sound of Death knocking to gain admittance. Sometimes the threat posed by such phenomena may be evaded by taking certain actions, but sometimes there is no escape.

When death approaches, various measures may be taken to ease the process of dying. Thus, in many countries of the world, friends and relatives of a dying person will open all the doors and windows (and often drawers and cupboard doors also) so that the unfettered soul may be allowed to escape unhindered. They may also open any locks and loosen knots in the sickroom for the same reason. Other precautions include never standing at the foot of the dying person's bed, in order to avoid obstructing the soul's passage; turning the mirror to the wall so as not to alarm and confuse the departing spirit; stopping the clock at the moment of death; and allowing a relative to inhale the last dying breath and thus inherit the dying person's talents. Many coastal communities believe that death will not occur until the tide is on the ebb.

In various societies it is deemed wrong to leave the newly-dead alone at any time between their death and their FUNERAL, and a constant vigil is kept by friends and relatives. Candles may also be lit so that the departing soul is not frightened by the dark. The ringing of bells is reputed to aid the departed by warding off evil spirits, and in Christian countries a 'passing bell' was commonly rung as the patient approached death.

A curiosity of British folk belief is the ancient notion of placing the dying person's bed under a beam to assure them of an easy death. Other largely neglected traditions include laying the table one last time for the dead person, so that the deceased may eat before his or her final journey. Another such tradition involves washing the dead person's clothing separately from that of the living, to prevent another death occurring in the family. The idea that one should never speak ill of the dead is still strong in many communities, and indeed in public life. This taboo dates back as far as the ancient Romans, and was observed originally not so much out of a desire for 'fair play' towards those who can no longer defend themselves, as from fear of provoking the dead into returning.

See also BURIAL CUSTOMS; DEAD HAND; GHOST; HAND OF GLORY.

Dee, Dr John English alchemist, geographer and mathematician, who became one of the most celebrated sorcerers of the Elizabethan age. Born in 1527, he was first accused of sorcery in 1546 when he built a mechanical beetle as a stage prop for a production of the Aristophanes play *Peace*. He then pursued the acquisition of further learning in Belgium and France under such authorities as Cornelius Agrippa and became fascinated in the realm of invention that lay between science and magic.

He was granted a pension by Edward VI and was subsequently appointed astrologer to Mary I, casting horoscopes both for her and for her intended husband, Philip of Spain, but he fell foul of his royal mistress in 1555 when alleged to have plotted her death by magic. Other charges included the suggestions that he had procured the death of children by witchcraft and kept familiars. He regained royal favour under Elizabeth I and was consulted by her as to the luckiest date for her coronation in 1559.

In 1563 Dee published the controversial *Monas Hieroglyphia*, which discussed the mystic science of numerology. In 1581 Dee teamed up with Edward Kelly and together they conducted numerous investigations into such activities as SCRYING and necromancy. Both Dee and Kelly stated that they had been granted interviews with angels through the agency of Dee's celebrated magic crystal (now preserved in the British Museum). Dee took down descriptions of the entities thus summoned from Kelly, as he alone could see them.

The two scholars and their wives travelled widely, becoming at various times the guests of the king of Poland, Emperor Rudolph II of Bohemia and the Czar of Russia. They finally parted company in 1589, two years after Dee had reluctantly agreed to a wife-sharing arrangement that Kelly said had been insisted upon by his supernatural communicants. Although Dee attempted further investigations into scrying, these were unsuccessful, as he could not find another assistant of Kelly's skill. In 1604, perhaps fearing for his welfare in the witchhunting hysteria then developing, he sought (but failed to get) a public refutation of his reputation as a magician from James I. This was a disappointment for Dee, who deeply resented the description 'magician' and maintained that he had always been a dutiful Christian. Despite the many extraordinary achievements of his life, the 81-year-old Dee finally died a pauper in 1608; he was buried in Mortlake, London, where he had been born.

deer The deer has special significance in numerous cultures around the world. Native Americans, for instance, regard the animal as sacred and totemic, venerating it with special dances and other rites. Celtic mythology, meanwhile, boasts a range of white stags and harts variously representing messengers from the gods and even Christ himself. There is also the famous story of David I of Scotland, who, while out hunting, was about to be gored by a stag but was saved when the creature's antlers turned into a cross. David showed his gratitude by founding the Abbey of Holy Rood (cross), among other pious deeds. Characters in a number of well-known legends and folk tales around the world are transformed by magic into the shape of stags or does, among them SADBH and GWYDION. Various nature deities are depicted with antlers, including CERNUNNOS and the WILD HERDSMAN.

Best known of the folk beliefs relating to deer is the wide-held belief that they cry on the loss of their horns or when mortally wounded. In former times many people were reluctant to eat venison on the grounds that deer were thought to consume snakes in the summer months, and that as a result their flesh was poisonous. In terms of folk medicine, epileptics were sometimes furnished with a ring containing a fragment of deer's hoof, which was alleged to cure the condition.

See also HORN DANCE.

Deirdre In Irish legend, the beautiful daughter of Fedlimid, harper to the high king CONCHOBAR. She features prominently as a heroine in the celebrated cycle of stories about the RED BRANCH. When the druid Cathbad foretells not only that the infant Deirdre (otherwise known as Deirdriu) will become the most beautiful woman in the whole of Ireland, but also that she will be the cause of much death and destruction in Ulster, becoming known as 'Deirdre of the Sorrows', many Ulstermen call for her to be killed. However, she is saved from this fate by being raised in secret on Conchobar's orders until she is old enough to become his wife.

Deirdre for her part is inspired by the sight of some ravens feeding on the blood of a newly killed calf in the snow to wish for a lover with skin as white as snow, raven-black hair and ruddy cheeks. She subsequently falls in love with NAOISE, who answers this description, and persuades him against his will to carry her off with him. The lovers then flee from Conchobar through Ireland and eventually seek refuge with Naoise's two brothers in Alba (Scotland). After several years together they are lured back to Ulster by FERGUS MAC ROICH, who promises them safety on Conchobar's behalf, but the lovers are betrayed. Naoise and his brothers are killed and Deirdre is forced to marry Conchobar, who then hands her over to his ally Eoghan, Naoise's murderer. Fergus, outraged that Conchobar has broken his word, rebels and many

Ulstermen are killed in the ensuing carnage. Unable to face life without her lover, Deirdre throws herself out of the chariot taking her to Eoghan and dashes her brains out on a stone.

Legend has it that two yews or pines grew from the graves of Deirdre and Naoise, their branches intertwining. In more recent times they have been commemorated in several notable works of literature, including plays by W. B. Yeats and J. M. Synge.

demon The study of demons and their attributes was a prime occupation of theologians and occultists in past centuries, and the mythology of the Christian world boasts a wealth of detail about these evil spirits. The Greek word *daimon* signified any spirit, evil or otherwise, but Christian doctrine demanded that all spirits other than God and his angels were by definition opposed to good, and thus 'demons' came to be understood as necessarily evil entities, and servants of the DEVIL. Learned experts argued that the Devil and his minions were fallen angels and remained in the service of God, being allowed certain powers in order to test the faith of humans and to punish those who subsequently veered from the path of righteousness.

Demons may belong to any one of a wide range of categories. These include the IMPS and FAMILIARS who served witches and sorcerers, INCUBI and SUCCUBI, and poltergeists (*see* GHOST). Some showed a predilection for tormenting priests and nuns, while others delighted in causing nightmares and other kinds of mischief among mortals in general.

The conventional idea of a demon in physical form was a miniature version of the Devil, complete with horns, wings, black or red skin, cloven feet and forked tail – although they were widely credited with the power to change their shape at will. In order to seduce young men, for instance, they might appear to them in the form of beautiful women. Demons were depicted in a host of paintings and engravings dating from both medieval and post-medieval times, issuing from the mouths of those undergoing exorcism and lurking in the vicinity of those they suspected might be vulnerable to their influence. It was widely believed that they could cover vast distances, always flying at night, and that they shared an unremitting hostility towards humanity – although (at great risk to himself) the cunning magician could use his powers to make such entities his slaves.

Among the most fearsome demons were Ashtaroth (who knew all secrets), Asmodeus (a demon of rage and lust), Baphomet (often identified as the goat of witches' sabbaths), Beelzebub (the prince of demons identified with the sin of gluttony), Belphegor (who made men slothful), Leviathan (the demon of envy), Lilith (a demoness who sucked the blood of sleeping men), Lucifer (the ruler of the underworld, otherwise synonymous with the Devil or Satan) and Mammon (who drove men to dreams of avarice).

Besides these, there was also a host of minor demons, whose powers varied. Alphonsus de Spina, writing in 1459, claimed that one third of God's angels had become demons, and that thus there were precisely 133,306,668 of them. Other estimates of their numbers suggested a total of 6,660,000 demons commanded by 66 princes, or 7,409,127 demons under the command of 79 princes. One authority, writing towards the end of the 16th century, claimed that the number of demons then active was equivalent to more than half the population of the world.

Possession by demons was conventionally tackled through exorcism of the victim. In the course of this the demon occupying the victim's body was asked various routine questions concerning its identity and its intentions. Once the demon's name was known, many believed this gave the exorcist control over it. Each demon had its opposing saint, to whom prayers might be addressed for assistance in expelling the demon in question.

Demons could be deterred by certain amulets and charms, and by anyone making the sign of the cross or the fig sign (*see* EVIL EYE), or defending themselves with holy water, firelight, spittle, bread, salt, iron or herbs.

Devil The ruler of the underworld, otherwise called Satan or Lucifer, who is the personification of evil in Christian demonology. Considered the arch-enemy of both God and humanity, he is conventionally depicted as the sponsor of all evil in the world, using such agents as demons and witches to plot against humans and to claim their immortal souls. Time was when many people were nervous of even speaking his name, referring to him instead as 'Old Nick' or 'the Old Gentleman' or by other euphemisms, so as to avoid invoking the powers of darkness. His other titles include 'the Prince of Darkness', 'the Horned One' and 'the Lord of the Flies'.

Terrifying as he may be, the Devil is often depicted as slow-witted, and many folk tales are based on how he is foiled by clever tricks played on him by mortals. This tradition strongly suggests a link with the fallible nature deities of pre-Christian pagan religions. He is described as manifesting in a variety of forms, his favourite guises including the cloven-hoofed satyr (half-man, half-goat and thus reminiscent of the Greek god Pan), the dog and the serpent. On other occasions he appears in human form, often being described in the confessions of witches, for instance, as a mysterious 'dark' man. The first theological definition of the Devil, ratified by the Council of Toledo in AD 447, described him as 'a large black monstrous apparition with horns on his head, cloven hoofs' with 'an immense phallus and a sulphurous smell'.

According to the Bible, the Devil's role was to afflict the faithful with various misfortunes so that the true nature of their faith in God might be revealed. His role was that of the malevolent accuser, roaming the earth looking for opportunities to expose weakness on God's behalf. Later, however, he was depicted as pursuing evil for his own ends, dedicating himself to the destruction of humanity and the overthrow of God. The story of the fall of the angel Lucifer through pride allowed demonologists to develop the mythology of the Devil as an arch-fiend ruling over his own kingdom and seizing the souls of wicked mortals. Another passage in the Bible explains how some two hundred of God's angels had lusted after mortal women, and as punishment had been imprisoned in the 'valleys of the earth' – Hell. These deposed angels became the nucleus of the Devil's cohorts (*see* DEMON).

The authority of the Bible was enough to convince the medieval and post-medieval mind that the Devil was an actual force to be reckoned with, and depictions of the Devil, a dark figure with horns and forked tail, undoubtedly did much to consolidate belief in his powers. If there was a God, then it followed that by the same authority there was also a Devil. Denial of the Devil's existence was therefore, in the eyes of the stricter church authorities, tantamount to a denial of God himself. The logical extension of this – that if the Devil, the source of all evil, was created by God, then all evil in the world was ultimately attributable to God – created some difficulty for early Christian scholars.

In return for their unqualified loyalty and ultimately their souls, witches were rewarded by the Devil with the gift of a FAMILIAR to serve their will, and also with promises of special magical powers for the rest of their lives. Members of covens reported their evil-doing back to the Devil when they met at their sabbaths, over which the Devil was said to preside, and those who did the most harm to their neighbours might be specially rewarded. According to some witches, the Devil played an active part in the revels that were a traditional highlight of important gatherings, and often revealed both his licentious nature and his taste for music (there are various folk tales in which the Devil pits his skill as a player of the fiddle against human players).

Devil worship reached a climax in Europe in the 15th century, with the rumoured development of orgiastic devil-worshipping cults. Ecclesiastical authorities claimed that the Devil was leading a campaign against the Christian world, recruiting witches and sorcerers to his cause and threatening to overthrow the church itself. Although belief in a real, persistently evil Devil has fallen off in modern times, a papal pronouncement of 1972 insisted that the Devil is still an actual functioning power in the world, and reports of Devil worship around the world continue to appear in the media on a fairly regular basis.

devolutionary theory Theory that claims that much of the world's surviving folklore and legends are relics of a single pre-Christian system. Formulated by the German folklorists the Brothers GRIMM, the theory suggests that these source legends and tales became fragmented as a result of attempts by the Christian church to obliterate earlier pagan traditions, hence the many variant forms in which some tales are known today. Later generations of folklorists tentatively traced the diverse folkloric tales and traditions of different cultures in the modern world ultimately to the mythology of ancient India and western central Asia.

diamond The most sought-after of all gemstones, which has inspired a variety of legends and folk beliefs over the centuries. Being uniquely enduring and brilliant, diamonds are particularly favoured as a choice for engagement rings, and have been widely prized since ancient times. In Western cultures they represent the notion of conjugal love, and are also believed to inspire courage in a man and pride in a woman. The superstitious particularly value diamonds that show flashes of colour inside the stone, as these are supposed to be proofs of a stone's magical properties, which will bring great good luck to the owner. Less desirable, though, is the ownership of such notorious gems as the Hope Diamond or the Koh-i-Noor Diamond (now part of the British royal regalia), on the grounds that both these stones bring bad luck or death to those who claim possession of them.

Diarmuid (or Diarmaid, Diarmid) Legendary Irish warrior who was one of the heroes of the FIANNA. Diarmuid ua Duibhne was the son of Donn and the nephew of FIONN MAC CUMHAILL, and as well as being very handsome was the possessor of a 'love spot', which made him immensely attractive to women.

Diarmuid's troubles began when GRAINNE fell in love with him and placed him under an obligation (see GEIS) to elope with her. On the day that Grainne was supposed to be getting married to the ageing Fionn, she and Diarmuid drugged the wedding guests, and then ran off together. Fionn set off in pursuit, vowing that the guilty lovers would never be able to spend two consecutive nights in the same place. For a time, conscious of his loyalty to Fionn, Diarmuid refused to sleep with Grainne, but eventually he gave in, and in due course fathered four children by her. After several years the two sides were uneasily reconciled, but Fionn harboured a grudge against Diarmuid and eventually ordered him to hunt a particular boar (actually Diarmuid's enchanted foster-brother), which he knew was fated to claim the life of the younger man. Diarmuid killed the boar, but in the struggle was mortally wounded. He begged Fionn for a drink of magic healing water to save his life, and Fionn seemed to comply. However, Fionn then twice deliberately allowed the water to drip from his hands, and, as he approached with the water a third time, Diarmuid finally expired.

Dick Whittington In English folklore, a young man who comes to London seeking his fortune, and after many adventures becomes lord mayor of the city. Richard Whittington was in fact a real person, who arrived in London around 1379. He subsequently became a rich textile merchant, married well, and served three times as lord mayor. He made large loans to Henry IV and Henry V, and performed various charitable acts, including the rebuilding of Newgate Gaol.

The legends surrounding the historical character dwell chiefly upon his early rise, describing how he nearly left London after initial disappointments, only to turn back after resting on Highgate Hill on hearing the city's bells, which seemed to say to him 'Turn again, Whittington, lord mayor of London'. He won fame and fortune with the assistance of a magical cat – a stock motif of such folk tales as PUSS IN BOOTS – but in this case perhaps a tradition inspired by a slang name for a coal barge (the real Whittington apparently having had a financial interest in the coal trade). The cat helps him to rid the city of a plague of rats and thus secures for him a large fortune, the hand of his employer's daughter and ultimately the position of lord mayor.

diffusion theory Theory which argues that variants of folk tales recorded in different parts of the world can all be traced back to single shared sources. Many European tales, for instance, are thus traced back to the folkloric traditions of Asia, communicated by travellers between the continents. The theory contrasts with that of POLYGENESIS, which argues that such variants develop independently of one another, with any coincidences between them being the inevitable consequence of similarities in social organization, and so forth. Modern opinion generally accepts that both processes had an influence.

divination The practice of using magic to learn secrets that may not be divulged by ordinary means. Men and women have consulted gods, demons and other spiritual entities for privileged knowledge for

as long as such beings have been conceived of and most cultures in the ancient world (including those of the Babylonians, Greeks and Romans) placed great faith in such practices.

In the ancient world people of all ranks consulted the oracles at the shrines of their gods, the most celebrated of which included the Greek oracles of Apollo at Delphi, Delos and Claros, of Diana at Colchis, of Aesculapius at Epidaurus and Rome, of Hercules at Athens and Gades, of Jupiter at Dodona, Ammon and Crete, of Mars at Thrace, of Minerva at Mycenae, of Pan in Arcadia, of Trophonius in Boetia and of Venus at Paphos and Aphaea. Here the augurs (generally women) delivered their responses to the queries put to them while seated on a tripod, usually after the making of appropriate sacrifices. Their answers were often obscure in meaning and were generally open to more than one interpretation. When Philip of Macedon, for instance, sought information from the oracle at Delphi about the fate of his planned Persian expedition he received the reply 'the ready victim crowned for death before the altar stands': he interpreted this as prophesying the imminent death of the king of Persia (although in fact the campaign culminated in his own demise).

In ancient Rome the political sensitivity of such oracular pronouncements meant that only commanders-in-chief were allowed to obtain readings of the 'auspices' (signs) of war. Those who interpreted such signs usually occupied a privileged place in society (in Rome they bore the title 'haruspex').

Some of the very earliest laws instituted against sorcerers and witches concerned the practice of divination, which could easily threaten the stability of the state. Consulting a diviner about the life expectancy of a monarch, for instance, could lead to the inquirer being accused of treason and being sentenced to death. Such a fate befell an English hermit known as Peter the Wise in 1213, after he unwisely foretold the death of King John.

More usual inquiries, about the whereabouts of hidden treasure or the prospects for success in love, were considered less dangerous, and for many centuries diviners who restricted themselves to such questions were subject only to relatively mild punishment.

There has always been money to be made from offering services as a diviner. Seers of various kinds were accorded some status in the ancient world (although they were also subject to periodic persecution), and in later centuries kings, generals and even prominent figures in the church thought it quite natural to consult a fortune-teller in times of crisis. Many notable scholars were famous for their skill at crystal-gazing (see SCRYING), and they would object strenuously to being labelled sorcerers or witches on these grounds alone.

There are various means by which diviners, sorcerers and witches might seek to reveal secrets about the past, present and future. These include studying the positions of the stars (see ASTROLOGY), examining the hands (chiromancy or palmistry), casting dice (astragalomancy), interpreting bird behaviour (ornithomancy), 'reading' numbers (arithmancy or numerology), tarot cards or tea leaves (tasseography), gazing into basins of water (lecanomancy), noting the shapes in burning flames (pyromancy) and listening to the noises made by the belly (gastromancy). Among more extreme means are inspecting the entrails of ritually sacrificed women and children (antinopomancy), raising the dead in order to quiz them about such matters (necromancy), and enlisting the assistance of a demon (demonomancy) – preferably from within the safety of a magic circle.

See also DOWSING; LOVE.

Dobrynja Kikitich In Russian folklore, a dragon-slaying hero who is the central character in a number of traditional tales. His adventures include postponing his wedding to kill a dragon, claiming his bride-to-be back from his blood brother who takes his place at the altar after he has been gone seven years, being turned into a bull as the result of a witch's spell, and ultimately meeting his death in combat with a giantess. He was based on a real character, a knight who died fighting the Turks in 1224.

dog The close relationship between humans and dogs is reflected in a wealth of folk traditions. Most cultures boast numerous stories about faithful dogs who give their masters valuable service (see GELERT), or who pine to death after the demise of their owners. Many of the legendary heroes are described as having a dog. The Celtic hero FIONN MAC CUMHAILL, for instance, was accompanied everywhere by his dogs Bran and Sceolan, while King ARTHUR had a dog called Cabal. By way of contrast, dogs are also often associated in folklore with the underworld, guarding the entrance to hell or accompanying various dark deities in their journeys about the earth (see WILD HUNT).

Various beliefs link dogs with death and the afterlife. This tradition appears to go back to pre-Christian religions, in which gods were often depicted in company with faithful hunting dogs. In later centuries dogs were often associated with the DEVIL. In the 1640s rumours abounded that Boye, the dog Prince Rupert draped over his saddle during his campaigns in the English Civil War, was really the Devil (the dog was killed at the Battle of Marston Moor in 1644). Perhaps in connection with this tradition it is still thought to be very unlucky for a dog to be allowed inside a church. Sailors, meanwhile, are reluctant even to mention the word 'dog' while at sea.

The way a dog behaves is alleged to reveal many things. If a dog scratches itself and seems sleepy then a change in the weather is in the offing. If it eats grass or rolls in the dust then rain may be expected. Dogs are widely believed to have psychic susceptibilities, and many dog-owners have stories about supposedly haunted locations where their dogs regularly refuse to proceed, hackles raised, alarmed by some apparition invisible to the human eye.

The howling of dogs for no apparent reason is dreaded by many people. In medieval Poland and Germany it was said that dogs howled incessantly en masse at the approach of the plague. Some maintain that there is no balking a dreadful fate if a dog is heard howling; people living in Staffordshire, however, have the option of taking off their left shoe, placing it upside down on the ground, spitting on it and then treading on it with the left foot, which will both quieten the dog and provide a measure of protection. Dogs that howl on Christmas Eve are said to be fated to go mad before the end of the year, and many otherwise healthy animals were formerly destroyed on these grounds.

The risk of rabies has made many people acutely nervous of dog bites, and some have resorted to bizarre remedies if bitten. These have included eating grass from a churchyard, consuming some of the 'hair of the dog that bit you' fried in oil with a little rosemary, and even eating parts of the dog itself (typically the heart or the liver). Destruction of a dog that has bitten someone was once automatic, as superstition had it that even if the dog was in good health at the time of the attack its victim would still get rabies if the dog happened to contract the disease at a later date. In Scotland, meanwhile, it is said that a dog will never bite an idiot.

In folk medicine, applying a poultice made from a dog's head mixed with a little wine is said to benefit those suffering from jaundice, while the lick of a dog's tongue will alleviate sores on the skin, and melted dog fat will help against rheumatism. Wearing a dried dog's tongue around the neck, meanwhile, will cure scrofula. Some authorities hold that removing a few hairs from a patient suffering from whooping cough, or various other complaints, and feeding these to a dog in some bread and butter will successfully cure the patient by transferring the problem to the dog.

See also BLACK DOG.

Dolorous Blow In Arthurian legend, the accidental blow sustained by the Grail King (*see* WOUNDED KING) that caused him severe injury in both thighs. The Grail King's physical injuries were reflected in a sympathetic decline in the state of his kingdom (*see* WASTELAND). The Grail King could only be healed by a pure knight asking the all-important 'Grail question' – that is, 'what does this mean?' or 'who does the Grail serve?' When PERCEVAL failed to ask the question he was rebuked, and it was left to GALAHAD to bring relief to the Grail King and his desolated lands.

dolphin The traditionally sympathetic relationship between dolphins and humans is reflected in the many legends in which dolphins are described rushing to the aid of people in distress at sea – a tradition that goes back to Roman times. According to ancient folkloric belief, dolphins have a weakness for human singing and also transport the souls of the dead across the sea to the ISLANDS OF THE BLEST. The identification of the creature as an emblem of Christ may have been inspired by the benevolence of the dolphin in folklore.

Like seals, dolphins are sometimes credited with the ability to adopt human form at will. The folklore of tropical South America incorporates various tales in which river dolphins transform into handsome young men in order to mate with local girls.

Other folk beliefs that have survived into modern times include the curious notion that dolphins change colour when death is near, and the general belief that dolphins playing in fine weather or close to shore are a warning of wind on the way, while the sight of dolphins at play in a turbulent sea indicates that a period of calm is in the offing. Similarly, good weather can be expected if dolphins swim north, and a deterioration in the weather will ensue if they are spotted swimming south.

See also SEAL MAIDEN.

domovik In Russian folklore, a species of domestic spirit that is traditionally supposed to live behind the stove or under the doorstep. The domovik keeps a wary eye upon all household matters, interfering if they are not properly looked after. If seriously displeased he may burn the house down. In order to avoid provoking him, it is customary to leave a little supper out for him on going to bed and, if moving house, to light the stove in the new house with brands from the stove in the old house so as to make him feel at home. He is said to have a wife (a domovikha) who lives in the cellar, and he may be just one of many domoviks living in a single house, each associated with a particular aspect of domestic life.

Don Juan Legendary Spanish lover who has appeared over the centuries as the central protagonist in numerous folk tales, plays, poems and operas. Born Don Juan Tenorio, he belonged to a noble family of 14th-century Seville and acquired a reputation for his many sexual conquests. In Mozart's opera *Don Giovanni* (1787), the libretto for which was provided by Da Ponte, the hero has some 2,500 mistresses, and similar excesses were attached to his name by others who reworked the Don Juan myth, among them Gabriel Tellez, Molière, Corneille, Shadwell, Byron, Dumas the Elder, Balzac, De Musset and Shaw.

The original legend tells how Don Juan murdered the commandant of Ulloa after seducing his daughter. He then demonstrated his arrogance by flippantly inviting a statue of the dead man, erected at a Franciscan convent, to dine with him – only for the statue to come to life at the end of the meal and hand him over to the Devil.

donkey See ASS.

door The door has great significance in many folkloric traditions, being a means of access by which not only humans but also evil spirits and other supernatural entities may enter or leave the home (other options include the windows and the chimney).

Now, as in former times, many householders around the world take precautions to protect themselves from evil by barring the door magically to malevolent entities. This can be done by various means such as hammering nails made of IRON into the door in the shape of a cross, hanging a HORSESHOE above the doorway, or concealing various witch-repelling objects, such as an open pair of scissors, under the threshold (once a place where sacrifices might take place). Another option is to chalk protective patterns on the doorstep, joining one door jamb to the other so that there is no place that the DEVIL and his minions can slip through. In parts of North Africa and the Near East these protective patterns often take the form of a red hand, which is supposed to ward off the threat of the EVIL EYE. Should these precautions fail and the house be invaded by evil spirits, solutions include hanging doors the other way round or bricking up existing doorways and creating new entrances elsewhere, a course of action that is bound to confuse any agent of misfortune.

In many cultures around the world doors may be opened at the time of childbirth and again at death to cut short prolonged suffering. In Germany it is considered particularly unwise to slam the front door in a house where someone has just died for fear of injuring the departing spirit. Another widespread belief, however, advises against going out leaving every door in the house open, and similarly never allowing the front and back doors to remain open together as this facilitates the free passage of malevolent spirits. However, doors and windows should be left open during thunderstorms to let LIGHTNING out again should it strike the house.

In some parts of the world coffins bearing the bodies of dead children leave the house via a window rather than through the front door, in the belief that this avoids prejudicing the chances of any woman subsequently passing through the door from having her own child. Generally, though, visitors to a house should leave by the door through which they entered in order to avoid taking the luck of the household away with them.

Once a coffin or a bride has passed through the front door on the way to church some people will immediately wash the doorstep to ensure the luck of those departing and to preserve the luck of those left behind. A new bride is further discouraged from walking over the threshold of her new home, and in order to guarantee a happy and long married life is traditionally carried over it by the groom (*see* MARRIAGE).

See also FIRST-FOOTING.

doppelgänger In German folklore, an apparition that is identical in every way to a living person. The appearance of such 'doubles' may cause great anxiety as they usually manifest at times when the person they resemble is in extreme peril and probably close to death. According to most eyewitness accounts, of which there are many, they appear almost exclusively to close friends or relatives.

See also FETCH; WRAITH.

dove The dove's association with the Holy Ghost of Christian teaching means that the bird is widely linked with the qualities of purity and holiness. The dove that returned to Noah's ark with an olive branch in its beak, meanwhile, has further promoted the bird's association with such concepts as salvation and peace. No evil spirit may assume the form of a dove or obtain control over one.

The dove, especially the turtle dove, is also commonly associated with love and sexuality. This tradition would appear to have its roots ultimately in the bird's links with the Greek goddess of love Aphrodite and also with Ishtar, the Babylonian goddess of love and war. Even today the murmured intimacies of courting couples may be referred to as 'billing and cooing', recalling this association.

Some people, though, fear the appearance of a dove as it may be associated with death (in Native American folklore, for instance, the dove is often identified as the reincarnated soul of a dead person). Welsh miners have been known to refuse to go underground on seeing a dove, and some say that a dove circling someone is a sure sign that the person concerned is fated to die in the near future. Another widely held folk belief, however, has it that no person can die while lying on a mattress or pillow that contains dove feathers, and in the past people deliberately laid the stricken on such feathers in order to delay the moment of death until various friends and relatives could be reached.

Scottish tradition advises that the innards torn from a living dove can be used as a laxative for cattle, although other authorities warn that great misfortune will befall anyone who kills a dove. US superstition advises that placing a dead dove on the chest will alleviate pneumonia, and further that turtle doves making their nests near a person's house will protect that person from rheumatism.

dowsing A form of DIVINATION used for finding hidden or lost objects through the use of rods, pendulums and other means. The theory is that the rod (often a V-shaped twig of hazel or rowan held in both hands) or the pendulum will quiver when brought close to the water, metal or precious stone that is being sought, thus revealing its whereabouts. Some modern dowsing rods incorporate a small holder in which a sample of what is being sought is carefully placed. According to some authorities, only one in ten people has the necessary gifts to dowse successfully. Scientists continue to dispute the claims made for dowsing, although thousands of apparently successful searches for underground streams and so forth through dowsing have convinced many people that the method must have some sound scientific basis.

Some dowsers specialize in rhabdomancy, the art of dowsing over maps rather than over the actual ground itself. Several skilful dowsers have been employed by the police over the years, sometimes with significant success, to conduct searches for the bodies of murder victims and missing people.

drac In French folklore, a species of demon that haunts watery caves. They are reputed to lure mortals into the water by manifesting as treasure and then drag their prey below the surface and drown them.

Dracula *See* VAMPIRE.

dragon Fierce reptilian beast that features in various guises in the mythology of many cultures. The classic dragon is a large scaly fire-breathing monster with a long forked tail and sometimes wings. It is immensely powerful and may ravage the countryside, killing and feeding on any knights or other heroes who challenge it to battle. Many dragons are more accurately described as water serpents, haunting certain lakes and pools.

Countless tales are told of brave knights who pit themselves against dragons to prove their valour and to steal the legendary hoards of treasure such beasts are reputed to guard. Among the most famous of these stories are the battle between BEOWULF and Grendel (and Grendel's mother), and the celebrated dragon-slaying feat performed by St GEORGE. Dragons also feature in the story of MERLIN, who as Merlin Emrys reveals two dragons that lurk underground beneath Vortigern's Tower, and in the NIBELUNGENLIED, in which Siegfried kills such a beast.

The fearsome reputation of the dragon meant that in former times many heroes adopted dragon emblems to emphasize their own prowess in battle. Similarly, carved dragons were fixed to the prows of

Viking longboats in order to spread terror among enemies, and subsequently dragons in various poses appeared on heraldic shields (as the red dragon still does on the Welsh flag). Dragons also featured prominently among the heraldic emblems of pre-Communist China, where the creature has particular significance as a symbol in Taoism. The parading of a huge dragon (actually a long body supported by scores of dancers) remains a well-known feature of the celebrations marking the Chinese New Year. The Chinese also fly so-called 'dragon kites', a reference to the dragon's identification in Chinese lore as a beast of the air.

See also LOCH NESS MONSTER; WORM.

Drake's drum *See* DRUM.

dream Folklore has always paid particular attention to dreams, offering a variety of interpretations about their origin and meaning. In the ancient world, long before Freud and Jung set about their analyses of the dream state, it was widely presumed that dreams contained messages from the supernatural world, and that much about the present and the future might be divined from their study. In many societies such analysis was placed in the hands of skilled seers and shamans.

Among the more commonly held beliefs are the notions that dreaming the same dream three nights in succession means it will almost certainly come true, and that it is lucky to forget the dream you had the previous night. If a dream is remembered its nature should not be divulged, according to British tradition, until after breakfast. Dreams experienced on a Friday night and discussed with others on a Saturday are sure to come true.

In both the West and the Orient it is said that if a person dreams something this means that exactly the opposite will happen in real life. If one dreams of death, therefore, this bodes well for the living, but if one dreams of a wedding a funeral is likely to follow. Dreaming of the future is promoted by sleeping with a horseshoe, a leaf or a key under the pillow. Various procedures, such as slipping the shoulder-blade of a sheep or goat beneath the pillow on retiring to bed, will enable the sleeper to dream of a future lover.

See also NIGHTMARE; ONEIROMANCY.

Dreamtime In Australian Aboriginal folklore, a time in the distant past when all things were created. Also known as the 'Dreaming', it witnessed the creation of the earth and all upon it by divine ancestral spirits. Souls are reputed to be fetched from the Dreaming at the moment of conception and return there after death.

drowned lands Legends of fabulous towns, cities and even whole continents that were inundated by the sea are common to many cultures around the world. The best known of these include the legend of ATLANTIS, which is supposed to have been destroyed around 1500 BC, the Breton city of Ys, Bomere in Shropshire, Kilgrimod near Blackpool, Caer Wyddno in Cardigan Bay and, in Arthurian myth, LYONESSE, an area off the coast of Cornwall from which TRISTAM is supposed to have come. Other tales suggest that two whole continents, called Lemuria and Mu, were similarly lost to the waves many centuries ago and vanished below the Indian Ocean, together with the civilizations that populated them. Both continents have been identified in various traditions as the biblical Garden of Eden.

drum Drums feature prominently in the rituals of many of the world's cultures, being beaten to summon up supernatural spirits, to frighten away demons, and to whip celebrants up into a state of ecstasy in which they will achieve communion with the spirit world.

Some particular drums have inspired their own legends. British folklore, for instance, boasts a number of spectral drums, which beat out warnings when dire events are in the offing. Most famous of these is Drake's Drum, which is said to beat a drum roll when war is about to break out. Formerly the property of Sir Francis Drake and now kept at Buckland Abbey, near Plymouth, it is said to have beaten a roll in 1914, at the start of World War I, again at the end of the conflict in 1918, when it was heard on board the British ships at anchor in Scapa Flow, and reportedly once more during the evacuation of Dunkirk in 1940. Another celebrated spectral drum was that which belonged to an itinerant drummer who was arrested for vagrancy in Tedworth (renamed Tidworth), Wiltshire, in 1661. After the drummer was parted from his drum and he had been sentenced to transportation, the drum continued to be beaten by an unseen hand, and the entire village was much troubled by poltergeist activity. In Scotland, the Airlie family of Cortachy Castle in Kirriemuir, Angus, claim their own 'drum of death', which is alleged to sound whenever the death of the head of the family is nigh.

dumb cake In the British Isles, a special cake that is prepared in complete silence so that it may be used for the purposes of DIVINATION. The ingredients of flour, water, eggs and salt are mixed by one or more persons and then placed on the hearthstone, the upper surface of the cake being pricked with the initials of one of those present. If all is done correctly and in complete silence, then the apparition of a future partner of the person concerned will appear and similarly prick his or her own initials on the cake. Variants of the tradition suggest that it may only be performed at midnight on Christmas Eve or on Hallowe'en or on other auspicious dates, and that portions of the cake must actually be eaten by those taking part. In some regions it is stipulated that the petitioners must walk backwards to their beds after eating the cake, and on so doing will be pursued by apparitions of eager lovers-to-be.

Dun Cow Mythical beast of English folklore that is supposed to have ravaged the countryside around Dunsmore Heath in Warwickshire until slain by GUY OF WARWICK. Described as massive in size, with huge horns and fiery dun-coloured eyes, it was said to produce an endless supply of milk and to have originally belonged to a giant who kept it at Mitchell Fold in Shropshire. It escaped after an old woman, having filled her pail with the Dun Cow's milk, tried to fill a sieve also. Incensed at the old woman's greed, the beast terrorized a wide area, destroying cattle and killing anyone who came near. Sir Guy himself only succeeded in killing the Dun Cow after a long and bloody battle.

Dunmow Flitch A flitch (side) of bacon that is presented each year to the most happily married couple living in the Essex town of Little Dunmow. To win the flitch a couple must be in a position to swear that they have not quarrelled or regretted the day they married at any time during the past year and a day. This well-known custom appears to have begun in the 12th century, and is still celebrated today, although there have been several interuptions in its continuity over the centuries.

duppy In the folk religions of the West Indies, a species of GHOST that can be raised from the grave through certain arcane rituals. These include pouring rum or tossing money onto a grave and then beating it with a stick. Once awakened the duppy will allegedly obey the commands of the person who has summoned it, however evil these commands may be. A person breathed on by a duppy will vomit uncontrollably, while the mere touch of a duppy can induce fits. Local folklore recommends various ways to keep duppies within the grave, and also advises that if prevented from returning to their graves by first light they will become harmless. Some people sprinkle tobacco seed over their doorways and windows to keep duppies out.

See also DAVY JONES; JUMBY; ZOMBIE.

dvergar In Scandinavian folklore, a breed of DWARF. They are supposed to live underground, where they fashion wonderful weapons, jewellery and other magical objects. Legend has it that they were created originally from maggots feeding on the corpse of the giant YMIR, and that they will turn to stone if exposed to sunlight.

dwarf A diminutive breed of FAIRY that figures in the legends and mythology of many cultures. The dwarf tradition was well-established in early Teutonic and Scandinavian mythology and was subsequently boosted by reports about the pygmy tribes of Africa. According to Norse legend, dwarfs were created originally from the flesh of the primordial giant YMIR, and have since then filled the role of guardians of the earth's underground regions.

Dwarfs are traditionally depicted as short, bearded old men, often wearing magic brown caps. In character they are variously supposed to be touchy and hot-tempered or else kindly and benevolent (as in the fairy tale 'Snow White and the Seven Dwarfs'). They make their homes in an underground kingdom (hence their legendary skill as miners) from which they rarely emerge. They dislike sunlight, and if trapped above ground during the day will be unable to return to their subterranean homes until nightfall.

Dwarfs are also said to be capable of fine metalwork, and invincible weapons and armour forged by dwarfs feature prominently in many heroic epics, notably the NIBELUNGENLIED. They are also reputed to be able to see into the future, and to have the power to make themselves invisible at will.

A minority of dwarfs are irredeemably evil, casting malevolent spells and seeking to cause harm to humans (as in the fairy tale 'Rumpelstiltskin'). Their crimes may range from minor acts of mischief to kidnapping human children to work in their mines.

See also ELF; KNOCKER; TROLL.

dybbuk In Jewish folklore, a wandering GHOST that roams restlessly from place to place looking for a susceptible human body it can possess. Tales about dybbuks caused much anxiety among Jewish people during the 16th and 17th centuries, and it was quite common for people displaying symptoms of mental illness to be subjected to exorcism in order to drive a dybbuk out. According to ancient authorities, dybbuks are the souls of those who have died with their sins unforgiven.

E

Eachtach In Irish Celtic mythology, the daughter of GRAINNE and DIARMUID. She took violent revenge upon FIONN MAC CUMHAILL, who had conceived a passion for Eachtach's mother and who had harassed her parents for many years. Her revenge took the form of inflicting wounds that were so severe they took four years to heal.

eachtra *See* ECHTRAI.

each uisge *See* KELPIE.

eagle The eagle has a strong folkloric identity in many cultures. In the mythology of several ancient peoples the bird was often associated with the sun, and it was commonly believed that the eagle alone had the power to gaze directly into the sun without being blinded. Scandinavian legend links the eagle with storms and melancholy, but also credits it with delivering warnings of danger to various folk heroes, including VÄINÄ-MÖINEN. To other peoples it has variously embodied courage and immortality, among other attributes. The ancient Egyptians believed that the human soul was transformed into an eagle after death, and the eagle-headed god Horus had special significance among the deities. The bird was also associated with the Greek Zeus and the Roman Jupiter.

Because of its imperious nature, the bird has figured prominently in the martial symbols of many nations, from the golden eagle standards carried by the Roman legions to its reappearance among the symbols of Nazi Germany. The bald eagle emblem of the USA was a somewhat surprising choice as American settler tradition linked the bird with such negative attributes as cowardice and immorality. Native American lore, however, views the bird in a more positive light, associating it with the Thunderbird or Great Spirit (hence the use of eagle feathers in headdresses, and the luck-bringing eagle dance common to many tribes). The two-headed eagle of the Holy Roman Empire was adopted to represent the eastern and western divisions of the empire. Imperial Russia also adopted the two-headed eagle, to symbolize the eastern and western parts of the Russian empire. In Christian symbolism the eagle represents St John the Evangelist, St Augustine, St Gregory the Great and St Prisca. An Irish legend claims that Adam and Eve still live today in the guise of a pair of eagles living on an island off Galway.

The Romans believed that every ten years the eagle soared up towards the sun until its feathers caught fire and then dived down into the sea, where it moulted and thereby enjoyed a new lease of life. A similar notion features in the legend of the Irish adventurer MAELDUINE, who once watched an eagle restoring its youth by immersing itself in a secret lake. In the story of MABON, meanwhile, the eagle was identified as the oldest of all the animals. Another old British folk tale describes how the eagle was deceived by the hawk into going on a fool's errand, while the hawk feasted on the eagle's eggs.

Superstitions concerning eagles are generally pessimistic. The cry of the eagle, for instance, is widely held to be a warning of death and disease to come, and the Welsh believe that when the eagles of Snowdonia flap their wings they raise whirlwinds. Because of the bird's reputation for immortality and sharp eyesight, the feathers, flesh and eggs of the eagle have all been used in spells by those variously hoping to enjoy a longer lifespan or better vision. The heart of an eagle was once supposed to be a powerful ingredient in love potions, while its marrow was supposed to have potent contraceptive properties.

eagle stone *See* HOLED STONE.

ear Like other openings to the body the ears have always been considered vulnerable to evil influence. The folklore of many European cultures includes various ways of protecting the ears. Because evil spirits may use the ears to gain access to the body it was once considered advisable to guard the ears with earrings made of such magical metals as gold and silver. This tradition has lasted into modern times, and was particularly popular with people engaged in dangerous occupations – notably sailors, who believe that if they wear earrings they will never be drowned. Today earrings continue to be worn by either sex in many parts of the world, even though the original reasons for this practice have been largely forgotten, and they now tend to be considered purely decorative.

Other traditions relating to ears include the long-standing northern European superstition that tingling ears are a sign that someone is talking about the person concerned. If it is the right ear that tingles then good things are being said, but if it is the left ear then the person concerned is being slandered. A ringing in the ears was sometimes regarded in

English superstition as a warning of the imminent death of a close friend or relation. According to the pseudo-science of physiognomy it is possible to discern much about a person's character from their ears: if they are small, for instance, the person concerned is very mean, but if they are long this is a sign of great wisdom.

earthquake Folklore inevitably has a number of explanations for earthquakes and why they happen. According to Indian tradition, earthquakes occur when Muhu-pudma, the huge elephant on whose head the universe rests, shifts a little. South American mythology claims that the earth rests on the back of an enormous frog, and earthquakes result when the frog moves about. Elsewhere the animal in question is identified as a turtle. In ancient Greek and Roman mythology earthquakes were blamed upon the various giants who were buried under high mountains by Zeus (Jupiter). Dreams of earthquakes are supposed to be a warning of trouble in store for the person concerned.

Easal In Irish legend, the King of the Golden Pillars, who owned seven enchanted pigs that were repeatedly restored after they were killed and eaten. Anyone who ate their flesh was supposed to be magically protected from disease. The Sons of TUIRENN set LUGH the task of obtaining the pigs.

Easter Christian festival commemorating the Crucifixion of Christ and his subsequent Resurrection. The precise dating of Easter has been debated for many centuries, and the Eastern and Western churches tend to celebrate the festival on different dates each year. The coincidence of the Christian festival with the celebration of earlier pagan rites marking the coming of spring, and the new life it represents, led to much confusion between the two traditions, and today's Easter festivities incorporate a wide variety of both Christian and pagan elements (as do CHRISTMAS celebrations). In the English-speaking world, for instance, some of the rituals that mark this time of year seem to owe more to the fertility rites once celebrated in honour of the Germanic goddess of the spring, Eostre or Ostera, after whom Easter is named, than to Christianity.

The more obvious religious rites include church services and processions as well as the bearing of flowers, the ringing of bells, the lighting of candles and the performance of devotional plays. The exchanging of chocolate Easter eggs and the elaborate decorating of eggshells reflects the fact that eggs are not eaten in some parts of the Christian world between Egg Saturday (or Egg Feast), the Saturday before Shrove Tuesday, and the end of Lent, the period of fasting leading up to Easter itself. However, the custom is also clearly influenced by much older pagan veneration of the EGG as a symbol of new life. There may also be links with the feudal practice of lords of the manor giving eggs as payment to their villeins at Easter, and with the ancient custom of colouring eggs red in remembrance of Christ's blood. The Easter RABBIT, who in the USA and to a lesser extent in the UK, is believed to deliver chocolate Easter eggs, is thought to have evolved from the rabbit with which the goddess Ostera was traditionally depicted, although attempts have been made to trace it all the way back via the HARE to an ancient Egyptian fertility symbol. German superstition claims that rabbits lay eggs on Easter Day.

In many parts of continental Europe Easter is also celebrated by the curious custom of men giving any women and girls they meet on Easter Monday a symbolic thrashing (actually a light tap) with a BIRCH twig – a practice known as the *Schmeckostern* in Germany and Austria. The women are usually allowed to return the 'beating' the following day. Other miscellaneous examples of Easter lore include the ancient belief that the sun

dances for joy each year on Easter Day, and the varied (and often very unruly) village sports such as EGG ROLLING and egg shackling (in which eggs are knocked together to see which breaks first) that are played throughout Europe at this time of year. Another ancient custom, found in the Welsh Marches and now of historical interest only, was that of 'Easter-lifting', which involved young men hoisting young women up in the air in specially decorated chairs and then claiming kisses from them.

The surviving tradition of wearing an 'Easter bonnet' and new clothes on Easter Day is thought to have originated in the custom of wearing just one set of clothes during the whole of Lent and then discarding these for new ones on Easter Sunday. People who do not observe this tradition, it is said, risk having their existing clothes soiled by passing birds.

Eber Donn In Irish Celtic legend, the brother of EBER FINN, and one of the leaders of the sons of MIL ESPAINE, who invaded Ireland and defeated the TUATHA DE DANANN. Eber Donn himself killed Mac Cuill, one of the Tuatha De Danann, but died before the question of who should rule Ireland in their stead came to the fore.

Eber Finn In Irish Celtic legend, the brother of EBER DONN and one of the leaders of the sons of MIL ESPAINE, who defeated the TUATHA DE DANANN. Eber Finn quarrelled with EREMON over who should rule Ireland, and in the end the country was divided in two, with Eber Finn ruling the south. When war broke out between the two realms Eber Finn was killed and Eremon became effective ruler of all Ireland.

echtrai A genre of Irish folk tale, usually describing how a mortal is invited to enjoy a privileged glimpse of life in the OTHERWORLD. In contrast to the IM-RAMA story-telling genre the emphasis is less upon the epic journey the hero makes to get there, and more upon tempting descriptions of the mythical land itself, and upon the means by which the mortal manages to get back home again. In some tales – such as that of Prince Coule, who is lured to an otherworld called the Land of the Living by a treacherous fairy and agrees to embark on the waters with her in a glass coracle – the hero disappears and is never seen again.

Eckhardt In German folklore, an apparition or spirit who manifests on Maundy Thursday to warn people to stay indoors, and thus to stay safe from the headless riders who roam the earth that night. The origins of the Eckhardt tradition are obscure: he may have evolved from a 13th-century Dominican friar called Meister Eckhardt, or else from Eckherdt the Faithful, one of the companions of TANNHÄUSER. Legend has it that the ghostly Eckhardt, whoever he really was, was originally snatched up from the mortal world as an old man by the train of the beneficent witch-goddess Mother HOLLE, and that he is fated to remain in her service until his release at the Day of Judgement.

eclipse The total or partial disappearance of the sun or the moon from the sky due to eclipses excited great fear in early times, and the phenomenon inspired a wide range of folkloric beliefs. It was usual to regard eclipses as bad omens, typically foretelling the death of a great leader (the deaths of Nero and Catherine of Aragon were among those preceded by an eclipse), or some other calamity (such as the Black Death of 1348 or the outbreak of World War I in 1914). Various explanations of eclipses have been offered in folklore. These include the theories that the sun and moon are quarrelling, that they are engaged in an incestuous relationship, or that they are being devoured by a great monster. According to the Chinese, the Lapps and the Persians, the monster in question is a DRAGON. Some peoples from the East

Indies, however, identify it as a black GRIFFIN. The usual remedy is to make sacrifices, dance, beat drums, fire guns or arrows into the air, and generally make a great racket in the hope of scaring the monster away.

Ector de Maris In Arthurian legend, one of the knights of the Round Table. Identified as the brother of Sir LANCELOT, he is sometimes confused with Arthur's foster-father ECTOR OF THE FOREST SAUVAGE.

Ector of the Forest Sauvage In Arthurian legend, the foster-father of King ARTHUR, who was entrusted with the future king's upbringing. On the instructions of MERLIN, he brought the young Arthur up in ignorance of his real identity and destiny.

Edain See ETAIN.

Edain Echraidhe See HORSE.

Eddas Two great works from the early Icelandic poetic tradition, in which are recounted various mythological tales. The word Edda may come from the Icelandic word *edda*, meaning 'great-grandmother', or from the Old Norse *odhr*, meaning 'poetry'. The Elder (or *Poetic*) *Edda* was discovered in 1643 by an Icelandic bishop, and has been dated to the 9th century. It has been tentatively attributed to Saemund Sigfusson (d.1133). Among its various tales are the story of the theft of Thor's hammer by the giant Thrym and the legend of SIGURD. The *Younger* (or *Prose*) *Edda*, which offers further mythological material as well as advice about writing poetry, was found in 1628, and has been credited to Snorri Sturluson (d.1242). Important episodes in this work include the journey of Gylfi, king of the Swedes, to ASGARD, and predictions of RAGNAROK, the end of the world.

Edmund, St English king of East Anglia whose violent death inspired a lasting cult. Born in 841, he was killed by the Danes after defeat in battle in 869, allegedly being tied to a tree and shot to death with arrows after he refused to abjure his Christian faith. The miracles of healing that allegedly took place at his shrine in what became Bury St Edmunds, established him as an object of veneration, his emblem being an arrow.

eel The unique and rather sinister appearance of the eel has guaranteed the fish a special place in world folklore. It was believed in some parts of northern England, for instance, that it was unwise to swim among eels, as they might suck the blood of the swimmer. Japanese folklore has a similar notion of eels, suggesting that eels are in fact disguised DRAGONS. People living in the Ozark Mountains of the USA used to claim that a fried eel left untouched would eventually become raw again. It was also rumoured among American anglers that eels have a particular weakness for human flesh, and that such bait will ensure the greatest catches. Elsewhere it was believed that witches and sorcerers sometimes wore eelskin jackets because these were thought to be impervious to gunfire.

Many superstitions built up surrounding the origin of eels: it was only relatively recently that it was discovered that eels migrate once in their lives to the Sargasso Sea, where they breed and die, leaving the young eels to find their way back to the rivers where their parents lived. Some said that eels were born from the slime of other fish, while others claimed that horse hairs immersed in water would eventually turn into eels.

Folk medicine had many uses for eels, although they are considered unsuitable as food in many parts of the world (maybe even poisonous). The liver of the fish could be powdered and applied to aid childbirth, and eel blood rubbed on warts was supposed to make them disappear. Eating a whole eel was believed to cure deafness, while slipping an eel into a drunkard's glass was reputed to be enough to cure the patient of addiction to alcohol. Eel skins were sometimes worn in the form of garters in the belief that this would counter the ague, rheumatism and other similar ailments.

Efnisien In Welsh legend, the half-brother of BRAN THE BLESSED. He attracted a reputation as a troublemaker. When Efnisien caused severe injury to 100 horses which king Matholwch had brought with him from Ireland when he came to seek the hand of Efnisien's sister BRANWEN, Matholwch took his revenge by maltreating Branwen after their marriage. Bran the Blessed set out on an expedition to recover Branwen, but the Irish, pretending to welcome him, planned to trick him by hiding 100 men in sacks of provisions until the signal was given to leap on him. Efnisien realized what was happening and killed the warriors while they were still in their sacks by crushing their heads. The quarrel was settled by Gwern, son of Matholwch and Branwen, being given the sovereignty of Ireland.

Efnisien did not approve of this arrangement, which compromised Britain's independence from Irish interference, and threw the lad into a fire, where he burned to death. A full-scale war now broke out between the Welsh and the Irish. The Irish enjoyed early success through their possession of a magic cauldron, with which they could restore slain warriors to life, until Efnisien managed to destroy the cauldron – sacrificing his own life in the process. At the end of the terrible war only seven of Bran's party were left alive to return to Wales, while the Irish forces were reduced to five pregnant women hiding in a cave.

egg The egg has special significance in world folklore. The notion that the earth itself is an egg hatched by the creator was shared by the Phoenicians, Egyptians, Hindus and Japanese, among others. Various other myths describe the earth being created as an egg laid in primordial waters. Other cultures describe the birth of the human race from a cosmic egg. The egg is one of the most widely understood emblems of life and fertility, and is also a potent Christian icon, widely revered as a symbol of the new life represented by the Resurrection.

Eggs are generally considered to be lucky, possessing a range of beneficial and protective properties. In England, farmhands were likely to present a pullet's first egg to their sweethearts, while those who ate eggs laid by black hens were thought to be immune to fever for the following 12 months. Moroccan folklore insists that men who eat an egg every morning for 40 days will enjoy greatly enhanced sexual powers. In France new brides were encouraged to break an egg on entering the marital home, in order to ensure their fertility. In many cultures eggs were considered appropriate for sacrifices, or were buried with the dead as a symbol of new life in the afterworld. To prevent eggs being interfered with by witches it was thought advisable to mark them with a black cross. Many people in former times also took care to smash empty eggshells, as witches were believed to use them as boats in which to set sail to wreck other ships.

Not all folkloric notions concerning eggs are positive, however. Finding an unusually small hen's egg was considered a portent of death, and the assumption was that it must have been laid by a cock. The remedy was to throw the egg over the barn roof – if it was allowed to hatch it was said that a serpent would emerge. In Japan, women are warned against stepping over eggshells, as it is believed that this could make them go mad. Fishermen at sea believe that it is very unlucky to have eggs on board their boats.

Perhaps the most contentious issue relating to eggs is the abiding question of which end they should be cracked open. Superstition claims that it is always best to crack open the larger end, as to open the egg at the smaller end threatens the disappointment of all the diner's hopes.

On various auspicious dates during the year, such as Midsummer's Eve, eggs may be used in ancient divination rituals, a practice known as oomancy. A typical example of these involves pouring three drops of egg white into water and then examining the shapes they form for clues about an enquirer's future.

See also EASTER; EGG ROLLING.

egg rolling A village sport celebrated in many parts of Europe at EASTER, in which eggs are rolled down sloping hillsides to see which reaches the bottom first. The sport was introduced to the USA in 1877 by the wife of President Madison, who allowed local children to use the grounds of the White House for the purpose (now an annual event). The rolling of hard-boiled Pasch or pace eggs (from the Middle English *Paschal*, meaning 'Easter') continues to this day in various parts of the world, including several towns in Scotland and northern England, among them Preston, Scarborough and Barton-upon-Humber. The eggs are usually painted before being rolled down grassy slopes, with small prizes on offer for the winner. Attempts to trace the origins of the custom have suggested links with the rolling aside of the stone sealing Christ's tomb, but the practice probably has pagan origins connected with the egg's role as a symbol of life and rebirth. At Dunstable, Bedfordshire, a similar ceremony takes place on Good Friday, with oranges taking the place of eggs.

Egil In Teutonic legend, a peasant who served as the keeper of the chariot and goats belonging to the god THOR. He was tricked by LOKI into breaking the leg bone of one of the goats so that Loki could feed on the marrow. When Thor saw that when he restored the goat to life it was lame he punished Egil by demanding his son and daughter as servants by way of compensation.

Another Egil features in Norse legend as the brother of the god WAYLAND THE SMITH. A great archer, he appears in the saga of Thidrik, performing a feat of marksmanship almost identical to that performed by WILLIAM TELL.

Eglamour Legendary knight, often referred to throughout European folklore as a model of chivalric behaviour. Having fallen in love with Chrystabell, the daughter of his lord Sir Prinsamour, the penniless Eglamour was told he would only be allowed to marry Chrystabell if he succeeded in completing three tasks. First he had to kill the giant Marrock, then a huge boar terrorizing the district and finally a dragon that was ravaging the area around Rome. Eglamour succeeded in his mission but was subsequently banished, as was his lover Chrystabell, after she bore him a son. Chrystabell spent many years wandering in search of their son after he was snatched away by a griffin, but the two lovers and their child were finally united after many further perilous adventures.

Einherier In Norse mythology, the host of slain warriors who spend eternity feasting with ODIN in VALHALLA. They are described as spending much of their time recounting their most famous triumphs and engaging in mock battles, defeated warriors being revived at the end of each day's conflict. In English folklore Odin's warriors were once identified with the WILD HUNT.

Eisert In Irish Celtic legend, a bard who persuaded IUBDAN, king of the dwarf Faylinn race, to visit the court of the giants of Ulster who, he claimed, enjoyed greater power than the Faylinn. Iubdan initially refused to believe Eisert's tales of a kingdom ruled by giants. However, after Eisert himself travelled to the court of Fergus Mac Leda of Ulster and returned with Aeda, Iubdan eventually allowed himself to be placed under a bond obliging him to go. The king's visit was fraught with peril, for the giants imprisoned both him and his wife, queen BEBO, and they were lucky to escape with their lives.

Eithne *See* ELCMAR; ETHLINN.

Elaine de Astolat In Arthurian legend, the daughter of the FISHER KING. She fell in love with Sir LANCELOT, and died when her love was not returned. Her sorry plight became known when her body floated in a boat down the river to Camelot, together with a lily and a letter identifying the reason for her demise. Her story is told in Alfred, Lord Tennyson's *Idylls of the King*.

Elaine of Corbenic In Arthurian legend, the daughter of King PELLES and the mother, by Sir LANCELOT, of Sir GALAHAD, finder of the Holy Grail. She used magic to dupe Lancelot into thinking she was his lover GUINEVERE, and lay with him one night.

Elatha In Irish Celtic legend, one of the early FOMORIAN kings of Ireland, whose realm predated the arrival of the Celts. He fathered BRES MAC ELATHA by ERI, one of the TUATHA DE DANANN women, and subsequently enjoyed his son's support in battle against the Tuatha. Bres himself in due course became king of the Tuatha de Danann.

El Cid *See* CID, EL.

Elcmar In Irish legend, the husband (sometimes the brother) of BOANN and the foster-father of ANGUS, who was actually the offspring of Boann and DAGDA. He is identified as the original owner of the otherworldly palace Brugh na Boinne (Newgrange, County Meath) that subsequently passed to Angus.

elder Many folk traditions and superstitions have evolved in association with the elder. In Christian tradition, the cross is reputed to have been made from elder wood, and it was from an elder tree that Judas is supposed to have hanged himself (hence the tree's bad smell). The tree is often linked with devil worship and witchcraft and its wood is preferred for the making of magic wands. Burning elder, in the hearth may result in the Devil himself coming down the chimney. If a man is murdered by a weapon made of elder, his ghost will rise from the grave to make the murderer known. Elder can, however, have beneficial effects. Elder may be rubbed on warts to make them disappear, and may also provide protection from witchcraft and vampires. It was once fixed over doorways in many countries to keep out evil spirits and to prevent the house being struck by lightning. Custom has it that elder should never be cut without first asking the permission of the 'Elder Mother', otherwise called the 'Old Gal', so that she does not take offence and strike the woodcutter down.

Dwarf elder, a separate species, is supposed in England to have sprung spontaneously from the ground wherever the blood of invading Danes had been spilled. Because of its red stems, suggesting the presence of real blood, the plant is sometimes listed as an ingredient in spells.

El Dorado Mythical 'golden' city in South America that was much sought by the Conquistadors, and which even today remains a metaphor for a source of immense wealth. The city was named after the fabulously wealthy king of the city of Manoa (or Omagua), on the Amazon. His name (meaning 'gilded') reflects the tradition that he was ritually coated in oil and gold dust before dipping himself in the Amazon in homage to the gods. A modern interpretation of the myth suggests it was made up by native Americans in the hope of persuading their European conquerors to move on elsewhere in search of riches.

Elen In Welsh folklore, the daughter of Eudaf (from whom the kings of Cornwall claimed descent) and the heroine of the ancient tale known as 'The Dream of Maxen Wledig'. The story goes that the Roman emperor Maximus (known as Maxen or Macsen Wledig by the Welsh) had a vision of Elen as he lay asleep and

immediately sent envoys to find her and bring her to him. In Wales, to which she later returned and where she became known as 'Helen of the Hosts', she devoted herself to Christian good works, including the building of many new roads (called the 'Sarnau Helen'). She is sometimes identified with Constantine the Great's mother St Helena.

elephant The elephant, with its reputation for long life, patient strength and great memory, is considered a lucky symbol in many parts of the world. Tiny elephant charms are worn in many countries to safeguard the good luck of the wearer and in the Western world elephants are often depicted on good-luck cards, whether these relate to weddings, driving tests or academic examinations.

Many of these traditions developed initially in the Indian subcontinent, where white elephants were considered sacred, and were transmitted to the English-speaking world during the days of the British Raj, when many elephants were brought to the West. The elephant-headed god Ganesh, who bestows riches and success upon those he favours, occupies a senior place in the Hindu pantheon. Indian mythology further claims that earthquakes result when Muhupudma, the great elephant on which the universe rests, shakes its burden. The ancient notion that an elephant has no knees and thus cannot regain its feet after falling over is not accurate.

elf According to Teutonic and Scandinavian folklore, a variety of DWARF possessing magical powers. In later times the word came to include many varieties of IMPS, FAIRIES and other supernatural beings, which may or may not harbour kindly feelings towards humans. Significantly, the word itself came originally from Old English *oelf*, which in turn was derived from the Teutonic *alp* (meaning 'nightmare'). In Welsh tradition elves were known as *ellylon*. In Scandinavian mythology the species was sometimes divided into light and dark races who differed not only in colouring but also in temperament. According to some accounts, the elves are delicate, lovely creatures, but in others they are described as squat and ugly. Elf women were said to be lovely when viewed from the front but their back view revealed a hollow body like a burnt-out tree or a long tail. The traditional home of elves is sometimes identified as ALFHELM, ruled over by the Norse god of vegetation Freyr. The modern understanding of the term elf owes much to the writer J. R. R. Tolkien, who linked the Scandinavian elves with the Celtic ALFAR or SIDHE, identified as the inhabitants of the BLESSED ISLANDS.

Fear of elves was once profound in rural areas throughout northern Europe. If babies were born with minor defects they were quite likely to be described as 'elf-marked', suggesting that the infants had been marked out for future mischief. Even worse, elves might be suspected of exchanging human babies with their own CHANGELINGS. If humans or livestock suffered any unexplained injury or sickness they were likely to be called 'elf-shot' and their ailment attributed to stone arrows fired at them by malicious elves. Actual examples of elf arrows preserved through the centuries are now understood to be, in most cases, Neolithic flint arrowheads. Less serious examples of interference by mischievous elves include the notion that tangled hair results from the toying of the elf queen MAB, whose favourite amusements were once said to include tying knots ('elf-locks') in the hair of unsuspecting humans.

See also BROWNIE; PIXIE.

elf arrow *See* ELF.

elf fire *See* WILL O' THE WISP.

Elfhame *See* ALFHELM.

elf locks *See* ELF.

Elidor In British legend, a priest who claimed to have made many visits to the underworld inhabited by the fairies. According to the writer Giraldus Cambrensis, Elidor's access to fairyland was abruptly cut off when he agreed to provide his mother with proof of his claims by stealing a golden ball with which the fairies played.

elixir vitae A magical potion or powder that has the power to prolong life. Elixirs of life have been long sought by alchemists, sorcerers and magicians throughout the world. Some claimed to have succeeded in their ambition and to have produced an effective elixir, but none of these claims proved convincing. Among those to claim success were the Comte de St-Germain, a favourite of Madame de Pompadour in the mid-18th century, who boasted that he was himself over 2,000 years old. Sir Francis Bacon (1561–1626) was rumoured to have discovered a similar potion, and to have lived for 1,000 years. Madame de Sévigné, in the 17th century, was supposed to have achieved immortality by drinking human blood and eating vipers. The Swiss physician Paracelsus was believed to possess a magical stone that turned any ordinary liquid into a potion that would prolong life and bestow other benefits.

See also ALCHEMY; PHILOSOPHER'S STONE.

ellyllon *See* ELF.

elm The elm tree featured prominently in Norse mythology as the source of the first woman, Embla, and subsequently became the focus of various beliefs. In the English-speaking world the tree was often associated with elves and thus avoided. Herdsmen once kept their livestock away from elms in the belief that falling elm leaves spread disease among the animals, while farmers in southwest England used to insist that barley should not be planted until the new elm leaves were the size of a mouse's ear. In the USA elm bark and leaves were formerly recommended as a poultice for the treatment of bed sores and burns.

Elphin In Welsh legend, the son of Gwyddno. He is usually remembered as the discoverer of the poet TALIESIN, whom he fished out of his father's salmon pool on the eve of May Day. Taliesin brought great luck to the penniless Elphin (or Elffin), rewarding him with a beautiful wife, swift horses and other riches. Such was his pride in his new acquisitions that King Maelgwn grew tired of his boasts and threw him into prison, bound with ironically appropriate silver chains. Taliesin rescued his patron, who escaped on the swift horses the poet had given him and was further compensated with a cauldron of gold.

Emer In Irish mythology, the lover of the great warrior hero CUCHULAINN. The daughter of Forgall, a wily chieftain, she won the love of Cuchulainn when he was just seven years old, but subsequently failed to prevent him embarking on numerous romantic liaisons with other women. Of these only Cuchulainn's attachment to FAND caused her particular distress, and in the end it required a magical potion to secure Emer and her lover freedom from Fand's enchantment. The legend goes that one day Cuchulainn rushed to Emer's side after he had a vision of her in terrible danger, only to find she was in perfect safety – he then rejected her pleas to stay and left to meet his own death (as warned of in his vision). Such was Emer's love for Cuchulainn that her heart broke at his death and, after loudly lamenting his demise, she fell dead with grief into his grave.

emerald Green-coloured gemstone that is usually associated with good luck. The birthstone for those born in May, emerald is said to safeguard chastity, ward off evil and protect the wearer against the threat of epilepsy. A sorcerer speaking with an emerald tucked under his or her tongue was supposed to have the power to raise up evil spirits. The stone is also believed to cure dysentery, to assist in childbirth, to negate the effects of snakebite and to improve poor eyesight. Emeralds were also occasionally placed in graves as symbols of life in the afterlife. According to ancient legend they could be obtained from the nests of GRIFFINS.

Emhain Macha The legendary palace of the kings of Ulster. It was supposed to have been founded by the warrior queen MACHA in the 4th century BC, and it was here that CONCHOBAR subsequently held court.

empyromancy The art of DIVINATION through the observation of how things burn in a sacrificial fire. This ancient form of prophecy is common to many of the world's cultures. Typical objects used for the purposes of empyromancy include eggs, flour, nuts and incense.

Endellion, St In Arthurian legend, the daughter of King Brychan and goddaughter of King ARTHUR. She was subsequently venerated as a saint. Legend claims that she put to death a man who had killed her cow but later repented and restored him to life. When she died she ordered her body to be laid in an ox-drawn cart and buried wherever the oxen came to rest.

Enid In Arthurian legend, the daughter of Yniol and the wife of Sir GERAINT, one of the knights of the Round Table. She incurred her husband's suspicion when he found her weeping over his failure to live up to knightly ideals and, presuming she was lamenting a lost lover, forbade her to speak to him. Consequently, she was barred from warning him of danger in the course of his subsequent adventures, to his cost, although they were eventually reconciled. Variously known as Enid the Fair and Enid the Good, she is the subject of Alfred, Lord Tennyson's poem 'Geraint and Enid' in his *Idylls of the King*.

97

Eochaid Airem Legendary king of Ireland who incurred the wrath of the SIDHE after claiming as his wife ETAIN, who was already married to Midhir, one of the SIDHE. Midhir subsequently visited Eochaid, agreeing to perform various miraculous tasks such as clearing a causeway (with the aid of fairy oxen) and then persuaded Eochaid to put Etain up as a stake in a game of fidchell (chess). Midhir won and, despite Etain's protests that Eochaid had not given his free consent to the deal, carried her off. Eochaid immediately declared war on the Sidhe and won Etain back, but in so doing earned the lasting emnity of the Sidhe, causing great suffering among his descendants.

Eoghan Mor In Irish mythology, a follower of NUADU, leader of the TUATHA DE DANANN. He married Beare and in due course became the ruler of southern Ireland.

Eostre *See* EASTER.

epilepsy In ancient times it was commonly believed that epileptics were in direct contact with the gods. The condition has always provoked feelings of curiosity and dread, inspiring a wide range of odd beliefs. In post-medieval Europe fits of epilepsy or 'falling sickness' were often blamed on witchcraft or possession by spirits. However, in other parts of the world epileptics were often respected as priests or seers. The folklore of every country offered cures for the ailment. These ranged from burying a black cock or hammering a nail in the ground where the fit took place, to wearing a ring fashioned from a half-crown given during a service of Holy Communion, drinking a potion based on MISTLETOE, or consuming the heart and blood of a CROW on nine days in succession.

Epona Celtic horse goddess, worshipped throughout Celtic Europe for her healing gifts. Her name means 'horse', and she appears in various ancient folk tales, described as a half-naked woman astride a mare, or as feeding two foals from her lap while seated upon her throne. She was one of the goddesses favoured by Roman cavalry regiments, and shrines dedicated to her were commonly placed in stables to provide divine protection for the horses. More ominously, it was also believed in the Celtic World that she escorted the dead to the next world.

Eremon In Irish mythology, the first king of all Ireland, from whom all subsequent Irish monarchs claimed descent. The son of MILED, he established control of the country after defeating and killing his brother EBER FINN in battle.

Ériu In Irish mythology, a goddess of sovereignty and queen of the TUATHA DE DANANN, whose name was perpetuated in the Gaelic name for Ireland, Erin or Eire. She was one of the three goddesses who promised the sons of MIL ESPAINE the rule of Ireland if they would agree to adopt one of their names as the title of their land. She was also the mother of BRES MAC ELATHA.

Erlking In German mythology, a terrifying GOBLIN, sometimes described as the king of the DWARFS, who ambushes and kills humans (especially children) in the forests. He became the subject of a poem by Goethe, in which the Erlking snatches the soul of a young boy from his father despite the latter's fierce resistance.

Estmere Scottish folk hero who is the central character in a late medieval romantic epic from Scotland. The story goes that Estmere was in love with the daughter of King Asland, but was initially rejected as a suitor. This all changed after Estmere, disguised as a Moorish harper, foiled a Spanish plot against King Asland and his daughter, and was rewarded with the hand of his beloved.

Etain (or Edain) In Irish mythology, the wife of Midhir, one of the SIDHE. Her abduction by EOCHAID AIREM provoked lasting emnity between the Sidhe and Eochaid's family. When still Midhir's wife, Etain suffered from the jealousy of Midhir's other wife Fuamnach, who transformed her rival into a fly. After seven years' adventures in the form of a fly she was restored to her normal shape nine months after falling into the cup of Etair's wife. She was then taken as wife by Eochaid Airem, but was reclaimed by Midhir as the prize in a game of fidchell (chess), and returned to TIR NAN OG in the form of a swan. Eochaid subsequently took arms against the Sidhe and eventually won Etain back.

Ethlinn (or **Eithne, Ethne**) In Irish legend, the daughter of BALOR. She was imprisoned by her father in a glass tower after it was prophesied that he would meet his death at the hands of his grandson. However, Cian, son of the medicine god Dian Cecht, managed to get into the tower, and in due course Ethlinn gave birth to their son LUGH. When Balor heard about the birth of his grandson, he tried to have the child drowned, but Lugh was rescued, entrusted to the protection of MANANNAN MAC LIR, and eventually fulfilled the prophecy.

Ethniu In Irish mythology, the foster sister of the daughter of MANANNAN MAC LIR. She was reduced to spirit form after one of the TUATHA DE DANANN attempted to rape her. She lived at Brugh na Boinne entirely on the milk provided by two magical cows, but one day left Brugh and found herself unable to return. According to later Christian legend she then converted to Christianity, and was administered the last rites by St Patrick himself, although she never forgot her former pagan companions.

euhemerism The theory that much of world folklore was based originally on real historical figures and events. Although it was probably first advanced at an earlier date by the Phoenicians, the notion is often credited to the Greek philosopher Euhemerus (4th century BC), who lived at the court of Cassander, king of Macedonia, and who suggested in his *Sacred History* that the gods and heroes of contemporary myth were once real earthly kings. Modern opinion argues that euhemerism can only account for a relatively small percentage of folk characters, and many more arose independently of any historical model.

evil eye The belief that certain people have the power to harm and even kill others – especially children and animals – through a mere look is very ancient, and common to many cultures. Anyone with a squint, green or blue eyes, or eyes that are unusual in any other way may be suspected of having the power of the evil eye, which today is particularly associated with gypsies.

Various gestures and other measures are supposed to counter the danger of being 'overlooked' by someone with the power of the evil eye. The most well-known of these include spitting in the eye of the person suspected of making such a threat, and gesticulating with the 'Devil's horns' or 'fig sign', made by holding down the middle two fingers of the hand with the thumb and directing the 'horns' thus produced at the person concerned. Children are thought to be particularly susceptible, and might be made to wear bits of coral, red ribbons or amulets to keep them safe. Protection can also be secured through charms and incantations, or the carrying of a knotted cord, four-leaf clover or a similar amulet. In former times people often hung 'witch balls' made of reflective glass in their windows in the belief that these would deflect the influence of the evil eye. It was also believed that the fleur-de-lis pattern used in heraldry could fend off such malevolent influence. Because the threat of the evil eye is often linked with envy, it is widely considered unwise to boast too loudly about the extent of one's riches, the beauty of one's wife, one's robust health and so forth, as this might attract such malevolent attention.

Fear of the evil eye has lasted into modern times. As late as the 1930s, for instance, King Alfonso XIII of Spain was widely suspected of possessing the power of the evil eye. The Italians in particular still have anxieties about the influence of the evil eye, which is sometimes referred to as the *jettatura*. To this day Mediterranean fishermen continue to decorate their boats with an eye device in order to ward off evil spirits.

Excalibur The magical sword of King ARTHUR that was given to him by the mysterious LADY OF THE LAKE. Today it is sometimes mistakenly assumed that Excalibur (meaning 'cut-steel') was synonymous with the sword that the young Arthur pulled from the stone, thus winning the throne, but this was in fact a different weapon, which Arthur carried until it was broken in battle. Excalibur was not the only name by which the sword was known – elsewhere it appears as Caliburn (Geoffrey of Monmouth) and Caledfwlch (in the *Mabinogion*). It may also have links with a magical sword of Irish legend called Caladbolg (meaning 'hard-belly'), which was said to have been forged in fairyland.

Excalibur guaranteed Arthur victory in battle, while the scabbard protected him from wounds (protection that ended when the scabbard was stolen by MORGAN LE FAY). When Arthur lay dying he ordered Sir Bedivere to return Excalibur to the Lady of the Lake. According to most accounts the sword was flung out over the water and caught by a hand appearing from the waves – an elaboration of Arthurian myth that was probably introduced by Malory.

exorcism The expulsion of evil spirits through the power of prayer and incantations. Such rituals have ancient roots, but even today most religions around the world have their own services of exorcism. Originally, it was supposed to be a special gift to be able to exorcize demons, but later the practice became the province of a certain class of the clergy, and later still it was carried out by any priest operating with the special permission of a bishop. Some priests today still specialize in exorcism. The Christian ritual, which may be directed at spirits or ghosts haunting persons, buildings or even animals or vehicles, usually incorporates the sprinkling of holy water and use of 'bell, book and candle' – the book being the Bible. Non-Christian exorcisms, as practiced in former times by local 'wise women' or aspiring sorcerers, ranged from relatively simple rituals involving the use of certain herbs and the recitation of charms to much more elaborate procedures necessitating the use of a magic circle and sacrifices of chickens or other animals. Another method required the victim to breathe in noxious fumes in the belief that these would drive out any demons lurking within the person's body.

F

Fables of Bidpai *See* PANCHATANTRA.

Faerie (or Faery) In Celtic mythology, the dwelling place of the fairies, usually located underground. In many tales mortals gain access to this otherworld, and there are taught various skills by the inhabitants, who mostly spend their time singing, dancing and feasting. Those who enjoy such privileges must be careful, however, not to eat or drink anything during their visit, as this will render them unable to return to their home above the earth. Time operates differently in Faerie to how it does in the mortal world, and many tales are told of humans who visit fairyland for a short time and then return to their own world, only to find that hundreds of years have passed, and that they themselves crumble to dust with age on coming into contact with the ground.

See also SIDHE; TIR NAN OG.

Fafnir In Norse mythology, the son of Hreidmar, king of the dwarfs. Legend relates how LOKI accidentally killed Fafnir's brother Otr, and was subsequently required to recompense Hreidmar with a large gift of gold. Fafnir then slew his father to get possession of the gold, but then had to transform himself into a dragon in order to prevent the gold being taken from him by his outraged brother Regin. He met his death at the hands of SIGURD.

fairy Diminutive supernatural being with magical powers. The term embraces a wide range of unearthly creatures, including brownies, elves, gnomes, goblins, leprechauns and pixies, which vary somewhat in character and appearance.

The fairy tradition is both ancient and detailed. The term itself comes from 'fay', itself ultimately from the Latin *fatum* ('fate') and suggests a link with the classical Fates. Fairies are popularly associated with pastoral landscapes of streams and woods and are generally considered to live underground within hills or 'fairy mounds' (often identified as barrows and other prehistoric burial mounds). Folklore claims that fairies are immortal and have the ability to make themselves invisible at will. It also warns that, although shy of mortals, they are naturally mischievous and vain, and may take delight in playing tricks on human beings. Other details of fairy lore include the belief that they are unable to count beyond five – larger numbers are reckoned in multiples of five. Explanations of the origin of the fairies include theories that they are fallen angels, the children of Adam by LILITH, the spirits of the prematurely dead, or the last survivors of a race of tiny beings who inhabited Celtic lands long ago.

The modern version of the fairy, influenced by such works of fiction as J. M. Barrie's *Peter Pan* (1904), is much more benign than was previously the case, and in past centuries fairies were greatly feared. Few people today worry about interference from the fairy race, although the Irish in particular continue to keep alive old stories and customs concerning what they call the 'little people'. Threatening small children that the fairies would come and get them was a favourite ruse of parents throughout Europe for many centuries, but adults themselves feared fairies, who were believed to have the power to injure their livestock and to cause terrible misfortune if crossed, whether accidentally or on purpose.

Among the most serious crimes laid at the fairies' door was the stealing of human babies and their replacement by CHANGELINGS. In the 17th century it was thought unlucky even to mention the word 'fairy', and such euphemisms as 'the good neighbour' were preferred. On occasion, however, the fairies might show favour to a particular human and put their magic at their disposal, or teach them something of the fairy arts. Tales were also told of occasional marriages contracted between mortals and fairies, but these usually ended tragically.

Inhabitants of rural areas learned to shun places where the fairies were reputed to gather, and took great care to avoid dark green 'fairy rings' in the grass, which were supposed to mark where the fairies had held a circular dance at midnight (the rings are actually made by a fungus). It was widely said that these rings indicated the whereabouts of a fairy village. It was thought to be very dangerous to sleep in a fairy ring or to step into one after nightfall – especially on the eve of May Day or on Hallowe'en, as the fairies were likely to seize any transgressors and carry them off to be their slaves in their underground realm, from which there is no escape. Livestock were also reputed to be nervous of these sites and to keep their distance from them. The more daring reported that after running nine times round fairy rings they could hear the sound of the fairies laughing and talking. This was a risky enterprise, and the runner always had to go in the direction the sun takes in order to remain immune to the fairies' power. Unsurprisingly, destruction of a fairy ring was considered extremely foolhardy. To be on the safe side, passers-by were recommended to reverse their hats to confuse any fairies who might attempt to make them join in their dread dance. Householders, meanwhile, habitually left presents of food, salt and other good things for the fairy folk in order to be spared their mischief.

See also BROWNIE; DWARF; ELF; FAERIE; GNOME; GOBLIN; LEPRECHAUN; MAB; OBERON; PIXIE; SIDHE; TITANIA.

fairy godmother In the European fairy tale tradition, a FAIRY guardian who uses her magic on behalf of the hero or heroine. Probably derived ultimately from the Fates of classical mythology, the fairy godmother is usually depicted as a kindly old woman who may watch over her charge from the day of his or her birth. Perhaps the most famous fairy godmother of them all is the one in 'Cinderella'. It is her magic that provides the heroine with the opportunity to go to the royal ball and meet Prince Charming. She puts herself at Cinderella's disposal after the girl does her the kindness of helping her gather sticks in a wood, although variants of the story in other cultures identify her as the ghost of Cinderella's mother. It appears to have been Charles Perrault who introduced the fairy godmother into the story in his 1697 version.

See also GUARDIAN SPIRIT.

fairyland *See* FAERIE.

fairy tale Genre of folk tale that has become well established in the oral and literary traditions of many of the world's cultures. In fact, relatively few fairy tales actually deal with FAIRIES, and the term can refer to a wide range of fabulous stories, many of which have ancient origins. The oldest recorded fairy tale, written on an Egyptian papyrus, has been dated to around 1250 BC. Common features include a marked emphasis upon magic and fantasy, strongly plotted story lines, the repeated use of stock motifs and characters, and the depiction of the perennial battle between good and evil. Good is typically represented by young lovers, and evil by demons or other wicked characters with access to supernatural powers. Most fairy tales have a happy ending, in which the good enjoy a moralistic victory over the bad.

Fairy tales have been variously interpreted as expressions of fear of and fascination with the supernatural, or as allegories on the theme of personal fulfilment, often with a disguised moral lesson (hence their relevance to the young). Characters in the tales include animals, dwarfs, giants, ogres, princes and princesses and witches. Most tales probably began as part of a purely oral folk tradition, but they were being collected and written down as early as the 9th century AD. Madame d'Aulnoy was a key figure in the early history of the more elevated literary fairy tale, writing her first story in 1690. Among her most illustrious successors have been Charles PERRAULT, the Brothers GRIMM, and Hans Christian ANDERSEN. Many stories enjoyed a wide readership through publication in inexpensive pamphlets called chapbooks, which circulated widely throughout northern Europe.

Fairy tales fell from favour somewhat in the early 19th century, but enjoyed a substantial revival by the middle of the century and have not faltered since then, providing the plots for books, pantomimes, plays, ballets, operas and other music and films.

Many fairy tales exist in variant forms in different cultures. 'Cinderella', for instance, is known in at least 500 different versions around the world. The stock of fairy tales continues to expand. Additions to the canon in the 20th century have included Frank L. Baum's fantasy *The Wizard of Oz* (1900) and J. M. Barrie's novel and play *Peter Pan* (1904).

Faithful John Archetypal servant character who plays a crucial role in numerous European and Asian folk tales. Loyal and trustworthy, he is usually identified as an ageing servant in the royal household, who acts selflessly to protect the best interests of his master. Sometimes his efforts are misunderstood and he is unfairly punished before his valuable service is finally appreciated. In some tales he is turned to stone after saving the life of his master or mistress, but is then restored to life through some blood sacrifice (which he then makes good). In one tale the king and queen sacrifice their own children to restore Faithful John to life, upon which he revives the children, to general rejoicing.

The tradition of the trusty servant would appear to have been imported originally from Asian folklore, but similar figures have long since become familiar characters in folk tales throughout the world. The trusty servant figure is known by a variety of names: for instance, in 'The Frog Prince', collected by the Brothers Grimm, he is known as Faithful Henry.

familiar The supernatural spirit agent of a witch or sorcerer. The familiar is a feature primarily of the witchcraft tradition of England and Scotland; few records exist of such unworldly assistants elsewhere. Familiars typically take the form of domestic animals, most often cats, dogs or black birds, but witches examined by witchfinders in the 17th century admitted to harbouring all manner of demons, which they were said to feed with their own blood. Admissions such as this were once sufficient 'proof' for a witch to be condemned to death, and many old and confused women died because they failed to deny associating with such IMPS.

The widespread fear of such familiars, which might enter a house and perform deeds ranging from souring the milk to committing murder, lay at the root of much superstition concerning various species of animal.

Fastnacht German festival descended from pagan rituals in honour of Hertha, the Germanic goddess of fertility. The festival of Fastnacht, which means 'eve of fasting' and which marked the end of a period of fasting, was subsequently Christianized and now takes place on Shrove Tuesday, with Mary replacing Hertha as the focus of the celebrations. Despite its incorporation into the ecclesiastical calendar, it has retained its generally uproarious character, with much music and the performing of special Fastnacht plays. One central feature of the festivity is the parading of the Fastnachtsbär, a man dressed in a bear's skin and otherwise covered in straw. He passes from house to house, dancing with the female occupants and thus promoting the chances of a good harvest and prosperity in exchange for gifts of food and money.

Fastnachtsbär *See* FASTNACHT.

Fata Morgana Italian name for the English MORGAN LE FAY, whose story may have come to southern Italy with the Norman conquerors of the 11th and 12th centuries. In Italian legend she is depicted as an underwater spirit, whose image is said to appear from time to time in the waters of the Straits of Messina. Identified as the lover of Ogier, the enemy of Orlando, she appears in the legends associated with CHARLEMAGNE and is today the subject of a semi-Christian folk cult still extant in parts of southern Italy.

Father Christmas The presiding spirit of Christmas, otherwise identified as Santa Claus. This modern bringer of gifts has ancient roots, and is thought to have been derived ultimately from St Nicholas of Patara, a 4th-century Bishop of Myra in Asia Minor whose feast day falls on 6 December. Legend has it that St Nicholas was touched by the plight of three poor sisters, and to save them from a life of prostitution dropped gifts of three gold balls into their stockings as they hung by the fire to dry. The developing lore surrounding the figure was imported to the USA by Dutch settlers, who called him Sante Klaas. Father Christmas's reindeer

and sleigh and the present-giving custom of modern times are a relatively recent US introduction, dating only from the 19th century. It was during this time that he developed into our modern image of the jolly, chubby, bearded old man dressed in fur-trimmed red.

Father Christmas's early development may owe something ultimately to the legends surrounding the Norse god ODIN. Each winter Odin was reputed to ride on horseback through the midnight sky to dispense punishment to the wicked and rewards to the deserving. In German folklore he is sometimes associated with Knecht Ruprecht, a knight of Christ similarly believed to bring gifts to good children. German children today put their shoes out on the night of 6 December for St Nicholas to fill them with sweets.

See also KRISS KRINGLE.

Faust Legendary German magician and sorcerer, whose dealings with the DEVIL were memorably brought to life by Christopher Marlowe and Goethe, among others. According to the legend and to the many plays and books based on it, Faust was a brilliant scholar who made a pact with MEPHISTOPHELES, selling his soul for a period of 24 years of pleasure and uninhibited knowledge-seeking on Earth. Among other excesses he was reputed to have swallowed a rival magician whole, to have summoned up Helen of Troy (among other spirits), and on another occasion to have attempted (unsuccessfully) to fly all the way to Venice. As the hour of his descent into Hell approached, however, he came to regret his decision – a salutary lesson to all those who might be considering a similar bargain with the devil.

The relationship between the literary Faust and a real historical figure is uncertain. It seems there was indeed a magician of the name in 16th-century Germany, but attempts to identify him as Johann Fust, a printer born in 1400 who died of the plague in 1466, are now dismissed by most authorities. Another contender as the model for Faust was one Georgius Sabellicu Faustus Junior, a necromancer, astrologer, alchemist, soothsayer and clairvoyant, recorded in Germany in the early years of the 16th century. This man was sacked as a teacher after being suspected of indulging in indecent behaviour with his pupils, and some years later he was banished from Ingolstadt for soothsaying. One Johann Faust, meanwhile, was awarded a theology degree in Heidelberg in 1509. Perhaps the Faust of fiction is an amalgam of several people. A book on demonology attributed to Faust was published in Germany in 1505, and in 1587 *The History of Dr Faustus, the Notorious Magician and Master of the Black Art* was published by Johann Spies at Frankfurt.

Christopher Marlowe's play *Dr Faustus* depicts the pact made between the learned doctor and Mephistopheles, and relates the wayward scholar's tragic end, carried off to Hell by the Devil himself. In subsequent works, including Goethe's poetic drama *Faust* (1808, 1832), the story of Faust is usually treated as an allegory of the possibilities and perils inherent in the search for knowledge.

fay See FAIRY.

Feast of Fools Medieval ecclesiastical celebration involving an uproarious reversal of roles between the powerful and the lowly, and the lampooning of religious rites. It was descended ultimately from the ancient Roman Saturnalia, a lively celebration held each December in honour of the god Saturn during which the usual social restraints were relaxed and participants indulged in all manner of debauchery and anarchy, ignoring the normal conventions and obligations of rank. The medieval incarnation of this tradition, which also absorbed the influence of celebrations marking the winter SOLSTICE, was observed in clerical circles throughout Europe during the Middle Ages, especially in France. It was usually centred on a cathedral or some other major religious site, and was celebrated on 26–28 December. It was often a riotous affair, complete with burlesques of the mass and various acts of obscenity and high spirits. The proceedings were presided over by a mock bishop or pope elected from the lowest ranks of the clergy. Sometimes the role was taken by a young boy or alternatively by an ass. Misgivings about the occasion eventually led to its prohibition during the Reformation.

See also LORD OF MISRULE.

Fenian cycle Cycle of Irish folk tales recording the heroic deeds of the FIANNA. It appears to have developed initially as an oral tradition, but later provided the basis for a large body of literature celebrating the heroic ideals of Celtic culture. It is distinguished by its more humorous and less elevated tone than that of the cycles recounting the legends of CUCHULAINN and the RED BRANCH, for example. This may reflect the origin of the tales in the oral tradition of the ordinary peasant population of Ireland. Many new tales were absorbed into the cycle between its first appearance in the 7th century and the 18th century.

fenoderee In the folklore of the Isle of Man, a species of BROWNIE that variously causes trouble or offers magical help to human beings. In contrast to other breeds of FAIRY, the fenoderee is depicted as being the same size as an ordinary person and is immensely strong, but shares in common with other fairy peoples a sensitive nature that is easily offended. Legend has it that the fenoderee was originally a fairy exiled from FAERY after falling for a mortal girl.

Fenrir (or **Fenris**) In Norse mythology, the son of the evil LOKI and the giantess Angrboda. Born in the shape of a terrible giant wolf, Fenrir was successfully bound to a rock with a slender magic rope made by the dwarfs. His struggles on being tied up were so fierce that the god Tyr lost a hand when helping to bind him. It was said that when he opened his mouth wide one jaw touched the earth while the other reached heaven. Fenrir is fated to break free during RAGNAROK and to devour ODIN, before Odin's son Vidar kills him by thrusting his sword into his vast mouth.

Ferdiad In Irish mythology, a close comrade of his foster-brother, the warrior-hero CUCHULAINN. He trained as a warrior alongside Cuchulainn at the court of Scathach in Alba, but was subsequently obliged to engage his friend in single combat during the War of the Brown Bull launched against Ulster by MEDB (*see* TAIN BO CUAILNGE). After three days' fighting, in which the two warriors broke off at nightfall to tend each other's wounds, Ferdiad fell to a mortal blow from Cuchulainn's legendary spear, the GAE BULG, leaving the latter grief-stricken.

Fergus mac Roich Legendary Irish king of Ulster and hero of the RED BRANCH, who lost his throne to CONCHOBAR. He had agreed to surrender the rule of Ulster to Conchobar for a year, at the request of his brother's widow NESSA, but Conchobar refused to hand back the reins of power at the end of the allotted time. Consequently, Fergus joined the forces of MEDB, which were ranged against Ulster (*see* TAIN BO CUAILNGE). He declined to engage in single combat with the mighty CUCHULAINN, on the grounds of having been the latter's teacher, but eventually met his death at the hands of his enemies after being surprised bathing in a pool with Medb.

fern The fern is widely regarded as possessing a range of magic powers. Sometimes referred to rather ominously as the 'Devil's brushes', ferns are variously reputed to be evil plants that will bring harm if cut or even touched, or else luck-giving plants that will ward off evil influences if used to decorate a horse's head or collar. If brought into the house they will provide protection against LIGHTNING, but if they are cut or burnt then rain will surely follow.

Walking on ferns is ill-advised as this will cause a person to lose his bearings and become lost. Plucking and carrying a fern leaf is also a bad idea, as the leaf will attract adders. In Russia it is believed that by tossing a sprig of fern in the air and observing where it falls the observer will learn the whereabouts of buried treasure. Carrying a fern flower about the person is widely supposed to offer a safeguard against the threat of witchcraft.

Particular folk beliefs are attached to the spores of the fern, which are said to bestow the power of INVISIBILITY if collected on Midsummer's Eve and carried about the person. Keeping some fern spores in a pocket or handbag will also promote the enduring faithfulness of a lover. Consuming spores crushed in water is said to be a sure remedy for stomach ache if they have been gathered from a fern growing on an OAK, and various other potions and lotions based on fern spores are recommended in folklore for the treatment of minor wounds, coughs, and inflamed eyes, among other conditions. Sleeping on a mattress or pillow containing ferns is alleged to cure rheumatism and rickets.

See also BRACKEN.

fetch In Irish and British folklore, a DOPPELGÄNGER or double of a person who is still alive (usually a relative or close friend). Reports of such sightings usually presage the death of the person concerned. Folklore also boasts reports of strange lights that appear when a person is close to death, called 'fetch lights' or 'fetch candles'.

See also WRAITH.

fetish A CHARM or AMULET that is supposed to have innate magical properties (rather than because it is possessed by some spirit or demon). African tribes have always treasured certain stone and wooden figures reputed to have magic potential, and European witches and occultists are similarly convinced that certain objects, such as HORSESHOES, HOLED STONES and four-leaf clovers, carry with them a natural magic force that may be tapped in their ceremonies. Witchcraft fetishes range from bones and chalices to mystic symbols, such as the hexagram. The word itself comes from the Portuguese *feitiço* ('something made').

Fianna In Irish mythology, a legendary court of some 150 warriors (or Fenians), each at the head of 27 men, about whom countless legends were told. Admission to the Fianna required proofs of great courage and skill in battle, as well as a chivalric nature and mastery of the poetic arts. To test a candidate's worthiness he had to go through such tests as having spears thrown at him. The members of the Fianna were renowned not only for their prowess as warriors, but also for their skills as physicians, druids and musicians. Their code of chivalry demanded observance of four specific injunctions or *geasa* (*see* GEIS): that they choose wives only for their virtue rather than on the grounds of their dowries; that they never withhold any gift asked of them; that they never retreat before less than ten opponents; and that they never show violence towards a woman. The most celebrated members of the Fianna included its legendary leader FIONN MAC CUMHAILL, his son OISIN, and DIARMUID. The court began to break up as a consequence of the feud between Fionn and Diarmuid over GRAINNE, and finally disintegrated completely following the slaughter of many of the warriors at the Battle of Gabhra.

Some of the legends surrounding the Fianna were later absorbed into Arthurian romance and inspired many of the legends of the ROUND TABLE.

field spirit *See* HARVEST CUSTOMS.

fig sign *See* EVIL EYE.

figurehead In SAILORS' LORE, a carved wooden figure (often depicting a naked woman) that in former times was mounted on the prow of seagoing vessels in order to protect the luck of the ship. Such figureheads were thought to embody the very soul of the ship itself and were thought by virtue of their beauty or their ferocity to calm rough seas. The custom of attaching such figureheads to boats probably had its roots in the ancient practice of dedicating ships to particular goddesses – the reason why the majority of figureheads were female figures (despite the tradition that it is unlucky to have women on board ship). Sailors always placed great faith in such figureheads, and they were consequently treated with great respect.

Although few modern ships are decorated with such figures, the idea has an echo in the assorted mascots, bunches of lucky heather and other emblematic objects that are attached by motorists to the front of trucks and cars.

Findabair In Irish Celtic mythology, the beautiful daughter of AILILL and MEDB. According to legend she fell in love with Fraoch, although her parents offered her hand to any warrior who would fight the invincible CUCHULAINN in the course of Medb's campaign against Ulster (*see* TAIN BO CUAILNGE). Fraoch alone presented himself against Cuchulainn, and was promptly slain. Findabair herself died of grief as a result of this loss.

Fingal Scottish name for the legendary Irish warrior hero FIONN MAC CUMHAILL. This Scottish rendering of the hero's name became widely familiar in the late 18th century with the publication of James MacPherson's celebrated 'Ossian' poems, purporting to be of ancient origin (though actually mostly by MacPherson himself). It is also familiar from Mendelssohn's 1830 overture *Fingal's Cave* (more properly *Hebridean Overture*), itself a reference to a large cave on the Hebridean island of Staffa where the hero is supposed to have sheltered.

finger The folklore of many cultures pays close attention to the fingers, which are widely considered to have great magical potency and to be closely linked to the soul. In some parts of the Pacific and Africa, for instance, the fingers of dead ancestors are carefully preserved and passed down from generation to generation. In medieval Europe the fingers of saints were among the most common sacred relics preserved in holy sites. Elsewhere fingers were once sacrificed as an appeal to the gods, or else to appease demons or the souls of the dead.

The shape of the fingers has great significance and reveals much about character. According to English folk belief, for example, short fat fingers suggest a person is dim-witted and intemperate, while long fingers are commonly said today to belong to 'artist's hands', suggesting intelligence but also financial incompetence and, according to the Scots, a tendency to steal. If the fingers are so short that a person cannot encircle their own wrists with thumb and forefinger then this is, according to Canadian lore, a sure sign that he or she is a glutton. Persons with long forefingers are also to be mistrusted, especially if this first finger is longer than the middle. The forefinger of the right hand is, incidentally, sometimes called the 'Poison Finger', and in former times was thought to be venomous, so was never used to rub ointment into a wound. The third finger of the left hand, usually the finger upon which wedding rings are worn today, is the luckiest of them all, and is deemed to have special healing powers. Tradition has it that a vein runs directly from this finger straight to the heart. A little finger that is crooked is said to indicate that its owner will die rich. Those born with extra fingers, meanwhile, will enjoy a lifetime of good luck (the legendary Irish hero CUCHULAINN was said to sport seven fingers on each hand).

Pointing a finger at something or someone has always been considered an act with aggressive magical potential. Pointing a finger at another person is considered rude in some circles, an attitude that may have its origins in the old notion that pointing a finger at another person risks causing them harm by invoking the power of the EVIL EYE. Pointing at a funeral or at a grave is especially to be discouraged, as this may lead to the premature death of the pointer.

Crossing the fingers (and thus making the sign of the cross) is a traditional countermeasure against the threat of evil, or against retribution for some minor transgression, such as the telling of a 'white lie' or the making of a promise that one has no intention of honouring. Pulling the finger joints to see if they 'crack' is a test of love: if they make the desired sound then the person concerned can be certain that he or she is in someone else's thoughts. Alternatively, pulling every finger and counting the cracks made will, according to superstition, reveal the number of one's lovers, or else the number of children one is destined to have.

See also FINGERNAIL.

fingernail In common with HAIR, the fingernails have particular significance in world folklore as, like other body parts, they are deemed to contain a trace of a person's magical life essence, or soul. This means that they can be used in a spell or other form of magic that has an effect (either benevolent or harmful) on the person from which they came. If buried beneath the person's doorstep, for instance, that person will be struck down at once by illness, which will continue until the parings are taken away. In former times it was thus considered vitally important to dispose of nails in such a way that a witch or other sorcerer could not make use of them. To be absolutely sure that parings are redundant for the purposes of witchcraft they should each be cut into three pieces or else spat upon.

In contrast, fingernail clippings also feature in many time-honoured remedies, being ritually burned or buried in the belief that in so doing a patient will be relieved of whatever ails them.

Nails should ideally be trimmed on a Monday or Tuesday, but never on a Friday or Sunday, as this is unlucky and risks interference from the Devil for the rest of the week. The fingernails of babies should not be cut until the infant is at least a year old or the child will become a thief in later life (it is, however, acceptable to bite them short). Sailors, meanwhile, claim that it is unwise to trim the nails while at sea for fear that this is bound to summon up a storm.

Finn mac Cool *See* FIONN MAC CUMHAILL.

Fionn mac Cumhaill (or **Fionn mac Cumhal, Finn mac Cool**) Irish warrior hero, famed as the leader of the legendary band of warriors called the FIANNA. He ranks among the most celebrated of all Irish Celtic heroes, renowned for his strength and skill in battle.

The son of Cumhaill and Muirne, Fionn mac Cumhaill was brought up by the druidess Bodhmall and was trained in warfare and the arts by the woman warrior Liath Luachra. One day, while helping to cook a salmon that had fed on hazel nuts from the tree of knowledge, he burned his thumb and sucked it. He thus unwittingly acquired all-seeing knowledge of the past, present and future. From that point onwards he could look into the future at any time simply by putting his thumb in his mouth. He is often described as being accompanied by two hounds, Bran and Sceolan (sometimes identified as his nephews).

Having claimed the leadership of the Fianna by virtue of his great knowledge and skills, Fionn had numerous adventures in company with the other heroes in the band. These included the slaying of the monster Aillen, which each year at the feast of SAMHAIN cast a spell over the soldiers guarding the royal palace of Tara and burnt it down. Fionn pressed his spear to his forehead so that the monster's spells had no effect upon him, and then beheaded the creature.

Fionn fathered OISIN by the deer-woman SADBH, one of his many wives and mistresses. As a relatively old man he failed (initially at least) to win the hand of GRAINNE in the face of the rivalry of DIARMUID, and spent years in pursuit of the lovers. After the death of many of the Fianna at the Battle of Gabhra, Fionn pined away, and according to legend retreated to the OTHERWORLD, where (like King ARTHUR) he sleeps with his knights awaiting the day he will be needed to save his country. Another tradition claims he eventually died at the advanced age of 230.

Fionnuala *See* LIR.

Firbolgs In Irish mythology, one of the early peoples to make Ireland their home. The Firbolgs (a name meaning 'people of the bags') are supposed to have come to Ireland from Greece, where they had been made to work as slaves transporting earth in bags. They made their escape from Greece by fashioning ships from the bags and arrived on Irish soil via Spain. They were eventually defeated by the FOMORIANS and subsequently driven out of the country by the TUATHA DE DANANN following the first battle of MAG TUIRED. Differing legends suggest they were allowed to settle in the Aran Islands or in the province of Connacht.

Fir Dhearga In Irish mythology, a race of supernatural beings that preceded the LEPRECHAUNS. Like leprechauns, they had a taste for playing tricks on human beings, but on occasion could be persuaded to lend mortals magical assistance. Their name translates as 'red men' – a reference to the red clothes they were traditionally said to wear.

fire As one of the four elementary forces once thought to govern the earth (alongside air, earth and water), fire – which imitates the life-sustaining action of the sun – has long represented such themes as renewal and life itself in world folklore. In ancient times it was generally agreed that fire was a gift from the gods, and thus many of the dead and living religions of the world feature fire in some way in their legends, liturgies and rituals. Examples of the symbolic importance of fire in Judaeo–Christian tradition include the story of the burning bush.

Much of the folklore relating to fire in the English-speaking world goes back to Celtic roots, recalling the bonfires that were lit during the festivals of BELTANE and SAMHAIN, and the rolling of burning 'wheels' of fire down hillsides at significant times of the year. Suggestions that live animals and people were sacrificed in these fires remain largely unsubstantiated. Such rituals were apparently intended to preserve the luck of livestock and crops. In the British Isles the tradition lives on in the annual Bonfire Night (*see* GUY FAW-KES NIGHT), which appears to have had its origins ultimately in the fires that were formerly lit to mark the end of summer.

The domestic hearth was formerly widely considered to embody the collective soul of the household, and innumerable folk beliefs and superstitions surrounded the business of anointing hearths and lighting fires. Even today some people will draw the curtains when lighting a fire, believing that it will not 'catch' in the direct light of the sun, which may be jealous of such imitation. In some households only residents of the house are permitted to poke the coals for fear of offending the gods of the hearth. The flames, smoke and ASHES in the hearth might also be carefully inspected for the purposes of divination.

In some cultures the rite of fire-walking has special religious significance. This involves celebrants walking barefoot over hot coals or glowing ashes in such a manner as to escape physical injury (through the use of trances or a variety of other means). Fire-walking is particularly associated with Indian and Far Eastern cultures, where it is typically undertaken to ensure a good harvest.

See also PHOENIX.

firebird In Russian folklore, a magical bird that features in a number of well-known folk tales. Several of these stories revolve around the mostly futile attempts of various heroes to capture the magnificently plumaged creature, which is described as having wings of gold and eyes of crystal. The firebird is today best known from Stravinsky's ballet *The Firebird* (1910), which drew extensively on these legends.

first-footing Traditional NEW YEAR ritual, originally a Scottish and northern English custom, that requires a dark-haired man to be the first person to cross the threshold after midnight has struck in order to guarantee the good luck of the household for the year ahead. He is usually expected to carry various propitious objects as he enters, among them a piece of coal, bread, salt and money, which represent the continuing prosperity of all present. Variants of the custom require the first-footer to enter with a gift, a kiss, a coin or some food. Having brought the New Year in with him by the front door, it is conventional for the first-footer to leave by the back door, thereby symbolically taking the old year out with him.

fish *See* ALADDIN; BEHEMOTH; BRENDAN THE NAVIGATOR; EEL; HADDOCK; MER-MAID; OTTER; SALMON; SHARK.

Fisher King In Arthurian legend, an alternative name for the keeper of the GRAIL. The title refers to an incident in which the Grail King is reputed to have fed a huge host of his followers with just a single fish – a story with clear echoes of the biblical story of Christ's feeding of the five thousand. Additionally, the title suggests Christ's reference to the 'fishers of men'. The Fisher King is variously identified by such names as Bron, Pelles or Amfortas, and in early French versions of the legend he is called the Rich Fisher. Having been wounded in both thighs (*see* WOUNDED KING), he needs to be healed by the pure knight destined to find the

Grail (PERCEVAL or GALAHAD) asking the all-important Grail question, 'Whom does the Grail serve?'

fleur-de-lis In heraldry, a stylized lily that features on many coats of arms, including that of French royalty. It is usually understood to represent purity, and is sometimes thought to refer to the lily from heaven that according to legend was given to Clovis, king of the Franks, when he was baptized. It often appears in groups of three, meant to symbolize the Holy Trinity.

floating islands Mythical group of moving islands that feature in a number of folkloric traditions. In some traditions the islands are identified as the location of a paradise inhabited by supernatural beings (see TIR NAN OG). In other traditions they are feared for the threat they present to seafarers, who may be crushed to destruction between their cliffs when they clash together (as described in the story of Jason and the Argonauts and in the mythology of the Inuits and several Native American groups).

Floral Dance See FURRY DANCE.

Flying Dutchman Legendary ghost ship whose appearance was greatly feared among seafarers. In former times it was believed that sightings of the vessel in the seas off the Cape of Good Hope were an omen of imminent disaster. Legend had it that the ship was doomed to sail forever after its master Hendrik Vanderdecken, cursed God during a storm or, alternatively, made a pact with the Devil in exchange for a safe passage. According to one version of the tale, Vanderdecken persisted in trying to round the Cape in terrible storms, ignoring the protests of his passengers and crew. When the Almighty himself appeared on the deck to ask him to turn back Vanderdecken blasphemed and fired a gun at him. The story is well known today from Wagner's opera *Der Fliegende Hollander* (1843).

flying ointment Magical ointment that witches are popularly supposed to smear on themselves in order to acquire the power of flight. According to widespread tradition, witches rub this ointment all over their bodies and then fly naked to their sabbaths on their broomsticks or other vehicles. Alleged ingredients of the ointment, which is usually described as being black or dark green in colour, include the fat of babies, the blood of bats, soot and samples of aconite, hellebore, hemlock and belladonna. It has been speculated that the potent and indeed highly toxic ingredients of the ointment may have induced hallucinations in some witches, who may really have believed they were flying.

According to German legend, a Frankfurt physician of the early 17th century once suspected his aunt of being a witch and spied on her when she was smearing herself with flying ointment. When she had gone the physician tried some of the ointment himself and was immediately whisked through the night sky, mounted on a calf and to his horror, witnessed the witches' sabbath. On his way back he was dumped unceremoniously in the Rhine, from which he had to be rescued by a friendly miller.

Fomorians In Irish mythology, a race of savages identified as the original inhabitants of Ireland. According to legend, the Fomorians were monstrous in appearance, with such distinguishing features as a single eye and missing limbs. Led by their king BALOR, they were a warlike people who were driven out of Ireland by PARTHOLON and took refuge in the Scottish Hebrides or the Isle of Man before returning to Irish shores to establish their tyrannical rule over the Nemedians (see NEMED). Subsequently they were obliged to share Ireland with the TUATHA DE DANANN, but were eventually defeated at the second battle of MAG TUIRED, in which both sides sustained many casualties. With Balor dead from a slingshot delivered by LUGH, the

Fomorians were routed and driven from Ireland for ever. Celtic myth associated the Fomorians with darkness and evil, and with all the dangers ranged against humanity.

Fool In northern European folklore and literature, a character of the MORRIS DANCE and other traditional dances and entertainments. A prancing jokester, sometimes identified as Malkin, Tom or by some other name, the Fool is best known today from the long-established tradition of court fools and jesters that were commonly employed to entertain at royal courts throughout medieval Europe. The most famous of these, who were renowned for their ready wit, physical buffoonery and acrobatic, poetic and musical skills included such performers as Henry VII's Patch, Henry VIII's Will Somers, Elizabeth I's Robert Greene and Charles I's Muckle John, who was often described as the last court fool in England.

Famous Fools of legend include DAGONET, the jester at the court of King ARTHUR. In the morris dance it is the Fool's role to ape the pretensions of the other characters and generally provoke ribald amusement among the audience. He traditionally wears a multi-coloured patchwork costume, complete with traditional belled Fool's hat and often carrying a Fool's bauble.

footprint According to the folkloric tradition of many cultures a footprint retains an obscure magical connection with the person who made it, and thus has considerable potential in magic making. In many parts of the world it was formerly believed that witches could cause their victims agony by the simple procedure of hammering a nail into a person's footprint, while soil from a person's footprint features in love spells all round the world. In Australia, Africa and elsewhere it was once thought to be a good idea for anybody fearing magical interference to scrub out their footprints behind them.

According to Irish folklore, tossing soil from a footprint at the fairies will oblige them to release any mortals they have kidnapped. Another ancient tradition common to Icelandic and other cultures claims that footprints may be used as LIFE TOKENS, and may be carefully examined for clues about the welfare of the absent person who made them.

All round the world indentations in rocks and elsewhere are commonly identified as the footprints of various supernatural beings, ranging from gods and saints to folk heroes and the Devil. On 8 February 1855 a trail of what appeared to be hoofmarks was discovered in the snow of south Devon: the trail, which extended some 100 miles and carried on over rooftops and haystacks, was widely attributed to the Devil.

Fortunate Islands In Irish Celtic mythology, an island paradise located somewhere off the west coast of Ireland. Sometimes identified as the Canary Islands or Madeira, they are described as being ruled over by MORGAN LE FAY and her court of muses.

See also FLOATING ISLANDS; ISLANDS OF THE BLEST.

Fortunatus In medieval European folklore, a legendary hero who features in a number of tales. Apparently inspired by Asian legend, he made appearances in German folklore in the 15th century, and was credited with the possession of an inexhaustible purse and a wishing cap, among various other magical items.

fortune-telling *See* DIVINATION.

fountain of youth Legendary spring that is supposed to bestow perpetual youth upon anybody who drinks from it. Tales about such fountains feature in many classical and folkloric traditions, although few heroes ever manage to locate them, for they are always located in some inaccessible place, and many obstacles must be overcome before their waters can be tasted. Often the only way to reach the fountain it is through supernatural assistance from friendly spirits or animals. When the first explorers arrived in the New World one of the treasures they sought was the fountain of youth, reportedly located in the Bahamas. In 1513 Juan Ponce de León discovered Florida while searching for it.

fox The fox is almost universally identified in folklore as an animal of great ingenuity and cunning. Foxes feature as central characters in numerous folk tales, in which they variously outwit more powerful animals (such as the bear, wolf or lion) or use their cunning to entrap their prey (as in the tale of the GINGER-BREAD MAN). In Oriental folk tales foxes are frequently credited with the ability to change their shape, transforming themselves at will into beautiful women in order to entrap gullible mortals. In this tradition they are often depicted as licentious and debauched.

Examples of folk traditions celebrating the fox's legendary cunning include the ancient belief that a fox troubled with fleas will swim into a river while holding a ball of wool or grass between its teeth. As the water rises the fleas climb onto the fox's head and then onto the ball of wool, which the fox then releases to float downstream.

Because of its alleged cunning and tendency to prey upon domestic livestock, the fox has a mixed reputation in many parts of the world. Witches were often alleged to have the power to turn themselves into foxes, and in Scotland farmers sometimes nailed a severed fox's head to the barn door to warn any prowling witches off. In Wales, it is still said to be lucky to spy a lone fox, but ominous to see several at once. Foxes are also unwelcome in the vicinity of the home as they signify the coming of disaster and death. In parts of eastern England it is claimed that a fox bite will have fatal consequences, and anyone thus bitten cannot expect to live more than another seven

years. Elsewhere it is claimed that if it rains while the sun is shining this is a sure sign that a fox's wedding is taking place (in other parts of the world the animal thus honoured may be the monkey, the jackal or poultry).

The fox is prized as a source of ingredients in folk medicine. The tongue of a fox may be laid on the skin at bedtime to extract a deeply embedded thorn, and can also be applied to the eyes to cure cataracts. It may also be cooked and eaten or else carried about the person to improve the courage of a person who is naturally shy. Carrying a fox's tooth will help to treat an inflamed leg, while the liver and lungs of a fox may be dried and sugared to prevent coughs. Fox fat rubbed into the scalp will apparently combat baldness, and finishing a bowl of milk partly drunk by a fox is reputed to be a cure for whooping cough.

See also FOX MAIDEN; REYNARD THE FOX.

fox maiden A beautiful woman who, in folk tales recorded in many parts of the world, is revealed to be a FOX. Similar to the tales surrounding SWAN MAIDENS and SEAL MAIDENS, these stories usually describe how a man spies a fox shedding its skin and changing into a woman and how, having hidden the skin, he claims her as his wife. Typically, after several years of happy marriage the fox finds its lost skin and changes back into its original form, or the man offends his wife by criticizing her musky odour and she leaves him.

Fraoch *See* FINDABAIR.

Freya In Norse mythology, the goddess of love and fertility. The daughter of the sea god NJORD and the fertility goddess NERTHUS, she bore two daughters, Hnoss and Gersemi, either by the sun god Odur or (through confusion with FRIGGA) ODIN himself. According to legend she could adopt the form of a falcon at will. When Odur deserted her she cried tears of amber and gold.

Friar Rush In German folklore, an equivalent of the English ROBIN GOOD-FELLOW. Properly called Bruder Rausch in German, this mischievous household spirit frequently disguised himself as a monk when playing his pranks, often trying to lead astray those bound by religious vows. According to some legends he was rather more ominous than other similar figures, working on behalf of the DEVIL.

Friar Tuck *See* ROBIN HOOD.

Frigga In Norse mythology, the wife of ODIN and thus the highest ranking of all Norse goddesses. Later Norse legend describes her as the mother of Odin's children Hermod, BALDUR, Hodur, and TYR, although another tradition claims she had seven children, each of whom founded a Saxon kingdom in England. Identified as a goddess of the clouds and sky, she was revered for her benevolence towards humanity, and was reputed to preside over 11 handmaids whose particular duty was to observe the course of human affairs.

frog The frog, with its curious amphibious lifestyle and glistening skin, features prominently in world folklore. Many of the folk beliefs and traditions relating to the frog associate the creature with the weather, especially with rain. Native American cultures, for instance, revered a Great Frog Spirit, to whom appeals were made in rainmaking ceremonies in times of drought. Elsewhere frogs were sacrificed or treated with special reverence in the belief that this would similarly promote the chances of rain falling. European superstition, meanwhile, claims that the skin of frogs becomes shiny when fine weather is in the offing, and dull if rain is on the way. Rain will soon fall in response to the croak of a frog and, before the development of adult frogs from tadpoles was properly understood, it was said that frogs themselves came to earth in showers of rain.

In times gone by some people placed great store in carrying a particular bone taken from a frog (or toad) that had been ritually killed. The procedure that had to be followed in order to obtain the bone involved burying a live frog or toad in an ant hill for the space of a month, until the next new moon, then stripping off the remaining flesh by placing the body in a stream. As the water did its work the sought-after bone would float upstream while uttering unearthly shrieks. The bone was then taken to a stable three nights in succession, on the last of which the owner might be required to do battle with the DEVIL himself before the spell was deemed complete. Possession of such a magic bone brought with it various gifts, including the power to control pigs and horses, and the ability to cure warts.

Other folk beliefs warn against killing frogs, as they are said to be the reincarnation of dead children (hence their sometimes childlike cry). Placing the tongue of a frog on someone while they sleep will oblige the sleeper to reveal his or her secrets, but some authorities warn that anyone who actually touches a frog will instantly become infertile.

Frogs feature in a number of outlandish folk remedies. Putting a live frog on a skewer and rubbing its body against a wart is supposed to cause the wart to disappear as the frog dies. Trapping a live frog in a bag and hanging the bag in the chimney until the frog perishes is reputed to cure whooping cough, as will feeding an unknowing patient frog soup. Holding a live frog in a patient's mouth will cure thrush by transferring the disease to the unfortunate animal. In times gone by, sufferers from consumption and cancer might be recommended to eat a few live baby frogs before breakfast.

See also FROG PRINCE.

Frog Prince, The celebrated European fairy tale that was among those collected by the Brothers GRIMM. The tale concerns an arrogant young princess who rashly promises a frog that he will be allowed to share her place at the table and sleep in her bed if he will rescue the golden ball she has dropped into a well. The frog retrieves the ball, and then insists upon her honouring her side of the bargain. The king obliges his daughter to keep her word, and thus the frog eats with the princess at her table and is placed on her pillow when she goes to bed. The princess finally loses patience and hurls the frog at the wall. This breaks a spell placed on the creature, which is instantly restored to its original form of a handsome young prince. They marry and live happily ever after. Variants of the tale have the frog being transformed into a prince on being kissed by the princess.

See also BEAUTY AND THE BEAST.

Frost Giants In Norse mythology, the sworn enemies of the AESIR. The reasons for the enduring feud between the giants and the gods is obscure, but legend has it that they are fated to invade ASGARD at the end of time, and to be destroyed along with the gods at RAGNAROK.

Fulk Fitzwarin Legendary English knight, who is supposed to have resisted the despotic rule of King John. Based on an actual historical character, he was the subject of a medieval romance which depicted him as the hero of many adventures, in the course of which he slays dragons and overcomes a variety of witches, demons and monsters. Like ROBIN HOOD, he was also supposed to have spent a good deal of time living the life of an outlaw.

funeral rites The sombre business of interring the dead is a focus of many folkloric and superstitious beliefs and traditions, most of which are concerned with ensuring that the deceased person is allowed to rest in peace, leaving the living to go about their daily lives untroubled by interference from GHOSTS.

Funeral customs vary greatly from one culture to another. Each society has its rituals and taboos when it comes to laying out bodies, disposing of corpses and honouring the memory of the dead. Many of the funeral customs of the English-speaking world are descended from ancient Roman rites, including the wearing of black by mourners (originally perhaps to make themselves less conspicuous to the dead), walking behind the coffin and carrying insignia on the bier. The Greeks customarily placed flowers upon graves, but this practice would appear to be very much older (a Neanderthal corpse discovered at Shanidar cave in Iraq, for instance, was found to have been laid on a bed of spring flowers).

In prehistoric and ancient times it was thought important in many cultures to provide the dead with all the tools and luxuries they might need in the afterlife, and thus rich stores of implements and treasure (and in some cases sacrificed servants, soldiers and concubines) have been found in archaeological sites all over the world. Some early societies made sacrifices in honour of the dead or poured libations over the tomb in order to appease their spirits. Stones might be piled up over the grave to prevent the dead rising to trouble the living (possibly the origin of today's gravestones). It was also customary (as it still is now) to make speeches praising the character and deeds of the deceased, again in the hope that this might dissuade the ghost of the dead person from returning.

It is widely held to be lucky if it rains during a funeral, but unlucky to postpone the date of a funeral once it has been arranged, as this might provoke Death into finding someone else to be buried. According to English superstition the coffin should always leave the deceased's house by the front door or by the window if these are alternatives to using the back door. If the back door is used then the deceased's soul is put in terrible jeopardy in the afterlife. Ideally, the body should be transported in an east-to-west (or 'sunwise') direction, and once the journey has been started it must not be delayed or abandoned. In times gone by, if a deceased woman was a virgin, this was marked by the mourners dressing in white and by a pair of symbolic white gloves being carried at the head of the funeral procession (*see* MAIDEN'S GARLANDS).

Care should be taken by mourners not to break certain taboos, which may mark them out as the next to die. In particular, they should keep behind the coffin as it proceeds to the church, avoid standing in a ray of direct sunlight during the ceremony, and finally be careful not to enter the home of the deceased before the next of kin go in after the service is over. If the mourners make an odd number then one among them will shortly be joining the deceased in the grave. In the USA it is very unlucky to go to a funeral uninvited, and pregnant women and children under the age of a year may not be welcome in the mourning party.

It is thought unlucky in many countries to meet a funeral procession in the street, particularly so if a bridal party and a funeral party come face to face. The only sure remedy is to walk a few steps with the funeral party. Other precautions include spitting after the hearse, crossing one's fingers and removing one's hat. It is also unlucky to count the number of cars following the coffin as, according to US folk belief, this determines the number of years the person counting has left to live. Irish superstition, however, suggests that some good can come of meeting a funeral procession, as a person may then wish his warts upon the corpse.

The tradition of feeding mourners at a wake in the home of the deceased after the funeral is also significant, and it was formerly believed that every mourner should wash and dry his hands in the house. The towel used was then thrown over the roof or otherwise given up to the wind. Even today it is often claimed that the happier the atmosphere at the wake, the better the prospects for living and dead alike.

See also BURIAL CUSTOMS.

Furry Dance Annual dance festival, otherwise known as the Floral Dance, that takes place in Helston, Cornwall, in May each year.

This ancient folk celebration is thought to commemorate the victory of St Michael, patron saint of Helston, over the Devil, but it may have its roots in obscure pre-Christian rites marking the coming of spring. The celebration is also sometimes linked to the Roman festival of Floralia, which took place in honour of the goddess Flora. The word 'furry' may derive from the Latin *feria* ('holy day' or 'festival'). The actual celebration involves pairs of dancers making their way through the town as the band plays the well-known Furry Dance tune.

fylfot *See* SWASTIKA.

G

Gabriel's Hounds Spectral pack of dogs, also known as Gabriel's Ratchets, that haunts the skies of northern Europe in company with the WILD HUNT. Anyone unfortunate enough to hear or see the hounds, who are particularly associated with stormy weather, is doomed to die in the near future.

See also SEVEN WHISTLERS.

Gae Bulg The formidable spear of the great Irish warrior hero CUCHULAINN. Fashioned from the bones of a sea monster, it was given to Cuchulainn by Aoife. The 30 notches on the spear inflicted terrible wounds upon Cuchulainn's victims. These included his own son Conla, whom he slew without realizing who he was, and his foster-brother Ferdiad. According to legend the spear was launched from between the toes. Cuchulainn himself was slain after being tricked into throwing the Gae Bulg.

Galahad In Arthurian legend, the knight of the ROUND TABLE destined to find the GRAIL. The son of LANCELOT and ELAINE OF CORBENIC, he is described as the purest of all the knights, and thus replaced his flawed father as the finder of the Grail. Welsh legend identifies him as Gwalchafed ('falcon of the summer'). He is alone among Arthur's knights in being able to sit safely upon the seat known as the Siege Perilous, which can only be occupied by the pure knight destined to find the Grail. Undefeated in battle, he dies after looking into the Grail, and is buried in the great abbey of Sarras, the holy city of the Grail.

Gamelyn Legendary English outlaw who, although largely forgotten today, was once as famous as his counterpart ROBIN HOOD. Like Robin Hood, he was identified as the dispossessed son of a noble and, having escaped from prison, became the king of the outlaws. He was renowned for his great strength and volatile temper, and had many adventures before finally being restored (together with his loyal brother Ote) to the possession of his lands. Early accounts of his life include a Middle English metrical romance that was recorded in the 13th century by Geoffrey Chaucer.

Gargantua In European folklore, a GIANT who is today best known from Rabelais' satire *Gargantua* (c.1535). According to legend, Gargantua had an inexhaustible appetite, on one occasion consuming five pilgrims, together with their staves, in a salad. It is thought that Rabelais' character, identified as the father of Pantagruel and the leader of a gang of similarly grotesque giants, came originally from Celtic mythology.

garlic According to folkloric tradition all round the world, garlic provides protection against a wide range of evils. Garlic was considered a gift from the gods by the ancient Egyptians, although Russian mythology by way of contrast had it that the first garlic sprung up where Satan's left foot stepped when he left the Garden of Eden (onions growing where his right foot fell). The plant is widely regarded as a counter to witchcraft and evil in many Oriental countries, and today is commonly identified as the best defence against VAMPIRES, being used to guard doors and windows and worn in the form of a necklace for personal protection. Garlic may also be fixed to a child's cradle to protect the infant from malevolent spirits, while Sicilians may slip garlic into the beds of women in labour to ease the pain of childbirth.

As a tool of the herbalist, garlic is prized for its effectiveness against infestations of worms, in treating sunstroke and dropsy, in relieving such life-threatening diseases as smallpox, plague and leprosy, and in easing relatively minor problems like toothache, earache and bedwetting. It may also be administered to calm hysterics, or placed in the socks of children afflicted with whooping cough. In remoter parts of the USA, garlic poultices are recommended for the treatment of rattlesnake bites and scorpion stings. Scientists, meanwhile, have identified garlic as one of the most effective natural mosquito repellents.

Gawain In Arthurian legend, the nephew and heir of King ARTHUR. The eldest son of Morgause and Lot of Orkney, he is usually described as being very strong, and appears to have been derived originally from a Celtic solar deity, his strength being at a peak at midday and fading towards the end of the day. Other details suggest the influence of the CUCHULAINN legends. In later accounts of Arthurian myth he is revealed as having a cruel and less than trustworthy character, as well as something of a reputation as a womanizer.

Known as Gwalchmai (meaning 'hawk of May') in the MABINOGION, he appears in some of the very earliest accounts of Arthurian myth, and the episode in which he engages in single combat with the monstrous Green Knight is among the most famous tales in the canon – as related in the long 14th-century poem *Sir Gawayne and the Green Knight*. In this episode, Gawain answers a general challenge to all Arthur's knights to strike off the terrifying Green Knight's head with a single blow, on condition that a year later he will submit to a return blow. Assuming he will easily be able to kill the Green Knight, Gawain accepts the challenge and chops off his head, only for the Green Knight to pick himself up and order Gawain to honour his part of the agreement in 12 months' time. Gawain, bound by his oaths of nobility, sets out to find the Green Knight. During his journey he undergoes various tests of his honour, including attempted seduction by the lady of a castle in which he is offered shelter (actually the wife of the Green Knight himself). He resists these temptations, with the single exception of the illicit keeping of a magic girdle. After many adventures he presents himself to the Green Knight to receive the return blow. The Green Knight, suitably impressed by Gawain's sense of honour, spares his life, only nicking his neck as punishment for the relatively minor offence of keeping the magic girdle.

geis In Irish folklore, a form of bond that could not be broken without risking extreme dishonour or even death. Many Celtic heroes were bound by such geasa and met their deaths after breaking these promises or taboos.

Gelert In Welsh legend the dog of the 13th-century Prince Llewelyn that met with a cruel fate after performing noble deeds on its master's behalf. Returning home one day from the hunt, Llewelyn was horrified to find his infant child missing and Gelert's jaws dripping with blood. The prince rapidly jumped to the conclusion that his child had been killed by the dog, which he promptly slew. Shortly afterwards, however, he found the body of a wolf killed by Gelert lying close to his peacefully sleeping son and understood the injustice of his act. What purports to be the grave of Gelert may still be seen in the village of Beddgelert in North Wales.

The basic story of a loyal animal slain by its master after performing some noble deed is common to folkloric traditions throughout Europe and Asia, although it is not always a wolf that features in the tale but a serpent or some other equally dangerous creature.

geomancy The art of DIVINATION by dropping seeds, fragments of soil, pebbles, sticks, bones and other small objects onto the earth and then observing their configurations upon the ground. Geomancy also includes the study of the patterns left in the ASHES of a fire, of the shapes made by leaves falling into a pool, and the marks made by ink blots. This method of divination is common to many cultures around the world, including those of Arabia, China and Europe.

George, St The patron saint of England, who is remembered chiefly for his dragon-slaying feats. The real St George would appear not to have been an Englishman at all, but a Christian martyred by the Roman emperor Diocletian at Lydda in Palestine around AD 303. He had become the subject of a cult by the 6th century and subsequently acquired particular significance in England during Richard I's crusade (1189–92) when the king captured the church at Lydda where St George's relics were preserved. Richard adopted St George as the patron saint of his army (he remains the patron saint of soldiers to this day).

The story of St George and the dragon seems to have been derived from the Greek legend of Perseus and his rescue of Andromeda from a sea monster. The legend tells how St George rises to the challenge of killing a dragon that has been ravaging the countryside far and wide and demanding human sacrifices. St George manages to overcome the dragon and, with his lance poised for the final kill, promises to despatch the monster if the people convert to Christianity.

Although he was also adopted as the patron saint of Venice, Genoa, Portugal and Catalonia, St George is best known as the patron saint of England, and his flag, a red cross on a white background, is well known as the English national flag, flying regularly from church towers throughout the country.

Geraint (or Gereint) In Arthurian legend, one of the knights of the ROUND TABLE. Identified as a prince of Devon and by the Welsh as the son of one Erbin, he features in the tale of 'Geraint and Enid', which was in turn derived from Chrétien de Troyes' *Erec et Enide*, written towards the end of the 12th century. This recounts Geraint's marriage to the beautiful Enid, and his subsequent misinterpretation of her regret that on marrying he had retired from his adventurous life as a knight. Mistakenly presuming his wife's unhappiness relates to the fact that she has taken a lover, Geraint forbids her from saying a word and insists that she accompany him on his quests. After many perilous adventures he realizes his mistake and is reconciled to Enid. Tradition has it that he eventually met his death fighting (presumably with Arthur) at the Battle of Llongborth (Langport, Somerset).

ghost The spirit of someone who is dead, which according to the folklore of virtually every culture in the world may return to earth to manifest itself to the living. A ghost may manifest itself as a visible apparition, as an invisible poltergeist who disturbs the furniture, or merely as a 'presence' felt only by those who are particularly sensitive to such entities. Most people are terrified at the thought of meeting a ghost, and fear what ramifications may follow from such an encounter. This fear has ancient roots, for humans have always felt anxiety about the possibility that the dead return to earth and interfere maliciously in the lives of those they leave behind. Tradition holds that spirits of the dead, which may include apparitions of animals as well as humans, return for a variety of reasons: some seek vengeance for their deaths, while others warn of danger, or come back to complete some unfinished business that must be put right before they can depart to enjoy eternal repose.

Ghost stories furnish a large body of myths in the folk tradition of numerous cultures. They range widely in character, and include tales of such phenomena as phantom coaches (complete with headless riders) and grey monks and nuns, as well as apparitions of the recently deceased, and even visions of people still living (see DOPPELGÄNGER). Most ghosts manifest in the hours of darkness in suitably gloomy, ominous locations such as ruins and deserted graveyards, but some are reported to have been seen during daytime in otherwise unlikely settings. Such stories have in turn inspired countless superstitions and taboos. Disregarding these may result in the calling up of the dead, and even lingering in the vicinity of such ominous locations as crossroads may be enough to summon the attentions of the supernatural. Protective measures include, according to Scottish tradition, wearing a cross of rowan wood fastened with red thread. Elsewhere the dead are understood to be incapable of returning to earth as ghosts if their bodies are either dismembered or cremated.

See also URBAN LEGEND.

ghost dance Native American folk religion that attracted a cult following among the Sioux tribes towards the end of the 19th century. Derived from the beliefs of the Shoshone peoples, it was taken up on a much wider scale following a dream that the Paiute prophet Wovoka had during an eclipse of the sun in the late 1880s. Wovoka reported seeing God in his dream, and passed on to his people the ghost dance that God had taught him. The dance, he told them, would make the white men disappear, bring the buffalo herds back and restore the Native American nations to their former glory, providing the celebrants gave up alcohol, farming and mourning rites. The cult of the ghost dance (itself a slow, shuffling, circular series of steps) spread quickly among the Plains Indians and was taken up by the Lakota in 1890. The Lakota added the detail of the ghost shirt, which was supposed to protect the wearer from all harm, including bullet wounds. The excitement engendered by the ghost dance led ultimately to the massacre that took place at Wounded Knee in December 1890, a calamity that effectively brought the cult to an end, although it is still occasionally revived among Native American peoples even today.

ghoul In Arabic and Oriental folklore, a variety of cannibalistic demon that feeds on both living and dead flesh. Although the term is now much more broadly used to refer to any loathsome spirit or person with a taste for the macabre, it was originally more specific. Ghouls are supposed to haunt various desolate places, from deserts and mountains to graveyards or the site of murders or other unpleasant events. According to Arabian lore they have the ability to change their shape in order to entrap their prey, often transforming themselves into beautiful women, but can still be identified by their hooved feet.

See also JINNI.

giant One of a breed of huge humanlike monsters, often many times the size of an ordinary person, which feature prominently in the folk traditions of virtually all the world's cultures. Variously credited with a range of magical powers, but also often described as slow-witted and ugly, giants generally appear as essentially evil characters, sometimes with a taste for human flesh. They often guard large stores of treasure in their great castles or lairs, which may be located underground or, sometimes, in the clouds. Because they are so physically powerful, it is usually up to the heroes of folklore to defeat them through cunning or the use of magic, as in such famous stories as JACK AND THE BEANSTALK and JACK THE GIANT-KILLER.

According to Celtic mythology, Britain was inhabited by a race of giants prior to the arrival of BRUT and his men, and many remarkable natural features, such as the GIANT'S CAUSEWAY, as well as many ancient megalithic monuments, such as Stonehenge, were commonly identified as having been built by these giants. Irish tradition maintained that the giants were in fact themselves gods who had been ejected from heaven and such legendary heroes as FIONN MAC CUMHAILL were commonly depicted as giants. In Norse mythology the giants battled against the gods until defeated by THOR and LOKI.

See also FROST GIANTS; GOG AND MAGOG; JOTUN; OGRE.

Giant's Causeway Natural geological feature on the Antrim coastline of Northern Ireland. According to ancient legend it was constructed by GIANTS. Comprising a unique landscape of hexagonal basaltic columns formed by rapidly cooling lava, the causeway was supposedly created by giants working together to build a road across the Irish Sea to Scotland. They fell out with one another, however, long before the task was completed, leaving the site as it is today.

Gingerbread Man European folk tale about a gingerbread man's flight from a wide range of animals and people trying to eat him. Familiar throughout Europe and North America, it culminates in the gingerbread man's demise when tricked and eaten by that wiliest of creatures, the FOX, which offers him safe passage across a river and then eats him in mid-stream.

ginseng Herb that has long been valued for its alleged medicinal properties. Prized especially in the herbal folklore of the East, ginseng probably owes its reputation to its physical resemblance to the MANDRAKE, long considered one of the most magically potent of all plants. Usually consumed in the form of wine or tea, ginseng is credited with a wide range of beneficial properties, and is believed by many to promote strength and guarantee a long life.

Glas Ghaibhneach In Celtic mythology, a magical cow that was the property of GOIBNIU, the smith of the gods. Remarkable for its never-ending supply of milk, it was stolen by BALOR, who took it to Tory Island, but it was then recovered by Cian. Tradition has it that the cow will manifest to any deserving person in need of its milk. However, it will disappear again if struck, milked into a leaky bucket or otherwise offended. A Welsh equivalent is called Fuwch Frech.

Glastonbury Thorn See JOSEPH OF ARIMATHEA.

gnome Variety of DWARF or GOBLIN typically described as living in underground caverns and mines. The term appears to have been coined originally by the 16th-century Swiss physician and alchemist Paracelsus, possibly from the Greek *genomos* ('earth-dweller). In the neo-Platonic theory of the elements they represent earth.

Gnomes feature in countless fairy tales and legends. They vary considerably in character, sometimes being depicted as benevolent and jolly bearded little men (as they are usually rendered today in the form of garden ornaments), but occasionally as short-tempered and even vicious. According to some traditions they guard great treasure, and are expert miners who have been known to guide human miners to rich veins of ore.

goat The goat has variously been associated in world folklore with virility, lechery and the darker supernatural forces, belying the creature's lengthy history as a domesticated animal. It was often identified in ancient times with the Greek god

Pan, who was half man and half goat, and subsequently with the DEVIL himself, who – like the horned gods of Celtic legend – is conventionally depicted with a goat's cloven hooves and goat's head. In some parts of Europe it is said that goats show their allegiance to the Prince of Darkness by visiting him every 24 hours to have their beards combed by him.

In primitive times it was often believed that sins and diseases could be transferred to a 'scapegoat', a single animal selected and ritually put to death in order to rid the whole flock of such evils. Even today in many parts of the world farmers sometimes keep a goat or two to absorb the physicals ills that would otherwise afflict his other livestock; it is said that the stronger the smell of a billy goat the less likelihood there is of any cows or horses falling sick.

Goats were often chosen as sacrificial animals, and the flesh, skin and milk of the animal is widely valued in folk medicine. Rubbing sore feet, eyes and heads with fresh goat cheese was recommended as a treatment in Anglo-Saxon times, and goats' brains, passed through a golden ring, were sometimes fed to children suffering from epilepsy. Some people carry goats' feet and hairs from goats' beards as lucky charms, and sailors have been known to fix a goatskin – or even a whole goat – to the mast to ward off foul weather. A goat's horn slipped under the pillow will cure insomnia.

goblin In European folklore, a mischievous breed of demon that delights in playing malicious tricks upon mortals. Variously depicted as inhabiting houses, mines or trees, goblins are closely related to DWARFS and GNOMES, but are usually regarded as a more malevolent species. Of generally grotesque appearance, they may be blamed for such trivial crimes as breaking things around the house and knocking on walls, but may also be accused of more serious crimes, such as the kidnapping of children, and even cannibalism. Making regular gifts of food and milk is recommended in several cultures to avoid causing offence to their kind. The word 'goblin' appears to derive from the ancient Greek *kobalos*, which signified a mischievous sprite.

See also BOGEY; HOBGOBLIN.

Godiva, Lady Wife of the 11th-century Leofric, Earl of Mercia, otherwise called Godgifu in Old English. She is the central character in one of the most famous of all English legends and her memory is still cherished in Coventry, where she lived, with annual processions in her honour.

According to legend, Godiva protested earnestly when her husband imposed heavy taxes upon the people of the city, realizing the hardship these demands would cause. Leofric jokingly agreed to lift the taxes if she consented to ride naked through the streets of the city on market day, little imagining she would consent to undergo such humiliation. With only her long hair to conceal her body, however, Lady Godiva accordingly rode through the city streets, the townspeople politely averting their eyes – with the exception of one 'Peeping Tom', who was appropriately punished for his temerity by being struck blind. Leofric obediently lifted the taxes he had announced, as he had promised. The detail of Peeping Tom would appear to be a later addition to the legend, probably dating only from the 17th century.

The existence of Leofric and Godiva is supported by historical documents, but the legend itself may owe more to ancient fertility rites and other folk rituals in which participants were often naked. According to Roger of Wendover, writing in the 13th century, the events took place in the year 1057.

Gog and Magog In English mythology, the only survivors of a race of giants born from demons who lived in England prior to the arrival of BRUT. Legend has it that they were taken to London as prisoners by Brut and his men and were there obliged to work as porters at the gate of the royal palace. Variants of the legend combine Gog and Magog as a single giant called Gogmagog, who attacks Brut and his men shortly after they land on the coast of Cornwall. He meets his match, however, in combat with Corineus, who throws him into the sea. Magog is sometimes identified with the goddess of a moon-worshipping cult, while Gog is said to have been her husband or son.

In the Bible, Gog and Magog are identified as representative of all the future enemies of the kingdom of God and it is generally assumed that it was from this biblical reference that all subsequent legends concerning the giants evolved.

Effigies of Gog and Magog were kept at London's Guildhall from the reign of Henry V, being replaced by new figures in 1708 following their destruction in the Great Fire of 1666, and again in 1953 following their obliteration during the Blitz in 1940. Statues of the two giants have been paraded in pageants and processions in London since at least the early 15th century, often appearing in the annual Lord Mayor's Show.

Goibniu In Irish mythology, the magic-working smith of the TUATHA DE DANANN. He made the weapons with which the Tuatha defeated the FOMOR- IANS and himself slew RUADAN, who had been sent to kill Goibniu at his armoury. The wounds he sustained in the struggle were healed with water from the well of Slane.

See also GLAS GHAIBHNEACH.

gold Universally prized for its monetary worth, gold is also important in world folklore for its intrinsic magical properties (presumably inspired by the metal's physical qualities, which include a high degree of malleability and resistance to tarnishing). Gold was widely used in the making of sacred objects in many of the world's early religions, and many legends developed about its origins. According to some, gold was distilled from the rays of the sun, while others maintained that it

should only be mined after the performance of various purifying ceremonies and acts of appeasement towards the gods to whom it properly belonged.

Gold has many uses in folk medicine. Records survive from a thousand years ago to the effect that gold is particularly efficacious in treating eye problems, and even today some people claim that rubbing a sore eye with a gold wedding ring will cause a sty to disappear. Rubbing the eyelids with gold even when one does not have a sty is said to bring good fortune to whoever tries it. When other treatments against illness prove ineffective, one option remaining is to pour a little water over a gold (or silver) coin and then to give the water to the patient to drink: the ailment is sure to disappear. Women having a difficult time in childbirth may be encouraged to remove any gold jewellery they have on, as this is sometimes blamed for such problems, and those who are troubled by warts may find that rapping them with gold will do the trick.

Another old tradition still honoured among the world's seafarers claims that those who wear gold earrings will never go down with their ship.

Goldilocks and the Three Bears European fairy tale about a young girl who trespasses in the house of three bears. It has been suggested that the story has its roots ultimately in a Scottish folk tale about a vixen that is devoured after entering a bears' den (a moral tale warning children to respect the laws of their community and to honour the rights of their neighbours). It was popularized through Robert Southey's retelling of the tale in his miscellany *The Doctor* (1837) and through a version recorded by the Brothers Grimm, which relocated the story in a forest. In these early variants Goldilocks (also known originally as Silverhair or Silverlocks) is not a young girl but an old woman.

The tale recounts how Goldilocks stumbles upon a small house in the woods and goes in, only to find no one at home.

She helps herself in turn to one of three bowls of porridge, in the process breaking the smallest of three chairs, and then goes upstairs to sleep in one of the three beds. The occupants of the house, three bears, then return, and Goldilocks flees in terror from the house. In early versions she tumbles out of the window after being discovered asleep in the bedroom.

golem In Jewish folklore, an artificial human being created by means of magic. Because the golem has a body but lacks a soul, it is regarded with loathing and fear. A 16th-century rabbi of Prague called Judah Loew (or Jodah Low Ben Bezalel) was supposed to have successfully created such a creature. It could be roused to life by quoting various formulaic words, and would revert to a lifeless state if these same words were spoken in reverse. It was said to have great strength and supernatural instincts.

goose Geese feature in numerous folk tales and legends, and many fairy-tale heroes benefit from the possession of a 'golden goose' that is either made of gold itself or lays golden eggs. These tales include several in which greedy villains foolishly kill the goose that lays golden eggs without realizing this will end the supply. There is also a European story in which those who try to steal a precious feather from the hero's golden goose become magically stuck to it. The resulting sight is so ludicrous that it provokes laughter in the princess, whose hand has been promised to any man who can make her smile, and thus the hero wins her.

In the British Isles, goose was traditionally served up on Michaelmas Day and was the staple Christmas fare before being replaced by turkey, and it was widely held that any household where goose was eaten on this day would enjoy prosperous times in the coming year. If the meat proved to have a brown tint this meant that a mild winter was in store; if it was pure white or bluish in colour then the winter would be severe. Geese were once seen in every farmyard, and in Wales it is still said that if the geese leave a farm this is a warning that there will shortly be a fire. Geese that fly high in the air, it is claimed, are a prophecy of good weather; if they fly near the ground then storms may be on the way.

In folk medicine, goose grease mixed with turpentine and rubbed on the chest is valued in the USA as a cure for coughs and colds, and is also used in the treatment of rheumatism and earache.

Gorlois of Cornwall See UTHER PENDRAGON.

Gotham, Wise Men of In English folklore, the dim-witted inhabitants of the village of Gotham, Nottinghamshire, who became renowned far and wide for their stupidity. Many hilarious stories about the folly of the Wise Men of Gotham were in circulation by at least the early 16th century (although some of these clearly came from foreign sources). Perhaps the best known of these concerns the villagers' attempts to catch a cuckoo by linking hands round the tree in which it has its perch, or else planting a hedge round it – only for the bird to escape over the top. On another occasion they try to drown an eel in the village pond.

Legend has it that Gotham acquired its reputation as the result of a ruse played by the villagers when it was learned that King John planned to build a hunting lodge there – a decision that would involve the local community in much expense and inconvenience. In order to put the king off, the villagers let themselves be seen engaged in all kinds of bizarre lunatic activities, thus successfully persuading the monarch to build his lodge elsewhere.

Grail, Holy The sacred cup or chalice that was used by Christ at the Last Supper, and was later employed to catch his blood as it dripped from his body on the Cross. The Holy Grail was the object of the Grail Quest pursued in Arthurian myth by the so-called 'Grail knights' of the ROUND TABLE. The Grail is first mentioned in Arthurian myth in Chrétien de Troyes' *Perceval ou Le Conte du Graal*, which was written towards the end of the 12th century. The tradition was also clearly influenced by older Celtic legends about miraculous cauldrons, and combines details drawn from both Christian and French romantic tradition.

Listed among the HALLOWS of Britain, the Grail was supposedly brought to the British Isles by JOSEPH OF ARIMATHEA, who was often identified as the first guardian of the grail, or 'Grail King'. His successors included BRAN THE BLESSED and PRYDERI (*see also* FISHER KING; WOUNDED KING).

Tradition insisted that the Grail could only be located by a knight of perfect virtue – the reason why the adulterous LANCELOT had to concede the honour to his son GALAHAD, accompanied by PERCEVAL and Bors. Only knights of spotless reputation stood to be rewarded by a glimpse of the Grail; if anyone of less than perfect character approached it, it vanished from view. The successful knight had to find the answer to the so-called Grail Question. Usually the knight concerned would be confronted with a procession of the Hallows, including the Grail, together with a great show of mourning. Any knight who failed to ask 'what does this mean?' was automatically debarred from being successful in his Grail quest. It was Sir Galahad who was destined to succeed in asking the question correctly.

Grail King *See* BRAN THE BLESSED; FISHER KING; GRAIL, HOLY; PRYDERI; WOUNDED KING.

Grainne In Irish mythology, the daughter of CORMAC MAC AIRT. She was promised in marriage to FIONN MAC CUMHAILL but subsequently, disappointed at Fionn's greying hair, eloped with DIARMUID. The couple escaped from Fionn and Grainne's wedding party after drugging the other guests, but were then pursued by the outraged Fionn. A reconciliation of sorts was eventually reached, and in time Grainne bore Diarmuid four sons and a daughter. When Diarmuid was mortally wounded by a boar, however, Fionn procrastinated in bringing him the water that would save his life, and he died. Grainne subsequently gave in to Fionn's wooing and dutifully married him. A variant legend offers a different ending, with the angry Fionn cursing the lovers so that they would fly forever, unable to spend two consecutive nights in the same place. Many stone circles and cairns throughout Ireland are identified as the temporary resting places of the unhappy pair.

Gram *See* BALMUNG.

Green Knight *See* GAWAIN.

Green Man In English folklore, a mysterious nature spirit of the woods often interpreted as the personification of summer. Otherwise known as Jack-in-the-Green, he is usually depicted bedecked in green foliage, with leaves for hair. Possibly a relic of ancient tree worship, he continues to appear as a character in MUMMERS' PLAYS and May Day processions, in which he is usually impersonated by a boy or young man wearing a wooden wickerwork frame covered with leaves, boughs, flowers and streamers. His likeness may also be seen in some English churches, usually in the form of a decorated roof boss, signifying a link with much older pagan beliefs. It seems likely that the character originated ultimately in pre-Christian tree worship.

Essentially a rural spirit, the Green Man acquired a new urban relevance in the 18th century when Jack-in-the-Green was taken up for obscure reasons by the chimney sweeps of London and other large English towns. Young sweeps gathered to march alongside Jack-in-the-Green every May Day, but the tradition had died out by the end of the 19th century following the prohibition of the employment of young boys in such work.

Equivalents of the Green Man elsewhere in Europe include the Slavic Green George and the Swiss Whitsuntide Basket.

See also ROBIN HOOD; WILD HERDS-MAN; WOODWOSE.

gremlin A diminutive variety of IMP whose interference with the workings of machinery is often blamed for any mechanical fault that develops. The gremlin was an invention of a British Royal Air Force bomber squadron stationed on the North West Frontier of India shortly before World War II. The squadron had been much plagued by minor technical problems, and the officers accordingly invented the gremlin as the source of these woes. The name was apparently devised as a combination of 'Grimm Brothers' and 'Fremlin's Brewery', whose beer (distinguished by a label depicting a GOBLIN climbing out of a beer bottle) was the only brand stocked in the squadron bar. The idea quickly caught on with Royal Air Force units during the war after the squadron was posted back to the UK, and the gremlin has since established itself as a familiar figure in the popular imagination, being blamed for breakdowns not only in aircraft but also in cars, trains, computers and virtually any other kind of machine or project. The only way to foil the activities of gremlins, apparently, is to lay an empty beer bottle nearby – the mischievous creatures will crawl inside and stay there.

Grendel *See* BEOWULF.

griffin Mythical monster born from the union of a lion and an eagle, and thus combining the head and wings of an eagle with the body of a lion (and sometimes also the tail of a snake). Stories about griffins were in circulation in the Mediterranean and Near East by at least the 14th century, and they were widely considered sacred to the sun, representing such qualities as nobility and power. They were also rumoured to guard vast treasures, which they defended from attack by the ancient Scythian tribe called the Arimaspians. In Christian tradition the griffin (or gryphon) was occasionally taken up as a symbol for Christ.

Grimm, Brothers The two German brothers Jakob (1785–1863) and Wilhelm (1786–1859) Grimm, who conducted pioneering work in the study of folklore. Their *Household Tales*, popularly known as 'Grimm's Fairy Tales', was an immensely influential collection of folk tales collected from such contacts as an old soldier, the old nurse who lived in the house next door and a tailor's wife. The brothers claimed to be passing on these stories in an unadulterated form, but it is clear that, although they refrained from expunging the gruesome scenes from such tales as *Bluebeard* to suit contemporary tastes, for instance, they did make many alterations of their own.

In all, the brothers published some 200 stories, the most famous of which included *The Frog Prince*, *The Golden Goose*, *Hansel and Gretel*, *Rumpelstiltskin* and *Snow White and the Seven Dwarfs*. The brothers' work in the field of folklore led them to devise their own theories about the origins and development of the tales, and they became convinced that many variant stories were descended from a single Indo-European source (*see* DEVOLUTIONARY THEORY). Although best remembered today for their fairy tales, which were translated into English in 1884, the brothers were also respected in their own time for their research into language and linguistics.

groaning cake A special cake (or sometimes a cheese) that was formerly made in English-speaking countries to celebrate the birth of a child and to ensure the good luck of the new arrival. Rarely seen in modern times, the groaning cake (so called in reference to the noises a mother makes in labour) had to be cut by the father, or else by the attending doctor, who had to take care not to cut himself as this was an omen that the baby would die before it was a year old. It was frowned upon for anyone to refuse to accept a piece of the cake, as this was thought to bring the infant bad luck and rob the child of charm.

In the case of a groaning cheese, the cheese was cut from the middle until the hole was large enough for the baby to be passed through it for luck (usually done on the day of the Christening). Unmarried girls may choose to keep their slice of cake or cheese and slip it under their pillow in the expectation of seeing a future lover in their dreams.

Groundhog Day In the USA, 2 February, upon which date the groundhog (or woodchuck) is said to emerge from its burrow after its winter hibernation. If the groundhog sees its own shadow it will return to its burrow for another six weeks, as spring has not yet arrived. If there is no shadow, then it will remain above ground, thus indicating that winter is nearly over. This tradition has its roots in much older beliefs that were apparently imported originally from Europe, where the animals concerned included bears and badgers.

guardian spirit A benevolent spirit or angel that watches over the welfare of a particular place, object, animal or individual. Belief in such spirits is ancient and widespread, and in the past many rituals were aimed at obtaining help from such beings. Guardian spirits are variously credited with giving warnings of imminent danger, with recommending particular courses of action and with providing protection more directly where necessary. They may appear in dreams or visions, or possibly in more material form, often as a bird or other animal. It is widely considered reckless to offend such guardian spirits, as they may punish transgressors.

See also FAIRY GODMOTHER; FAMILIAR.

Gudrun In Norse and Germanic legend, the wife of King SIGURD. According to the *Völsungasaga*, she is married to Sigurd after her mother Grimhild administers a love potion to him, making him forget his lover BRYNHILD. After Sigurd's death, she marries Attila, the king of the Huns, and bears him two children. Attila, however, kills her two brothers, and she in revenge murders their own two offspring, feeds their hearts to her husband and then slays him as well.

Another Gudrun features in the 13th-century German epic romance called the *Gudrun Lied*. Derived from the *Prose Edda*, the tale relates how Gudrun's hand is sought by three royal princes and how she is seized and imprisoned for 13 years by one of them, Hartmut of Norway. After years of abuse by her captor she is rescued by another of her suitors, her lover Herwig of Zealand.

Guillaume d'Orange French folk hero whose adventures are related in *La Geste de Guillaume d'Orange*, one of the most famous of the CHANSON DE GESTE cycles of the medieval period. The cycle recounts the noble role of Guillaume d'Orange's family in the wars against the Moors. He may have been modelled upon the historical Wilhelmus, cousin of the 9th-century emperor CHARLEMAGNE.

Guinevere In Arthurian legend, the faithless wife of King ARTHUR. The daughter of Leodegrance of Cameliard, she would appear to have inherited some of the attributes of MORRIGAN and other pagan goddesses, particularly those associated with SOVEREIGNTY. Her name, given in Welsh as Gwenhwyfar, means 'white one' or 'white ghost'.

According to legend, Guinevere betrays Arthur by becoming the lover of Sir LANCELOT, and thus precipitates the break-up of the knights of the ROUND TABLE. Other legends tell how she is abducted by Arthur's nephew MORDRED (the enemy responsible for informing Arthur of his wife's adultery), and also by

Meleagraunce, from whom she is rescued either by Arthur or Lancelot. Tradition claims that Arthur sentenced Guinevere to be burned at the stake for her infidelity, but that Lancelot saved her from this fate and took her to the castle of Joyous Gard in France, which Arthur subsequently besieged. Ultimately all three were reconciled, with Guinevere being sent as a nun to the monastery of Amesbury. Lancelot for his part agreed to his exile from Britain, but was at Guinevere's side when she died. Legend has it that she was eventually buried alongside Arthur at Glastonbury, their graves supposedly being discovered by monks there centuries later.

Gunnar *See* GUNTHER.

Gunther In the NIBELUNGENLIED, the king of Burgundy, who is the brother of Siegfried's wife KRIEMHILD. Identified as Gunnar in Norse legend, he sought the hand of BRUNHILD, but could not break through the ring of flame that surrounded her castle. Siegfried dutifully disguised himself as Gunther and, having got through the flames, claimed her on Gunther's behalf. Gunther and Brunhild were married, but when Brunhild learned the truth of what had occurred she ordered the killing of Siegfried and committed suicide herself. Gunther in turn was slain by Attila (or Atli) the Hun after refusing to reveal the location of the hoard of the Nibelungs.

Tradition has it that the legend of Gunther was modelled originally upon the life of the historical King Gundaharius of the Burgundians, who died fighting the Huns in 436.

Guy Fawkes Night Annual British festivity, also known as Bonfire Night, commemorating a foiled attempt made on the life of King James I by Guy Fawkes on 5 November 1605. Celebrated with bonfires and firework displays, this traditional event is among the few communal folk gatherings still widely observed in Britain on an annual basis.

The so-called Gunpowder Plot was a Catholic conspiracy to blow up the Houses of Parliament while James I was in attendance. Guy Fawkes and the other plotters were discovered in the cellars below Parliament shortly before the allotted time, and were subsequently tried for treason. Fawkes himself was tortured and finally executed. Effigies of Guy Fawkes are today placed on the top of the bonfires that burn on 5 November, the anniversary of the famous plot.

The festivities enjoyed on Guy Fawkes Night probably derive ultimately from much earlier bonfire rituals held at much the same time of year, marking the end of summer (*see* SAMHAIN).

Guy of Warwick English folk hero whose adventures were celebrated in Anglo-French romances of the 12th century. Identified as a 10th-century knight, he is supposed to have fallen in love with the beautiful Félice, the daughter of the Earl of Warwick, and in order to win her hand performed many feats, which included the slaying of a terrifying boar, and the fearsome DUN COW and a dragon. In the process he saved the life of a lion, which consequently became devoted to him. Repentant for having spent so many years in the pursuit of love, he also performed many noble deeds while on pilgrimage to the Holy Land. On his return to England he came to the support of King Athelstan in his wars against the Danes, killing the Danish champion Colbrand and thus saving Winchester from capture. He ended his life as a hermit near Warwick, begging bread at his castle gate from his own wife, who did not recognize him in this guise. On his deathbed he sent his ring to his wife, who was reunited with him just before he died. Various miraculous cures were attributed to his body, which was interred within his hermit's cell after magic prevented its removal.

Gwalchmai *See* GAWAIN.

Gwydion In Celtic mythology, a sorcerer who features prominently in Welsh legend. The son of the magician Don, he served as steward to his uncle, Math, but subsequently provoked war between Gwynedd and Dyfed by cheating PRY-DERI of his celebrated pigs, the only domesticated pigs in the world. In the fighting that followed, Gwydion killed Pryderi, but was then turned by the magic of Math successively into a stag, a sow and a wolf. After three years he was restored to his original human shape, and subsequently used his magic to win LLEU LLAW GYFFES the recognition of his mother (and Gwydion's sister) ARIAN-RHOD, with whom he was also reputed to have had an incestuous relationship. When Lleu was killed, it was Gwydion who brought him back to life again.

gwyllion In Welsh mythology, a breed of mischievous female FAIRY suspected of committing such relatively minor crimes as luring travellers from their way. They are also credited with the ability to change their shape, commonly taking the form of a GOAT. Like other fairies the gwyllion have to be treated with great courtesy and care as they are easily offended and may seek retribution. They can be warded off, however, by brandishing anything made of IRON.

gyromancy Method of DIVINATION that involves walking in circles until the person concerned falls down with dizziness. The direction of the fall is then analysed for its significance.

gytrash In the folklore of northern England, a spirit that haunts lonely roads at night. Variously identified as malevolent or kindly towards lost travellers, the gytrash may manifest in a range of forms, including those of large dogs or horses.

H

haddock Various folk beliefs have attached themselves to the haddock, most of which attempt to explain how the fish acquired its black gill spots. According to one of these, the spots are the fingerprints of Christ himself, imprinted on the fish when he held it aloft at the feeding of the five thousand. Another tradition links the haddock to St Peter, the marks of his fingers being left on the fish's skin after he held it to receive the tribute money that the fish brought. One Yorkshire legend claims that the haddock acquired its spots after it was seized by the Devil, who picked it up by mistake after he dropped his hammer in the sea while constructing the rock outcrop at Filey Brigg (otherwise known as the Devil's Bridge).

The Scots refrain from burning the bones of the haddock, which is considered a lucky fish, because the fish once warned that if they did so it would cease to frequent Scottish shores.

hag A loathsome old woman commonly identified as a witch or as some variety of supernatural demon. World folklore is rich with tales of hideous old women who prey on innocent young men and others, taking the form of beautiful girls in order to seduce them, or tormenting sleeping mortals with nightmares (*see* SUCCUBUS). According to ancient superstition, men or animals who wake apparently exhausted after a troubled night's sleep may have been 'hag-ridden' – that is, mounted and ridden around the countryside by such hags as they work their evil.

It has been suggested that the hag tradition may have its roots ultimately in various pagan fertility goddesses.

See also CAILLEACH BHEURE; LOATHLY LADY.

Hagen *See* NIBELUNGENLIED.

hair Folklore insists that hair retains a mystical link with the body even after it is cut off and it thus has great potential in folk magic, playing a role in numerous traditions, legends, and folk tales (such as that of RAPUNZEL).

To begin with, the colour of the hair is said to communicate much information about character. A red-haired person is widely held to have an irascible temper (perhaps in reference to the red-haired Judas Iscariot or else to the fierce red-haired Norse invaders of Britain), although he or she may also be courageous, and it is considered lucky to run one's fingers through a head of red hair. Fair hair is a sign of a weak nature, while black hair suggests great strength and virility, and is also lucky. Whatever the hair's colour, however, it remains unwise to pluck out any odd grey hairs that appear, as ten more will grow for every one thus removed.

People with straight hair are said to be cunning, while those with curly hair are of good temper. Those whose hair forms a 'cowlick' curl are said to be naturally lucky, but any woman whose hair grows down into a point fairly low on the forehead is said to have a 'widow's peak', an ill omen that indicates that she is destined to become a widow herself. People desirous of curly hair, meanwhile, are advised to eat the crusts of newly baked bread. Girls with exceptionally long hair were once warned that a girl 'with hair below the knee ne'er a bride will she be', and too bushy a growth of hair suggests that the wearer may be dim-witted, because the hair is diverting nourishment that should go to the brain.

In men, a hairy chest or luxuriant facial hair is widely held to be a sign of strength and is thus lucky (the reason why in ancient times victorious soldiers hacked the beards off defeated enemies). Those with a lot of hair on the arms and on the backs of the hands are destined to enjoy considerable wealth, although hair on the palm of the hand is widely considered to be a sign of madness.

Looking after the hair involves the observance of various taboos. The Scottish say that a woman must never comb her hair after dark if she has friends and relations at sea, as this will bring them into terrible danger. Hair that is trimmed when the moon is waxing will grow back quickly, but hair that is cut when the moon is on the wane will stay short and may lose its shine. On no account should hair be trimmed on Good Friday, and in some areas hair cutting should also be avoided on Thursdays, Fridays, Saturdays and Sundays. Cutting one's own hair is unlucky, and seafarers are warned that cutting the hair while at sea will summon up a storm. In some societies the hair may be shorn very short as a sign of grief after someone dies, or else as part of a ceremony associated with INITIATION.

Disposal of cut hair is of paramount importance for, in common with nail clippings and various bodily fluids, the smallest amount may be used by a witch to obtain control over the person from whom it came. Simply boiling a strand of hair will oblige the owner of it to come to the witch or sorcerer responsible. By burning the hair in a ritual ceremony a witch might also cause excruciating pain

to the person from whom it has come. One variant of this involves using a few strands of hair in the making of a wax image representing the person from whom the hair has come and then holding the figure in a flame, thus inflicting intense burning pains and even death. One defence against such a threat is to cut off some hair, or more drastically part of a finger, as a sacrifice, thus warding off further harm. Witches themselves were sometimes shorn by their accusers of all their body hair so as to deprive their familiars of a place to hide. Even in modern times lovers sometimes exchange locks of each other's hair, originally to show their trust that the other will not misuse it as a witch might.

The safest way to dispose of cut hair is to bury it. This is better than burning it, as the soul of the person to whom it belonged will have need of hair on Judgement Day. Perhaps because of the threat of witchcraft many people formerly chose not to preserve locks of their own hair or that of their children, although others favoured keeping a single lock in the form of a LIFE TOKEN. If a bird obtains so much as a single human hair to make its nest, the person concerned will be afflicted with a severe headache; if the bird is a magpie, according to the folklore of the English county of Devon, that person will die within the year. Other miscellaneous myths concerning hair include the persistent idea that hair will continue to grow in the grave: this is entirely untrue as both hair and nails cease to grow at the moment of death, when the blood supply to the cells ceases (although shrinkage of the skin after death may expose a minuscule length of hair previously hidden).

Hallowe'en Pagan festival of the dead, descended from the ancient Celtic festival of SAMHAIN, that is celebrated each year on 31 October (the end of summer in the old Celtic calendar). According to longstanding tradition this is a night when ghosts revisit their earthly homes, witches hold their sabbaths and malicious spirits of all kinds seek to do mischief.

It was once widely believed that the sun passed through the gates of hell on this date, providing an opportunity for evil spirits to slip out and to menace the earth for a period of some 48 hours – hence the ominous associations of the modern version of the festival. Attempts to Christianize the festival by making it the eve of All Hallow's Day or All Saints' Day, when Christian saints and martyrs are commemorated, have failed to obliterate the essentially pagan character of the event, with the now ubiquitous imagery of broomstick-riding witches and grotesque hollowed-out turnips or pumpkins (originally intended to scare demons away). The modern 'trick-or-treat' custom, whereby children disguised as ghosts, demons, or witches go from house to house demanding sweets, was clearly inspired by the ancient belief that multifarious spirits wander the world on this special night of the year. Although commonly thought of as a relatively recent US invention, similar practices have been a feature of Hallowe'en rituals for centuries: Scottish folklore, for instance, has the still-observed tradition of 'guising', in which children go from house to house begging for treats (but without the threat of retribution if these are not forthcoming).

In former times communities often gathered on Hallowe'en to light big bonfires in order to ward off evil spirits, and in many rural areas farmers circled their fields with lighted torches in the belief that this would safeguard the following year's harvest. Others drove their livestock between branches of rowan to keep them safe from evil influences.

Hallowe'en marks the one time when the supernatural holds sway over the earth, and is thus an ideal date for spell-casting and divination of the future. According to Welsh tradition, for instance, anyone going to a crossroads on Hallowe'en and listening carefully to the wind may learn what the next year has in store and, when the church clock strikes midnight, will hear a list of the names of those who are to die in the locality over the next 12 months.

Several of the most widely known Hallowe'en divination rituals relate to apples. Superstition suggests that if a girl stands before a mirror at midnight on Hallowe'en while eating an apple and combing her hair she will see her future husband's image reflected in the glass. Moreover, if she peels an apple in one long piece and then tosses the peel over her left shoulder (or into a bowl of water) she will be able to read the first initial of her future partner's name in the shape assumed by the discarded peel. Alternatively the peel is hung on a nail by the front door and the initials of the first man to enter will be the same as those of the unknown lover. Yet another Hallowe'en custom involving the fruit is the game of ducking (or in Scotland, 'douking') apples, in which children attempt to take bites out of apples floating in a bowl of water or suspended on a string without using their hands; tradition has it that are fated to marry the owner of the apple they manage to bite. A popular variant involves players kneeling on a chair above the bowl and dropping a fork held in the mouth in an attempt to pierce an apple.

Other Hallowe'en customs involve blindfolded girls pulling cabbages up and examining the shape of the root to make conclusions about a future spouse, sprinkling letters cut out from a newspaper onto water to see what name they form (the name of a future lover), and throwing nuts into the fire to see if they jump (if they do a lover will prove unfaithful) – hence an alternative name for the festival, Nutcrack Night.

Hallows In Celtic Irish mythology, the kingly regalia that were widely recognized as symbols of true SOVEREIGNTY. They comprised: the Stone of Fal, upon which kings were inaugurated; the spear of LUGH, which was believed to be invincible in battle; the sword of NUADA, which could inflict wounds on any foe; and the cauldron of DAGDA, which had the ability to satisfy any hunger. Possession of the Hallows was much sought by contenders for the throne, as they could be used to indicate who had the right to power. They were brought from the OTHERWORLD by the TUATHA DE DANANN, and subsequently appeared as the sword, spear, cup and pentacle of conventional magic. Arthurian legend reworked the Hallows in the form of a broken sword, the spear of the DOLOROUS BLOW, the dish on which the head of the former guardian of the GRAIL is carried and the Holy Grail itself. The regalia of modern British royalty includes the royal sceptre, the swords of state, the ampulla of holy oil and the crown itself.

See also THIRTEEN TREASURES OF BRITAIN.

hand of glory The hand of an executed criminal, which was once reputed to have various magical powers. Possession of a hand of glory was prized by witches throughout Europe as part of the paraphernalia of black magic, and also by thieves, who valued its alleged ability to make the occupants of a house fall into a deep entranced sleep while they went about their nefarious business.

A hand of glory was prepared by severing the hand of a hanged felon while the body was still on the gallows, pickling it for 15 days, drying it till it was hard, and then fixing between the fingers a candle made from unused wax mixed with the fat of a hanged man and Lapland sesame. When the candle thus mounted was lit, everyone in the vicinity, with the exception of the owner of the gruesome object itself, would fall into a profound slumber from which they could not be roused, however much noise was made. Records exist of such a hand of glory being employed during a foiled burglary in rural Ireland as late as 1831. In some cases no candle was fixed in the hand, but one of the fingers was lit instead; if the finger would not light this was a warning that someone in the house was immune to the candle's influence.

handsel The giving of a small amount of money or some other favour to the other party at the outset of a business deal or some other transaction to guarantee the luck of one or more of the parties involved. According to ancient and widespread tradition it is good policy to start the day's business with such a gift or favour, as this will promote good fortune in the rest of the day's affairs. In times gone by traders of all description kissed or spat on the first money they made each day for the sake of luck, and the first customers in a pub or bar even today may be treated to a free drink for the same reason.

hangman's rope The rope used to hang a man was in former times considered to have its own special magical properties. As far back as the ancient Romans it was claimed that wrapping such a rope round the temples would relieve a headache, and this tradition persisted in Britain almost as long as capital punishment. Possession of such a rope or even a single strand of it was also reputed to fend off all manner of fits and fevers, the rope being worn somewhat ironically around the neck. Gamblers also much prized such ropes in the belief that they improved their luck. Hangmen used to make a tidy profit from selling off portions of their rope, although pieces of rope used by suicides were considered almost as effective.

Hansel and Gretel German fairy tale that was among those collected by the Brothers GRIMM. The tale appears to have ancient origins, and is also known in variant forms in many other parts of the world, including India, Japan, Africa, the Americas and the Pacific. It is unclear, however, whether these all came from a single source or developed independently.

Hansel and Gretel are the children of a poor widowed woodcutter who has recently married for a second time. The children's wicked stepmother persuades her husband that as there is only enough food in the house to feed two, he should take Hansel and Gretel deep into the woods and abandon them there. Hansel, however, overhears the plot, and as they set off leaves a trail of pebbles in their wake. After their father has abandoned them the children follow the pebbles back home. The outraged stepmother persuades her husband to try once again, and Hansel looks for more pebbles to make another trail. He cannot find any, however, and instead creates a trail by dropping crumbs of bread. Unfortunately, birds eat the crumbs, and when the children attempt to find their way home there is no trail to follow.

The children then happen upon a house made entirely of gingerbread, actually the home of an evil witch. The witch welcomes them inside, but then locks Hansel in a cage where she can fatten him up to be eaten, and makes Gretel perform the household chores for her. The witch has poor eyesight, and when she demands that Hansel stick out his finger for her to decide if he is fat enough to eat he fools her by holding out a thin bone. Eventually the witch loses patience and orders Gretel to crawl into the oven to see if it is hot enough to cook the boy. Gretel pretends she does not understand and the witch pokes her own head into the oven to show her how, upon which the girl pushes her in and she burns to death.

Gretel then releases her brother and, having helped themselves to the witch's treasure, they make their way home with the aid of various animals. There they discover that their wicked stepmother has died, and they live happily ever after in the company of their repentant father.

Happy Hunting Ground The paradise of Native American folklore, in which the souls of the dead spend eternity feasting, dancing, singing and gambling. Accounts of the location of the Happy Hunting Ground vary from group to group, but it is often described as lying beyond a great ocean. As elsewhere in the world, there are many tales of this supernatural land being visited by mortals, who have subsequently returned to the land of the living to tell what they have seen. It would appear that the souls of all the dead were permitted to enter the Happy Hunting Ground, regardless of how well they had behaved when alive.

hare The folk beliefs associated with the hare mark it out as an ominous creature closely linked with the moon, and thus with the dark forces of nature. The hare was worshipped in Britain in pre-Christian times and this, together with the animal's eerie cry, habit of standing on its back legs almost like a human and 'mad' behaviour during the mating season, may have contributed to the otherworldly reputation of the animal that has persisted into modern times.

The hare was formerly widely regarded as a favourite disguise of witches, and in rural communities many people accordingly feared the appearance of a hare anywhere in the vicinity of their livestock. Countless stories survive of hares that have been shot at with silver bullets (ordinary bullets having no effect) and of some crone in the district shortly afterwards appearing with a fresh bandage on the relevant part of her body. Witches disguised as hares were alleged to milk cattle dry, and the sight of a hare crossing someone's path was considered deeply unlucky, to the extent that if this happened fishermen would turn back for home and brides would postpone their weddings. Storms, mining disasters and fires (which are sure to follow if a hare runs down the main street of a village) have all been blamed on sightings of hares, and sailors traditionally will not suffer even the word 'hare' to be mentioned while at sea for fear of what might follow.

Dreaming of hares is similarly said to warn of imminent catastrophe, often a death. In some regions, however, it is only white hares – the reincarnations of lovers who have died of grief according to the

Cornish – that are unlucky, and seeing a brown hare is actually said to be a good omen. In modern times, indeed, most people have somewhat perversely come to associate the hare with good luck, chiefly through the time-honoured tradition that carrying a hare's or rabbit's foot, now usually in the form of a key-fob, is very lucky. Other miscellaneous superstitions connected with hares include the notions that they change their sex every year, that killing them is unlucky, that they never sleep and that they will cause deep melancholy and timidity in anyone who consumes their flesh. It is also said that any pregnant women who is startled by a hare is likely to give birth to a child with a harelip (so named from the resemblance to the cleft upper lip of a hare).

In folk medicine, hare's blood rubbed into the skin is recommended as a cure for freckles and carrying a hare's foot will ward off rheumatism. One very ancient English remedy suggests eating hare's brains in wine will effectively stop a person oversleeping.

harvest customs The celebration of the successful gathering in of crops at the end of the summer has long had an important place in the calendar of many cultures. Because the fate of the harvest depends so intimately upon the unfathomable workings of nature it was formerly considered imperative to show gratitude to the various nature gods or field spirits through a variety of festivities, ceremonial dancing, and other rites. The performance of these acts of homage further guaranteed the prospects of the next crop to be planted, and ensured the continued fertility of the fields.

In some societies the celebration of the harvest included sacrifices to the vegetative spirits of a particular tribe or people, and might also include feasting and indulgence in sexual licence.

The harvest festival of the modern Christian church absorbed many of these ancient pagan traditions, and because of this non-Christian element it was only in relatively recent times that the Church of England among other denominations eventually recognized the festival as an official date in the church calendar. In the Church of England it was sanctioned as late as 1843, at the instigation of the Cornish poet and vicar Robert Stephen Hawker. Many churches in the English-speaking world now celebrate the occasion with collections of fruit, vegetables, tinned food and flowers, which are subsequently distributed among the needy. Churches are also decorated with sheaves of corn, loaves of bread and other appropriate products of the season.

See also CORN DOLLY.

Havelock the Dane Legendary Danish prince whose story became well known in both British and Scandinavian myth. Born the rightful heir to the Danish throne, he was sentenced to death by Godard the Usurper, but was taken in secret to England by a fisherman named Grim (the founder of Grimsby). In England, where his royal identity remained unknown, he was forced to marry Princess Goldborough, heir of King Athelstan, as part of a plan to humiliate her. Princess Goldborough subsequently recognized the signs of kingship in her new husband's character and appearance. In due course Havelock defeated Godard, and was acknowledged the rightful king of both England and Denmark.

hawk Like other birds of prey the hawk has special significance in the folklore of many cultures. It is frequently described as a messenger of the gods and is also associated with the sun. In Celtic mythology the Hawk of Achill, which tricks the eagle into giving up its warm nest, is identified as the oldest animal of them all (although the salmon is also considered a contender for this honour).

hawthorn In common with other thorn trees, the hawthorn has dark supernatural associations, largely because the crown of thorns placed on Christ's head at the Crucifixion was widely supposed to have came from the hawthorn. Accordingly, hawthorn blossom should never be brought into the home, because it brings death with it, and spikes of hawthorn are sometimes used in black magic rituals intended to bring pain to some unwitting victim, the thorns being pressed into the heart of a sheep or bat. The sickly smell of the hawthorn blossom is said to be exactly like that which accompanied the Great Plague in London in 1665, and many people claim that the smell of the plant is the smell of death itself.

It is most unwise to sit under a hawthorn on Hallowe'en or on one of the other dates in the year when malevolent spirits roam the earth, as this risks enchantment by fairies, who are apparently often found in the vicinity of the tree. According to the Irish, it is very unlucky to cut a hawthorn down unless the permission of the fairies has been requested first.

Hawthorn blossom (sometimes called May blossom) is, however, also linked with the more optimistic ceremonies traditional to MAY DAY, and is believed to protect livestock and people from evil influences as well as from lightning. In times gone by the taboo against bringing hawthorn into the home does not seem to have applied, and many people decorated their rooms with hawthorn blossom in order to protect the household, the theory being that witches would get tangled up in the spikes. Newly married couples were once offered boughs of hawthorn for protection, and the Romans adorned babies' cradles with hawthorn cuttings as a charm against sorcery. In the English Midlands a 'globe' of hawthorn was suspended in farmhouse kitchens at New Year, and kept there for a year before being burned over the ridges in the fields to guarantee a good harvest in the succeeding year. Hawthorn trees also symbolize fertility, and the scent of the hawthorn is considered an aphrodisiac in some parts of the world.

Legend has it that the very first hawthorn to grow in the British Isles was the one that took root at Glastonbury when JOSEPH OF ARIMATHEA struck the ground with his staff.

hazel European folklore credits the hazel with a variety of protective properties, and the tree is traditionally thought to be particularly effective as a defence against witchcraft and other evils. According to Norse mythology the tree was sacred to THOR, and thus could be relied upon during storms to provide protection from lightning. The Celts identified the hazel as the tree of knowledge, and legend described how a salmon that fed on the hazel nuts that fell into Conla's well became the wisest creature in the world (knowledge that subsequently passed to FIONN MAC CUMHAILL). The Celts also used the hazel for the treatment of rheumatism and lumbago among other ailments. Because of the tree's varied magical powers, forked hazel twigs are among the favoured tools of dowsers and diviners, and both sorcerers' wands and royal sceptres were once made of hazel wood. In former times the tree also symbolized fertility and immortality, and its foliage was thus frequently carried by those attending weddings.

Welsh tradition has it that anyone who wears leafs and twigs of hazel in their cap will enjoy particularly good luck and have all their wishes granted. Sailors, meanwhile, remember the link with Thor and believe that taking a bit of hazel to sea with them will protect them from storms and shipwreck. Hardened drinkers once believed that if they cut a piece of hazel on midnight on Hallowe'en and kept it in their pocket they would never succumb to the effects of alcohol, however much they consumed.

Hazelnuts may be used for the purposes of divination at Hallowe'en, the nuts being placed in the fire to see if they jump in the air (if they do a lover is unfaithful). The nuts, like the tree itself, represent fertility, and years when there is a good crop of nuts are said to be good years for the birth of many babies – and also for large numbers of prostitutes.

healing *See* MEDICINE.

hedgehog European folklore tends to regard the generally endearing hedgehog as an unlucky animal, and furthermore as a favourite disguise of witches. In times gone by farmers throughout Europe believed that hedgehogs robbed milk from their cows and thus sought to exterminate the creature as they would any other vermin. In other traditions it was claimed that the creature exhibited its sinister cunning by such tricks as rolling on apples in order to impale the fruit on its spikes.

According to an ancient British weather superstition the hedgehog emerges from hibernation at Candlemas (2 February) to see if the winter is over: if the animal returns to its den then at least another six weeks' worth of severe weather is in store. In the USA the same traditions apply to the groundhog or woodchuck. Eating hedgehog meat, a delicacy that is usually associated with gypsies, is said to cure fits, while consuming the left eye fried in oil is alleged to counter insomnia. In former times hedgehog blood was sometimes rubbed on warts in the belief that this would make them disappear. According to another European tradition it was once claimed that pregnant women who accidentally trod on a hedgehog would be fated to give birth to one of the creatures.

Heimdal In Norse mythology, the guardian of BIFROST who defended the bridge against the invading FROST GIANTS. The son of ODIN and nine sea maidens, he was renowned for his acute hearing and far-seeing eyesight, and it was prophesied that it would be his job to rouse the other gods to battle on the day of RAGNAROK. Dressed in white armour and wielding a flashing sword and a magic horn, he resided in the castle of Himinbiore.

Hel Norse goddess of the underworld, after whom Hell was named. The daughter of the evil LOKI and Angrboda, she was depicted as presiding over the entry of the sick and the old to her kingdom.

hen Folklore generally associates the hen with fertility and motherhood, but also infers from its behaviour that it is both fussy in character and rather slow-witted. When it appears in folk tales, for instance, it is usually as a gullible victim of more cunning creatures, such as its mortal enemy the FOX. The blood of a hen has long been thought to have special magical potential, reflecting the frequent sacrifice of hens since ancient times. Black hens have always been particularly prized for ritual sacrifice.

Other traditions concerning hens include the notions that a hen coming into the house may be interpreted as a warning that an important visitor is about to call, and the now archaic practice of taking a cackling hen into the home of newlyweds to guarantee their happiness. Perhaps best known is the general belief that if hens gather together on a mound and start to preen their feathers then rain is in store.

See also ALECTRYOMANCY.

herbs *See* MEDICINE.

Herla Legendary British king who is traditionally supposed to have enjoyed access to the underworld. An ancient legend, recorded by the 12th-century Welsh writer Walter Map, tells how King Herla was allowed into the underground realm of a dwarfish goat-hoofed king in order to attend his wedding (the underworld king having already done Herla the honour of coming to his wedding in the mortal world). While in the underworld Herla was presented with a small bloodhound, together with the warning not to put it down on the ground before the dog leapt down of its own accord. On returning home Herla and his party discovered that hundreds of years had passed since their departure. When the rest of the knights dismounted the years caught up with them and they were turned to dust. Only Herla, remembering the warning, remained on his horse, and according to some he rides it still, waiting for the dog to jump down.

Herne the Hunter Supernatural spirit of English tradition that is said to haunt Windsor Great Park and to escort the dead to the underworld. Folklore has it that Herne the Hunter was a keeper of the park in the reign of Henry VIII in the early 16th century. According to this version, he was hanged from an oak – identified thereafter as Herne's Oak – after being found guilty of dabbling in the occult. Many tales were subsequently told of his ghost, clad in deerskin with forehead surmounted by a magnificent set of stag's antlers, thundering through the park on a fire-breathing horse with a company of spectral hounds. Anyone who saw the ghost was fated to misfortune (although this did not prevent Henry VIII, for one, claiming to have witnessed the apparition).

An alternative version of the legend places Herne in the 14th century. This version suggests that as a keeper Herne the Hunter saved the life of Richard II by killing an injured stag that was attacking the king. In the process Herne was badly wounded himself, but a mysterious stranger appeared and by binding the stag's antlers to Herne's head brought him back to health. The king promised to make Herne headkeeper, but this offended the other keepers, who threatened to kill the stranger unless he did something to prevent Herne taking the office. The stranger agreed, after extracting the keepers' consent to accepting Herne's curse. Soon after, Herne found all his knowledge of hunting had deserted him and the king reluctantly dismissed him, upon which the luckless keeper hanged himself. His vengeful ghost subsequently hounded each one of the other keepers to their death.

Scholars have since made the obvious connection between Herne the Hunter and the Celtic Cerne or Cernunnos, the horned god of the 'old religion' (and the prototype Devil of witchcraft tradition). There are similar figures associated with the forest of Fontainebleau in France and the Black Forest in Germany.

See also WILD HUNT.

hex A CURSE or SPELL, the aim of which is usually to bring harm to a person or to his or her livestock or property. The word was taken up by German and Dutch settlers in Pennsylvania and was originally used to describe both positive and negative magic-making, although it has since become identified primarily with black magic.

Fear of hexes has lasted into modern times, with accusations being made against persons suspected of such activity in Pennsylvania well into the 20th century. Conventional safeguards against such ill-intentioned magic include the wearing of amulets bearing certain mystic symbols, and protecting entrances to the house or barn with various designs and patterns supposed to deter evil. Victims also have the option of seeking out a 'hex doctor' specializing in the business of removing curses and lifting the power of the EVIL EYE.

Hiawatha Legendary Native American hero whose story is best known today from Henry Wadsworth Longfellow's celebrated poem *The Song of Hiawatha* (1855). According to Longfellow, Hiawatha was the son of Mudjekeewis (the west wind) and Wenonah, and was the chief of the Onondaga tribe around the 15th or 16th century. Educated by his grandmother Nokomis, he married the beautiful Minnehaha (meaning 'laughing water'), and when the first white men arrived did much to persuade his people to listen to the words of Christian missionaries. He was revered for his many skills and for his efforts to bind rival tribes into a confederacy of Iroquois nations.

Hildebrand German folk hero whose story is told in the celebrated romance *Das Hildebrandslied*, written around AD 800. An old man renowned for his considerable skills as a magician, Hildebrand returns home after spending years with his master King Theodoric fighting the Huns, but is then challenged to a duel by his own son Hadubrand, who does not recognize him. The ending of the poem is not explicit about the outcome of the duel, but the implication is that Hadubrand is killed by his father in the ensuing conflict. Hildebrand also appears as a character in the NIBELUNGENLIED and other epics.

hobbyhorse Character in English MUMMERS' PLAYS, MORRIS DANCES and a variety of other folk celebrations, primarily those associated with MAY DAY. The hobbyhorse is usually played by a masked actor or dancer wearing an outlandish, colourful costume, sometimes supported by a wickerwork frame, which as often as not bears little actual resemblance to a horse. The costume commonly features a pair of snapping wooden jaws, with which the performer threatens other characters or onlookers.

The hobbyhorse tradition survives in a number of English towns and villages, among them Padstow in Cornwall (famous for its 'Obby Oss') and Minehead in Somerset (where the hobbyhorse has a nautical flavour, designed in the shape of a boat and locally dubbed the 'Sailor's Horse'). Both the Padstow and Minehead horses are reputed to have driven off foreign invaders, the former frightening off the French in 1346–47 and the latter scaring off Danish attackers in the 9th or 10th century.

The hobbyhorse is typically paraded through the streets with great revelry on May Day morning, accompanied by dancers and musicians, who collect money from onlookers. From time to time it sinks to the ground as though dead, but then rises up again in response to the beating of drums, symbolizing the extinction and revival of life with the cycle of the seasons.

hobgoblin In English folklore, a mischievous breed of sprite, usually described as small, ugly and of an often cheerful but occasionally unreliable temper. Both PUCK and ROBIN GOODFELLOW are sometimes identified as hobgoblins, which according to tradition are quite distinct from other similar beings such as the more openly malevolent GOBLINS. They are usually understood to include such subspecies as the BROWNIE.

Hogmanay In Scotland, New Year's Eve. The word itself is of uncertain origin but is in wide use today, being frequently applied to New Year's Eve festivities (which often have a distinctly Scottish flavour) throughout the English-speaking world. Features of the Hogmanay festivities include feasting and drinking and the ritual of FIRST-FOOTING. The evening usually culminates today in the singing of Robert Burns's song 'Auld Lang Syne'. In former times it was customary for children to demand gifts of oatcake or oat bread.

See also NEW YEAR.

holed stone Stones – and even trees – with natural holes in them have long been credited with healing properties.

Holed stones, usually made of clay ironstone, were commonly believed to have come originally from eagles' nests, hence their alternative name 'eagle stones'. Large numbers of such stones were imported to western Europe from the Far East in the 17th and 18th centuries and were worn as amulets by women in labour in the belief that they would make delivery easier. Records of eagle stones being used in childbirth seem to have come to an end during the first half of the 19th century.

All around the world the idea persists that passing a sick person through a hole in a large stone or tree, with appropriate ceremony, will cure that person of their ailment, which may range from rickets or whooping cough to boils. Barren women passed through such a hole, it is alleged, will find themselves at once made fertile. Once a person has been passed through such a hole and been cured, it is important that they act to protect the stone or tree in question in the future, as their fates are now linked, and any misfortune that befalls the stone or tree will be reflected in their own well-being.

Smaller holed stones, also known as hagstones, witchstones or fairystones, were formerly carried about the person to ward off witchcraft and other evils. Keeping one of these on the bedstead was said to prevent nightmares and also to guard against rheumatism.

Holle, Mother In German folklore, a sky goddess who according to tradition flies through the night sky at the head of an army of witches and the souls of unbaptized infants. Also known as Holde, Hulda or Hulle, she would appear to have inherited many of her attributes from the Roman goddess Diana, who was also given to such night flights. Despite the ominous nature of her night rides, she is sometimes depicted as a fairly benevolent witch, and when it snows there is a tradition that the flakes are actually feathers shaken from her bedclothes. Legend has it that an old man named ECKHARDT was accidentally swept up in the train of Mother Holle as she dashed across the night sky, and that he is consequently doomed to ride with her party for eternity. According to tradition the realm of Mother Holle can be reached by descending to the bottom of a well.

holly Tradition credits holly with a range of protective powers, and it is generally considered a lucky plant. It has particular significance in Christian tradition, and sprigs of holly are traditionally hung in homes around the English-speaking world as part of the Christmas decorations to keep evil at bay (a relic of much older pagan reverence for the plant). It is

claimed that holly wood was used in the construction of Christ's cross and that the berries of the holly were previously yellow, but took on their red colour in remembrance of Christ's blood. The evergreen leaves, meanwhile, are widely understood to represent eternal life.

Hanging holly in the house protects all within from witchcraft and other misfortunes. Some say the holly must be picked before Christmas Eve (but not taken inside until that day), and that the prickly variety is especially lucky for men while the smooth-leaved version is lucky for women. One English tradition has it that if the holly is male then the man of the house will get his way at home over the coming year, but if it is female his wife will rule the roost for the next 12 months.

When the festive season is over some people will retain just one small sprig of holly, which is kept indoors for the rest of the year to protect the house from lightning. Discarded holly boughs must not be burned while the leaves are still green as to do so is the extremely unlucky and may bring about a death in the household. It is also unlucky to step on a holly berry, and risky in the extreme to cut down the tree itself.

A very well-known weather superstition associated with the holly is that the tree will bear many berries if severe winter weather is in the offing. Leaves from the plant may also be used in a variety of charms intended to reward young girls and boys with glimpses of their future mates. Young girls may also divine their future by counting off the number of prickles on a holly leaf while reciting 'girl, wife, widow, nun' and noting at which word they reach the last prickle.

Drinking milk from a cup made of holly wood is said to cure whooping cough in children, and placing a garland of holly round a horse's neck will prevent the animal suffering nightmares. Finally, thrashing the feet with sprigs of holly is alleged to be an effective, if painful, cure for chilblains.

See also IVY.

Holy Grail *See* GRAIL, HOLY

horn Animal horns have been commonly interpreted since ancient times as symbols of fertility and good luck and feature widely in folklore both as headwear and in the form of musical instruments, drinking vessels and so forth. Many pagan deities, including the Celtic Cernunnos, sported horns or antlers, signifying a war-like nature as well as virility. Various folk-loric warrior heroes are described carrying horns with which they may summon up supernatural aid or achieve feats of magic. Among the most famous drinking horns is the Horn of Fidelity of Arthurian legend, which Morgan le Fay gave to King Arthur, explaining that no lady who was untrue to her husband would be able to drink from it without spilling the liquid inside.

Although it is traditionally considered unlucky to allow a horn into the house, possession of a horn may help to give protection against the Devil (the 'horned god'), especially – in the USA – if it has come from an ox. The effects of the EVIL EYE, moreover, will be negated if a person keeps the horn of a stag, at least according to a shared British and Spanish tradition, while 'making horns' (or the 'fig sign') by pointing the index and little fingers towards another person is said to ward off similar evil influence. Making this gesture may also imply that the man being point-ed at is a cuckold – possibly a reference originally to the rutting of stags, which customarily select several females as their mates after using their antlers to defeat other males in combat, or else to the ancient custom of engrafting the spurs of a castrated fighting cock to the root of its excised comb so that they might grow into horns.

Powdered horn remains a common ingredient of potions widely supposed to counter impotence and sterility – best known today through the controversial use of powdered rhino horn in traditional Chinese medicine.

See also HORN DANCE.

horn dance Folk dance that is per-formed by dancers carrying sets of antlers or other animal horns. The horn dance was once a common feature of pagan festivities throughout Europe, and is still performed in a handful of places even today. It is thought that the dance began as a fertility rite linked to the winter solstice, a theory supported by the fact that the dancers performed their luck-bringing dance several times during the day in the course of visiting local farms and estates. A more prosaic version of the dance's ori-gins suggests it may have begun in Anglo-Saxon times as part of the rejoicings marking the granting of hunting rights in a particular locality.

The best-known modern example is probably the horn dance performed annually at Abbots Bromley, Staffordshire, on the first Monday after the Sunday fol-lowing 4 September (the week of the local 'wakes'). Originally part of the fes-tivities that marked Twelfth Night, and still being performed at Christmas, New Year and on Twelfth Night until well into the 16th century, the Abbots Bromley version of the dance is performed by 12 male dancers, of whom six carry reindeer antlers (hence the alternative name, the 'Antler Dance'). The same set of antlers is always used, and these are thought to be many years old (the last wild reindeer in Britain having disappeared by the 12th century). Three of the six sets of antlers are mounted on wooden deer heads painted blue, while the other three are mounted on heads painted white. When not in use they are kept in the local parish church. The other performers comprise an accordion player, a triangle player, a boy carrying a crossbow and arrow, a jester, a man dressed as ROBIN HOOD mounted on a HOBBY HORSE and anoth-er dressed as a woman, tentatively identi-fied as Maid Marian. All wear costumes vaguely Tudor in style (a relatively recent innovation, as the dancers continued to wear contemporary dress until the late 19th century).

See also MORRIS DANCE.

horse The horse has been widely associated with magic since ancient times. Archaeological finds have provided evidence for horse-worshipping cults existing throughout Europe in pre-Christian times, and many pagan gods, such as the Celtic goddess EPONA or RHIANNON, were routinely depicted on horseback. Other finds indicate that horses were sometimes sacrificed in the course of important rituals, or killed and buried with their warrior masters. The most visible reminders of the reverence inspired by the horse in ancient times in the British Isles are the huge white horses carved into chalk hillsides in various parts of the country, notably on White Horse Hill near Uffington in south Oxfordshire (supposedly cut to commemorate King Alfred's victory nearby over the Danes but probably much older). Similar horse worship was also a feature of the ancient folklore of China and Japan.

The search for a divine horse wearing a magical bridle features in numerous legends and also in Arthurian romance, with Gawain and other knights going in quest of the creature. On being found it typically changes into a beautiful woman. The black horse of many other tales may be interpreted as a guise of the DEVIL.

The horse was widely linked with the notions of fertility and protection, and horse bones were often buried in the foundations of new houses to guarantee the prosperity of the inhabitants. Horses also appear as characters in ancient mummers' plays and other ceremonies marking auspicious dates in the folk calendar, notably May Day (*see* HOBBYHORSE).

The economic value of the creature in former times meant that horse-owners were especially nervous of any threat posed by witches against their animals, which had to be defended with horse brasses and other charms and amulets. Black horses and horses with white 'stockings' on their legs are considered especially lucky. Horses that were found to be sweaty in the morning were rumoured to have been 'hag-ridden', that is, used as mounts by witches going to sabbaths during the night. This was regarded as a serious calamity, and horse-owners often placed a HOLED STONE or some other magical safeguard in the stable to prevent this happening. Alternatively, the horse's tail might be carefully plaited with ribbons to deter witches. Horses are also widely supposed to be able to see ghosts, and there are many stories of horses refusing to proceed when they reach a supposedly haunted location.

White horses are often thought to be harbingers of ill fortune, particularly (in the USA at least) if ridden by a redheaded girl, and anyone who encounters one is advised to spit immediately on the ground. This dread of white horses probably owes much to a passage in the Book of Revelations in which Death is described riding upon a 'pale horse'. Piebald horses are generally considered lucky, and a wish may be made on seeing one. It is also said that the riders of piebald horses are excellent people to consult regarding folk cures: whatever treatment they suggest will prove infallible, however implausible it may seem.

Going to a stable and inhaling horses' breath is recommended as a cure for a host of ailments, including whooping cough. Eating a single hair taken from a horse's forelock with bread and butter will cure anyone suffering from worms, while one taken from the tail can be bound round a goitre to make it disappear. A preparation of horse hoof is said to alleviate fever, and horse teeth may be used to counter nightmares and to treat chilblains, while powdered horse spur (a horny growth on horses' legs) drunk with warm milk and beer was once said to combat cancer. Least appealing of all is the remedy for sore throats that advises the sufferer to drink a concoction comprising the juice of live crabs combined with foam from a horse's mouth.

Other miscellaneous folk beliefs relating to horses include the notions that horses standing in a group with their backs to a hedge are a warning that rain is imminent, and that a journey will turn out well if the horse one is riding snorts a lot. Last but not least, it is deemed very bad luck to change a horse's name.

horseshoe Of all lucky charms and amulets guaranteed to ward off evil, the horseshoe is perhaps the best known in European and North American folklore. The origins of the beliefs surrounding the horseshoe are uncertain, but they may be linked to ancient HORSE worship. Alternatively, the special properties of the horseshoe may have been derived from its crescent shape, revered by pre-Christian MOON worshippers, or else from the fact that it was made from IRON, one of the most magical of metals.

Finding a horseshoe by chance is very lucky. Horseshoes lose their lucky properties if bought with money, however. Especially lucky is a horseshoe that has been cast from the near hind leg of a grey mare and that has seven nail holes, particularly if some of the nails are still in place. Horseshoes found by chance can either be spat upon and tossed over the left shoulder while making a wish, or taken home to be nailed above a doorway to bring good luck to anyone passing beneath. Opinion is divided over which way up the horseshoe should be fixed, although most people hold that the prongs should point upwards in order to keep the good luck from falling out. Others, however, have been known to allow the prongs to point downwards in order, they explain, to direct the good luck at those passing beneath. In some parts of the USA they may even be placed sideways so as to direct luck towards the home. Once in place, the horseshoe will not only protect the good luck of the household but will also deter witches. According to an old English legend, the Devil, who was subjected to great agony on being forcibly shod by St Dunstan, promised never to enter a house protected by a horseshoe.

The horseshoe is now one of the most widely recognized emblems of good luck, being particularly associated with weddings. It is also commonly depicted on good-luck cards relevant to many other undertakings, such as school examinations and driving tests. Many athletes, performing artists and others carry miniature horseshoes for luck. Horatio Nelson was just one of many Royal Navy commanders past and present who have had a horseshoe nailed to the mast of their ship (in his case, the *Victory*) to safeguard the luck of the ship's company and keep the vessel safe from storms.

Other folk beliefs associated with the horseshoe relate to folk medicine. It is said that the water in which newly made horseshoes are dowsed has the power to cure impotence, while in Germany food served on a plate branded by a horseshoe is said to cure patients with whooping cough. Nailed in groups of three to the bedstead, horseshoes are also alleged to fend off the threat of fever.

hot cross bun Small buns marked with a cross, which are traditionally eaten at EASTER. In fact, the hot cross bun has its origins in the buns that were eaten at various pre-Christian pagan festivals, the cross being added later to make the link with the Crucifixion and also to keep evil spirits at bay. If baked on the morning of Good Friday, these buns are supposed to have special magical properties, and in the past some were always kept aside to be hung up in the house to preserve its luck through the year (it was said they would never go mouldy). If someone fell ill, a little of the bun was grated off and mixed with milk or water and administered to the patient. It was believed that this would cure such ailments as whooping cough and dysentery. Sailors in former times often took a hot cross bun to sea with them as a lucky charm, and farmers have been known to keep them to protect their granaries from rats.

houri In Islamic mythology, one of a race of beautiful black-eyed virgins who tend to the needs of the righteous after their entry into paradise. It is said that those who have lived good lives on earth will be rewarded with all manner of luxury and sensuality in the afterlife, in which the houries will satisfy all their bodily desires. Houries are supposed to be able to renew their virginity on demand, and to remain ever young and lovely for the delight of their charges.

household spirit *See* BOGGART; BROWN-IE; GOBLIN; GUARDIAN SPIRIT; PIXIE; PUCK; ROBIN GOODFELLOW.

hunting magic Because success in hunting was crucial to survival, most hunter-gatherer cultures, both past and present, have observed a wide range of rituals and taboos in relation to hunting. Hunters honoured relevant deities with sacrifices, ceremonial dances and other rites, and also sought to promote their fortune by fasting, abstaining from sex before setting out and respectfully asking permission of the gods to take their prey. Once successful, hunters generally offered ritual thanks for the kill, and might even offer up some of the best parts as sacrifice. The animal itself would be praised for its courage in the hunt, among other gestures of respect intended to placate its spirit. It was widely thought to be reckless to kill any animal for sport, or to take more than was required for food. Such traditions linger on even today, as witnessed by the ritual 'blooding' of first-time hunters following a successful fox hunt: after the fox is killed its tail is cut off and the animal's blood is smeared on the new hunter's face.

World mythology boasts many hunter-gods, typically depicted carrying bow and arrow, and often accompanied by a hunting dog. Some, such as the Celtic god Cernunnos, are commonly depicted wearing horns or the skins of their prey.

hunting the wren *See* WREN.

I

Idris In Welsh Celtic mythology, a GIANT and prince who lived on the mountain of Cader Idris (meaning 'chair of Idris') in Gwynedd. Idris was more gifted than the average giant, and could claim proficiency in astronomy, philosophy and poetry. Legend claims that any person who spends the whole night on top of Cader Idris will die, go mad or benefit from sublime poetic inspiration.

Iduna In Norse mythology, the goddess of spring. The daughter of the dwarf Svald and consort of Bragi, the god of poetry, Iduna preserved the youth of the gods by feeding them her golden apples of immortality. She was tricked into leaving ASGARD by the evil LOKI, but the latter was subsequently obliged by the other gods to bring her back, taking the form of a falcon and seizing her in his beak.

Igraine (or **Igerna**) In Arthurian legend, the Duchess of Cornwall and mother of King ARTHUR. Igraine was the wife of Gerlois of Cornwall, but subsequently attracted the attention of UTHER PENDRAGON, who besieged Tintagel Castle, and with the help of MERLIN stole into the castle disguised as Igraine's husband. Gerlois was killed, and the next day Uther married Igraine, who later gave birth to Arthur. Uther could not be sure, however, that he was the baby's father, and the upbringing of the infant Arthur was entrusted to ECTOR OF THE FOREST SAUVAGE, who brought him up in ignorance of his real parenthood.

Ilmarenin In the Finnish KALEVALA, one of the three sons of Kalewa, whose adventures alongside his brothers LEMMINKÄINEN and VÄINÄMÖINEN, established their place among the most celebrated of heroes in Finnish legend.

Ilya Muromets Russian folk hero, whose adventures are the subject of many Russian folk tales. Ilya was born into a humble peasant family, and for the first 33 years of his life was confined to his bed through ill health. Everything changed, however, when two pilgrims called at the cottage of his parents and paid for the hospitality they received with a draught of honey for the sick man. On drinking the honey Ilya was at once endowed with amazing strength, and set out on a series of adventures, defending his homeland against pagan invaders. He could destroy oak trees with a single arrow from his bow, and soar through the sky on his magical horse. At Kiev he destroyed a huge pagan idol and single-handedly erected a vast cathedral. Unfortunately he became boastful of this last feat and was punished for his pride by being turned to stone. His statue was placed carefully inside the cathedral he had built.

The history of Ilya Muromets bears some resemblance to the legends surrounding the pre-Christian god Pyerun, on which the Russian tales were probably based. The persisting popularity of the Ilya Muromets story was shown in World War I, when the name was given to a very large type of bomber aircraft.

Imbolc One of the four major festivals in the Celtic calendar, celebrated each year on 1 February. Also called Oimelc (meaning 'sheep's milk'), the festival was linked with the lactation of ewes, and in Ireland was identified with the Celtic goddess BRIGID. When the Christians absorbed the Celtic festivals into the church calendar Imbolc became Candlemas and the feast day of St Brigid.

See also BELTANE; LUGHNASADH; SAMHAIN.

imp In medieval folklore, a demon and servant of the DEVIL. Imps were often sent by the Devil to serve the whims of the witches and wizards who swore allegiance to him. They were reputed to be responsible for many malicious acts, from the harming of livestock to child murder. During the later medieval period the distinction between imps, frequently depicted as diminutive horned versions of Satan himself, and fairies and other supernatural beings became confused, although all were treated with dread and loathing.

imrama A genre of Old Irish epic folk tale, in which the story of a long voyage of adventure is told. The most celebrated examples of these folk tales include *The Voyage of Bran* and *The Voyage of Brandon*. Christian details were frequently intermingled with pagan elements. The heroes of these tales typically travel from island to island, encountering supernatural beings of one kind or another, and learning much about the world of spirits.

See also ECHTRAI.

incubus In medieval folklore, a demon who has illicit sexual intercourse with women as they sleep. Any children resulting from these unions were thought likely to be deformed or monstrous, or to enjoy remarkable magical powers. In Arthurian romance, for example, MERLIN was allegedly the result of an incubus coupling with his mother. Accepted thinking on the subject claimed that incubi were incapable of producing their own semen,

and so transformed themselves into succubi in order to seduce young men and thus steal their semen for their own uses. It was rumoured that mortals who had sex with incubi and succubi found the experience much more satisfying than normal intercourse. Some witches were reputed to enjoy nightly intercourse with incubi, who typically took the form of dark and handsome young men.

In 1275 reports that Angela de Labarthe, of Toulouse, had given birth to a monster with a wolf's head and a serpent's tail was considered proof that she had slept with an incubus, and she became the first person known to be executed for such an offence.

Defences against the threat of interference by incubi included the wearing of St John's wort, vervain or dill.

See also SUCCUBUS.

industrial lore The Industrial Revolution produced its own mythology, some of it representing developments of older lore associated with agricultural societies (especially that surrounding blacksmiths) and some of it entirely new. In ancient times various metals, notably iron, gold and silver, were considered magical in nature and this tradition has survived into modern times, expressing itself in a variety of superstitions, taboos and beliefs associated with the working of such materials and those who handle them.

Certain trades quickly developed their own tales and taboos, from coal mining and railway building to shipping and engineering. Among the most enduring of these were the many legends of dwarfs, elves and other supernatural beings who helped in the completion of onerous tasks, so that they were finished with remarkable speed to the highest standards. Miners around the world, for instance, put great faith in various supernatural beings that were supposed to live deep inside the earth, tapping to indicate the whereabouts of rich seams or else to warn of imminent danger. These and other workers in equally perilous industries also placed great store in the observation of various natural 'omens' as they travelled to work (typically a glimpse of a certain species of animal or bird) and were prone to interpret these as signs of how their shift was fated to go.

Workers in the new industries on both sides of the Atlantic quickly invented their own mythology, complete with folk heroes and legends associated with their particular trade. The most famous of these included tales about fellow workers celebrated for their superhuman strength and other qualities (such as JOE MAG-ARAC, a hero of the steel mills, or JOHN HENRY, the railway labourer).

Such legends served to cement a sense of communal identity and to add a human dimension to what were otherwise almost exclusively technical endeavours. Even today many industrial companies feature animal or human characters (often drawn from legend) in their names, logos or slogans in an apparently unconscious attempt to add a human dimension to their work.

Another manifestation of the mythologization of industry was the emergence of various INITIATION rites that in many ways aped the rites and rituals of pre-industrial society. These typically involved (and still involve) sending the new worker on some impossible errand, such as fetching a jar of elbow grease.

The products of industry and technology are themselves sometimes considered subject to magical influence even today. Motorists throughout the world commonly attach charms (sprigs of heather, dice, medallions bearing images of the patron saint of travellers St Christopher, etc.) to their vehicles for good luck, while air pilots during World War II habitually overlapped the belts on empty seats to form a cross and thus prevent any unseen spirit from occupying them. Similar practices have been recorded in association with numerous other products of manufacture, from railway trains and telephones to televisions and computers.

Ing In Norse mythology, a stranger from across the sea who founded the Saxon race. He later vanished once more into the east – perhaps a suggestion that he joined the gods and heroes in ASGARD on his death.

initiation The rituals surrounding the entry of an individual into a particular social grouping or organization, often on the attainment of a given age. Such rites of passage have been celebrated in virtually all societies in human history, although they can take varying forms. They typically mark a crucial change in the life of an individual, such as the onset of puberty or adulthood. Alternatively, they may mark entry into a select group of some kind (such as a club, trade or secret society) and the sharing of secret knowledge that comes with it.

The actual ceremony may involve some form of ritual humiliation, isolation, or even physical mutilation. Occasionally the initiate may be required to perform an act of symbolic or actual sexual intercourse – a custom closely associated in the public imagination with witches' covens. Sometimes the initiate must endure (without complaint) considerable physical pain, as in various Native American societies. This may leave scars that the initiate will never lose. Examples of initiation involving ritual humiliation include the traditional ceremony of 'crossing the bar' (celebrated when a seaman crosses the equator for the first time), in which initiates are shaved, dunked in water, pelted with eggs or otherwise abused. Initiates may be given new names or be required to take solemn oaths and to sever connections with their family. At the close of the ceremony all present may indulge in feasting and drinking, which the initiate may be obliged to pay for. In modern society such customs are generally reserved for celebrations of baptism, circumcision, coming of age, weddings, anniversaries and funerals. More minor rites of passage, such as entry to clubs or societies, are more perfunctory, being marked with little more than brief hand-shakes and occasionally the speaking of certain promises, although some long-established groups, such as the Free-masons, still jealously guard more complicated and arcane procedures.

The business of initiation often involves the notion of the initiate experiencing a symbolic death and rebirth. This is particularly true of religious initiation, as in the baptismal rites of the Christian churches or the Jewish Bar Mitzvah. Such ceremonies are often confined to male initiates only, although many societies have some form of ceremony to mark the onset of MENSTRUATION (typically involving pain and isolation).

See also INDUSTRIAL LORE.

insects The insect world has a special place in the folklore of many societies. The huge variety of species is reflected in the diversity of the superstitions and beliefs associated with them. Some species, such as ladybirds and bees, are considered benign and, if treated with respect, are believed to be harbingers of good fortune. Other species, such as beetles and lice, are more menacing and may be portents of disaster. The ticking of the death-watch beetle, for example, is thought throughout the English-speaking world to be a warning of a coming death in the house.

Folklore suggests numerous ways of fending off the threat posed by plagues of insects. The more exotic of these include the staging of full funeral ceremonies, in which the corpse of a locust or caterpillar is accompanied to the grave by a train of human mourners in full mourning regalia. The thinking here is that through sympathetic magic the death of the individual insect will bring about the demise of all the others.

Ancient Egyptian mythology gave the scarab beetle divine status, as representative of the sun god Ra, and many folk traditions claim that insects may be consulted in various magical ways to learn from them secrets about the future. Later societies may not have ranked insects among the gods, but readily credited them with human traits and failings. This is most vividly illustrated by the extraordinary trials of beetles and other insect miscreants that took place in all seriousness from time to time in medieval Europe and the Middle East.

Folklore finds many uses for insects in traditional potions and remedies. These range from the superstition that smearing a paste of ants mixed with honey onto a wart will cause it to disappear, to the contention that a patient may be relieved of an ailment by allowing gnats free access to and from the sick-room at sunset.

Insect characters crop up occasionally in folk tales around the world. Examples include the giant fly of Sardinia, several stories belonging to the genre of the URBAN MYTH and the ant and the grasshopper in one of Aesop's fables, in which the grasshopper fails to profit by the ant's example of making preparations for the winter.

See also SPIDER.

invisibility The plots of numerous folk tales around the world rely upon the device of invisibility. Heroes learn the trick of making themselves invisible in order to gain entry to guarded palaces, overhear private conversations, obtain treasure and generally foil their enemies, and numerous species of spirits, fairies and other supernatural entities are credited with the power of making themselves invisible at will.

In most cases the person concerned can only enjoy the power of invisibility through the possession of a magical object, which is most often a cap or a cloak (although it might also be a ring, a stone or something else). In JACK THE GIANT-KILLER it is a cloak, as it is in the well-known tale of the princess's dancing slippers, while in the tale of REYNARD THE FOX it is a ring of three colours. European superstition also advises that the gift of invisibility can be enjoyed by anyone who carries a piece of agate about their person, who gathers FERN or BRACK- EN spores in a certain manner on St John's Eve, or who obtains a magic ointment from a witch, fairy or other cooperative spirit. More bizarre methods include possession of a HAND OF GLORY, carrying the right eye of a bat and digging up a dead body and exchanging shirts with it. English witches, meanwhile, confessed to making themselves invisible by mixing the spittle of a toad with the sap of a sow thistle and smearing this on their body in the shape of a cross.

The idea that a person can enjoy the power of invisibility is a beguiling one and has resurfaced in relatively recent times in the such stories as H. G. Wells' *The Invisible Man* (1897), in which the same end is achieved through chemical means.

iron The special role of iron in world folklore probably reflects the impact that the discovery of iron had upon ancient stone- and bronze-using societies. The metal itself was considered to have magical powers, particularly as it often came from meteorites – literally gifts from the heavens. Such 'elemental' iron was rare but was used long before people learnt to smelt iron ore to extract the metal; this latter process began in the Near East and southeast Europe around 1200 BC.

Articles made of iron were long valued as defences against the EVIL EYE and against fairies, witches and other supernatural entities (although they were ineffective against DWARFS due to their mastery as iron-workers). Iron was also supposed to ward off lightning (despite the fact that in reality it actually attracts it). It was once quite commonplace to put knives made of iron in babies' cradles to keep evil influences at bay, and also to put iron objects in coffins to prevent demons making use of the corpses. Thousands of homes today are still protected by iron HORSESHOES nailed above front doors to prevent evil spirits entering (relying upon a combination of iron and horse magic), and it was once quite common in

rural areas to leave a pair of scissors or something else made of iron under the front doormat in the belief that witches would not be able to walk over them. Iron could, however, also be a cause of trouble. A long-established superstition, for instance, insists that friends should never exchange knives as gifts as this will sever the friendship. The only remedy is for the recipient to hand over a few coins, in the pretence that the knives are actually being bought, not given.

Even rusty iron has magical potential. A rusty sword kept beside the bed was formerly supposed to ward off cramp. Dulled iron, however, could attract misfortune. It was believed to be important to prevent iron ever coming into contact with MISTLETOE, as this would rob the metal of its magical properties.

Islands of the Blest (or Islands of the Blessed) Mythical islands in the folklore of many cultures that are often identified as the abode of the dead, or as paradise. The islands were called the Hesperides or Elysium in Greek legend. Usually described as a series of islands in the west, they are rarely visited with impunity by mortals, although some heroes successfully reached them. The island paradise of pagan Celtic mythology, visited by BRAN MAC FEBAL among other mortal heroes, reported that they spent their time there feasting and basking in the company of beautiful, willing maidens. The Islands of the Blest as described in later Celtic folklore combined Celtic and Christian imagery. When St BRENDAN THE NAVIGATOR came to them he described a paradise that bore a marked similarity to the biblical heaven.

The notion of the Islands of the Blest was boosted by tales told by seafarers about remarkable islands that they were utterly unable to find again in later voyages. The ceaseless quest to find them may have played some part in the eventual discovery of land on the western side of the Atlantic, including America. Other places that may have helped give rise to the mythical islands included the Azores and the Canary Islands.

See also AVALON; FLOATING ISLANDS; FORTUNATE ISLANDS.

Isolde of Brittany In the story of TRIS-TAM and ISOLDE OF IRELAND, the woman who became Tristam's wife after Isolde of Ireland was reconciled with her husband. Otherwise called Iseult, Isolt or Isolde of the White Hands, she fell deeply in love with Tristam and, having heard him singing of his love Isolde (although he meant Isolde of Ireland), thought her love was returned. As Tristam lay dying from a poisoned wound he sent for the other Isolde, and Isolde of Brittany realized her mistake. Subsequently she denied the truth that Isolde of Ireland was hurrying from Cornwall to see him, thus hastening his death, upon which both Isoldes also died of grief and remorse.

Isolde of Ireland In Arthurian legend, the wife of King MARK of Cornwall and the lover of his nephew TRISTAM. Having healed Tristam of the wounds he sustained in battle with a dragon, Isolde of Ireland (otherwise called Iseult, Isolt or Ysolde the Fair) agreed to marry Tristam's uncle King Mark but while being escorted to Cornwall by Tristam the pair accidentally drank a love potion meant for her and the king, administered by her maid Brangaine. Subsequently Isolde secretly arranged for a girl to take her place in the marriage bed and continued her illicit liaison with Tristam. The guilty lovers hid themselves in the forest, but Isolde was restored to the king's favour after Tristam exiled himself from Cornwall. Subsequently she heard that Tristam was dying from a poisoned wound and hurried to save him. She arrived too late and died of a broken heart. The story very closely resembles the legends of GRAINNE and GUINEVERE.

Ith In Irish Celtic mythology, the head of the family from which came the first human rulers of Ireland. Ith is supposed to

have got his first glimpse of Ireland from the top of a tall tower in Spain, his homeland, and decided to visit the country. On his arrival he was welcomed by the TUATHA DE DANANN, the gods who ruled Ireland. He was even asked to decide which of the gods he thought had the best claim to the Irish throne, but suspicions grew that he wanted to rule the country himself and he was murdered. His corpse was returned to Spain, following which his nephew MILED invaded Ireland and the gods were replaced by human rulers.

Iubdan Legendary Celtic elf ruler of the mythical Irish fairy kingdom of Faylinn, who features in a well-known Irish folk tale. Iubdan and his wife, Queen Bebo, decided to visit the kingdom of Ulster in order to inspect the humans who lived there, but were captured and held prisoner by King Fergus mac Leda. They were only released after payment of a ransom of various treasures, which included a harp that played itself and a pair of shoes with which a person could walk on water. The tale is known in several different versions.

ivy Evergreen plant that has strong folkloric associations in many parts of the world. Sacred to Dionysus, the god of wine and vegetation in general in ancient Greece, to the ancient Egyptian god Osiris and to the Roman pleasure-seeker Bacchus (the Roman equivalent of Dionysus), ivy came to represent immortality to the Christians (hence its use in funeral wreaths). Ivy was frequently planted in graveyards, and it was often said that it would not grow if the souls of the dead buried nearby were restless. It was reputed to grow in particular abundance on the graves of those who had died for love, and consequently became for many a symbol of constancy.

If slipped under the pillow, ivy is supposed to inspire dreams of future lovers. It should, however, never be brought into the house for fear of the bad luck it will bring with it or exchanged as a gift between friends as this will endanger the friendship. An exception to this general rule is the practice of bringing ivy into the home as part of the Christmas decorations: according to Christian tradition ivy guarantees the good luck of women in the house, while HOLLY protects the good fortune of the men.

Folklore, recalling the link with Dionysus, insists that ivy can be used medicinally as a defence against inebriation, and also in various other applications, for instance, to soothe burns, corns and wounds. The berries can be used to make medicines to treat the plague, gangrene, toothache and jaundice.

J

Jack The archetypal hero of many European folk tales, including such well-known stories as JACK AND THE BEAN-STALK and JACK THE GIANT-KILLER. Variously called Jack, Juan, Jean, or Hans, he is usually depicted as a lazy but rather sly-witted peasant lad who is not always particularly deserving of the rewards he wins. The archetypal trickster beloved of folk tales worldwide, he triumphs not through virtue but rather through good luck and low cunning (sometimes abetted by supernatural assistance). He is thought to have had his origins in a legendary Cornish hero, or alternatively in the equally legendary Coroneus, said to have been one of the Trojan companions who accompanied BRUTUS to England (see also GOG AND MAGOG). Another theory links him with an East Anglian peasant who fought a celebrated battle with a seven-foot Viking.

Today Jack is regularly brought to life on the English stage each Christmas as a central character of various pantomimes, usually played by a woman (a tradition dating back to 1819).

Jack and the Beanstalk Fairy tale that exists in variant forms in several European cultures. In the English version of the story, JACK is berated by his penniless mother after he exchanges their cow for a handful of supposedly magic beans. His mother tosses the beans out of the window, but they take root and produce a huge beanstalk that reaches to the clouds. Jack climbs the beanstalk and finds himself outside the castle of a GIANT. He gains access to the castle, but the giant quickly senses his presence: 'Fee-fi-fo-fum, I smell the blood of an Englishman; / Be he alive or be he dead, I'll grind his bones to make my bread.' The giant's kindly wife, however, hides Jack from her husband and distracts the latter with a huge meal. The giant falls asleep and Jack successfully steals the giant's hen (or goose), which lays golden eggs and escapes with it back down the beanstalk.

Jack goes up the beanstalk again, and this time steals the giant's bags of gold. On a third visit, he steals the giant's magic singing harp, but the harp calls out to its master and the giant wakes. The giant pursues Jack down the beanstalk, but falls to earth and is killed when the lad quickly chops it down with an axe. Jack and his mother are left to enjoy their new-found wealth in peace.

The story is well-known in Britain as the basis of a popular Christmas pantomime, and is familiar throughout the English-speaking world as a nursery tale. In the 19th century the apparent immorality of Jack's behaviour was justified in some versions of the story by the additional detail that the giant had killed Jack's father many years before and thus deserved his fate.

In many respects the tale combines elements common to many other European folk tales. These include the central trickster hero, the magical access to a supernatural world, the sequence of three thefts and the talking harp that threatens to betray the hero. Variants of the tale include a traditional US version in which Jack steals a gun, a knife and a coverlet from the giant.

Jack-in-the-Green *See* GREEN MAN.

Jack-o'-Lantern *See* WILL O' THE WISP.

Jack-o'-Lent A stuffed puppet that is ritually abused throughout continental Europe as part of the observance of LENT. The puppet is widely identified with Christ's betrayer Judas Iscariot, but the custom probably has its roots in much earlier pagan spring rites. In most places the puppet is dragged through the streets at the beginning of Lent to be mocked and then publicly burned.

Jack o' the Bowl In Swiss folklore, a household spirit or BROWNIE. The spirit gets its name from the long-standing rural custom of leaving a bowl of fresh cream on the cowhouse roof each night for him to enjoy. The bowl is usually found to be empty in the morning.

Jack the Giant-Killer English folk tale, thought to have come originally from a French source. Jack is the son of a poor Cornish farmer, who kills his first giant, the fearsome CORMORAN, by luring him into a deep pit and chopping off his head. Subsequently, imprisoned by the giant BLUNDERBORE and locked up in a high tower, he strangles his enemy by looping a noose round his neck, and escapes with his treasure. His third triumph comes after visiting the house of an unnamed Welsh giant. Suspecting that the giant will try to kill him while he is asleep, Jack places a log in the bed, which the giant duly batters with a great club. In the morning Jack presents himself, and to the giant's consternation complains only of flea bites during the night. He then challenges the giant to an eating contest and makes a play of cutting open his own stomach to let out some of the food he has eaten so that he has room for

more (in fact, he has concealed a bag of oats under his shirt). The giant attempts to do the same and thus kills himself.

In other episodes Jack convinces a giant of his superior strength by squeezing water from a stone (actually a slab of cheese), and dispatches two more by cleverly tricking them into stoning each other to death.

Jack the Giant-Killer also makes an appearance in Arthurian myth, helping one of Arthur's knights rescue a damsel who has fallen victim to an evil spell. The knight needs money for his quest, so Jack goes ahead of him to the castle of a giant and warns the giant of the approach of a strong army. The giant flees to the cellar, leaving Jack and the knight to help themselves to his riches. In return for his apparent salvation, the giant gives Jack a number of presents: a magic coat, which makes him invisible; a magic pair of shoes, which enable him to outrun everyone; a magic cap, which gives him knowledge of anything he wishes; and a magic sword, which can cut through anything. Thus equipped, Jack helps the knight complete his quest and is rewarded with a seat at Arthur's ROUND TABLE. His adventures come to a satisfactory conclusion with his marriage to a duke's daughter, whom he has rescued from imprisonment by the giant Galigantus.

Some of the giant-killing episodes would appear to have been taken from Scandinavian mythology, and the tale continued to evolve from the late 17th to the 19th century, becoming a particular favourite of the chapbooks of popular tales that circulated widely throughout the English-speaking world. The story was first rendered as a pantomime on the English stage in London in 1773, in an adaptation by the celebrated actor-manager David Garrick.

jackal The jackal features prominently in the folklore of Africa, India and other parts of Asia, and had strong religious significance in the ancient world. Worshipped in the form of Anubis by the ancient Egyptians, the jackal symbolized death and destruction in Hebrew lore, and its howling was feared in India as an omen of misfortune. The creature has a reputation for cowardice, and in many tales it relies upon the stronger LION for its livelihood, scavenging whatever is left after its master has finished eating (just as in real life the jackal will help itself to the kills of lions and other more powerful predators after they have satisfied their hunger). Like the FOX, the jackal is thought to have a cunning nature, and appears in many tales in the role of deceitful trickster.

jackdaw Being primarily black in colour, the jackdaw is widely associated in folklore with mischief-making and death. It is supposed to be an omen of imminent death if a jackdaw settles on a rooftop, and even more threatening if the bird comes down the chimney. In some areas the sight of a single jackdaw is feared as much as that of a lone MAGPIE.

The bird has a particular reputation as a thief, and is alleged to steal anything shiny. In the story of 'The Jackdaw of Rheims', a jackdaw steals the cardinal's ring, but is subsequently revealed as the thief after the cardinal curses the unidentified culprit by 'bell, book and candle', upon which the guilty bird is revealed to him, reduced to the bedraggled condition in which it still appears today.

The gloomy associations of the jackdaw are not universal, however. In parts of Europe a jackdaw settling upon the rooftop may be interpreted as a prophecy of a coming birth within the family. Other traditions include the superstition that jackdaws fly noisily in circles when rain is on the way, and will return to their roosts later in the evening than usual if severe weather is in store.

jade Semiprecious gemstone that has magical significance in many cultures. Most traditions view the stone in a fairly positive light. In the Orient, for instance, jade is regarded as lucky, while Africans

prize it as a rain-bringer. In New Zealand the gem is often fashioned into a fertility symbol. Native American lore claims that the stone will guard against snakebite if worn in the form of an amulet.

Jade has particular importance in folk medicine, and was once believed to ward off colic if pressed against the side (the word jade itself comes from the Spanish *piedra de ijada*, meaning 'stone of the side'). In South America jade is also used to cure spleen problems.

jaguar According to Mesoamerican and South American folklore, the ghostly and seldom seen jaguar is closely associated with the world of the spirits. Worshipped as a god in Mayan mythology, it was formerly believed that the jaguar was responsible for eclipses. It was also said that shamans liked to prowl the jungle in the form of jaguars and might attack their enemies while in this shape. Various folk tales from the northern parts of South America describe marriages between jaguars and humans.

jalpari In Punjabi mythology, a malevolent female water spirit that drowns young men whenever she feels hungry or desires company in her watery home. In order to placate this dangerous demon it is thought wise to leave regular gifts of flowers at the waterside.

Jataka A compilation of tales about the Buddha that incorporates many ancient folk stories as well as the thoughts of Buddha himself. Resembling the ARABIAN NIGHTS in terms of structure, the 500 tales include animal fables and tales of heroic deeds, together with commentaries (which are generally thought to have been the work of a single writer). Most depict the Buddha in his various incarnations, in the guise of such animals as elephants. Some of the stories also appear in Aesop's *Fables* and elsewhere.

jay A wild bird that features in many folk tales around the world. Because of its noisy, social character the jay is frequently depicted as a boastful creature who is given to gossip, and the bird also has a reputation as a deceitful trickster. Several Native American tales revolve around the tricks of the jay, and the bird is also identified as a favourite disguise of shamans.

Jersey Devil A demon that is supposed to haunt the southern shores of New Jersey. According to legend, the Jersey Devil was the 13th child of a New Jersey witch, who had prophesied that her 13th child would be a demon. The monster is described by witnesses as having the head of a horse, dog or ram, bat-like wings and a long thin tail. Both serious crimes (including brutal murders) and trivial misdemeanours attributed to the Jersey Devil have been reported at irregular intervals in the US press for well over 100 years. Today the character is an established part of local cultural heritage. It has even been marketed as a tourist attraction: in 1909 one entrepreneur went so far as to exhibit a green-painted kangaroo fitted with fake wings as the Jersey Devil itself. One theory suggests that the tradition may have had its origins in the birth of a severely deformed child, which its mother tried to keep secret from the rest of the world.

Jethart Ba' Traditional Shrovetide ball game played in the Scottish Border town of Jedburgh every year on Candlemas Day (2 February) and on Fastern's E'en (the eve of Lent). The best-known traditional ball game in the Scottish folk calendar, it is a fairly rough contest played through the streets of the town, and even into the waters of the River Jed. The ball, decorated with streamers, can be thrown and passed by hand but not kicked (the game appears to have developed after street football was prohibited). The two sides comprise the Uppies – those who live above the Mercat Cross – and the Downies. Local legend claims that the game has its roots in the days of Border warfare, specifically in a gruesome incident when the Scottish victors played football with the severed heads of their vanquished English foes.

jettatura See EVIL EYE.

jinni (or djinni, genie) In Arabian mythology, a spirit that may be either malevolent and very ugly, or else very beautiful and kind, granting anything that a human may desire. According to legend, the jinn came from the mythical mountains of Kaf and were created some 2,000 years before the creation of Adam and Eve. They are credited with the power to change their shape at will, and may assume such forms as cats, dogs, old men, serpents and monsters. The most famous jinn include those of the lamp and of the ring in 'Aladdin and the Lamp' and other stories incorporated in *The Arabian Nights*. In these tales, control over a jinni is usually won through possession of a particular talisman, such as Aladdin's famous lamp. Even then a jinni may show great reluctance to grant its new master's wishes, and only agree to do so in exchange for a promise of freedom. If a jinni is offended in any way it may well punish the person responsible.

In English pantomime versions of *Aladdin*, a Good Genie often takes on an Evil Genie and the characters are variously played by muscular brown-skinned men or curvaceous women.

See also OLD MAN OF THE SEA.

Joe Magarac Literary character who acquired folkloric significance as a hero of modern US industrial legend. Joe Magarac, whose name means 'jackass' in Slovak, is seven feet tall and made of steel. He works with superhuman strength and stamina in a steel mill, making rails by squeezing molten metal with his bare hands and pausing only to eat huge meals. When some high-quality steel is needed to build a new mill he willingly melts his own body down as raw material.

The creation of the writer Owen Francis in the 1930s, the legend of Joe

Magarac is strongly reminiscent of earlier mythical worker-heroes, notably JOHN HENRY and PAUL BUNYAN.

John Barleycorn In English and Scottish folklore, the personification of malt liquor. To this day alcohol is often jokingly referred to by this name, and it has been suggested that the character may have roots in obscure rural tradition, possibly even with veneration for ancient nature gods. Robert Burns promoted use of the name by quoting it himself in his celebrated poem *Tam o' Shanter* (1791).

John Bull Fictional character who is widely understood to be a personification of Englishness. Although of earlier origin, the name became well known through the satires of Dr John Arbuthnot in the early 18th century, published as *The History of John Bull* (1712). He is usually depicted as a stout, red-faced yeoman farmer in top hat, tailcoat and union jack waistcoat, the epitome of the rural middle class as it once existed. In Arbuthnot's pamphlets he represents the sturdy, patriotic and conservative politics of the rural landowning classes of England, optimistic but impatient towards those who do not deal plainly and honestly with him. He is constantly at odds with such fellows as Nicholas Frog (France), Lord Strutt (Spain) and the aristocratic Humphrey Hocus (the Duke of Marlborough). In character he is honest and bold and a good companion, although his hot temper and fondness for a good drink frequently get him involved in quarrels with his friends or anyone who seeks to govern his ways.

John Henry Legendary black American railroad worker, whose great strength is celebrated in a famous traditional US ballad. According to this, he was persuaded to pit his fabled strength against that of a modern steam drill. Wielding a hammer in each hand he managed to outpace the drill breaking up rocks, but ultimately the effort killed him. Many variants of the legend developed through constant repetition of the story, some of them concentrating upon his renowned sexual prowess. In some versions he was even depicted as white.

The tale would appear to have been inspired by tests that are thought to have been made in Virginia in the 1870s to compare the efficiency of new rock-crushing machines with that of ordinary human workers.

John o'Groat In Scottish legend, one of three brothers who lived in a large house west of Duncansby Head, Caithness, during the reign of James IV of Scotland (1488–1513). John o'Groat (or Jan de Groot) was originally Dutch, but, together with his brothers Malcolm and Gavin, decided to settle in northern Scotland, where in due course the three brothers became the heads of eight families bearing the same name. The families met for an annual celebration, but repeatedly fell out over the question of who should have precedence at the table. To solve the problem John o'Groat built an eight-sided room, each with its own door, and sat the guests at an octagonal table. A mound in the village near Dunnet Head in Caithness (the northernmost point of mainland Britain) is supposed to mark the place where this remarkable house stood, although it is Duncansby Head, the northwestern point of mainland Britain, that is now generally known as John o' Groats in his honour.

Johnny Appleseed In modern US mythology, a folk hero who in many respects resembles the nature gods of ancient times. He was, in fact, based upon a real person – a missionary called John Chapman (1774–1845), who wandered the northern states of the USA preaching and planting appleseeds wherever he went. He had collected the seeds from the waste produced by the cider presses of Pittsburgh, and also used them to barter for the few necessaries he needed to keep body and soul together.

Over the years Chapman planted enough seeds to cover some 1,200 acres of land with apple orchards, and consequently entered popular mythology as a personification of nature. He was eccentric both in character and appearance, described as looking like a tramp, with long hair, a wide-brimmed hat, holed trousers and an old coffee sack as a shirt. He also had a reputation as a herbalist, and was revered as a healer by both settlers and Native Americans. Many legends became attached to his name, most of them emphasizing his identification with animals and the natural world. Among these was the story that he once put out his own fire in order to stop mosquitoes being burnt in it. Legend has it that he died of exposure.

Jormungandr In Norse mythology, a huge serpent that wrapped its body round Midgard (the earth) by biting on the end of its own tail. Also called the Midgard Serpent, it was created by LOKI, but was thrown into the sea by ODIN while still relatively small. According to tradition, Jormungandr lashes storms up by beating the water with its tail. It is fated to perish during RAGNAROK.

See also KRAKEN.

Joseph of Arimathea In the New Testament, the wealthy Jew in whose tomb the body of the crucified Christ was laid. Although the Bible has little more to say about him, Joseph of Arimathea has special folkloric significance in Britain. A tradition apparently of 13th-century origin claims that Joseph of Arimathea had links with the Cornish tin trade and made many visits to England, possibly bringing the young Jesus (sometimes identified as his nephew) with him – hence the line in William Blake's 'Jerusalem': 'And did those feet in ancient time / Walk upon England's mountains green?'. After the Crucifixion Joseph of Arimathea is said to have been entrusted with the keeping of the GRAIL, the cup used at the Last Supper. Another tradition claims that the

Grail kept Joseph alive during his 12 years' imprisonment by the Romans. Once out of prison, he brought the Grail with him to Glastonbury, where he built England's first Christian church. He also brought with him the spear with which Longinus was said to have pierced the side of the dying Christ.

Joseph's staff, itself cut from the thorn bush from which came Christ's crown of thorns, is supposed to have burst immediately into flower when he planted it in the ground on Wearyall Hill, Glastonbury when he paused for a rest. For many centuries a hawthorn tree growing on the hill was reputed to be Joseph's staff. It was cut down by a fanatical Puritan during the English Civil War, but cuttings from the tree had already given rise to new plants, which remain today. The trees are reputed to flower each year on Christmas Eve, and some of the flowers are sent in tribute to the Queen.

jotun In Norse mythology, a race of giants that represented the forces of nature. The jotun had their home in Jotunheim, located in the northeast of ASGARD. Many Norse myths concerned relationships between the jotun and the gods, some of whom intermarried. Today the name Jotunheim is borne by a mountain range in Norway that incorporates the country's highest peaks.

Jotunheim *See* JOTUN.

Joyeuse The sword of CHARLEMAGNE, with which he was ultimately buried. According to legend the sword bore the legend *Decem praeceptorum custos Carolus*. The same name is sometimes given to the swords of other heroes in medieval European romance.

Judon In British mythology, the wife of Gorboduc, the legendary king of Britain who claimed descent from Brutus. After their son Porrex murdered his brother Ferrex, Judon killed him in his turn, and the line of Brutus came to an end.

Julian the Hospitaller Legendary Christian hero whose well-known story appears to have been first written down by Vincent de Beauvais in the 13th century. A young nobleman, Julian was one day warned by the stag he was hunting that he was fated to kill his own mother and father. Shocked by this revelation, he fled to a distant land, where he hoped he might escape his dreadful destiny. There he married well and was knighted and given a fine castle for his service to the king. One day, while Julian was away, his sorrowing parents arrived at his home in search of him. They were admitted by Julian's wife, who gave them their own bed to sleep in. When Julian returned home he went to his room and was outraged to see two people in his bed. Mistaking his mother for his wife and his father for her lover he killed both parents and stormed from the castle, only to meet his wife coming back from church. Realizing what he had done, Julian and his wife abandoned their home in horror and sought to do penance for the terrible deed by building a hospice for travellers and the poor at a spot where a ford crossed a wide river.

In consequence of the legend, Julian was recognized by Christians as a saint and became the protector of travellers, in much the same way as St Christopher. He is also regarded as the patron of ferrymen, innkeepers, itinerant musicians and circus performers.

jumby In Caribbean folklore, a spirit of the dead. It is sometimes related to the ZOMBIE of Haitian folk religion.

See also DUPPY.

juniper The evergreen juniper tree is widely respected for its protective powers. In the Christian world this tradition has its roots in the legend that the infant Christ was hidden from pursuing soldiers in the foliage of a juniper tree. Ever since then such animals as foxes and hares are said to have sought shelter in the tree when chased by the hunt. Juniper boughs were often hung up in cowsheds to protect livestock from evil spirits, and the smoke of burning juniper was believed to ward off evil spirits and disease. The berries, meanwhile, are supposed to repel snakes. Not surprisingly, in view of the respect felt for the juniper, Welsh folklore claims that anyone who is rash enough to cut a juniper tree down will die within the year, or else lose a close relation.

Rather less positive is the warning that dreams about juniper trees will be followed by a decline in a person's luck or health. Dreams about juniper berries, though, are supposed to advise the dreamer concerned of the imminent birth of a male child.

Juniper has a number of uses in folk medicine. Potions of juniper may be used to treat rheumatism, toothache, epilepsy and liver complaints. They are also said to be effective in rejuvenating the elderly.

One of the folk tales collected by the Brothers Grimm, 'The Juniper Tree', is based on an ancient story common to the British, French, German, Magyar and Scandinavian cultures. It concerns the treachery of a wicked stepmother who feeds her husband with the flesh of his own son, whom she has murdered. The murdered boy's sister wraps the bones that are left in a white handkerchief and puts them in a juniper tree, from which emerges a bird. The bird tells the story of the boy's death to a goldsmith, a shoemaker and a miller, who reward it with a gold chain, a pair of red shoes and a millstone. The bird, actually the reincarnated spirit of the son, tells his father what has happened and places the chain round his neck as proof. He then rewards his sister with the red shoes and kills the wicked stepmother by dropping the millstone on her head, upon which he is magically restored to life in his original form.

K

kachina In Native American folklore, a breed of ancestral spirit revered by many tribes, including the Pueblo Indians of the southwestern USA. Also variously identified as nature spirits, kachinas are supposed to spend their winters on earth and their summers in the land of the dead. Ceremonies are held to mark the times when they make their journeys between the two worlds, with masked dancers attempting to achieve commu-nion with the spirits they portray. In return it is believed that kachinas protect each tribal group, safeguarding their health and prosperity. Children are often given small kachina dolls to grant them the special protection of the spirit world.

kakamora In Melanesian folklore, a supernatural being who dwells in caves and forests. Described as dwarfs distinguished by their long nails and great strength, they are of an unpredictable nature and are reputed to have killed humans from time to time. People fearful of falling victim to the kakamora can protect themselves by wearing white, a colour that is supposed to have the power to drive them away.

kalau In Russian folklore, a species of demon greatly feared by the people of Siberia. The kalau delight in bringing misery to human beings by inflicting disease and death.

Kalevala The national epic of the Finns, which was assembled from oral tradition in the middle of the 19th century by Elias Lönnroth (1802–84). Named after the three sons of Kalewa (VÄINÄMÖINEN, ILMARENIN and LEMMINKÄINEN) and sometimes interpreted as meaning 'land of heroes', the epic bears the influence of both Teutonic and Scandinavian mythology, as well as that of the Christian church. The epic describes how the seer Väinämöinen bids to win the hand of the Maiden of Pohjola with the aid of Ilmarenin, but is then thwarted by Ilmarenin taking her for himself. The jealous Lemminkäinen causes havoc at the subsequent wedding, but the three heroes reunite to retrieve the magic mill they built for the Maiden's mother Louhi, and ultimately successfully defeat her forces in battle.

See also KULLERVO.

kappa In Japanese folklore, a water demon that preys on any living creatures that venture into the water where it dwells, devouring their bodies from the inside. Depicted with a monkey's head, the body and shell of a tortoise, and the legs of a frog, the kappa depends for its strength upon the pool of water it carries in a pit on the top of its head. The best defence humans have is to bow to the creature, thus obliging it to bow in return and thus spill the water from its head, forcing it to go back to its pool for a refill and allowing the intended victim time to escape. The kappa will, however, spare any person who has previously thrown a cucumber with their name written on it into the monster's pool, as it has a particular taste for them.

karawatoniga In Melanesian folklore, a sky spirit associated with the seashore. The karawatoniga are depicted as human in appearance, with long hair, and are usually considered harmless.

kasha In Japanese folklore, a demon that preys upon the bodies of the newly dead. Fear of interference by kashas resulted in the tradition of friends and relatives of the dead keeping watch over the corpse until the appointed time for cremation. In order to frighten away the kashas the mourners usually make a good deal of noise throughout their vigil.

Kay, Sir In Arthurian legend, the son of ECTOR OF THE FOREST SAUVAGE and the foster-brother of King ARTHUR. Despite his outspoken, boorish and rather ill-tempered nature, he became the king's steward and featured in most of Arthur's early adventures. According to the Welsh he was a heroic warrior, but in later Arthurian writings he is accused of the murder of Arthur's son Llacheu (or Lohot) and described as resenting the greater fame of his foster-brother. Together with Sir BEDIVERE he tracks down and rescues MABON from imprisonment in Gloucester, carrying him to freedom on his back.

keening See FUNERAL RITES.

kelpie In Scottish mythology, a species of water horse that haunts certain lochs, awaiting the opportunity to prey upon passers-by. It is also known in Gaelic as the *each uisge*. The magnificent-looking horse allows strangers to climb onto its back, but then rushes with them into the water where it drowns and devours them. On a more positive note, the kelpie was also said to go out of its way to help millers by keeping their mill wheels turning at night. It was sometimes claimed that any mortal who could place a bridle on a kelpie would be able to make the creature his slave.

Kempe Owen Legendary British hero who undertook the rescue of a maiden who had been transformed by magic into the shape of a fearful DRAGON. In order to restore the maiden to her previous form he had to kiss the dragon three times. Having succeeded in the task, however, he found that his own stepmother in her turn had been transformed into a dragon, only to return to her human shape upon the arrival in Britain of St KENTIGERN.

Kentigern, St The first bishop of Strathclyde and the patron saint of Glasgow, otherwise called St Mungo (meaning 'dearest' or 'dear friend'), whose life is shrouded in legend. According to Scottish tradition, he was born in the early 6th century, possibly the grandson of URIEN of Rheged. He had an early adventure when he and his mother were set adrift in a coracle, and only a miracle saved them. Subsequently he played a celebrated role in protecting the good name of Queen Langoureth when she was suspected of adultery. The queen had taken a lover and had rather rashly given him a ring that had been a present from her husband, King Roderick. The king learned about the affair and stole the ring back when his wife's lover was asleep and threw it into the Clyde. He then commanded his wife to produce the ring within three days or else to suffer dire consequences. The distraught queen rushed to Kentigern for help, who prayed for divine assistance. Shortly afterwards he fished a salmon out of the Clyde and found the ring firmly clasped in the fish's mouth, thus bringing about a reconciliation between the royal couple.

There is also a legend that Kentigern baptized MERLIN before his death. He died around 603 and his relics are supposed to lie in the Cathedral of St Mungo in Glasgow, which he founded in 573. A ring and salmon feature today in Glasgow's coat of arms.

key Keys and keyholes are among the many everyday objects that have strong folkloric significance. They have had special importance in mythology since the earliest times, usually representing power: Celtic goddesses, for instance, were frequently depicted with a key, probably symbolizing their ability to open the gates to the OTHERWORLD.

The fact that keys were traditionally made from IRON, a magical metal, also promoted their magical associations. People once touched their keys for protection if they thought they were under the threat of the EVIL EYE, and throughout Europe keys were slipped under children's pillows to ward off evil while they slept. The sick were commonly encouraged to carry a bunch of keys to aid recovery and even today a folk remedy recommends slipping a key down the back of a patient suffering a nosebleed to staunch the flow. Mothers in childbirth were formerly given the key to their own unlocked door in the belief that this would avoid a difficult labour. In some cultures of the Mediterranean region a key is still laid on corpses to symbolize their admission to the afterworld.

In the English-speaking world today keys are widely associated with 18th and 21st birthdays, when a person is said to get the 'key to the door' (in other words, the right to come and go from the parental home as they wish, and thus in a more general sense admission to the adult world). Cards celebrating the event often depict keys, and small plastic keys are often given as keepsakes.

There are numerous superstitions concerning keys. It is thought to be very bad luck, for instance, to drop a key, and even worse to break one. Keys that go rusty, however, are a good omen, and in the English Midlands this is sometimes interpreted to mean that the person concerned is about to be left an inheritance in someone else's will. When not in use, keys should be left in the keyhole, as this bars the way to the Devil, fairies, and other supernatural spirits that may seek access to the home by this route. A rather more obscure tradition warns against jangling bunches of keys on Wednesdays, as this will make their owner go mad.

See also BIBLIOMANCY.

Khidr, El In Arabian folklore, a supernatural entity who was revered for his great wisdom. Otherwise described as the Green One, he appears in Islamic tradition as an equivalent of the Hebrew Elijah and numbers Moses among his followers. In other non-Islamic traditions he is depicted as a water spirit who comes to the aid of travellers in peril when crossing water and, in Syrian folklore, as the dragon-killing St GEORGE.

kikimora In Russian folklore, a household spirit who takes a particular interest in domestic chores. Tradition has it that the kikimora will work to make the life of the diligent housewife easier, but will cause problems for any housewife who fails to do her work properly.

See also DOMOVIK.

k'ilin In Chinese mythology, a legendary creature understood to represent the virtues of piety and self-restraint. It is usually described as having the head and legs of a horse, the body of a deer, the horn of a UNICORN and the tail of a lion.

Kilkenny cats In Irish legend, two wild cats that fought each other until all that was left of them were their claws and tails. In Norman times Kilkenny consisted of two townships, Englishtown and Irishtown, and the cats are usually understood to have represented these two rivals, which were constantly at odds with one another in the 12th century. Another explanation links the legend to the Irish rebellion of 1798, when Hessian troops at Kilkenny derived amusement by tying two cats together by their tails and watching them fight. The soldiers' sport ended when an officer approached and a trooper hurriedly separated the cats by cutting their tails with his sword. When the officer asked for an explanation of the two bloody tails he was told that this was all that remained of two cats that had fought themselves to death.

Any opponents who fight with unusual ferocity or until both sides have lost everything are often described as 'fighting like Kilkenny cats'.

kilyakai In the folklore of Papua New Guinea, a breed of forest spirit that delights in causing harm among humans. Described as small, wrinkled hunters, they are routinely blamed for many misfortunes, from the disappearance of human babies to outbreaks of malaria, which they spread by shooting mortals with poisoned arrows.

kingfisher This colourful wild bird figured prominently in the legends of the ancient Greeks, who called the bird the halcyon, and it has resurfaced many times in folklore since then, often in the role of messenger of the gods.

In medieval times the bird was widely believed to be lucky (especially in business matters), and it was further claimed that its dead body would never decay: the corpses of kingfishers were sometimes placed in cupboards to keep clothing fresh and free of moths. It is also on record that the body of a dead kingfisher was sometimes suspended from the roof of a house to act as a weathervane, its beak infallibly turning to point into the wind.

The kingfisher, originally grey according to legend, was the first bird to be sent out from Noah's ark, and acquired its bright plumage after accidentally flying too close to the sun. It then tried to return to the ark, but the boat had floated on elsewhere, and it is said that the kingfishers since seen skimming low over lakes and rivers remain in search of it. Women formerly wore kingfisher feathers in the belief that they magically promoted beauty in the wearer, and they were also known to sew them into their clothing for good fortune.

See also SAILORS' LORE.

King of Misrule *See* LORD OF MISRULE.

King o' the Cats In English folklore, the legendary ruler of the cats. The character appears in a famous folk tale in which a gravedigger encounters a mourning party of black cats, who ask him to pass the message to Tom Tildrum that Tim Toldrum (or a similar name) is dead. The gravedigger hurries home to tell the story of the extraordinary meeting to his wife. Their cat, Old Tom, also hears the story and with the shout 'Then I'm the king o' the Cats!' escapes up the chimney and is never seen again.

king's touch The touch of a reigning monarch that for centuries was believed to have special healing powers, particularly in the treatment of the 'king's evil' (scrofula). Reminiscent of the healing power of Christ's touch, the idea of the 'king's touch' was familiar in ancient Rome, and subsequently came to be associated with several of the great ruling families of Europe.

The first English king credited with the power of the king's touch was Edward the Confessor, although it was not until the reign of Henry VII that it evolved into a formalized ceremony. The last such ceremonies were held in the reign of Queen Anne in the early 18th century, when those who received the royal touch included the young Samuel Johnson in 1712 (apparently without result). Charles II is reputed to have bestowed the king's touch upon around 100,000 scrofula victims (including 8,500 in 1682 alone). On one occasion several people died in the crush to reach him – although the promise of a small gold or silver medallion (which was known as the 'touch-piece') to each person may have done something to promote the hysteria in this instance. The usual procedure in each ceremony was for the monarch to touch the sufferer while speaking the words 'I touch, but God healeth.' The medallion then presented had to be worn round the patient's neck for the remainder of his or her days.

Although faith in the king's touch died out long ago, even at the end of the 20th century parents have been recorded bringing their babies to the royal seat at Windsor 'for luck'.

kiss The act of kissing has always been considered more than a simple expression of affection or greeting. Because the breath has since ancient times been considered magical, containing something of a person's soul, the exchange of breath in a kiss has special folkloric significance.

The kissing of hands or rings is a traditional feature of various civic and religious ceremonies, representing declarations of loyalty and humility. By kissing an amulet or some other luck-giving object a person also promotes their own good fortune, hence the habit gamblers have of kissing betting slips or lottery coupons and so forth in the belief that this will improve their chances of winning. Indulgent parents still tell children complaining of minor injuries that they will 'kiss it better', the relic of the old custom of sucking poisons from wounds.

Other miscellaneous superstitions concerning kissing include the notions that it is unlucky to kiss babies (contrary to modern assumptions), to kiss anyone on the nose (as this will lead to a quarrel) or to lean over someone's shoulder to kiss them on the cheek (as the kiss will shortly be followed by a knife in the back).

See also MISTLETOE.

kissing bough *See* MISTLETOE.

Knecht Ruprecht In German folklore, the Servant Rupert, who is usually described as a knight of Christ, and appears to have been to some extent an early equivalent of SANTA CLAUS. The character appeared in the course of Christmas celebrations of the 18th and 19th centuries, going from house to house and handing out gifts to children who had been good over the past year,

and switches to the fathers of those who had misbehaved. He was usually depicted in white robes, with a wig and mask.

knife Knives have always had special folkloric significance, in part because of their use in a wide range of rituals and in part because they are made of IRON, traditionally thought of as a metal with great magic potential.

The importance placed upon the protective power of knives is illustrated today in the occasional finds in old houses of knives hidden beneath doorsteps or windowsills, where it was believed they would prevent the entrance of the Devil or witches into the building. In much the same way Scottish tradition recommended concealing a knife under the pillow to prevent the sleeper being carried off by fairies during the night. Seafarers formerly stuck knives into the mast of their ships in the belief that this would summon up a favourable wind and generally safeguard the luck of the vessel. In many folk tales, special magic knives are used to kill a variety of monsters and demons when other means have failed.

Superstitions relating to knives include the taboo against making gifts of knives (as these will sever the friendship of the people concerned), and the prohibition against allowing knives to cross each other when laying the table (as this presages a quarrel in the household). If a knife falls from the table this may be interpreted as warning of the imminent end of a love affair, or else of the arrival of a stranger, and is generally a bad omen, unless the blade happens to stick upright in the floor. Tradition also warns against leaving knives lying with the sharp edge of the blade upwards, reasoning that they will cut the feet of fairies and thus incur their wrath.

Other superstitions emphasize the trouble that may arise from careless handling of knives. An old proverb, for instance, advises cooks against stirring the pot with a knife: 'Stir with a knife, stir up strife.' Even in modern times some people will hide knives and other items of cutlery during thunderstorms, believing they will attract lightning.

knocker In Cornish folklore, a species of FAIRY that dwells in tin mines. It is said that the knockers will guide miners to rich veins of ore, or alternatively warn them of imminent danger by the tapping noises they make. They are variously identified as the souls of the dead or as a breed of DWARF.

knot The notion that there is magic in the tying of knots is ancient and common to many cultures. The Celts, to name but one example, saw great magic in knots, and knotwork figured prominently in Celtic art of all kinds. Even today, the tying of knots is often a feature of important religious ceremonies, notably marriage services (hence the expression 'tying the knot', meaning 'getting married').

For centuries people (especially gamblers) were in the habit of tying knots in their clothing for luck, and even today the ruse of tying a knot in a handkerchief in order to remember something is widely familiar. The underlying reasoning in the latter case is that the intricacy of the knots will distract the Devil or any other demons intent upon making the person concerned forget whatever it is they are trying to remember.

The tying of knots featured in many spells and curses. By tying nine knots in her garter and speaking a special rhyme a girl was supposed to be rewarded with a glimpse of her future lover. By tying knots in a piece of string while reciting curses on the marriage bed a rival could deprive a newly-wed couple of the pleasures of sexual union (which was why some bridegrooms went up the aisle with their shoelaces untied in days gone by). In medieval times, indeed, anyone found guilty of tying knots to bring a curse to bear upon a newly married couple risked excommunication. By the same token women were rumoured to use knots to prevent pregnancy.

Knots also had a role in folk medicine. A long-established treatment for warts, for instance, involved rubbing the affected part with a knot and then ritually burning the knot (and thus causing the wart itself to fade to nothing).

In some circumstances it was important that every knot in the vicinity was untied. It was feared that allowing knots to remained tied in the bedclothes or nightgown of a woman in labour would make the birth more difficult, while knots left tied anywhere in the room of a person in their death throes would impede their passage to the next world.

See also WIND.

kobold In German folklore, a species of mischievous household spirit or, alternatively, a variety of GNOME who dwells in mines and forests. It is a German equivalent of the English ROBIN GOODFELLOW or BROWNIE. Easily offended and made irritable if not kept well fed, kobolds delight in hiding things from their human owners and committing other minor acts of mischief, but if given food will offer such services as singing children to sleep at night. A kobold called Goldemar is supposed to reserve his malevolent attention for clergymen, delighting in learning and then broadcasting their secrets.

kornwolf In French, German and Slavic folklore, a nature spirit that is supposed to dwell in the last sheaf cut in a field of corn. The person who cuts this last sheaf will enjoy the power to adopt the shape of a wolf at will in order to keep his rebellious children under control. Effigies made from the sheaf might be ritually destroyed or else carefully preserved over the winter to ensure a good crop the following year (*see* CORN DOLLY).

Kraken In Norse mythology, a huge sea monster over a mile in circumference that dwells in the waters off the coast of Norway. Possibly inspired by early sightings of giant squids, the Kraken was believed to be responsible for pulling large ships under the waves and sucking other vessels into the whirlpool it caused when it dived.

kravyad In Hindu folklore, a frightening man-eating GOBLIN. It is supposed to dwell in the flames in which bodies are cremated at funerals.

Kriemhild In the NIBELUNGENLIED, the wife of SIEGFRIED. Celebrated for her great beauty, she was the daughter of King Dankrat and the sister of Gunther, Gernot and Giselher. After the end of her marriage to Siegfried she married Attila, king of the Huns.

Kriss Kringle A central character of German CHRISTMAS lore who is now considered an equivalent of SANTA CLAUS or St NICHOLAS. Originally called Christkindl (from the German for Christ-child), this representation of Christ was supposed to deliver gifts to children on Christmas Eve in the wake of St Nicholas, who travelled in advance to ask the children what they hoped to get. The distinctions between these various Christmas characters have largely broken down in modern times, and the name Kriss Kringle is today often regarded as synonymous with that of the more familiar FATHER CHRISTMAS.

See also KNECHT RUPRECHT.

k'uei In Chinese folklore, the spirits of the dead that remain on earth after being refused admission to the afterworld. Trapped in the world of men, frustated k'uei look for opportunities to wreak their revenge upon mortals. Their weakness lies in the fact that they move in straight lines, so they cannot gain access to any home in which the front door does not open directly into other rooms in the house.

Kulhwch *See* CULHWCH.

Kullervo In Finnish folklore, a tragic hero whose tale is related in the KALEVALA. Having been taken into the household of ILMARINEN as a slave, he helped to bring about the death of the Maiden of Pohjola and subsequently sought the safety of his mother's house. Here he raped his own sister, whom he did not recognize, causing her to kill herself. The incensed Kullervo then waged war against his uncle Unatamo, whom he blamed for his troubles, but returned to find the rest of his family dead, and ultimately committed suicide himself.

Kvasir In Norse mythology, the god of wisdom and poetic inspiration. He is supposed to have been born from the spittle of the AESIR and the VANIR, and thus inherited the knowledge of both. He wandered the earth providing answers to the many questions posed by mankind, but was eventually murdered by two jealous dwarfs. The dwarfs used his blood to make a magical brew that bestowed the gift of poetic inspiration.

L

ladder The taboo against walking under ladders is common to many cultures and persists in superstition even today, being encountered in both Christian and non-Christian countries. Many people who reject more archaic superstitions will still cross the road or choose another route if a ladder propped against a wall blocks their path (although they may protest that they are simply nervous of something being dropped on them).

In fact, this taboo is thought to have had its roots ultimately in primitive fears of contact with the blood of menstruating women (*see* MENSTRUATION) and the importance that was formerly given to the avoidance of accidental contamination. In many cultures it was thought unwise to walk under ladders or anything else that a woman could climb, as blood from her might drip down upon anyone passing beneath. In the Christian world, however, this ancient fear has been redefined on the basis that a ladder leant against a wall completes a triangle with the wall and the ground. The triangle is a symbol of the Holy Trinity, and thus anyone who walks straight through it is showing disrespect for God and is likely to incur divine wrath. Alternatively, as in the biblical story of Jacob's ladder, a ladder offers a means of ascent to heaven. Because of this, great care must be taken when approaching a ladder for fear of obstructing or offending any invisible spirits mounting it.

The usual punishment for those who ignore the taboo can range from a bout of unlooked-for misfortune to the postponement of marriage hopes and, in the Netherlands and formerly in parts of the British Isles, the death by hanging of the person concerned. This last notion probably dates from times when condemned felons might be executed on impromptu gallows comprising a ladder leant against a tree.

In cases where there is no alternative to walking under a ladder folklore does, however, offer a safeguard, advising that crossing the fingers and keeping them crossed until a dog is sighted will afford the transgressor some protection from misfortune. Similarly, spitting on one's shoe and allowing the spittle to dry may negate any ill effects.

Those who work on ladders are not immune to their powers. In the USA it is said that anyone who climbs a ladder under which a black cat has just walked will experience bad luck, and in many European countries it is also unlucky to pass anything through the rungs of a ladder – as it also is at sea. Danger lurks even if the ladder is resting horizontally on the ground, as bad luck will plague any person who treads between the rungs.

In many non-Christian countries the taboo against walking under ladders can be simply one aspect of a wider superstition that applies to walking under any other kind of object, the notion being that it is disrespectful to allow anything to be placed over the head, as the head is the seat of the spirit and should never be thus overshadowed. In Japan, for instance, it is thought that anyone who walks under a telegraph wire will be possessed by devils.

Ladders play an important role in a number of folk tales and legends. Various heroes gain access to heaven or the other-world by means of a ladder of some kind, and in 'Jack and the Beanstalk' it is by climbing the beanstalk like a ladder that Jack reaches the giant's castle.

ladybird The distinctive colouring of the ladybird (otherwise known as the ladybug, or by some as God Almighty's cow) has long distinguished it in folklore. Associated with the Virgin Mary for obscure reasons, it is regarded as a harbinger of good fortune in many parts of the world (the principle being the redder the insect the better the luck). It is widely considered to be particularly lucky for a ladybird to land on someone, as long as it is not brushed off.

On no account should the creature be harmed: if a ladybird is accidentally killed the body should be buried and the ground over it stamped on three times, according to East Anglian superstition. In southern England, the number of black spots on a ladybird is supposed to reveal to the observer the number of happy months that lie ahead, thus making ladybirds with an abundance of spots particularly welcome. Hebridean folklore, however, has it that the five spots that distinguish the local ladybirds are symbolic of the wounds of Christ, while rural mythology of the West Country used to advise that the number of spots on the ladybirds indicated the number of shillings a bushel of wheat would fetch that season. In the USA a ladybird landing on a dress or some other item of clothing indicates that the owner will soon acquire a new garment of the same kind. Elsewhere a ladybird landing on the hand is a sign of good weather to come. German folklore claims that the ladybird is a bringer of babies (a role otherwise associated with the stork).

Children throughout the UK are familiar with the rhyme 'Ladybird, ladybird, fly away home; / Your house is on fire and your children are gone.' By chanting this couplet to a ladybird and noting the flight path the insect then takes, information may be gleaned about the direction from which a future true love will come. This particular tradition may be linked to the practice of burning fields after the harvest to prepare them for replanting, a practice that poses a particular threat to the ladybird population.

Lastly, those suffering from toothache are recommended by folk medicine to collect the yellow liquid exuded by the insect when alarmed; this is then rubbed on the teeth to lessen the pain.

Lady of the Lake In Arthurian legend, a shadowy enchantress who lives in a castle in the middle of a lake, surrounded by her attendants. Also known as the Dame du Lac and variously identified as Vivien, Niniane, or NIMUE, she was the foster-mother of LANCELOT, preparing him for membership of Arthur's Round Table. According to Malory's *Morte d'Arthur* she presented Arthur himself with his magical sword EXCALIBUR. She is also supposed to have deceived MERLIN into revealing the secrets of his magic to her, after which she trapped him forever in a stone or inside a tree. When Sir BEDIVERE returned Excalibur to the lake, on Arthur's orders, the arm that rose from the water to take it is usually assumed to be hers.

Some details of her description, such as her guardianship of the HALLOWS, suggest links ultimately with the ancient Celtic goddess of SOVEREIGNTY.

La Fontaine, Jean de French poet who is today remembered primarily for the fables that he collected and published between 1668 and 1694. Born in 1621, he studied law in Paris before following his father as superintendent of the waters and forests of Château-Thierry in Champ-agne and establishing a reputation as a poet. The first six books of his *Fables choisies mises en vers* were published in 1668. In all he published around 250 fables before his death in 1695, drawing to a large extent upon the tales of Aesop and other writers from much earlier times, as well as contributing fables of his own invention. The first English translation of his fables appeared in 1734.

Lambton Worm Legendary monster that is supposed to have ravaged the countryside around Lambton Castle in County Durham at an unspecified date during the early medieval period. This most famous of English WORMS was eventually destroyed by the son of Lord Lambton, who was advised by a witch to wear a suit of armour studded with razors: when the beast emerged from the well in which it lurked and wrapped itself around him it was ripped to pieces. In exchange for the witch's advice the knight had promised to kill the first living thing he met on returning, but instead of the dog he had arranged to meet he was confronted with his own father. He refused to kill his father and as a result the witch cursed the whole family, many of whom met bad ends.

Lammas Day Christian festival celebrated on 1 August each year. A day of thanksgiving for the year's harvest, dating back to the reign of King Alfred or beyond, it is traditionally marked with a special mass in which bread made from the first-ripened corn is consecrated. The name Lammas itself comes from the Anglo-Saxon *hlafmaesse* ('loaf-mass'). Lammas Day is also important in Scotland as one of the quarter days on which rents become payable, and it was formerly a Scottish custom to sprinkle livestock with menstrual blood on this date in the belief that this would ward off evil in the months ahead. To this day Lammas Day processions take place at Lanark and elsewhere.

Lancelot du Lac In Arthurian legend, the most prominent of the knights of the ROUND TABLE. The son of King Ban of Benoic in Brittany, he was stolen as an infant and brought up by the LADY OF THE LAKE before being admitted to Arthur's court. Although respected as the strongest of the knights, he was nonetheless flawed. Having rescued Arthur's wife GUINEVERE from her kidnapper Meleagant, he was unable to resist becoming her lover, thus precipitating the eventual downfall of Arthur's court. As a result of this crime, he failed in his quest to be the perfect knight destined to find the GRAIL (although he twice caught sight of it), that honour going instead to his son GALAHAD. On another occasion he was guilty of the accidental killing of his best friend, Gareth of Orkney. Following the departure of Arthur, Lancelot took up the life of a hermit, and in due course died at his castle, Joyous Gard, which has been tentatively identified as Alnwick in Northumberland.

Details of Lancelot's story suggest that he may have developed under the influence of the Celtic sun god LUGH. His quest to rescue Guinevere from Meleagant has been interpreted as an allegory of the battle between summer and winter over the goddess of fertility.

langsuir In Malayan folklore, a species of female demon believed to be the spirit of a woman who has died in childbirth. These hags return to earth to suck the blood of other women's children by means of a hole in the back of their necks. Other distinguishing features include long, tapering fingernails, green dresses and long black hair. They become harmless if their hair and nails are cut and the trimmings packed into the hole in their neck. The corpses of women who die in childbirth may be buried with glass beads, eggs and needles in the belief that such measures will prevent their transformation into langsuirs.

Lanterns, Feast of Chinese festival celebrating the New Year. Held during the first full moon of the year, it is marked by general rejoicing, firework displays and the hanging of ornate paper lanterns on both houses and graves. According to tradition, the festival was inspired by the story of a famous mandarin's daughter who fell into a lake one dark night, but was subsequently rescued after her father and his neighbour looked for her by the light of their lanterns. The light and heat of the lanterns is supposed to ward off evil spirits.

lapwing (or peewit) The eerie high-pitched cry of the lapwing has inspired a range of folk beliefs in the regions where the bird is commonly seen, and it is generally considered unlucky. The Welsh and the Scottish claim that its call – reputed to bring bad luck – consists of the words 'Bewitched! Bewitched!' In Scotland there is a legend that when the Covenanters were in hiding from the king's men, lapwings betrayed their hiding places to their pursuers. The Irish curse the bird for leaving them only its droppings while the Scots get all the eggs, and the English nervously speculate that the birds are the incarnation of restless spirits. The mere sight of the bird is feared by many people, and in some areas it is thought extremely reckless to handle the body of a dead lapwing.

Swedish folklore claims that the first lapwing was formerly a handmaid to the Virgin Mary until transformed into a bird as punishment for stealing a pair of Our Lady's scissors (hence the bird's vaguely scissorlike tail). Elsewhere it is commonly believed that old women who die unmarried are reincarnated as lapwings after death. In parts of Africa the bird is said to demonstrate its fearlessness by snatching food from the mouths of crocodiles.

lark Songbird whose musical talents have inspired a number of curious folk beliefs. Revered for the sweetness of its voice, the lark was formerly said to sing best if blinded with a red-hot needle (blinded larks were often sold as pets in cages). Humans could share in the lark's musical gifts by eating three larks' eggs before the church bells rang on Sunday, a procedure

that was guaranteed to benefit the voice. Eating the lark itself did not necessarily help improve one's singing, but consuming a dish of crested lark was once recommended as a cure for colic.

Offending against the well-being of a lark or its nest should not be undertaken lightly, however: inhabitants of the Shetland Islands believe the three black spots under a lark's tongue are curses that will be directed at anyone who shows malicious intent towards the bird. German folklore cautions against the action of pointing at a lark, as a sore will consequently appear on the outstretched finger. Welsh superstition adds that larks singing joyfully high in the sky are a certain sign of fine weather to come.

The lark is closely associated with the cause of lovers in many different cultures. One love spell suggests that concealing a lark's eye wrapped in wolf skin in the right pocket will make the wearer overwhelmingly attractive to the opposite sex. Likewise, a lark's eye surreptitiously slipped into someone else's drink will certainly provoke passionate feelings of love in the drinker.

In folk medicine, a lark brought into the bedroom of a sick person will avert its gaze if the patient is fated to die, but will stare without flinching if the patient is going to recover.

laurel *See* BAY.

lead Of all metals, lead is the one most closely associated with death. In former times coffins were frequently made of lead, and various ancient spells designed to deliver death curses against an enemy involved the employment of a piece of lead bearing the victim's name. The lead had to be hidden somewhere in the victim's home or else buried in the ground to make the curse effective. To determine whether someone suffering from illness was under the influence of witchcraft, a little molten lead might be held over the patient and then dropped in water: if the lead congealed into a definite image then evil spirits were clearly at work. A little of the lead thus formed might then be given to the patient to wear over his or her heart in the belief that this would counter any spell. More cheerfully, in different circumstances observing the shapes formed by molten lead immersed in cold water may reveal some symbol, such as an anchor or book, that identifies the occupation of a future lover.

The link with witchcraft is reflected in the tradition that vampires and witches cannot be killed with lead bullets, but are vulnerable only to bullets made of silver; according to Scottish tradition, if a lead bullet is used it may even rebound and kill the person who fired the shot. Conversely, the density of the metal made it the favoured material from which to make caskets to preserve important religious relics, the idea being that the lead would keep the relics safely sealed from any malevolent spirits and prevent their dissipation into the air.

Lead was also widely used in ALCHEMY in the belief that it was the metal most susceptible to being converted to gold in conjunction with the use of a PHILOSOPHER'S STONE.

Leanan Sidhe In Irish mythology, a FAIRY enchantress who brings inspiration to poets and musicians. She appears in visions to encourage mortals to create works of art based upon the lost glories of Ireland's past. She is also supposed to seek the love of mortal men and then to steal both their bodies and their souls. Anyone who falls victim to her allure may enjoy the poetic inspiration she bestows, but is not likely to live very long.

Lear Legendary king of Britain, whose story subsequently provided the basis for William Shakespeare's tragedy *King Lear*. The son of BLADUD, the aged Lear set in train a tragic sequence of events after deciding to divide his kingdom among his three daughters according to the intensity of their love for him. His daughters Goneril and Regan delivered the flat-tering expression of devotion that he expected, but Cordelia was more honest and was consequently sent into exile with nothing. Goneril and Regan subsequently took everything from their father but one last servant. Finally, driven mad through desperation, the repentant Lear sought out Cordelia in France. With her help he raised an army to regain his kingdom before dying and being buried beside the River Soar. In Shakespeare's version of the legend Lear dies across Cordelia's body after she is captured and slain by her sisters.

It is unclear whether Lear was based upon a historical king or was a fictitious invention, as recorded by Geoffrey of Monmouth in the 12th century. It is thought that Lear was modelled upon the Celtic LLYR, the father of BRAN THE BLESSED, while Cordelia was originally the Celtic Creiddylad.

See also LIR.

leek Appropriately enough, as it is a national symbol of Wales, Welsh folklore in particular sets great store by the magical properties of the leek. According to ancient tradition any warrior who smears himself with the juices of a leek (or alternatively with garlic) will be invulnerable to his enemies in battle. Legend has it that the armies of the Welsh king David wore leeks in battle in order to distinguish their comrades from their Saxon foe.

Lee Penny A coin belonging to the Scottish Lockhart family of Lee that is reputed to have miraculous healing powers. A groat dating from the reign of Edward I, the Lee Penny incorporates a dark-red pebble that is supposed to have been brought back from the Holy Land in the 14th century and is among the most celebrated of several coins, stones and other objects considered to have similar powers. Legend has it that when dipped into drinking water the Lee Penny has proved most effective in the treatment of various livestock diseases, as well as against such human ills as rabies and haemorrhages. In 1645 the coin was borrowed to curtail an outbreak of the plague in Newcastle-upon-Tyne.

Lemminkäinen Finnish folk hero, whose adventures are related in the KALE-VALA. Possibly inspired by an earlier sea god, he is depicted as both cheerful and amorous. The most notable episodes in his story include his marriage to Kyllikki and her subsequent betrayal of him; his death at the hands of an aged Laplander whom he had offended; his resurrection after his mother collected the bits of his body; and his interruption of the marriage ceremony of his brother, the smith Ilmarinen, and the Maiden of Pohjola, with whom he had fallen in love. The tale culminates in the attempt of Lemminkäinen and his brothers Ilmarinen and Väinämöinen to retrieve Ilmarinen's inexhaustible mill (eventually lost in a lake).

leprechaun In Irish folklore, one of a supernatural FAIRY race also known as the 'little people'. The modern idea of the leprechaun is a dwarfish old man with a strong sense of mischief. Usually depicted all in green, he delights in playing jokes upon mortals and features in countless humorous stories. In these the leprechaun often offers to grant a gullible human three wishes or to reveal the whereabouts of hidden treasure in return for being released from a bottle or other trap. Often, the instant the human lays eyes on the promised hoard of gold it disappears. Similarly, as soon as the human looks away the leprechaun will vanish.

Historically, the leprechaun appears to have developed out of the FIR DHEARGA or the Red Men, and was usually depicted as a fairy shoemaker.

leshy In Slavic folklore, a forest demon who is reputed to waylay travellers and lure them off their path. Supposedly the offspring of mortal women and demons, the leshy is credited with the power to change its shape. It is generally believed to have a lecherous nature, often attempting

to rape young women in the forest. Another tradition suggests the leshy hibernates in the underworld during the winter months.

lettuce Since Roman times the lettuce has been credited with a wide range of magical properties. Eaten in large quantities at Roman banquets because it was supposed to prevent drunkenness and at wedding celebrations because it was believed to be an aphrodisiac, it was subsequently used in various love potions in medieval times. A further folk belief had it that young women who ate plenty of lettuce would have little trouble giving birth, although an English variation on this notion warns that too many lettuces in a garden will prevent a woman having any children at all. Wild lettuce is used to treat insomnia and headaches among other minor ailments, although long-standing tradition also claims that it will induce sleep.

Leviathan In Old Testament lore, a huge sea monster who is identified as one of the prime demons of Hell. Linked with the sin of sloth, Leviathan was variously depicted as a crocodile, whale, serpent or dragon, echoing a long Judaeo-Christian tradition of equating dragons and snakes with the DEVIL.
See also BEHEMOTH.

life token An object believed to respond magically to the changing circumstances of its absent owner, thus revealing his or her fate. Life tokens were often carefully preserved by the families of seafarers and others who embarked upon long journeys as the only means of knowing how they were faring. Such life tokens could include a wide variety of objects, from knives and rings to phials of the person's urine or a garment of clothing. The theory ran that if the ring or the urine clouded, the knife tarnished or oozed blood, or the clothes rotted, these were sure signs that the erstwhile owner was similarly in decline or even dead. In some parts of

Africa and North America an animal or plant might serve the same purpose.

In times when communication over long distances was more problematic than it is now, whole families would unquestioningly go into mourning if the condition of the life token indicated that the absentee was no more.

lightning The age-old fear of thunder and lightning, once credited to the anger of the gods, has inspired a wealth of folk beliefs and superstitions, many of them designed to offer comfort to the nervous. Many cultures have shared the notion that the gods hurl lightning bolts at mortals to punish their trangressions, and several supreme gods, including the Greek Zeus, were traditionally depicted with a streak of lightning in their hand. When someone is struck down by lightning it is common for their demise to be blamed on some offence they have caused the gods.

Christian tradition claims that it was the Virgin Mary who created lightning as a means of warning against Satan's thunder, allowing people on earth just enough time to cross themselves for safety's sake. In gratitude to the Virgin Mary's intervention, people in some parts of the world click their tongues three times each time the lightning flashes.

The tradition that lightning never strikes twice in the same place is, unfortunately, demonstrably untrue (the Empire State Building was once recorded as having received 68 lightning strikes in just three years), but this remains a universally popular assumption. Opinions differ over which trees offer the safest shelter in a storm, with some recommending the oak and others preferring the beech or the walnut. A Sussex rhyme rejects all these species in favour of the hawthorn: 'Beware of the oak, it draws the stroke; avoid the ash, it courts the flash; creep under a thorn, it can save you from harm.' This last advice is probably the most sensible, as the thorn does not grow as tall as many other species and is thus less likely to attract lightning bolts.

The custom of opening doors and windows in a thunderstorm in order that any lighting bolt that does enter the house will be able to get out again is advised in many areas, as is the covering up of mirrors and metal objects like scissors as these are said to attract the stroke. Keeping acorns or various plants (such as elder, hazel, Christmas holly and the houseleek for example) in the house is also supposed to deflect lightning. If further reassurance is required, tying a snakeskin around the head will provide added protection, as will keeping a fire going in the grate, wearing natural silk and sleeping on a feather mattress. Keeping one's distance from the family dog is also a good idea, as dogs' tails are sometimes suspected of attracting lightning.

In times gone by it was considered foolhardy to look directly at a lightning flash as this was reputed to cause a person to go mad. Neither is it advisable for a person to draw someone else's attention to lightning, as this will draw the bolt, and the old custom of counting the seconds between the flash and the thunder to determine how many miles away the storm is should also be discouraged, according to some.

Wood taken from a tree that has been struck by lightning is widely understood to have special magical properties and may be fashioned into a luck-bringing amulet. US folklore insists that such wood should never be burned on the domestic hearth as this will draw lightning towards the house.

Close inspection of any site where lightning has struck may be rewarded by the discovery of 'devil's pebbles' or 'lightning stones', fragments in the shape of hatchets or arrowheads. These are believed to have very strong magical properties: placed in an open wound they will, according to the folklore of Alsace, bestow great strength upon the injured party, who henceforth will be able to strike his enemies dead by simply threatening them with the words 'May lightning crush you.'

likho In Russian folklore, a fearsome ogress who represents the malevolent aspect of Fate. She is usually depicted as an old hag, sometimes described as having only one eye.

lilac The lilac, with its soporific perfume, is considered an unlucky plant in certain parts of the British Isles, especially in the case of the white-bloomed variety. It is among the plants that are least welcome in bouquets for hospital patients, although some say that lilac blossoms with five petals will bring luck to those who find them.

Lilith Night demon and vampire identified in Jewish, Christian and Islamic folklore as the chief of all demonesses, who murdered young children and had intercourse with men as they slept.

Probably descended from the Assyrian Lilitu, a hideous monster with wings and long hair, Lilith was supposedly the first wife of Adam. She deserted Adam, however, in order to indulge herself with demons, producing 100 demon offspring every day. According to Islamic tradition she coupled with the DEVIL to give birth to the race of jinn (*see* JINNI). By way of consolation for his loss, God created Eve as Adam's new companion. Lilith herself was punished through the slaughter of her children, which inspired in her a deep and lasting hatred of mankind. She continued to terrorize humanity, often being attracted to couples having intercourse in the hope of stealing a few drops of semen with which to create more evil spirits. She was also reputed to prey on children and to attack travellers venturing into the desolate wildernesses where she resided.

Those fearing attacks by Lilith were advised in former times to scrawl a magic circle on the bedroom wall, completing it with the words 'Adam and Eve, barring Lilith'. Lilith was the subject of cult worship among some Jews until the 7th century AD.

See also SUCCUBUS.

lily The lily is associated with the Virgin Mary, and is widely understood to represent the qualities of purity, virginity and innocence. Another ancient Judaeo-Christian legend claims that the first lilies sprang up from the tears shed by Eve upon her expulsion from paradise.

It is thus considered unwise in many countries to spoil the blooms in any way, one superstition warning that any man who does this will be punished by the discovery that virgins within his own family have been similarly defiled. The lily (sometimes with stamen and pistils removed) has long been thought a suitable flower for the decoration of churches, and these religious connotations have promoted the idea that the lily provides protection against the forces of evil. The lily may be employed in spells designed to counter witchcraft, and will deter ghosts from entering the house if planted in the garden.

The use of lilies at funerals, symbolizing the restored innocence of the soul at death, has led to a more profound linking with the afterlife, and as a consequence many people will refuse to allow lilies into the house (although they are often seen at weddings as a symbol of purity). Dreaming of lilies may be thought to be ominous, but is in fact supposed to signify good fortune. In parts of eastern Europe the notions that lilies represent innocence and death are brought together in the tradition that lilies will spring from the grave of any person who has been executed for a crime he did not commit.

In folk medicine, lilies are used for the treatment of boils, venomous bites, burns, sores and various growths.

Clusters of bell-shaped lilies-of-the-valley, meanwhile, are commonly said to be the cups of the fairies, hung on stalks and forgotten by their owners. This particular variety of lily may be used to treat headaches and sore eyes and to improve the complexion.

See also FLEUR-DE-LIS.

lime *See* LINDEN.

linden (or lime) Deciduous tree that has a variety of magical associations in European folklore. Swedish tradition identifies the tree as a favourite haunt of wood spirits, while Germanic myth claims that it may provide a home for dwarfs or dragons – although another German belief suggests the presence of a linden tree guards the local community from evil. The tree plays an important role in the NIBELUNGENLIED: Siegfried was made invincible when showered in dragon's blood, but in just one place where a linden leaf settled on his shoulder he was rendered vulnerable.

Linden tea may be administered to treat hangovers, head-aches and insomnia.

lion As the king of the animals and a symbol of kingship, the lion has inspired many legends and folk beliefs. It is said to be virtually fearless, and most traditions connected with the lion refer to its strength and regal bearing (feeding a little lion heart to a child, for instance, will make it grow up healthy and courageous). Any warrior going into battle dressed in a lion's skin might congratulate himself on the certain knowledge that no harm could befall him. The animal is also respected for its reputed magnanimity towards its defeated enemies.

Tradition claims that a lion will never kill a fellow king, and the lions formerly kept in the menagerie at the Tower of London were said to be mysteriously attuned to the well-being of the English sovereign: if one of them died then an ailing monarch's days were surely numbered. Only when faced with a game cock, which refuses to acknowledge the lion's rank, will the animal betray anything like trepidation.

Lionesses are said to breed every seventh year, an event that is marked by a larger number of stillbirths among other species, including humans. Other traditions state that lions sleep with their eyes open, and that lion cubs are born dead and remain so until their parents breathe life into them.

Lions make many appearances in folk tales, sometimes as noble warrior heroes but occasionally, by way of contrast, as monstrous but slow-witted creatures easily duped by such wily lesser beasts as the fox, hare or jackal.

Lir In Irish mythology, the sea-god father of MANANNAN MAC LIR. His story bears some resemblance to those of the English LEAR and the Welsh LLYR. Lir sired four children – Fionguala (or Fionnuala), Aed (or Hugh), Conn and Fiachra – by his wife Aobh, but after she died he married her evil sister Aoife. Aoife, jealous of the love Lir had for his children, secretly turned them into swans and convinced Lir that they were disloyal to him. When Lir finally learned what Aoife had done he visited her father Bodh Bearg, king of the SIDHE, to ask him to punish her. After 900 years as swans the children were eventually restored to their human form when a woman from the south (Deac, a princess from Munster) married a man from the north (Lairgrén, king of Connacht). Their great age quickly overcame them in their human form, however, and all four died shortly afterwards and were buried together. In consequence of this legend it is considered a most unlucky act in Ireland for anyone to injure or kill a swan.

Little John *See* ROBIN HOOD.

little people *See* FAIRY; LEPRECHAUN.

Little Red Riding Hood Well-known European fairy tale about a wolf that seeks to devour a little girl and her grandmother. Absorbed into the oral storytelling tradition of many European countries, the modern version of the story can be traced back via the Brothers Grimm to Charles Perrault's *Tales of Mother Goose* (1697), although it may have come originally from an Italian source. A tale about a little girl wearing a red cap being devoured by a pack of wolves was in circulation in France as early as 1023.

The story begins with Little Red Riding Hood setting out to take food and drink to her ailing grandmother at her cottage in the forest. She is warned not to wander from her path but loiters to pick some pretty flowers by the wayside. While she is thus delayed the wolf devours Little Red Riding Hood's grandmother and then disguises itself in her clothes and awaits the girl's arrival. In the original version of the tale Little Red Riding Hood herself is devoured, but later variants introduced a woodsman who, hearing Little Red Riding Hood's cries, bursts in and kills the wolf. Little Red Riding Hood and her grandmother are then released unharmed when the wolf's stomach is slit open. This now generally accepted happy ending is in fact a later German addition.

The most famous episode of the tale features Little Red Riding Hood's arrival at her grandmother's, where she finds the disguised wolf in her grandmother's bed and marvels at the size of her ears ('All the better to hear you with'), eyes ('All the better to see you with'), and teeth ('All the better to eat you with!').

lizard The lizard has always been regarded in a somewhat equivocal light in folklore, as reflected in the range of positive and negative superstitions that have accumulated concerning the creature. Among Pacific peoples the creature is sometimes regarded with awe as a messenger of the gods, but elsewhere it is associated with the dead or with demons.

In medieval England many people feared lizards, thinking they were venomous (although another belief had it that lizards would warn sleeping humans of the approach of poisonous snakes). Accordingly, lizards became linked with the mythology of witches, as ingredients, familiars, and even as the progeny produced by couplings between witches and the DEVIL. A lasting relic of this mistrust is to be found in the surviving pan-European tradition that it is an ill omen for a lizard to cross the road in front of a

traveller. It is also most unlucky for a bride to see a lizard while on her way to the church, for her marriage will not be happy. In contrast, a woman who allows a lizard to run over her hand will enjoy increased skill at her needle.

Lizards are reputed to go blind during their long winter hibernation but to recover their sight on looking into the rising sun in the spring. The fact that lizards can regrow their tails has always inspired superstitious respect, and Italian tradition places special store by a lizard that is discovered to have two tails. The tails themselves are widely considered lucky talismans, and the tails of green lizards are occasionally worn in the right shoe to promote chances of happiness and prosperity. German folklore dictates that no one should kill a lizard, as it was a lizard that licked up Christ's blood when on the Cross.

Sleeping in a field with the mouth open is considered an open invitation for a lizard to crawl inside, but no lizard will do this if it is first licked all over, according to the Irish. A person who can bring himself to do this will be rewarded with a tongue that has remarkable powers of healing, particularly in reference to burns. Other beliefs around the world variously credit lizard-based medicines with the power to treat syphilis, impotence, warts and skin diseases, among sundry other complaints.

Lleu Llaw Gyffes Welsh folk hero who represents a Welsh equivalent of LUGH, and who was possibly the original for the LANCELOT of Arthurian myth. The son of ARIANRHOD and an unknown father, he was rejected by his mother, who only conceived him as the result of submitting to a test of her virginity. When he was born Arianrhod cursed him, saying he would have no name until she chose to give him one, would not bear arms unless she gave them to him, and would never win a human wife.

The baby was then raised in secret by Arianrhod's brother, the magician

GWYDION, who duped his sister into giving her son the name Lleu Llaw Gyffes ('the bright one of the skilful hand') by engineering a situation where she admired the lad's dexterity with a sling without realizing who he was. Lleu subsequently deceived his mother to the effect that her castle was under attack, thus persuading her to present him with weapons with which to defend it – there proved to be no attacking army but Lleu now had the right to bear arms.

When it came to countering Arianrhod's curse that Lleu would never win an earthly wife, Gwydion and Lleu's great-grandfather King Math used magic to provide Lleu with a wife by creating Blodeuwedd from blossom. She, however, proved faithless and was persuaded by her lover Gronw Pebr to bring about Lleu's death, having learned that her husband was fated to die as the result of a wound inflicted by a spear made during Sunday mass over a year and a day, and when he was neither inside nor outside and neither on horse nor on foot. Blodeuwedd accordingly coaxed Lleu to demonstrate how he might be vulnerable in this way. Lleu obligingly put one foot on a roofed bathtub and the other on a goat and was swiftly slain by Gronw using a specially made spear. Lleu's spirit escaped in the form of an eagle, but was reunited with his body by Gwydion. Thus restored, Lleu returned to kill the treacherous Gronw. Blodeuwedd was transformed into an owl for her crime.

Llyn y Fan Fach, the Lady of In Welsh mythology, a beautiful young woman who lived in the lake of Llyn y Fan Fachh near Llanddeusant. When the son of a local farmer sought her hand in marriage, she agreed to become his wife with the warning that if he hit her three times she would return immediately to her lake. After several years of marriage the husband had forgotten the warning and hit his wife three times, upon which she disappeared into the lake together with the oxen that came with her as her dowry, but leaving behind their three sons. One version of the legend has the heartbroken farmer trying to follow her into the water and drowning. Another adds that the wife returned from time to time to administer treatment to her sons when they were ill. They in their turn became famous physicians.

Llyr In Welsh mythology, a god of the underworld who was the equivalent of the English LEAR and the Irish LIR. Also known as Lludd Llaw Ereint ('Silver Hand'), he was identified as the father of MANAWYDDAN, BRAN THE BLESSED, BRANWEN, EFNISIEN and Nissien.

Loathly Lady In Celtic mythology, a supernatural figure often interpreted as representing the concept of SOVEREIGNTY. Usually depicted as a loathsome hag who is transformed into a lovely young woman upon being kissed, she appears in many legends as well as in Arthurian romance. Typically, she is encountered by several heroes all with a claim to the throne, and demands a kiss from them. Only one of their number consents to kiss her loathsome face, upon which she changes into a fair maiden, signifying the rightful claim of the hero to kingship. In Arthurian romance she tests those knights who seek the GRAIL, and among other deeds rebukes PERCEVAL for failing to ask the all-important Grail question. She is also sometimes identified as the wife of Arthur's heir GAWAIN, thus legitimizing his claim to succeed.

Loch Ness monster Legendary sea creature that is supposed to lurk in the depths of Loch Ness, one of the deepest bodies of fresh water in Scotland. Tales of the monster go back to the 7th century, when St Adamnan recorded how St Columba banished such a beast to the waters of Loch Ness. Further reports of sightings of a monster in Loch Ness were made over succeeding centuries, but it was not until 1933 that the legend became the subject of intense fascination following the publication of a photograph of what appeared to be a large unidentifiable creature in the loch. This most famous of many alleged photographs and films of the monster has, however, since been discredited as a hoax.

Most descriptions of the monster suggest something like a prehistoric reptile, with a long snakelike neck and one or more humps projecting above the surface of the water. Attempts to search the loch using sonar and other forms of modern technology have proved inconclusive, and scientists insist that there is insufficient food in the loch to support a community of such large creatures, unless they have access to the sea.

The legend has clear links with ancient tales about Celtic water horses of various kinds (see KELPIE). Similar traditions are associated with other bodies of water around the world, including Loch Morar in Scotland and Lough Nahooin in Ireland, as well as lakes in Canada, Siberia, central Africa and Scandinavia. Among the most well-attested of these is the water demon Ogopogo that is said to live in Lake Okanagan in British Columbia.

lodestone A rock with strong magnetic properties that has consequently been much valued for its apparent magical power. Lodestones, actually magnetite, were particularly prized in ALCHEMY and were formerly commonly worn as love charms or amulets, thought to bestow courage and determination. They were also worn by men to promote virility and by women to make childbirth easier. In Cornwall, where lodestones have frequently been found, such rocks were formerly carried as a cure by those suffering from sciatica.

See also MAGNETIC MOUNTAIN.

Logan stone A large stone that is so balanced that it may actually be rocked to and fro at the slightest touch. There are several such stones in Cornwall, among other places. Folklore inevitably places some importance on these rare natural phenomena. Such is the latent power of these stones, they are reputed to be favourite meeting places for covens, and it is said that merely touching one of them nine times at midnight is enough to transform a person into a witch. Rocking a child suffering from rickets at midnight on the Logan stone at Nancledra, St Ives, is supposed to effect a cure (although the treatment will not work if the child was born out of wedlock).

Lohengrin German folk hero, called the Knight of the Swan, whose story is today best known from Wagner's opera, first produced in 1850. Identified as the son of PERCEVAL and brought up among the knights of the ROUND TABLE, he arrives in Antwerp in a boat drawn by a swan and agrees to marry Elsa of Brabant on condition that she does not ask him his name or lineage. She does so, however, on their wedding night and he, after answering her questions, vanishes forever. The swan returns to fetch him and is restored by Lohengrin to its original form as Elsa's brother Gottfried, who had been turned into a swan by the sorceress Ortrud.

Loki In Norse mythology, the wicked trickster god of the AESIR. Identified as the son of the giant Farbauti and Laufey and as the brother of ODIN himself, he was credited with helping to create the first humans. However, he was also guilty of bringing about the death of BALDUR, and became associated with evil. The other gods assembled against him and he was eventually chained to a rock in an underground cavern, guarded over by a dragon, whose poison dripped continually upon him. His struggles to break free from this imprisonment were said to be the cause of the earthquakes that periodically shook the world. Married first to Glut, who gave birth to two daughters, and then to the giantess Angrboda, who bore HEL, FENRIR and JORMUNGANDR the Midgard Serpent, he was fated to die during the final battle of RAGNAROK at the hands of HEIMDAL.

Lord of Misrule British medieval and Tudor tradition that involved the mock crowning of some lowly person, who then had licence to wield power over everyone high and low for a specified period (usually a single day). The crowning of the Lord of Misrule (alternatively called the King of Misrule or, in Scotland, the Abbot of Unreason) was usually associated with the Christmas festivities, and this reversal of the usual order of rank was often treated as an occasion for general anarchy and uproar. The reign of the Lord of Misrule might last the entire 12 days of Christmas or else extend from All Hallows' Day (1 November) to Candlemas (2 February). Sometimes an entire court was appointed, complete with HOBBYHORSES, DRAGONS and musicians. The custom, which was observed in royal courts, noble houses, law courts and elsewhere throughout Britain, was probably derived ultimately from the Roman Saturnalia.

It is possible that in early times the person chosen to be the Lord of Misrule was actually sacrificed at the end of his reign in order to guarantee the continued prosperity of the community through the remainder of the winter.

See also FEAST OF FOOLS.

lotus Name shared by several species of plant that have been credited from ancient times with a range of magical properties. The lotus of ancient Egyptian myth was a variety of water lily, while the Hindus and Chinese identified it as a form of water bean, and the Greeks applied the name to a North African shrub that produced edible fruit. Islamic tradition describes a lotus tree standing in the seventh heaven, on the right hand of God's throne, while Egyptian and Hindu belief claimed that God himself was born from a lotus flower. Lotus flowers were also reputed to spring up from the footprints of the Buddha. Chinese Buddhist tradition depicts paradise as a lake in whose waters the souls of the dead are reincarnated as lotus flowers.

The Greeks, meanwhile, emphasized the soporific properties of the plant, and the legend that those who ate lotus fruit would forget their friends, homes and everything else about their past life has persisted through the centuries (as described in Tennyson's famous poem 'The Lotus-Eaters', itself based on an episode in Homer's epic poem *The Odyssey*.

love The folklore of all the world's cultures is rich with charms, potions, spells, superstitions and taboos catering for the multifarious needs of the lovelorn. These items may be grouped roughly into three categories: magic that may be used to learn the identity of a future partner; magic that may be employed to win a specific person's love; and magic that may be applied to keep or test a partner's love.

In order to glean information about – and perhaps even a vision of – a future partner, folklore recommends a range of possible courses. These vary from throwing the peel of an apple over the shoulder to see what initial may be discerned from the shape it assumes on the floor (the first initial of the future partner's name) to chanting various charms on going to bed, and sleeping with certain flowers, pieces of wedding cake or a mirror beneath the pillow. Other procedures will reveal the direction from which a future lover will come, and even what trade he or she is likely to be engaged in.

Measures that may be taken in an attempt to win over a particular person by magic include stealing their hat band and wearing it as a garter, feeding them certain foods or potions noted for their aphrodisiac properties, and casting a spell over a sample of their hair, blood or nail-parings. The magic of knots may also be employed, or the help of certain saints or demons invoked. Alternatively, simply reciting the name of the loved one over and over may have the desired effect.

Once focused on one particular potential lover, their fidelity may be checked by such means as exchanging LIFE TOKENS or plucking the petals off a daisy while alternating the phrases 'He/she loves me' and 'He/she loves me not'. In order to avoid the accidental risk of a break-up, couples might also observe such taboos as refusing to be photographed together at any time before the wedding, not kissing when one partner is seated, not exchanging gifts of shoes or knives and, in the case of girls, not taking the last piece of bread and butter from a plate (unless it is specifically offered to them).

See also HALLOWE'EN; ST VALENTINE'S DAY.

luck The role of luck, that indefinable governing factor in virtually every field of human activity, is recognized and respected in every culture throughout the world. Inevitably, much folklore is concerned with the preservation and improvement of one's luck, and many taboos, such as avoiding walking under LADDERS or putting up umbrellas indoors, are observed to avoid bad luck.

Many people believe themselves to be naturally lucky or else fated to misfortune, or at least admit to believing in lucky or unlucky streaks, in which fate seems to be temporarily either for or against them. In either case they may place great store by 'lucky' charms, amulets and talismans personal to themselves, ranging from the ubiquitous horseshoe, rabbit's foot and four-leafed clover to treasured items of clothing and ritualistic actions (such as always getting out of bed on a particular side or touching wood when ill fortune has been risked). Superstition claims that black cats and certain other animals can confer excellent luck in given circumstances, while others, such as single magpies, take luck away. There are also 'lucky' or 'unlucky' buildings, ships, roads, plays, alignments of the planets and times in the cycle of the moon. Other traditions include lucky or unlucky numbers (notably the ominous thirteen), colours, gemstones and dates in the calendar.

People throughout the world commonly wish their friends 'good luck' when undertaking a challenge, be it a driving test, a sporting contest or a business deal, but there are circumstances when somewhat perversely this is seen in itself to be tempting fate. Actors and actresses thus do the opposite, expressing the traditional hope that a colleague will 'break a leg'. Others nervous of being wished good luck include fishermen and gamblers.

Psychologists have often noted the irony that in an age when rationality is the ruling credo, people should commonly place such reliance upon the random and largely uncontrollable actions of fate. The wisest observers, however, see this as entirely healthy, an acknowledgement of unknown possibilities and influences. Scientific exploration of the concept of people's perceptions of luck seems to suggest a psychological process at work: 'lucky' people are generally more confident in facing challenges, while those who complain of being fated to failure are by nature less sure of their abilities, and thus more likely to be unsuccessful.

ludki In Slavic folklore, a breed of little people, resembling DWARFS. They are generally believed to be benevolent towards humans. They enjoy music and singing, but are reputed to detest the sound of church bells.

Lugh (or **Lug**) In Irish mythology, a sun god who represented the victory of light over dark. The grandson of BALOR and the son of ETHNIU and Cian, Lugh sided with the TUATHA DE DANANN in their war against the FOMORIANS, led by Balor, and took up the leadership of their army after NUADU was wounded. Acclaimed for his many skills in both the arts and in warfare, he was acknowledged king of the Tuatha after Nuada's death. It was a blow in the eye from Lugh during the second battle of Mag Tuired that brought about the death of Balor and thus ended the war. Lugh also gave succour to CUCHULAINN, fighting on his behalf at one point to allow the hero some rest. According to some accounts, Lugh was actually Cuchulainn's father.

See also LLEU LLAW GYFFES; LUGH-NASADH.

Lughnasadh One of the four major festivals in the Celtic calendar, celebrating the yearly harvest. Dedicated to the god LUGH and to his foster-mother Tailtiu, the goddess who died from exhaustion after clearing the plains of Ireland for agriculture, it was celebrated on 1 August and has strong historical links with Teltown on the River Boyne (itself named after Tailtiu). The date was marked by various sacred games, and by livestock sales and the hiring of farm hands. In some parts of Ireland it was also a time when couples might enter into officially recognized temporary marriages without becoming bound legally to their partner. After the coming of Christianity, Lughnasadh was redefined as the festival of Lammas (*see* LAMMAS DAY).

See also BELTANE; IMBOLC; SAMHAIN.

lycanthropy *See* WEREWOLF.

Lyonesse In Arthurian legend, a lost land located somewhere between the west coast of Cornwall and the Scilly Isles. Apparently influenced by ancient legends about the drowned city of Atlantis, it was reputed to have been the birthplace of TRISTAM, and was sometimes claimed to be the location of what remained of the court of King Arthur following Arthur's departure, the sea surging over the knights to prevent ordinary mortals joining them. Tradition claims that it included the City of Lions and no less than 140 churches.

M

Mab In British folklore, the queen of the FAIRIES. The origins of her name are obscure, but it may be a development of Maeve (*see* MEDB) or else the Welsh *mab* (meaning 'baby'), from the belief that she acts as the fairies' midwife. She is also believed to be the creator of mortals' dreams, but is also sometimes accused of mischief-making and with exchanging human babies for CHANGELINGS. *See also* TITANIA.

Mabinogion Celebrated post-medieval compilation of Welsh legends, and one of the most important repositories of Celtic folk history. Many of the tales were told originally in two 14th-century sources, *The White Book of Rhydderch* and *The Red Book of Hergest*, themselves probably reflecting a much older Celtic oral tradition going back at least to Roman times. The title of the collection, the *Mabinogion* (roughly meaning 'tales of childhood'), is a relatively late detail going back only as far as Lady Charlotte Guest's 1849 English translation of the work.

The *Mabinogion* comprises 11 tales, belonging to three groups. The first and probably the oldest of these groups is divided into four 'branches', and includes legends surrounding the mythical Welsh Prince PWYLL, BRANWEN, MANAWYDDAN, and Math, lord of Gwynedd. The second group includes the story of CULHWCH and OLWEN, and incorporates some of the earliest accounts of Arthurian myth in Welsh literature. The last three of these tales, 'The Lady of the Fountain', 'Gereint Son of Erbin' and 'Peredur the Son of Evrawc' (which includes an early version of the GRAIL legend), betray Norman-French influence and have been attributed on occasion to Chrétien de Troyes. At this early stage in its evolution, Arthur's court is attended by warriors from ancient Irish Celtic legend and fairytale heroes as well as more familiar names from later Arthurian stories. The 1849 English translation also includes a tale entitled 'Taliesin', about the 6th-century bard of that name.

Mabon In Welsh mythology, a 'Wondrous Youth' who became a cult figure among the Celtic peoples of the British Isles. According to an account of his life in the story of CULHWCH and OLWEN, he was the son of MODRON and would appear to have inherited many of the attributes of the Greek god Apollo, being represented as a hunter and harpist. The legend goes back to the beginning of time and describes how Mabon (whose name means 'son') was seized from his mother when just three days old. The search for him is led by Sir KAY and BEDIVERE, who question many animals and birds and are ultimately informed by a salmon of Mabon's whereabouts (in a prison in Caer Loyw, understood to signify the otherworld). Culhwch effects his rescue and in return Mabon helps Culhwch find Olwen and win her as his bride.

Macha In Irish mythology, one of the three aspects of MORRIGAN. Macha herself was considered to have three separate guises – those of Macha, wife of Nemed (leader of the third invasion of Ireland); Macha the Red; and Macha, the secret wife of Crunnchu. Despite the fact that she was heavily pregnant, Macha was obliged to race against the king's horses after Crunnchu boasted that she was faster. She won the race but then died giving birth to her two children. As she breathed her last she cursed the kingdom of Ulster, prophesying that henceforth its warriors would be as weak as women in the advanced stages of labour and unable to fight for five days and four nights. Because of this Ulster sought the aid of CUCHULAINN, whose origins lay outside the kingdom. In her guise as Macha the Red, she was a goddess of battle, and warriors once stuck the heads of their defeated enemies upon the Pole of Macha. According to another legend, she met her death at the hands of BALOR.

Madoc ap Owain Gwynedd In Welsh mythology, a prince who was famed for his legendary voyages across the Atlantic Ocean. Tradition claims that Madoc, the son of Owain Gwynedd, reached America in the 12th century, making a landfall at Mobile Bay in Alabama in the year 1170. A lost Native American tribe called the Madon were reputed to be his descendants, and fortifications north of Mobile Bay have been claimed to have a passing resemblance to pre-Norman Welsh castles. The legend of Madoc's discovery of America appears to date from the 15th century.

Maelduine In Irish mythology, a legendary hero who embarks on a long voyage of adventure seeking vengeance for the murder of his father AILILL. During the course of his voyages in a skin boat he explores the ISLANDS OF THE BLEST, but he and his crew eventually become homesick for Ireland, and after three years and seven months return home, having spared the lives of Ailill's murderers on the advice of a hermit.

Maeve *See* MEDB.

magic The harnessing and employment of supernatural forces either through special knowledge of the occult arts or innate natural power. The notion that sorcerers, wizards and others can gain access to elemental forces is very ancient, possibly predating the development of the first religions, and is common to virtually all the world's cultures. It is often believed that only certain individuals can exercise magical skills, and that these practitioners must observe certain taboos and purification rituals in order to work magic effectively. These commonly include sexual abstinence and fasting.

There are many different kinds of magic, some directed towards the protection of the whole community (influencing the weather, promoting the fertility of livestock and so forth) and some towards the fulfilment of an individual sorcerer's own desires or those of their clients. Activities grouped under the general heading of magic range from ALCHEMY and the casting of SPELLS to the ability to foretell future events and converse with spirits through a wide range of rituals, sacrifices, potions and such devices as magic circles. The practice of magic is sometimes categorized as 'black' or 'white', black denoting mal-evolent magic (typically worked with the assistance of evil spirits) and white denoting magic of a more benevolent nature. Many sorcerers were reputed to keep books called grimoires, in which the ingredients and procedure of their spells were recorded.

Magic plays a significant role in countless fairy tales and folk myths. Sometimes the ability to succeed through magic is attributable to a particular god, fairy godmother or supernatural being who feels sympathy for the hero. On other occasions the source is left unclear, creating the impression that the hero enjoys access to magic solely by virtue of his own moral strength or other inborn qualities.

See also SYMPATHETIC MAGIC; WITCH-CRAFT.

magic carpet In Arabian and Asian folklore, a flying carpet that will transport its owner instantly to any place he or she chooses. Flying carpets figure as plot motifs in numerous tales, most famously in the *Arabian Nights*, in which Prince Houssain owns such an object. Others credited with the possession of such carpets include King Solomon, who was said to own a carpet of green silk large enough to seat his entire court, the men and women standing to the right of his throne and his vassal spirits to the left. As Solomon and his court flew through the air flocks of birds sheltered them from the glare of the sun with outspread wings.

magnetic mountain Mythical mountain island that draws ships towards it apparently through the power of magnetism. Tales of such mountains go back at least to medieval times, and are mentioned in such works as the 14th-century *Travels of Sir John Mandeville*. It was feared that any ship venturing too close to such a mountain would have its iron nails pulled out by magnetic force, leading to the wreck of the vessel, and thus many seafarers reported sailing on ships that were held together with wooden pegs and cord rather than iron fixings. The notion was probably inspired originally by unexplained variations in compass bearings, although the presence of magnetic rocks in the Black Cuillin mountains of Skye and elsewhere has long been known to affect compasses on passing ships.

See also FLOATING ISLAND.

magpie The magpie is widely thought to be dishonest, unlucky and vain, and has evil associations in many cultures. According to legends associated with the biblical story of Noah, for instance, the magpie was ejected from the ark for chattering too much, while another Christian tradition blames the bird for refusing to wear full mourning at Christ's Crucifixion. The bird's piebald colouring suggests its perverse nature, which combines the white of the blameless dove and the jet black of the more ominous raven, both of which left the ark before the other animals and were thus left unbaptized by the waters of the Flood.

Popular superstition holds that it is most unlucky to see a single magpie, but less alarming to encounter a pair. Particular dread is associated with seeing a lone magpie when setting out on a journey (particularly if one is setting out for church), and the sight of one of the birds circling a house and croaking is thought to be a portent of death. Protective measures that may be taken on seeing a lone magpie include bowing to it and politely wishing it good morning, taking off one's hat to it, or immediately making the sign of the cross.

There are several variations in the interpretations that may be placed on the sight of a given number of magpies, of which the following English rhyme is perhaps the best known: 'One for sorrow, two for joy; three for a girl, four for a boy; five for silver, six for gold; and seven for a story never to be told.' A traditional variant of this runs: 'One for sorrow, two for mirth; three for a wedding, and four for a birth; five for a christening, six for a dearth; seven for heaven, eight for hell; and nine for the Devil's own self.' Coming across a large group of magpies busy chattering away to each other is an ill omen, for the birds are probably plotting some evil or other (Scottish tradition, indeed, claims that every magpie holds a drop of the Devil's blood under its tongue). To understand what the birds may be saying, one course of action is to scratch a magpie's tongue and drop into the scratch a drop of human blood, which will reputedly enable the bird to speak.

In China, however, the bird is actually considered to be a harbinger of good fortune, in marked contrast to the mixed reputation it enjoys in Europe, and it is said that dire misfortune will befall anyone who kills it (a belief that is also shared throughout Europe). In North America, meanwhile, the bird is respected for its hardiness, being one of the few species that do not migrate in the cold season, and it appears as a trickster hero in a number of folk tales.

Mag Tuired In Irish mythology, the site of two legendary battles fought by the TUATHA DE DANANN. The first battle resulted in victory over the FIRBOLGS, but also left NUADA, leader of the Tuatha de Danann, with severe wounds. Nuada was either slain or forced to abdicate following the second battle of Mag Tuired, which was settled by single combat between Nuada's successor LUGH and the one-eyed giant BALOR. Lugh secured victory for the Tuatha de Danann by killing Balor with a shot from his sling.

Mahabharata Sanskrit heroic epic that along with the RAMAYANA is one of the two great epic poems of ancient India. Written around 400 AD and attributed to the scribe Vyasa, it was probably derived from much older oral tradition. It relates, at great length, episodes that occurred during the war between two rival families, the Kauravas and the Pandavas. The events upon which it was based are thought to have taken place as early as 1500 BC. Comprising some 100,000 couplets, it is divided into 18 sections, and includes the *Bhagavadgita* among its most sacred passages.

Celebrated episodes include the romance of NALA AND DAMAYANTI, the marriage of Santanu and Satyavati, and the climactic battle in which the Kauravas are finally destroyed. A final appended section details the genealogy of Krishna (an incarnation of the god Vishnu).

maiden's garland A garland of white paper or linen, often embellished with streamers and a single white glove, which was formerly carried at English funerals of unmarried women of blameless reputation. Such garlands were hung on display in the church for many months or even years after the funeral. Tradition had it that they should not be removed but allowed to rot gradually to pieces, and

then be buried in the graveyard. To remove them at any earlier stage was deemed very unlucky.

Maid Marian *See* ROBIN HOOD.

Manannan mac Lir In Irish mythology, a god of the sea who is sometimes included among the company of the TUATHA DE DANANN. The son of LIR and one of the oldest of all the gods, he constructed the SIDHE for the Tuatha after their defeat by the MILESIANS. He is sometimes identified as the guardian of the ISLANDS OF THE BLEST and of the GRAIL, and as one of the early keepers of the HALLOWS. His wife FAND was stolen by CUCHULAINN, but he himself sired Mongan, the future king and warrior, by Caintigerna, wife of Fiachna, the king of Ulster, and was reputed to have seduced many women by coming to them at night in the guise of a seabird or heron. His home was said by some to be located in the Isle of Man, of which he was the first king.

See also MANAWYDDAN.

Manawyddan In Welsh mythology, the son of LLYR who represents a Welsh equivalent of MANANNAN MAC LIR. Having married RHIANNON, he lifted the curse laid upon Dyfed by LLWYD in revenge for the cruel treatment meted out to Rhiannan's former betrothed, Gwawl, by her first husband PWYLL. A number of tales are told about the adventures shared by Manawyddan, Rhiannon, his cousin PRYDERI and Pryderi's wifes, Cigfa He is depicted as a shrewd and skilled craftsman.

mandrake (or mandragora) The distinctive root of the mandrake, which to many eyes resembles a human figure, was one of the most valued ingredients in medieval medicine, and has been credited in folklore with all manner of magical properties. The somewhat grotesque root of this member of the potato family was reputedly used in witches' brews, and was alleged to have various soporific, aphrodisiac and purgative powers (the root does, in fact, contain an alkaloid that can suppress pain and promote sleep).

The Egyptians called the mandrake the phallus of the field, while the Arabs called it the devil's testicles, clear evidence that the plant had long been recognized as a potent influence upon sexual drive and appetite. The English, meanwhile, nicknamed the plant the love apple. In the Bible, Jacob's two wives – one barren and the other too old to conceive – both become pregnant after acquiring some mandrakes. The mandrake may also be used in spells and potions to increase one's wealth by magic, to fix broken bones, to ease the pain of toothache or rheumatism, as an anaesthetic before operations, to cure depression, to enable the dying to recover, to prevent fits and even to give up smoking. Overdoses of mandrake will, however, drive the patient insane.

In witchcraft, a mandrake root dug up, watered with human blood and embellished with berries for eyes and mouth is said to acquire the power of speech, and will reveal the future, open locks and locate gold. Mere possession of a mandrake root was, in consequence, enough evidence to have a suspect condemned to death as a witch in former times.

Care has to be taken in pulling up the root of the mandrake, for any person who attempts this with their own hands will be struck down dead shortly after, or alternatively will never be able to have children. Thus, the conventional method for gathering the roots is to get a dog to dig them up. As the root leaves the soil it is said to utter a terrible shriek, which is enough to kill or drive any living thing mad. Adding to the rather sinister image of the plant is the ancient European belief that the mandrake only grows naturally under a gallows, springing from the semen falling from the decomposing bodies of executed felons.

Man in the Moon Mythical figure whose face can, according to tradition, be made out in the shadows on the surface of the MOON. Interpretations of his identity vary from culture to culture. Judaeo-Christian tradition claims that he is a man punished for collecting sticks on the sabbath: he can be seen still, leaning on his fork, on which his bundle of sticks is still lodged. Some observers claim that he is also accompanied by his dog. Another explanation claims that he is Cain and that the dog who accompanies him is the Devil himself. Variants elsewhere in the world include the notion that the Man in the Moon is actually an old woman at her cooking, or is otherwise a hare or a frog. Scandinavian legend, meanwhile, identifies two figures, claiming them to be Hjuki and Bil (possibly the originals of Jack and Jill), who together with their pail found refuge on the moon from their cruel father.

Superstition warns that it is inadvisable to point at the Man in the Moon, as he may take offence at this and seek retribution in some way. If the crime is committed nine times then the offender risks not being allowed into heaven.

manta In the folklore of South America, a species of monster that is reputed to lurk in various Chilean lakes. Unless appeased with suitable offerings it will thrash the water and attack any mortal who ventures too near the lake's edge. It can only be killed by piercing it with the thorny branches of the quisco bush.

marigold The golden-flowered marigold, allegedly so named because the Virgin Mary wore one on her breast, has been credited with various properties over the years. Some say that the flower can be used as a love charm (hence the alternative names husbandman's dial and summer's bride), and it is sometimes included in wedding bouquets because it represents fidelity and endurance in love. Others claim that the yellow petals will ward off malevolent interference from witches, while dreaming of marigolds signifies approaching riches.

A note of caution about the plant is sounded by one West Country superstition, which claims that anyone who picks marigolds – or even so much as looks at them – runs the risk of developing a weakness for strong drink, and the plants themselves are sometimes known by the alternative name 'drunkards'. Elsewhere in Europe, though, the marigold is variously associated with unrequited love, sorrow, pain and anger. In Mexico it is said to have sprung up from the blood of those slaughtered by the Spaniards under the conquistador leader Cortés.

The flower of the marigold is alleged to be effective in easing the pain of wasp and bee stings when rubbed on the skin, and powdered marigold was formerly used to ease the ague. Inhaling the scent of the marigold or taking a little distilled water of the blossoms is reputed to cure headaches and depression.

Mari Lwyd In Welsh folklore, a HOBBY-HORSE (actually a garlanded horse skull, real or wooden, mounted on a be-ribboned pole) that is traditionally paraded through the streets at Christmas time. During the course of the ceremony, the hobbyhorse is taken from house to house, and the occupants are challenged to cap the lines of a riddling dialogue song performed by the Mari. If they fail the Mari and the bearers must be invited inside and given refreshments. The custom is thought to have developed out of the legend that Mari Lwyd was the horse that had to be put out of the stable in which Christ was born. Ever since then she has wandered the earth looking for another place to shelter. The name Mari Lwyd may be variously interpreted as meaning 'Grey Mary' or 'grey mare'.

Mark In Arthurian legend, the king of Cornwall, who is one of the main characters in the story of TRISTAM and ISOLDE. Mark sends Tristam to Ireland to fetch his betrothed, Isolde, to him in Cornwall. Unfortunately, a love potion meant for the bridal couple is accidentally drunk by

Tristam and Isolde and they fall in love. Subsequently Mark is deceived into thinking Isolde is faithful to him through the ruse of substituting the virgin Brangaine in Isolde's place in the wedding bed. One version of the legend has Mark eventually realizing that he has been betrayed and consequently ordering the death of Tristam.

marriage As one of the crucial rites of passage, marriage has special folkloric significance in all the world's cultures. Marriage ceremonies are often elaborate, emphasizing the social importance of the event, and are often celebrated by the whole community as well as the bridal couple themselves and their families.

Marriage customs vary considerably from culture to culture, but most procedures include a variety of symbolic acts, such as the exchanging of rings or the drinking of wine together, as well as the speaking of special set words. In some societies child marriages are widely accepted, and it is recognized practice for partners to be selected by the parents, usually from the same social rank or tribal unit (endogamy). In others, marriage is discouraged before middle age, and partners ideally come from outside the immediate social unit (exogamy). Mutual attraction may play a major role, or none at all. Often women are advised to marry early, while men are recommended to delay getting married because this can entail a loss in hunting prowess. In some parts of the world it is expected for people to take more than one spouse at a time. Usually this relates to a man taking several wives (polygyny), although elsewhere, but much more rarely, it is the woman who is expected to take more than one partner in marriage (polyandry). Sometimes scores of couples may get married in mass ceremonies.

The whole procedure of finding a partner, getting engaged and then finally marrying is surrounded with a wealth of superstitions, taboos and customs. Many cultures have taboos warning against marriage to blood relatives, although these taboos often go beyond what is genetically inadvisable to include marriages between sets of brothers and sisters, for instance. In former times, if a man faced a choice between two sisters, he was often put under pressure to marry the elder as to do otherwise was considered to be tantamount to an insult.

Choosing a date for the wedding is the first hurdle a newly engaged couple must cross. This should not be lightly undertaken as certain months and, indeed, days are luckier than others for getting married. May is a month particularly to be avoided, as this has been associated with rites honouring the dead since Roman times. The periods of Lent and Advent are also deemed to be unlucky. June, however, is ideal, particularly if the wedding is timed to take place when the moon is on the wane. Even the day of the week is important, as an old English rhyme explains: 'Monday for wealth, Tuesday for health, Wednesday the best day of all; Thursday for crosses, Friday for losses, Saturday for no luck at all.' Once the date of the wedding has been decided it should not be changed, as this is very bad luck. Neither should the happy couple attend church to hear their banns read as this is also thought to be a bad omen.

The intervening weeks or months between the engagement and the wedding is the time for making the many preparations that are usual for the big day. Folk belief is full of suggestions about the selection of bridesmaids, of the wedding dress, of flowers for the bouquet and so forth, and few women choosing 'traditional' weddings in the English-speaking world make their way to the altar without the required 'Something old, something new, something borrowed, something blue'. Further superstitions surround the making of the wedding cake and the choosing of wedding rings.

As the bride leaves the house, it was once common in England for the doorstep to be washed with boiling water in the belief that this would hasten the marriage of the first single girl whose dress was thereby dampened (usually one of the bridesmaids). In times gone by, wedding parties generally made their way to the church on foot, and various superstitions concerned their route and events that might happen on the way, such as meeting certain animals or, if things went badly wrong, cross-eyed people and others suspected of having the power of the EVIL EYE. Among the most inauspicious persons to meet on the journey were clergymen, policemen, doctors, lawyers, blind men and funeral mourners. In previous centuries, to keep evil spirits at bay attendants fired guns into the air at regular intervals, or else a charge of powder was set off on the local anvil as the wedding party passed. The bride's face was covered with a veil, so as to conceal her beauty from evil spirits who might otherwise interfere with the ceremony. A version of the 'first foot' custom now confined to New Year also used to be observed by such wedding processions. This involved the groom giving a coin or a gift of some food to the first person he met on the way to the church (and the bride doing likewise on leaving it).

According to weather lore, it is a good omen for the sun to shine on a bride on her wedding day and also if it snows. If it is windy, then the marriage will be plagued by misunderstandings, and if it rains the couple concerned will be anything but happy. This tradition dates back to the days when marriage ceremonies were often conducted at the entrance to a church and brides risked getting a thorough soaking.

During the service itself a few tears from the bride are considered a good omen (although confusingly an alternative tradition warns that a bride who cries on her wedding day is fated to cry throughout her married life). Once safely in church, the couple may take heart if the service is interrupted by a child crying, as this is generally held to be a good omen for the marriage. The groom and the best man should take care, however, not to drop the wedding ring, as this is deemed to be unlucky.

The throwing of confetti (or, in former times, rice) as the couple leave the church is meant to promote their chances of having children in due course. The couple should not take the same route that they took on arriving at the church and, in former times, were discouraged from walking through a lych gate, where coffins were once laid. Bad luck will also follow if they should happen to encounter a funeral procession or a pig on their way to the reception, but good luck is certain if they encounter a chimney sweep (who is entitled to give the bride a kiss), a black cat, a grey horse or an elephant.

The giving of presents to a newly married couple at their reception has its roots in the ancient custom of presenting the bride and groom with fruit as a symbol of fertility. Certain presents, particularly knives, should not be given though, as they are unlucky.

When the time comes for the newlyweds to depart on their honeymoon it is usual for the bride to toss her bouquet to the bridesmaids and other unwed females. This is a relatively recent tradition, probably invented in the USA in the early years of the 20th century (in some regions the bride throws one of her shoes). The idea is that the girl who catches the bouquet (or shoe) will be the next to marry. Similarly, in the days when few couples went away after their wedding, before retiring for the night the bride used to allow one of the young men present to remove her loosened garter, which he would then wear in his hat before offering it to a girl of his choice.

Bridegrooms to this day carry their new brides over the threshold, even if they are not entering their own home but are spending their first night in a hotel somewhere. This tradition dates from Roman times, when it indicated that a bride sacrificed her virginity with becoming reluctance, although it has since become a more generally 'lucky' act. One suggestion is that it dates from much earlier times when grooms were given to snatching and carrying off wives against their will and had actually to carry them kicking and screaming into their future home.

mascot An emblematic design or object that is taken to represent the luck of a particular ship, team, regiment and so forth. Motorists often prize the mascots that adorn their bonnets or dashboards, while ships' crews show the profoundest respect for FIGUREHEADS and ships' cats, and sports teams may put their faith in an animal or small child paraded in the team colours. Similarly, army regiments throughout the world proudly parade such mascots as goats and dogs on ceremonial occasions. In the last case, the totemic role of such mascots links them with the standards that were once carried by the Roman legions and other armies of the ancient world, objects that had a very clear purpose as rallying points and that could also provide magical protection in times of crisis. In all cases, mascots are considered repositories of luck, which may be kissed or touched for psychological reassurance. The loss of a mascot may be considered very serious and thereby actually trigger a decline in the fortunes of those who value it.

The word 'mascot' itself is thought to come originally from the Provençal *masco* (meaning 'sorcerer').

mask Masks have been used in ceremonial and religious rituals throughout the world since ancient times. Cave paintings suggest prehistoric people used masks in celebrating the elemental forces governing nature, and in several early civilizations such as that of ancient Egypt the dead were buried with masks representing the deceased as they were in life in the belief that this would assist in their reincarnation in the afterworld. Masks have also long been used both in dramatic performances and in religious rites in many Asian cultures, including those of Burma, China, Japan, Java, Thailand, Sri Lanka and Tibet. In New Guinea masks were formerly carved in the likeness of dead relatives and covered in the skin of the deceased person so that they might be worn by descendants as protection from evil. Elsewhere terrifying masks may be worn during initiation rites or during services of exorcism in the belief that they will frighten away any demons present. Wearing a mask may also be an attempt to identify (or be identified) with a particular god or spirit and thus gain access (or be understood to have access) to their supernatural power.

In the West masks have survived in use chiefly in dance and drama, recollecting their use in ancient Greek theatre and in medieval religious plays, for example. They are still used in a variety of folk dances. Masks are also worn throughout Europe in the course of various carnivals and festivals celebrating the summer and winter solstices, as well as in witchcraft, often taking the form of grotesque animal heads complete with horns.

master thief Archetypal folk hero who is the central character in numerous folk tales around the world. He is usually depicted as a good-for-nothing young man who establishes a reputation as a cunning master thief through successfully meeting a series of challenges. In one of the best known such tales, for instance, he faces the challenge of stealing in succession his master's horse, the sheets from his bed and the ring from his wife's finger.

Often little attempt is made to justify the nefarious feats of the central character – it is the ingenuity with which he overcomes the most difficult of challenges that is the focus of interest. Among the most notable master thieves of folklore are ALI BABA and the eponymous hero of 'Jack and the Beanstalk'.

May Day The first day of May, formerly the Roman Feast of Floralia and Celtic fire festival (*see* BELTANE). It is widely considered to be one of the most magical days of the year, and is still marked in many countries by a public holiday. The day is associated with a host of folk beliefs and customs, most of which celebrate the return of the sun and summer's victory over winter.

In years gone by, the date was marked by large processions of people making their way in the early hours to nearby woods, drinking and blowing horns as they went. Street parties still take place in villages and cities throughout Europe, and include dancing round the MAYPOLE, MUMMERS' PLAYS, music and other forms of riotous entertainment with their roots in ancient fertility rites. Decorations of green foliage and garlands of flowers – symbols of fertility – are carried or arranged in honour of the continual rebirth of nature. Symbolic battles were once fought to represent the struggle between winter and summer, summer always coming out the victor and taking the place of glory (now occupied by the May Queen, a girl chosen for her wholesome beauty who is ceremonially crowned with flowers). Today this old tradition is kept alive in the many folk games that are played around this time of year. In the past, English May Day festivities were often presided over by celebrants dressed as the GREEN MAN or else as ROBIN HOOD and Maid Marian. The aim of all these elaborate festivities is generally to ensure the good luck of the coming harvest and to protect the welfare of both livestock and humans.

The May Day festival, with its pagan origins, was temporarily abandoned in England in the mid-17th century after the Puritans banned it and burned all the maypoles, but the popularity of the event ensured its revival after the Restoration.

May Day has always been considered a prime date for the purposes of divination and for the practice of love magic. Unmarried boys and girls may gaze into wells at noon on May Day and discern therein the face of their future partners. Washing the face in the dew on May Day morning is particularly recommended for keeping the complexion clear and generally promoting personal beauty. Singeing cattle with a lighted straw, meanwhile, will grant them protection against evil over the coming year, and cows should also be bled on this day. Boiling cuttings taken from herbs on the first day of May together with a few hairs from a cow's tail will ensure that the butter will be invulnerable to interference from witches throughout the year. If it rains on May Day then a farmer must expect to lose half of the milk yield of his herd. An old Irish tradition advises against selling or giving away fire, salt or water on May Day as this is guaranteed to bring ill luck down on the house.

Other folk customs formerly associated with May Day included 'May birching', which involved the hanging up of sprigs of green foliage at each house – the choice of tree reflecting local opinion of the residents (greenery from a hawthorn, lime or pear was a compliment, but a bough of thorn, holly or plum could be interpreted as insulting). In some places, notably Oxford, dawn is greeted on May Day with the singing of a traditional hymn (delivered in Oxford by the choristers of Magdalen College).

See also HOBBYHORSE.

maypole Tall wooden pole around which dancers perform a variety of folk dances on MAY DAY and other notable dates in the folk calendar. The use of maypoles goes back to Celtic times, and in medieval England a maypole stood on virtually every village green. Some of these were permanent and could be actual living trees with their branches stripped back. Because of the often riotous nature of May Day celebrations in general, the Puritans prohibited dancing round maypoles in the mid-17th century, but the custom returned following the Rest-oration. Maypoles are still danced round today, the dancers weaving intricate patterns with the long streamers they hold, the other end of each streamer being attached to the top of the pole. The tallest surviving maypole in England is the 26-metre (86-feet) pole danced round at Barwick-in-Elmet in Yorkshire on Whit Tuesday each year.

meadowsweet The heavy scent of meadowsweet means that the plant is regarded with some mistrust in folklore. The scent itself is reputed to have the power of inducing sleep from which a person cannot be roused. Many people are reluctant to allow flowering meadowsweet into the home, though records from past centuries suggest that there was a time when the plant was welcomed into the house as a decoration at summer feasts, and that its strong perfume was believed to be conducive to a cheerful atmosphere. It was also strewn on floors in many countries. In ancient times, meadowsweet was, with water mint and vervain, one of the three most highly valued herbs used by the Druids.

Medb In Irish folklore, the goddess-queen of Connacht. Also known as Maeve, she deserted CONCHOBAR for AILILL, and subsequently, motivated by jealousy of Daire's Dun Bull, launched the attack upon Ulster known as the TAIN BO CUAILNGE. Having enlisted the help of FERGUS MAC ROICH, she seized the bull and engineered the death of CUCHULAINN, who led the resistance of the Ulstermen, but her forces were eventually driven back home. One legend claims that she was herself killed by a piece of cheese shot from the sling of her nephew Furbaidhe, who sought vengeance for the death of his mother. Tales emphasize Medb's her insatiable lust for mortal lovers. She is sometimes interpreted as a symbol of SOVEREIGNTY.

See also MAB.

medicine Before the development of modern medical science the treatment of disease and other physical ailments depended almost entirely upon traditional folk remedies. The folk traditions of many different cultures have provided a wealth of cures, some of which have proved to have a sound scientific basis. The medicinal lore of the Celts, for instance, was widely respected throughout Europe in the Dark Ages, and even today Chinese herbal medicine, largely based upon ancient folklore, has a worldwide reputation (although science strenuously refutes the claims made for treatments depending upon such outlandish ingredients as rhino horn and various body parts of the tiger). These traditions commonly emphasized the importance of maintaining the internal balance of the body, blaming all manner of ills upon imbalances of one sort or another.

Physical problems were formerly widely blamed upon the action of evil spirits, and thus treatment was often through appeals to these spirits or through their expulsion from the patient's body. Methods used by skilled medicine men or shamans might vary from the performance of ritual dances and the making of sacrifices to attempting communication with the spirit world through trances or the use of powerful natural drugs. Alternatively, the spells of a malevolent sorcerer or witch might be assumed to be the cause, and action might be taken against any suspected party, either through the use of charms, amulets and counter-spells, or more directly. Considerable emphasis was put upon preventative medicine, and those seeking to guard their health had a vast range of protective charms and amulets to choose from.

One large category of folk remedies relied upon the working of SYMPATHETIC MAGIC. These treatments commonly depended upon the transference of the physical symptoms to an animal, which was then driven away, or to an inanimate object (such as a slice of bacon or a piece of bread and butter) which was then buried, sealed up in the bark of a tree, or otherwise disposed of, taking the disease with it. Perhaps because it had so many obvious dangers, actual physical surgery does not play such a big role in folk medicine, although there are exceptions and such practices as trepanning (making a

small hole in the skull) have a surprisingly long history.

Many folk remedies were relatively simple and did not require the assistance of a medicine man or other expert. Herbal remedies are still in common use today, and many are accepted as medicinally sound. The belief in treating the whole body of the patient in order to treat a specific problem is of particular interest to modern medical science, which is increasingly coming round to accepting such a 'holistic' approach.

Of the countless concoctions suggested as effective by folk tradition, the most useful include a relatively simple recipe including branches of rue, nine juniper berries, a walnut, a dried fig and some salt: properly prepared while the sun is at its zenith and taken on a regular basis, this medicine is alleged to cure virtually any ill. Many experts in the field apparently realized that the more outlandish the remedy they suggested, the more they could charge, and thus the folklore of many cultures is replete with medicinal treatments making use of such bizarre ingredients as snail slime, mouse droppings and bear fat.

Melusina In French folklore, the FAIRY wife of Raymond de Poitiers, Count of Lusignan. Her legend inspired many important French medieval romances. Known in France as Mélisande, she enclosed her father inside a mountain after he offended her mother, and was consequently herself punished by having her lower half transformed into a serpent every Saturday. She married Count Raymond on condition that he promised never to come to her on a Saturday, but he could not resist the temptation to discover his wife's secret, and one Saturday witnessed her transformation after hiding himself nearby. One tradition claims that once he realized his wife's terrible secret the count imprisoned her in his castle, but in other versions Melusina was doomed to abandon her husband and wander the earth in the form of a spectre until the end of time.

Several famous European families, including the royal houses of Lusignan, Rohan, Luxembourg, and Sassenaye, claim descent from Count Raymond and Melusina, and it is said that her cries can be heard whenever one of her descendants is close to death.

menstruation Menstruating women have always been regarded with some misgiving in folklore. In various societies women were considered natural, if unwitting, harbingers of evil, and were deemed to be doubly dangerous when menstruating. They were consequently disbarred from many important ritual events or completely isolated from normal human contact at this time. Other precautions over the centuries have included elaborate measures taken to prevent the feet of a menstruating woman from resting on the earth, as this polluted it, and careful avoidance of eye contact, as the briefest glance was reputed to be lethal. In Roman times menstruating women were said to cause fruit to fall from trees, to make seeds infertile, to kill swarms of bees, and to cause plants to wither and die; their mere look blunted swords and dulled mirrors. Menstrual blood in particular has always been viewed as a dangerous substance, which in some cases has been interpreted as a sacrifice to the moon.

Various taboos limit the involvement of a menstruating woman in everyday domestic affairs in rural European areas even today. It is said that such a person should never attempt to make mayonnaise or jam, as the eggs will curdle and the jam will not set. Neither should she be allowed to participate in the baking of bread, as this will prevent the dough from rising, nor should she be permitted to handle meat, milk cows or approach hams hanging to mature. In parts of Africa menstruating women are prohibited from having any role whatever in the preparation of meals for fear that the food will in some way be contaminated and those who eat it will fall ill. The presence of a menstruating woman will also prejudice the luck of hunting parties.

The folkloric associations of menstruation are not entirely negative, however. In parts of Africa newly menstruating girls may be invited to touch everything in the house in the belief that this somehow promotes the fertility and thus the prosperity of the whole household.

Mephistopheles In Christian mythology, one of the chief demons of Hell, usually depicted as the FAMILIAR of the DEVIL himself. Mephistopheles, whose name means 'he who loves not light' in Greek, originated in ancient Mesopotamian religion, and is conventionally depicted as half animal and half human. In Germany he is referred to as 'the knight with the horse's hoof'. He is now best known for his role in the FAUST legend, offering the central character a lifetime of pleasure and knowledge in exchange for his mortal soul. His name is frequently invoked in black magic.

Merlin In Arthurian legend, the master-magician who acts as adviser to and patron of King ARTHUR. Originally identified in Welsh legend as Myrddyn, he was renamed Merlin by the chronicler Geoffrey of Monmouth, and has since become one of the most familiar figures in the Arthurian canon, although myths about Myrddyn appear to predate Arthurian romance. Myrddyn was himself an historical character, namely a 6th-century Welsh poet. He is reputed to have lost his sanity and retreated to the woods of southern Scotland after his master King Gwenddolau was defeated in battle against RHYDDRECH HAEL at Arfderydd in 575 – although this legend appears to confuse details from the lives of what may have been two distinct historical characters of the same name. This period of madness was the subject of several early stories about Merlin.

According to legend, Merlin was born the child of an otherworldly father and a mortal woman, and was thus technically fatherless. The young Merlin (often called Merlin Emrys or Ambrosius) revealed his magical nature when, threatened with sacrifice because of his unique fatherless origins, he explained to King VORTIGERN the reason why a tower he was building kept falling down. The answer, Merlin told him, lay in the fact that the tower's foundations rested on a lake in which there were two dragons, one white, and one red. The dragons – representing the British and Saxon races – were dug out and fought a mighty battle in the skies. Following Vortigern's death Merlin became adviser to UTHER PENDRAGON and thus, in time, of his son Arthur. It was apparently on Merlin's advice that the ROUND TABLE came into being. Merlin was also associated with the building of Stonehenge and identified as the keeper of the THIRTEEN TREASURES OF BRITAIN, which he was reputed to preserve from harm in a glass tower on Bardsey Island off the coast of North Wales.

There are many versions of Merlin's downfall. One tradition claims that after being tricked by NIMUE or Vivien (*see* LADY OF THE LAKE) into revealing the secrets of his magic he was imprisoned forever by her in a glass tower, or alternatively under a heavy stone or inside a hawthorn tree.

mermaid Legendary sea creature described as half human and half fish. Typically depicted as female, they may also be encountered less commonly as males (called mermen). According to most accounts, mermaids have the upper body of a beautiful woman affixed to a fish's tail. They are sometimes depicted holding mirrors, symbols of their traditional association with the moon. Mermen, in contrast, are often described as hideously ugly.

Merpeople appear in a variety of guises in different cultures, and are the subject of many tales, particularly in Celtic folklore from Cornwall and elsewhere. Sometimes they fall in love with mortals and yearn to become fully human (as in the fairy tale 'The Little Mermaid' collected by Hans Christian Andersen), exchanging their fish's tail for human legs and a mortal soul, but on other occasions they are depicted as malevolent enchantresses, enticing seafarers with their beauty and their singing and then drowning them or carrying them off to their home beneath the waves. Many sailors feared seeing a mermaid, and believed that such a sighting might presage a storm, shipwreck or some other calamity. In some tales, however, they show kindness towards humans and might grant three wishes.

The only way to gain influence over a mermaid is to steal one of her possessions, namely her mirror, her cap or her belt. Stories have long been told of mortals who married mermaids after gaining magical influence over them in such a way. Among the most famous of these legends is that of Cornishman Matthew Trewhella, whose tuneful singing at the parish church of Zennor in Cornwall lured a mermaid out of the sea. He in his turn fell in love with the mermaid, and was lured beneath the waves. According to local myth his singing could be heard coming from the sea for many years after.

It is commonly assumed that tales of mermaids were inspired originally by sightings of seals, dugongs, manatees and other creatures.

See also MERROW; SEAL MAIDEN.

merrow Irish equivalent of a MERMAID. Merrows are usually spotted shortly before storms and are said on occasion to take mortal husbands. A number of old Irish families claim descent from such beings, as revealed by webbed hands and feet in their young.

Midgard Serpent *See* JORMUNGANDR.

Midsummer Day The Feast of St John the Baptist (24 June) that has been celebrated since pre-Christian times as marking the height of the summer. Falling just three days after the summer SOLSTICE (21 June), it is widely held to be one of the most magical times in the year, marking the moment when the power of the SUN starts to diminish. In order to bolster the strength of the sun, people throughout Europe once lit huge bonfires on Midsummer's Eve. Celebrants at these festivities often leapt through the flames in order to promote by magic the welfare of their crops and to purify their own souls. Herds of cattle were driven through the ashes or smoke of these fires to purge them of any diseases they might be carrying, and burning torches might be carried through the fields to ward off evil spirits. In some places burning straw wheels or tar barrels were rolled downhill or through the streets in imitation of the sun on its course through the heavens. The date still has significance today, and until the authorities placed restrictions on the site at this time of the year large crowds used to arrive each Midsummer to watch modern-day Druids conduct ritual ceremonies at Stonehenge.

Because Midsummer marks the start of a gradual decline in the sun's power, it is a time when the forces of darkness are believed to be especially active. It is therefore one of the best times to cast spells. Witches favour Midsummer's Eve as a date for holding covens, and are said to break open hens' eggs to divine what the future holds in store. It is also on this evening that anyone who sits patiently in a church porch may be rewarded by seeing a procession of the apparitions of all those souls who are fated to die in the parish over the next 12 months. The nervous are advised to keep their distance from walnut trees on this date as these are said to be meeting places for demons and other spirits bent on a night of revelry and mischief making. Inhabitants of Cornwall claim that this is also a time when snakes gather together in huge writhing masses. Children born on Midsummer's Eve, furthermore, are reputed to have the power of the EVIL EYE.

Midsummer's Eve is the traditional time for the gathering of St John's wort, which is much valued for its efficacy in treating nervous disorders, and is also put up over doorways (as is fennel) to prevent the passage of malevolent spirits. It is also one of the best times of the year for the performance of love magic. Any woman who is unable to conceive is advised to pick a St John's wort from her garden on Midsummer's Eve in order to become fertile (although this will only work if she is entirely naked at the time). A rosebud picked on Midsummer Day and carefully wrapped in white paper will stay fresh until Christmas Day if a girl's lover is true to her; if the rose withers she should find herself a new partner. One option is to wear the rose to church – the man who takes it from her is almost certainly destined to become the girl's husband.

In order to conjure up a vision of the man a girl is to marry one procedure is to prepare a meal of bread, cheese and wine on Midsummer's Eve and to leave the door open: the man concerned will enter, bow, and raise a glass to his future wife. To dream of a future lover, girls should gather yarrow growing on the grave of a young man and place it under their pillow on this night.

See also NEED-FIRE.

Mikula Russian folk hero celebrated for his great strength. An equivalent of the American PAUL BUNYAN, he is depicted as a peasant possessed with the ability to outstrip all others in his work as a lumberjack. Many tales have gathered around his name. Among other things, it was said that he could lift his great cart with a single hand, although scores of ordinary men could not shift it at all. Legend also identified him as the lover of Maki-Syra-Zemlya, Mother Earth.

Miled In Irish mythology, the king of the MILESIANS. He is supposed to have sailed to Ireland from Spain intending to avenge the death of his uncle (or brother) ITH. However, he did not himself reach the country, and it was left to his sons to complete the invasion. The attempts of the TUATHA DE DANANN to conceal Ireland with mist led the frustrated Miled to dub the country Muic Inis ('Pig Island').

Milesians In Irish mythology, the sons of MILED, who are identified as the legendary founders of the Gaelic race. Also known as the Sons of Mil Espaine, they came to Ireland from Spain, but before that are supposed to have resided in Egypt and Scythia. The fifth invaders of the country, they wrested control of Ireland from the TUATHA DE DANANN, renaming their new homeland Eire in honour of the goddess Eriu, who helped them in their quest. They eventually agreed a truce with the Tuatha de Danann, who were allowed possession of the underground part of the country (see SIDHE). At first the country was ruled by different kings, but Eremon ultimately united the whole land under his own rule.

Mil Espaine, Sons of See MILESIANS.

milfoil See YARROW.

Mimir The Norse god of the sea. Having tasted the waters of the sea he was said to enjoy all-seeing knowledge of both the past and the future. When ODIN sought similar knowledge by drinking from the sea (sometimes referred to as 'Mimir's Well'), Mimir demanded one of the god's eyes as payment. Another legend claims that when Mimir's head was cut off Odin kept it safely so that he could consult it when he wished to know more about future events.

miners' lore In common with others engaged in dangerous occupations, miners are renowned for their stock of time-honoured superstitions and taboos, many of which are still observed. Like sailors, who are traditionally highly sensitive to ominous signs as they make their way to the harbour, many miners will show extreme reluctance to go underground in certain circumstances. These include catching sight of a dove or a robin flying around a pithead (a prophecy of imminent disaster below), encountering a woman, a rabbit or a cross-eyed man on the way to the pit, having to turn back home for something once one has started out, and dreaming the previous night about broken shoes. The sight of flowering beans may also be unwelcome, as accidents are said to be more frequent when these plants are in bloom. In the USA the sight of rats deserting a mine is said to presage some catastrophe.

Once underground, miners can be very nervous of marking anything with a cross, as this may provoke interference by pagan spirits. They will also bewail the presence of a cat or the sound of a person whistling. Should any of these taboos be broken, a miner may touch iron in the hope that this will avert disaster. On re-emerging from the pit, some miners will avoid bathing their backs, as this is supposed to lead to a weak spine, and may also cause the roof of a mine to collapse.

Miners working underground throughout Europe have always been wary of meeting dwarfs, the magical masters of all subterranean excavations. Rock falls and other setbacks are often attributed to dwarfs, who are presumed to have been angered in some way. By way of contrast, it is said that kindlier dwarfs, in return for offerings of food, warn human miners of danger by making tapping sounds, and may also help in the digging. Numerous reports have been made of the sound of the dwarfs' picks at work, and over the centuries some miners have even recorded eye-witness accounts of these diminutive fellow workers.

mirror Mirrors have always been regarded as magical objects. Before mirrors were conceived of, many myths surrounded the reflections that men and women saw in pools and lakes. The theory developed that what a person saw was not a mere reflection but a visual representation of the soul, which was thus temporarily divorced from the body and vulnerable to interference by evil spirits. Such reflections could be asked questions about the future, and if they trembled or broke up the prognosis was generally considered bad. In some remote parts of the world it is still maintained that if any 'harm' befalls a reflection, it is inevitable that the owner will also come to grief.

Those fearful of witchcraft formerly purchased small 'witch balls' of reflective glass, which were reputed to ward off sorcerers, and mirrors were credited with the power to deflect the influence of the EVIL EYE, a notion that led to a 17th-century fad for the wearing of hats decorated with small mirrors. Witches themselves are said to favour mirrors framed on just three sides, as these enable them to see over immense distances. Mirrors may also be consulted to discover the answer to various questions, such as the identity of a future lover. This last tradition is well known today from such fairy tales as 'Snow White', in which the wicked queen inquires of her mirror 'Who is the fairest of them all?', only to receive the displeasing reply that Snow White is the fairest of all. Other magic mirrors feature in the legends surrounding MERLIN and REYNARD THE FOX, among others.

Belief in the mystical power of mirrors has survived into modern times, not just in the taboo against their breakage (which is widely believed to result in seven years' bad luck). Some mothers nurse a prejudice against allowing their babies to see their own reflection before they are a year old, for fear that the shock will retard their growth or that they will be doomed to suffer epilepsy, develop cross eyes or a stutter, or even be fated to an early death. Brides are commonly warned not to look at their reflection when trying on their complete wedding outfit (particularly if they are wearing a veil), as this is likely to endanger the happy outcome of the marriage plans.

Many people admit to being wary of looking into a mirror over someone else's shoulder, as this threatens the luck of the person thus 'overlooked', or otherwise signifies a quarrel between the two parties. No one, incidentally, should look into a mirror by candlelight, as this is also thought to be unlucky, and neither should they look into one for too long, as the face of the DEVIL will surely appear in the glass in response to such vanity.

If someone lies ill in a household then the mirror may be covered up to prevent the invalid seeing his or her reflection. The theory is that in a weakened state the patient may be unable to re-establish contact with the soul after it has been thus temporarily separated from the body and trapped in the glass. If the patient dies it is doubly important that the mirrors be covered or turned to the wall, as failure to do so not only risks the well-being of the deceased's spirit, but also threatens the welfare of anyone who then looks into the glass, as their own soul may be snatched by that of the dead patient to provide company on the journey to the hereafter. Some people will also turn the mirrors to the wall or cover them with a sheet during thunderstorms, for fear that they attract LIGHTNING. The chilling tradition that a VAMPIRE, having no soul, has no reflection is well known from 20th-century cinema. If a normal person looks into a mirror and finds no reflection this is a sign that the soul has already departed, and is thus an omen that the person in question is about to die.

Bearing in mind the magical nature of mirrors, it is not so surprising that their breakage should be attended by such dire consequences. These apply even if a mirror breaks by itself, in which case the death of a close friend or a loved one must be expected. Should the unthinkable happen, however, all is not lost, according to one relatively little-known English superstition: if the pieces of the broken mirror are buried in sacred ground or thrown into a swift-flowing stream or river one's luck will remain intact.

See also SCRYING.

mistletoe Parasitical evergreen plant, which was revered for its magical properties by the Druids and has retained to this day certain mystical associations. The

Druids held that mistletoe – preferably growing on an OAK – had to be cut with a golden sickle during the summer or winter SOLSTICE. On no account was it allowed to fall on the ground as this would rob the plant of its magical powers; instead it was caught in the lap of their robes. Norse mythology also placed special importance upon the mistletoe, the plant with which the evil Loki killed the sun god BALDUR. Throughout Scandinavia, enemies meeting beneath a bush of mistletoe were supposed to lay down their weapons, as the plant was considered to be a symbol of peace.

Allegedly the wood of which Christ's cross was made, and also the 'burning bush' in the story of Moses, the mistletoe is ironically unwelcome in churches because of its pagan history, and it will be carefully removed if accidentally included in decorative greenery. However, mistletoe used to be carried in solemn procession to the altar at York Minster in medieval times, and was allowed to remain there throughout the Christmas season as a symbol of the general pardon that was then in force. The plant, which bears berries in the winter, has nonetheless come to be identified with Christmas; in the English Midlands it is said to be unlucky to cut mistletoe at any other time of year.

English people have kissed beneath boughs of mistletoe since Saxon times, a man having the right to demand a kiss from any female who passes (either inadvertently or on purpose) beneath a bough of mistletoe hung from the ceiling. Until relatively recently, the men plucked a berry with each kiss, and no more kisses could be claimed after the last berry was gone. This superstition derives from the days of the Druids, when the plant was considered to have strong sexual potency. Another suggestion has it that the practice originated in a curse placed on the mistletoe as a punishment by pagan gods, to the effect that it would always have to look on while pretty young girls were kissed beneath its leaves.

Once Christmas is over, some people insist on burning the mistletoe, maintaining that if it is not burnt on TWELFTH NIGHT then the couples who kissed beneath it are fated to quarrel before the year is over. Others, however, claim that there is some virtue in keeping the bough carefully in place till the following Yuletide before it is ceremonially burnt. Keeping the cut bough through the year is said to preserve its luck-giving qualities, and farmers formerly fed the first cow to calve after the New Year a sprig of the plant in the belief that this would promote the welfare of the whole herd over the coming 12 months. A little mistletoe hung over a cradle, meanwhile, is supposed to ward off fairies and to prevent the child's replacement by a CHANGELING.

Also known by the name all-heal, the plant is credited with various healing powers, being beneficial (usually in the form of a tea) in the treatment of epilepsy, heart disease, nervous ailments, snakebite, toothache and St Vitus's Dance. The plant does in fact contain the drug guipsene, which can indeed be used to help sufferers of hypertension and nervous disorders, but is poisonous in large quantities. Mistletoe is also said to have the power to mend quarrels, to ward off lightning and to promote fertility. Not surprisingly, in view of the plant's varied properties and magical associations, anyone who is reckless enough to take the whole bush or actually cuts down a mistletoe-bearing tree is warned to expect a particularly grisly and premature end.

Modron In Welsh mythology, the mother of MABON. The story of the loss of her son bears some similarity to the legend of RHIANNON and MACHA, and would appear to be just one variant in a wide class of 'lost son' legends. Her name sometimes appears as an alternative for MORGAN LE FAY.

mole A small, burrowing, nearly blind mammal, rarely seen above ground, that has inspired a large number of folk beliefs.

Attitudes to the creature vary from culture to culture. Some people claim it is lucky to see a mole, while others rather fancifully believe that moles only emerge from their tunnels at night in order to listen to the angels singing. Others again claim that the animal represents greed.

The sudden appearance of molehills in a garden that was previously free of them is open to more than one interpretation. It may indicate that someone will soon be moving elsewhere, or, more ominously, it may be a portent of illness or death (intensified if the molehills surround the house, according to the Scots). If the animals dig close to a bathroom or kitchen then it is the woman of the house who is threatened. US tradition predicts that bad weather is in the offing if there are more molehills than usual.

Among the cruellest folk remedies is one recommended for those suffering from toothache, rheumatism, cramp or other ailments. This involves cutting the paws from a living mole and carrying these about the person; if the problem is in the arms then the front paws must be carried, while if the problem is in the legs then the back paws are needed. Sleeping with the affected part wrapped in moleskin – or else in the two halves of a mole's body – may also prove beneficial. Hands that have been used to strangle a mole are said to have the power to give relief to anyone suffering from pains in the chest. People troubled with warts might try bathing them in the still-warm blood of a freshly killed mole, while blood taken from a mole's nose and swallowed on a lump of sugar will cure fits. The skinned and powdered body of a male mole, consumed with gin, will ward off fever. Owners of moleskin purses, meanwhile, may be comforted by the thought that they will never run out of small change.

Momotaro Japanese folk hero who is the central character in a well-known folk tale. According to legend, Momotaro was born from a peach and was brought up by two well-meaning elderly peasants. As an adult he left home and defeated the demon Akondoji, whose treasure he seized with the assistance of a dog, a monkey and a pheasant.

moon The moon occupies a prominent place in world folklore, and was an object of worship in many ancient cultures. While the SUN represents the life essence and the more positive aspects of existence, the moon, ruler of the tides and other elemental forces, is generally taken to symbolize darker, more mysterious and often negative influences. The reverence felt for the moon in ancient cultures is reflected in the mixed feelings many people still have for the earth's nearest neighbour in space.

Perhaps the oldest and most widely-known of the folk beliefs connected with the moon is that those who gaze too long at the full moon risk becoming 'lunatic', that is, mad, and will henceforth be subject to attacks of insanity whenever the moon is full. (Alternatively, if they happen to be werewolves, the sight of a full moon may be enough to transform them into their wolf state.) The moon's disorientating influence is also to be seen in the erratic behaviour of animals at certain times in the lunar cycle, and has long been linked with the cycle of MENSTRUATION in human females.

The awe felt for the moon in ancient times has never quite died away, and it continues to be treated by the more superstitious with the utmost respect. In the past, for instance, young girls in particular were warned against sleeping in the moonlight, lest they become 'moonstruck' and beget monsters. To be on the safe side, many adults will greet the new moon with a respectful bow or curtsey (in which case they believe they will be granted a wish). Witches and other sorcerers, meanwhile, have long been credited with the power to 'draw down the moon', attracting and harnessing the malevolent power of the moon so that they may employ it towards their own nefarious ends.

Although the Gregorian calendar is based on the solar cycle, the Jewish, Islamic and Hindu calendars are all based on the lunar phases, and there have been many attempts to determine from the moon's cycle when the optimum times are for the inauguration of various enterprises. Broadly speaking, the waxing of a new moon is a time when lovers may divine what the future has in store for them, when new projects may be safely begun, and when journeys may be best undertaken. Farmers will choose whenever possible to do their planting and sowing when the moon is waxing (although such plants as runner beans, which grow anticlockwise, are sown on the wane), and this is also the best time for weddings, childbirth and convalescence. Livestock that is slaughtered when the moon is waxing will give better meat.

Bowing to the new moon and turning over any silver coins in one's pocket will guarantee a doubling in the amount by the end of the next cycle. If in company, the first person to see the new moon should kiss one of his or her companions without delay, as they may then expect a gift in the near future. It is important, however, that the new moon should not be seen for the first time through glass or through the branches of a tree, as this is a bad omen (similarly if it is first seen to the left side of the observer). Ideally it should be sighted in the open air via a glance over the right shoulder (in which case a wish may be made).

The monthly period when the moon is at its fullest has special magical significance in many cultures, particularly when it coincides with the autumn equinox (the 'harvest moon') and the following 'hunter's moon'.

A waning moon exerts a generally baleful influence, and is a particularly bad time for births and weddings. Anything cut in this period will not grow again, including the hair and fingernails, although it is apparently a good time to move house, to let blood, to pick fruit, to cut down trees, and to stuff feather mattresses.

Worst of all is the period between cycles, when there is no moon at all. It was formerly believed in many parts of the world that the moon was consumed by demons and other monsters at this time, and it was said that children born in this dark period would come to nothing, as an ancient English proverb warns – 'No moon, no man'.

Should two new moons fall within the same calendar month, extremely bad weather is sure to follow, and may extend to flooding and various other natural catastrophes. If this happens in May it will rain for a year and a day. A full moon that falls on Christmas Day, meanwhile, is lamented by farmers as a prophecy of a poor harvest in the year ahead.

The colour of the moon is also significant. A red moon is widely interpreted as an ominous sign, while 'the new moon with the old moon in her arms' (denoting a full moon just visible in the light of a new moon) is considered by seafarers worldwide to be an omen of an approaching storm.

In folk medicine, there is a remedy from northern England which recommends blowing on one's warts in the light of the full moon to cure them, while many regions boast the tradition of 'washing' hands affected by warts in a shiny metal basinful of moon's rays. Many herbs valued for their medicinal properties should ideally be collected under the light of the moon.

See also ECLIPSE; MAN IN THE MOON.

moonstone A variety of feldspar, whitish in colour, that is associated in folklore with the MOON. According to Hindu folklore it is formed from crystallized moon rays and is believed to have many special magical properties, including the power to excite feelings of love. It is reputed to wax and wane in sympathy with the moon, and if placed in the mouth, it will bestow the gift of prophecy.

Mordred (or **Modred**) In Arthurian legend, the treacherous nephew of King

ARTHUR or, according to French tradition, the result of the king's incestuous relationship with his half-sister Morgause. Mordred is usually depicted as a villain, and legend has it that Arthur – perhaps conscious that the child's incestuous origin gave him a strong claim on the throne – attempted to secure his death by casting him off in a boat, along with all the other children born at the same time. Mordred survived to become a knight of the Round Table, and, according to Geoffrey of Monmouth, Arthur entrusted him with the rule of England when he visited Rome. While Arthur was away Mordred demonstrated his untrustworthiness by attempting (unsuccessfully) to seduce GUINEVERE. He was eventually slain by Arthur at the Battle of CAMLAN, during the course of which Arthur himself received a mortal wound.

Morgan le Fay In Arthurian legend, the sorceress half-sister of King ARTHUR. The daughter of GORLOIS OF CORNWALL and IGRAINE, she learnt the arts of sorcery while a girl and subsequently used her magic against Arthur and the knights of the Round Table. Her crimes included the theft of EXCALIBUR and its scabbard (only the sword was recovered), and the attempted seduction of Sir LANCELOT among others. She brought Arthur further woe when she revealed to him, by means of a magic draught, knowledge of the adulterous affair between Lancelot and Guinevere. When Arthur lay dying it was Morgan le Fay who escorted his body to AVALON.

Details of the legends surrounding Morgan le Fay suggest that she may be descended ultimately from the Celtic war goddess MORRIGAN, although descriptions of her may also have been influenced by the traditions surrounding the MERMAID. According to Geoffrey of Monmouth she ruled over a magical kingdom in company with her 12 sisters. Later medieval writers depicted her as the queen of the fairies, referring to her by the name FATA MORGANA. Her reputation as a sorceress has also linked her name with witchcraft.

Morgiana *See* ALI BABA.

Morrigan (or Morrighan) In Irish mythology, a war goddess sometimes also regarded as a mother goddess associated with fertility. She was either a single goddess, or had three separate aspects – those of MACHA, Nemainn, and BADB. As a war goddess she assisted the TUATHA DE DANANN in their struggle against the FIRBOLGS, and prophesied the end of the world. She offered herself to CUCHULAINN, but when he rejected her advances she attacked him, first in the shape of an eel and then as a she-wolf. Her usual guise was that of a crow or raven. She was also said to have mated with DAGDA, standing with one foot on each bank of the River Unius. The legends surrounding her name link her to the stories of other notable mythological characters, notably MODRON and MORGAN LE FAY.

morris dance English folk dance celebrating fertility and the cycle of the seasons. It is performed during the spring and summer months throughout England, particularly upon such notable dates as MAY DAY. Derived from the Spanish morisca, which depicted the battles fought between Moors and Christians, it appears to have been introduced to England from Spain during the reign of Edward III (1327–77).

The morris (or 'Moorish') dance is traditionally performed by a troupe of six, eight or ten men dressed in white, with bells tied to their knees. In some places the dancers also black their faces (a reference to the Moorish aspect of the dance), and hold sticks or handkerchiefs in their hands. The sticks may be rapped together or else tapped on the ground, mimicking the planting of seeds, so presumably intended to promote the success of the coming harvest. The steps mostly comprise a repeated series of springs and hops danced in unison, although there is also scope for solo jigs.

The dances sometimes incorporate a HOBBYHORSE and such stock characters as ROBIN HOOD, Maid Marian and the FOOL. The most famous dances include 'Bean Setting', 'Constant Billy' and 'Country Gardens'. The music is usually provided by a fiddle or accordion. In recent years many women's teams have been formed, although these have sometimes met with heated opposition from troupes of male dancers.

See also HORN DANCE.

mosquito Contrary to what might be expected, the mosquito is generally considered a harbinger of good luck. Mosquitoes may even be welcomed in the bedroom of a sick person on the grounds that as they fly out again they will take the illness with them. They may also be used as indicators of the weather to come: if they fly close to the ground then rain is coming, but if they fly high in the air then the weather will be fine.

Mosquito bites may be treated, it is said, by applying butter, garlic, lemon peel, oil, onion, or vinegar, and then blowing on them. Less positive is the African and American tradition of man-eating mosquitoes, and the central European folk belief that mosquitoes are born from the Devil's pipe.

Mother Goose *See* NURSERY RHYMES.

Mother Holle *See* HOLLE, MOTHER.

Mothering Sunday A specified Sunday in the year on which children and adults throughout the English-speaking world present their mothers with cards, flowers and gifts. Otherwise known as Mother's Day, in the UK the date falls on the fourth Sunday in Lent, which was formerly known as Simnel Sunday or Refreshment Sunday as it was on this date that servants were allowed the day off to visit their families, usually taking small gifts with them. This custom had its roots in pre-Reformation times, when the devout brought small offerings to the Mother Church of the diocese on this date.

Mothering Sunday had become a celebration of motherhood by the middle of the 17th century, but the tradition had suffered a marked decline by the late 19th century, when it was more or less ignored by most people. Its upsurge in popularity in the UK since the 1940s owes much to the influence of US servicemen arriving in the country during World War II: they confused the British Mothering Sunday with their own Mother's Day, a chiefly secular celebration of motherhood reserved (since 1914) for the second Sunday in May. The US Mother's Day can be traced back only as far as 1907, when one Anna Jarvis of Philadelphia (who had recently lost her own mother) suggested that one day in the year should be set aside for the special honouring of all mothers. This celebration originally included religious services at which each member of the congregation wore a carnation – red if the person's mother was still living, white if she was dead.

mouse Mice, though timid and not loathed with the same ferocity as rats, are nonetheless viewed with considerable suspicion in folklore. They are even believed by some to be an invention of the DEVIL himself. Their appearance in houses previously free of them is regarded as a warning of the imminent death of a family member (as is their sudden disappearance from a house for no apparent reason). There is also a widely-held belief that mice are in fact the souls of murder victims that have returned to the world, or else the souls of the sleeping, which have temporarily left the body. Another theory suggests that they are created by witches from scraps of cloth.

Discovering damage done by mice to clothing is itself an unlucky act, redolent of further evil to come, and the sound of a mouse squeaking near the bed of a sick person may cast doubt on the patient's recovery. Anyone who has a mouse run over them is sure to die soon, and the sight of a white mouse crossing the floor is also a portent of death. Many travellers dislike meeting mice when on a journey for fear of the bad luck they bring, and seafarers will not suffer the word 'mouse' to be uttered while at sea. In Scotland one measure that may be taken to clear a house of mice is to capture one of their number and to roast it slowly before the fire, suspended by the tail: the other mice will apparently take the hint and vacate the premises. White mice are said to be a favourite disguise of witches' imps; nonetheless, mice are considered lucky in Germany, where few people will kill a mouse for fear of provoking bad fortune.

Folk medicine has several uses for the mouse. A meal of roasted, boiled, stewed, baked, or fried mouse – or a drink made with powdered mouse – is especially recommended for the treatment of those suffering from whooping cough, small-pox, coughs and colds, fever, or measles, and it will also cure children of bedwetting. Dropping mouse blood on a wart will cause it to disappear, while stroking the cheek with a dead mouse will, it is claimed, relieve the pain of toothache.

Mice appear as characters in a number of folk tales, usually tricking much more powerful animals or alternatively coming to a sticky end themselves after forgetting their own vulnerability. One of the most famous fairy tales concerning mice is 'The Town Mouse and the Country Mouse', in which the country mouse visits his urban cousin and is initially impressed by his high standard of living, but returns quickly to the country after he appreciates the risks of life in the city. Another well-known story is Aesop's fable of the mouse and the lion, in which a mouse, having been freed by a lion, belies its diminutive size by managing to gnaw through the bonds with which the lion has been restricted, thus repaying the lion for its kindness.

Much the Miller's son *See* ROBIN HOOD.

mugwort Herb that is reputed to have considerable power as a defence against witchcraft and other evils. Mugwort is traditionally held to be among the most effective weapons against poisons, spells and various illnesses, and, if placed care-fully in the shoe, will also prevent tired-ness on long journeys (a notion that was commonplace among travellers up until the 17th century). Also known as the motherwort, it is said to be particularly efficacious in preventing disease in women, and was formerly much respect-ed as a means of treating consumption. German folklore advises that any person who digs up a mugwort on Midsummer's Eve will find a small coal hidden in the soil; this has its own special magic properties, being able to protect its owner from burns, the plague, carbuncles and fever, and also from being struck by lightning.

mummers' play Traditional dramatic entertainment that has been performed at Christmas or Easter or on other notable dates at various locations through Eng-land, Northern Ireland and other parts of Europe since medieval times or even ear-lier. Descended originally from early dumb shows and from 16th-century Italian masquerades, mummers' plays were passed on from generation to gen-eration through oral tradition, and gener-ally tell stories with a strong religious theme, usually celebrating the triumph of good over evil. Characters in the plays include FATHER CHRISTMAS, ST GEORGE, the Doctor, the Turkish Knight and Little Johnny Jack. A typical plot depicts how St George is mortally wounded fighting the Turkish Knight but is then revived by the Doctor (a mock resurrection with obvious reli-gious associations).

The mummers themselves sometimes dress in the costume of the character they are playing, but alternatively may appear in a traditional mumming outfit, com-prising a shaggy suit of clothes covered with strips of torn paper, streamers and ribbons. They may hide their faces with masks or with black make-up.

Muspellsheim In Norse mythology, the realm of fire identified as the homeland of the fire god Surtr. It represents the opposite of the frozen wastes of NIFLHEIM, with which it combined to create the world. The name Muspellsheim means 'Home of Brightness'.

Myrddyn *See* MERLIN.

myrtle This evergreen shrub or tree is generally considered to be lucky, and is associated with love, marriage and fertility. In Jewish lore, a myrtle was the one tree Adam brought with him when he and Eve were expelled from paradise, and it was widely understood to symbolize God's promise that he would keep faith with humanity.

Planting a myrtle on both sides of the front door will, according to the Welsh, promote the peace and happiness of the household. However, the plant should be carefully looked after, for if it withers and dies through neglect, or is actually dug up, only misfortune will follow. In several European countries myrtle blooming abundantly in the garden is interpreted as a sign of a coming wedding in the household, and it was formerly common for brides to carry myrtle bouquets.

The plant will prosper best if put in the ground by a woman, who must take care to spread her skirt over the plant and look as proud as she can while doing this. German authorities, however, warn that if a girl who is engaged plants myrtle, then the wedding will be called off (the same authorities advise that a bride decked out with myrtle will avoid becoming pregnant on her wedding night).

Young girls who drink myrtle tea will enjoy greater beauty – in which case they might have need of an old English superstition that employs myrtle to discover the identity of a future husband. This advises girls to lay a sprig of myrtle against the words of the marriage service in their prayer book, and then to sleep with the book under their pillow: if the myrtle has disappeared in the morning then their lover is destined to marry them.

N

naga In Buddhist and Hindu folklore, one of a species of supernatural half-human, half-snake creatures that were banished to an underground realm by the god Brahma when they became too numerous on earth. Here they live in regal style in splendid palaces, under the rule of their king Mucalinda, spreading their hoods to provide shade for the gods and guarding over a great hoard of treasure. Nagas (whose name means 'serpent' in Sanskrit) are variously described as having many heads or else as having the upper body of a human appended to the long tail of a serpent. Sometimes they have a miraculous jewel embedded in their head. They generally leave mortals alone, except when the latter have angered the gods, in which case they may use their poisonous bite to deadly effect. The nagas are held in great respect, and many noble Indian families claim descent from them.

Closely associated with water, nagas may be called upon to bring relief in times of drought. The theory that the Indian nagas may have been inspired originally by the snake-worshipping cults of the ancient Scythians, located to the north of the Black Sea, has yet to be substantiated. They may instead be simply an expression of an almost universal reverence for snakes and serpents, as recorded in many of the world's cultures.

Naglfar In Norse mythology, the ship of the GIANTS. Constructed from the nail cuttings of the dead, it is fated to transport the army of the giants at RAGNAROK, when the world will end. Because of this, it was once thought wise to trim short the nails of the newly dead so that it would take the giants longer to complete the vessel and thus delay the final battle.

nagual In Aztec folklore, a species of animal spirit. It was in the form of a nagual that shamans were believed to work their evil against mortals. The naguals were said to wander abroad at night, spreading sickness and causing harm to the vulnerable. Occasionally, though, they were treated as guardian spirits, and it was believed that every person had their own personal nagual. It was customary for the young to spend a night in the open so that their nagual could present itself to them in its chosen animal form, or else for ashes to be sprinkled around cradles to make visible the tracks of any nagual that visited the infant during the night.

nail Iron nails were once widely recognized in European folklore as effective charms against evil by virtue of the fact that iron was itself a magical metal. Hammering iron nails into the wall or lintels of a house was believed to keep evil spirits and disease at bay, particularly if the nails were rusty, had been taken from an old coffin or were arranged in the form of a cross. Similarly, it was supposed to be lucky to find a nail lying in the road and carrying a nail about the person was believed to ward off the threat of the EVIL EYE. Superstition also made use of nails in a test for witchcraft: this involved an iron nail being driven into a footprint made by the suspect who, if a witch, would shortly appear to remove it and thus reveal his or her guilt.

In folk medicine, a nail might be hammered into the ground at the spot where an epileptic suffered a fit, in the belief that this might provide a cure, or else would be rubbed on an ailing part of the body and then likewise driven into the ground to treat the problem. In Ireland it was claimed that headaches could be alleviated by driving nails into an old skull.

The notion that hammering a nail into something is somehow magical recalls the ancient Roman custom of hammering nails into the wall of the temple of Jupiter in Rome, originally an annual ceremony that was meant to count off the years but which later developed into a religious ritual that might be performed at any time of national distress. As recently as World War I the German public was encouraged to buy nails to hammer into a large wooden statue of Field-Marshal Hindenburg to help raise funds for the war effort.

The symbolism of the nail in the Christian world was subsequently reinforced by the nails by which Christ was affixed at the Crucifixion.

See also FINGERNAIL.

nain rouge In Norman French tradition, one of a race of temperamental household spirits who are usually thought to be beneficent towards mortals (especially fishermen) but who can cause trouble if offended. The name translates as 'red dwarf'. The tradition travelled to the USA at an early date: the malice of a nain rouge was blamed, for instance, for the inferno that destroyed Detroit in 1805.

nakh In Estonian folklore, the spirit of a drowned mortal. Nakhs are variously described as human or horselike in form or, if female, similar in appearance to a MERMAID. The nakh lures humans into the water with its singing, or else uses magic to force mortals to dance until they

are exhausted, whereupon it drowns them. Anyone who sees a nakh may take this as an omen that he or she will shortly suffer death by drowning.

Nala and Damayanti One of the best known of the tales that make up the MAHABHARATA. The tale begins with the betrothal of the young king Nala and the beautiful Damayanti, daughter of King Bhima. At the wedding, Damayanti successfully distinguishes Nala from four gods who have assumed the young king's appearance in order to test her. After several years of happy marriage, the wicked Kali, goddess of death and destruction, enters Nala and causes him to gamble away his kingdom, upon which he reluctantly sends his beloved Damayanti back to her father. After many adventures Nala becomes a cook and charioteer in the service of the king of Kosala, in which guise Damayanti eventually recognizes him – despite the fact that his identity is now magically disguised. The king of Kosala is so impressed by Nala's skill as a charioteer he agrees to bestow upon him his own luck as a gambler, and thus Kali is driven out. Nala is restored to his original appearance by the use of a magic robe and the lovers are reunited. Together they reclaim their kingdom, making good use of the gambling skills Nala now enjoys to regain his former wealth.

names Personal names have always been considered to have strong magic potential. In the working of black magic, for instance, it was believed that simply calling a particular demon repeatedly by name was sufficient to cause the spirit to manifest itself. Similarly, it was thought that witches could use their knowledge of their victim's name to direct malevolent magic at them. Because of this, it was thought unwise in many rural areas to bandy names about too freely, and in some parts of the world people rarely used their real names but chose to be known by nicknames in order to forestall any interference by evil spirits. By the same token, it was thought reckless to let others know what name had been chosen for a baby before the baptism took place, as unbaptized children were deemed to be especially vulnerable to supernatural threats. Records exist of anxious fathers who did not tell even their wives their approved choice until all were assembled at the font.

Some names are never to be spoken at all for fear of inviting the attention of malign spirits. An example of this is the Jewish taboo against referring openly to God by his name Yahweh or Jehovah, who is instead referred to by such euphemisms as Adonai (meaning 'lord'). Similarly, in the English-speaking world many people formerly feared mentioning the DEVIL by name and preferred to use such nicknames as Old Nick. Other taboos have operated against speaking the names of the newly deceased (commonly referred to by such euphemisms as 'the recently departed'), certain animals (such as snakes, bears and pigs), and even wives and mothers-in-law. The idea that a personal name has great magical potential can work either way, however: in the well-known German fairy tale 'Rumpelstiltskin', for example, finding out the demon's name is enough to drive him into a self-destructive rage.

Most personal names have a specific meaning, and a select few are believed to be lucky, or unlucky, in themselves. English folklore claims, for instance, that no one called George has ever been hanged, and also that girls called Agnes are destined to go mad. If a man called Joseph marries a girl called Mary, meanwhile, the couple will, for obvious reasons, be blessed with the power of healing, particularly with reference to whooping cough. More generally, it is thought to be very unlucky among many people to name a new child after a dead sibling or an older relative, apparently because the fates may confuse the two. By the same token, it is a good idea to name a new baby after some great or successful person as the infant may share in that person's luck.

European folklore recommends a variety of methods for parents unable to settle upon a name for their new offspring. These include opening a Bible at random and reading until the first name is reached, or naming the child after a saint, in which case it will enjoy that saint's protection. In most circumstances superstition advises against changing a name once it has been settled upon, but women have the opportunity to change their surname at least on getting married. Here again tradition warns that certain changes may be unlucky – a cautionary English rhyme runs: 'Change the name and not the letter, change for the worse and not for the better.'

The names of animals and such inanimate objects as ships are hedged in by similar notions all around the world. In the case of ships it was formerly thought to be fatal to change the name of a vessel and even worse to choose a name ending in the letter 'a', a superstition that was greatly boosted by the loss of the *Lusitania* in 1915.

Nanna In Norse mythology, the goddess of flowers and vegetation. The wife of BALDUR, she died of a broken heart when he was killed and accompanied him to the Underworld. When Hermod, son of ODIN visited the Underworld in a bid to rescue Baldur, Nanna had the opportunity to return to the world, but elected to stay in the Underworld with her husband, who could not leave. She did, however, give Hermod a beautiful piece of embroidery to take back as an expression of her steadfast love for the world.

Naoise In Irish Celtic mythology, one of the three sons of Usnech, and the lover of DEIRDRE. There was a prophecy that Deirdre, the most beautiful woman in Ireland, would cause great suffering to whoever became her lover. She had also been betrothed to King CONCHOBAR since birth. Despite the misgivings caused by these circumstances, Naoise fell deeply in love with her and promised to rescue her and carry her off to Scotland. The deed accomplished, he and his brothers were eventually lured back by Conchobar's message that he had forgiven the lovers, but they were treacherously deceived and killed by King Eoghan, an ally of Conchobar's.

narcissus Spring flower named in honour of Narcissus of Greek legend, who fell in love with his own reflection and, unable to tear himself away from it, wasted away and died. After his death the sympathetic gods reincarnated him as the flower that now bears his name. The poisonous bulb of the narcissus has many uses in European folk medicine. It is said to have the power to induce headaches, madness and even death, while the roots have been used as poultices or to remove splinters. Some authorities also recommended combining narcissus bulbs with honey as a painkiller.

Nasciens In Arthurian legend, a hermit who appears on several occasions in connection with the quest for the GRAIL. Originally identified as a knight called Seraphe, he came to Britain with JOSEPH OF ARIMATHEA and advises the knights on their quest but is himself struck blind when he looks into the Grail. He is subsequently healed by the Grail Lance.

Nasnas Islamic demon who lies in wait beside river crossings to murder unwary travellers. Manifesting in the form of a feeble old man, the demon asks to be carried across the river but then latches onto any mortal who lets him climb onto his back and drowns him in the water.
See also OLD MAN OF THE SEA.

nat In Burmese folklore, a class of demon that encompasses a variety of nature spirits, supernatural beings and the souls of the dead. Dating back to before the development of Buddhism, nats may belong to either sex. They have to be appeased with regular offerings of food and flowers and other expressions of

respect as otherwise they will take revenge by harming the health and prosperity of an individual or community. Even the weather will respond to their influence. Special shrines dedicated to nats can be found in many Buddhist pagodas. Particular reverence is shown for the Thirty-Seven, an elevated rank of nats who are variously identified as the spirits of celebrated warriors or legendary heroes.

Nechtan In Irish Celtic mythology, the husband of BOANN. Only Nechtan and his cupbearers were allowed to go to the fabled well of knowledge. When Boann attempted to do the same the well uprooted itself and chased her, becoming the River Boyne.

need-fire The sacred fire that was lit to celebrate MIDSUMMER'S EVE and other important festivals in the pagan calendar. The need-fire symbolized the notion of renewal and the cycle of the seasons and was venerated throughout pre-Christian Europe. When the main bonfire, ignited by friction, was lit worshippers leapt through the flames to be purified by them, while livestock was subsequently driven through the embers to ensure they enjoyed supernatural protection from disease or the effects of witchcraft. Such fires might also be lit at times when a community felt itself to be threatened by some calamity in the expectation that this would bring some relief.

Brands from the fire were traditionally taken from house to house to rekindle the fire in the domestic hearth, which would then burn continually until the next festival. Whoever carried the need-fire from hearth to hearth had to be innocent of any crime, and was prohibited from carrying anything made of metal as he went about his sacred duty.

The Christian church forbade the lighting of such fires in the 8th century, but the practice continued in various parts of Europe into relatively modern times. Records exist of such fires being lit to counter cattle disease in England as late as 1785.

Nemed Legendary conqueror of Ireland, who is identified in the ancient *Leabhar Gabhala Eireann* (Book of Invasions) as the leader of the third invasion of the country. Nemed is said to have taken over the country after the previous inhabitants (the followers of PARTH-OLON) had been wiped out by plague, but after he too died of the plague his people were overwhelmed by the FOMORIANS, the race of monstrous demons named as the original inhabitants of Ireland before Partholon's invasion. The remaining band of 30 Nemedians eventually left Ireland to find a new home elsewhere.

Nerthus In German and Scandinavian mythology, a goddess of fertility who was venerated as a Mother Earth figure. Also known as Hertha, she is often confused with the Norse NJORD.

Nessa In Irish mythology, the mother of King CONCHOBAR. Also the lover of Fergus Mac Roth, she conceived Conchobar either by her husband Fachta or by the druid Cathbad.

Net In Irish mythology, an early war-god identified as the consort of NEMAINN. The grandfather of BALOR, he was killed at the second battle of Mag Tuired.

nettle Stinging weed that has long been credited with a variety of magical properties. According to British folklore the plant grows only where human urine has spilled on the ground and is deemed to have particular magical potency if growing in locations where sunlight never falls. Together with the thistle, it is sometimes identified as the plant of the DEVIL.

Northern European tradition makes numerous claims for stinging nettles. Not only will they ward off lightning (recalling the Norse identification of the plant with Thor, the god of lightning) but they will also bring courage to those in danger

and instantly cure fever in any patient who pulls up the weed while intoning their name and those of their parents. Consuming nettle seeds will negate the effects of various poisons and stings and will also heal damage done by the bite of a mad dog. Nettle tea is supposed to purify the blood, and is widely considered good treatment for colds or toothache.

British folk medicine claims that packing the nose with stinging nettles will staunch nosebleeds and that combing the hair with nettle juice will restore thinning hair. Sufferers from rheumatism, meanwhile, are recommended to thrash the affected parts with stinging nettles to get relief from the problem.

The relieving of nettle stings by rubbing the site with a dock leaf while intoning 'In dock out nettle' ranks among the best known of all folk remedies.

New Year The beginning of the year is celebrated as a time of special magic significance all round the world (even though the date may differ from culture to culture). Some celebrations are strongly religious in character, while others are secular social gatherings during the course of which a variety of traditional customs are observed, usually symbolizing the notions of death and rebirth.

In the modern English-speaking world the event is usually celebrated in the form of parties, with highlights including the counting down of the last seconds to midnight and the singing of 'Auld Lang Syne' (to the words of Robert Burns). In Britain this may be followed by a FIRST-FOOTING ritual. Church bells throughout Europe and the USA are rung at midnight on New Year's Eve and it was formerly thought advisable to make as much noise as possible as midnight strikes in order to scare away evil spirits. If the alcohol runs out at New Year's Eve parties tradition advises that WELL water turns to wine as the year changes. The first person to drink from a well at New Year, incidentally, will thereby enjoy great good fortune over the next year. In times gone by there was great competition to be the lucky person to taste this so-called 'Cream of the Well'.

It is widely believed that whatever happens on New Year's Day will set the pattern for the rest of the year. Thus, it is unlucky to have no money or food in the house on the first day of the year, and many people will insist upon getting up early and doing something active, even perhaps some work, to ensure they have a productive year. By the same token, the fire must not be allowed to go out during the first night of the year, as otherwise the hearth will be cold for the next 12 months. It is also unlucky to throw anything away on New Year's Day, lest all good luck is accidentally thrown out with it, and financially reckless to pay money or make a loan on this date. It was formerly believed that it is also a bad day to wash clothes, as this might mean one of the family will be 'washed away' in the months to come.

The state of the weather on New Year's Day is also significant. If the wind blows from the north, for instance, the year will see much bad weather, while if it blows from the south the weather will be good. If it blows from the east the world must expect famine or some other calamity. If it blows from the west then the year will see good supplies of milk and fish but also the death of a famous person. Best of all is a New Year's Day when the wind does not blow at all, as this signifies a year of joy and prosperity.

See also HOGMANAY.

nhang In Armenian folklore, a malevolent demon that lures mortals to their deaths at sea. The nhang appears as a beautiful female, not unlike a MERMAID.

Niall of the Nine Hostages In Irish legend, a king of Tara, possible a semi-historical figure living in the 4th century AD. He won his throne in a competition with his four step-brothers. Promised the throne by his father Eochu Muigmedon, he was obliged to go through various tests

of his suitability as king. For the first test the prophetic smith Sithchean set fire to his forge to see which tools the brothers rescued from the flames – the young Niall retrieved the hammer and anvil that were of all the things inside the most important of the smith's tools and thus won the contest. To confirm Niall's suitability Sithchean sent all four boys into the forest to test their survival skills. Desperate to find a drink, the boys happened across a well guarded by an ugly hag, who insisted upon a kiss before she would allow them to slake their thirst. Niall alone stepped forward to kiss her and she was transformed instantly into the goddess of SOVEREIGNTY, thus proving once and for all his right to the crown.

Niamh In Irish mythology, the lover of OISIN, who kept him in TIR NAN OG for some 300 years before conceding to his request to revisit his old haunts on earth. She instructed him not to let his feet touch the ground, but he dismounted from his horse and was instantly turned into an old man and died. The name is also borne by two other characters in Irish myth, one being the lover of CUCHULAINN and the other the wife of one of the sons of CONCHOBAR.

Nibelungenlied German medieval epic poem that was based upon tales from Norse mythology. Many of the legends retold in the *Nibelungenlied* by an unidentified author in the 13th century were recorded originally in the VÖLSUNGASAGA and the EDDA.

The Nibelungs are a race of dwarfs, the possessors of a fabulous hoard of gold, who are ruled over by their king Nibelung. The Hoard, forged by the dwarf ALBERICH, subsequently passes to other guardians, including SIEGFRIED. Siegfried's story is the subject of the first part of the epic, which describes his marriage to Gunther's sister KRIEMHILD and his murder by Hagen (who runs a spear through Siegfried's one vulnerable spot, on his back) at the wish of BRUNHILD.

Gunther and Hagen then deprive Kriemhild of the Hoard and hide it in the Rhine, but both are killed before telling anyone where they have put it. It therefore remains the eternal responsibility of the Rhine Maidens.

The second part of the epic follows the marriage of Kriemhild to Etzel (or Attila) of the Huns and her subsequent revenge over Gunther and Hagen, both of whom she kills before herself dying at the hands of Hildebrand.

The *Nibelungenlied* has had a profound influence upon German culture over the centuries, inspiring numerous works of art as well as major works of literature and Wagner's renowned cycle of four operas, *The Ring of the Nibelungen*.

Nicholas, St *See* FATHER CHRISTMAS.

Nich Noch Nothing Celtic folk tale about the adventures of a young hero who is set a series of seemingly impossible tasks by a GIANT. Knowing that if he fails any of the tasks he will die, Nich Noch Nothing is faced initially with the challenge of clearing out a stable seven miles long (reminiscent of the stable-cleaning feat of Hercules in classical myth). This he achieves with the aid of an army of animals and birds summoned by the giant's sympathetic daughter. Next he is ordered to empty a large loch, seven miles cubed. Once again he is helped out by the giant's daughter, who commands the fish in the loch to drink all the water. The third challenge is to climb a seven-mile-high branchless tree and to bring down the eggs he will find at the top. The giant's daughter accordingly cuts off all her fingers and toes to build Nich Noch Nothing a flight of steps to the top of the tree, but he drops one of the eggs on the way down and has to run away before the giant catches him.

Nicka-Nan Night *See* SHROVE TUESDAY.

Niflheim In Norse mythology, a northern land of eternal cold and ice ruled over by the goddess HEL. It comprises nine worlds, to which the spirits of those who have died of disease or old age are destined to go. According to legend, this is where the world was originally created.

nightingale Sweet-voiced European songbird around which a number of well-known folkloric traditions have accrued. According to medieval superstition, the nightingale is terrified of snakes and fears it will be bitten by one while it sleeps: thus it sings out of pain as its presses its breast against a thorn in order to stay awake all night long. Alternatively, it is in love with the rose and presses itself against a thorn in order to fight this passion. Medieval tradition also had it that if the nightingale sings before the cuckoo then the person who hears it can expect success in love. Other beliefs concerning the nightingale include the notion that anyone who dines on nightingale tongues will enjoy greatly enhanced powers of eloquence, and that anyone who eats nightingale flesh will find they can overcome sleepiness.

nightmare Folklore offers a variety of explanations for bad dreams. Most of these blame them upon the influence of the Devil or of some other evil spirit (*see* INCUBUS) or witch seeking to cause distress in the sleeper. These demons are reputed to steal into bedrooms and once inside squat upon the sleeper's breast, thus creating the stifled sensation often associated with bad dreams. They are sometimes described as appearing in the guise of spectral horses, hence the term 'nightmare' (although the word would actually appear to have come from the Old English *mare*, meaning 'evil spirit').

Folk remedies for those plagued by nightmares include pinning one's socks in the shape of a cross to the end of the bed, keeping a knife or something else made of iron near the bed, and sleeping with the hands crossed on the breast. In some parts of the Christian world sleepers attach small straw crosses to the four corners of the bed for the same reason. Any lingering ill effects resulting from nightmares may be dismissed on waking up by spitting three times.

Nimue In Arthurian legend, a maiden with whom MERLIN falls in love. Merlin meets Nimue while out in the woods, situated according to Breton tradition in the Val Sans Retour in Brittany. Nimue asks Merlin how to make a tower of air, and then imprisons the adoring Merlin within it. In English romance Nimue is sometimes regarded as synonymous with the LADY OF THE LAKE. Other versions of her name include Niniane and Vivienne.

Nine Worthies A band of nine legendary heroes who were celebrated as emblems of courage and virtue in medieval times. They comprised the biblical figures of David, Joshua and Judas Maccabaeus, the classical heroes Alexander, Hector and Julius Caesar, and the Christian leaders Arthur, Charlemagne and Godfrey of Bouillon (a leader of the First Crusade). Shakespeare's partial list of the Worthies in *Love's Labour's Lost* includes Pompey and Hercules.

Niniane *See* NIMUE.

nisse In Scandinavian mythology, household spirits similar to BROWNIES. They have unpredictable tempers, and if not appeased with suitable offerings of food may take offence and cause trouble, although on other occasions they can also be very helpful to mortals.

nix In Norse mythology, a malevolent water spirit found in various bodies of fresh water. Also known as a nicker, it is variously described as half-child and half-horse, with backwards-pointing hoofs, or else as an old man who sits on rocks while wringing the water from his hair. Nixes, which may belong to either sex, have a great love of dance and music and may be tempted to go in disguise to village celebrations to enjoy dancing with mortal maidens and perhaps engage in romantic liaisons with them. However, nixes are not to be trusted as they sometimes seize mortals and drown them. In former times it was widely thought to be unwise to attempt to rescue someone drowning for fear of incurring the wrath of a nix, who might get revenge by drowning the rescuer. Like various other types of evil spirit, they were also believed to exchange human babies with their own loathsome CHANGELINGS.

Njord In Norse mythology, the god of the ocean. One of the VANIR, he was subsequently admitted to the ranks of the AESIR. In constant strife with the earth goddess NERTHUS, he married the ice giantess Skadi, in whose house in the mountains he spent part of each year (she disliked his home on the seashore because the noise made by the seagulls prevented her from sleeping). He was venerated as the protector of wealth and ships.

nocnitsa In the folklore of several Eastern European countries, a variety of HAG that takes delight in frightening small children. In order to protect their infants from interference by such hags as they prowl around human habitations at night, mothers may place a knife in the cradle or else use a knife to draw a protective circle around the child's bed, thus employing the magic of IRON to ward off the threat of evil.

Nodens *See* NUADU.

Norns In Norse mythology, the three goddesses who control the fate of mortals. Variously taking responsibility for the past, the present, and the future, the Norns were variously depicted as giantesses or dwarfs, and had equivalents in many other cultures. They lived at the foot of the ash-tree YGGDRASIL, which they tended each day with water from the fountain of Urd. The Anglo-Saxons knew them as the Wyrdes.

nose Because the nose is associated with the life-sustaining process of breathing it has always been regarded as significant in folklore. In primitive times the nose was even venerated by some people as a symbol of life itself. To prevent evil spirits gaining access to the body via the nose it was widely thought to be desirable to decorate it with an amulet or ring made of some deterrent metal. In some cultures, especially in the Far East, the noses of corpses are traditionally sealed up with pieces of jade or other objects to keep them safe from such interference.

According to the pseudo-science of physiognomy much may be divined about a person's character from the shape of their nose. The French say that a short nose, for instance, is indicative of a lazy nature, while a long nose suggests a proud and courageous temperament. A pointed nose is a sign of a hot temper and a good memory, while a fat nose signifies a loyal and honest character. Turned-up noses suggest daring and lustfulness.

The size of the nose is traditionally supposed to be indicative of the size of male genitalia. Blue veins running across or down the nose, meanwhile, may be interpreted as portents of death.

An itching nose may be interpreted as meaning a variety of things. A Canadian rhyme advises: 'You'll be mad, see a stranger, kiss a fool or be in danger'. Folk remedies for nosebleeds range from dropping a cold iron key down the sufferer's back or inhaling the ashes of a vinegar-soaked rag, to wearing a dried toad in a bag around the neck or, according to one rather bizarre US tradition, poking a cat's tail up the nostril.

Nuadu In Irish legend, the king of the TUATHA DE DANANN. He lost a hand in the first battle of MAG TUIRED against the FIRBOLGS and thus lost his throne to BRES MAC ELATHA under the law that a rightful king of the Tuatha must not be physically imperfect. The Medicine god Diancecht and Credne the smith subsequently made him a silver hand, thus allowing him to reclaim his throne, and Diancecht's son Miach ultimately created for him a hand of flesh. Nuadu appointed LUGH king in his stead while he devised a plan to beat the FOMORIANS, but was himself killed in the second battle of Mag Tuired. He was also known as Airgetlam (Silverhand) and Nodens, the name by which he was venerated at a shrine at Lydney, Gloucestershire, and was also by some identified as a god of the waters not dissimilar to the Roman Neptune.

numbers The folklore of many cultures has attached particular magical significance to certain numbers, particular those between 0 and 14.

Most of the world's cultures consider odd numbers to be luckier than even numbers, perhaps because they will not yield to exact division. Many people have their own 'lucky' numbers, which they favour when gambling or otherwise chancing their luck. Among the most generally agreed propitious numbers are one (God's number), three (the number of the Holy Trinity), seven (possibly because ancient civilizations knew of seven planets but also because of its frequent appearance in the Bible, as in the Seven Virtues and the Seven Deadly Sins), and nine (which, being thrice three, amounts to a trinity of trinities). The number three is perhaps the focus of the largest body of superstitions shared around the globe. People in many parts of the world are familiar with the notion of being 'third time lucky', for instance, although it is also said that accidents and funerals happen in threes. In the Christian world this negative aspect of the number is linked to Peter's three denials of Christ, although the same taboos also crop up in non-Christian cultures. The number nine is especially linked with health matters and appears many times in legend, as for instance in the nine worlds of NIFLHEIM and the nine lives that every cat is supposed to have.

Less propitious numbers include four (which represents death in the folklore of the Far East and is also ominously significant in Christian tradition through the Four Horsemen of the Apocalypse) and the infamous 13 (the number of diners at the Last Supper, but also regarded with mistrust in pre-Christian times). Another is 666, the biblical 'number of the Beast' which is mentioned in the Book of Revelations and is today considered the Devil's number.

Counting was itself regarded as a magical act in many ancient cultures. Simply by counting one's warts, for instance, and telling the number to a stranger was thought to be enough to make them disappear. However, counting up one's money, children, cattle or other assets was frowned upon in many societies as this could be interpreted as questioning God's bounty and thus likely to invite divine displeasure. Not dissimilar is the legend associated with many stone circles in northwest Europe to the effect that the stones themselves cannot be counted and that anyone who attempts to do so will be struck down or taken ill before the task is completed.

The pseudo-science of numerology attempts to apply the magic of numbers directly to human existence by employing them as a means of divination or character analysis. Methods used to such ends include adding up the numerical value of the letters in a person's name or alternatively their date of birth and breaking the total down to a number between one and nine, each of which has its own characteristics. Thus, a person whose name relates to the number one has a dominating and ambitious personality, while two denotes a kind and gentle nature, and three signifies intelligence and an artistic temperament. Four suggests dependability, five indicates intelligence, impatience, sociability and sexuality, six bespeaks a harmonious nature, seven suggests intellectuality, eight denotes wealth and power, and nine suggests idealism and high achievement.

numerology *See* NUMBERS.

nure onna In Japanese folklore, a malevolent spirit that causes trouble among mortals. It is usually described as having long hair and a long tongue.

nursery rhymes Rhymes, poems and couplets that are recited or sung to and by young children throughout the world. These traditional metrical jingles form the basis of many old games, dances and songs, and are still in common use today, widely recognized for their value in teaching language and social skills.

It is possible to group nursery rhymes of the English-speaking world into various categories. Many, such as 'Rock-a-bye, baby' and 'Bye, baby bunting' are lullabies, designed to lull fractious children to sleep. Others, such as 'Oranges and lemons', are accompaniments to simple children's games. Some, such as 'Eenie, meenie, minie, mo' and 'One, two, buckle my shoe', are used to count out time at the start of a game and may have had their origins in the rhymes once used by shepherds when counting their sheep. Other rhymes, such as 'This little pig went to market' and 'Pat-a-cake, pat-a-cake, baker's man', are accompanied by physical actions and are intended purely for the delight of young charges. Other categories include riddle-rhymes and moralistic proverbs aimed at children.

Some nursery rhymes have ancient origins rooted in folklore or superstition, while others (such as 'Old Mother Hubbard' and 'The Grand Old Duke of York') grew out of relatively recent historical personages or events. Among those with traceable historical roots are 'Ride a cock-horse', which may have referred to Elizabeth I or to Lady Godiva; 'Mary, Mary, quite contrary', apparently a reference to Mary I; 'Little Boy Blue', which is supposed to have been a reference to Cardinal Wolsey; 'Hot cross buns', which developed out of a street cry; and 'Lavender's blue', which was based on a 17th-century ballad. The historical background of 'Little Jack Horner' is particularly detailed, supposedly referring to one

Thomas Horner, steward to the Abbot of Glastonbury, who is alleged to have helped himself to the title deeds of the manor of Mells when told to take the title deeds of 12 properties 'baked in a pie' as a present to Henry VIII. The nursery rhyme 'Ring-a-ring-o'-roses', meanwhile, is often associated with the Black Death or the Great Plague, apparently referring to the symptoms of the illness (which included red rashes and sneezing bouts), but it may in fact have originated quite independently of this, with 'falling down' perhaps signifying a curtsey.

The first serious collections of nursery rhymes were compiled in the early 18th century, many of the best known being collected under the name of such mythical storytellers as Mother Goose, Mother Bunch, Old Mother Hubbard and Tom Thumb.

nut Widely regarded as symbols of life itself, nuts are generally considered to be emblems of good luck and most folkloric traditions connected with them are positive in character. Brides were formerly presented with bags of nuts as a symbol of fruitfulness as they left the church (a practice that was later replaced by the tossing of rice and, in more modern times, paper confetti). Lovers may also employ the magic of nuts in order to divine the future of love affairs. The most popular method (closely associated with HALLOWE'EN) is to name a nut after each partner and then place them in the fire or on the bars of the grate: if the nuts burn together with a bright flame this is a sure sign that the affair will prosper.

Tradition claims that a good harvest of nuts will be followed in due course by a bumper crop of babies. This notion may relate to an ancient ruse many wives used to deceive their husbands – meeting their lovers on the pretext of gathering nuts. No one, incidentally, should go out nut-gathering on 14 September, as this is the day the Devil goes a-nutting.

Nutcrack Night *See* HALLOWE'EN.

nutmeg Like other spices, nutmeg is widely believed to have various luck-giving properties. Sprinkling nutmeg upon a lottery ticket or gambling slip, for instance, is supposed to promote the chance of winning. Dreams of nutmeg signify coming changes in the sleeper's life. Nutmeg also has its uses in folk medicine, being worn as a charm against rheumatism and boils. In the West Indies powdered nutmeg is sometimes administered to women in the throes of childbirth. Elsewhere it is used to eradicate freckles and improve the eyesight.

Nutter's Dance English folk dance that is performed annually at Bacup, Lancashire, on Easter Saturday. Similar to the MORRIS DANCE, it is danced by eight men wearing black costumes, with white skirts and stockings. The main feature of the dance is the rhythmic clapping together of wooden 'nuts' worn at the hands, knees and waists.

O

oak The oak tree, known in England as the 'monarch of the forest' and venerated in many European cultures, has been widely considered among the most sacred of all the trees since ancient times. Its longevity, combined with its ability to throw up new shoots from the roots of the old tree, probably accounts for its special folkloric significance.

The oak was regarded with awe and reverence in various pagan cultures and was particularly associated with the Norse god THOR and with the Celtic Druids (the word 'Druid' itself possibly coming from the Greek *drus*, meaning 'oak'). Certain 'holy oaks' were identified as magical places and oak wood was widely favoured as material for carved idols. Pagan marriages often took place beneath oaks, as did many other ritual events. Veneration of the tree in pagan Germany was such that any man found guilty of damaging an oak tree might to put to death by having his navel nailed to the tree itself and then being forced to walk round the trunk so that his intestines were pulled from his body and wrapped round the tree. Centuries later, it was still considered ill-advised to fell an oak, and it was widely maintained that the screams of an oak being cut down could be heard up to a mile away.

The sacred reputation of the oak survived the introduction of Christianity, and many churches were built close to oak trees that were already a focus of local veneration. Oak-leaf decorations may still be seen in many churches today. Open-air gospel readings and religious meetings were until relatively recent times often held under well-known 'gospel oaks' in each locality. The pagan connections of the tree were not extinguished by Christianity, however, and it is still widely associated with the GREEN MAN and, since medieval times, with WITCHCRAFT. Legend has it that MERLIN sometimes prepared his spells under the shelter of an oak to ensure their effectiveness.

Boughs of oak were carried at weddings in former times as a symbol of fertility, and were also kept in houses in the belief that these would safeguard the occupants. According to a long-standing tradition rooted originally in the link with Thor, the Norse god of thunder, lightning never strikes oak trees. This is, however, erroneous (as recognized by the old English rhyme warning 'Beware the oak, it draws the stroke'). Nonetheless, as a result of this belief oak boughs or ACORNS were often placed on window sills to protect houses during storms.

The oak has a prominent role in folk medicine. In Cornwall, for instance, it was once believed that by hammering a nail into an oak tree a patient might enjoy relief from toothache. According to Welsh folklore it was supposed that rubbing sores with oak bark on Midsummer Day would quickly clear up the problem.

Some oaks are famous for their historical or folkloric associations and still stand today (or at least were still in existence into relatively modern times). In Britain the most celebrated have included the

Boscobel Oak near Shifnal, Shropshire, in which Charles II is supposed to have hidden from the Parliamentarians; the Ellerslie Oak near Paisley, in which Sir William Wallace and his men once sheltered; Herne's Oak in Windsor Great Park, which is reputed to be the haunt of HERNE THE HUNTER (replaced by a new tree planted by Queen Victoria after the old one blew down); and the Major Oak in Sherwood Forest, which – like the now vanished Robin Hood's Larder in the same area – is intimately connected with the ROBIN HOOD story.

See also MISTLETOE; OAK APPLE DAY; YULE LOG.

Oak Apple Day In the English folk calendar, a traditional celebration held each year on 29 May – Charles II's birthday – in honour of the king's escape from his Parliamentarian enemies in 1651 after the Battle of Worcester, when he hid from his pursuers in an OAK tree. Also known as Royal Oak Day, Oak-and-Nettle Day and, in some places, Shick Shack Day, it was introduced after the restoration of the monarchy in 1660 to celebrate the king's deliverance, and was for a time a more widely observed holiday than MAY DAY itself. In former times, anyone who failed to wear a sprig of oak leaves on Oak Apple Day risked being beaten with stinging nettles by way of punishment.

A variety of customs connected with oaks and acorns were observed on Oak Apple Day, some of them predating Charles II's adventures by many centuries. These included processions in which honour was paid to a person paraded in the guise of the 'Garland King'. The Garland King was lavishly decorated with flowers and with sprigs of oak, as were houses, church towers, war memorials, horses, vehicles and even fishing boats. Even today the people of Castleton in Derbyshire celebrate 29 May as Garland Day, with a procession featuring marching bands and a flower-laden Garland King and his Lady, both dressed in Stuart costume.

In London 29 May is also celebrated as Founder's Day at the Royal Hospital, Chelsea (home of the Chelsea Pensioners), which was founded by Charles II allegedly at the suggestion of his mistress Nell Gwynne: during the course of the celebrations a statue of the king in the main court is appropriately decorated with oak boughs in front of the assembled veterans themselves, all proudly wearing sprigs of oak.

Oakham horseshoes See HORSESHOE.

oath In the folklore of most cultures, a solemn promise that must be observed on pain of dishonour or of divine or supernatural retribution, or else the invoking of some powerful totemic being, person or object to witness the truth of what is being claimed.

The notion of the oath as the motive force behind many folk tales and legends is ancient and common to virtually all folkloric traditions. The most sacred oaths are usually made either in the name of a god or physically over some object of ritual importance. These objects may range from warriors' swords or the grave of a parent or loved one, to water from a holy river or a sacred book, such as the Bible.

Often the person who has bound himself by such an oath denies that he is free to change his mind at a later date, however much he may wish to do so, and once made there is no unmaking of an oath. In many folk tales the news that an enemy has taken a solemn oath of revenge is rarely taken lightly and may be enough to cause great misgiving in the intended victim.

Often oaths are taken to demonstrate the veracity of what a person is alleging, the theory being that if he or she is actually lying this will be quickly revealed in the form of some act of divine retribution, typically the death of the person concerned. Even today people may attest the accuracy of what they claim with such formula oaths as 'May God strike me down if I am lying' or the similar 'Cross my heart and hope to die'. Although the wording might vary from culture to culture the underlying reasoning is the same: a liar who breaks his oath must expect his guilt to be revealed by his suffering the consequences he himself predicted.

A striking (and apparently true) example of the consequences of a broken oath that was once widely repeated was that of the suspected English witch Joan Flower who declared on oath in court at Lincoln in 1618 that she was no witch, and that if she was then God would choke her as she ate the piece of bread she now put in her mouth. Before the eyes of the startled judges she promptly swallowed the bread, choked on it and died.

Obeah In Africa and the West Indies, a tradition of magic that in many ways represents an equivalent of the VOODOO folk religion of Haiti. Like voodoo, obeah is usually associated with the conjuring of black magic with the intention of harming others. The spells of the obeahmen are said to make use of human corpses, parts of animals, blood and graveyard soil, and the word itself has the connotation of putting something in the ground in order to cause harm to someone else. The obeahmen are much respected among the local people, particularly the poor, who see their magic-making as a means of retaliation against those who oppress them.

Oberon The legendary king of the fairies. Best known in the English-speaking world from William Shakespeare's depiction of Oberon and his queen, Titania, in his play *A Midsummer Night's Dream*, Oberon may have been imported originally from a French romance called *Huon de Bordeaux*, in which he is identified as the son of Julius Caesar and MORGAN LE FAY. The French source gives his name as Alberon, suggesting a link with German legends about the dwarf ALBERICH, king of the elves.

Varying accounts depict Oberon as being just three feet tall and as having an angelically beautiful face. At his birth the fairies bestowed upon him insight into the thoughts of mortals and the power to transport himself instantly from one place to another. According to Shakespeare's account of him he also had the power to make himself invisible.

Ochain The magic shield of the great Irish warrior CONCHOBAR Mac Nessa. Legend had it that the shield would moan whenever its owner was in danger.

Octriallach In Irish legend, one of the FOMORIANS, the early inhabitants of Ireland who warred with the TUATHA DE DANANN. It was Octriallach who found out how Diancecht, physician to the Tuatha de Danann, was reviving the dead by taking them to the Well of Slaine. Octriallach led the other Fomorians to the spring and filled it in to prevent any further resuscitations. He met his death at the hands of the warrior OGMA.

Odin In Norse mythology, the king of the gods, who holds court in VALHALLA. Also known among Anglo-Saxons as Woden, Wotan or Votan, he sees everything and knows everything, having exchanged one of his eyes for a drink from the fountain of MIMIR, the source of all wisdom, and having learned the secrets of the Runes by hanging on YGGDRASIL for nine days and nights. He is also described as the god of agriculture, poetry and war, dispatching the VALKYRIES to bring the bravest Viking warriors to his hall.

Odin was the son of the god Bor and a giantess called Bestla. He is often depicted as a one-eyed wanderer, dressed in a cloak and wide-brimmed hat and leaning on a staff that was in reality his spear Gungnir. Sometimes he appears on his horse, called Sleipnir. His one remaining eye is the sun. He is sometimes depicted presiding over the feasting at Valhalla from his throne Valaskialf, with his two ravens, called Hugin (Thought) and Munin (Memory), perched on his shoulder. At his feet lie the two wolves Geri and Freki.

It was Odin who constructed the earth from the body of the giant YMIR and who created the first men from the ash and the elm. On the whole, he is described as generally benevolent towards humanity, his own creation, although he often finds the deeds of mortals peculiar and sometimes positvely laughable.

The Vikings respected Odin more than any other god. The 'promise of Odin', in which a person passed their hand through a huge silver ring or else through a sacrificial holed stone while making a vow, was the most serious promise that could be made. In the Orkneys there is still a holed oval stone called the Stone of Odin that is thought to have been used for such promises, particularly marriage vows.

Oenghus *See* ANGUS MAC OG.

Ogier the Dane Legendary Danish hero whose adventures were celebrated in French medieval romance. The son of Geoffrey, King of Denmark, his birth was said to have been attended by fairies, including MORGAN LE FAY. According to legend his own son was killed by Charlot, son of CHARLEMAGNE. In a rage, Ogier wreaked revenge by killing Charlemagne's nephew and was only narrowly prevented from putting Charlemagne himself to death. He spent much of his life in exile and is also recorded as having defended France against the Saracens. The fairies then carried him to AVALON, where he lived for some 200 years before returning to France to fight off another invasion. Morgan Le Fay then took him back to Avalon. He is still celebrated in Denmark as a national hero, known in Danish as Holger Danske.

Ogma In Irish mythology, one of the heroes of the TUATHA DE DANANN, also the god of eloquence and of literature. The son of the DAGDA and the father of TUIRENN, he was humiliated by BRES, who forced him to gather firewood, but he subsequently led the Tuatha de Danann to victory against the FOMORIANS,

capturing Orna, the talking sword of King Tethra in the process. According to some accounts, he guided the dead to the OTHERWORLD. He was also identified as the inventor of the Ogham alphabet used in ancient inscriptions in Ireland (possibly a relic of an earlier system of forgotten druidic writing).

See also OGMIOS.

Ogmios In Celtic mythology, a god who was the subject of a cult following in Gaul. Equivalent to the Irish OGMA, he was considered to be a sun god and was sometimes depicted as a muscular old man carrying a whip and a bow, and with his hair sprayed out like the rays of the sun (re-miniscent of the Greek Hercules). Like Ogma, he also guided the dead to the OTHERWORLD.

ogre A malevolent GIANT that feeds on human flesh. Ogres may be of either sex, and some are credited with the ability to change their shape, often assuming the guise of an animal. Most are greedy and not very intelligent, and are readily fooled by the heroes of the folk tales in which they appear.

The word 'ogre' is thought to have been first used by Charles Perrault in the fairy tales he collected in 1697 as *Histoires ou contes du temps passé* (translated as *Tales of Mother Goose*). It has been suggested that Perrault took the name from Orcus, an alternative name for Pluto or Hades.

Oimelc *See* IMBOLC.

Oisin (or Ossian) In Irish mythology, a bard and warrior who was one of the heroes of the ill-fated FIANNA. The son of FIONN MAC CUMHAILL and SADBH, he survived the disastrous Battle of Gabhra but was then lured by the beautiful NIAMH to the supernatural world of TIR NAN OG, where he remained for several hundred years (although it seemed but a short time to Oisin himself). He eventually persuaded Niamh to allow him to revisit Ireland, riding a white horse, but was warned that he must not allow his foot to touch the ground while he was there. Unfortunately he dismounted to help some peasants move a heavy stone and was at once transformed into an old man. Before dying he told the story of the Fianna to St Patrick (who tried unsuccessfully to persuade Oisin to be baptized as a Christian), thus passing the legends on to later generations.

The fact that Oisin was also a bard gave some credibility to the poems purportedly by him that were published to great acclaim by the Scottish poet James MacPherson (1736–96). The poems were subsequently revealed to have been the work of MacPherson himself, but in the meantime many people (including Goethe and even the French emperor Napoleon) had read them with great interest and expressed their admiration. Sir James MacGregor published a more reliable collection of Ossianic ballads as *The Book of the Dean of Lismore* (1512–26).

Old Man of the Sea In the *Arabian Nights*, a pernicious old man (actually a JINNI) who latches onto the unsuspecting SINBAD during his travels. He persuades Sinbad to lift him onto his shoulders to reach some fruit but then holds on tightly so that Sinbad cannot put him down again. After many days and nights carrying this burden about Sinbad finally succeeds in making the Old Man of the Sea loose his hold by getting him drunk. He shakes the demon off and dashes out his brains with a stone.

Equivalent characters in the folklore of other cultures include the Burr-woman of Native American myth – an old woman who similarly persuades the hero to lift her onto his back and once in place cannot be dislodged.

Old Nick See DEVIL.

olive The slow-growing olive tree has long had special folkloric significance in Mediterranean countries, representing such virtues as peace, friendship, beauty,

prosperity and strength to the Arabs, Carthaginians, Cretans, Egyptians, Hellenes, Greeks, Phoenicians and Romans, among other ancient civilizations. In the Bible it is an olive leaf that the dove brings back to the Ark as a sign that the waters of the Flood have receded. The Garden of Gethsemane, where Jesus was betrayed is sometimes described as an olive grove. The tree is supposed to provide protection against lightning, witchcraft and other forms of evil. The olive is also closely associated with fertility, and is said to flourish when tended by innocent young children.

Oliver One of the most famous of the knights who attended the court of CHARLEMAGNE. The son of Regnier, Duke of Genoa, his adventures with his companion ROLAND were much celebrated in medieval romantic literature. According to these accounts, his sword was called Hauteclaire, while his horse had the name Ferrant d'Espagne.

Olwen In Welsh mythology, the daughter of the giant Yspaddaden. She eventually became the wife of the hero CULHWCH after the latter completed the many apparently impossible challenges set him by her father. Olwen was noted for her great beauty and courage, and was also known as White Track, because white trefoils sprang up where she walked. She did not, however, give any assistance to Culhwch in the difficult tasks he had to fulfil, as it had been prophesied that whoever she married was fated to kill her father – a prophesy that was realized when Culhwch completed the 39 challenges, claimed Olwen as his own, and put Yspaddaden to death.

omen A portent of good or bad fortune that is usually revealed by some event beyond human control. Over the centuries omens have been read into a wide range of natural phenomena, from the appearance of comets or the blooming of flowers out of season to the birth of two-headed calves and the spitting of household fires. The behaviour of birds has always been interpreted as being especially significant: if a black bird settles on a house, for instance, this foretells the death of one of the occupants, while even today many people worry about seeing a single magpie as this is similarly understood to be a warning of misfortune.

Some portents come in more overtly supernatural guises. Such portents range from meeting a DOPPELGÄNGER to hearing inexplicable rappings or the unearthly wail of the BANSHEE – all foretelling an imminent death.

oneiromancy The pseudo-science of DIVINATION through the analysis of dreams. The interpretation of dreams has a long history, going back to ancient times, although conclusions about what each detail of a dream means vary hugely from culture to culture and from era to era. Today, many practitioners of oneiromancy favour the notion that dreams express the direct opposite of what is going to happen. Since the 19th century the influence of Freud has meant that many interpretations dwell on the sexual relevance of dreams. Despite the less-than-scientific basis of the practice, oneiromancy remains one of the most popular forms of divination in modern Western society, and there are numerous publications offering guidance on the subject. One method of analysis links dreams to a particular card of the Tarot pack, each of which has its own detailed symbolic meaning.

oni In Japanese mythology, a class of demons or ogres. Depicted with large monstrous heads, complete with fangs and horns, they could also change their shape, and might appear to mortals disguised as old women or beggars. Several folk tales describe how an oni is overpowered by a devout Buddhist, who then saws off the demon's horns. A feature of Japanese New Year rituals is the ceremonial ejection of the oni from the house.

onion The pungency of the onion, together with its powerful eye-watering properties and strong taste, has made it the object of a wide variety of folkloric beliefs. Among other things, onions are supposed to ward off snakes and witches, who detest the smell, and if placed under the pillow will cause sleepers to enjoy dreams of their future partners. Another tradition insists that if onions are found to have thicker skins than usual this is a sure sign of a severe winter in store.

The onion has many roles in medicinal lore. It is supposed to prevent colds and generally promote a healthy atmosphere – the reason why onions were often hung up in rooms in times of plague. Onions may also be used in the treatment of dog bites, hangovers, insomnia, earache, warts, toothache and fever, and if carried about the person, will generally safeguard health. In some parts of the southern USA it is maintained that rubbing the scalp with onion will help to counter the threat of baldness.

See also GARLIC.

onyx Black and white gemstone that has a generally ominous reputation in folklore. Traditionally associated with sorcery and WITCHCRAFT, the gem is reputed to have uses in some of the most potent death-dealing spells. Those who own onyx may find themselves prone to nightmares and plagued by worry in their waking hours. Others, however, may find that the stone promotes their love life and keeps them in an optimistic frame of mind. Indian lore claims that onyx calms lust and can also be used to restore the immune system.

opal An iridescent gemstone that has the reputation of being perhaps the unluckiest of all precious gems. Tradition advises that it is risking grave misfortune for anyone to wear opal, unless they were born in October (opal being the birthstone for that month) – although another superstition suggests that if the stone is worn next to a diamond the latter will negate any malevolent effect. If an opal is inadvertently set in an engagement ring this may be interpreted as an omen of premature widowhood for the wearer.

The stone's reputation for bad luck was much boosted in the 19th century when King Alfonso XII of Spain gave an opal ring to his wife on their wedding-day. She died shortly afterwards, as did the king's sister and sister-in-law when the ring passed to them in their turn. When the startled and dismayed Alfonso then took to wearing the ring himself, his death also followed within a very short time. To prevent any further harm resulting from ownership of the ring the Queen Regent placed it round the neck of the Virgin of Almudena in Madrid.

On a more positive note, it was once believed that opals dipped in wine would reveal the presence of poison by turning pale or going cloudy – a property that made them popular among rulers in Renaissance Italy in particular. Science agrees that opals may indeed go cloudy if water is present. Another ancient tradition claims that opals will make their wearers invisible, hence their popularity with thieves in various stories.

Folk medicine claims that people who wear opals will enjoy better eyesight and, if blond, will find their hair keeps its colour much longer.

Open Sesame *See* ALI BABA.

orange The orange has long been prized for its effectiveness as a fertility charm, and is widely associated with love. It is said that lovers who exchange gifts of oranges will find they are drawn closer together, and brides today still carry orange blossom at their weddings in the belief that this will bring them luck and promote their chances of having children (a notion apparently inspired by the fact that the orange tree remains green and bears fruit and blossom throughout the year). They are also appropriate at weddings as they symbolize the virtues of chastity and faithfulness.

All British children are familiar with the nursery song 'Oranges and lemons', thought to have been originally a reference to the import of oranges, lemons and other exotic fruit at the London docks in medieval times. A special Oranges and Lemons ceremony of early-20th-century origin, is observed today at the Church of St Clement Danes in London on 31 March each year. This takes the form of a religious service, at the close of which all the children attending are presented with an orange and a lemon. During the course of the service the 'Oranges and lemons' tune is played on handbells.

Orc Triath In Irish legend, a boar that belonged to BRIGID, the daughter of the DAGDA. An Irish equivalent of TWRCH TRWYTH, it is thought to have been revered as an emblem of kingship.

Orfeo British incarnation of the Orpheus of classical Greek mythology, who journeys to the underworld in a doomed attempt to recover his beloved Eurydice. The story was retold in a number of medieval English and Scottish folk tales, in which Orfeo similarly descends to the underworld to rescue his lover, variously identified in Scottish tradition as Isabel and in English versions as Meroudys or Herodis. The Orpheus story also inspired the Welsh legend of PWYLL and RHIANNON and the Irish myth of Midhir and ETAIN.

Orlando *See* ROLAND.

Orvandil In Norse mythology, a legendary seafarer who was visited by THOR at his home in the land of Jotunheim. Called Earendel by the Anglo-Saxons, he lost a toe when it became frozen and was broken off by Thor, who flung it into the heavens where it formed the constellation of Orion (also known as Orvandil's Toe).

Oscar In Irish mythology, the son of OISIN. Like his father, he was famed as a warrior. He won fame by killing a massive boar, a task that many before him had failed to complete, and in his first battle killed three kings (although he also killed his best friend Linne by accident). Leading a band of fearsome warriors known as the 'Terrible Broom', because they swept aside everyone they came up against, he was also noted for his skills as a negotiator. He was advised of his imminent death by a meeting with the WASHER AT THE FORD. Shortly afterwards he was killed at the Battle of Gabhra by the High King of Ireland, who also died in the encounter. When the news reached his wife Aidin she died of a broken heart.

Ossian *See* OISIN.

Otherworld In Irish Celtic mythology, the kingdom of the dead. It is in the Otherworld, or Tech Duinn, that the souls of the dead are reborn. Once a year, according to legend, on the feast of SAMHAIN, the gates of the Otherworld are opened and the spirits of the dead revisit earth, bringing vengeance down upon any erstwhile enemies still living. The Otherworld is also described as the home of the gods. According to Irish folklore, the gods feast in the Otherworld around inexhaustible cauldrons (it was to the Otherworld beneath Ireland that the TUATHA DE DANANN were dispatched by the Sons of MIL ESPAINE). The Welsh, meanwhile, knew the Otherworld as Annw and located it on islands off the western coast of Wales.

In some folk tales privileged mortals gain access to the Otherworld while still alive and while there do not age at all, but on returning to the land of the living revert to their proper age (as was the case with OISIN when he returned from the Otherworld after a period of some 200 or 300 years). In some accounts the Otherworld is described in terms of a paradise, a land of perpetual happiness and pleasure, but according to others it is a dark and ominous place inhabited by demons and monsters.

See also UNDERWORLD.

otter The otter was the subject of great fascination to the Celts, who had many outlandish ideas about its nature and magical properties. The creature's semi-aquatic lifestyle led to arguments over whether the animal was flesh or fish (and thus, incidentally, acceptable as food during Lent). It was also believed that the animal changed its form as it moved between land and water.

The otter features in a number of folk tales. In Welsh legend, for instance, CERIDWEN adopts the guise of an otter when pursuing TALIESIN. In other tales from northern Europe otters offer assistance to a variety of heroes, such as MAELDUINE and BRENDAN, usually by offering them food.

overlooking *See* EVIL EYE.

ovinnik In Russian folklore, a supernatural spirit that inhabits the kilns used for drying and seasoning timber. The spirit must be treated with respect and thanked for his cooperation, as if he is displeased he may burn down the kiln. In former times cocks were regularly sacrificed to these important domestic spirits.

See also DOMOVIK.

Owain In Arthurian legend, the son of URIEN and MORGAN LE FAY who also appears in the *Mabinogion* and Chrétien de Troyes' poem 'Yvain', among other works. Based on a shadowy historical figure who fought with the British against the invading Angles in the 6th century, Owain was identified in 'The Dream of Rhonabwy' as the leader of a band of supernatural warriors called the Ravens, who fought Arthur's knights while the two leaders played a game of chess. His other adventures included defeating the Black Knight, finding the mythical Castle of the Fountain, and marrying the Lady of the Fountain. However, his subsequent desertion of this lady provoked her into driving him from Arthur's court and forcing him into seclusion in a remote country. On his deathbed he was magically revived by a noblewoman and went on to slay a lion and a serpent before rescuing Luned, the servant of the Lady of the Fountain from death by fire. He also rescued several other maidens in distress and killed a giant before finally returning to his lover, the Lady of the Fountain.

owl Being a largely nocturnal bird, the owl has always been regarded with mistrust in folklore. Seeing an owl, or hearing its call, is considered a bad omen in many cultures, and may be interpreted as a portent of imminent death – particularly if it is seen during daylight. Looking into an owl's nest, according to one tradition, sentences the person concerned to a life of melancholy, while the sight of an owl settling upon a rooftop threatens ill luck to all within. French superstition claims that if an owl hoots in the vicinity of a pregnant woman she will give birth to a girl. In Wales an owl hooting among houses reveals that the virginity of an unmarried girl nearby is in danger.

In keeping with the bird's generally ominous associations, transformation into an owl is greatly feared in folklore. In Welsh legend, for instance, BLODEUWEDD is transformed into an owl by the outraged GWYDION as a punishment for betraying her husband LLEU LLAW GYFFES.

The bodies of owls are supposed, however, to have their uses as safeguards against evil. The corpses of dead owls were in former times sometimes nailed to barn doors to protect the livestock and to keep the building safe from lightning strikes. Like other birds of prey, the owl was associated with courage, and warriors once carried owls' hearts when going into battle. More often, however, the bird is associated with wisdom.

In folk medicine, owl soup was recommended for the cure of whooping cough and the restoring of grey hair to its original colour. Eating charred and powdered owls' eggs was supposed to help those with weak eyesight. An obscure German remedy, meanwhile, suggests that if a person is bitten by a mad dog they should carry the heart and right foot of an owl about their person to prevent the onset of rabies.

oyster The oyster is perhaps the best known of all aphrodisiac foods. This tradition goes back to Roman times, perhaps inspired by a fancied similarity in appearance between the oyster and the female genitals. According to a long-established British custom, oysters should only be eaten in months that have the letter 'r' in them (thus confining their consumption to September to April), although this habit has substantially broken down in recent times with the import of oysters from other parts of the world all year round.

The English town of Colchester boasts a unique folk custom relating to oysters – the Oyster Feast held every year on or near 20 October. This large gathering of invited guests consumes around 12,000 oysters in celebration of the beginning of the oyster season, which has brought wealth to fishermen in the area since at least the 13th century.

According to US folklore, oyster shells are lucky and should be carried about the person to ensure good fortune. Another tradition claims that oysters 'wax and wane' with the moon. In folk medicine, a cure for deafness is to drop into the ear saliva that has been kept in an oyster shell buried in manure for two days.

P

pace-egging *See* EGG ROLLING.

Palm Sunday The Sunday preceding EASTER, on which Christ's entry into Jerusalem is commemorated throughout the Christian world. In early Christian iconography palms were carried by martyrs as a symbol of their martyrdom, and palm fronds are still carried by worshippers during Palm Sunday services. In past centuries, in regions where palms did not grow, people often substituted sprigs of hazel, willow and other native plants. It is said to be most unlucky to allow palms or their substitutes into the house before Palm Sunday itself, but once in the house these will protect the occupants from evil over the coming year. Similarly they may be hung up in stables to protect livestock.

The weather on Palm Sunday itself should be carefully noted: if it is fine then a good harvest will surely follow later in the year.

Palomides In Arthurian legend, a Saracen knight who was among the most respected of the knights of the ROUND TABLE. He sought the hand of ISOLDE OF IRELAND, and took the place of PELLINORE in the search for the QUESTING BEAST, although without success. He was honoured by LANCELOT with the title of Duke of Provence.

Pancake Day *See* SHROVE TUESDAY.

Panchatantra, Book of Indian fables, also known as the *Fables of Bidpai*, many of which have long since passed into European literature and folklore. This celebrated compilation of legends is thought to be between 1,500 and 2,000 years old, although the original Sanskrit version has only survived through translations in a range of other languages. It would appear to have become familiar to European readers by the 14th century, and some of the tales were subsequently reworked by such writers as LA FONTAINE and the Brothers GRIMM.

Similar in style to the *Fables of Aesop*, the stories that make up the five books of the *Panchatantra* are mostly animal tales, supposedly narrated by a wise brahmin to three rather slow-witted princes in order to illustrate to them simple moral truths and the benefits of a shrewd approach to life. One of the best known episodes is the tale of the hares who trick a lion into attacking its own reflection in a well and thus to drown itself. Another well-known episode is the legend of the crow that rids itself of a snake that has been eating its eggs; it does this by secreting a necklace from the royal palace in the creature's lair, which results in the snake being discovered and killed by palace servants.

pansy Brightly coloured flower, also known as heartsease, johnny-jump-up, love-in-idleness and (in Germany) stepmother, which has long been prized for its efficacy in love magic. In Shakespeare's *A Midsummer Night's Dream*, for instance, Puck drips the juice of a pansy into Titania's eyes to make her fall in love with the first living thing she sees on waking. The flower is also used in folk medicine to treat chest complaints and epilepsy. English lore advises that picking a pansy when the weather is fine will bring on a rainstorm, while another tradition warns that picking a pansy when it is wet will cause the death of a lover.

See also VIOLET.

paradise A heavenly AFTERWORLD to which the souls of the good may be admitted after death. The notion of an otherworldly paradise is common to many cultures, including most of the world's major religions. The Biblical paradise called the Garden of Eden is typical in that it is described as a place of harmony, innocence and ease where there is no suffering or death and the surroundings are those of a pleasant natural garden. The paradise or heaven to which the dead go is, however, regarded as distinct from this paradise and is little described but is often presumed to be similar in nature.

The paradise of Islam tradition is similar, although there is a much stronger sensual element, with the rewards of the faithful including the attentions of beautiful young virgins (see HOURI). The Buddhist paradise, Nirvana, is less focused upon physical well-being and is envisaged rather as a state of perfect spirituality.

The whereabouts of paradise was a source of much debate in medieval times. European authorities generally placed it somewhere in the east, variously located in China or on a circular island off India. According to a letter purported to have been written by the shadowy PRESTER JOHN it lay within three days' journey of his own kingdom. When the giant seed of the coca de mer was first found washed up on beaches in the Indian Ocean it was thought to be the fruit of paradise (the trees actually grow in the Seychelles).

parsley Like most other herbs, parsley is credited with various magical properties. Ancient tradition links parsley with the DEVIL (perhaps a relic of the Roman cus-tom of planting parsley on graves), and it is said that only wicked people can grow good parsley. Furthermore, the seeds must be sown nine times before they will come up because the Devil claims the first eight sowings, while the long period of germination is attributed to the fact that the seeds go to hell and back before sprouting. Parsley must never be planted by a stranger, and it is always best for the seed to be sown by a woman, as this will encourage its growth. A garden where the parsley flourishes is deemed by some to belong to a household where the woman rules the roost.

Parsley was once considered an antidote to poison, and adding a sprig of parsley as decoration to a dish was originally intended as a gesture of good faith. Care should be taken in bringing parsley into contact with glass, however, as this may mysteriously weaken the glass and cause it to shatter. In folk medicine, parsley seeds sprinkled on the head will cure baldness, and if consumed before a bout of drinking will enable a person to resist the effects of drunkenness. Chewing parsley will relieve rheumatism and a little parsley fed to livestock will cure disease. Carrying dried parsley is reputed to fend off nausea.

Lastly, by old British tradition, curious children are sometimes informed that baby girls are found in parsley beds, while baby boys are born under gooseberry bushes or alternatively in beds of nettles. Really persistent children are further enlightened with the information that the doctor digs up the new babies with a golden spade.

Partholon In Irish mythology, the leader of the first invasion of Ireland. Renowned for his mastery of every craft, he drove out the FOMORIANS and did much to bring civilization to Ireland. Among other things, he introduced such crafts as the brewing of ale, and established a code of laws. He also helped to prepare the landscape for agriculture, and is sometimes identified as the reaper of the last sheaf.

Unfortunately his efforts did not prevent the demise of his people through plague.

Patrick, St The patron saint of Ireland, whose name has become associated with many legends over the centuries. Born in mainland Britain around AD 390, he was captured by Irish pirates at the age of 16 and spent six years as a slave in Ireland. He eventually escaped to Britain and may have travelled subsequently to Gaul, but around 435 is thought to have returned to Ireland as a missionary. He did much to repress paganism and sun worship among the Irish as well as organizing the Christian church there and generally spreading the faith, in the process himself acquiring a legendary reputation. He is perhaps best known in legend for driving all the snakes from the country (explaining why there are none there today). Irishmen all over the world mark his feast day, 17 March, by wearing the three-leafed shamrock, which Patrick is supposed to have used to illustrate the Trinity to his congregation.

See also OISIN.

Paul Bunyan American folk hero celebrated for his remarkable strength. A huge man with a massive appetite, he put his physical prowess to good use in the course of his work as a lumberjack in the northwestern regions of the USA. His extraordinary feats included the single-handed damm-ing of rivers to create lakes, breaking up log jams, building the Black Hills of Dakota, and he is also said to have cut the Grand Canyon in south-western USA by dragging his pick behind him. Stories about his deeds were popular among the lumberjack community by the end of the 19th century, and first appeared in print early in the 20th century. Some versions of his adventures introduce such companions as Babe the Blue Ox and Johnny Inkslinger.

pea The humble pea is a harbinger of good luck and was formerly widely used for the purposes of love divination.

Finding a peapod with just one pea inside is supposed to be very lucky. It is similarly fortunate to find a pod with nine peas inside, in which case the pod may be thrown over the right shoulder while a wish is made. Such a pod may also be used to glean information about a future partner. A girl places the pod over her door and the first unmarried man to enter is destined to become her husband (a variation of this advises that the man who enters merely shares the same first name as the husband-to-be). Placed in a fire, two peas that burn enthusiastically together signify that two lovers will have a happy life together, but if one jumps away then the marriage will not be a good one. A pod containing nine peas may also be employed to cure warts, being rubbed against them and then tossed away with the words 'Wart, wart, dry away'.

See also PRINCESS AND THE PEA.

peach Chinese folk belief gives the peach an exalted place, interpreting the fruit as a symbol of fertility and immortality and crediting it with the power to ward off evil spirits. In Chinese legend, the tree that supports the world is identified as a peach tree, and anyone who feeds on its fruit can expect to live 3,000 years in the prime of life. In the Western world, the peach tree is said to give warning of cattle epidemics by shedding its leaves early. The wood of the peach tree is widely prized for the making of dowsing rods. *See also* MOMOTARO.

peacock Although revered by Hindus as sacred, the peacock is widely regarded as unlucky in Western folklore. The Indians believe that the peacock eats snakes, and this idea has been absorbed in other cultures; one English superstition from Tudor times (when the peacock was considered a 'royal' bird) claims that the cry of the peacock scares off venomous animals.

In art, the splendour of the peacock's tail feathers have given it a role as a symbol of heaven. However, the 'eyes' on its tail have also inspired more ominous associations. One legend claims that the eyes belong to the Seven Deadly Sins, plucked out as a punishment by God. The Seven Deadly Sins are, therefore, thought to lurk in the vicinity of the peacock, trying to get their eyes back, and the bird itself is consequently a harbinger of intense bad fortune. Another tradition links the eyes to the Classical story of the giant Argus, whose 100 eyes were given to the peacock by the goddess Hera after he was slain by Hermes.

Peacock feathers should on no account be allowed indoors or worn as decoration as they may inflict the magic of the EVIL EYE. Another suggested derivation of this taboo links it with the tradition that peacocks were kept in the temples of ancient Greece, where the illicit removal of their tail feathers was a crime which was punishable by death.

Other folk beliefs concerning the bird include the notions that peacock flesh never decays (thus linking the bird with immortality), and the tradition that, although proud of their plumage, peacocks are ashamed of their feet and scream with disgust whenever they catch sight of them.

pearl The link between pearls and the sea means that the stone has a somewhat dubious reputation in world folklore. Giving a baby the gift of a pearl – the birthstone for June – is said to guarantee the infant a long life, but to others pearls symbolize tears and are thus unlucky, especially if worn at weddings. Powdered pearls are, however, supposed to have aphrodisiac properties, and sleeping with a pearl beneath the pillow is reputed to help childless couples to conceive. They also have their uses as LIFE TOKENS, becoming cloudy when an absent partner is in trouble or dying. According to folk medicine, wearing a pearl will cure madness and prove beneficial in the treatment of epilepsy, jaundice and snake and insect bites. A tradition with its tongue perhaps in its cheek adds that pearls will also cure depression in females.

The origin of pearls has long exercised the imagination. The Chinese claimed that they were spat out by DRAGONS, while the Hindus said they could only be found inside the bodies of elephants. Others suggested that they were crystallized teardrops, or else the result of raindrops swallowed by oysters.

Pecos Bill Folk hero of the American Wild West, famed for his many remarkable feats. Actually the creation of the journalist Edward O'Reilly in the 19th century, he soon passed into folklore and inspired similar legends outside the USA itself, notably in Australia and Argentina. Weaned on moonshine and reared by coyotes, Pecos Bill used his prodigious strength to halt a train with his massive lasso, to ride a mountain lion and to harness a twister (tornado), in the process creating the Rio Grande. He is said to have died after eating a meal of barbed wire and nitroglycerine. The songs he is supposed to have sung are still commonly heard today, and in the modern West any teller of tall tales is likely to be dubbed a 'Pecos Bill'.

Peeping Tom *See* GODIVA, LADY.

pelican Large water bird that has come to represent the themes of resurrection and maternal devotion. The pelican became especially popular among Christians as a symbol for charity and for Christ himself. At the root of this tradition was the erroneous belief that female pelicans habitually kill their young and then, after three days' grieving, revive them with blood from their own breast (just as Christ shed his own blood for mankind and was resurrected on the third day after his death).

Pellam *See* PELLES.

Pelles In Arthurian legend, the WOUNDED KING who suffers the DOLOROUS BLOW. Identified as the king of the Grail Castle, he is wounded in both thighs by the spear of BALIN and through the magical connection between a sovereign and his land (*see* SOVEREIGNTY) his kingdom is reduced to a wasteland. He is eventually healed by GALAHAD, the son of his daughter ELAINE OF CORBENIC, who treats his wounds with blood from the GRAIL. In other legends he appears variously as Pellam, Pellean and Pellinore, although these are sometimes assumed to be different people (all versions of the name appear to come from the Cornish *peller*, meaning 'wise man'). He may also be synonymous with the Welsh PWYLL.

Pellinore In Arthurian legend, the King of the Isles, who was also one of the most distinguished of the knights of the ROUND TABLE. Identified as the brother of PELLES, the WOUNDED KING, and occasionally treated as synonymous with him, he was the son of PERCEVAL, and was one of the knights to go in pursuit of the QUESTING BEAST. By killing Lot of Orkney, he incurred the enmity of GAWAIN, who together with his brothers eventually killed Pellinore in an ambush.

pennyroyal *See* MINT.

peony English folklore values the peony, named after Paeon (the Greek god of healing), for its protective properties. Sailors are advised to burn a peony to cause storms to subside, while the sick are recommended to wear a necklace made from peony roots as this will relieve such ailments as epilepsy and cramp, and in children will also encourage the development of healthy teeth. The seeds of the peony are reputed to ward off evil spirits. Chinese folklore, meanwhile, associates the flower with imperial power, joy and spring.

pepper Though less important in folkloric terms than SALT, pepper nonetheless has its significance. Supposedly an aphrodisiac if consumed in large amounts, it should not be eaten by anyone suffering with a fever as it will only cause the problem to intensify. Otherwise it may be used to treat a vast array of complaints, from headaches to the plague. A US tradition holds that applying cotton wool dipped in black pepper to the ear will cure earache, and that eating whole chilli peppers will see off a cold. Finally, sprinkling a little pepper on the chair of a guest will ensure that he or she does not overstay their welcome.

Perceval In Arthurian legend, one of the most prominent of the knights of the ROUND TABLE. Variously called Perceval, Parzival, Perlesvaus or Peredur, he was the subject of numerous legends. Born in north Wales, he settles on a life as a knight, against the wishes of his mother, after meeting some of Arthur's knights while still a youth. Despite his lack of familiarity with the notions of chivalric behaviour, he joins Arthur's court, where his lack of knightly training acquires him a reputation as a guileless fool. Having become a fully fledged knight, he goes in pursuit of the GRAIL, but is so wary of breaking his newly learned rules of chivalry that he neglects to ask the FISHER KING the all-important 'Grail question' that will lead to the discovery of the Grail itself. According to Wolfram von Eschenbach's *Parzival* (*c.* 1212), he subsequently makes amends for this mistake and becomes the finder of the Grail, although most other versions identify GALAHAD as the eventual Grail hero, with Perceval playing only a supporting role.

peri In Islamic mythology, a beautiful female spirit who escorts the souls of the dead to paradise. Peris appear to have had their origins in a breed of evil female demons of Persian mythology who were considered much more malevolent in nature, plaguing mankind with eclipses, droughts and other natural disasters.

Perilous Bed In Arthurian legend, an enchanted bed upon which those who seek the GRAIL are invited to rest. Once upon the bed, the sleeper is attacked by invisible spear-hurling demons and wild beasts. Among those to face the terrifying dangers of the Perilous Bed and to survive was GAWAIN.

Perilous Seat In Arthurian legend, a place at the ROUND TABLE that could only be occupied with safety by the Grail Knight, usually identified as GALAHAD. When anyone else (such as PERCEVAL) sat upon it the chair would either break or swallow up the trespassing knight. Also known as the Siege Perilous, it appears to have symbolized the place taken by Christ at the Last Supper.

periwinkle Evergreen plant with a blue or white flower, which has a somewhat dark reputation in folklore, being traditionally linked with witchcraft and death. The Italians used to adorn dead babies with garlands of periwinkle, and in former times heretics burned at the stake were given periwinkle crowns. Maintaining the link with death, a Welsh tradition warns that anyone who picks a periwinkle from a grave will suffer from nightmares about the dead person buried there for a whole year. In Germany, the periwinkle is considered the flower of immortality. A more cheerful English tradition advises that if a man and a woman eat the leaves of a periwinkle together they will fall passionately in love.

In folk medicine, periwinkle leaves may be chewed to treat haemorrhages, poisoning and toothache. The plant may also be used in treatments for diabetes, and scientists have verified that it is in fact rich in valuable alkaloids.

Perrault, Charles French poet and author who was among the first to produce written versions of many of the most famous fairy tales, published as *Contes de ma Mère L'Oye* (1697) and subsequently translated into English in 1729 as *Tales of Mother Goose*. Born in Paris in 1628, Perrault was the first author to attempt a comprehensive compilation of such tales, which had previously existed only in the oral tradition. His versions of such stories as *Bluebeard, Cinderella, Hop o' my Thumb, Little Red Riding Hood, Puss in Boots* and *The Sleeping Beauty* thus became established as the standard form of these tales, which were otherwise known in many variant forms. The success of Perrault's publication inspired many other folklorists and his stories enjoyed a wide and influential readership – although when the tales first appeared they were attributed to his son Pierre in order to safeguard Charles' literary reputation after criticism from members of the Académie française (of which he was himself a member). He died in 1703.

philosopher's stone Magical stone or other substance, the discovery of which was one of the chief aims of ALCHEMY. If red, the stone was supposed to have the power to produce gold; if white it could be used to make silver. The term came to be used more generally for any element that could supposedly be employed to convert base metals to gold or silver, or to provide cures for a wide range of illnesses and complaints (*see also* ELIXIR VITAE). Although some alchemists claimed success, no one managed to prove possession of such a substance, although many agreed that a mixture of sulphur and mercury might work if combined in the right proportions. It was while searching for the philosopher's stone that Roger Bacon learned much about the nature of gunpowder in the 13th century, and others made breakthroughs leading to the foundation of the science of chemistry.

The symbol of the philosopher's stone is a hexagram, representing the union of the triangular symbols of fire and water.

phoenix Legendary bird that featured widely in the mythology of the ancient world, common to the folklore of Greece, India, Egypt, China, Japan and Arabia. Representing the sun and the concept of resurrection, the phoenix was generally supposed to be immortal, renewing itself every 500 years or so by setting fire to its own nest and then rising with new life from the ashes in which it had burnt itself. The Romans adopted the phoenix as an emblem of their state and the creature was also taken up as a symbol by early Christians. In medieval times it was described in various BESTIARIES as being the only creature that remained free of sin after the fall of Adam and Eve. It was also associated with ALCHEMY, as a result of which it came to be adopted as a sign put over chemist's shops.

Pied Piper of Hamelin Medieval German folk tale about the deliverance of the town of Hamelin, Westphalia, from a plague of rats. It is familiar to the English-speaking world from the poetic version of the tale by the English poet Robert Browning in the 19th century. The tale is very specific in terms of location, and may have originated as an allegory either of the disastrous Children's Crusade of 1212, when Nicholas of Cologne led some 40,000 German children over the Alps to their deaths, or of the emigration of many young Germans following the expansion of German territory in the east.

The Pied Piper is a mysterious musician who promises to relieve the town of Hamelin of its many rats if the authorities agree to pay him a certain amount. Subsequently he uses the magic sound of his pipe to lead all the rats out of the town and to their death by drowning in the River Weser. The elders of the town then quibble over the fee they have previously agreed, and the angry Pied Piper plays his pipe once more. In answer to his music all the children in the town follow him out to nearby Koppenberg Hill, where the children disappear inside, never to return. Only two small children, one lame and unable to keep up and the other blind, are left behind to tell the tale of the children's disappearance.

pig Many cultures consider the pig to have an elevated status, and the animal also has various occult associations. Pigs were sacrificed to the gods of ancient Greece, worshipped in Crete and Egypt, and credited by the Chinese (who think the pig lucky) with psychic powers. The Jews and the Arabs will refuse to eat its meat on the grounds that the animal is 'unclean'. The pig has special significance in Celtic folklore, appearing in numerous legends. It is after being surprised by pigs, for instance, that Goleuddydd gives birth to the Irish hero CULHWCH (whose name means 'pig-sty'), and one of Culhwch's greatest feats is the slaying of the monstrous boar TWRCH TRWYTH. In the *Mabinogion*, meanwhile, GWYDION'S theft of the pigs that PWYLL has received from ARAWN, the King of the Underworld, leads to war and the killing of Pwyll's son PRYDERI. Pigs also feature in Arthurian legend, specifically in the theft by ARTHUR and his knights of pigs belonging to King MARK.

In the British Isles rural tradition claims that the DEVIL often takes the form of a pig, and there are many legends of demon pigs that terrorized whole localities. A variety of demon pig, the 'yird swine' or earth pig, was reputed to scavenge in graveyards for newly buried bodies. The Isle of Man, meanwhile, boasts its own stories of 'fairy pigs'.

The runt of a litter is said to be protected by St Anthony, and thus some farmers will be reluctant to slaughter what is sometimes called the 'pantony pig'. Pig farmers are also careful not to hit their pigs with sticks of elder as this is reputed to cause immediate death. When pigs are slaughtered for food it is always best to kill them when the moon is waxing, as this means the meat will swell in the pot rather than shrink. Pork soup has various medicinal properties, and washing warts with pigs' blood or rubbing them with bacon will make them disappear. According to the Irish, children suffering from mumps and other ailments should rub their heads on a pig's back and the disease will be transferred to the animal.

Pigs make relatively few appearances in folk tales, and when they do they tend to be depicted rather negatively as greedy or slovenly. The one famous exception is the fairy tale 'The Three Little Pigs', in which three little pigs seek to build houses in which they can shelter from the ravages of the Big Bad Wolf. The first builds a house of straw, which the wolf easily blows down, while the second fares little better with a house of sticks. The third pig, however, builds a house of bricks that the wolf cannot blow down. When the wolf tries to come down the chimney he perishes in a cauldron of boiling water.

piskie *See* PIXIE.

pixie In English folklore, a variety of ELF. Also referred to as piskies, they are considered a distinct race to FAIRIES and are sometimes identified as the souls of unbaptized children. They are particularly associated with the folklore of the southwestern counties of England, notably Cornwall and Devon.

Pixies are usually depicted as mischievous spirits dressed in green, who delight in dancing in the moonlight and playing practical jokes upon mortals, including leading travellers astray. Other bits of mischief attributed to pixies include blowing out candles, moving furniture about, kissing pretty girls in the dark, pinching idle servants, and chasing horses in circles until they are exhausted. Anyone who fears they are thus 'pixie-ridden' should turn their coat inside out or back-to-front, as this is supposed to bring any such interference to an end. Pixies are, however, reputed sometimes to offer mortals help with domestic chores.

See also BROWNIE.

plantain Plant of the banana family that has special significance in the folklore of the Americas and is widely valued in folk medicine for its healing properties. Magical uses of plantain include wrapping two bare spikes of the plant in a dock leaf or otherwise secreting them under a stone and leaving them overnight: if they have blossomed in the morning this is a sign that a love affair will prosper. The plantain is notable chiefly, though, for its usefulness in folk medicine. Native American lore, for instance, recommends preparations of plantain for the treatment of bee stings, wounds and snakebite. Elsewhere it is used to relieve headaches, sore eyes, earache and, in the form of tea, to cure the measles.

In a tale collected by the Brothers Grimm the plantain is represented as a young woman who patiently awaits at the roadside for the return of her absent lover: every seven years she turns into a bird and flies away in search of him (thus explaining the plant's distribution to many parts of the world).

Plough Monday The first Monday after TWELFTH NIGHT, which for centuries past has marked the return of the farmer to his plough after the Christmas holiday. The date is still celebrated in many rural places with special religious services in which a plough is taken to church to be ceremonially blessed. These rituals are thought to have had much earlier pre-Christian roots.

Other folk customs associated with Plough Monday include the ceremonial dragging of a plough from village to village, as was formerly done in certain parts of Yorkshire. During the course of this various SWORD DANCES would be performed along the way, the dancers begging for money to spend on a celebration at the end of the day. Sometimes a traditional 'Plough Play' (a variety of MUMMERS' PLAY) might be performed. This might be followed by an evening feast or lively dance presided over by Betsy, the festival queen.

plum The plum tree is well known in China as a symbol of immortality, and is also associated with the NEW YEAR because of its early blossom. According to Chinese legend, it first sprang up from the blood that spilled on the ground when a dragon's ear was cut off. The blossom of the plum tree can have ominous significance, according to the Welsh, however:

an old tradition claims that if a plum tree produces blossom in December someone in the owner's family is doomed to die in the near future.

Drinking tea brewed from the bark of a plum tree is recommended by Native American folk medicine as a means of settling upset stomachs.

poltergeist *See* GHOST.

polygenesis Theory that superficially similar folkloric tales and customs around the world have developed independently of one another and are not the result of simple dissemination of one core tradition. Such coincidences are explained as natural consequences when different cultures move independently from one stage in their development to another. Although most authorities accept the fact that all cultures will naturally concentrate on certain themes (such as fertility and death) in the evolution of their folk lore, few experts accept the theory in its entirety, given the extraordinary number of shared themes and motifs in world folklore. The fact that the fairy tale 'Cinderella' has been traced in some 500 separate versions all round the world, for instance, argues a strong case for such cultural cross-fertilization.

Pooka *See* PUCA.

Pope Joan Legendary female pope, supposedly born in Germany of English parents, who succeeded to the office in the guise of a man in 855 and remained in it for some three years before exposure of her true sex. According to tradition, Joan followed Benedict III as John VIII after demonstrating her suitability in junior posts under the name Johannes Anglicus. The fact that she was a woman was finally realized when she gave birth during a papal procession in Rome and was stoned to death. This version of her life appears to have been current by the 13th century, although she was sometimes referred to by such alternative names as Gilberta and Agnes. The legend was taken up with glee by Protestant reformers in the 16th century, who presented it as literal truth, but subsequently doubt was cast upon the whole story, for which there appears to be no hard historical evidence.

poplar Like the aspen, the poplar is renowned for its trembling leaves, and shares the same reputation as a tree with special powers of healing. It is also revered in many cultures as a symbol of life after death. Witches may use poplar leaves in the preparation of the flying ointment they smear on themselves before taking flight on broomsticks and so forth. Theories accounting for the shivering of the poplar's leaves variously attribute it to the traditions that wood from the tree was used to make Christ's cross, that Christ prayed under a poplar in the Garden of Gethsemane prior to the Crucifixion, or that the poplar was the only tree that refused to mourn at the Crucifixion.

poppy As a symbol of the dead of two world wars, the blood-red poppy is now recognized primarily as a symbol of remembrance. This identification recalls the poppies that sprang up on the battlefield of Flanders during World War I (the flower prospering where earth has been disturbed). The modern association between poppies and dead soldiers was first established in the poem 'In Flanders Fields' by John McCrae (1872–1918), but it neatly evokes a much older tradition that the plant sprang up from the blood of dead warriors (hence its colour). Since ancient times, indeed, the flower has been associated with sleep and death, presumably because of its famed narcotic powers. Christian tradition, meanwhile, claims that the flower first sprang up from the blood of the crucified Christ.

The flower has also long been associated with fertility, and farmers in the ancient world maintained that corn would not grow unless there were a few poppies amongst the crop. This association may have its origin in the fact that if a field has not been well tilled, no poppies will appear. English tradition, however, insists that the poppy is an unlucky plant, and in parts of the Midlands there are those who claim that it should never be brought indoors because it will cause illness. Looking into the bright red centre of the flower is reputed to be enough to rob a person of their sight, and the poppy's scent is supposed to bring on headaches. If pressed against the ear, a poppy will allegedly cause earache. Simply picking a poppy, moreover, may trigger a thunderstorm.

More positively, poppies made into a poultice are alleged to relieve the pain of toothache, earache and other ailments, and in former times they were an ingredient in potions for insomnia. With their narcotic properties, poppies have long been prized for purposes of divination, and it is also possible for lovers to use them to confirm a partner's interest: if a dried poppy petal snaps with a distinct noise when pressed between the fingers, the other party's love is genuine. For those bewitched into love, spells involving poppies are said to offer an antidote.

potato Since its introduction to Europe in the 16th century, the potato has inspired a variety of folk beliefs. In the early days, it was much prized as an aphrodisiac and credited with the power to cure impotence. Much later, having lost this reputation as a food of love, the potato developed a new standing as a cure for rheumatism, being carried in the trouser pockets of sufferers far and wide; as the potato (which according to some has to be stolen) slowly shrivels and hardens it is said to absorb the poisons that caused the problem in the first place. The fact that the drug atropine, which is reputed to cure rheumatism, can be found in small quantities in potato 'eyes' suggests that this tradition may not be entirely without foundation.

Other superstitions connected with the potato include the notion that it is ideally planted on Good Friday, in which

case it will prove immune to interference by the DEVIL (although other authorities claim exactly the opposite), and the quaint custom that allows anyone eating a new potato for the first time in the season to make a wish. To make sure harvested potatoes keep well, every member of the family should share in the eating of the first few that are prepared. US superstition adds that if a cook allows a pan of potatoes to boil dry there will be a rainstorm.

potlatch Native American folk custom involving the lavish distribution of gifts as a demonstration of the wealth and social status of the donor. Associated chiefly with tribes on the northwestern seaboard of the USA, it generally took place during the course of a feast held to welcome guests or chiefs of other tribes. The hosts sought to impress with the quality and quantity of their gifts, and might even take the step of destroying prized possessions to prove their magnanimity. Similar displays might also be staged at social gatherings, including weddings and funerals. Such was the extravagance of such ceremonies that some donors were reduced to poverty in the attempt to match the generosity of their neighbours. In response to such undesirable consequences the US government took steps to ban the practice by law towards the end of the 19th century.

Potter Thompson In English legend, a Yorkshireman who, while exploring the passages beneath Richmond Castle, discovered King ARTHUR and his knights as they lay asleep, awaiting the day they will be needed to save England. He picked up a horn but fled, terrified, when the knights began to stir. As he ran away he heard voices telling him that if he had sounded the horn or drawn one of the knights' swords 'he would have been the luckiest man e'er born'.

See also SLEEPING LORD.

Prester John Legendary Christian King of the East, identified in the medieval period as a much-needed ally of the Christian crusaders in Palestine. He became absorbed into Arthurian legend as one of the keepers of the GRAIL, the son of Repanse de Joye and Feirefitz, but also claiming descent from the Magi who attended the infant Christ.

The earliest mentions of Prester John appear to date from the 12th century. According to Marco Polo he was the ruler of the Tartars; subsequently, he was variously described as the Emperor of Abyssinia (Ethiopia) and identified as the Great Khan of the Mongols. In the 13th century a letter supposedly written by Prester John in 1165 came to light, providing details of his kingdom, which took on all the aspects of an earthly paradise. In the letter he also claimed to be a master of magic, enjoying influence over the weather and providing tame dragons for his citizens to ride.

For several centuries the Christian church accepted the existence of Prester John as literal truth, but failure to locate his kingdom eventually undermined belief in his reality.

Princess and the Pea European folk tale that was among those collected by Hans Christian ANDERSEN in the mid-19th century. A prince seeking a true princess for his bride doubts that a girl who arrives at the town gates dripping with rain can really be nobly born. He decides to test her by making her sleep upon a deep pile of 20 mattresses and 20 eiderdowns under which he secretes a single PEA: only a person from a very privileged background could be expected to notice such a minor annoyance. Sure enough, when questioned the following morning the girl complains bitterly of the uncomfortable night she has just spent. She thus proves her royal identity and becomes the prince's bride.

Andersen said he had taken the story from native Danish sources, although he would in fact appear to have drawn upon a variety of Swedish folk tales, as well as adding his own polishing touches, as he so

often did. In older versions of the tale the princess is usually alerted to the presence of the pea by a dog, cat or some other helpful intermediary.

proverb A short and often pithy traditional saying expressive of a commonplace truth or generally perceived fact of experience. A good proverb neatly summarizes what might otherwise be difficult to express and is immediately understood by the person to whom it is addressed. Proverbs represent a shorthand route in conversation, adding colour to plain exchanges and often expressing complicated or sensitive truths in an acceptable stylized form.

Every culture has its store of proverbs, many of them ancient, revealing much about its beliefs, roots, character and folklore. The wealth of proverbs in the English language which are based upon observation of animals and nature, for instance, speaks strongly of a rural past, even though they are still in common use in a modern technological context. Many are international, as is the case with the sayings quoted in the Book of Proverbs in the Bible. Others are unique to a particular people, and different cultures may have totally different proverbs expressing identical thoughts.

Proverbs vary in their directness: many are blunt recommendations about how to act, while others are so metaphorically obtuse their meaning has been long forgotten. Others again are apparently obscure but are in fact widely understood (for instance, 'Don't put all your eggs in one basket', meaning 'spread your risk so as not to lose everything'). All too often the water is muddied by one proverb confusingly recommending exactly the opposite of another.

A cursory trawl of proverbs from different nations might produce gems as diverse as: 'Faint heart ne'er won fair lady' (English); 'Every invalid is a physician' (Irish); 'If you can't beat them, join them' (US); 'The absent are always wrong' (French); 'Apples, pears and nuts spoil the voice' (Italian); 'What belongs to everybody belongs to nobody' (Spanish); 'He who begins too much accomplishes little' (German); 'If vinegar is free it is sweeter than honey' (Serbian); 'It is better to wear out one's shoes than one's sheets' (Genoese); 'Watch the faces of those who bow low' (Polish); 'He who has no bread has no authority' (Turkish); 'As a tree falls, so shall it lie' (Hebrew); and 'Your neighbour's apples are the sweetest' (Yiddish).

Pryderi In Welsh legend, a folk hero identified as the son of RHIANNON and PWYLL. His adventures start with his birth, when he is threatened by a giant claw as he lies in his cot. Alternatively he mysteriously disappears while still a baby, but is found by TEYRNON, who subsequently brings the child up as his own son until finally realizing the likeness between Pryderi and his real father and returning him to his parents.

Pryderi's adventures as Lord of Dyfed include his marriage to Cigfa, a curious episode in which he becomes stuck fast to a golden bowl until rescued by MANAWYDDAN, and the conflict that follows the theft of his father's pigs by GWYDION. This last turn of events culminates in a duel between Pryderi and Gwydion, which ends with Pryderi's death.

Prydwen In Arthurian legend, the ship in which King ARTHUR sails to ANNWN to bring back the HALLOWS. Alternatively rendered as Pridwen, it is sometimes also identified as the name of Arthur's shield.

psychological theory Theory that the folklore of a culture should be interpreted primarily in terms of the collective preoccupations of a particular society together with behaviouristic factors. This approach to the study of folklore has gained acceptance since the early years of the 20th century, largely through the work of Sigmund Freud, who analysed many fairy tales and other folkloric material with particular reference to their sexual symbolism. The work of Carl Jung, meanwhile, built upon Freud's ideas and laid new emphasis upon the role of folk tales as expressions of what became known as the collective unconscious.

puberty rite *See* INITIATION.

Puca Irish equivalent of the English PUCK. Puca (or Pooka) is depicted as a mischievous spirit with a generally benevolent attitude to mortals. Able to transform his shape at will, Puca may bestow the gift of animal speech upon mortals or perform a variety of domestic chores on their behalf, but will also punish those who commit crimes.

Puck In English folklore, a mischievous spirit who delights in playing on human foibles. Best known today from his depiction in William Shakespeare's *A Midsummer Night's Dream*, he has a malicious streak and in medieval times was regarded as a demon or hobgoblin. Shakespeare's Puck is playfully mischievous rather than downright wicked, which is how he is depicted in Edmund Spenser's *Epithalamion*. Among his favourite tricks are luring travellers from their path and changing into a horse and then ditching his mortal rider in a river. Later he became virtually synonymous with the more generally benevolent ROBIN GOODFELLOW, helping mortals with domestic tasks and so forth. The association is explicit in the closing lines, spoken by Puck, of Shakespeare's *Dream*: 'Give me your hands, if we be friends, And Robin shall restore amends.' His equivalents in other countries include the Welsh Pwca, the Scandinavian Pukje and the Irish PUCA.

pumpkin Revered by the Chinese above all other plants, the pumpkin is widely respected as an emblem of fertility, presumably because of its generous size. Associated throughout the English-speaking world primarily with the celebration of HALLOWE'EN, pumpkins hollowed out and carved into grotesque faces and then illuminated from within by a candle are reputed to scare away the evil spirits that roam abroad on this particular night. In keeping with their reputation as a protection against evil, pumpkins are best planted on Good Friday. Once growing they should never be pointed at, as this will allegedly cause them to rot. Pumpkin seeds may be consumed to quieten an excessively passionate nature, and if mixed into a paste with oil and rubbed on the skin will eradicate freckles.

The pumpkin plays an important role in the fairy tale 'Cinderella', as it is a pumpkin that is transformed by the fairy godmother's magic into the magnificent coach that carries Cinderella to the royal ball. This would appear to be a detail first added by Charles Perrault in his 1697 version of the tale that was translated into English in 1729. Perrault may have been prompted by an earlier Italian version of the story in which one Zezolla is sprinkled with 'pumpkin water' (a cosmetic oil) by the fairies before she goes to the ball.

Puss in Boots European folk tale featuring the adventures of a remarkable cat. Although recorded in many other versions, the tale is most familiar today from Charles Perrault's *Contes de ma mère l'oye* (1697, *Tales of Mother Goose*), based in turn upon a 1534 rendering by the Italian writer Gianfrancesco Straparola.

The story begins with a young man whose only inheritance from his miller father is a cat. The cat, however, turns out to have great magical power, and when wearing a pair of enchanted boots enjoys the power of speech. The cat promises to help the young man by deceiving the royal family into thinking he is a dispossessed prince, by name the Marquis of Carabas. To do this he persuades the young man to bathe in a river that the royal coach is due to pass. When the coach appears the cat hails it and tells the occu-

pants that his royal master is drowning and has lost all his fine clothes. The young man is rescued and as he travels in the royal coach the cat goes on ahead and persuades shepherds in the fields to tell the king that the fields they are working belong to the Marquis of Carabas. To complete the deception the cat tricks an ogre into changing into a mouse and then devours him so that the young man can claim the ogre's castle as his own. The king, suitably impressed by all this evidence of the young man's wealth, gladly grants him the hand of his daughter in marriage. At the close of the tale the cat is revealed in his true form to be a prince, who is now transformed back to his original human shape.

In variant forms of the tale the role of the cat is taken by such animals as a fox, a jackal or a monkey.

Pwca *See* PUCK.

Pwyll In Welsh legend, the Lord of Dyfed whose adventures include a year spent in the guise of ARAWN, King of the Underworld. He incurs the wrath of Arawn by accidentally insulting him while out hunting but repairs the rift by agreeing to spend a year in the form of Arawn, and by promising to defeat Arawn's enemy Hafgan, another lord of the underworld. Subsequently Pwyll becomes the husband of RHIANNON, whom he wins in the face of the rivalry of her former suitor Gwawl. Having recklessly agreed to grant Gwawl any favour he desires, he finds himself obliged to grant Gwawl Rhiannon's hand in marriage. When the time for the marriage comes, however, Pwyll's men throw Gwawl into a sack and beat him until he agrees to release Pwyll from his promise. Pwyll and Rhiannon are duly married, but later experience grief through the loss of their son PRYDERI in the bitter fighting that follows the theft of Pwyll's pigs by GWYDION.

Q

quail Game bird that features in medieval English folklore as a symbol of sexual love. Such was the link between the quail, which was supposedly to have an insatiable sexual appetite, and the pursuit of love that in times gone by prostitutes were commonly referred to as 'quails'. It was formerly believed that quails were the only species apart from humans that was vulnerable to EPILEPSY, but despite this the consumption of quails' brains was sometimes recommended as cure for various ailments.

quest Many of the world's most famous folk tales revolve around a central quest upon which the hero is engaged. Sometimes the quest is undertaken as a punishment or in a bid to save the hero's own life (as in Geoffrey Chaucer's 'The Wife of Bath's Tale' in which the central character travels far and wide to identify what it is that women desire most) or else to prove the hero's honour (as in *Sir Gawain and the Green Knight*), or to win riches or the hand of the woman the hero desires. Often the quest serves as a running plot linking various otherwise unconnected episodes. The most celebrated of all the quests is the quest for the Holy GRAIL, which is one of the central themes of Arthurian legend.

Questing Beast In Arthurian legend, a mythical creature that was described as being in constant search of water to satisfy its endless thirst. Also known as the Beast Glatisaunt, it had the head of a serpent, the body of a leopard, the rump of a lion and the legs and hooves of a deer, and as it ran the howling of 30 pairs of hounds echoed from its stomach. According to a French romance it was born from a mortal woman who later met her death when ripped apart by hounds. It was pursued fruitlessly by King PELLINORE and subsequently by PALOMIDES. In Malory's *Morte d'Arthur*, ARTHUR meets the beast, a symbol of incest and lawlessness, at a fountain shortly after being crowned king. It was the model for the 'blatant beast' in Edmund Spenser's *Faerie Queene*.

R

rabbit Rabbits have a mixed reputation in world folklore. Renowned for their fecundity and thus widely associated with the notion of fertility and procreation, they are also, like the HARE, traditionally linked with WITCHCRAFT, and have been connected with the powers of darkness since pagan times. Because of their tendency to play in the light of the MOON, they were once widely identified with the moon god. It was also believed that witches could disguise themselves as rabbits, and various parts of the rabbit's body (especially the ears, the kidneys and the genitals) feature in mischief-making spells and potions.

The rabbit is a central character in folk tales from many parts of the world. Typically it defies its small size and evident vulnerability by being unsurpassed as a trickster well able to deceive such enemies as the FOX and the WOLF. This tradition is illustrated by, among others, folk tales from Africa, India, Burma, Tibet, the USA (notably Joel Chandler Harris' *Brer Rabbit* stories) and the UK (where vestiges of the same notion reveal themselves in Beatrix Potter's *Peter Rabbit*).

Today, because of its ancient identification with fertility, the rabbit is widely recognized as a symbol of EASTER, personified by the figure of the Easter Bunny, who delivers Easter eggs to children according to modern US tradition. Perhaps because rabbits are born with their eyes open and are thus deemed capable of warding off evil, they are often considered harbingers of good luck.

Some people claim that it is lucky for a rabbit to cross a person's path, and carrying around an amulet in the form of a rabbit's foot has long been thought a guarantee of good fortune. Women who carry a rabbit's foot are likely to have large families in consequence.

It is, however, unlucky for a miner to see a rabbit on the way to the pit, as this presages disaster, and equally unfortunate to dream of rabbits. Farmers worry if they see rabbits in close proximity to their livestock, as they may be witches in disguise or the reincarnated souls of dead ancestors. White rabbits are portents of particular dread (although saying 'white rabbits' before anything else on the first day of the month or on the first day of a new moon is supposed to bring good luck). 'Rabbit' is also one of the taboo words that must never be spoken on board ship, according to sea-going lore.

The rabbit has a number of uses in folk medicine. These include wearing rabbit-skin socks to ward off the threat of pleurisy. Dorset folklore insists that feeding rabbits' brains to a fractious child will result in an immediate improvement in the child's behaviour.

Ragallach In Irish mythology, a king of Connacht who was fated to meet his death at the hands of his own daughter. In panic at this prophecy of his ultimate destiny, Ragallach made his wife put their infant daughter in a bag and hand her over to a swineherd for destruction. The swineherd, however, deposited the bag at the door of a poor woman, who reared the girl in secret. She eventually became her own father's mistress and in due course fulfilled the prophecy by bringing about his death.

Ragnarok In Norse mythology, the end of the world in which everything will be destroyed during a battle between the gods (the AESIR) and the FROST GIANTS. The final confrontation will be preceded by three severe winters (the Fimbulwinter) and three years in which humanity will become steadily more self-destructive and finally die out. Given new strength by the rising tide of evil, Loki's offspring Fenris and Hel will break free and instigate rebellion among the giants, culminating in a furious onslaught against ASGARD. It was foretold that certain gods will survive the final battle, namely BALDUR, Odin's sons Vidar and Vail, Odin's nephews Vili and Ve, Thor's sons Magni and Modi, and Odin's companion Hoenir. These gods will retreat to Gimli, the highest of the Norse heavens, while those who have behaved the worst will be sent to Nastrond, the Norse hell.

Ragnell In Arthurian legend, the real identity of the LOATHLY LADY. Transformed into a hideous old hag by the magic of her own sister, Gromer Somer Joure, she features in the story of Sir GAWAIN, agreeing to tell him what women most desire if he will consent to marry her. He overcomes his repulsion at her appearance and seals the contract. When he kisses her, however, she turns into a beautiful woman. Ragnell tells Gawain that he must choose between having her beautiful during the night (when only he will see her) but ugly during the day (when the whole world will see his bride), or vice versa. Gawain says he will leave the decision to her, upon which he discovers he has found the answer to the original riddle he has been set by Gromer Somer Jaure – that which women most desire is sovereignty over their husbands.

ragwort Common weed, also known as ragweed, groundsel or (in the USA) as stinking Willie, that is widely credited with a variety of magical properties. According to Cornish folklore, witches use stalks of ragwort to fly through the air, while Irish tradition identifies the ragwort as a favourite mount of the fairies. Although the plant is notoriously poisonous, its juice is used in folk medicine to soothe sore eyes and the plant itself can be pulped for use as a poultice.

Rahu In Hindu folklore, a demon who is the sworn enemy of the sun and moon. He was beheaded by Vishnu after illicitly tasting the magic nectar of the gods that bestows immortality, but his head remains alive, awaiting the opportunity to take revenge upon his enemies, who betrayed him to Vishnu. Consequently, when an eclipse occurs, Hindus often attribute it to the evil Rahu.

Railroad Bill In the black folklore of the southern states of the USA, a folk hero who robs from the rich to help the poor, rather in the style of the English ROBIN HOOD. Credited with the power to change his shape at will to escape his enemies, Railroad Bill became the focus of a small body of legends and the subject of many tales and ballads. He was, in fact, based upon a real 19th-century outlaw named Morris Slater, who is recorded as having avoided arrest by shooting a deputy and escaping on a freight train, from which he then (reputedly) stole goods to distribute among the poor.

rain The crucial importance of rainfall to the successful rearing of crops and livestock, and indeed to the maintenance of life itself, has made it the focus of innumerable superstitions and folk beliefs throughout the world.

Predicting the onset of rain has always been a prime preoccupation, and folklore is rich with portents of coming rain. Many of these depend upon close observation of animal behaviour (for instance, a cat washing behind its ear or spiders seeking shelter). Others refer to the state of the observer's own body, noting such phenomena as aching limbs or painful corns (a notion that has in fact been backed by modern science). Yet more depend upon minor happenings around the house: if a piece of bread and butter falls face down on the floor when accidentally dropped, or if soot comes down the chimney, or the salt sticks together in lumps, or the bread goes soft, then wet weather is clearly in the offing.

Conclusions may be drawn about rain that falls on certain days of the year. Rain on St Paul's Day (25 January) signifies poor supplies of corn, while rain at Easter indicates that grass later in the year will be lush, but also that there will be little hay. If it rains on St Peter's Day (29 June), the saints are deemed to be sending water for the apple orchards, and it is predicted that the apple crop will be a good one. If it rains around St Mary Magdalen's Day (22 July), this is said to be because the saint is washing her handkerchief ready to weep on St James's Day (25 July).

See also ST SWITHIN'S DAY.

As well as predicting when rain will fall, folklore is replete with suggestions about how rainfall can be invoked artificially. Rainmakers were held in awe in many societies, and are still highly respected in some parts of the world. Most rainmaking methods operate on the principle of SYMPATHETIC MAGIC, often accompanied by appropriate sacrifices to the gods or calls for help from the spirit world. The simplest of these procedures vary from burning some ferns or some heather, or sprinkling water or blood on the ground, to dipping a cross or some other religious relic in holy water. Formerly, in various parts of Europe, statues of the saints were routinely dipped in lakes and rivers in times of drought. Another solution is to step on a beetle or ant. If it rains too much, one English remedy suggests that persuading a first-born child to undress and then stand on his head in the rain will cause it to cease.

In folk medicine, rainwater is supposed to be excellent for the hair and for the treatment of eye problems. In times gone by, people often collected rainwater that fell on Ascension Day in the belief that, as long as it had not come into contact with rooftops or trees or with the ground, it had special healing properties. Welsh tradition claims that a baby bathed in rainwater will learn to talk much sooner than other infants of the same age, and also that money washed in rainwater will never be stolen.

Finally, a bizarre German superstition insists that couples who make love when it is raining will conceive girls, whereas those who make love when it is fine will have boys.

rainbow The mysterious nature of the rainbow, which appears to link the heavens with the earth, has ensured it a special place in the folklore of many cultures. To some it is a phenomenon evoking dread, whereas others think a rainbow lucky and will make a wish on seeing one.

In Judaeo-Christian tradition the rainbow is a visible reminder of God's promise that He will never again flood the earth as happened in the story of Noah's Ark. In other traditions, though, the appearance of a rainbow is an omen of death – an idea that is perhaps a folk memory of BIFROST, the celestial bridge of Norse folklore over which the dead get to VALHALLA. In the Shetland Islands, for instance, the sight of a rainbow arching over a house is taken as a portent of imminent death, and elsewhere numerous superstitions are concerned with negating the evil influence of rainbows. In various other cultures throughout the world the rainbow is interpreted in terms of a supernatural serpent that reaches up periodically to the sky in order to take a drink from the clouds. As such it is often the subject of veneration, and may appear as a character in folk tales.

In some areas it was once accepted practice to chant rhymes to make a rainbow disappear, while in others it was understood that laying down two sticks or straws in the form of a cross would 'cross out' the rainbow. It was widely considered reckless to point at a rainbow, as this might cause the rain to start again or invite even worse luck. Rather more positive, though, is the popular tradition that a crock of fairy gold may be found at the end of the rainbow – if only that spot can be located. Not dissimilar is the old European notion that a person who drinks from the well at the end of the rainbow will thereby change sex.

Other folk beliefs about rainbows include the contention that they suck water from rivers and lakes to feed the clouds, the sailors' theory that a rainbow can swallow up a whole vessel, and the warning that water that has been touched by a rainbow is thereby made poisonous.

The appearance of a rainbow is supposed to allow the observer to glean a certain amount of information about the weather to come. As is the case with red skies, a rainbow in the morning signifies wet weather on the way, while one in the afternoon or evening suggests that the following day will be fine.

rakshasa In Hindu folklore, a variety of demon that preys on mortals by night. Rakshasas may appear in a range of forms, having the ability to disguise themselves as animals, monsters or even humans. Although they can be of either sex, they are often described as beautiful women. Most traditions concerning rakshasas emphasize their evil nature and their need to feast on human flesh. They are said to lurk in graveyards and, rather like VAMPIRES, lose their power each dawn.

Ramayana Sanskrit epic that recounts the legends associated with the life of Rama, the seventh incarnation of Vishnu. Written by the poet Valmiki around 300 BC, it traces the life of the semi-divine Rama from his youth to his eventual ascent to heaven.

The early episodes include Rama's victory over the demon Taraka, his marriage to SITA after successfully meeting the challenge of bending Shiva's mighty bow, and his exile to the forest as a result of plots against him at court. In exile Rama and Sita suffer from the malevolent attentions of various RAKSHASAS, who try to drive them apart by various ruses. Rama recruits the aid of Sugriva, king of the monkeys, to rescue Sita but then, doubting her fidelity to him, abandons her in the forest. Sita seeks shelter with the hermit Valmiki, author of the *Ram-ayana*, and in due course gives birth to Rama's twin sons. Ultimately, Rama and Sita are successfully reunited and take their rightful place in heaven.

Details of the stories contained in the *Ramayana* vary from one account to another, having been relayed largely by oral repetition over the centuries. They have inspired many celebrated works of art, from dance and theatre to paintings and films. Today, the *Ramayana* still has considerable religious importance among Hindus, and its recitation may be regarded as an act of purification. Rama himself, usually depicted as a prince armed with bow and arrow, is honoured at a major festival held each year at Varanasi (formerly known as Benares).

Ran In Norse mythology, the wife of AEGIR, who rules over a dreadful underwater realm. The goddess of storms and whirlpools, she was believed to whip up storms to sink the ships of mortals and drag the sailors down to her underwater palaces. In an attempt to appease her, Norse sailors often tossed gold into the waves when storms blew up.

Rapunzel Fairy tale heroine whose imprisonment by a wicked witch and subsequent rescue has furnished pan-European folklore with one of its best-known stories, as recorded by the Brothers Grimm.

The story begins with the imprisonment of the beautiful Rapunzel in a tall tower as the price of her father's life after he has accidentally offended a witch. The tower has no door, and each day Rapunzel has to let down her fine long hair so the witch can climb up. One day, however, a prince is attracted by the sound of Rapunzel's singing and persuades her to let down her hair so that he can climb up. The witch is incensed when she learns of this interference with her prisoner and as punishment cuts off Rapunzel's gorgeous hair and abandons her in the desert. The prince returns, but when he asks Rapunzel to let down her hair the witch lowers the severed locks. The prince realizes what has happened just in time and leaps to safety, but is blinded in the process. The two lovers are eventually reunited, and when Rapunzel's tears fall on the prince's eyes his sight is magically restored.

The tale is often interpreted today as an allegory on the theme of virginity, and it clearly incorporates elements common to a wide class of fairy tales, among them the demand of the girl in exchange for the father's life and the abandonment of the girl in the desert.

rat Perhaps because the rat has always been feared as a carrier of disease it has long been considered with a jaundiced eye in the folklore of most cultures. Rats are almost universally loathed, and almost all the traditions concerning them point to their association with death and disaster. Rats are said to have a sixth sense when it comes to predicting death, and various cultures credit the creatures with knowing when a calamity of some kind is nigh. According to one of the most widely known superstitions, shared by seafarers worldwide, rats will desert a sinking ship long before the crew realize there is anything wrong with the vessel (accordingly, it is actually lucky if rats are seen boarding a new vessel). It is no surprise, then, to learn that it is deemed most unlucky even to mention the word 'rat' on board ship.

On land, it is claimed that rats will vacate a house that is in imminent risk of collapse or where one of the occupants is close to death. The death of a resident must also be expected if rats gnaw at a person's clothing or damage the bedroom furniture. A sudden invasion of rats for no apparent reason may be interpreted as a prediction that the residents will soon be on the move (though a variation of this recorded in Scotland suggests this signifies that someone in the house will shortly come into some money).

Infestations of rats may be ended by various magical means, several of which depend upon writing a curse on a piece of paper and then leaving it where the rats will find it. The Irish in particular boast a long tradition of rat-cursing poetry. Alternatively, sitting beside a rat hole and politely requesting the occupants to move on, without resorting to actual curses, is sometimes reputed to have the desired effect. The idea that rats are peculiarly susceptible to the charms of music is reflected in the legend of the PIED PIPER OF HAMELIN, and also in the fact that rat charmers still working in remote areas in modern times have been known to lure rats from their hiding places by whistling or singing.

Other folk beliefs concerning rats include the notion that an explosion in their numbers constitutes a suitably macabre warning that war is about to break out. In folk medicine there is the belief that a concoction of dried rat's tail may be used to treat a bad cold. Lastly, parents anxious that a child should develop strong teeth are advised to leave one of the infant's lost milk teeth by a rat hole and to request of the resident rat that he accept this in exchange for a really good new one.

rattle Percussion instrument widely used in ritual ceremonies in many parts of the world. Ranging from relatively modest handheld gourds to elaborate drums made from such varied materials as animal skins, bones and tortoise shells, rattles were probably first taken up as a means of frightening off evil spirits, but are also used to summon friendly spirits to attend ritual gatherings. Their use features in a huge variety of ceremonial occasions, from initiation ceremonies and marriages to funerals and exorcisms. They may be worn by dancers at these ceremonies or else played by the person officiating or by other participants in the events. In shamanistic ceremonial, rattles may be rhythmically shaken to help a shaman achieve a state of trance.

raven Like other black birds, the raven (an attendant upon the gods in both ancient Greek and Norse legend) is widely considered a bird of ill omen. It makes many appearances in folklore, particularly in Norse, Celtic and Arthurian mythology and is also important in Native American lore, appearing as the creator god of the Alaskan Inuit and nearby Siberian and Native American tribes and also as a trickster in folk tales originating in the Pacific Northwest.

In keeping with the general prejudice against black birds of various kinds, ravens are particularly disliked in the vicinity of the sick, and the croak of the bird – sometimes interpreted in the English-speaking world as 'corpse, corpse' – is widely understood to be an omen that the patient will not recover.

In times gone by, it was suggested that the bird was a favourite disguise of the DEVIL, and also that it carried disease around the countryside on its wings. Scientists suggest that this association with death may have some root in the bird's extremely sensitive powers of smell, which draw it to decaying flesh, even though some distance away. Another explanation harks back to the Norse invaders of England, who carried the raven as an emblem on their banners, thus linking the bird in the minds of the English with the ravages of war. For centuries after the end of the Norse raids, naughty children throughout northern England were warned to mend their ways 'or else the black raven will come'.

The raven is not always so ominous. The Welsh go so far as to suggest that if a blind person shows kindness to a raven then the bird will repay this by helping the person to regain his or her sight (a tradition presumably derived from the habit ravens and other birds of prey have of plucking out the eyes of their prey and the belief that they thus enjoy excellent vision themselves). The Welsh also welcome the sight of a raven perching on a rooftop, as this presages good luck to everyone within. In the English West Country, ravens are saluted by the raising of the hat, and anyone who robs a raven's nest will be punished through the death of a baby in his or her home village. Similarly, the Cornish warn against harming a raven, explaining that the bird is the reincarnation of King ARTHUR.

The royal connection is expanded in London, where it is said that the British monarchy and the United Kingdom itself will last only so long as there are ravens at the Tower of London. Even today, the Tower ravens are carefully fed and protected (aided perhaps by another tradition that anyone who kills one of the Tower ravens will die soon after). This well-known superstition is thought to have evolved from the story of BRAN THE BLESSED, whose head was allegedly buried on Tower Hill facing France to ward off any invasion of England (the name Bran means 'raven'). Legend has it, however, that Arthur dug the head up, thus reserving the salvation of England to himself.

In folk medicine, raven soup is recommended for the treatment of gout. Raven eggs, meanwhile, may be used to dye the hair black – with the warning that they should only be applied to the hair while the mouth is full of oil, lest the teeth are turned black as well.

In the business of weather prediction, ravens flying towards the sun are a sign of fine weather on the way, but ravens preening themselves on the wing are a sure portent of rain. Should they fly recklessly at one another this may be taken as an omen of war.

Red Branch In Irish mythology, the warrior companions of the legendary

King CONCHOBAR. Their adventures were recounted in the ULSTER CYCLE. Famed for their prowess in battle, they were so unpredictable in temper that they were forbidden to wear arms when they sat down to eat in their castle at Emain Macha, as a quarrel was sure to erupt sooner or later. Among the most redoubtable of their number were CUCHU-LAINN, FERGUS MAC ROICH, and the three sons of Usnech. The origin of the company's name is disputed: it may have referred to the red room where they congregated, or else to Ross the Red, king of Leinster.

Redcap In Scottish folklore, a malevolent GOBLIN who preys on mortals in lonely ruins and other desolate places with ominous associations in the Borders of Scotland. His name refers to his practice of dipping his cap in the blood of his victims. Travellers fearful of being attacked by him can protect themselves by carrying a cross.

Renauld de Montauban The hero of a medieval French romance, later celebrated in Torquato Tasso's 16th-century epic *Rinaldo* and other classic works. Having slain the nephew of CHARLEMAGNE following an argument over a game of chess, Renauld was besieged in the castle of Montessor but managed to escape against all odds on his magical horse BAYARD. Subsequently he devoted himself to good works, helping to build the cathedral at Cologne before being murdered by some of his fellow workers, who tossed his body into the Rhine.

revenant The spirit of a dead person that may return to earth in a variety of supernatural forms. Revenants include GHOSTS, VAMPIRES and SPEAKING HEADS, although on many occasions they are reported to manifest themselves in human form. Sometimes these spirits are kindly in nature and protect the living, but occasionally they are motivated by a desire for revenge and seek to do harm to the living (as in the case of vampires). Often they have been themselves the victim of some terrible wrong and return to earth only for as long as it takes to set things right. It was one of the prime techniques of ancient sorcerers to attempt to contact revenants to enjoy supernatural assistance in their magic-making.

See also LANGSUIR.

Reynard the Fox Animal hero who appears in numerous well-known folk tales popular throughout medieval Europe. The epitome of the cunning FOX, Reynard uses his native wit to outmanoeuvre such rivals as the WOLF and the BEAR. He appears as the central character in a cycle of stories first recorded in France towards the end of the 12th century, although many of the tales may be much older. Subsequently versions of the cycle were produced in Italy, Germany and the Low Countries, with Reynard's name being rendered variously as Renard, Rainardo, Reinhart and Reinaert. In the 15th century the printer William Caxton furnished an English version of the Reynard tales. Reynard's popularity among the French was such that the animal itself was renamed the *renard* rather than the *goupil* as it had been previously known.

Rhiannon In Welsh legend, the daughter of Hefaidd Hen, ruler of the underworld. She attracted the attention of PWYLL, the king of Dyfed, who rode hard in pursuit of her. However, either by riding a fine white horse or else by adopting the form of a horse herself, she easily outpaced both him and his men. Suitably impressed by her beauty and by her turn of speed, Pwyll claimed her as his bride, overcoming the rival claim of Gwawl. Subsequently their son PRYDERI was kidnapped by demons, and the nursemaids, fearing they would be blamed for the crime, smeared Rhiannon's face with blood, thus making it appear that she was responsible for her own offspring's disappearance. As punishment for her apparent crime, she was forced to let all visitors to the court ride on her back and was obliged to repeat to them the story of her guilt. All was made well, however, when Pryderi, who had been found and brought up by a chieftain named TEYRNON, returned home. After Pwyll died, Rhiannon married MANAWYDDAN, who subsequently rescued both her and her son after they became magically affixed to a golden bowl they had found in a supernatural castle.

In many respects Rhiannon resembles the Gaulish horse goddess EPONA, the Celtic war goddess MACHA, and MODRON, the mother of MABON. The Birds of Rhiannon appear in various legendary tales: anyone who listens to them is cast into an unearthly trance.

Rhydderch Hael In Arthurian legend, a sorcerer who owns a magic cauldron that provides an endless supply of sustenance to various heroes. He is depicted as the victor of the Battle of Arfderydd, in which Merlin's master Gwenddolau was defeated, and he then marries Merlin's wife Guendolena. It has been suggested that he may have been based upon a shadowy historical 6th-century king who held court at Dumbarton.

rice The role of rice as a staple food across Asia and in other parts of the world has ensured it special significance in world folklore. Several cultures in the Far East boast a Rice Goddess or Rice Mother who oversees the crop and has to be honoured with solemn ceremonies and gifts. In Java and elsewhere couples traditionally had sex in the paddy fields in the belief that this would promote the harvest, although some cultures declare that any kind of impure behaviour within the rice fields is strictly forbidden for fear of offending the resident gods. Women may also be excluded if they are menstruating. There is a belief among some Arabs that every grain of rice is a drop of sweat from the brow of Muhammad. The Japanese honour the rice crop with plays

and prayers, and rice cakes feature prominently in Japan in the course of many important ceremonies. In former times, anyone who harmed the rice crop in various eastern countries was likely to suffer extreme punishment, either at divine or human hands.

The Western tradition of throwing rice at wedding ceremonies is a reference to its time-honoured status as a symbol of fertility, and in essence constitutes the wish of the guests that the new marriage be blessed by the birth of children in due course. Before rice became commonly available, newlyweds were customarily presented with bags of nuts as they left the church, with much the same intentions. Rice, in its turn, has largely given way in recent times to paper confetti.

riddle The riddle, in which a question is posed in a cleverly disguised form, has a long history in world culture. The oldest known riddles appear in ancient Babylonian writing. The most famous riddle in the classical world was that of the riddle of the Sphinx, solved by Oedipus. In the Bible riddles set by Samson are solved by 'the men of the city'. Riddles are occasionally posed in the celebration of various rites such as initiation and marriage – often the success of the event depends upon the riddle being successfully answered. In some parts of Europe riddles are often of an obscene nature, suggesting their distant origin in orgiastic festivals of such events as the winter solstice.

Many folk tales revolve around a hero's quest to solve a riddle set by a god, the Devil, a wise man or a witch, often at the risk of losing his or her own life or immortal soul. In many cases he only succeeds in answering it with supernatural assistance. A common device in folk tales is the riddle that must be solved by a common-born suitor in order to win the princess's hand in marriage.

riding the marches Traditional ceremony that has been observed annually at a number of locations in the Borders of Scotland since medieval times. A Scottish equivalent of BEATING THE BOUNDS, the ceremony involves a large band of riders traversing the marches (or boundaries) of their town on horseback and inspecting boundary stones, usually on a specified date in June, July or August. In former times, when the area was riven by a seemingly endless series of border wars, such ceremonies had a very serious purpose. Today, the event is the occasion not only for a good ride but for colourful processions and civic ceremonials. The fact that only men are traditionally allowed to take part has caused considerable controversy in recent years, with many women riders insisting upon their right to participate.

Rigru Roisclethan In Irish mythology, the queen of the otherworldly land of Benn Edair. Representing the concept of SOVEREIGNTY, she is identified as the mother of Segda Saerlabraid. She rescued her son from the high king Conn Cetchathach, taking the form of a weeping woman leading a cow (symbolizing milk and plenty). She advised Conn to give up the goddess Becuma as otherwise Ireland would never prosper.

ring Rings symbolize many things, according to their design and composition, and are widely credited with supernatural powers. These include various healing properties and the ability to act as LIFE TOKENS, conveying through the maintenance of their lustre or any deterioration in their condition the fortunes of the absent wearer.

Rings bearing inscriptions, which might range from certain magic words to the names of the Holy Family or the three Magi, are supposed to be effective against the threat of the EVIL EYE, and were once said to ward off the plague. If made of metal that is in some way 'holy', a ring will have redoubled powers of healing. Edward the Confessor owned a ring (now preserved in Westminster Abbey in London) that was reputed to have the

power to heal cramp, and many subsequent English monarchs obliged in bestowing their blessing upon so-called 'cramp rings' that would then be given to loyal subjects suffering from the problem. It was also once quite commonplace to take the first five silver coins offered at communion and to melt them down, while saying prayers, to form similar rings for the same purpose.

In cases where neither the monarch nor the church could help, healing rings were sometimes made from coins or other small silver objects donated by five different unmarried members of the opposite sex, and such rings were regarded as equally beneficial. Tradition has it that some of the best cramp rings are those made from the melted-down handles and metal fittings of old coffins. Rings and bracelets, usually made of copper, are still advertised by jewellers for their efficacy in healing the ravages of rheumatism. Such is the magic of rings that one West Country superstition claims that simply running the ring finger of the left hand along a wound will heal it.

Swearing oaths on rings is a practice dating from at least Anglo-Saxon times, and is reflected in the giving and receiving of wedding rings during modern marriage services. The idea underlying this custom is the fact that a ring, being a circle with neither beginning or end, represents the concepts of eternity, unity, and perfection.

Rip Van Winkle Legendary character who falls asleep for 20 years and wakes to find his surroundings greatly changed. He was the invention of the US writer Washington Irving, who published the story of Rip Van Winkle in his *Sketch Book* (1819–20). Irving's character is a rather idle, happy-go-lucky man who suffers from the continual nagging of his wife. While walking in the Catskill Mountains he assists a curious stranger in carrying a heavy keg up the hillside and catches a glimpse of the stranger's peculiar, otherworldly companions playing at nine-pins.

However, when he drinks from the keg he is magically overcome by sleep and loses consciousness. When he awakes after what he thinks is but a brief time he finds that 20 years have passed and that his house is deserted, his children have grown up and his shrewish wife is dead. The strangers he met in the mountains are identified as the spirits of the explorer Henry Hudson and his crew.

Irving drew upon several old legends for his tale. In particular he borrowed ideas from the Scottish legend of Thomas the Rhymer and similar Germanic tales about a blacksmith and a goatherd called Peter Klaus; these two also stumble upon games being played by supernatural beings while out in the mountains, and are also subsequently overcome by sleep. Almost identical tales are told in China and other parts of the world.

rites of passage Crucial moments in an individual's life that are formally celebrated by the community as a whole. Every society marks such important events as CHILDBIRTH, INITIATION, MARRIAGE and DEATH, although the ceremonies held at such stages in life may differ widely in character. Typical rituals include the ceremonial washing of the person concerned, the revealing of sacred secrets hitherto withheld, and such symbolic acts as the lifting of the bride's veil during the wedding service.

roane In Scottish folklore, a variety of FAIRY described as taking the form of a seal. Roanes were considered friendly to humans and said to enjoy coming ashore to dance in the form of beautiful women. Tales are still told of fishermen who claimed roanes as their wives after stealing their discarded sealskins.

See also SELKIE.

robin The robin ranks among the most sacred of all the birds in a number of traditions, though in others it is not so beneficent. A time-honoured saying dictates that the robin and the WREN are God's 'cock and hen' and thus enjoy divine favour. According to the Welsh the bird acquired its distinctive red breast when it was singed while carrying drops of water to souls tormented in the fires of hell, although others suggest it scorched itself when extinguishing the burning feathers of the wren after it had fetched fire from hell as a gift for mankind. Another widely heard tradition, however, accredits the bird's red breast to the legend that it was splashed with Christ's blood or else was pricked when it attempted to pull the thorns from his brow. As a consequence of this kindly act, it is supposed to be extremely unlucky to kill a robin, to cage it or to destroy its eggs. Such is the dread of harming the bird that even cats are said to refrain from attacking robins. The religious associations of the bird may account for its popularity as a choice of subject on Christmas cards, although this may owe as much to the bird's continued presence in gardens and woodland in Britain through the winter months, long after many other species have migrated. The bold and inquisitive character of the bird, combined with its relatively tame nature, may explain its traditional adoption as the 'gardener's friend'.

Among the more ominous superstitions attached to the bird is the widely held belief that if a robin flies into a house or sings close to it someone within will die shortly thereafter. The same conclusion may be drawn if a robin taps at the bedroom window of anyone who is sick, and some people are reluctant to send ailing friends and relatives get-well cards that bear pictures of robins. If a robin flies into a church then the life of a parishioner is deemed to be drawing to a close, and should one appear near a mine shaft this is a portent of disaster below. This association with death is extended by the age-old tradition that the robin, like the wren, will not suffer a corpse to remain unburied but will cover the body with leaves (a superstition kept alive through the fairy tale 'Babes in the Wood').

A more cheerful tradition has it that a person can make a wish when they see their first robin of the year, but they must take care to complete their wish before the bird flies away, as failure to do this means a whole year of bad luck.

In terms of weather prediction, spotting a robin deep within a hedge or tree suggests that rain is in the offing, but if it is seen in the open then it may be expected that the weather will be fine.

Robin Goodfellow In English folklore, the son of OBERON, king of the fairies, by his union with a mortal woman. Able to change his shape at will, he punishes the wicked and rewards the good on the orders of his father. He is sometimes described as having an irrepressibly mischievous character. According to tradition, he will help deserving mortals with the household chores in exchange for a little bread and milk.

See also PUCK.

Robin Hood Legendary English outlaw, who as the central character in numerous ballads, plays, children's stories and, more recently, film and television adventures, retains his status as one of the most celebrated of all English folk heroes. A dispossessed nobleman and unrivalled archer, Robin leads a band of fellow outlaws in the depths of Sherwood Forest, robbing the rich to help the poor and dedicating himself to resisting the injustice and cruelty imposed by corrupt representatives of church and state. After many adventures, in which he repeatedly outwits such enemies as the evil Sheriff of Nottingham and Sir Guy of Gisborne, both henchmen of the royal usurper Prince John, he is united with his lover, Maid Marian, and ultimately is pardoned by the rightful king, Richard I, on his return from the Crusades.

Debate continues over whether the legendary Robin Hood was based on an actual person. The earliest certain references to him are made in William Langland's *Vision of Piers Plowman* (1377) –

although a 'Robin Hod, fugitive' is recorded in the York assizes of 1225. Sometimes described in retellings of the legends as 'Robin of Lockesley', it is popularly supposed that he was in reality the outlawed Earl of Huntingdon, Robert Fitzooth, although it has also been suggested that he may have been a member of the more humble Hood family of yeomen, who were tenants of the manor of Wakefield. In the earliest versions of Robin's adventures, the action is set in the region around Barnsdale, Yorkshire. A link is also made with Robin Hood's Bay, also in Yorkshire, where legend has it that Robin kept a fishing boat in order to escape his pursuers.

Various 14th-century ballads tell of Robin's prowess with a bow, and also celebrate his flouting of the unpopular laws against the killing of deer in the royal forests and his defiance of the evil Sheriff of Nottingham. In *A Lytell Geste of Robyn Hode* (c.1495), for instance, Robin kills the Sheriff and is subsequently visited in his forest home by the king. These early versions, however, place the adventures in the time of Edward II (1307–27) rather than during the reigns of Richard I (1189–99) and King John (1199–1216) as was later usually the case. Furthermore, in early versions there is no theme of English resistance to the Norman nobility or mention of the outlaw robbing the rich to help the poor.

It is likely that the legend, passed on in the oral tradition, absorbed the influence of other similar hero tales. Folklorists have detected elements in common with the stories of Hereward the Wake, FULK FITZ-WARIN, and ADAM BELL. Similarly, Robin's band of Merry Men has changed over the years. In the earliest tales he is accompanied by Little John, Will Scarlet, Much the Miller's son, Allen-a-Dale and George-a-Green, but the familiar figures of Friar Tuck and Maid Marian were added much later. Marian was a 13th-century import from French folklore who featured in various May Day revels long before she was identified as Robin's wife or mistress. The fact that Robin always wears a 'Lincoln green' tunic may also be a borrowing from May Day customs, in which the GREEN MAN played a prominent role.

Another late addition to the story of Robin Hood was the episode dealing with the hero's death at Kirklees Priory, near Halifax in Yorkshire. According to this, in 1247 Robin was treacherously bled to death by a nun acting on the orders of his aunt, the prioress at Kirklees. As his last act he shot an arrow through the open window and requested that he be buried where it landed. A mound in Kirklees Park is traditionally identified as his grave, and what are said to be his bow and arrow are preserved at Kirklees Hall. Another relic of Robin Hood's life is said to be the oak called 'Robin Hood's larder' in Sherwood Forest. It was within a hollow in this tree that the hero is said to have hidden the deer he poached. The tree blew down in 1966, when it was reputed to be over 1,000 years old.

Robin Hood remains a potent and much-loved symbol of English resilience and courage. It is speculated that back in the 14th century he was popularly taken up as a hero by oppressed peasants whose frustrations culminated in the Peasants' Revolt of 1381, and it was only later that he was transformed from a humble yeoman to a dispossessed aristocrat in keeping with Romantic notions of chivalry. Modern interpretations of the Robin Hood legend generally follow this latter pattern, as consolidated by Sir Walter Scott in the novel *Ivanhoe* (1818). Alternative theories include the suggestion that the real Robin Hood was one of Simon de Montfort's supporters, forced into outlawry after de Montfort's defeat at Evesham (1265).

As well as playing a starring role in ballads, novels and films, Robin Hood has also established himself on the stage as a late addition in the pantomime story of 'Babes in the Wood', and is sometimes identified, alongside Maid Marian, as the May King during May Day celebrations.

roc In Arabian folklore, a monstrous white bird that carries off humans and other large prey (even elephants) to eat in its mountain nest. In the ARABIAN NIGHTS, SINBAD is carried aloft by a roc, having tied himself to the foot of the bird in order to escape from an island, and subsequently his ship is smashed by boulders dropped by a pair of rocs after his crew cook their egg for food. Others reputed to have encountered the creature included Kublai Khan, as reported by the Italian traveller Marco Polo. In some writings the huge luminous egg laid by the roc is interpreted as an emblem of the sun.

Roland In French legend, one of the most celebrated of the 12 paladins who attended the court of CHARLEMAGNE. Roland's story was told in the 11th-century *La Chanson de Roland*, the most famous medieval CHANSON DE GESTE. In this he is depicted as the epitome of the noble knight-hero, who behaves with great courage even in the most perilous situations, armed with his great sword called Durandel (or Durindana).

The tale recounts Roland's betrayal by his stepfather Ganelan, who gives the Saracens information enabling them to ambush Roland's army in the pass of Roncesvalles in the Pyrenees. Roland stubbornly resists the urgings of his friend OLIVER to sound his horn Olivant, which would summon armed assistance from Charlemagne. By the time reinforcements arrive Roland and all his men have met a heroic death. To prevent his enemies gaining his sword Roland throws it into a stream, where it is said to remain intact and undiscovered to this day. A variant version of the tale suggests that Roland did eventually sound the horn, but that Ganelan told Charlemagne to ignore it as it was only the sound of the hero out hunting.

Italian versions of the legend, in which Roland is referred to as Orlando, include such great literary works as Ariosto's *Orlando Furioso* (1532) and Boiardo's *Orlando Innamorato* (1487).

romancero Spanish ballad genre based on real historical events and characters. Many historical subjects were reworked in romancero form, with the addition of many folkloric elements. The most famous included the story of EL CID and others celebrating Spanish resistance to the Moors. The romancero tradition has a stronger literary character than the ballad traditions of many other cultures, and as such has had a profound and lasting effect upon national identity and art throughout the Spanish-speaking world.

Ronan In Irish mythology, a king of Leinster, whose tragic end was related in the *Book of Leinster*. The husband of Ethne and the father of Mail Fothartaig, Ronan goes on to marry the young daughter of EOCHAID AIREM, only for her to make advances to Mail. When she is rejected by Mail, she takes revenge by telling Ronan that his son has tried to rape her. The outraged Ronan has his son and his foster-brother Congal put to death, but is horror-struck when he learns the real truth. Congal's brother has his revenge by killing the queen's parents and brother, upon which she takes poison and dies. Ronan himself meets his death at the hands of Mail's two sons.

rose Of all garden flowers, the rose is perhaps the most significant in terms of folklore. Allegedly introduced to the West from India by Alexander the Great, it has long been identified as the quintessential flower of love, its blood red bloom signifying passion and its thorns symbolizing the agonies of the lovelorn. It was also taken up as the emblem of many Christian saints, as an emblem of England and in heraldry as the badge of a seventh son and, famously, as the family symbol of the rival houses of Lancaster (a red rose and later a red and white rose) and of York (a white rose) who in the 15th century waged the lengthy civil conflict now remembered as the Wars of the Roses.

The rich and varied symbolism of the rose was well-established in European folklore by at least medieval times, when the flower's adoption as a symbol of the Virgin Mary was extended until the bloom came to represent the feminine sex in general. Examples of medieval reverence for the rose include the late 13th-century French epic love poem *Roman de la Rose*, in which a poet falls in love with a rose, and the spectacular rose windows of the cathedrals of Chartres, Notre Dame and elsewhere.

In Victorian times specific interpretations were placed by lovers upon gifts of roses of certain colours – red roses symbolizing passion and white roses purity of love, for instance. This association with secret passions also made the rose the emblem of discretion and silence. In ancient Greece a rose suspended from the ceiling signified that nothing said in that room would be revealed – hence the image of the rose found set into the ceilings of council chambers and other meeting places as a reminder that what is discussed there should remain private (or *sub rosa* – 'under the rose').

The red rose is said to have got its colour either from the spilt blood of Christ (whose crown of thorns was made of rose stems), Venus or Adonis or, according to a Muslim legend, from the sweat of Muhammad's brow. Alternatively, the original white rose that grew in the Garden of Eden blushed red after being kissed by Eve. Another tradition claims that the nightingale is in love with the rose and cannot resist pressing its body against its thorns, its blood thus staining the flower red. According to medieval legend the first rose sprang up miraculously at Bethlehem in response to the prayers of a lovely young girl, who had been falsely accused and sentenced to death by burning: when the fire was kindled the burning brands turned into red roses, while the unlit branches turned into white roses. As a result of this remarkable divine intervention the girl was spared and set free.

In Roman times, roses were often planted at gravesides in the belief that they had the power to protect the dead from evil. In former times white roses, symbolic of innocence, were often planted at the graves of virgins, while red roses were planted on the graves of lovers or philanthropists renowned for the love they showed their fellow human beings. This association with death probably lies at the root of the body of generally pessimistic folk traditions now linked to the flower. Thus, superstition warns that if a rose drops its petals while someone is holding it this is an omen that the person concerned is soon to die. Roses that bloom out of season, meanwhile, are looked upon with a jaundiced eye, as these are supposed to presage misfortune in the year to come. Dreaming of roses may be interpreted as a prediction of success in love, but if they are white in colour then misfortune lies in store.

On a more cheerful note, girls may use roses to identify their husband-to-be by wrapping a rose in white paper on Midsummer's Eve and keeping it until Christmas. Then it is unwrapped and if still fresh worn by the girl on her dress; the first man to admire the rose or remove it is destined to become her spouse. To determine how sincerely one is loved, a person has only to snap the stem of a rose – the louder the noise produced, the stronger the passion. Anyone plucking a rose should, incidentally, ask permission from the fairies or little people first.

The rose plays a role in many folk tales. In 'Beauty and the Beast', for example, the plucking of a rose from the Beast's garden by Beauty's father arouses the former's anger. There is also a Turkish legend in which the rose and butterfly argue over which is superior – only for the rose to be plucked by a passing woman and the butterfly to be swallowed up by a bird.

The rose has various uses in folk medicine. In England in the 18th century it was alleged that the rose could promote fertility, and women wishing to bear children sometimes wore red roses in small bags round their necks. The gall of the rose, meanwhile, is supposed to be an effective cure for whooping cough and toothache, if worn around the neck, and will combat insomnia if placed beneath the sufferer's pillow. In medieval times people sometimes carried posies consisting of rose blooms in the belief that these would ward off the plague. The tradition that the nursery rhyme 'Ring a' ring o' roses' was inspired by the arrival of the Black Death in England in 1348 and that it describes the rosy rash and sneezing symptoms of the disease is, however, probably fanciful as the rhyme did not appear in print before the 19th century and is thought to have evolved as a chant accompanying a simple 'falling down' game for young children.

rosemary Like many other herbs, rosemary is widely respected for its alleged supernatural properties. Sacred to remembrance and friendship, sprigs of rosemary were formerly tossed onto the coffin by mourners at funerals as a sign that they would not quickly forget the deceased person. Rosemary was also drunk in wine by newlyweds at their wedding breakfast celebrations as a symbol of lasting fidelity in love. Rosemary is further said to ward off the EVIL EYE, to cure madness, to guard against nausea and nightmares, and to prevent storms. It may also be carried about the person or pinned up by the front door to keep witches and disease away. It is, moreover, a crucial ingredient in many love charms and in spells intended to reveal the future: sleeping with a sixpence and a sprig of rosemary under the pillow on Hallowe'en, for instance, will vouchsafe visions of a future partner in one's dreams. Wearing a sprig of rosemary in the buttonhole is reputed to aid the memory, and will also generally promote the wearer's good fortune.

It is said that rosemary, like parsley, will only grow in households where a woman holds sway. There is also a belief that the plant grows upwards for 33 years until it reaches the height Christ was at the time that he was crucified, after which it grows outwards only. Another ancient tradition claims that, in common with the Glastonbury Thorn, rosemary flowers at the hour of midnight on Old Christmas Eve (the eve of 6 January, upon which date Christmas was celebrated under the old Julian calendar).

Other miscellaneous traditions associated with rosemary include the notion that a little rosemary added to a barrel of beer will rob it of its intoxicating properties, and the idea that spoons made of rosemary wood add taste to even the most unpalatable dishes, as well as negating the effects of poison. Similarly, combs made of rosemary wood are reputed by the French to combat dizziness, while others claim that applications of lotion containing rosemary will restore thinning hair.

Round Table In Arthurian legend, the huge round table around which the knights of the court of King ARTHUR assembled at CAMELOT. According to tradition, Arthur either ordered the making of the table to eradicate bickering over the issue of precedence when it came to seating his knights, or else accepted it as a gift from Leodegrance of Cameliard, the father of GUINEVERE. Accounts of how many people could sit at the table vary – some claim that 25 knights could be accommodated, while others insist that as many as 50, 150, or even 1,600 could be comfortably seated. One seat, the Siege Perilous, was left empty as only a sinless knight could occupy it in safety (a tradition apparently inspired by a similar legend concerning a table made by Joseph of Arimathea to commemorate the Last Supper, the empty seat being that of Judas Iscariot). The Knights of the Round Table, as they became known, met twice a year to tell the stories of their adventures and to demonstrate how they had adhered to the court's chivalric ideals.

The Round Table now displayed at the Great Hall in Winchester is not in fact old enough to have been the table used at Camelot, assuming such a table ever existed. It dates instead from the 13th century,

probably made on the orders of monarchs who hoped to benefit by associating themselves with Arthurian kingship.

rowan The rowan, or mountain ash, was sacred to the Druids and continues to be respected in folklore for its protective properties. This tradition was reinforced by the identification of the rowan as the tree from which the wood for Christ's cross was taken.

Planting rowan trees in the garden was formerly a recommended defence against WITCHCRAFT, while nailing rowan branches over the doorway to cow sheds and houses was likewise reputed to keep evil spirits from entering. In many English counties these branches were formerly gathered on 3 May (Holy Rood Day or Rowan-tree Day) and were then left in place for a whole year before being renewed. To be absolutely sure of keeping cattle free from the influence of witches one alternative was to tie a twig of rowan to the animals' tails with a length of red thread. In the case of horses, it was thought advisable for the rider to carry a whip made of rowan or to wear a few sprigs of rowan in his or her hat. Carrying rowan about the person and attaching a small piece to the bedhead was supposed to furnish further protection from interference by witches, and had the added benefit of preventing rheumatism. According to a Scottish tradition, touching a witch with a rowan stick was said to result in the witch being immediately dragged off by the Devil.

Rowan trees are often to be found in graveyards, where they are said to prevent the slumber of the dead from being disturbed. Rowan wood is also a traditional choice for the making of divining rods, water wheels, farm tools and crossbeams in houses.

Ruadan In Irish mythology, the son of BRES MAC ELATHA and BRIGIT, who fought on the side of the FOMORIANS at the second Battle of Mag Tuired. Ordered to spy on the forces being assembled by their enemies, the TUATHA DE DANANN, he became involved in a fight with the legendary armourer GOIBNIU. He managed to wound his adversary but was then himself slain by Goibniu using the very spear that he had been making.

ruby The birthstone for the month of July, the ruby is said to be one of the luckier gems. Hindu folklore advises that those fortunate enough to own a ruby may wear it in the happy knowledge that it will safeguard them from evil of all kinds and ensure a peaceful and successful life. It will also prevent the wearer from having impure thoughts. The association of the ruby with the blood is reflected by the tradition that a ruby will change colour according to the state of health enjoyed by the wearer. The stone may also be used in folk medicine to treat haemorrhages and blood disorders.

rue Herb that is widely understood to represent bitterness, sorrow and repentance. It was often listed among the ingredients of witches' brews, although it could also be used as a deterrent against WITCH-CRAFT and the threat of the EVIL EYE. It has particular significance in Arabic countries, where it is said to have been the only herb blessed by Muhammad.

In times gone by it was customary for someone who felt he had been wronged to throw a handful of rue in his enemy's face and to curse him with the words 'may you rue this day' or something similar (hence the phrase 'rue the day', meaning to regret some past action). In contrast, rue is said to bring luck to anyone who wears a sprig of the plant in their buttonhole, and is also credited with certain healing properties, being particularly valued in treating eye problems and as an antidote for poison. It is also reputed to counter vertigo and epilepsy, to promote chastity, and to act as a painkiller in combination with other ingredients, although in reality many people suffer severe skin reactions after touching the plant. During plague epidemics in the 16th and 17th

centuries rue was often sprinkled on the floor in the belief that it would combat infection, and judges carried posies of rue to prevent them catching gaol fever from the criminals brought before them.

The plant is said to grow best if it has been stolen or roughly treated.

Rumpelstiltskin Well-known European folk tale, possibly of British origin, that was among the stories retold by the Brothers Grimm.

Rumpelstiltskin is a malicious DWARF who comes to the aid of a miller's daughter imprisoned and threatened with death by the king unless she demonstrates her gift for spinning flax into gold (as her father has boasted). The dwarf agrees to complete the seemingly impossible task in exchange for the girl's necklace, and when the king returns in the morning he is delighted to find a pile of gold in the girl's cell. He immediately transfers her to another room and insists she repeat the performance, this time with a larger pile of flax. Once again the dwarf helps out, this time in exchange for the girl's ring. When the king sees the girl has met his demand once more, he takes her to an even larger room containing an even bigger heap of flax, and this time promises to make her his wife if she will repeat the feat one last time. When the dwarf appears in the girl's cell that night she has nothing more to offer him, but he agrees to spin the flax to gold if she will promise to give him her first-born child. The girl agrees and the dwarf completes the task. The king honours his bargain and marries the miller's daughter, making her his queen.

A year later, the queen gives birth to their first child, and the dwarf reappears to demand the infant as originally agreed. The queen begs him not to take the baby, and the dwarf consents to allow her one last chance to keep it: if she can guess his NAME within three days he will release her from her promise. The royal couple send messengers out far and wide to collect every name in the kingdom, but none of them prove correct. Eventually, however, a messenger reports having overheard a strange man resembling the dwarf singing a little ditty of self-congratulation in which he revealed his name as – Rumpelstiltskin. When the queen suggests that this is the dwarf's name Rumpelstiltskin stamps the floor so hard with rage he becomes firmly wedged in it. When he tries to wrench himself free he pulls himself apart, leaving all who remain to live happily ever after.

rusalka In Slavic folklore, a variety of water spirit usually identified as the spirit of a dead woman. Some rusalki are benign and become the wives of mortals, but others are viciously malevolent, luring victims with their beautiful singing and then drowning them.

See also VODYANIK.

rush-bearing Annual festival that is still celebrated in a few northern English towns and villages. Before the 18th century, when wooden flooring became more common, it was usual for the floor of most churches to consist of stone flagging or else of beaten earth. The feet of the congregation were kept warm and dry by strewing these floors with cut rushes, grass or hay, which was renewed annually on a specific date, sometimes the festival of the church's patron saint. The fresh rushes and grasses were brought in with some ceremony, being carried in procession into the church accompanied by children carrying garlands of flowers and sometimes also by Morris dancers. Today rush-bearing ceremonies are still performed in Grasmere, Ambleside and other places in the English Lake District (and occasionally elsewhere in Britain). At the Ambleside festival the celebrants also parade two tall pillars of rush and various rush-decorated wooden frames through the town and sing hymns before entering the church for a short service, after which all the children present are given a piece of gingerbread.

Ryons In Arthurian legend, a king of North Wales who was famous for lining his cloak with the beards of his defeated enemies. Shortly after King ARTHUR was crowned, Ryons (or Riance) demanded his beard for his cloak, but the young king declined the demand, adding that he was too young to have a substantial growth of beard, and proceeded to defeat Ryons in battle. Legend has it that Ryons died some time later when his own warriors rebelled against him.

S

sacrifice An offering to a deity, which often takes the form of the ritual slaughter of an animal upon an altar but which can also encompass gifts of plant material or metal artefacts such as cauldrons or weaponry thrown into sacred lakes or rivers and so forth. The practice of sacrificing animals and even humans to win divine favour dates back to the very beginnings of human history. In some cultures the thinking behind such acts seems to have been that by presenting a deity with the finest gifts the community has to offer (such as the life of a young man) the group as a whole will benefit, while in others the sacrifice takes the role of a scapegoat in the belief that by killing a chosen animal or person the rest of society is relieved of its collective guilt and may thus escape divine retribution.

The theme of sacrifice is central to Christian philosophy, culminating in the sacrifice of Christ on behalf of humanity. The celebration of the Eucharist similarly runs parallel with the tradition shared by many cultures of eating a sanctified meal and thus becoming one with the gods. At one extreme it was believed that the gods would only be satisfied with mass sacrifices, as illustrated by the bloody rituals of ancient Mesoamerican civilizations. Often though, a single life would suffice: the Pawnee Indians, for instance, developed the custom of choosing one young girl, providing her with everything she desired for six months, and then killing her and distributing the parts of her body throughout the corn fields in the belief that this would promote the crop and give the earth new life. The selection of a single girl for sacrifice seems also to have been practised by some of the pre-Columbian Andean civilizations, as attested by the discovery of their mummified remains. By way of contrast, other cultures appear to have made relatively little use of human sacrifice at any stage in their history. The degree to which the Celts, for instance, observed such practices is still debated, although the discovery of ritually killed bodies preserved in European bogs suggests that they may have been more active in this regard than was previously generally accepted.

Blood sacrifices are rare in the modern world, although they continue in VOODOO and a small number of other folk religions. However, many folk customs around the world have their origins in blood sacrifice, and the same notion of making gifts to the supernatural forces that govern nature in order to gain divine protection, promote fertility or safeguard crops and so forth lies behind countless relatively innocuous rituals.

Sadbh In Irish mythology, the mother of OISIN. She was turned into a deer after rejecting the advances of Fear Doirche, but found she could escape his influence while under the protection of the FIANNA. She married FIONN MAC CUMHAILL but subsequently fell back into the clutches of Fear Doirche after unwisely venturing out of Fionn's house. Seven years' later Fionn's hounds found her son Oisin (which means 'little fawn').

saga Prose epic of medieval Icelandic and Scandinavian literature. It is possible to group sagas into three main categories: family sagas, which depict the first settlers of Iceland and their descendants; kings' sagas, which are biographical works about the kings of Norway; and the legendary or heroic sagas, which recount the adventures of great heroes. It is debatable to what extent the sagas relate actual history, and modern scholars conclude that the bulk of the material is probably literary invention dating from the 13th century. The plots generally typically revolve around epic quests or blood feuds. The most famous sagas include the early *Egils saga* (c. 1220) attributed to Snorri Sturluson (1178–1241), the *Njals saga* (a 13th-century family saga), the *Grettis saga* (c.1320, relating the adventures of the Icelandic outlaw Grettir), and the celebrated VÖLSUNGASAGA (c. 1270).

sage Like many other herbs, sage is prized as a lucky plant, and has many uses in folk medicine. Legend has it that sage was introduced to the British Isles by the Romans, who dropped bits of it while marching along the roads they constructed (said to be the reason why the plant is often spotted growing on grass verges). Credited with promoting wisdom and improving the memory, sage is said to flourish in gardens where a woman holds sway, and also responds well when tended by someone who is very wise. It is important, however, that the sage is picked before it can bloom, as flowering sage brings bad luck to the household. Hanging a sprig of sage in the kitchen will enable occupants of the house to know how a missing member of the family is faring when away from home: if the sage wilts and perishes then the person concerned is in trouble of some kind.

For the purposes of love divination, a girl is advised to pick 12 leaves of sage at midday on 25 April (St Mark's Day) or at midnight on Midsummer's Eve, plucking one leaf at each stroke of the clock: the first unmarried man she sees after doing this is supposedly destined to become her husband.

The plant, which was used widely in herbal medicine, has a strong reputation for its curative properties, as indicated by the etymology of its name, ultimately from the Latin *salvia*, from *salvus* (safe, in good health); hence also 'salve'. Eating sage on seven (or nine) mornings in succession before breakfast will cure the ague, according to one ancient Sussex belief. It may also be used in treatments for sore throats and weak eyes, in healing wounds, in promoting fertility and in facilitating childbirth. In the days before the introduction of toothpaste, many people rubbed their teeth with a sage leaf to keep them clean.

An old proverb heard in various forms in several different countries suggests that eating sage in May, when the plant is deemed to be at its most potent, may have benefits for those seeking to extend their life span: 'He that would live for aye must eat sage in May.'

sailors' lore Seafarers around the world, because of the perilous nature of their work, are among the most superstitious of all groups of individuals, and marine folklore is remarkably rich and varied. Much of it seeks to provide reassurance to the anxious sailor that he will return home safe, magically preserved from the threat of drowning.

In former times seafarers from many cultures placed great importance upon placating the gods of the sea through sacrifices and offerings. Viking sailors, for instance, were said to run their longboats over the bodies of captive enemies to ensure divine favour, and even today many crews observe special 'crossing the line' ceremonies when those crossing the equator for the first time are symbolically 'sacrificed' through ritual humiliation (usually a playful ducking before the assembled crew impersonating Neptune and his court).

Sailors all over the world are well known for their faith in a variety of AMULETS, CHARMS and other guarantees of magical protection. In times gone by, for instance, every ship had a FIGURE-HEAD, often in the form of a naked woman, which was believed to calm the seas over which it sailed. Not dissimilar is the age-old Mediterranean custom of painting large staring eyes on the prow of a boat in the belief that this will ward off the threat of the EVIL EYE. Seamen of all nationalities have for centuries sought to protect themselves through magic by adorning their bodies with TATTOOS and gold earrings (which are supposed to prevent evil spirits gaining access to the body via the ears). Other charms taken very seriously until at least the early years of the 20th century included the careful preservation of CAULS (the amniotic membrane covering some babies' heads when they are born) in the belief that these would guard the owner against the threat of drowning. When they sailed many sailors left behind a model of their ship in a glass bottle, believing that as long as this was carefully preserved, no harm would befall the real ship in which they departed.

By the same token, seamen are especially sensitive to signs that might threaten trouble ahead. Bad omens include meeting a clergyman, someone who is cross-eyed or red-haired, or certain birds and animals on the way to their ship. It is also unlucky if a voyage is scheduled to begin on a Friday or on certain specific dates in the calendar, namely 2 February (Candlemas Day), the first Monday in April (Cain's birthday) and 31 December (when Judas committed suicide). On safely reaching the ship many sailors will be careful to board with the right foot rather than the left in order to avoid the bad fortune that might otherwise be invoked. They will not be reassured if well-wishers watch the ship until it is out of sight and point after it, thus threatening it with the evil eye, but they may be heartened if the same friends and relatives hurl old shoes after the vessel for luck. They will also be pleased to find the ship has a CAT, as this will promote the luck of the vessel.

Sailors may express reservations if they find corpses, women or clergymen on board during a voyage, and they may also be prejudiced against anything that is black in colour. Welsh crews formerly disliked transporting spinning wheels, for some obscure reason. In the case of corpses, these must either be given a burial at sea at the first available opportunity (carefully weighted so that they do not follow the ship), or else carried 'athwart' the planks and never parallel with the line from bow to stern. On reaching port the body must leave the ship before any living person. Conversely, the birth of a child on board a ship is universally greeted as a stroke of the greatest good fortune for ship and crew alike.

Disaster will be confidently predicted if certain animals – or even traces of them – are found on board a vessel. These include dogs, hares, horses and pigs. It is TABOO even to mention such animals by name. It is considered a particularly ill omen if the rats suddenly vacate a ship (a sure sign that the vessel will sink). Most dangerous of all, however, is the ALBATROSS, which if recklessly killed will bring dire misfortune down upon the vessel and its hapless crew. Sailors will also show a certain nervousness if a ship is tailed by sharks, as these creatures are supposed to have a sixth sense concerning the approach of imminent death.

Other portents of disaster include such accidents as losing a mop and bucket over the side, tearing the ship's colours, or absent-mindedly passing something through the rungs of a ladder. It is also extremely unlucky to play cards at sea, to do any sewing, to throw salt overboard or to whistle.

Various folk traditions offer seafarers ways in which they can influence the WEATHER while at sea. Apart from the risky remedy of whistling to raise a wind when lying becalmed, which may result in a destructive gale, sailors may scratch the foremast with the fingernail, in which case a helpful breeze will soon spring up. Alternatively, the wind may respond if asked politely to oblige, or else burning an old brush may have the desired effect. When the wind does come, a dead KING-FISHER nailed to the mast will prove useful in indicating the quarter from which the wind is blowing. This particular tradition harks back to the Classical belief that the seas remain calm for seven days before and after the winter solstice to allow the eggs of the kingfisher (formerly called the 'halcyon') to hatch. Even today any period of calm weather (especially following or preceding a storm) is likely to be dubbed a time of 'halcyon days'. Tradition further claims that cutting the hair at sea or trimming the nails is unwise as this will blow up a gale. Tossing a coin into choppy water, however, may cause the waves to subside.

Should the worst actually happen, a French tradition rather ghoulishly advises that the sweetheart of a sailor lost at sea will be made aware of the awful truth by the sound of dripping water beside her bed.

Sailors themselves are sometimes considered harbingers of good luck. A well-known custom (more often encountered away from the coast, where sailors in uniform are a rarer sight) claims that good luck will befall anyone who touches a sailor's collar.

See also FLYING DUTCHMAN; KRAKEN; MERMAID.

saining Ancient folk tradition, recorded in various parts of the British Isles, involving a ritual ceremony through which a newborn baby or a recently deceased body is offered special supernatural protection. The more or less defunct practice of saining requires the whirling of lighted candles in a sunwise direction around the bed in which the baby or the body lies. A variation of this procedure involves the midwife circling the bed nine times while reading from the Bible.

saint Pious individual who has been formally honoured by the Christian church through canonization and may be the object of veneration. Hundreds of saints have been recognized by the church over the centuries, their number ranging from popes and monarchs to evangelists, martyrs and ordinary mortals who have distinguished themselves by their piety.

Many are shadowy figures whose names have become the focus of legend. During the medieval period the saints largely replaced pagan deities and surviving local gods as the supernatural protectors of certain areas, countries, trades or other communities and took over their roles as the divine spirits associated with various important activities, such as childbirth and travel. Every profession, it seems, can lay claim to its patron saint, from the bricklayers' St Stephen and the dentists' St Apollonia to the tax collectors' St Matthew and the yachtsmen's St Adjutor.

Many accounts of the lives of the saints (some first compiled in the 13th century) stress the supernatural element, with numerous stories of miraculous events. Often these were clearly borrowed from existing folkloric sources, and it is not unusual to find that the life of a particular saint bears a marked resemblance to that of a well-known folk hero or pagan deity. The Irish St Brigid (or Bridget, or Bride), for instance, is closely related to the Celtic goddess Brigit and, because the latter was a goddess of fire a fire was customarily kept burning at shrines dedicated to the Christian saint descended from her. Stories about miraculous phenomena associated with the preserved relics of certain saints are similarly reminiscent of many ancient folk tales.

It would appear that in many parts of the world saints were venerated alongside pagan deities and frequently made their appearance in tales alongside pagan heroes. Many saints' festivals were similarly based upon much older feasts that dated from pre-Christian times.

See also GUARDIAN SPIRIT.

St Elmo's fire Glowing electrical discharge that is sometimes observed around the mastheads of seagoing vessels or church spires and so forth. This curious phenomenon has been known for many centuries, and was once considered a divine sign that the vessel or building concerned enjoyed the protection of St Elmo (otherwise known as St Erasmus), the patron saint of sailors. In Germany the phenomenon was interpreted by sailors as being the soul of a deceased fellow seaman advising the crew about the weather in store – if the light grew in strength good weather lay ahead.

St John's wort Yellow-flowered wild plant, which is reputed to have various healing and protective properties. The flower is traditionally linked with the festivals marking Midsummer's Eve. Named after St John the Baptist, at whose festival the flower was once ceremonially burned, St John's wort is supposed to ward off evil spirits and witches, and was formerly often kept indoors or hung above doorways for exactly this purpose. The red spots that may sometimes be discerned on its leaves are said to represent the blood that was spilled when St John the Baptist was beheaded, and are alleged to appear each year on 27 August, reputedly the anniversary of the saint's death.

Women experiencing difficulty in becoming pregnant are promised by superstition that they will overcome the problem if they take off all their clothes and venture into their gardens during the hours of darkness on Midsummer's Eve and there pick a St John's wort. Midsummer's Eve is also the best time to gather St John's wort for use in treating people suffering from nervous disorders such as depression and insanity. Sleeping with a St John's wort secreted under the pillow, meanwhile, will vouchsafe the sleeper visions of a future marriage partner.

Lastly, regional traditions warn that it is dangerous to step on a St John's wort, as the guilty party may find a fairy horse rears up and carries the person concerned off on a wild ride that will last all night, before the hapless rider is unceremoniously dumped in some far-off spot.

St Swithin's Day A well-known English tradition claims that if it rains on St Swithin's Day (15 July) it will rain for another 40 days in succession. This belief dates back to an attempt that was made to move the remains of St Swithin, a 9th-century bishop of Winchester, to a more prestigious location in Winchester cathedral on 15 July AD 871. Heavy rain lasting 40 days prevented the disinterment being completed and was taken as a sign of the saint's disapproval of the proposed move. The plan was eventually abandoned, leaving the saint in the humble spot in the open graveyard that he had chosen for himself on his deathbed (although in the year AD 963 his remains were successfully moved regardless of what he had requested for himself). His shrine within the 11th-century Norman cathedral was restored in 1962.

Weather forecasters admit that mid-July often sees a fundamental change in weather patterns, but deny that it is possible to discern distinct annual 40-day droughts or downpours following this particular date.

St Valentine's Day The feast of St Valentine celebrated on 14 February, when, according to time-honoured custom, lovers exchange cards, flowers and gifts. Cards are traditionally left unsigned, and much of the day is spent by recipients in delicious speculation about the identity of their admirers (originally the cards were designed and drawn by the senders themselves).

St Valentine was a Christian martyr executed during the reign of the Roman emperor Claudius II around AD 269, apparently for opposing a ban on the marriage of young men of soldiering age. However, the tradition may owe more to the Roman fertility festival of the

Lupercalia, which was celebrated on 15 February. During the course of this a lottery was held, with boys drawing from an urn the name of their sweetheart for the next year. According to medieval folklore, 14 February also marks the first day of the mating season among birds.

St Valentine's Day is, according to folklore, a good time to use magic to find out the identity of future partners. One tradition has it that if a girl leaves her house early in the morning on 14 February and the first person she meets is a man, then she will be married within three months (quite possibly to that particular man). Her chances of meeting the love of her life may be enhanced if she wears a yellow crocus in her buttonhole, and further information may be gleaned about a future spouse by noting which species of bird she sees first. A blackbird, for instance, signifies marriage to a clergyman, while a robin suggests a sailor, a sparrow a farmer and a woodpecker nobody.

Less romantic is the tradition from eastern England that St Valentine's Day is an auspicious occasion for the preparation of EELS for the purposes of magic.

salmon The salmon had particular significance in ancient Celtic mythology, in which it represented wisdom. Legend has it that FIONN MAC CUMHAILL became immensely wise after burning and then licking his thumb while cooking a salmon that had eaten magical nuts growing on hazel trees at the bottom of the sea. It was also as a salmon that TALIESIN escaped from CERIDWEN. According to Scottish superstition, the salmon is an unlucky fish in many circumstances. It is thought particularly unfortunate for fishermen to find a salmon in their first haul of the day, and many of them regard the word 'salmon' as a TABOO word that should never be uttered while at sea.

salt Sodium chloride was once considered one of the elementary substances, and as such has considerable significance in folklore. Vital to the maintenance of life

and apparently magical in its properties of food preservation, salt has always been highly valued – Roman soldiers were sometimes paid in salt. Some folk beliefs connected with salt may date back to pre-classical times, when salt was frequently used in sacrifices to placate the gods, to ratify important agreements and to solemnify other social transactions. The Aztecs boasted a salt goddess, while the Judaeo-Christian tradition has the story of Lot's wife and her transformation into a pillar of salt after she turned to look back at the evil city of Sodom. Salt has also been used around the world in some of the major religious ceremonies, including baptism and exorcism.

The most commonly observed superstition concerning salt is the assumption that evil spirits are roused when salt is accidentally spilt – in some areas it is said that a tear will be shed for every grain thus scattered. This notion undoubtedly has its origins in the high value that was once placed on salt, although some authorities also link it to the legend that Judas overturned the salt cellar at the Last Supper. The tossing of a pinch of the spilt salt over the left shoulder is regarded as an antidote to any ill luck thus risked, in the belief that it will drive away the DEVIL before he can whisper in the ear of the person concerned (variations in this tradition add that a cross should then be traced in the salt that is left on the table). Similarly, a pinch of salt thrown after a gypsy is believed to nullify any CURSE he or she may have just pronounced.

Other less well-known traditions are based on the luck-giving powers of salt. Fishermen have been known to sprinkle their nets with a little salt, while boatbuilders traditionally spill salt between the planks of a craft under construction in the expectation that this will safeguard the crew on future voyages. Salt is also carried over the threshold in many British homes as part of the NEW YEAR celebrations, as this brings the promise of prosperity. Once inside the house salt should never be lent out again, particularly on

New Year's Day, as this constitutes giving away one's good luck.

Salt is reputed to have considerable power as a protective against evil influences. A little salt held in the palm of a woman giving birth is said to be of great benefit to mother and child, and newborn children were once given gifts of salt or bathed in salty water to ward off the threat of WITCHCRAFT. Dairymaids in former times often sprinkled a pinch of salt in their pails and in the butter churns to prevent interference by witches. In some cultures, a saucer of salt, sometimes mixed with soil, may be laid on the chest of a dead man, ostensibly to prevent the body swelling, but more probably to scare away evil spirits.

Samhain Celtic festival celebrating the start of the New Year. Held each year on 1 November, Samhain was believed to be a time when the gates of the underworld were opened and the dead roamed freely in the mortal world. It was also possible for mortals to gain access to the otherworld at this time. Mythology claimed that Cailleach, the goddess of winter, was reborn each year during the festival, which featured the burning of ritual fires among other acts of celebration. In practical terms the feast marked the beginning of winter and was the time when some animals were slaughtered for food in the cold months ahead and the rest were brought indoors or moved to winter pasture. The modern equivalent of Samhain is HALLOWE'EN.

Sand Man Folkloric character of European and US nursery lore, who brings sleep to tired children by sprinkling magical sand in their eyes. A benevolent spirit who brings good dreams to the sleeping, he was formerly also known as the Dust Man, until this title became associated with refuse and lost much of its attractiveness.

See also BOGEY.

Santa Claus *See* FATHER CHRISTMAS.

sapphire The birthstone for September, reputed to promote love and happiness in those who possess one. Oriental folklore claims that there is a captive spirit inside every sapphire, while according to Buddhist tradition, the sapphire has special powers to induce trances. It also repels witches and evil spirits, and promotes health in general.

Sasquatch *See* BIGFOOT.

Satan *See* DEVIL.

Scathach In Irish mythology, the Scottish woman warrior who trained CUCHULAINN in the arts of war. She declared his training to be complete after a year and a day when he successfully beat her in combat and, predicting his future as a great hero, rewarded him with an invincible spear and the hand of her daughter UATHACH. The island of Skye, where she may have kept her training school, was named after her.

Scheherazade In the ARABIAN NIGHTS the beautiful young wife of King Shahryar, who preserves her own life by narrating an exciting tale to him each evening. Scheherazade knows that as soon as he tires of her the king will have her executed (the fate of his many previous wives) and thus resolves to tell him an exciting story each night, leaving it unfinished until the following evening. She goes on like this, keeping the king fascinated in her tales, for 1,001 nights, until the king finally relents and promises not to order her execution.

Schlaraffenland *See* COCKAIGNE, LAND OF.

Scot, Michael Scottish wizard, who is still remembered for his legendary skills as a sorcerer and occultist. Scot, who was born at Balweary near Kirkcaldy in Fife around 1175, was renowned for his learning. He studied Arabic, astronomy and alchemy at Oxford, mathematics and theology at Paris and the occult at Padua in Italy and in due course was appointed tutor and astrologer to Frederick II, the Great, at Palermo. His reputation was international, winning him a mention in Dante's *Inferno* and in the poetry of Sir Walter Scott, who dubbed him 'the wondrous Michael Scot, a wizard of such dreadful fame'.

Though relatively little is now known of his career beyond his achievements as a translator of key Arabic texts, various legendary feats are still attached to Scot's name. Among other achievements, he taught the witches of Glenluce how to plait sand (a trick they still perform judging by the curious ropelike patterns the sands naturally form in Luce Bay), was once transformed by a rival witch into a hare (in which shape he was pursued by his own hounds), and used his magic to cleave the Eildon Hills in three. He died around 1235 and is supposed to lie buried in Melrose Abbey.

screaming skull One of a number of skulls preserved around the English-speaking world that are reputed to utter unearthly screams if moved or otherwise interfered with. The tradition is particularly associated with the British Isles. The most famous examples include the notorious skull of Bettiscombe Manor in Dorset, which is said to have belonged to a black servant who died there of consumption in the 17th century, and that of Ann Griffith at Burton Agnes Hall in Yorkshire. Not only will these skulls utter piercing shrieks if moved, but they may also roll back to their original position under their own volition.

scrying The art of DIVINATION by gazing into a MIRROR, a crystal ball or some other reflective surface, such as a brightly polished sword blade. The reflection was considered magical in classical times and according to some theories it was a visible manifestation of a person's soul (thus the tradition sometimes encountered that anyone who has sold their soul to the

DEVIL has no reflection at all). Such reflections, in mirrors or in water, could be asked questions about the future, and if they trembled or broke up the prognosis was generally considered very worrying.

Some experts employed scrying, or crystal gazing, to root out witches and thieves, revealing the face of the culprit in their mirror to any inquirer. The method could also be employed to trace lost property or missing persons or to contact spirits. Only the pure in heart were said to be able to communicate with good spirits, and thus many young children were employed as scryers.

By medieval times scrying, or catoptromancy, had become very sophisticated and was highly regarded even by royalty. Not everyone could master the art, and those who claimed to have such powers were much sought after. Expert practitioners of the art of scrying became famous and mixed with the highest in the land, though they risked being accused by their enemies of dealing with the Devil, and might acquire a popular reputation as a witch or sorcerer.

Pre-eminent among these individuals in the Elizabethan and Jacobean ages, when scryers were much respected, was Dr John DEE, who performed such services at the English court and, among other events, foretold the Gunpowder Plot of 1605. Like many others, Dee was unable himself to see anything in the mirror or, in his case, the crystal, and so had to employ someone else with such gifts to act as an intermediary.

It was widely believed that the crystal ball or mirror used for scrying purposes should never be handled, as this reduced its effectiveness, and that passing the right hand over it several times helped to cause images to appear.

seal maiden The curiously human appearance of seals basking on rocks may well have accounted for the legends of seal maidens that captivated the imagination of European folklore in ancient times. According to Scottish legend, seals were fallen angels, and many tales were told of seal maidens who married mortals and became the source of famous Scottish families. The only evidence of these origins was said to be the webbed hands or feet of children of these families. Other traditions identified seals as enchanted kings. An alternative name for seals in Scots Gaelic is *Cuilein Mairi* ('Mary's Whelps').

See also ROANE; SELKIE.

sea serpent *See* WATER SPIRIT.

Sedna Heroine of Inuit legend, who is also identified as the ruler of the underworld. The legend describes how she is thrown into the sea by her own father in response to her marriage to what is variously identified as a seabird or dog. She clings to her father's boat in a desperate attempt to save herself, but her merciless father hacks off her fingers and she drowns. The fingers turn into sea monsters and avenge her by killing her father. A great feast is held in her honour every year.

seelie court In Scottish legend, the court of the fairies. The fairies attending the seelie court were thought of as being generally benevolent, in contrast to those belonging to the UNSEELIE COURT, although they might be quick to avenge any offence. Periodically, they issued out from their court to inspect the boundaries of their kingdom, specifically upon the feasts of OIMELC, BELTANE, LUGHNASADH and SAMHAIN.

selkie (or silkie) In Scottish legend, a species of SEAL capable of disguising itself in human form. Selkies can remove their skins to go about undetected among mortals, although if a mortal finds the sealskin of a female selkie he can thus force her to live with him as his wife. Various tales recount how humans ensnare selkie wives in this fashion and how they bear human children before finally retrieving their sealskin and

returning to the sea. As with MERMAIDS, it was said that if anyone killed a selkie and allowed the blood to drip into the sea their own ship would be lost in a storm.

serpent *See* SNAKE.

Seven-League Boots Magical boots that allow their owner to cover seven leagues (21 miles) with each step. They appear in several European folk tales, usually having been stolen from a GIANT. They are said to shrink by magic to fit the foot of mortal wearers.

Seven Whistlers A flight of seven spectral birds, whose appearance was formerly much dreaded by sailors, fishermen and miners across Britain. Usually encountered at night, the Seven Whistlers utter eerie high-pitched calls and are said to be an omen of death or of some other calamity. According to some witnesses, the birds are actually six in number and they fly in constant search of the seventh: when the seventh bird finally joins them the world will end. Another tradition concerning the birds claims that they are the spirits of drowned seafarers, or else the souls of unbaptized babies (although the less superstitious may identify them as flights of curlews, plovers or other birds with distinctive whistling calls).

See also GABRIEL'S HOUNDS.

shaitan In Islamic folklore, a variety of JINNI. Described as extraordinarily ugly, shaitans (or sheitans) are irredeemably evil in nature and spread disease and other ills among mankind. They are said to be descended from the demon Ali-Shaitan and take pleasure in luring mortals into sin. They dislike daylight and are said to feed on excrement. In Christian lore the term was taken up as the name of the arch-fiend Satan.

shamanism The belief that gods and spirits, responding to the influence of privileged individuals called shamans, are behind all good and evil in the world.

Shamanistic religions can be found in many parts of the world and are particularly associated with the Siberian, Inuit and Native American peoples, but are also found in places like Korea, India, southeast Asia and Oceania and to a lesser extent in parts of Africa.

The shaman is credited, by virtue of his access to supernatural forces, with the power to persuade spirits to cure disease and with the knowledge to conduct various important rituals. They typically enter a trance state through the use of dancing, music, hallucinogenic drugs or other means and while in this condition travel to the spirit world to negotiate or struggle with the spirits they encounter there. It is also widely believed that shamans have the ability to change their shape, to leave their bodies at will, to foretell the future, and to kill their enemies at great distances. They may inherit these skills from their elders or else be marked out as shamans by their unusual appearance, odd behaviour or some disability or by the fact that they are known to have undergone some mystic experience, such as being struck by lightning without suffering injury. They may have to go through an elaborate initiation ceremony before they can practise their arts. In many cultures it is believed that shamans live several lives.

shamrock See PATRICK, ST.

shanty See WORK SONG.

shape shifting The ability to use magic to change one's physical form, usually to that of an animal. This ability has been widely credited to all manner of supernatural beings as well as to sorcerers and witches over the centuries. The idea of shape-shifting spirits appears to have been common to virtually all the world's cultures at one time or another, and the theme features in numerous folk tales, with heroes being transformed into such animals as wolfhounds, swans, crows, ravens and a vast array of other forms.

Many supernatural beings were deemed capable of changing their shape at will, but mortals usually had to have the use of a magical cloak or some other device. In some parts of the world it was thought sufficient simply to don an animal skin to assume its characteristics; elsewhere, the sorcerer had to perform an elaborate ritual or smear the body with magic ointment in order to change shape. In some cases, the ability to change shape was unlooked-for and was the result of a spell or of a curse placed on a family. Celtic legend, for instance, had it that certain ancient Scottish and Irish families were descended from seals or wolves and that the descendants were perforce obliged to take those forms from time to time.

Shape shifting was dismissed as an impossibility by the medieval church, but belief in the phenomenon revived considerably in the 16th and 17th centuries when the witchcraft hysteria was at its height. Usually under torture, many witches confessed to using magic ointments given to them by the Devil and then in the form of wolves or other wild beasts savaging livestock and attacking men so as to feast on their flesh. In many other cases, they admitted to adopting animal shape in order to spy on their neighbours or to escape pursuit (hares and cats were favourite disguises, although tales were also told of witches who turned into bees, birds and other creatures). In rare cases some witches claimed to be able to change themselves into inanimate objects, especially wheels. Often injuries suffered by sorcerers and witches while in their transformed shape would still be evident when they returned to their human form.

See also LYCANTHROPY.

shark With their uncanny ability to detect prey from great distances and their reputation for attacking the victims of shipwrecks and swimmers, the shark is feared and loathed by seafarers around the globe. Superstitions associated with them include the notion that sharks (often three in number) tail a vessel when someone aboard is close to death. The sight of porpoises near a ship may, however, offer some reassurance as these are reputed to ward sharks off. Polynesian folklore, meanwhile, identifies sharks as the spirits of the dead and thus considers them sacred. Elsewhere in Oceania sharks inspire both reverence and abhorrence, as they do in many modern cultures.

sheitan *See* SHAITAN.

shivaree *See* CHARIVARI.

shoe Of all items of clothing, the shoes are perhaps the most significant in terms of folklore. They make frequent appearances in folk tales around the world – examples including the glass slipper in 'Cinderella', and the SEVEN-LEAGUE BOOTS of fairy tale fame.

Shoes and the feet have long had strong sexual symbolism, as evidenced by the Chinese custom of foot-binding, which was still practised in relatively recent times. This particular tradition was explained by an old legend that claimed that the fairy wife of an early emperor hid her cloven feet by wearing a pair of tiny shoes, thus starting the fashion for such footwear and establishing small feet as a requisite of great beauty. In reality, the practice probably had its roots in the belief that by binding a girl's feet and thus making her incapable of physical work the parents indicated her superior social status.

Similar thinking may lie behind the otherwise obscure modern link between shoes and boots and weddings. Old shoes, which are deemed to be lucky, are often tied to the rear bumper of the car in which newly-weds depart after the ceremony, and it is sometimes suggested that this will ensure the couple's fertility. It would appear that shoes have been associated with wedding ceremonies as far back as biblical times. In Anglo-Saxon England, for instance, the father of the bride handed a shoe to the groom as a sign of the transfer of responsibility.

For the purposes of love divination, placing the shoes in the shape of a letter T beside the bed on Midsummer's Eve and reciting the rhyme 'Hoping this night my true love to see, I place my shoes in the form of a T' may be sufficient to vouchsafe to the sleeper visions of a partner-to-be. Putting one's shoes under the bed with the soles turned upwards is said in parts of southern England to be a cure for cramp, and leaving them by the bedroom door so that one shoe is coming into and the other going out of the room will confuse the demons that cause nightmares.

Different traditions conflict concerning gifts of new shoes, some claiming that such presents are harmful to the luck of the recipient, while others see only good luck in the act. A third variation on this theme advises that gifts of new shoes are perfectly acceptable, provided that the recipient gives a small coin in return. All agree, though, that it is inviting bad luck to give shoes as presents at Christmas. Should a person never give someone else a pair of new shoes as a present, however, they are doomed to go barefoot after they die, according to another tradition. In times gone by it was thought unwise to wear new shoes at a funeral, for fear of exciting the jealousy of the deceased.

Shoes should never be placed upon a table as this is symbolic of death (either because condemned prisoners were usually hanged with their shoes on or because bodies still wearing shoes might be laid out on tables). At the very least this risks an argument breaking out in the household.

When putting shoes on it is a bad omen to try to put one on the wrong foot, and in any case unwise to put the left shoe on first (although some people claim it is the right foot that is unlucky). One superstition has it that a person who makes a habit of always putting the left shoe on first will never suffer toothache. It is also unlucky, as well as perilous, to walk with just one shoe on. An old and rather mischievous English superstition claims that if a new pair of shoes squeaks when a person is wearing them this betrays the fact that the shoes have not been paid for. By the same token, superstition warns that people with expensive-looking shoes that never seem to get dirty or worn are probably cheats and thieves. The Japanese, incidentally, think it unlucky to put on a new pair of sandals before five o'clock in the afternoon.

Shrove Tuesday The eve of the first day of Lent (Ash Wednesday), which is the occasion of numerous folkloric celebrations in the English-speaking world. Falling in late February or early March, it is also known as Pancake Day as people traditionally eat pancakes on this date (originally a useful way of using up any eggs and butter, which are forbidden foods during the Lenten fast). Most people toss their pancakes in the air while cooking them, and in some parts of Britain pancake races, in which contestants rush through the street while tossing pancakes, are held. One such race, the origins of which go as far back as 1445, is held annually in Olney in Buckinghamshire. Local names for Shrove Tuesday include Guttit Tuesday, Bannock Night and Doughnut Day.

Shrove Tuesday is also the date when a variety of boisterous village sports take place. These include various games of Shrovetide football, which have been played on this date in Ashbourne, Derbyshire, and other towns and villages for many hundreds of years (despite attempts to ban this often dangerous pastime in the 19th century). The Ashbourne game can continue for many hours as the two teams (from the upper and lower parts of the town) struggle to get a football into one of the two goals, which are situated some two miles apart. The scorer of the winning goal gets to keep the ball. Similar games are played at Alnwick in Northumberland, Sedgefield in Durham and Atherstone in Warwickshire among other places.

In Cornwall the eve before Shrove Tuesday used to be known as Nicka-Nan Night and was an occasion for pranks and the playing of practical jokes.

shvod A variety of BOGEY in US folklore. The attentions of these household spirits are sometimes used as a threat to naughty children.

sidhe Irish name for the FAIRY race. The name was given originally to the share of the otherworld that each member of the TUATHA DE DANANN was allotted when they retreated underground to escape the MILESIANS, but it later came to be used of fairies and sprites in general, as well as to the otherworld itself, which may be entered via various secret gateways in natural land features and burial mounds.

Siegfried *See* SIGURD.

Sif In Norse mythology, the wife of THOR. Famous for her long golden hair, she fell victim to the mischief-making of LOKI, who cut it all off while she slept. Thor ordered Loki to replace the hair, obliging him to seek out dwarfs who had the skill to make real hair out of gold.

Sigurd Germanic hero who features in both Old Norse legend and, as Siegfried, in German mythology. His story is related in the Norse VÖLSUNGASAGA, in which he is identified as the son of Sigmund and Hjordis, the last of the Völsungs. He falls in love with BRUNHILD but then marries GUDRUN after taking a love potion. His adventures include killing FAFNIR the dragon and the treacherous dwarf Regin. His tale ends with his slaying by Gunnar, at the instigation of Brunhild, who subsequently throws herself on his funeral pyre.

The German version of his life, related in the first part of the NIBELUNGENLIED, is markedly different in many respects. The youngest son of Siegmund and Sieglin, the king and queen of the Netherlands, he slays Fafnir and subsequently gains possession of the gold of the Nibelungs. Using his cloak of invisibility, he helps Gunther to win Brunhild as his wife and then himself marries Gunther's sister Kriemhild. The two queens later fall out and procure Siegfried's death at the hands of Hagen.

Sigyn In Norse mythology, the wife of the wicked LOKI. She remains faithful to Loki even after he is imprisoned for his crimes in an underground cavern. By draining off some of the venom of the serpent set to watch him she relieves him of the worst of his torments.

silkie *See* SELKIE.

silver Folklore considers silver to be one of the most useful of all precious metals, and the metal above all others that is associated with the MOON. Although silver is invulnerable to magical influence from outside, it transmits the power of other magical objects more perfectly than any other material, making it ideal for the making of TALISMANS and other magical objects. Because of this property, bullets made of silver were considered ideal for the killing of VAMPIRES, WEREWOLVES, witches and demons. The link with the moon, however, means that silver does have uses in ALCHEMY, WITCHCRAFT and other occult practices. One of the aims of alchemy was to create a 'white stone' that would turn any metal into silver.

Silver is generally considered to be lucky, and many people carefully preserve silver sixpences or other silver coins to use in Christmas puddings or simply to ensure continued prosperity. Turning over any silver coins in the pocket on first sighting a new moon is widely recognized as a sure way to attract more money. Boatbuilders may place a silver coin under the mast of the boat they are constructing in order to ensure its luck, and in the past householders often buried silver coins under the threshold for similar reasons. As well as wearing 'something old, something new, something borrowed and something blue' some brides even today will go through their marriage service with a silver sixpence in their left shoe for luck.

Anyone who encounters a gypsy and fancies they would like to make use of their services in divining the future must first 'cross their palm' with silver, a custom that was recorded before the birth of Christ and that is still pursued today, only the amount of silver differing. Other miscellaneous traditions relating to silver include the superstition that if a piece of silver jewellery becomes tarnished this is a sure omen that its owner is about to die.

simnel cake Fruit cake topped with marzipan that is traditionally baked for eating on the fourth Sunday of Lent or at Easter. Simnel cakes used to be made by servant girls to take home to share with their families on MOTHER'S DAY. It is usual for the cake to be decorated with 12 marzipan balls representing the 12 Apostles, although the number is sometimes reduced to 11, with Judas Iscariot being left out. The word 'simnel' comes originally from the Latin *simila*, the name of a fine wheat flour.

Sinbad A hero of the ARABIAN NIGHTS, whose adventures are among the most celebrated episodes in the whole cycle. During the course of Sinbad's seven voyages he has numerous hair-raising escapes. These include disembarking on an island only to discover it is the back of a whale, being carried off to the nest of a giant ROC, being captured by dwarfs, being attacked by a one-eyed monster, falling into the hands of cannibals, being set upon by the OLD MAN OF THE SEA and being sold into slavery as an elephant hunter, before finally returning home loaded with riches. His adventures have been retold in numerous forms, including several films.

sin eating The practice of magically transferring the sins of a dead person to a person still living so that the deceased's soul may have an easier journey to the afterlife. This archaic custom was once found in various forms in many societies, both Christian and pagan, and was still being revived on an occasional basis in the British Isles as late as the 19th century. Typically, some food was placed on the breast of the corpse or passed over it to the sin eater, who would normally have been specially hired for the purpose and received a small payment for his services. By eating the food thus offered, this volunteer was deemed to take on some of the dead person's sins and thus increase the latter's chances of gaining entry to heaven. In other cases food that had been placed on or near a corpse was surreptitiously fed to a beggar or to some other person otherwise unaware of the ramifications of the situation.

As the hired sin eater gradually disappeared in common practice, so mourners gathered instead to drink a symbolic glass of wine in the presence of the dead person, the bottle and glasses being placed on the coffin itself. To decline a glass thus offered would be deeply resented.

singing bone Musical instrument constructed from the bone of a murdered person. When the instrument is played it reveals in song the details of the crime that has been committed. This macabre notion appears in a large number of folk tales of Eurasian origin. One of the best-known stories was that collected by the Brothers Grimm. Two brothers seek to win the hand of a princess, who has been promised to anyone who kills a fierce wild boar terrorizing the land. The younger brother succeeds in the task, but is then killed by his brother, who claims the credit for the boar's demise and wins the princess. A shepherd subsequently finds a bone from the young brother's body in the forest and unwittingly turns it into a pipe, upon which it sings of the elder brother's guilt.

Sita The heroine of the RAMAYANA, who becomes the consort of Rama himself. She is depicted as the epitome of wifely

loyalty, remaining faithful to her husband even after being abducted by Ravana. When Rama falls prey to suspicion that she has been unfaithful to him he sends her into the forest, where she is swallowed up by Mother Earth. By the time Rama realizes the allegations made against her are untrue it is too late.

Skidbladnir In Norse mythology, the fabulous ship of the AESIR. Constructed by dwarfs for the weather god Freyr, it could fly through the air as well as upon water, and did not depend upon the wind to go directly to its destination. It was large enough to transport all the gods and their arms, but could also be folded up small enough to be carried in a pocket.

sky people In Native American folklore, a race of divine beings who live in the sky. According to the mythology of several tribes the first humans resulted from a female member of the sky people falling through a hole in the sky and landing on the earth. In order to break her fall, all the animals quickly spread out the landscape on the back of a turtle. Similar notions may be found in the mythology of various parts of Africa and Asia.

Sleeping Beauty European folk tale known in a variety of forms in different cultures. It is best known today from the 'Little Briar Rose' story collected by the Brothers Grimm, although Charles Perrault also published a version of the tale as 'La Belle au bois dormant' as early as 1697. Even earlier was the 14th-century French romance *Perceforest*, in which the prince Troylus discovers and rapes the sleeping Zellandine. The story may have come from Persian legend.

'Little Briar Rose' relates how a Wise Woman takes exception when inadvertently omitted from the guest list for a celebration to mark the birth of the king and queen's daughter. She curses the child, prophesying that she will die at the age of 15 after pricking her finger. Another guest changes the sentence of death to a sleep lasting 100 years, but the curse cannot otherwise be lifted.

Despite attempts to remove all sharp points from the kingdom, the princess (now aged 15) pricks her finger on the spindle of a spinning wheel, and immediately she and the entire royal household fall into a deep sleep from which they cannot be roused. The palace is surrounded by an impenetrably thick thorn hedge that prevents anyone gaining entry from the outside world. After 100 years a prince manages to get through the thorn hedge and wakes the sleeping princess with a single kiss.

sleeping lord The legend of a heroic leader lying asleep under the hills, awaiting the day when he will be needed to save his people, is common to many cultures. Among the sleeping lords of Britain are King ARTHUR (variously said to lie sleeping beneath Glastonbury Tor or Arthur's Seat in Edinburgh), BRAN THE BLESSED and Robert the Bruce. A similar legend involves CHARLEMAGNE. Sir Francis Drake is similarly believed to be awaiting the day when he will be needed to sail against England's foes again, summoned by the beating of his drum (preserved at Buckland Abbey near Plymouth). The sound of spectral drumming, attributed to Drake's drum, was reportedly heard in 1914 at the start of World War I, and again in 1918, when the German fleet surrendered (*see* DRUM).

sluagh In Gaelic legend, the host of the unforgiven dead whose appearance may inspire great dread among the living. Mortals may encounter the sluagh returning to their old haunts on earth, or else hear them warring in the heavens. Their appearance is particularly feared by those who believe that they may be snatched up by the sluagh and forced to remain in their ranks for ever.

snake Folklore has always regarded the snake with fear and respect, crediting the creature with various supernatural pow-

ers. Snake-worshipping cults have thrived in many different parts of the world, and snakes occupy a prominent, if not always positive, position in world mythology. In the Christian world they are particularly associated with the DEVIL, who took the form of a snake in the biblical story of Adam and Eve. Other cultures have associated the snake with healing, fertility and rain-making (as celebrated in the snake dances of various Native American tribes), or have emphasized the protective properties of the creature. It was believed in some parts of the British Isles, for instance, that hanging a snakeskin from the rafters would prevent the house burning down. The fact that snake designs are popular as TATTOOS is another illustration of this tradition. Hindu folklore associates snakes with a variety of positive attributes, identifying them with benevolent gods, although elsewhere they are more usually regarded with loathing and dread. In the southern USA a Christian snake-handling sect advocates the handling of venomous snakes as a test of faith (inspired by a passage in the New Testament).

Folklore has cherished a number of misconceptions about snakes. These include the widespread beliefs that all snakes hypnotize their prey and that they inject their venom via their forked tongues. Another popular tradition shared by several cultures has it that snakes cannot die until the sun goes down.

Seeing a snake crossing one's path is unlucky, as are dreams about snakes, and a pregnant woman who is frightened by a snake may give birth to a child with a constricted neck (although it is also said that snakes will never bite pregnant women). Tying a snakeskin around the waist of a woman in labour will ease childbirth, and carrying a snakeskin is generally supposed to be beneficial to the health, being effective against headaches and also in extracting thorns from the skin. In the USA it is said that women in labour who are fed a drink made from the powdered rattle of a rattlesnake will have an easier time of it. Carrying a snake's tooth will ward off fever, and these may also be carried for luck in gambling. Other uses of snakes in folk medicine include an old English treatment for swollen necks, which requires that a live snake be drawn across the affected part three times and then buried alive in a bottle. Another tradition claims that anyone who eats snake flesh will thereby be able to converse with animals.

Folk medicine recommends a host of animal and plant preparations for the treatment of snakebite. The more bizarre of these include the rubbing of crocodile blood into the bite. Should crocodile blood be unavailable, another course is to tie the dead body of a snake around the wound. To avoid getting bitten by a snake in the first place the simplest course is to wear an emerald.

sneeze In times gone by sneezes were considered more than mere symptoms of a bodily ailment. According to Parsee belief, for instance, sneezes should be interpreted as a sign of evil spirits being abroad in the vicinity, and similar notions surround the sneeze in the folklore of Africa and North America.

The custom of saying 'bless you' has been credited by Christians to St Gregory. Many people, however, believe inaccurately that the practice of saying 'Bless you' dates only from the Great Plague of the 17th century, when blessing someone who had just sneezed had serious intent, sneezing being one of the supposed early symptoms of the dread disease. In fact, records exist of similar traditions as far back as the ancient Greeks. One theory behind this convention claims that whenever a person sneezes they are temporarily deprived of their soul, which will only return to the body when someone says 'Bless you'. While the soul is absent malevolent spirits may gain access to the body and there work their evil unimpeded. The explosive sneeze therefore marks the passage of various spirits to and from the body.

Sneezing before one has put on one's shoes is reputed to be a bad omen. Sneezing just once or three times in a row is unlucky, but two sneezes in quick succession are said to bestow good luck (a variation of this suggests one for a wish, two for a kiss, three for a letter and four for 'something better').

Care should be taken as to the direction one sneezes in, as sneezing to the right is lucky but sneezing to the left is unlucky, particularly if one is at sea or in the vicinity of a grave. Sneezing straight ahead presages the arrival of good news. Two people sneezing simultaneously will result in both parties enjoying good luck. A tickling nose that refuses to culminate in a sneeze may be interpreted as an indication that the person concerned is the object of another's secret longing.

Another tradition concerning sneezing relates to the first sneeze of a baby: this should be welcomed as until it happens the baby is held to be in the power of the fairies. This first sneeze also indicates that the child is mentally normal, as a long-held superstition has it that a fool cannot sneeze. Other miscellaneous traditions include the notion prevalent in the USA that someone who sneezes while talking is undoubtedly telling the truth.

Snegurotchka In Russian folklore, a snow maiden who is the daughter of Frost and Spring. She lives in the dark recesses of the forest, but is finally enticed into the sunlight by her fascination with humans and her desire to experience mortal emotions. She falls in love, but the sun destroys her the instant she steps out of the shadows cast by trees.

snow *See* SNEGUROTCHKA; WEATHER.

solstice One of two dates in the year when the sun is at its northernmost or southernmost point when viewed from the equator. These significant dates in the folkloric calendar fall on 21 or 22 June (the summer solstice; the longest day in the northern hemisphere) and 21 or 22

December (the winter solstice; the shortest day in the northern hemisphere). The dates are marked in many cultures with a variety of rituals, many of which feature the lighting of bonfires in imitation of the sun's heat. Celebrants often wear masks and dance round the fires on these dates, hoping to ensure the sun's continued cycle and to frighten away any evil spirits at these magical times of the year.

The solstices were important dates to many early civilizations and it has been observed that many notable prehistoric sites, such as stone circles and burial mounds, were aligned in such a way as to capture the first rays of the sun on these significant days. It is thought that these structures may originally have had a practical purpose as well as a mystical one, being used to confirm the accuracy of early calendars.

Because of their ancient significance both these times of year became the focus of later ritual celebrations, including (in June) the marking of MIDSUMMER'S DAY and (around the time of the winter solstice) the ancient Roman Saturnalia, the medieval FEAST OF FOOLS and, today, CHRISTMAS and NEW YEAR.

Sons of Mil Espaine See MILESIANS.

soothsaying See DIVINATION.

sortilege See BIBLIOMANCY.

soul cake A small round flattened loaf of the sort that was formerly baked in many parts of England for luck on 2 November, All Soul's Day. This now defunct custom involved children being given such soul cakes as a special treat as they sang traditional songs while going from house to house ('souling'), although many people kept their soul cake carefully by, often for many years, in order to preserve the luck it brought them.

sovereignty The concept of sovereignty had particular significance among the Celtic peoples, whose legends often featured a goddess personifying the idea. In many of these tales pretenders to various thrones prove their right to kingship by winning the approval of the goddess of sovereignty, who was often interpreted as representing Ireland itself. Typically, she would appear initially in the guise of a hideous hag, but reveal her true identity after winning from the hero a kiss or some other token of nobility or kindness, as in the story of NIALL OF THE NINE HOSTAGES. If a king lost the right to sovereignty, for instance through injury, then the land itself would betray this fall from favour, being transformed into a wasteland. Names by which the goddess of sovereignty was identified included Brigit and Brigantia, who was subsequently replaced by BRITANNIA.

See also WOUNDED KING.

speaking head A severed head that remains alive long after being separated from the body. Tales of severed heads are particularly associated with Celtic mythology. The most famous include that of BRAN THE BLESSED, whose head was eventually interred to await the day when it would be needed to rescue England in its hour of need. Like others it was reputed to offer useful advice to the living, and also to entertain friends with songs and stories. English folklore, meanwhile, is replete with tales of ghosts carrying their heads under their arms.

Speewah Mythical Australian cattle station that is supposed to be bigger and better than any other ranch in the world. The Speewah has become the setting for a large number of tall stories resembling those of Baron Münchausen in character.

spell The casting of magic through a charm, incantation, or other magical act. The idea that spells can be used to achieve influence over others is very ancient and common to all the world's cultures. Its practitioners over the ages have included a wide variety of witches, wizards, sorcerers, magicians, demons and fairies. These might employ FAMILIARS to perform various deeds on their behalf, but on the whole the public imagination cherishes the image of a witch or sorcerer bent over a bubbling cauldron, muttering weird incantations and cackling hideously at the thought of the consequences of the spells being prepared.

Spells threatening physical incapacity or even death, as well as the destruction of livestock and property once inspired great dread, and are still the subject of anxiety in many parts of the world today. All manner of means may be employed to such ends, ranging from the use of waxen images or puppets of wax to poisons and 'overlooking' (see EVIL EYE). The simplest procedures to ensure the death of someone, for instance, include burying something belonging to or representing the intended victim in an existing grave. To blight a farmer's fields and to steal his crops one spell involves the assembling of a miniature plough drawn by a team of toads (a spell detailed in the confession of Scottish witch Isobel Gowdie).

Other malevolent spells are of a less serious nature, designed to bring inconvenience of a more trivial kind to an enemy. Typical of such mischief-making spells was that which a Suffolk witch named Alicia Warner admitted to casting against two women she disliked back in 1645. By her spell Alicia Warner hoped to send evil spirits to the women in order to infest them with lice, and the court found that the two women were indeed 'lousy according as she confessed'.

Many spells are designed to provoke love in a reluctant partner. As well as preparing love potions, witches and sorcerers might also offer other forms of spells to achieve the same end. One of the oldest of these requires the making of a poppet of wax mixed with the desired partner's bodily secretions (blood, semen, saliva and so forth). The name of the person is written on the forehead of the image and the name of the aspiring lover on the breast, using blood from the third finger of the left hand. The figure is then

pierced in the back, the head, the heart and the pelvis with four new needles and subsequently laid in a fire after being sprinkled with salt and mustard seed. The fire has to be kindled using a piece of paper bearing a sample of the handwriting of the desired person. When the fire dies down the person's name is inscribed once more in the ashes, to make doubly sure that the magic is directed at the right party.

Other spells are designed to solve the problems that might arise from realized desire, specifically, to procure the abortion of unwanted babies. These usually work by virtue of being so disruptive of the body's system that the pregnant woman will be taken seriously ill and thus be more than likely to have a miscarriage (there is, however, the ever-present risk that the expectant mother will die). Among the noxious substances that were once commonly included in such spells were the poisonous pennyroyal, rye ergot and oil of tansy.

Spells might also be cast to read the future (see DIVINATION), to spread the plague by poisoning the air, to influence the weather (see STORM), to start fires, to make men mad, to render husbands impotent, to spoil butter and beer and to steal milk from cows. To achieve the latter feat, European witches were rumoured to 'milk' lengths of rope or straws or, according to some reports, the handle of an axe stuck in a wall.

The preparation of spells can be simple or exceedingly complicated, requiring extensive knowledge of the magic arts and access to a book of spells (called a grimoire) detailing procedures to follow. The ingredients of spell-making brews are likewise many and various. They include herbs, plants, roots, animal organs and bits of human corpses (especially those of babies and hanged men). Among the more exotic ingredients are deadly nightshade, bats' blood, mandrake root and snakes' venom. Typical of the more arcane recipes is a 17th-century remedy for the healing of wounds, the ingredients of which include powdered worms and bloodstones, stale boar fat and moss taken from an old human skull.

For a spell to work it is important that together with the right ingredients the spell maker establishes a connection between the magic being made and the intended victim. This is especially necessary in the case of using waxen figures to attack intended victims (as in the case of the love spell already described). The most effective way to make this connection is to incorporate in the figure or spell physical traces of the person to be bewitched. Such traces may range from purloined samples of nail trimmings, teeth and locks of hair to bodily fluids, pieces of clothing and the straw the victim sleeps on. Even a footprint can be used against the person who made it, a typical procedure being to bang a nail from an old coffin into the print, thus causing the victim terrible pain until the nail is removed. The connection can also be made by identifying the person against whom the magic is to be directed by simply repeating their name several times during the preparation of the spell.

As witches rely upon the DEVIL for their magic powers, it is usual for an appeal to be made to the spirit world for assistance in ensuring a particular spell works as desired. This is best done from within the safety of a magic circle, for the spirits raised might easily turn their evil upon the magician responsible for disturbing them.

spider The spider, with its unique web-spinning ability, has its own place in world folklore. Spiders are generally regarded as lucky creatures, although many people in the modern world regard them with loathing and even fear.

Legend claims that the creature saved the lives of Christ, Muhammad and Frederick the Great when they were infants. In Christ's case the spider spun a web across the entrance of the cave in which the Holy Family was hiding from Herod's soldiers, thus making it appear that no one had passed by recently. Even better known is the Scottish legend of Robert the Bruce and the spider, whose stubborn attempts to construct a web are supposed to have inspired Bruce to renewed resistance against the English. The spider also appears in the folklore of many other cultures, for instance, in the West African and Caribbean folk tales relating the adventures of the cunning spider god Anansi.

Tradition insists that it is most unwise to kill a spider, as one ancient rhyme makes clear: 'If that you would live and thrive, / Let the spider run alive.' This notion probably dates from medieval times or before, when it was realized that spiders in the home helped to keep down the numbers of flies. Killing a spider will, superstition adds, cause it to rain or, according to a Scottish belief, will result in the accidental breaking of crockery before the day is over.

Although the idea of a spider dropping onto a person's face from the ceiling may be viewed with horror by arachnophobes, superstition claims that this is supposed to be a very lucky thing to happen. Similarly, if a spider is seen running over a person's clothes this constitutes a promise that the wearer will receive a set of new clothes, as does the sight of a spider actually spinning a web. If kept in the pocket or in a purse, the tiny red money spider will similarly attract money to the person concerned.

Folk medicine has many uses for the spider. Eating a live spider in a pat of butter is highly recommended for anyone fearing an attack of jaundice, and a spider eaten in an apple or in jam or treacle will ward off fever. Various other remedies for a range of ailments such as ague involve suspending one or more live spiders in a small bag around the neck until they are all dead. Spiders' webs also have their uses in medicine, being rolled up into pills and swallowed to alleviate fever, asthma and whooping cough, or being laid on open wounds to help in the healing process (a custom that has a good scientific basis).

spirit General term describing a supernatural entity. Spirits may vary considerably in nature and appearance. Inhabitants of the spirit world may be identified as friendly, malevolent or unpredictable in nature, capable of great acts of kindness towards humans as well as the darkest treachery. Among the benevolent spirits may be included angels, FAIRY GODMOTHERS and other species of GUARDIAN SPIRIT associated with particular places, TREES or plants and so forth. Spirits that are often considered openly hostile towards humans include a wide range of DEMONS, GHOSTS, POLTERGEISTS, VAMPIRES, WATER SPIRITS and WEREWOLVES. Examples of spirits that may be either friendly or otherwise mischievous or threatening include BROWNIES, HOBGOBLINS and other breeds of FAIRY as well as a host of nature gods and the souls of the dead. Sometimes spirits take on a substantial corporeal appearance, often manifesting in animal or even human form; more often, though, they are airy, insubstantial beings of relatively unknown character. Communication between the spirit world and the human world is the theme of innumerable folk tales, and has been a source of lasting fascination through the ages.

See also DEVIL.

spitting Saliva is widely thought, in common with other bodily fluids, to have various supernatural properties, and thus the act of spitting has considerable magical significance. Since ancient times it has been believed that in spitting a person expresses a little of the essence of their soul, which thus becomes a sacrifice to the gods and likely to attract divine favour. Many cultures are familiar with the practice of spitting for luck, and people will spit on playing cards, gambling slips, letters, exam papers, footballs, fishing nets and sometimes on their own palms when shaking hands to seal a business deal. Spitting on the fists before a fight is another ancient idea, thought to harden the skin in preparation for the coming

conflict (hence the reason why boxers often do it), and many manual workers will spit on their hands before undertaking a task – not so much to improve their grip as to make the work easier by magical means. Spitting while saying an oath, meanwhile, has long been supposed by many people to be as binding as swearing an oath on a Bible.

Spittle is credited with the power to ward off evil demons, and some people will spit to protect their luck on seeing a cross-eyed person, a magpie or someone or something else suspected of having the power of the EVIL EYE. To keep witches from using cut fingernails or hair trimmings in their spells, the safest course is to spit on this debris before disposal. Parents, meanwhile, should spit on their newborn children for luck and also whenever someone compliments their offspring, in order to protect them from misfortune. Other precautions include spitting on fields before reaping a crop, spitting on new clothes before putting them on, spitting on the right shoe before setting out on a journey or entering a dangerous place and, if at sea, spitting with the wind to prevent a storm developing.

Spittle is also alleged to have certain curative properties and many people will automatically spit on insect bites to get relief. Smearing spittle on warts, ringworm, birthmarks and other skin blemishes is said to be an effective treatment, especially if the spittle is that of someone who is fasting. Less well known is the idea that spitting on a finger will help to restore a foot that has gone to sleep. Lastly, tradition insists that human saliva is poisonous to snakes.

spring *See* WELL.

squirrel According to a widespread European superstition, it is very unlucky to kill a squirrel. This belief is thought to have originated in the legend that the squirrel hid its eyes with its tail when it saw Adam and Eve eating the forbidden fruit in the Garden of Eden, and thus acquired the bushy tail it has today. Anyone who kills a squirrel will henceforth lose all their skill at hunting. The squirrel also features in Norse legend, in which it is depicted as a mischief maker, and in Celtic mythology, in which it is the symbol of MEDB.

stag *See* DEER.

star The folklore of virtually every culture has its own explanations for the presence of the stars and other celestial bodies, and a collection of beliefs and superstitions associated with them. The observation of comets and other events in the heavens were commonly interpreted as warnings of earthly catastrophes, and the study of the alignments of the planets has long been undertaken in the 'science' of ASTROLOGY, with all it portends for the everyday fortunes of individuals on earth. In some early societies, the stars were supposed to be departed souls or else the homes of the gods, although early Christians reinterpreted this belief in the idea that they were simply rocks set in place to deter men from trying to enter heaven by artificial means. Other cultures discerned in the pattern of the constellations the shapes of animals or people, and devised legends to explain their presence. The constellation identified as Taurus, for instance, was variously interpreted as having the shape of a bull by the ancient Babylonians, Greeks and Hebrews, while the Chinese saw it as part of a Great White Tiger, which had quite different origins and attributes. Many of the world's folk heroes ascend to heaven as stars, rather than suffering an ordinary mortal death. Examples of these in ancient Greek legend included Hercules, the nymph Calisto, the hunter god Orion and the seven daughters of Atlas and Pleione, now immortalized as the Pleiades. Although they had many successors in other cultural traditions the scientific establishment now largely ignores these associations in favour of these early Classical identifications and legends.

Numerous pagan sites, including burial places and stone circles, were apparently laid out with reference to a particular star or constellation, illustrating the importance that the stars had in pre-Christian mythology. The most notable of these range from the Great Pyramid of Cheops in Egypt (aligned with Orion) to Stonehenge in England, which according to one theory may have been laid out so as to function as a prehistoric observatory.

Miscellaneous beliefs concerning stars that are still current today include the taboo against pointing at stars, on the grounds that this offends the gods and will result in the guilty party finding that their finger remains permanently pointed by way of punishment. There is also the quaint notion that counting the stars will lead to the person concerned getting white spots under their fingernails. Running somewhat counter to this last tradition is the belief, recorded in Wales and other places, that a person who counts 9 (or 99) stars on 9 nights in succession will be granted a wish.

A person will also be granted a secret wish if it is made on the first star seen after dark and while reciting the following lines: 'Star light, star bright, first star I see tonight; I wish I may, I wish I might, have the wish I wish tonight.'

Lastly, the Milky Way is traditionally supposed to be a celestial road along which departing souls make their way from earth to heaven.

See also ECLIPSE; MOON; SKY PEOPLE; SUN.

stone circle Prehistoric monument of a type found throughout the British Isles and, less commonly, elsewhere in Europe. They are now known to date from the Neolithic and early Bronze Age. The origins of these curious relics have inspired countless legends, although the exact purpose of these sites remains shrouded in mystery. Such notable sites as Avebury and Stonehenge continue to excite fascination, and the ancient legends concerning them remain in circulation. According to

Celtic tradition, Stonehenge was created by the Welsh wizard MYRDDIN, using stones from Ireland. These stones had been carried to Ireland from Africa by the GIANTS, who were the earliest inhabitants of the earth. Other circles are said to owe their existence to the activities of sorcerers, dragons, and as in the case of the Rollright Stones in Oxfordshire, the petrification of a royal army.

Stone of Destiny *See* STONE OF SCONE.

Stone of Scone A slab of sandstone, also known as the 'Stone of Destiny' or the 'Fatal Stone', on which Scottish kings were traditionally enthroned. Legend has it that the stone was actually Jacob's Pillow, or else Columba's Pillow, and was first brought to Scotland by Gaythelus, one of the founders of the Scottish nation. Another tradition claims that it came to Scotland via Ireland, where it had served as the seat of the high kings of Tara since around 700 BC. The stone was kept originally at Dunstaffnage Castle, but was transferred to Scone, the ancient Pictish capital of the country, in around AD 840, and was subsequently used in the coronations of every Scottish king until 1292. It was taken to England by Edward I in 1296, and for many centuries it remained in Westminster Abbey as part of the Coronation Chair upon which monarchs sat when they were crowned. The stone was kidnapped by Scottish nationalists in 1950 but was later recovered in Arbroath Abbey and taken back to London. It was finally returned to Scotland, to rest in Edinburgh Castle, in November 1996.

Stoorworm Legendary Scottish sea serpent that inspired great fear among the early inhabitants of Scotland. Apparently modelled upon the Norse serpent Nidhoggi, which wrapped its body around the world, the Stoorworm was so huge it drowned whole islands in its wake and brought great destruction to life and limb despite attempts to appease it through the sacrifice of maidens. Eventually, the hero Assipattle rose to the challenge and, in exchange for the hand of the king's daughter and possession of his famous sword (a present from ODIN), he managed to kill the monster by piercing its liver with burning peats. As it died the creature spat out its teeth, which became the Faroe, Orkney and Shetland Islands, while its thrashing tail created the Skaggerak and its torso became the island of Iceland. The fires of Iceland are ignited by its still burning liver.

stork It is widely acknowledged that the stork is a lucky bird, particularly associated with childbirth and the young. In biblical tradition, the stork flew around Christ's cross to express its sympathy, and the Romans regarded the bird as sacred to Venus. Since ancient times it has been considered most unlucky to kill a stork, and a good omen if storks build their nest on one's rooftop (not least because they will protect the house from the threat of fire). The mere sight of two storks is said to be enough to cause girls to become pregnant, and modern nursery superstition frequently depicts the stork carrying babies to their mothers direct from God. German folklore claims that if a stork flies over a house someone inside will shortly give birth. This link with fertility probably originated with the bird's association with water, although storks are also celebrated for the care with which they rear their young, and also, so tradition claims, for their kindnesses to the old.

Other miscellaneous folk beliefs concerning storks include the notions that in the fullness of time they are transformed into men; that it is lucky to see them returning to their old nests each year; that the bird will weep human tears if injured; that the male will kill its mate if she proves unfaithful; and that they will peck out the eyes of any humans who betray their marriage partners. Storks are also supposed to have a great loathing for snakes, and will prey on them at all opportunities. In terms of forecasting the weather, fine days are in store if the storks arrive late in the spring, but rain will follow the appearance of a black stork and droughts will accompany a white stork.

In the folk medicine of lands where the stork is indigenous, various parts of the bird are said to have useful healing properties. Wrapping the sinews of a stork around feet stricken by gout will lead to a marked improvement in the condition of the person concerned, while Jewish tradition claims that the gall of a stork may be used in treating scorpion stings.

Storks appear as characters in folk tales from many countries. One of the best known of these is a tale collected by the Brothers Grimm, in which the king of the storks is despatched to earth to punish some frogs that have offended Zeus by complaining about the log he has provided for them.

storm Storms, particularly thunderstorms, have aroused the deepest forebodings in people throughout the ages, and countless folk beliefs have evolved concerning both their causes and their consequences. Storms have been variously blamed upon the anger of the gods, upon witches, demons and other malevolent spirits, and also upon ordinary mortals who have broken some TABOO or other. Taboo activities that are said to provoke storms at sea include cutting one's fingernails or one's hair while on board ship, or whistling. If a storm breaks out while a person is being buried this is likely to be interpreted in parts of Scotland as a sign that the deceased sold his or her soul to the DEVIL.

The coming of a storm may be forecast in a number of ways, in particular by observing that the marigolds have not opened before seven o'clock in the morning and by noting that the cat turns its back to the domestic fire. Particularly violent storms, or storms that happen out of season, are widely believed to be linked to important happenings in earthly affairs, often the imminent death of a prominent person

or a reigning monarch. In former times, it was often claimed that if a storm blew up when the assizes were being held this was a sure sign that more prisoners than usual would be condemned to death for their crimes.

To make a storm cease, one Austrian tradition suggests that hurling a handful of meal out of the window will be enough to appease the spirits that caused it in the first place. Elsewhere in Europe it is said that ringing the church bells offers some protection against storm damage.

Sorcerers, witches and other magic makers were once widely suspected of having the power to raise storms through their spells. By this means they were accused of wrecking ships, destroying crops and inflicting a host of other calamities upon their enemies. Such was the belief in the power of witches to control the elements, in fact, that it seems that whenever a strong wind caused damage in a locality the blame would be laid almost as a matter of course at the door of some elderly and little-loved crone. To raise a storm these magic makers were variously alleged to thrash water with a wand, toss magic powders, sacrificial pullets or sea sand into the air, fling pieces of flint over the left shoulder towards the west, shake wet brooms, pour water or urine into holes in the ground, boil hog bristles or eggs, lay sticks on a dry river bank, recite charms, boil babies in cauldrons, or bury leaves of sage in the soil to rot. One Scottish variant, described at a witch trial in 1662, was to beat a 'cursing stone' with a wet rag while reciting a storm-raising rhyme.

Belief in the magic of storm raising was such that in 1563 the king of Sweden allegedly enlisted four witches when fighting the Danes so that he might influence the weather in his own favour. Accusations that witches raised storms in order to sink ships were especially common in Scotland and the seafaring Scandinavian countries. One celebrated instance of alleged storm raising was the case of the North Berwick witches, in which the accused admitted tossing into the sea a cat bound up with the limbs of a corpse in order to threaten the ship carrying James VI to Denmark (the king's ship survived, but another vessel bound for Leith went down). As late as 1707 a storm that struck the fleet of Sir Cloudesley Shovel off the Scilly Isles, resulting in the loss of 2,000 lives including that of Shovel himself, was widely blamed upon a CURSE laid by a sailor unjustly hanged on the Admiral's orders.

See also KNOT.

Stormalong Legendary hero of sea lore, whose extraordinary feats were celebrated in numerous tall tales and sea shanties. He was said to be the master of the *Courser*, a ship so huge he had to coat its sides with soap in order to get it through the English Channel. When the *Courser* was caught up in a hurricane it hit the coast of central America so hard the collision created the Panama Canal. According to legend, after many adventures Stormalong died and was appropriately buried at sea.

succubus In Judaeo-Christian lore, a demon who seduces mortal men while they sleep (the female equivalent of an INCUBUS). According to the earliest legends about succubi, they were half human and half demon in appearance, and by seducing mortals they gave birth to monsters. Not all offspring of such couplings were demons, though: many notable men – including Alexander the Great and Merlin – were rumoured to be the product of these affairs. Anyone found guilty of having a sexual liaison with a succubus, however, committed the sin of bestiality and was held to be doomed to an eternity in the fires of hell.

According to the demonologists, succubi are organized into their own hierarchy, at the head of which stood Princess Nahemal (otherwise identified as LILITH). Tradition has it that succubi commonly manifest in the form of very beautiful women or even assume the appearance of wives or lovers so as to 'steal' the semen of the men thus tempted. Particularly susceptible to assault from succubi are monks and others dedicated to a life of celibacy (suggesting that these demons were invented in order to explain uninvited erotic dreams and nightmares with sexual overtones). Several early saints, notably St Anthony of Egypt, were tormented by succubi, who tempted them with lascivious thoughts. Another saint, St Victorinus, was reputedly overcome by the temptation and had intercourse with a succubus, and the future Pope Sylvester II (10th century) admitted to being tempted as a young man by a succubus calling herself Meridiana.

Many men in former times claimed that sex with a succubus was far superior to any pleasure that might be had with a mortal partner. One entrepreneur of the 15th century claimed to have staffed his brothel in Bologna entirely with succubi, to the evident satisfaction of his clients (he was put to death in 1468 for his pains). The scholar, philosopher and demonologist Pico della Mirandola, meanwhile, told a story about a man who enjoyed a sexual relationship with a succubus over a period of some 40 years and could not be prevailed upon to give her up.

sukusendal In Finnish folklore, a variety of night demon that preys upon mortals as they sleep. A Finnish equivalent of the INCUBUS and SUCCUBUS, it is also reputed to ambush humans who venture outside alone late at night, and to substitute CHANGELINGS for human babies. Placing objects made of IRON in the bed is supposed to be effective in warding off any sukusendal in the vicinity.

Sulis Celtic goddess who was venerated at Bath and associated with the healing thermal waters there. The goddess of the underworld and of knowledge and prophecy, she was equated by the Romans with their own Minerva, becoming known as Sulis Minerva. Legend has it that the spa at Bath (called Aquae Sulis by the Romans) was founded by BLADUD, who got relief from a skin disease by rolling in the hot mud there, having observed how pigs did the same thing to ease their sores.

sun As the source of light and the sustainer of life on earth, the sun was worshipped in many early religions, and has always occupied an important place in world folklore, typically representing power and wisdom. The Celts were typical in regarding the sun with particular interest, developing such symbols for its power as the wheel, and depicting the sun as a character in various folk tales. However, unlike many other cultures, the Celts do not appear to have identified particular sun gods. Numerous societies around the world include sun deities among their most important and beneficent gods, and observe elaborate rituals in their honour. The best known of these include the sun dances and other ceremonial rites of the Native Americans of the Great Plains of North America, the most extreme of which included hanging worshippers up by strips of skin hanging from their lacerated bodies. This theme of self-mutilation has echoes elsewhere in the world, the general belief being that the sacrificial spilling of blood will encourage the sun to continue in its usual cycle.

Perhaps the clearest link today with primitive sun worship is in the bonfires that are still lit to celebrate such festivals as Midsummer's Eve. These conflagrations were originally intended to mimic the sun and thus to bring luck to local communities and to promote the fertility of crops and livestock. Christianity has added its own sun myths, which include the quaint notion that the sun dances for joy early on Easter morning, when the holy image of the lamb and flag may also be discerned on its surface.

The sun is said to shine brightest on the righteous, and will hide its face if some catastrophe is in store. Brides who are married in bright sunshine are especially blessed and may look forward to a happy marital life, but anyone who feels the sun on their head while attending a funeral is warned that they too will soon be dead. It is widely held to be unlucky to be caught pointing at the sun, as this is interpreted by many as an insulting gesture and may be punished by instant death. Only the EAGLE can stare directly into the sun in safety. One of the most curious traditions concerning the sun is the old idea that its rays will put a fire out; even in relatively modern times people have been known to shield the domestic fire from sunshine, in the belief that the flames will otherwise fail to catch as desired.

In terms of predicting the weather, one course is to study the sun's rays reflected in a bucket of water on Easter Day. If the rays shine bright and clear in the water then the season will be a fine one, but if they tremble and are unclear then foul weather lies in store. There will also be many fires if the sun shines strongly on Christmas Day, and a good crop of apples if the sun shines through the apple trees then or on Easter Day. A rather obscure English tradition also holds that the sun always shines on Saturdays, even if only for a few seconds.

Surtr In Norse mythology, one of the GIANTS. The ruler of Muspellsheim, the kingdom of fire, he is destined to set fire to the world during the final cataclysmic battle of RAGNAROK.

Svart Alfar See ALFAR.

swallow The swallow is widely welcomed as a herald of summer, and more generally as a bird of blessing. A Christian legend claims that the swallow won divine favour by calling out 'Dead! Dead!' to the Roman soldiers at the Crucifixion in an attempt to prevent them inflicting further torture upon Christ. A Swedish version of this story has the swallow circling the crucified Christ calling out 'Cheer up! Cheer up!'. As a result it is thought to be very unlucky to kill a swallow or to damage its nest. Allowing a swallow to nest in the roof will guard the house from lightning, fire and other evils, but if it then deserts this nest ill luck will befall the household.

By way of contrast, some societies associate the swallow with death. In Russia, dead children are reputed to take the form of swallows, and in parts of eastern England groups of swallows that gather on church roofs are said to be plotting the deaths that will occur in the parish over the coming year. In Scotland it is alleged that the swallow carries a drop of the Devil's blood in its veins – a hint perhaps of an ominous character – while the Irish claim that if a swallow plucks out a certain hair from a human head the unfortunate victim is doomed to go to hell. If a swallow alights on someone then all are agreed that the person concerned is fated to die shortly.

Other miscellaneous folk beliefs relating to swallows include the notion that they carry small sticks with them when they migrate so that they can snatch a quick rest on the waves; that they hibernate underwater in a huge mass; that their red feathers recall the fact that they brought fire to mankind; and that they spend the winter in caves. In terms of weather prediction, it is said that storms will accompany the arrival and departure of the swallows each season.

Authorities in folk medicine have claimed over the centuries that swallows carry inside their bodies small stones that have various magical properties, specifically a red stone with the power to cure the mad and a black stone that promotes luck. In addition, anyone who puts such a stone under their tongue will enjoy great eloquence. Other body parts may be used variously in the treatment of alcoholism, fractures and sprains, epilepsy, toothache, snakebite and rabies.

swan The swan is the focus of a wide range of folk beliefs. Considered to be semi-divine in the classical world, the bird had particular significance in Celtic mythology, in which it represented the SUN and thus healing and fertility (its feathers were commonly used for ceremonial cloaks among other ritual purposes). In other traditions, however, swans are generally considered to be unlucky birds. Presumably because they seem equally at home on land, on water and in the air they are also widely credited with SHAPE-SHIFTING abilities and may manifest in the form of beautiful women (see SWAN MAIDEN). This latter property recalls the erotic reputation of the swan, as embodied in the classical legend in which Zeus takes the form of a swan to seduce Leda, a beautiful mortal woman.

Other folk beliefs concerning swans include the inaccurate notions that they only sing for the first time when dying, and the theory that they can only hatch their eggs during thunderstorms, when the shells are broken by the thunder.

Swans have been protected in England as a 'royal' bird since medieval times, and no one may kill a swan without special dispensation from the crown. Killing a swan is in any case the height of folly according to superstition, and will be followed by the death of the guilty party (or else of someone else in the parish) within the year. In Scotland and Ireland this idea is strengthened by the supposition that swans are in fact the reincarnation of human souls (according to the Irish, the spirits of virtuous maidens). Scottish fishermen regard the very sight of swans as unlucky, and there is also an old Scottish belief that three swans flying together presage an imminent national calamity.

Observing the behaviour of swans reveals much about coming weather. If the birds stretch their heads backwards over their wings during the daytime this is said to be a warning of foul weather in the offing. If they take to the air then strong winds should be expected – galeforce conditions are in store if they fly directly into the wind. Heavy rain may be expected if swans start building a nest unusually high up.

See also LIR.

swan maiden In northern European folklore, a beautiful young woman who has the magical ability to change her shape at will to that of a SWAN. Sometimes identified as a variety of FAIRY, the swan maiden usually depends upon a magic garment of swan feathers (her 'swan shift') to achieve the transformation. If this is stolen then she must obey the wishes of the thief until the day when she can retrieve it.

Swan maidens appear in numerous folk tales. Typical of these is the legend in which a mortal man spies upon a flock of swans landing on a lake, and is startled to find himself instead watching a group of beautiful young women bathing in the water. He steals one of the cloaks they have left at the water's edge and thus makes one of them his wife. She bears his children, but then, years later, recovers her cloak, puts it on, and escapes in her swan form, never to return. Variants of the story outside Europe include Native American tales in which the maiden manifests in the form of a goose or vulture.

See also FOX MAIDEN; SEAL MAIDEN; SELKIE.

swastika Variety of CROSS with four crooked arms, now universally reviled as the symbol of the Nazis in the mid-20th century. In fact the symbol has a long history as a magical emblem. Across Celtic Europe the swastika represented the SUN, and evoked the ideas of good luck and well-being. Accordingly, swastikas have been found on many stone altars and other relics. It also has special magical significance in the mythology of Buddhists, Jains, Hindus, Navajo Indians and other cultures. Otherwise known as a fylfot, the swastika owes its name to the Sanskrit *svastika* ('of well-being').

sword In the days when swords were the chief weapons of warriors in battle they were widely regarded as magical objects, with their own mystic names, emotions and supernatural properties, sometimes including the power of speech. Many folk heroes are credited with the ownership of magic swords received from supernatural sources; in most cases such a sword can only be wielded by the hero. The most famous swords of legend include the Arthurian EXCALIBUR, Charlemagne's Joyeuse and Flamberge, Oliver's Glorious, Roland's Durandel and Siegfried's Balmung and Gram.

An oath made on a sword was once considered as binding as one made on a Bible. Among the various folk beliefs that have survived are the notions that a sword that falls out of its scabbard is an omen of approaching death, and the tradition that a sword may be used in the place of a wand in witchcraft. Skilled practitioners of magic might use swords as a defence against hostile spirits, and also, by looking into the brightly polished blade, for the purposes of SCRYING. Some swords were believed to operate as a LIFE TOKEN, becoming rusty or shedding tears of blood on the death of their owner.

For the purposes of love divination, a man should walk three times round a church at the hour of midnight and then thrust a sword into the keyhole with the words 'Here is the sword, but where is the sheath?' – and if all goes well, he will be rewarded by the appearance of his future wife. Women may follow a similar procedure, with the words 'Here is the sheath, but where is the sword?'.

See also SWORD OF CHASTITY.

Sword Bridge In Arthurian legend, the bridge that links the world of mortals with that of the otherworld. In the tale of 'Culhwch and Olwen' Osla Big-Knife lays his knife over a river in order for Arthur and his army to cross the water. A similar scene is repeated in the story of LANCELOT, when he has to cross a river on his way to rescue GUINEVERE from the underworld. Constructing a sword bridge is one of the skills taught by SCATHACH to CUCHULAINN.

sword dance English folk dance that is still, to this day, performed at various locations in northern England. Dancers wield long flexible 'swords' made of wood or steel and perform a complicated series of steps culminating in the 'lock', when the swords are meshed together in an intricate star-shaped pattern that the leader of the dance then lifts in the air. The dance is often performed together with a play, in which a character called the Fool pokes his head through the locked swords. The swords are then withdrawn and the Fool falls apparently lifeless to the ground, and is then revived by Besom Betty or the Doctor. The play evokes notions of death and rebirth, suggesting that the whole performance was original-ly intended to celebrate the cycle of the seasons.

Sword dancing is today usually associ-ated with Scotland, where the tradition of dancing over and around two crossed broadswords or a broadsword and scab-bard laid on the ground still continues at Highland gatherings. Properly called the Gillie Chalium, this dance appears to date back to the Jacobite rebellions of the 18th century, and may have begun as a victory celebration.

sword of chastity The custom of keep-ing apart two people sleeping in the same bed by laying a sword or some other object between them. The theme surfaces in a number of folk tales and legends, notably the Old French romance AMIS AND AMILES, and would appear to have been a fairly widespread device to ensure that taboos against intercourse in certain significant situations (such as before a hunt or after childbirth) are not broken. Other objects used in the place of swords included crosses.

sympathetic magic A variety of spell casting that depends upon the apparent link between two objects or actions. Also referred to as image or imitative magic, it often depends upon the fashioning of a likeness or effigy of a living person. The theory is that whatever happens to the image will be duplicated in real life. The

image itself is often shaped out of wax or clay, although sometimes carved from wood or taking the form of a rag doll. Some authorities insist that in order to work a figure has to incorporate certain magically potent ingredients, such as soil from a fresh grave, human bones reduced to ashes, black spiders or the pith of elder. The usual stipulation is that the image must also incorporate some trace of the real person if it is to work effectively. Thus, such images might include a few strands of the victim's hair, their fingernail clippings, threads from their clothes, their handkerchief, their saliva, blood, sweat, tears, or sexual fluids – or anything else that has been produced by, or has been in close contact with, their body. Even soil taken from the centre of a person's foot-print might be enough to establish the magical connection. In days gone by, to counter such malevolent magic, people were very careful about the disposal of their personal belongings and meticu-lously burned trimmed fingernails, locks of hair and so forth, to prevent them falling into the wrong hands. Even water used for washing the body had to be care-fully disposed of because of the traces it carried of a person's soul.

Once made, such images might be stuck with pins, nails or thorns, or melted, placed in water or buried, in order to bring pain and even death to the victim. Penetrating the figure's head with a nail will make the person it represents go mad, while driving one into the heart inflicts instant death. Burying the figure in the ground means the victim will slowly and painfully waste away as the likeness itself rots. A refinement of the practice observed by VOODOO sorcerers is to send the actual figure to the person concerned, thus heightening their fear and laying them open to further mali-cious magical interference.

The only defence against image magic is for the victim to find the image and to burn it, or else to rely upon the witch concerned relenting from causing further harm. Time was when mere possession of a waxen image, or something that resembled one, was enough to condemn a suspect to the gallows or the stake.

Typical targets of image magic over the centuries have included rivals in love, opponents in business affairs and those in positions of power and prestige. Several notable cases hinging on the use of malevolent image magic concerned members of royal families or the nobility. Among the monarchs and nobles who allegedly found themselves the target of image magic were Elizabeth I, Philip VI of France (who levelled charges at Count Robert of Artois) and Pope Urban VIII, who had the nephew of one of his cardinals executed for the crime of sticking pins into a wax figure.

As a tool of the sorcerer, the use of waxen images can be traced back all the way to ancient Egypt. Their use has continued into modern times. In 1900 a critic of President McKinley burned his pin-studded effigy on the steps of the American Embassy in London, while during World War II an effigy dressed in the uniform of a WAAF officer was found in Gloucestershire, with a pin driven into one of the eyes.

Such image magic was not, however, always directed against someone's well-being. White witches also used such images in casting spells designed to benefit a person's financial prospects, their health or their love life. They were also used to promote fertility and in some services of EXORCISM.

The same principles may also be detected in a wide range of other folk customs and superstitions, such as the loosening of knots and unlocking of doors throughout the house when a women is in labour, in the belief that this will make the birth easier. The notion of sympathetic magic is especially important in folk medicine. Many cultures can still boast 'cures' in which a patient is treated symbolically, for instance by treating samples of their blood or saliva after it has been taken from their body.

T

taboo A ban or prohibition dictated by folk custom that often has no clear rational meaning or explanation. Every culture has its taboos, which may vary from speaking forbidden words to widely accepted prejudices limiting actions in relation to cultural, artistic, social or religious matters. Sometimes they are based upon notions of 'sacredness' – a word or object being held subject to pollution by reckless physical contact or use. On other occasions a taboo is based upon notions of 'uncleanliness' – a word, action or object being deemed likely to pollute anyone who comes into contact with it or breaks any prohibition concerning it. If a taboo is broken the guilty party risks not only the opprobrium of the community but also the threat of supernatural retribution, possibly at the hands of the gods themselves.

The word 'taboo' itself comes from Polynesia, where it specifically evokes the threat of evil influence and operates in a manner closely akin to a CURSE. A taboo was placed, for instance, by native Polynesians upon Captain James Cook when he offended them by attempting to set up an observatory on the Sandwich Islands. Similar notions are common to all the world's cultures and are apparently of ancient origin. They were certainly in currency in several early pre-Christian civilizations, including those of the ancient Egyptians and the Jews.

Examples of the strongest taboos include bars against certain incestuous relationships (which vary from culture to culture), the mouthing of the name of God or other supernatural entities, the eating of certain proscribed foodstuffs and the handling of food by women while they are menstruating. More unusual taboos encountered in certain cultures around the world include strict prohibitions against social contact between men and their mothers-in-law, and bars against touching the body of the chief or leader of a tribal group or community.

The 20th century has witnessed the erosion of many social and sexual taboos, except those associated with incest and paedophilia, which retain a unique aura of moral repugnance. In an attenuated form, taboos also operate on an everyday social level, in the form of socially restrictive codes of behaviour, as seen in the persistent attachment of succeeding generations to notions of 'good manners', which are commonly interpreted to encompass such matters of everyday concern as simple table manners, politeness towards elders or the opposite sex and avoidance of a variety of slang words. Anyone who fails to adhere to such codes of behaviour today, however, is more likely to risk social ostracization rather than divine retribution.

Tain Bo Cuailnge Irish heroic epic, which forms the longest episode in the celebrated ULSTER CYCLE. Otherwise known as the *Cattle Raid of Cooley* or *The War of the Brown Bull*, it is among the oldest of all Celtic epics and was supposedly told originally by the ghost of the hero FERGUS MAC ROICH. It recounts the events that transpire after Queen MEDB of Connacht conceives a desire to possess the magnificent Dun Bull of DAIRE MAC FIACHNA, having become jealous of the fine bull owned by her husband Ailill. When Daire declines to lend the Dun Bull to her, Medb launches an attack on Ulster with the aid of such notable warriors as Fergus Mac Roich. The expedition meets with disaster at the hands of CUCHULAINN, who slaughters many of Medb's soldiers, including (after a ferocious single combat lasting many days) his half-brother Ferdiad. Ultimately, King CONCHOBAR inflicts defeat upon Medb's remaining forces at the Battle of the Tain, and the survivors return to Connacht. To complete the humiliation of Medb's army, the Dun Bull, which Medb has managed to seize, breaks free and kills Ailill's bull before escaping back to Daire's court in Louth.

See also BOOK OF THE DUN COW.

Taliesin Semi-legendary 6th-century Welsh bard who foretold the reign of King ARTHUR and became himself the subject of many tales.

Legend has it that he was born originally under the name Gwion Bach and was only later transformed into Taliesin. This transformation occurred after the young Gwion had been ordered by the sorceress CERIDWEN to stir a cauldron in which she was brewing a drink of knowledge and inspiration for her own son, the hideously deformed Afagddu. When some of the brew splashed onto Gwion's fingers he immediately put them into his mouth to cool them, and thus enjoyed the gifts intended for Afagddu. The furious Ceridwen pursued Gwion, who changed his shape from one form to another in a desperate attempt to escape. In the end he turned himself into a grain of wheat, and was immediately eaten by Ceridwen, who had assumed the form of a hen.

Ceridwen then found she was pregnant, and in due course Gwion was born again. Adamant not to keep the child, but reluctant to kill him, Ceridwen set the baby afloat in a bag. He was subsequently rescued from a salmon weir by ELPHIN, who took the infant into his care and gave him the name Taliesin (meaning 'radiant brow'). Taliesin subsequently repaid Elphin for his kindness by freeing him from prison, and later sailed with Arthur when he attacked the underworld of ANNWN. The many places and people Taliesin met are listed in the famous *Book of Taliesin* (c.1275). Further tales were attributed to Taliesin in the *Mabinogion*, although these do not appear to have been associated with his name before the 16th century.

talisman A tangible object that is usually carried about the person to ensure magical protection from supernatural threats. A talisman differs from an AMULET, which provides continuous general all-round protection, in that its properties may be directed to perform a specific task (often an act of healing). Examples of widely revered talismans include wands, cloaks of invisibility, pieces of jewellery bearing a person's astrological sign or other magical planetary characters, and the Jewish Star of David. Often talismans will have been obtained from someone who claims to be able to invest such objects with magic potential.

See also PHILOSOPHER'S STONE.

Tam Lin Legendary Scottish hero, whose story was related in a famous Scottish ballad. The ballad recounts how the knight Tam Lin is kidnapped by the fairies when he falls from his horse while out hunting and is himself transformed into a fairy. Subsequently, still in fairy form, he falls in love with the king's daughter, called Janet, and makes her pregnant. Tam Lin fears he will be handed over to the Devil as the tithe the fairies pay him every seven years. He asks Janet to help him regain his human form by holding tightly onto him at HALLOWE'EN when he is summoned by the fairy host as it rides by. The fairies attempt to make her release Tam Lin by transforming him into a series of terrifying shapes, however they cannot make her loose her hold, and he is saved.

tangie In the folklore of Orkney, a species of water spirit that variously takes the form of an old man or a horse covered in seaweed. The tangie is not feared as much as the KELPIE, but may nonetheless be suspected of minor acts of mischief. It is likely to ditch anyone who attempts to ride it into the water.

Tannhäuser German poet whose life became the subject of legend after his death around 1270. The historical character was a Minnesinger, the German equivalent of the French troubadours. He travelled widely, reciting his own poetry, and took part in the Crusade of 1228. This figure later became confused with a legendary knight-hero, and became the central figure in numerous tales.

According to a 16th–century ballad version of his life, Tannhäuser comes under the influence of the mythical Frau Holde (or Venus) and abandons himself to the debaucheries of her court in Hörselberg in Thuringia. Ultimately, however, he finds this life of pleasure no longer pleases, and he travels to Rome to obtain the pope's forgiveness. The pope is outraged at the tales of excess that Tannhäuser repeats to him and refuses him absolution, saying that his own staff will bud before Tannhäuser will get his blessing. Tannhäuser leaves Rome in a state of desolation. But three days later the pope's staff breaks miraculously into flower, and messengers are sent after the wanderer to bring him back. Unfortunately, Tannhäuser is nowhere to be found.

Today, the legend of Tannhäuser is best known from Richard Wagner's music drama *Tannhäuser* (1854), in which the hero makes his way back to his loyal lover Elizabeth, only to find that she is dead – upon which he dies himself just before the papal envoys catch up with him.

Tara The capital, in County Meath, of Celtic Ireland, and the traditional seat of the high kings of Ireland. Its history as an important political and religious site goes back to around 2000 BC, and it may have been considered sacred in Neolithic times. It makes an appearance in many Irish legends, both as the capital of the TUATHA DE DANANN and as the traditional home of King CONCHOBAR and the fabled RED BRANCH.

Taranis In Celtic mythology, the god of thunder. Considered by the Romans an equivalent of their own Jupiter, he is usually depicted with his symbol, a spoked wheel. Altars dedicated to Taranis have been found in Britain, France, Germany and Croatia.

tar baby Plot motif of many folk tales, in which the hero becomes firmly stuck to a figure made of pitch, wax or some other very sticky substance. Best known today from the *Uncle Remus* stories of Joel Chandler Harris, in which Brer Rabbit is tricked into becoming stuck to a tar baby set up to trap him, the motif is also encountered in folk tales from Africa and the West Indies. In Brer Rabbit's case, he takes offence when the tar baby fails to return his cheery greeting and gets stuck when he then strikes the figure in anger with his hands, feet and head. In African and Caribbean folklore much the same tale is told, with the role of Brer Rabbit being taken by the spider Anansi. Native American equivalents have the coyote and the skunk suffering similar humiliation at the hands of their enemies. The motif would appear to have reached the Americas with slaves brought from Africa, although it may ultimately be descended from a European or Indian source, and have been absorbed by virtue of its similarity to extant native stories. The tradition could be said to continue today, though in a somewhat reworked form in various URBAN LEGENDS involving the mischievous use of superglue on lavatory seats and so forth.

tase In Burmese folklore, a variety of evil spirit identified as one of the dead. These ghosts are greatly feared, as they are believed to return to earth specifically in order to take revenge upon their enemies. They may take the form of monsters or fierce wild animals, but will be frightened off by loud noises – hence the tradition of making as loud a racket as possible at funerals through the use of drums, cymbals and shouting.

tattoo The tradition of adorning the body with tattoos is very ancient, and has strong folkloric significance. In many societies young men (and sometimes women also) were tattooed as a visible mark of their transition to adulthood, but in many more tattoos were prized for their magical protective properties. The use of tattoos in the Western world was revived in the late 18th century following contact with Pacific peoples who traditionally covered the entire body with tattoos (the word 'tattoo' is itself Polynesian in origin).

The practice proved particularly popular among seamen, who were eager to enjoy any promise of supernatural protection when facing the perils inherent in long voyages. Anchor tattoos have always been common among seafarers, the notion being that this will ensure that any sailor falling overboard will remain close to his ship. Sailors' lore also claims that tattoos ward off evil spirits and keep the bearer safe from sexually transmitted diseases. In the days when flogging was a frequent punishment, many sailors had tattoos depicting the Crucifixion etched on their backs in the belief that the lash would flinch at the prospect of flogging the image of Christ – probably a good move, as any person of religious leaning would be likely to lay the lash on much more lightly if confronted with such a sacred image.

The same notion of tattoos providing supernatural protection ensured their popularity in many other spheres. In the 19th century many performing 'strong men' in fairground booths covered their body with tattoos in the belief that their strength would thus be magically protected, and this tradition has doubtlessly contributed to the lingering popularity of tattoos among those engaged in manual labour, whose very livelihood may depend directly upon the maintenance of robust health.

Otherwise, in the modern Western world the tattoo is usually encountered in use as a fashion statement or else as a declaration of love or allegiance, whether it be to a partner, pop group, football club or make of motorbike and so forth. The fact that tattoos can only be removed with some difficulty invokes the notion of permanence and persuasively suggests considerable sincerity on the part of the bearer (although the advent of removable tattoo stickers may have weakened this tradition somewhat in recent years).

taxim In Eastern European folklore, a corpse that reappears after death to take revenge on its mortal enemies. Reports of such manifestations dwell upon their revolting appearance, complete with rotting flesh and accompanying stench.

teeth Like most body parts, the teeth are associated with a wide variety of folkloric beliefs. Best known of all traditions associated with teeth is that of the 'tooth fairy', who will pay a coin to any child who sleeps with a newly lost milk tooth under the pillow. Variations in this tradition suggest that a little SALT should also be left for the fairy, and that it is unlucky for the tooth not to have disappeared by midnight, as this might harm the child's luck.

Because it was once believed that witches could make use of any body parts to direct evil magic at the person concerned, proper disposal of lost teeth was formerly taken very seriously. The first molar to be lost, for instance, had to be sprinkled with salt and thrown onto the fire. If this was not done, the tooth might end up being eaten by a dog, and the child would get dog's teeth as a result; or else after death the luckless individual would be doomed to search for the tooth in a bucket of blood. Alternatively, leaving discarded milk teeth at the entrance to a MOUSE or RAT hole is a good way to ensure that the replacements are strong and sharp.

It is thought to be very unlucky for a baby to be born with any teeth already through, and in some regions this is supposed to prophesy that the child will grow up a murderer. If a child's first tooth comes through in the upper jaw this is also unlucky, and may be interpreted as an omen that the infant will die in childhood. Children that teethe early are either highly intelligent or doomed to die early. Alternatively, they are developing that bit faster because they have advance warning that their mother will soon be having another baby – as indicated by the proverb 'Soon teeth, soon toes'. By the same token, the number of teeth a child has at the age of one year is said to predict the number of brothers and sisters that are yet to be born.

People with gaps between their front teeth are widely thought to be lucky, and destined to enjoy great riches and to travel widely (although in Scotland it is believed that such people are prone to lechery). Many people also carry 'lucky' animal teeth as a matter of course, believing that they are among the most beneficial of all lucky charms.

tempting fate The fear that by openly anticipating something happening one tempts the spirit world to intervene to make sure it does not happen is the motivating force behind numerous well-known taboos and superstitions. In many cultures it is thought wise never to sing the praises of children, livestock, good health or anything else that is held precious too loudly, as this may offend the spirits, who may feel their cooperation is being taken for granted. People from many parts of the world may show distinct unease if someone directs lavish praise in the direction of themselves, their families or their possessions, and may attempt to ward off the resulting threat of evil interference by immediately touching wood or iron, making the sign of the cross, spitting and saying 'God bless', or by taking some other precautionary measure recommended by long-standing tradition.

Specific examples of actions to be avoided include never bringing a cradle or pram into the house before an expected baby is safely delivered, never asking a fisherman where he is going when he about to set sail, never admitting to being very well if someone inquires after one's health and never wishing actors and actresses good luck when they are about to go on stage.

tengu In Japanese mythology, a species of tree spirit believed to inhabit mountainous regions. Tengus were believed to hatch from eggs, and were often depicted with the beak and wings of a bird. They were frequently described as threatening and aggressive entities, and were sometimes identified as the ghosts of people who had been noted for their arrogance while alive.

tennin In Buddhist lore, a race of lovely maidens who live in paradise. They make occasional visits to the mortal world – as related in the tale of the maiden Hagoromo, who dances for joy when she sees how beautiful the sea is, but when spied by a fisherman, she flees, leaving behind only her magnificent robe.

Teyrnon In Welsh mythology, the lord of Gwent Is-Coed, who was the foster-father of PRYDERI. He brought up Pryderi after finding him on his doorstep, calling him Gwri, but later discovered the boy's real identity on noting the resemblance between him and PWYLL.

Thirteen Treasures of Britain In Welsh legend, an assortment of magical objects associated with the concept of

SOVEREIGNTY. According to tradition, they will only work properly when in the possession of a rightful king and thus reveal who that person might be. Legend has it that they remain in the safekeeping of MERLIN on Bardsey Island, off the coast of North Wales.

One surviving list of the treasures includes the magical sword Dyrwyn; the inexhaustible hamper of Gwyddno Garanhir; the horn of Bran, which will serve any drink requested; the chariot of Morgan the Wealthy, which will take its master anywhere; the halter of Clyno Eiddyn, which will summon any horse wished for; the knife of Llawfronedd the Horseman, which will carve for 24 men at a sitting; the cauldron of Diwrnach the Giant, which will only boil the food of brave men; the whetstone of Tudwal Tudglyd, which will make a brave man's sword deadly; the coat of Padarn Red-Coat, which will only fit a nobleman; the crock and also the dish of Rhygenydd, which will serve up any food desired; the chessboard of Gwenddolau, which will play a game by itself when set up; and the mantle of Arthur, which will make the wearer invisible.

thistle Prickly weed that has long been revered as the national emblem of Scotland. The thistle's Scottish connection goes back to the 10th century, when a party of Danish invaders sought to stage a night attack on Staines Castle. The Danes attempted to wade across the moat, but the moat was dry and full of thistles. Their cries of pain alerted the defenders, and they were driven off.

The plant is also associated with the Virgin Mary, reputedly having sprung from one of the nails from Christ's cross after she planted it in the soil. Another tradition, however, links it with the Devil, because of its vicious prickles.

The thistle has various uses in folk medicine, being used in former times to treat such disorders as toothache, stitches in the side, jaundice and (in the form of thistle wine) depression.

Thomassing Traditional English folk custom celebrated upon the Feast of St Thomas the Apostle (21 December). Also known as 'mumping', 'curning' or 'gooding', the practice involved poor women in a particular district begging from door to door. This long-established tradition carried no taint of shame about it, as ordinary begging did, and most relatively wealthy people happily handed over small amounts of money or gifts of wheat, candles or meat in the saint's memory. Sometimes callers were treated to a round of hot spiced ale. The recipients in their turn rewarded the donors with good wishes for Christmas, and perhaps a sprig of holly or mistletoe. The custom seems to have died out towards the end of the 19th century.

Thomas the Rhymer Legendary Scottish poet who is supposed to have enjoyed privileged access to Elfland. Identified with Thomas of Erceldoune, who lived in Scotland in the 13th century, he was said to have been escorted by the queen of Elfland herself to the land of the fairies, and there to have spent seven years. The queen's presents to him included a set of clothes in elf-green, and the gift of prophecy. Many of the prophecies he subsequently made were recorded in the 15th-century *Romance and Prophesies of Thomas of Erceldoune*. A good number of them were reported to have come true, among them the death of Alexander III of Scotland (who died when his horse fell over a cliff), the Battle of Bannockburn and the accession of James VI to the throne of England.

Also credited as the author of the romance *Sir Tristram*, he is best known from the ballad 'Thomas the Rhymer', included by Walter Scott in his *Minstrelsy of the Scottish Border* (1802).

Thor In Norse mythology, the god of thunder and lightning. Depicted in horned helmet and carrying a huge hammer, he was venerated throughout the Norse world and was among the most popular of the AESIR. Fiery and hearty in temperament, he was a great favourite with Norse warriors, and was reputed to have fought many battles with GIANTS. He presided over his followers at his great hall, Belskirnir, one of the most magnificent in the whole of ASGARD. His worshippers often carried talismans in the shape of his famous hammer.

Three Golden Sons A well known European folk tale that appears in numerous variant forms around the world. Although the details of the story vary from one culture to another, most share the basic theme of a king who has to choose a bride from three sisters and, having married the youngest sister, sires three fine sons by her. The rejected sisters toss the three baby boys into a river and make it look like the queen is responsible, with the result that she is sent into exile or otherwise punished. The babies are, however, rescued and reared by a peasant. When they are old enough, the first two sons go off in turn in search of the bird of truth, the singing tree and the water of life, hoping thereby to find out the identity of their parents, but both fail and are turned to stone. The youngest son wisely enlists supernatural aid and succeeds in the quest, thereby securing the release of his two brothers and the reunion of the whole family. The queen is restored to the king's favour, and her two wicked sisters are punished.

Three Little Pigs See PIG.

Three Old Women European folk tale that was among those collected by the Brothers Grimm. This well-known tale, which bears more than a passing resemblance to RUMPELSTILTSKIN, revolves around a beautiful young girl who, through the idle boasts of her mother, has the reputation of being able to spin flax to gold. The prince hears of the girl's talent and promises that if she spins three roomfuls of flax into gold he will marry her. The girl is cast into despair, but is then offered assistance by three deformed old women, one of whom has a massive foot, while another has a vast lower lip, and the third has a huge thumb. In return for spinning the flax to gold all they ask is to be invited to the royal wedding. They complete the task and subsequently attend the wedding. The king, curious about the women's appearance, asks how they came to look as they do and is told that their deformities resulted from their long years' working at the loom, one of them working the treadle, another feeding the thread through her fingers and the third moistening it. The king, suitably impressed and somewhat chastened, promises that he will never ask his beautiful new wife to spin for him again.

thunder The sound of thunder has always inspired feelings of awe, and even terror. In many earlier cultures it was likely to be interpreted as the anger of the gods, possibly provoked by the deeds of mortals, or else as the sound of battle between supernatural forces in the skies overhead. Often it is identified with a particular deity, such as the Norse God THOR or the Native American Thunderbird, and great importance is placed upon winning the god's favour through gifts and sacrifices. Other cultures have their own explanations for the phenomenon. Some Native American tribes, for instance, associate it with the sound of a rattlesnake shaking its tail. The imitation of thunder through the beating of drums and other instruments is a common feature of rainmaking ceremonies throughout the world, based upon the theory of SYMPATHETIC MAGIC.

The commonplace reaction of pulling the bedclothes over the head when thunder is heard at night has support in time-honoured superstition, which dictates that no one will suffer harm during a thunderstorm if they pull their bed into the middle of the room, cover themselves with the sheets and recite a Paternoster. In contrast, travellers should welcome the sound of thunder in the distance as they set off, as this is supposed to bode well for their journey.

In weather lore, the time of day that thunder is heard is significant in forecasting the weather to come, according to one old English rhyme: 'Thunder in the morning, all the day storming; thunder at night, is the sailor's delight.' According to a tradition recorded in Tudor England, conclusions may also be drawn from the day upon which thunder is heard: thunder on a Monday signifies the death of a woman; on Tuesday it is a promise of a good grain harvest; on Wednesday it means the death of a prostitute or is a warning of approaching violence; on Thursday it bespeaks a good harvest and plentiful supplies of livestock; on Friday it forecasts the death of a great man or the fighting of a battle; on Saturday it threatens an epidemic; and on Sunday it predicts the death of a leading scholar, judge or author. Another British tradition claims that the sound of thunder between November and the end of the year heralds the imminent death of a prominent person in the area, while thunder that is heard on the first Sunday in the year is a warning of the death of someone in the royal family.

See also LIGHTNING; STORM.

thyme Herb that is traditionally associated with death, and in particular with murder. The scent of thyme is said to linger in places where murders have been committed, and the flower is said to provide a resting place for the souls of the dead (as well as for fairies). Reinforcing this connection with death, thyme was often brought into the house in parts of England when there was a corpse awaiting burial and not removed until the body was taken away (perhaps originally because it helped to disguise any smell given off by the corpse). Other folk beliefs relating to thyme include the notions that it bolsters courage, and that it may also be used in treating depression or in love divination. The link with courage dates back to the medieval period, when jousting knights were sometimes presented with sprigs of thyme by the ladies of the court.

tiger Like the LION, the tiger has inspired numerous myths and legends. Many of the folkloric associations of the tiger are similar to those of the lion, both representing such qualities as courage and nobility. However, the tiger also appears in folk tales in which it reveals a more sinister, cunning side. In some tales it is even credited with the ability to change its shape at will. The animal is regarded with particular dread in Malaysia, where it is said to be a favourite disguise of sorcerers, or else the reincarnated form of dead souls seeking vengeance for wrongs done them when alive.

In recent years the tiger has been threatened with extinction both through loss of habitat and as a result of hunting – primarily for its body parts, which are highly valued (although illegal) in Oriental medicine. It is alleged that those who dine off the gallbladder or flesh of the tiger will share the creature's great courage, and also benefit from a boost in virility, while its claws, whiskers and bones may promote strength.

Tigernmas Legendary king of Ireland, who introduced the worship of Cromm Cruach, a gold and silver statue. The name Tigernmas means 'lord of death', and human sacrifice played a large part in the rituals he instituted, notably at the feast of SAMHAIN. He is said to have perished himself at one of these bloody festivals. He is credited with having introduced mining, gold smelting, silversmithing and the weaving of tartans to Ireland.

Till Eulenspiegel Legendary trickster whose pranks are celebrated in many medieval German tales. He appears to have been based upon a real historical character, a peasant from Brunswick who died around 1350 after a lifetime of mischief making. The targets of his sometimes cruel jests included local tradesmen, innkeepers and other representatives of the bourgeoisie. Details of the jokes he played appear to have been written down for the first time in the 16th century, and subsequently provided the basis for major works by composer Richard Strauss and poet Gerhard Hauptmann.

Tintagel (or Tintagil) A castle in Cornwall that is linked to Arthurian legend. According to local belief it was here that ARTHUR was both conceived and born. The castle ruins visible today date, in fact, from the 12th century, although the site of an older Celtic monastery is located nearby, and this may well have been standing in Arthur's day. It is also identified in some writings as the castle of GORLOIS of Cornwall, or alternatively as the home of King MARK of Cornwall.

Tir Nam Ban (or Tir Na m'Ban) In Irish mythology, the land of women. Tales describe this magical place as being inhabited by a race of beautiful women who offer all manner of comfort to mortals who arrive there, including entertainment, music, female companionship and the gift of immortality. Most human visitors, however, find such delights too much to bear, and in most tales soon elect to return home. Among those to gain access to this otherworld were BRAN MAC FEBAL and MAELDUINE.

Tir Nan Og (or Tir Na n'Og) The OTHERWORLD of Irish mythology, a land of youth where mortals and gods live in surroundings of peaceful harmony and beauty without ever growing old. Several legendary heroes, including OISIN, gain access to this paradise and describe it on their return to the mortal world. Typically these visitors believe they have only spent a short time in the otherworld, but when they return to their homes find that many years have passed, and they themselves become instantly old as time catches up with them. The TUATHA DE DANANN took refuge in Tir Nan Og after the invasion of the MILESIANS, and it was subsequently identified in legend as the home of the fairies.

Titania In English legend, the wife of OBERON, king of the fairies. She is best known today from her depiction in William Shakespeare's *A Midsummer Night's Dream*. The name made its first appearance as one of the alternative titles of the Roman goddess Diana.

See also MAB.

toad Presumably because of its ugly appearance and the poisons secreted by its warty skin, the toad has a negative reputation in many cultures. As well as being closely associated with witchcraft and the Devil, the toad is widely thought to be a harbinger of bad luck. In China, lunar eclipses were often blamed upon a cosmic toad devouring the moon. In pre-Christian times so much as looking at a toad was reputed to be fatal. Witches were often alleged to keep FAMILIARS in the form of toads, and to include toads among the ingredients of their evil spells. If cattle fell ill the bite of toads was often considered the cause, and many people habitually spat or threw stones if they happened upon one of the creatures. It is, however, unlucky to kill a toad, as this is reputed to bring on rainstorms.

In some circumstances the toad is a lucky creature, whose appearance means the end to drought and general good fortune, possibly in the form of unexpected wealth. It is thought to be particularly lucky if a toad crosses the path of a bride on her way to church, as this means the union will be both prosperous and happy. Other miscellaneous superstitions concerning toads include the curious notion that if a thief carries a dried toad's heart he or she will never be caught, and the suggestion that a man who equips himself with a dried toad's tongue will enjoy success with the opposite sex. Toads are also said to detect distant thunder long before it is audible to humans, and are believed to have got their beautiful eyes by exchanging their old ones with the lark.

In terms of folk medicine, wearing a dried or powdered toad in a bag around the neck was supposed in the 17th century to ward off the plague and other diseases. Rubbing a live toad on the skin was said to cure cancer of the breast, according to a superstition from eastern England, and wearing the legs ripped from a living toad was supposed to be effective against epilepsy and scrofula. Handling toads is discouraged by another widely held folk belief, however, which warns that this will cause warts.

According to another old saw every toad has a precious jewel secreted within its head. This has various magical properties, including the ability to detect the presence of poison (which it reveals by changing colour). Long-preserved 'toadstones' have since been identified as fossilized fish teeth.

Tom Thumb English folk hero of tiny size, who undergoes numerous adventures as a result of his diminutive stature. He appears to have made his first appearance in print in 1579, and in 1584 was listed among other elves, imps and goblins with which servants threatened naughty children. The first full versions of his adventures were published in the early 17th century, when they were set in the days of King ARTHUR.

According to the best-known versions of the tale, Tom Thumb is born to an old couple after they beg MERLIN for a baby, even if it is no bigger than their thumbs. Though destined never to grow any larger, Tom proves a wilful and mischievous child who is always in trouble. Among other adventures, he falls into his mother's pudding mix, rides out on a mouse to do battle with a wasp, and is eaten in quick succession by a cow, a giant and a fish. In the original versions of the story he escapes from the cow by means of a laxative, but this was later modified in the interests of delicacy so that he simply drops from the cow's mouth. When the fish is served up at Arthur's court, Tom pops out, to everyone's amazement. He ends his days a greatly loved and respected knight of Arthur's court.

Similar tales are told in many non-European cultures, including those of India and Japan. In German variants he hides from danger in a snail shell, among other adventures, and finally meets his death in a spider's web.

topaz Gold-coloured gemstone, the birthstone for November, which is widely held to be one of the luckier stones, suggesting good fortune in making money and winning friends. Representative of the sun, topaz has the property of making its wearer both courageous and wise. It will also counter madness and bestow a degree of control over wild animals. In Hindu folklore it is thought to promote beauty and to guarantee a long and successful life. In folk medicine it is said to lift depression, sharpen the mind and cure such complaints as flatulence, haemorrhoids and the plague.

tortoise Largely because of its longevity, the tortoise is considered a lucky creature, associated with strength, persistence, patience and immortality. The tortoise is sacred in Chinese culture, one of several cultures in which the world is supported on a giant tortoise or turtle. The tortoise also enjoys the protection of folklore in that it is said to be very unlucky to kill one. Wearing a tortoiseshell bracelet is said to provide a defence against evil. In parts of Africa the tortoise is closely connected with femininity, and thus has a role in a variety of fertility rites. Suspending a tortoise foot from the matching foot of a person suffering from gout, meanwhile, is reputed to bring some relief, and tortoise oil is supposed to have some value as a painkiller.

Attitudes to the tortoise are not universally positive, however. The Aztecs scorned the creature's tendency to withdraw into its shell in times of danger, and thus associated it with cowardice.

The tortoise appears as a character in a number of folk tales. In many of these the action revolves around the creature's attempts to fly, sometimes with the aid of an eagle, as in one of Aesop's *Fables*. Another of Aesop's stories depicts the race between the tortoise and the hare, which the tortoise, despite its slow speed, wins through the hare's complacency – it thinks victory is so certain it pauses for a nap and wakes to find the tortoise is just crossing the finishing line.

See also TURTLE.

totemism Belief that different kinship groups or clans each have a spiritual link with a particular totem. The totem itself may be a natural object, an animal or a plant, and both the totem and its image are treated as a subject of veneration in the belief that there exists some magical affiliation between it and the community in question. Totemism appears to have been an important feature of many pre-historic societies, and has played a role in countless cultures around the world through the ages. The mystical unity of a clan is generally considered a benevolent, protective force that must be revered and respected. Thus any object or animal identified as totemic must be carefully treated, and it may be considered a serious crime against the clan to kill, eat or even touch it. In some cases a community may venerate more than one totemic object, with individuals choosing which one they will adopt as their own (and they may consequently be barred from marrying anyone else within their own totemic group, as this may be considered tanta-mount to incest).

Today, the term totemism is particular-ly associated with veneration of carved wooden totem poles among the tribes of the northwest Pacific coast of North America. These poles are supposed to be magically linked with the tribe's guardian spirits or protectors, although they were often actually grave markers or had a range of other practical or social func-tions. Native American totem poles usu-ally combine a variety of animal and bird images, in which forms tribal ancestors are believed to have been reincarnated. Sometimes a whole tribe may adopt the name of its totemic animal or object for themselves (as in the case of the Crow Indians of the Sioux nation).

touching wood The time-honoured tradition of touching wood (or iron) to counter the threat of evil is known in many different cultures. This measure is most often taken when someone fears that something they (or someone else) has said may be interpreted as TEMPTING FATE. According to some authorities, underlying the tradition is the idea of making an appeal to the wooden cross on which Christ was crucified, although others suggest that the help of pre-Christian nature gods is thus invoked. Originally, it was considered essential that the person actually touch a piece of wood, preferably that of a sacred tree such as the OAK or ASH, but this notion has gradually been modified so that many people today think it sufficient just to say the words 'touch wood' after expressing some hope about their future affairs.

See also TREE.

touchstone A hard, dark siliceous stone, such as basalt or jasper, that was tradition-ally used in ALCHEMY to test the quality of GOLD and SILVER. It was believed that the purity of the metals could be tested by rubbing the touchstone against them and then examining the colour of the streak thus produced.

transference healing *See* MEDICINE.

transformation *See* SHAPE SHIFTING.

tree Trees have a special place in European folklore, echoing the import-ance of trees in pre-Christian religions, in which every tree was believed to have its host spirit. The emblem of the tree was central to Norse mythology (*see* YGGDRASIL), and veneration of trees seems to have been among the very earli-est forms of worship in human society.

The raising of maypoles in the course of spring festivities is an example of how relics of ancient tree worship have been preserved into modern times.

Many cultures boasted sacred groves or particular trees that were believed to be places of great magical potential, where connections could be made with the supernatural world. The notion of a Tree of Life is widespread, and trees have always been associated with regeneration and fertility magic. Often they are depicted as having the whole universe resting on their branches. In Germanic folklore it was claimed that the first men were created from the wood of the OAK. As a result of such associations, the felling of trees was commonly punishable by death in many early societies.

The fact that people still place some magical significance in trees is reflected in such practices as TOUCHING WOOD when evil threatens, tree-hugging (originally a Native American custom through which an individual could gain access to the latent magical energy of a tree) and in the custom of planting a tree to mark the birth of a child or other important events in life.

Certain trees, such as the YEW, are associated with death and are often planted in graveyards, while others, such as the ASH and the oak, are respected for their protective powers.

Trees are also central to the custom of 'transference healing', with sufferers of various complaints either hammering nails into the trunk of a given type of tree, or else sealing up a lock of their hair (or a piece of bacon that they have previously rubbed on their skin) in the wood of the tree in the belief that the tree will thereby absorb the poison and thus relieve them of the problem.

See also ASPEN; BAY; BIRCH; CHERRY; ELDER; ELM; HAWTHORN; HAZEL; LILAC; MYRTLE; OAK; OLIVE; PLUM; ROWAN; WILLOW.

tree spirit *See* GREEN MAN; TREE; WILD HERDSMAN; WOODWOSE.

Tristam (or **Tristan**) In Arthurian legend, the nephew of King MARK of Cornwall. His tragic romance with IS-OLDE OF IRELAND constitutes one of the best-known tales in the Arthurian canon. In fact, the tale would appear to have had an independent existence long before the compilation of the Arthurian cycle in the 13th century, and may have evolved originally from legends about the Pictish king Drostan (or Drust).

Named Tristam (meaning 'sorrow') after his mother died giving birth to him, he was born the son of King Melodias and Queen Elizabeth of LYONESSE. With Lyonesse sinking beneath the waves, Tristam joined the court of his uncle King Mark and fought on his behalf against the Irish giant Morholt and slew him. Grievously wounded by the giant's poisoned sword, Tristam was nursed back to health by Isolde of Ireland and on his return to Mark's court lavished such praise on her that his uncle decided she would make an ideal queen for him. Accordingly, he sent Tristam to fetch Isolde from Ireland. Unfortunately on their way to Cornwall Tristam and Isolde accidentally drank a love potion prepared for Isolde and her husband-to-be and were immediately attracted to one another. A maid was persuaded to take Isolde's place in the bridal bed and the lovers continued their illicit affair. Inevitably, King Mark began to hear rumours of the liaison and sought to test Isolde's loyalty to him, but failed to substantiate the stories. When he discovered the guilty pair asleep together in the forest, for instance, he found they had placed Tristam's unsheathed sword between them as a guarantee of chastity: the king was unable to take action against them beyond replacing Tristam's sword with his own as a sign of his disapproval.

Driven to despair by the impossibility of having Isolde to himself, Tristam ultimately went into exile at the court of King ARTHUR, where he rivalled Sir LANCELOT as the strongest of the knights of the ROUND TABLE. Later he moved to

Brittany, where he married ISOLDE OF BRITTANY, otherwise known as Isolde of the Fair Hands, but was then fatally wounded by a poisoned arrow (fired at him on the orders of King Mark, according to some versions). As he lay dying he sent for his lover Isolde of Ireland, thus revealing his true feelings. The captain of the ship dispatched to fetch her was carefully instructed to fly a white sail if Isolde agreed to come, but a black sail if she refused. Tristam's outraged wife Isolde of Brittany lied when the ship came in sight, telling Tristam that the sail was black. Tristam expired in his grief, as did Isolde of Ireland when she landed and found her lover no more. Isolde of Brittany subsequently committed suicide, overcome with remorse at what she had done.

As a final footnote to the legend, it was reported that after the two lovers were buried next to each other two trees sprang up from their graves and grew with their branches entwined.

troll Demonic being of Scandinavian folklore, noted for its malevolence towards humans. Originally depicted as GIANTS, trolls were subsequently redefined as squat, ugly DWARFS with rather slow but vicious natures. Because they hate sunlight, which makes them burst or else turn to stone, they are usually to be found in dark, gloomy places such as the shadows beneath bridges. Sometimes they are described as having their own castles, where they may guard fabulous hoards of treasure. Many tales are told of folk heroes who are threatened by trolls but manage to outwit them. The best known of these include the tale of the 'Billy Goats Gruff', who manage to fool a troll into letting them pass over his bridge unmolested to reach the sweeter grass on the other side of the stream.

See also TROW.

trow Equivalent of the Scandinavian TROLL that was formerly much feared in Shetland and the Orkneys. Generally described as vicious dwarflike creatures inhabiting caves or hillsides, they were believed likely to molest any mortal who entered their domains. If treated with respect, though, they might (unlike trolls) be persuaded to provide assistance with domestic chores.

Tuan mac Carill In Irish mythology, one of the warriors who accompanied PARTHOLON (his uncle) in the first invasion of Ireland. He alone of all Partholon's army survived the plague that brought their invasion to an end and lived to pass on what he knew of the early history of Ireland. Having been reborn as a stag, a boar and an eagle, he was transformed into a salmon, in which form he was ultimately devoured by his own wife. She then gave birth to him in human form.

Tuatha de Danann In Irish mythology, the godlike rulers of ancient Ireland who secured control of the country in the 15th century BC after defeating the FIRBOLGS at the first battle of MAG TUIRED and the FOMORIANS at the second battle of Mag Tuired. According to legend, they hailed originally either from heaven or else from northern Greece, and were believed to be wise, handsome and skilled in the magic arts. The king of the Tuatha de Danann, NUADA, lost an arm during the first battle and thus had to pass on the right of kingship to BRES MAC ELATHA. Subsequently, however, he was fitted with an artificial silver arm and regained his throne. The deposed Bres joined the Fomorians and raised a new army against his former allies. The Tuatha, now under the leadership of LUGH, overcame Bres at the second battle of Mag Tuired (the result of which was decided by single combat between Lugh and the giant BALOR).

The Tuatha were finally themselves defeated by the MILESIANS, after which they retreated to the underground realm of TIR NAN OG. They are often identified in Irish legend as synonymous with the fairy race called the SIDHE.

See also HALLOWS.

Tuiren In Irish mythology, the wife of Iollan, son of FERGUS MAC ROICH. She was turned into a hound by her husband's jealous lover, one of the SIDHE. While in this form she gave birth to two pups, BRAN and Sceolan, who became the hounds of FIONN MAC CUMHAILL (Tuiren's nephew). She was restored to her human form after her husband promised his love to his mistress alone.

Tuirenn In Irish mythology, the father (possibly by the goddess BRIGID) of three sons: Brian, Iuchar, and Iucharba. He killed Cian, the father of LUGH. When his sons faced death at the hands of Lugh, Tuirenn begged Lugh to spare them, but Lugh would give them no mercy and Tuirenn died of grief upon the bodies of his slaughtered offspring.

Turpin, Dick English highwayman whose life became the subject of legend. Born the son of a butcher in Hempstead, Essex, in 1706, Turpin abandoned his father's trade when he became involved with a gang of housebreakers in the mid-1730s, and was soon a wanted man. After an accomplice turned king's evidence, Turpin took to the life of a highwayman, operating on the roads leading out of London. Having murdered a forest keeper's servant in Epping he was forced to go further north, and eventually found himself in York, where he was arrested in 1739 for horse stealing. His guilt in many other crimes was then realized, and in due course he was hanged.

Even before his death Turpin had captured the public imagination, and crowds flocked to see him in York prison. It was the publication of Harrison Ainsworth's novel *Rookwood* (1834), however, that really established the legend of Dick Turpin, in particular his celebrated ride from London to York on his mare Black Bess to establish an alibi. In fact, Turpin never made such a ride, and the story may have been based upon a similar feat performed by another highwayman, John Nevison, who had been hanged at York in 1685.

turquoise Greenish gemstone, the birthstone for December, which is supposed to have various occult powers. Because the colour of the turquoise may become gradually greener, thus losing much of its value, the stone is associated with the idea of corruption and decay, and may be regarded as unlucky, often being used in the black arts of necromancy and alchemy. More positively, some say the turquoise symbolizes unselfishness, prosperity and happiness, adding that wearing it also increases sexual passion. Changes in the colour of a turquoise may, it is alleged, warn of imminent danger for its owner. In some parts of the Far East it is worn as protection against the EVIL EYE, and also to preserve riders from injury should they fall from their horses.

turtle The turtle features prominently in many folkloric traditions, and is widely understood to represent the virtues of wisdom and patience. It is sometimes identified, like the tortoise, as one of the animals that support the world itself (on the back of its shell). It also appears as a character in many folk tales, in which it typically triumphs through perseverance over otherwise superior animal opponents, such as the jaguar. It is often associated with femininity, and is thus widely linked with fertility.

Because of its longevity, the turtle has considerable significance in folk medicine. According to US superstition, fever may be assuaged by rubbing the patient with oil obtained from a turtle that has been killed while the moon is on the wane. Another tradition from the same part of the world, meanwhile, claims that rheumatism can be greatly relieved by rubbing the affected parts with the yellow meat of a turtle.

See also TORTOISE.

Twelfth Night The last day of the CHRISTMAS season, which falls on 6 January, otherwise known as Old Christmas Day as this was when Christmas was celebrated prior to the switch from the

Julian to the Gregorian calendar in the early 18th century. The date, which appears in the modern church calendar as the feast of Epiphany (commemorating the visit of the Wise Men to see the infant Jesus), is usually noted today as the time when all the Christmas decorations must come down. Superstition decrees that it is very unlucky to leave the decorations up beyond Twelfth Night – and conversely that it is also unlucky to anticipate the date by taking them down any earlier, as this symbolizes throwing away prosperity and even the life of a family member. Interestingly enough, this date has changed over the centuries, as it was once considered acceptable to leave decorations up until Candlemas, which falls at the very end of January.

In former centuries Twelfth Night's role as the last day of Christmas had more significance, and the date was the occasion for a last outburst of merriment before life returned to its usual mundane course. In many countries the feast was celebrated with a variety of revels that might include the lighting of bonfires, dancing, the eating of special Twelfth Night cakes, and the election of an Epiphany King or King of the Bean, who would oversee the festivities. Other miscellaneous folk traditions relating to Twelfth Night included the Faroese belief that seals take human form on this date, and the ancient custom of marking the close of the Christmas festivities by killing a WREN and then parading its body in procession (for some obscure reason a ritual supposed to protect local seafarers from shipwreck).

Formerly, Twelfth Night was welcomed across Europe as marking the end of the dark midwinter period when spirits of all kinds were believed to roam throughout the world. It was during this time of year that the WILD HUNT was most likely to be spotted, as well as WERE-WOLVES and TROLLS and other supernatural beings, including fairies and the ghosts of the dead. In many regions few people ventured outdoors unless they really had to before Twelfth Night was over, for fear of encountering other-worldly entities that might threaten them with harm.

See also HORN DANCE.

twins Twins have usually been regarded with mistrust in folklore, as they are believed to be in some way closer to the spirit world than other children. Thus, in many tribal societies, twins may be ostracized, and everything they touch will be declared TABOO to other children. In former times twins were sometimes greatly feared and risked being put to death immediately, along with the mother.

The superstitious will suggest various reasons as to why a woman gives birth to twins, speculating perhaps that she has at some point during her pregnancy consumed a 'double' fruit (that is, two fruits that have grown as one) or a fruit that normally grows in pairs (such as cherries). Twins will also result if husbands spill the pepper while their wives are pregnant, and women with a red line down the middle of their stomachs are said to be naturally prone to giving birth to more than one baby at a time. A rather pernicious tradition holds that a man may only father one child at once, and that therefore the second child must be the result of the wife's infidelity or of the action of spirits.

It is widely believed that twins, particularly identical twins, enjoy telepathic sympathy with one another, knowing when the other twin is in pain and so forth, and it has been speculated that there may be some as yet unproved scientific basis for this. According to one ancient tradition twins share only one soul between them, and if one dies and rigor mortis does not set in as might be expected this is a sign that the dead twin is waiting for its partner to join it in the afterlife. If the remaining twin survives the demise of its sibling it is supposed to acquire new vitality as well as supernatural healing powers, being able to cure thrush by breathing into the patient's mouth (though only if the patient is of the opposite sex). As regards livestock, farmers are inclined to see the birth of twin calves as an unlucky event, and may seek to sell one of them without delay.

Twins appear as central characters in many folk tales, often representing opposite qualities. Thus, while one is good, kind and clever, the other is revealed to be wicked, vicious and slow-witted.

Twm Shon Catti Semi-legendary Welsh folk hero who is regarded as a Welsh equivalent of the English ROBIN HOOD. He was born around 1530, and after many adventures ends up marrying an heiress and attaining the rank of squire and magistrate.

Twrch Trwyth In Welsh legend, a mighty BOAR who ravages Britain and Ireland with his seven piglets until slain by CULHWCH.

Supposedly a king prior to his transformation into a boar as the result of a spell, he is eventually hunted down by Culhwch as one of the 39 daunting tasks he is set by the giant Yspaddaden. With the help of other knights of King ARTHUR, Culhwch drives the creature off a high cliff and into the sea, also managing to snatch the scissors, razor and comb that the boar keeps between its ears. His equivalent in Irish mythology is called Torc Triath.

tylwyth teg In Welsh mythology, an alternative name for the FAIRY race meaning 'the fair family'. Like fairies elsewhere, they engage in all manner of mischief making, and, although sometimes friendly to mortals, are prone to steal human babies and replace them with their own CHANGELINGS (called crimbils by the Welsh). Sometimes they intermarry with humans and produce young by them. They are generally described as short and ugly.

Tyr In Norse mythology, the god of war. He was customarily called upon in battle by Viking warriors. He ranked alongside ODIN and THOR as one of the three most important gods in the Norse pantheon. He was sometimes identified as the son of Odin and FRIGGA. According to one legend, he lost a hand when helping to bind the wolf FENRIR to prevent him running amok prior to RAGNAROK. It was said that in the final battle he would die fighting Garm, the watchdog of HEL.

Tyrfing In Norse folklore, a magical SWORD made by the dwarfs. It was supposed to be unconquerable and capable of fighting on its own. It was also said, however, that once drawn it could not be replaced in its sheath until it had tasted blood, and furthermore that it would always eventually bring about the death of its possessor.

U

Uaithne In Irish mythology, the magic harp belonging to the DAGDA. It played only at the command of the Dagda but was subsequently stolen by the FOMOR-IANS. The Dagda discovered the harp's whereabouts when it answered their calls, killing nine as it leapt forward. Uaithne was also the name borne by a harpist who played for the Dagda.

Uathach In Irish legend, the daughter of SCATHACH who became the mistress of CUCHULAINN. Through her Cuchulainn received training in arms from her warrior mother at her home in Alba. Shortly after his arrival Uathach brought Cuchulainn some food and the latter, forgetting his own strength, accidentally broke her finger when taking it from her. She screamed with pain and Cuchulainn was immediately challenged to single combat by her lover Cochar Crufe. Cuchulainn killed his opponent and subsequently won Uathach as his mistress, possibly also as his wife.

Uath mac Imoman In Irish mythology the judge in the contest between Conall, CUCHULAINN and Laoghaire to decide which of them was the best warrior in Ireland. Uath ordered each of the rivals to cut off his head and then return the next day for him to return the blow. According to one version of the story, only Cuchulainn accepted the challenge. He severed Uath's head, only for the latter to pick it up and replace it, apparently none the worse for wear. The next day

Cuchulainn duly presented himself to receive Uath's return blow. Impressed by Cuchulainn's courage, Uath spared his life by striking him with the blunt edge of his axe and declared him champion (although the other two contenders refused to recognize the legitimacy of this decision).

UFO *See* UNIDENTIFIED FLYING OB-JECT.

Ugaine Mor In Irish mythology, a 6th-century AD king who was ruler of Ireland and Gaul. Possibly modelled on a real historical character, he fathered many children by a Gaulish princess, and on his death Ireland was divided into 25 regions, each ruled by one of their offspring – a system of government that remained in place for some 300 years.

Uigreann In Irish legend, a warrior who met his death in combat with Cumhaill, father of the celebrated FIONN MAC CUMHAILL. Uigreann's sons avenged their father by killing Cumhaill with spears.

uldra In the folklore of Lapland, a FAIRY race whose contacts with humans include both benevolent and hostile encounters. Like fairies in other parts of the world, the uldra live underground. They are rarely seen except in the winter, when they venture out into the frozen wastes to tend to hibernating animals. Usually they behave with shyness and kindness towards humans, but tales are also told of the uldra poisoning livestock and replacing human babies with CHANGELINGS.

Ulfius In Arthurian legend, a knight who served as chamberlain to King ARTHUR. He lived alongside MERLIN in the court of UTHER PENDRAGON before devoting himself to Arthur.

Ulster cycle The oldest and most celebrated of the Irish story cycles, telling the story of the reign of CONCHOBAR and the knights of the RED BRANCH. The events described in the cycle took place in the 1st century BC and the stories seem to have been first written down in the 1st century AD. The oldest extant texts go back to the 12th century. Important episodes in the cycle include descriptions of Conchobar's palace, called the Red Branch (where he keeps the heads of his defeated enemies), the adventures of Conchobar's nephew CUCHULAINN and other knights of the Red Branch, and the tragedy of DEIRDRE.

Uncle Remus The storyteller created by the US author Joel Chandler Harris in his *Uncle Remus, his songs and his sayings; the folk-lore of the old plantation* (1880). Harris's narrator appears in the guise of an old black former slave whose tales, with their animal characters and themes of trap-laying and trickery, reflect his African roots. The most famous of his tales include those featuring Brer Rabbit and his enemies Brer Fox and Brer Wolf. The author's avowed intention to produce faithful retellings of his African originals was more plainly revealed in his sequel *Nights with Uncle Remus* (1883), which also incorporated a number of folk tales (including tales of witchcraft and ghosts) contributed by his readers. Further Uncle Remus collections followed.

Uncle Sam Cartoon figure who is widely recognized as the personification of the United States of America. Employed in a similar way to England's JOHN BULL, Uncle Sam is a lean white-haired man with a straggly goatee beard, long-tailed coat and tall top hat, dressed entirely in a stars and stripes motif. He first appeared in political cartoons in the 19th century and quickly established himself as a visual expression of the archetypal Yankee character. The original Uncle Sam is thought to have been one 'Uncle Sam' Wilson, a businessman who worked from the Troy district of New York, supplying the US army – then engaged in the War of 1812 – with beef. His barrels were marked with the initials US to distinguish them as army property, and contemporary wags readily transferred Wilson's nickname to the government, and thus the country itself (a link that was officially acknowledged by Congress in 1961).

The most celebrated realization of the Uncle Sam character came in World War I when artist James Montgomery Flagg designed his famous recruiting poster of an earnest and somewhat cadaverous Uncle Sam pointing directly at the observer over the legend 'I want you for US Army', somewhat after the manner of Britain's Lord Kitchener poster with the slogan 'Your country needs you.' In later decades artists chose to satirize the Uncle Sam posters to great effect. An example during the Vietnam War features a bloodied and bandaged Uncle Sam pleading with the observer over the caption 'I want out'. In another example, Uncle Sam's image is ripped away to reveal a beckoning skeleton.

See also BROTHER JONATHAN.

undead Corpses that rise from the grave to threaten harm to the living. The tradition that some bodies somehow escape the normal processes of death and decay and break free from the grave to terrify living people is very ancient, and found in many of the world's cultures. Most societies have ritualized death and developed detailed funerary customs and procedures, with the evident purpose of formalizing the natural gulf between the living and the dead. Thus any suggestion that some souls can override such processes has always been particularly disturbing, and a perpetual source of horrified fascination. The VAMPIRE superstition is perhaps the best-known incarnation of the tradition in modern times. Other manifestations of the same idea have included the greatly feared ZOMBIES of the voodoo folk religion.

In order to ensure the bodies of the newly deceased remain in the grave various precautions have been recommended over the centuries. These have ranged from such drastic measures as transfixing the corpses of suspected vampires with a wooden stake through the heart and placing iron bars over the graves of executed witches, to the simpler acts of placing sharp objects such as scythes in coffins, and making sacrifices of red wine or blood to assuage the supposed lust that the undead are reputed to have for the blood of the living.

underworld The realm where the spirits of the dead reside. The exact nature of the underworld varies from culture to culture. The hell proposed by Christianity, for instance, is a place where evil souls are punished for their misdeeds in life, but other versions of it, such as the Norse Niflheim, are more vague about what goes on there. Access to the underworld is usually prohibited to mortals except in very special circumstances, although many cultures include tales in which courageous adventurers have found their way in and managed to return to the land of the living.

See also OTHERWORLD.

Undine Water sprite who appears in a famous French folk tale. She subsequently became well known through Friedrich de la Motte Fouqué's rendering of it in his story *Undine* (1811). Like other supernatural beings, Undine was born without a soul, but unlike other spirits had the option of obtaining a soul by marrying a mortal and bearing his child. Brought up in the humble cottage of a fisherman, she

fell in love with a knight called Huldbrand, and on marrying him gained a soul, thus experiencing for the first time all the pains and difficulties of a mortal existence. Unfortunately, Huldbrand subsequently fell in love with the fisherman's long-lost daughter Bertalda, provoking Undine to rise up from the water to which she had returned to kill her husband with a poisoned kiss. The story later provided the basis for several operas, among them works by Hoffmann (1816), Lortzing (1845), Mori (1865) and Sporck (1877) and a ballet by Henze (1958), with choreography by Frederick Ashton.

Undry In Irish mythology, the magic CAULDRON of the DAGDA, which was listed among the revered HALLOWS of Ireland. It had the invaluable property of always being full of food, however much was taken out of it. It was further said that people got as much food from it as accorded with their worth.

unicorn Mythical one-horned creature, representing both purity and strength, that has played a prominent role in folklore since classical times. Variously interpreted as a magical HORSE, an antelope, the extinct giant aurochs or a rhinoceros, the unicorn is now thought to owe its existence to a simple mistranslation by Greek translators of the Old Testament, perhaps supported by finds of narwhal horns washed up on shorelines. It appears in several medieval bestiaries and is sometimes described as having the legs of a buck, the tail of a lion and the head and body of a horse, while the horn may be depicted as white, black or red in colour.

Myths concerning the unicorn include the notion that it can only be subdued by a virgin, who has the power to cause the creature to lay its head in her lap and go to sleep, allowing it be killed with ease. If a girl who is not a virgin attempts to capture the beast in this way she runs the risk of being killed for her presumption. The powdered horn of the unicorn was said to have aphrodisiac properties and also to be an effective antidote to poison, hence the use of drinking horns constructed from what purported to be unicorn horns by a number of wary rulers in former times. Such beliefs remained in fairly common currency until well into the 17th century.

The presence of the unicorn in the British royal arms reflects its role in the heraldry of the Scottish royal house. It replaced the red dragon of Wales on the British royal arms when James VI of Scotland became king of England in 1603.

unidentified flying object (or **UFO**) Reported sightings of 'flying saucers', allegedly of extraterrestrial origin, are largely an invention of 20th-century folklore, although people have always been perplexed by odd things happening in the heavens. The phenomenon first began to attract massive interest in the late 1940s, since when many thousands of reports have been made of strange disc or cigar-shaped machines seen in the sky around the world. Photographs and film of purported UFOs have often been proved to be hoaxes, but many have confounded photographic experts, intensifying speculation about the reality of visitors from other planets. Some sightings are readily explained away as natural phenomena, such as cloud formations or the northern lights, or flights of experimental aircraft, and so forth, but the large number of unexplained sightings has inspired the growth of a whole industry revolving around UFOs, from books to Hollywood blockbuster movies.

Tales of abductions by aliens and rides aboard flying saucers are strongly reminiscent of much older folkloric tales about mortals being snatched away to some fairy underworld, and to many authorities the UFO craze of today is very much a modern reincarnation of a well-established folk tradition.

unseelie court The kingdom of the fairies in Scottish mythology. The fairies who belonged to the unseelie court were more malevolent towards mortals than those who belonged to the SEELIE COURT, and were always on the lookout for an opportunity to harm people and their livestock with their arrows. Their numbers were said to include the souls of those who died unsanctified, sometimes called the sluagh.

Up-Helly-Aa Annual fire festival that is celebrated at Lerwick in the Shetland Islands on the last Tuesday in January. Dating back to the times when the Shetlands were a Viking stronghold, the festival originally marked the end of the pagan Yuletide festivities, and was intended to provide a warm welcome to the returning sun. In former times, barrels of burning tar were pulled through the streets by gangs of local people in fancy dress, but this practice was prohibited in 1874 because of the risks involved and because of the mess caused by the tar. The main feature of the event since then has been the ceremonial burning of a mocked-up Viking longboat (a re-enactment of the ancient custom of cremating deceased Viking chiefs with their ships). Local people still dress up for the event, led by a chief celebrant called the Guizer Jarl, who takes pride of place in the longboat as it is dragged through the streets to the place where it will be burned. As the ship burns the crowd sing 'The Norseman's Home'. Another aspect of the celebration, introduced in 1931, is the Guizer Jarl's Proclamation, a large board carrying satirical verses about local people and events of the past year.

urban legend Species of modern folk tale reflecting contemporary neuroses but directly descended from much older storytelling traditions. Such tales have been accepted as a genre in their own right, and are often retold as allegedly true stories, usually described as having happened to 'a friend of a friend', but hardly ever to the actual narrator. A small percentage of the tales can be traced back to an actual event reported in the media or directly from a much older source, but the origins of the vast majority of legends are unknown. With each retelling the stories acquire new details, and may be relocated to places more familiar to the narrator's audience. Many of these features echo the way in which many much older forms of folk tale evolved over the course of centuries.

Some of the stories have an underlying moral message to impart, typically warnings against promiscuity or poor personal hygiene. Others simply reflect widely shared anxieties about such topics as violent crime, Aids, cannibalism, incest and social embarrassment, and probably serve to some extent to exorcize such worries. Another class of tale has its origins in the conventional ghost story, usually updated to include a modern element, as in stories about haunted stretches of road and disappearing hitchhikers.

Examples of the best-known urban legends, retold countless times, include such stories as those of the poodle dried off in a microwave oven (with predictably tragic results), the motorist who gives a lift to a young woman with suspiciously hairy hands (actually a deranged murderer), the holidaymaker bitten by a spider in some exotic country (the resulting sore eventually bursts open under the pressure of hundreds of baby spiders), the child who breathes in a tomato seed (and is later found to have a tomato plant growing in his nose) and the yucca plant bought in a well-known supermarket that when brought home turns out to be sheltering deadly tarantulas. Many of the tales are frankly shocking, including such gruesome topics as mutilation by axe-wielding maniacs, but others are more openly comic. Examples of this latter category include the story of the businessman invited home by his secretary, actually for a surprise birthday party in his honour: the man misinterprets his secretary's intentions when asked to wait for her in a darkened room and excitedly strips off all his clothes – only for the lights to snap on, revealing his naked form

to an assembled crowd comprising his family, friends, and work colleagues …

Urban of the Black Thorn In Arthurian legend, the guardian of a ford who tried to bar the way to PERCEVAL. Supported by several female spirits in the shape of ravens Urban did battle with Perceval but conceded defeat when one of his retainers was killed. The legend would appear to have been influenced by the myths surrounding the Irish battle goddess MORRIGAN and the ravens of OWAIN.

Urien In Arthurian legend, the king of the land of Gorre and the husband of the sorceress MORGAN LE FAY. Having fathered Morgan le Fay's son OWAIN he parted from her and pledged himself to the service of King ARTHUR, eventually dying in battle against Arthur's enemy MORDRED. Attempts have been made to identify the legendary Urien with a 6th-century king of Rheged, who defeated the Saxons at Argoed Llwyfain, although his reign does not appear to have coincided with that of Arthur.

urine In common with other bodily fluids, urine is widely held to retain a supernatural link with the body and therefore has certain magical properties. Measures should be taken against witches obtaining a person's urine, for instance, as this might be used in spells to threaten the welfare of the person concerned. Spitting into one's urine or washing the hands in urine are accepted ways to ward off such interference, as is sprinkling the doorposts of one's home and every member of one's family with urine.

In times gone by, friends and relatives could follow the fortunes of a person away from home for a prolonged period by keeping a bottle of their urine and examining it from time to time for any changes: if the urine clouded or otherwise deteriorated this could be interpreted as a sign that the missing party was ill, in trouble or even dead.

Beneficial uses of urine include wiping the face with a baby's first wet nappy to ensure a good complexion, pouring urine over snakebites or into the ear of someone with hearing problems to effect a cure and adding the urine of a patient suffering from fever to a few nettle leaves in order to make a prediction about the outcome of the illness: if the leaves stay green the patient will recover, but if they dry out the person will die. There is also a general prejudice against two people urinating together, as this means they will soon quarrel.

Uscias In Irish mythology, a wizard who lived in the city of Findias in the original homeland of the TUATHA DE DANANN. It was Uscias who gave NUADA the Sword of Light that defeated all enemies.

Usnech, Sons of *See* AINLE; NAOISI.

Uther Ben *See* BRAN THE BLESSED.

Uther Pendragon In Arthurian legend, a king of Britain identified by Geoffrey of Monmouth in the 12th century as the father of King ARTHUR. Through the magic of MERLIN, he assumed the outward appearance of King Gorlois of Cornwall and thus gained access to Gorlois' wife IGRAINE, with whom Uther had fallen in love. After the death of King Gorlois, Igraine and Uther were married and she gave birth to Uther's son Arthur. Shortly after the birth, Uther died, having been poisoned by his Saxon enemies. Before he died, worried by rumours that the baby had been fathered by Gorlois (whom Uther had killed in battle), Uther entrusted the upbringing of the infant Arthur to Merlin. He himself is reputed to have been buried at Stonehenge.

V

Väinämöinen Finnish folk hero whose adventures are told in the KALEVALA. He was born in the sea, and became famous as a magician and the protector of his people. He also invented the harp and the art of poetry.

His adventures include his resurrection by his mother after being cut to pieces by a Lapp enemy, and victory over his rival the Laplander Joukohainen in a singing contest. Described as a wrinkled old man, he failed in his various attempts to obtain a wife, and at the end of the *Kalevala* he bids farewell to his people, apparently recognizing there would be no place for him following the introduction of Christianity.

valerian Strongly perfumed plant, also called allheal, that was formerly prized for its healing properties. It was used in the cure of such ailments as coughs, rickets, sleeplessness and nervous complaints. In medieval times its powerful perfume (reminiscent of tomcats) was very popular, and was thought to be highly effective as an aphrodisiac, particularly in the Arab world. In England, girls were recommended to slip a sprig of valerian into their underwear to attract members of the opposite sex.

Native Americans were among those to value the plant for its sedative properties, and they also used it in the form of a poultice for sprains and bruises. Botanists have established that the root of the Eurasian *Valerian officinalis* does indeed have sedative properties.

Valhalla In Norse mythology, the OTHERWORLD to which Viking heroes were taken by the VALKYRIES after death in battle. Presided over by ODIN, Valhalla was usually described as a great hall with a roof made of spears and walls of polished shields. It had 840 doors, each of which was wide enough for 800 men to pass through line abreast. Only the bravest warriors were permitted to enter. Here they could pass eternity feasting, drinking, singing epic songs about their victories, and indulging in mock battles, attended throughout by the Valkyries, dressed in white. The word Valhalla came from the Norse *valr* ('the slain') and *hall* ('hall').

See also ASGARD.

Vali The Norse god of light and spring. Born the son of ODIN by the giantess Rinda, he is said to have avenged the death of BALDUR by killing HODUR when he was still only one night old.

Valkyries A race of beautiful golden-haired warrior maidens who appear in Norse mythology as attendants upon the slain Viking heroes dwelling at the court of ODIN in VALHALLA. The name originally meant 'choosers of the slain', and it was the Valkyries who selected and accompanied slain heroes to Odin's court. Here, dressed in white robes and shining armour, they waited upon the dead warriors, serving them mead and ale in human skulls. According to different versions they were 7, 9, or 12 in number.

Reported sightings of Valkyries speeding through the sky mounted on fine white horses were widely understood to be portents of imminent battle, although the maidens were also said to be able to adopt the guise of ravens or wolves. The Valkyries appear in the NIBELUNGENLIED cycle and were the subject of Wagner's opera *Die Walküre* (1870), the second part of his Ring cycle.

See also BRYNHILD.

vampire Supernatural being that feeds on the blood of the living and is universally identified with evil. The vampire tradition has a long history, with tales of blood-sucking monsters common to many of the world's cultures, although it is chiefly associated today with Transylvania (now part of Romania) and other parts of eastern Europe. It may go back ultimately to the ancient Greek and Roman lamia, a species of female monster that returned from the grave to prey on young men by night. According to some authorities vampires are the reincarnated dead corpses of suicides or excommunicated heretics, who need fresh blood to maintain themselves, while others believe they are the victims of other vampires' infectious bites. In southern Europe it was once supposed that babies born with teeth were destined to become vampires.

World folklore boasts a rich and detailed body of myths concerning vampires. It is said that vampires can be distinguished by their long pointed incisors and by the fact that they have no reflection or shadow (because the reflection is an embodiment of the soul, and the vampire has no soul), that they have a strong aversion to sunlight (which can destroy them), and that they must return to their coffins, lined with soil from their birthplace, during the day. They also enjoy a tremendous sexual hold over women, and have the power to transform themselves into bats when going in search of prey.

Although vampires are by definition already dead, there are several generally agreed ways in which they can be destroyed. As well as exposing a vampire to sunlight, it can also be destroyed by driving a stake through its heart as it lies in its coffin, or by shooting it with a silver bullet (a counter-measure that was formerly reserved for witches). It is also possible to protect oneself against vampires through the presence of garlic or iron, or by carrying a crucifix.

The vampire superstition enjoyed a major boost in the late 19th century through the classic Bram Stoker horror novel *Dracula* (1897), which referred obliquely to the semi-legendary Vlad Dracula of Transylvania, otherwise known as Vlad the Impaler, a 15th-century prince whose misdeeds included impaling 20,000 Turkish prisoners on stakes. Stoker's creation has inspired countless movies over the years. The superstition may originally have been inspired by misconceptions about certain rare blood disorders, which render sufferers unable to stand sunlight, or else to misunderstandings about the symbolic drinking of Christ's blood in the Mass. Modern fascination in vampires probably owes something to reports concerning the blood-drinking vampire bats of South America, although psychologists often suggest it may have gathered strength in response to repressed eroticism and sadomasochism in contemporary society.

See also LYCANTHROPY.

Vanaheim *See* VANIR.

Vanir In Norse mythology, an early race of gods (mostly fertility gods) who predated ODIN and his court (*see* AESIR). They presided over the universe at their palace Vanaheim.

Ve *See* VILI.

vervain Flowering plant of the verbena family that has been credited with a range of magical properties since Roman times, when it had special significance in various religious rites and was believed to ward off evil. It was also venerated by the ancient Persians and the Druids, to whom it was the 'enchanter's plant'. Over the centuries it has been widely used in love potions, in divination, and in spells to open locks by magic. It was also valued as a charm against the EVIL EYE and WITCH-CRAFT. Children were often made to carry vervain in the belief that it would ensure they grew up both intelligent and friendly, and brides formerly carried sprigs of vervain at their weddings (although it was also said that a man who drank vervain juice would be untroubled by thoughts of lust for seven years). Like other magical plants, it had to be gathered in a certain way if it was to retain its effectiveness, usually by moonlight.

Vervain had many uses in folk medicine. Among other things, it was traditionally supposed to be effective as a treatment for cancer, snakebite, piles, the plague and epilepsy. Native Americans consumed vervain to alleviate nightmares and to soothe upset stomachs.

vetala In Hindu mythology, a frightening spirit that haunts graveyards and preys on corpses. A character in a range of folk tales, it can be distinguished by its backwards-pointing hands and feet.

vila (or veela, willi) In eastern European mythology, a variety of spirit feared for its malevolence towards the living. They were usually identified as the ghosts of unbaptized children or of virgins, fated to roam the earth forever, and were rumoured to force mortals they came across to dance to death. A more positive and contrasting tradition claims that they may offer mortals supernatural assistance, or even bear them offspring.

Vili In Norse mythology, the son of ODIN. He and his brother Ve constructed the earth using the flesh and blood of the giant YMIR, and then made the first humans out of ash and elm trees.

violet Flowering plant around which numerous folk myths have arisen. Like several other wild flowers, violets are often considered to be fairly ominous and may bring bad luck if brought into the house in anything less than generous bunches. It is also thought to be a bad omen if violets bloom out of season, in particular a portent of the imminent death of the person who owns the land on which they grow. This omen may also be interpreted as a portent of an approaching epidemic. Violets are said to grow especially plentifully on the graves of virgins and young lovers. These rather gloomy associations may owe something to the Christian tradition that the shadow of Christ's cross fell on the violet, causing it to droop permanently. Dreams of violets are, however, supposed to be lucky, and the flower has also been listed as an ingredient in many love potions. Violets also have their uses in folk medicine, being recommended for fever, jaundice, pleurisy and other ailments.

virginity Chastity has always had special folkloric significance around the world. Not only was virginity often a crucial issue in marriage negotiations, but it also bestowed various degrees of magical status. Virgins were supposed to be able to subdue UNICORNS, stare directly into the sun, walk through swarms of bees without getting stung and restore the flame of an extinguished candle, among other feats. They were also believed to have special powers of divination and healing – the mere touch of a virgin was supposed to make warts disappear. If a girl or woman died while still a virgin it was customary in the British Isles for many centuries for the funeral decorations in church to include white paper cut into the shape of a woman's glove, to represent their celibacy.

The social importance of virginity meant that folklore provided various theories about how its loss might reveal itself. These included rapid development of the breasts, and an irresistible urge for the woman to urinate if tricked into drinking a little powdered coal. A rather bizarre central European tradition claims that a woman regains her virginity after giving birth to seven illegitimate children. Virginity is not universally prized, however – in parts of southern Africa, for instance, it is considered a social embarrassment for a girl to be still a childless virgin when she gets married.

Vivien *See* LADY OF THE LAKE.

vodyanik In eastern European folklore, a water spirit that was often blamed for drownings and other mishaps suffered by fishermen and others on or near water. Other misdemeanours committed by these spirits included the tangling of fishing nets and the upsetting of boats. They were commonly depicted as fat old men wearing caps of woven reeds.

See also RUSALKA.

Volkh Russian folk hero who appears in many traditional tales. Also known as Volga, he was celebrated for his immense strength, and was also credited with the power to change shape.

Völsungasaga German prose epic depicting the history of the Völsung dynasty. Written in the 13th century, it can in many respects be traced back to the Norse EDDAS.

See also NIBELUNGENLIED.

voodoo Haitian folk religion combining elements of Christianity, magic, snake worship, superstition and witchcraft. Of largely African origin, but also influenced by Christian ritual, it incorporates the veneration of a range of demons and ancestral spirits, referred to collectively as the loa. Rituals, which often include animal sacrifice and hypnotic possession, are held chiefly at night in conditions of great secrecy. The name 'voodoo' is variously thought to have been derived from the French *vaudois* (a title given to the Waldensians, a Christian sect once sus-

pected of sorcery), from the Ashanti *obosum* (denoting a fetish or tutelary spirit), or from *vadu*, a word of the African Ewe people meaning 'gods'.

See also ZOMBIE.

Vortigern A semi-legendary 5th-century king of Britain, whose name means 'overlord'. It was at the invitation of the historical Vortigern that Saxon mercenaries came to England to help fight the Picts and Scots, but stayed to take over the kingdom. Vortigern's attempts to appease his Saxon mercenaries, who were joined by ever-increasing numbers of companions from continental Europe, culminated in a peace gathering between the Britons and the Saxons at Stonehenge, but the Saxons proved treacherous and murdered the British negotiators. Vortigern's life was spared, and he escaped to Wales. Here, according to the legends surrounding Merlin Emrys (*see* MERLIN), he tried to build a great tower, only for it to collapse due to the shifting of two dragons (one red, one white) who lay buried beneath the foundations. Representing the opposing armies of the Britons and the Saxons, the two dragons broke out of the ground and engaged in fierce combat. Vortigern eventually met his own death at the hands of the warrior AMBROSIUS and UTHER PENDRAGON, whom he had originally usurped.

vulture Like other carrion-eating birds, the vulture is regarded as a bird of ill omen, and is loathed and feared in many cultures. Because they feed on dead flesh, vultures have always been associated with death, and their appearance is often greeted with alarm. However, this reputation is somewhat offset by the belief that vultures are good parents – a notion that may have come about through confusion between the similar Hebrew words for 'vulture' and 'compassion'. The bird also featured in the mythology of ancient Egypt as an emblem of the goddess Isis.

W

Walpurgisnacht The German name for May Eve, one of the two nights of the year when it was formerly believed that evil forces held sway over the earth (the other being HALLOWE'EN). Walpurgisnacht (30 April) – named after St Walpurga (or Walburga), the English-born abbess who founded a Benedictine convent at Heidenheim, near Munich in the 8th century – was one of the nights when witches were thought to gather for the casting of spells and other magic-making activities. The most famous of these ominous gatherings was the annual meeting of German witches attended by the Devil himself that was supposed to take place on the Brocken, the highest peak of the Harz Mountains.

Wandering Jew In pan-European folklore, a Jew who insulted Christ as he carried his cross to the place of Crucifixion and in punishment was condemned to wander the earth until Judgement Day. The legend became well known in late medieval times, when the Wandering Jew was variously identified as Cartaphilus, the doorkeeper of Pontius Pilate (who is supposed to have taunted Christ to walk faster and was warned that he himself would 'tarry till I come again') or Ahasuerus (a cobbler who prevented Christ resting for a moment at his door). He is occasionally also identified as the leader of the WILD HUNT.

The legend claims that the Wandering Jew falls into a trance every 100 years and wakes up as a young man of around

30 and is thus obliged to recommence his ceaseless journey. Reports of the Wandering Jew have been recorded all over Europe, promoted over the centuries by anti-Semitic feeling. Towards the end of the 16th century he was reported to have been seen in Venice, bearing the name Salathiel ben-Sadi, and it was this sighting that did much to disseminate the legend throughout Europe. In Germany and the Low Countries he was identified as one John Buttadaeus, who turned up in Antwerp in the 13th, 15th and 16th centuries, and resurfaced once more in Brussels in 1774. In France he went by the name Isaac Laquedom (or Lakedion). Reports of the wanderings of this mysterious figure seem to have ceased during the 19th century.

Equivalents of the Wandering Jew in other cultures include the British King HERLA, doomed to wander the earth forever, unable to dismount from his horse, and the FLYING DUTCHMAN.

Wantley, **Dragon of** A dragon that wrought havoc in the region of Wantley (now Wharncliffe) in Yorkshire until slain by More of More Hall. As related in Thomas Percy's *Reliques of Ancient English Poetry* (1765), More equipped himself with a suit of armour studded with spikes and killed the dragon by kicking it from behind (the one area where it was vulnerable). One theory has it that the dragon represented a rapacious agent of the Wortley family who was notoriously greedy in collecting tithes from poor parishioners until hauled up in court by a man named More.

war dance *See* DANCE.

War of the Brown Bull *See* TAIN BO CUAILNGE.

Washer at the Ford In Celtic mythology, a mysterious spectre, variously described as an ugly hag or a beautiful young woman, who may be encountered washing bloody linen beside a river. According to some authorities, she was the spirit of a young woman who had died in childbirth and now roamed the earth grieving over her fate. Any knight seeing her, it was believed, was thereby warned of his own imminent death in battle. Among the heroes to see her were the great Irish warriors OSCAR and CUCHULAINN, who both came across her while riding to their last battles.

See also BANSHEE.

wassailing The custom of honouring crops or livestock during the Christmas season in the expectation that this will promote the harvest in the coming year. This chiefly English tradition has ancient roots (the word 'wassail' means 'be whole' in Old English), but was still being widely observed in rural areas well into the 20th century, often being performed on Christmas Eve or alternatively at New Year, Twelfth Night or on Old Twelfth Night (17 January). Typical features of the ritual included drinking the health of fruit trees, cattle or corn (usually with cider), lighting fires in the fields and orchards, and firing with shotguns into the branches of the best apple trees in order to scare away any evil spirits lurking there or to awaken the god or goddess protecting the trees. Sometimes the ritual was performed in the hope of promoting the prosperity of the local community, with revellers going from house to house while drinking from special wooden wassail cups or bowls filled with spiced ale or cider. The modern tradition of carol singing is descended from this old custom.

In Scotland, where many people relied upon fishing for their livelihood, the sea was sometimes honoured in a similar fashion, with a glass of ale being poured onto the waves in the hope that this would ensure good catches for local fishermen in the months ahead.

Wasteland In Arthurian legend, the land surrounding the Castle of the Grail that was laid waste when the GRAIL KING received the DOLOROUS BLOW. Representing SOVEREIGNTY, and thus magically linked to the ruler's physical well-being, the land remained desolate and barren until the WOUNDED KING recovered. In the Grail cycle the Wasteland is personified by such characters as the LOATHLY LADY before her beauty is restored.

water divination *See* DOWSING.

water of life *See* FOUNTAIN OF YOUTH.

water spirit *See* KELPIE; KRAKEN; LOCH NESS MONSTER; MERMAID; NAKH; OLD MAN OF THE SEA; ROANE; RUSALKA; SEAL MAIDEN; SELKIE; TANGIE.

Wayland the Smith In Norse mythology, the smith of the gods, who was also identified by some as king of the elves. He fashioned the gods' weapons and armour and in Arthurian legend was also credited as the maker of EXCALIBUR. Other remarkable objects produced by his hand included a boat made of feathers, and winged cloaks. According to legend, he was lame (as was the Greek god of the forge Hephaestus) from an injury inflicted by King Nidud of Sweden when the latter stole one of his swords and tried to make Wayland his slave. Wayland escaped to VALHALLA by flying away in a feather robe first tried out by his brother EGIL. Wayland took his revenge by murdering Nidud's two sons (whose skulls were turned into drinking bowls and sent to their father) and by raping Nidud's daughter.

Wayland the Smith is mentioned in several early writings, including *Beowulf* and the *Eddas*. His name is also associated with Wayland's Smithy, a mysterious prehistoric burial chamber in Oxfordshire, near White Horse Hill. According to local legend anyone who leaves their horse there, together with a payment of sixpence, will return to find the horse freshly shod.

weasel The weasel is widely regarded as one of the most ill-omened of all creatures, and in former times was commonly associated with WITCHCRAFT. Witches were often suspected of disguising themselves as weasels, and any contact with the creature was greatly feared, especially if the animal was white in colour, in which case the person concerned would die within a year. Even the cry of the weasel was considered a harbinger of bad luck. In Dorset it was claimed that weasels would turn into fairies if approached. In China weasels were thought able to cast spells over men, while in Greece even mentioning the animal in casual conversation was considered very unwise.

On a more positive note, it was said that anyone who kept their coins in a purse made of weasel skin would never run out of money, and also that its flesh could be consumed as an antidote to snake venom. In medieval Christian iconography Christ was occasionally depicted as a weasel overcoming the Devil, possibly a reference to the classical belief that the weasel and the cock were the only creatures capable of killing the dreaded basilisk.

weather The crucial importance of the weather and its prediction has guaranteed it a central place in world folklore. Since early times it has been believed that the weather is subject to divine influence, and great store is still placed in some parts of the world on appeasing the gods through sacrifice and so forth in the hope that this will persuade them to bring good weather. By the same token, thunder was widely interpreted as the anger of the gods, while rain was said in some cultures to be poured out from a vast celestial jug.

A vast body of superstitions has evolved over the centuries inspired by the urge to divine what the weather has in store. Some of these are universal beliefs, while others are peculiar to people working in a particular profession, such as farmers or seafarers. Much weather lore appears to have had its origin in observation of the weather itself. Examples of this include the well-known English rhyme 'Red sky at night, shepherd's delight; red sky in the morning, shepherd's warning'. This particular saw is relatively reliable, as a red sun setting in the west (from which direction weather systems affecting Britain usually come) indicates that there is little moisture in the air and thus that the following day is likely to be dry.

Other superstitions depend upon the examination of animal behaviour. Predictions of bad weather may be made from, among other things, house martins flying low, cows or horses sitting or lying down in the field, seagulls flying inland, cats sneezing or washing behind their ears, crows cawing, donkeys braying, ants and spiders rushing for shelter and bees staying in their hives. Indications of fine weather include bats flying in the early evening and ants busily clearing out their anthills.

Nature also provides other coded messages about the weather. If the oak trees produce leaves before the ash trees, for example, the coming summer will be good. If fruits and vegetables have unusually thick skins, however, this means the coming winter will be severe. A piece of seaweed kept beside the front door will shrivel up when warm weather is on the way, but will become moist when rain is about to fall. In the USA the best-known weather superstitions include the notion that on GROUNDHOG DAY (2 February) the groundhog, or woodchuck, emerges from its burrow to test the weather: if the groundhog casts no shadow, it remains above ground and spring has begun.

Sometimes the clues may be found within the inquirer's own body. Many people believe that when their limbs ache or their corns become painful then wet weather is in store – a notion that is supported to some extent by modern science, which has linked changes in atmospheric pressure with the occurrence of such symptoms.

The state of the weather at certain moments is thought to exert something more than a purely physical influence upon human affairs. Thus it is still said to be a good omen if the sun shines on a bride and, conversely, if rain falls during a funeral. In Germany a rather bizarre tradition claims that if couples make love in the rain then they are sure to conceive a girl. Christian tradition, meanwhile, insists that a 'white Christmas', when snow falls on Christmas Day, is a sure sign of a happy and prosperous year ahead.

Given the primary importance of such events in human society it is not surprising that people should have sought ways in which they might dictate the behaviour of the weather through magic. In various parts of the world it is believed that the weather will respond to a variety of ritual dances, incantations, and other ceremonial acts. Rain-making dances are widely known in parts of the world where drought is a serious threat, although other methods of inducing wet weather over the centuries have ranged from burning bits of fern or heather to dipping religious statues in water. If a storm becomes too violent it can be tempered, according to Austrian folklore, by tossing a handful of meal out of the window, or else by ringing the church bells.

See also RAIN; RAINBOW; ST SWITHIN'S DAY; SNEGUROTCHKA; STORM; SUN; THUNDER; WIND.

wedding *See* ANNIVERSARY; MARRIAGE.

well As a source of vital water supplies wells have always been a focus of veneration and local folklore. In bygone times every well or spring was believed to have its own guardian spirit, to whom respect was due. Some wells, it was said, occasionally made strange noises or were reported to fill and empty repeatedly to warn of imminent disaster. Others were believed to have special healing properties, and anyone who drank the 'cream of the well' (water from the first bucket hauled up at the beginning of the year) was supposed to enjoy great good luck over the year to come. In order to prevent a well running dry it was once customary to offer a piece of bread to it at New Year. Wells could also be used for the purposes of divination: the usual procedure was to drop a stone into the water – if the stone created lots of bubbles things would go well, but if it made the water cloudy then it might be concluded that trouble lay in store.

The belief that some wells are wishing wells, which will grant any wish made if a coin or pebble is tossed into the water, is still alive and well, and today virtually any pool accessible to the public may be adopted as a wishing well, the coins thus collected being donated to charitable causes. This custom is thought to have had its origins in the practice of making sacrifices to the pagan deities that were once believed to live in the vicinity of wells and springs. A rather different kind of wishing well is the well of St Elian at Llanelian-yn-Rhos in Wales, which has a long-standing reputation for making curses come true. The curses are written on pieces of paper that are then lowered into the well in a lead casket.

The universal reverence for wells survives today in the ancient custom of well-dressing. In this custom, common to villages in various parts of northern England, people decorate their local wells with elaborate flower arrangements and pictures made from berries and pebbles and so forth. In the Derbyshire village of Tissington, where the practice is thought to have originated, it is explained that the tradition is kept up in gratitude for the village's five wells remaining pure during the Black Death, which devastated neighbouring regions in 1348. The ceremony now has a quasi-religious aspect and usually takes place on Ascension Day, when rival groups of locals endeavour to outdo each other, creating wonderfully detailed pictures with a religious theme on a wooden frame placed over the well itself. A procession led by church and civic dignitaries then visits each well in turn to bestow a blessing upon it.

wendigo *See* WINDIGO.

werewolf A person who periodically changes into a wolf and then feeds voraciously on human flesh. Such transformations are also known as lycanthropy. Belief in werewolves goes back to ancient times, and occurs in many parts of the world. Early theories about werewolves included the suggestions that men born out of wedlock or on Christmas Eve were particularly prone to such transformation, although others were supposed to have developed the condition after being bitten by another werewolf (resembling VAMPIRE mythology), or through contact with demons or black magic. The condition of the werewolf contrasts to that of the vampire, however, in that the sufferer is not actually dead.

In Germany it was believed that sorcerers could change their form at will by donning a wolf's pelt, and equally could return to their human shape when they chose. Other werewolves, however, were believed to be unable to choose the time when they were transformed, the change being effected by, for instance, the sight of a full moon. They could be detected when in their human guise by their unusually hairy hands, flat fingers and eyebrows meeting above the nose.

Fear of werewolves was formerly much more intense than it has been in modern times, when it has only rarely caused a commotion outside the movie industry. In 1521, for instance, two men were burned alive at Besançon, France, after confessing that they could assume the form of child-eating wolves by rubbing a special ointment over their bodies. In this instance it was clearly thought that a werewolf could be destroyed by fire, but elsewhere it is maintained that the only certain way in which a werewolf can be killed is to shoot it with a silver bullet, ideally one that has been blessed by a priest. Any wound inflicted upon a werewolf will still be evident when it reverts to its human shape.

In parts of the world where wolves are unknown similar traditions have evolved concerning such animals as foxes, hyenas, jaguars, leopards and tigers. West African lore even boasts werecrocodiles.

See also SHAPE SHIFTING.

whale The whale by virtue of its prodigious size has always occupied a central place in marine folklore. It has long been considered a lucky animal, and for centuries seafarers, with the notable exception of whalers believed that misfortune would befall any person who killed a whale. It was also said to be unlucky to spot whales where they were not usually seen. Ancient mythology, meanwhile, proposes the whale as one of the creatures upon whose back the whole of the earth rests.

Whales feature prominently in a number of famous folk tales. These include the story in the *Arabian Nights* in which SINBAD disastrously mistakes the back of a whale for an island. There are several other tales, apparently inspired by the biblical story of Jonah and the whale, in which humans are swallowed whole by whales and find themselves trapped inside their huge stomachs.

whistling Many cultures harbour misgivings about whistling, which is taboo in many circumstances. In English-speaking countries it is considered foolhardy in the extreme to whistle in theatres, down mines or while at sea, as this invites disaster. This prejudice may have its origins in the old superstition that witches have the power to 'whistle up' storms. In the theatre a more pragmatic explanation refers to the old system of signalling scene changes by whistling. Christians in former centuries particularly resented the idea of a woman whistling, as this was believed to be unlucky, recalling the tradition that a woman stood idly by, whistling, as she watched the nails to be used at Christ's Crucifixion being made.

white horses *See* CHALK HILL FIGURES.

White Lady In German and French legend, a species of ghost whose appearance is supposed to be an omen of imminent death. She is possibly descended from the Teutonic goddess Hulda or BERCHTA, to whom the souls of young children came. First recorded in the 15th century, when she was given the name Bertha von Rosenberg, she is usually depicted all in white with a bunch of keys at her side. In Normandy, White Ladies of various descriptions haunt numerous bridges, fords and ravines. Here they command any passing mortals to dance with them – and if they are refused they fling the traveller into the nearest ditch.

Whitsun The seventh Sunday after Easter, on which Christians celebrate the feast of Pentecost – although it is likely that this was already a date for pagan festivals celebrating the coming of summer. A popular time for fairs, feasts and village gatherings throughout Europe, it is marked by the observation of many old customs. Traditions attached to the day itself include an old English superstition that it is unlucky not to wear at least one new item of clothing on Whitsun – those who ignore this will have their clothes soiled by passing birds. It is also thought to be an unlucky date on which to be born, and it was once feared that Whitsun babies would grow up to kill or be killed.

Wild Edric Legendary English hero, from Shropshire, who abducted an elf maiden and was allowed to marry her on condition that he never criticized her or her kin. However, It was not long before Edric broke his promise and she promptly disappeared. Legend has it that William the Conqueror was fascinated by the story and made Edric one of his closest companions. Local tradition claims that Edric lies imprisoned under the hills of west Shropshire but patriotically rides forth against his country's enemies whenever war breaks out.

Wild Herdsman In Welsh legend, a black giant of the forest who appears in such folktales as 'The Lady of the Fountain'. He is depicted as the guardian of the beasts of the forest, which he summons to him by beating with his club upon the belly of a stag. Wise but also somewhat belligerent in character, some aspects of his personality appear to have been subsequently absorbed into early legends about MERLIN.

Wild Hunt A band of spectral riders, complete with ghostly black hounds (the Wish Hounds) that has long been supposed to career noisily through the sky on dark and stormy nights. The legend of the Wild Hunt was once familiar throughout northern Europe, and may have had its roots ultimately in Norse mythology: the leader of the hunt, mounted on a fire-breathing horse, was originally equated with ODIN. Others, however, associated the Wild Hunt with the Devil, and believed the hounds to be the souls of unbaptized children. Sometimes the head huntsman was identified as a particular legendary or semi-legendary character, including HERNE THE HUNTER, King ARTHUR, Sir Francis Drake (in the Dartmoor region), King Herod, the WANDERING JEW and (in Bohemia) King Wenceslas. In Welsh legend he is identified as Gwynn Ap Nudd, the greatly feared lord of the dead.

The Wild Hunt goes by different names in different cultures: it is known as the Yule Host in Iceland, and the Raging Host or Furious Host in Germany. The Wish Hounds, which are sometimes described as headless, are also known as the Yeth or Yell Hounds (southern

England), the Gabriel Hounds (northern England), the Ratchets (Lancashire) and the Hell Hounds or Night Hounds (central England).

It was considered very ominous indeed for a person to catch a glimpse of the Wild Hunt, whose approach was signalled by the sound of blowing trumpets, baying hounds and rushing winds. Anyone who heard these warning signs was recommended to throw themselves on the ground and to hold onto a tree or something else firmly planted in the earth in case they were swept up and carried off to the underworld.

wili In Slavic mythology, a species of female GHOST that preys upon young men. The tradition identifies the wili as the vengeful spirit of a young woman who lived just long enough to become engaged but died before her wedding day arrived. These spectres are said to haunt lonely roads and to force young men passing by to dance with them until they die.

William of Cloudesly English folk hero whose legend bears strong similarities to that of WILLIAM TELL. William of Cloudesly hailed from the north of England and was an outlaw famous for his skill as an archer. He was captured and sentenced to be hanged after stealing into town to visit his wife, but was rescued by his fellow outlaws ADAM BELL and CLYM OF THE CLOUGH and subsequently sought a pardon from the king in London. To demonstrate his skill as an archer he shot an apple off his son's head at a distance of 120 paces – as in the William Tell legend (although in this instance it appears there was no element of coercion involved). The king was suitably impressed by the feat and granted the outlaw his freedom.

William Tell Swiss folk hero who appears in a number of myths and legends known throughout Europe. Although there seems to be no historical basis for the story of William Tell, the legend is fairly specific about when and where he lived. It is said that he was a peasant from Bürglen in the Swiss province of Uri and was a great shot with the crossbow. Having refused to salute the cap of Herman Gessler, steward of Albert I of Austria (d.1308), which had been hoisted up on a pole in the town square for the purpose, he was challenged to shoot an apple off the head of his own son. Tell managed to hit the apple without hurting his son, but when Gessler asked why he had removed two bolts from his quiver replied that had he missed he would have used the second bolt to kill Gessler himself. In punishment for his insolence, Tell was immediately despatched by ship to Küssnacht castle, but during a storm the prisoner managed to leap from the ship to a nearby rock and made good his escape. Subsequently he killed Gessler in an ambush, precipitating a general uprising that secured Swiss independence from Austria (hence Tell's lasting fame).

It seems probable the legend had its roots originally in Norse legend, specifically the story of the 10th-century Tokko, who was obliged to perform a similar feat of marksmanship at the order of Harold Bluetooth. Other parallels include the legend of the English outlaw WILLIAM OF CLOUDESLY. The Tell legend became widely known initially in ballad form, and received a major boost in the early 19th century through Schiller's celebrated drama *Wilhelm Tell* (1804).

will o' the wisp A glowing light of the type occasionally seen on marshy ground or near graves. The result of burning marsh gases (specifically the methane produced by decaying organic matter), these lights – also called ignis fatuus ('foolish fire'), Jack-o'-lanterns, elf fire or will o' the wykes – were once thought to be of supernatural origin, and might be identified variously as ghosts, witches, demons or the wandering spirits of unbaptized children. They are almost universally regarded as omens of disaster, and may be interpreted as warnings of imminent death. Unwary travellers who are foolish enough to try to follow the lights are, it is claimed, likely to be lured into bottomless bogs – although tales are also told of such lights leading mortals who have lost their way back to safety.

willow The willow tree has long had special significance in folklore. Over the centuries it has become identified with sadness, and become an emblem of grief, melancholy, and lost love. In times gone by it was common for sprigs of willow to be worn as a symbol of grief, and even today many people have reservations about taking willow catkins indoors because of their gloomy associations (except on May Day). On a more positive note, however, willow wood was believed to have strong magical potency, and was a popular choice for the making of magic wands. Travellers were formerly known to carry willow rods for magical protection and luck. A bitter infusion derived from willow bark was also recommended for treatment of the ague (fever), and in the 19th century salicin (the source of the modern aspirin) was isolated from willow.

Will Scarlett *See* ROBIN HOOD.

wind Like other aspects of the weather, the wind has often been interpreted as an expression of divine will, and has consequently become the focus of many folkloric traditions. Christians claimed that the winds were controlled by four angels located at the four points of the compass, while other cultures assigned control of the wind to specific deities, or maintained that the winds had escaped from a cave or bag after being loosed by some mischief-making spirit or god. In some parts of the world winds that blew from a particular direction were likely to be identified as 'sick', pestilence-bearing winds full of evil, while gales were often attributed to the activities of witches or demons.

Superstition offers a number of ways in which mortals may try to influence the behaviour of the wind. Sailors becalmed at sea, for instance, may try scratching the mast of their ship with their fingernail to raise a breeze, or else toss a coin or brush into the water to produce the desired change in the weather. Witches and 'wise men' of former times commonly sold lengths of knotted string, claiming that when each knot was loosened a wind would blow up – a soft breeze with the first knot, a strong wind with the second and a gale with the third.

Whirlwinds are the subject of particular dread in America and elsewhere, being interpreted as forces of evil or as the spirits of the dead. Recommended precautions to be taken on the approach of a whirlwind include hiding, talking to the wind, clapping at it and stamping one's feet. Whirlwinds also appear as characters in a number of folk tales.

See also STORM.

windigo In Native American folklore, a man-eating monster who haunts the desolate forests and icy wastelands of the northern USA and Canada. The windigo (or wendigo) is supposed to have been human originally, but was transformed into a terrifying monster upon tasting human flesh for the first time.

Wish Hounds *See* WILD HUNT.

wishing well *See* WELL.

witchcraft The practice of magic by witches, warlocks, wizards and sorcerers. Legal definitions of witchcraft in former times emphasized the anti-Christian nature of witchcraft and the importance of a pact between the practitioner and the Devil. This pact involved the witch acquiring the power to cast spells and so forth in exchange for his or her immortal soul. If no such pact was proved then the person accused was not technically a witch. If the pact was proved then the modern distinction between 'black' and 'white' magic (black magic being malicious spell-making against others) was irrelevant, as the important issue was the pact itself. If evidence of such a pact was produced, the accused person was liable to be put to death. This was particularly common in many European countries during the witchcraft hysteria of the late 15th, 16th and 17th centuries.

In many respects witchcraft was a post-medieval invention, although it absorbed elements of much earlier ideas about sorcery and spell-making. The word 'witch' appears in the Bible, but only as a later interpretation of a word that more accurately meant 'pythoness' or 'poisoner'. The archetypal witch in the modern imagination is an old hag, hated and feared by her neighbours, who works with various IMPS or FAMILIARS (a largely British elaboration) to harm others through magic. In reality, unpopular old women were not the only suspects – in Catholic Europe, where the authorities often had the right to confiscate the wealth of convicted witches, accusations were just as likely to be levelled at the middle and upper classes, and to include both sexes. In so far as anyone actually did pursue such practices, they seem to have been confined to the deranged (such as the self-confessed Scottish witch Isobel Gowdie) or the 'wise men' and 'wise women' whose knowledge of herbalism and folk medicine was liable to be mistaken for something much more sinister.

As well as threatening humans and their livestock with their magic, witches were widely supposed to be able to change their shape, travel vast distances on broomsticks, and to attend regular covens or sabbats at which they indulged in all manner of sinful excess at the command of their demonic master. In fact, very few accused persons confessed willingly to such activity, and evidence for organized witchcraft, implicit in rumours of large-scale covens, was virtually non-existent before modern times.

There were supposed to be various recognized ways in which a suspect could be detected. Every witch, for instance, was believed to have a Devil's mark – a skin blemish or other abnormality (such as a mole) that indicated where the Devil had marked the suspect out as one of his own. It was claimed that these marks were impervious to pain, and thus developed the practice of 'pricking' accused persons with sharp points to see if they felt any pain. Tales were similarly often told of suspects who were 'swum' to establish their guilt: in this procedure suspects were bound hand and foot and thrown into a pond – if they floated they were guilty as charged, if they sank they were innocent (but likely to drown anyway).

How many people were put to death during the witchcraft hysteria is a matter of some debate, although it would seem certain that the figure was among the tens of thousands (some estimates go much higher). Fear of witches was at its height in the fragmented states of Germany in the late 16th and early 17th centuries, although the hysteria spread as far as America (scene of one of the most famous outbreaks of all, that involving the Salem witches at the relatively late date of 1692).

Witches play the role of chief villain in numerous European folk tales, from 'Hansel and Gretel' to 'The Tinder Box'. Some of the most famous witches in literature and legend have included the Russian BABA YAGA, MORGAN LE FAY in Arthurian romance and, in more modern times, the Wicked Witches in L. Frank Baum's classic children's story *The Wonderful Wizard of Oz* (1900) and the White Witch in C. S. Lewis' *The Lion, the Witch and the Wardrobe* (1950).

Attempts to associate post-medieval witchcraft with the religious practices of pre-Christian times, as 'revived' in the modern folk religion called 'Wicca', do not appear to have much basis in historical fact.

See also SHAPE SHIFTING.

wivern Mythological creature, also called the wyvern, that combines the attributes of a DRAGON with a long snake-like barbed tail. It became well known chiefly as a heraldic emblem.

wizard *See* WITCHCRAFT.

Woden *See* ODIN.

wolf The wolf has always inspired a mixture of dread and reverence. The link between wolves and evil is particularly strong and well-established. The Devil was often suspected of disguising himself as a wolf, and Welsh legend insisted that the animal was created not by God but by Satan himself. In Germany it was believed that the Devil squatted between the creature's eyes. Elsewhere the wolf was identified as the lord of the dead. The creature was commonly assumed to have a cunning, rapacious but also cowardly character, and to have little compunction about preying upon humans when the opportunity arose (as illustrated in the story of 'Little Red Hiding Hood'). This did not mean, however, that the animal had no weaknesses: according to some authorities it was supposed to have an apparently irrational fear of crabs and shrimps.

In some cultures, though, the wolf was viewed in a more positive light. According to the Celtic peoples, wolves often came to the assistance of travellers who had lost their way, guiding them back to safety. Native American folklore includes a number of stories in which wolves appear as the hero (several tribes claim descent from wolves).

The creature also had its uses in folk medicine. Wolfskins were once wrapped round epileptics to alleviate their condition, and were also recommended in the treatment of rabies. Wolves' teeth were particularly useful, being rubbed against the gums to relieve toothache, and in France being worn round the necks of young children to keep them from harm.

The wolf appears in folk tales all over the world, usually being depicted as treacherous and threatening. Many tales, such as the animal fables of the Brothers Grimm and the *Uncle Remus* stories of Joel Chandler Harris, revolve around the outwitting of the wolf by his potential prey. Sometimes the wolf works in concert with the FOX, hoping to profit by the latter's cunning.

See also WEREWOLF.

woodwose In English legend, a wild man of the woods. Otherwise called ooser or wooser, the woodwose was widely believed in during medieval times, and made frequent appearances in art of the period. He wore no clothes, but was often described as being very hairy.

work song Genre of folk song associated with manual labour. These songs mostly developed originally as a means of keeping workers moving together in situations where it was important that each kept to the same rhythm, as in rowing, hauling rope or hammering spikes on a railroad. They also served to make tedious work less wearisome, and encouraged labourers to keep working beyond the point when they might otherwise stop. Some of the oldest examples of the genre include the songs of agricultural workers and the shanties sung by seamen around the world. Often the mass of workers sing out simple repetitive refrains while one or more leaders of the group sing short interconnecting verses. Sometimes the songs are about the work itself, but they may equally be about any other kind of human experience. Occasionally the narratives relate the history of well-known folk heroes.

Some of the most famous work songs were those of black slaves working on plantations in North America in the 19th century. These typically dealt with the harsh experiences suffered by the slave populationp, and also provided a rare outlet for deep-seated resentment at centuries of ill-treatment at the hands of white masters.

The work song tradition has more or less died out in the Western world during the course of the 20th century, with rare exceptions, but study of the genre still reveals much detail about the lives and experiences of past generations of manual workers.

worm In British legend, a variety of DRAGON that has some of the characteristics of a giant earthworm. There are numerous tales of such creatures causing terrible devastation in their immediate locality, recorded throughout the length and breadth of England, Ireland and Scotland (where they were often described as retreating to the bottom of deep lochs in between attacks on their victims). Among the most celebrated of these creatures was the LAMBTON WORM, which justified its name through its alleged ability to rejoin its body after being cut in two. Various folk heroes came face to face with such monsters, and Bram Stoker subsequently drew on the tradition for his blood-curdling horror novel *The Lair of the White Worm* (1911).

Wotan *See* ODIN.

Wounded King In Arthurian legend, the title bestowed upon the GRAIL KING (or FISHER KING) after he receives the crippling DOLOROUS BLOW. Injured in both thighs, the Wounded King's claim to power was severely undermined because of an ancient Celtic custom that prohibited anyone with such debilitating wounds from enjoying the right to rule, the theory being that the ruler's physical impairment would be reflected in a disastrous decline in the fertility of his land and people (*see* WASTELAND).

wraith An apparition or phantom that may appear as the double of someone still living but in immediate danger, or else of someone who has only recently died. Sometimes the wraith is insubstantial and immediately identifiable as a ghost, but often it appears to be solid flesh, and it may not be until later that the truth of its nature is realized. The word is also used more loosely for any spectre or ghost.

wren Despite its diminutive size, the wren is traditionally known as the king of the birds and has a special place in the folklore of the bird world. According to an old Danish tale, the bird is supposed to have won this lofty accolade after it outwitted the eagle in a contest to see which bird could fly nearest the sun: the eagle flew higher than all the other birds, only to find the wren perched on its back. Ancient tradition identifies the wren as the wife of the robin, and the bird has always been considered lucky (perhaps because it was considered sacred by the Druids) – although it was also associated with WITCHCRAFT. It is said to be extremely unlucky to kill a wren, an act of recklessness that could result in anything from a broken bone to being struck by lightning. Sailors prized the bird's feathers as they were supposed to safeguard them from death by drowning.

In former times the Irish observed an otherwise obscure folk custom called the 'wren party' each year upon St Stephen's Day (26 December), also known as Wrenning Day. This involved young boys stoning to death a wren in commemoration of the stoning of St Stephen. They then paraded the body (or a substitute for this) from house to house, where demands would be made for a few coins to help in paying for a party at the end of the day.

Wyrdes *See* NORNS.

Wyvern *See* WIVERN.

Y

yakku Native American demon that is traditionally believed to spread sickness among humans. The yakkus are malicious spirits, who also have the power to change their shape at will, and have to be appeased with sacrifice.

yaksha Indian nature spirit of a type that inspired numerous cults in early Indian history. Although generally friendly in nature, they might occasionally steal human children for food. Yakshas were usually linked with a specific locality, such as a particular hill or well. They were supposedly ruled over by a chief yaksha called Kubera, who held court at Alaka in the Himalayas. They were often depicted in the form of bejewelled naked women.

Yama–uba Japanese demon that was believed to prey upon mortals in mountainous regions of the country. The monster, usually depicted as female, seized its prey by means of its long hair, which transformed itself into a mass of serpents.

yarrow Herb that is widely credited with various magical properties. Also known as soldiers' woundwort, nosebleed, milfoil, devil's plaything, thousand weed and bad man's plaything, yarrow has long had a role in divination and folk medicine, being used to staunch bleeding, to soothe upset stomachs and to promote hair growth and menstruation. It is also supposed to protect a person's luck and to ward off witchcraft. Slipped under the pillow it will guarantee a sleeper dreams of a future partner (particularly if the sprig has come from the grave of a young man). In times gone by it was often carried at weddings to ensure the faithfulness of the happy couple. In Christian countries its special powers are associated with the legend that yarrow was the first herb held by the infant Christ.

yawning Because the breath is thought to have magical significance around the world, the action of yawning has always been thought significant. In ancient times it was feared that anyone opening their mouth very wide risked evil spirits slipping inside their bodies (as similarly when SNEEZING), and even today people cover their mouths when yawning in an unconscious echo of this belief. Various cultures recommended a range of precautions to be observed when yawning. In the Christian West, for instance, making the sign of the cross was widely considered a sensible countermeasure. In other parts of the world people will snap their fingers if someone yawns, as otherwise the yawn may be interpreted as a death omen.

yeck In Indian mythology, a kind of mischievous demon that leads travellers astray. Described as a small furry creature with a magic cap capable of bestowing invisibility upon anyone who steals it, the yeck is actually very powerful, and is supposed to be able to raise up whole mountains. Tales are told of resourceful adventurers who manage to capture yecks and enslave them as their servants.

Yell Hounds *See* WILD HUNT.

yeti Large, hairy, human-like creature that is supposed to live in remote parts of the Himalayas. Tales of the 'abominable snowman' have been in circulation for many years, promoted by alleged sightings by Western climbers in the Tibetan region since the 1950s. The creature, which inspires great fear among the local people, is described as hairy and walking erect. Investigators have found what they claim to be the creature's footprints, and photographs have been taken of what is supposed to be the yeti in the far distance. Physical evidence of the creature collected by locals has included pieces of skin and tufts of hair, although most of these have turned out to have belonged to bears and other known fauna. One of the most remarkable sightings occurred in 1974, when a 19-year-old girl reported seeing a yeti kill five of her yaks before being knocked unconscious herself.

The tradition appears to have had its origins in the Sherpa legend of a monkey king who converted to Buddhism and decided to live as a hermit in the mountains. It was his union with a female monster that resulted in the birth of the first yeti.

Reports of similar creatures have also been made in other remote parts of the world, including Canada (*see* BIGFOOT) and the Caucasus, home of a creature known as the almas.

yew Evergreen tree that is widely associated with immortality and life after death, hence its presence in countless churchyards in the Western world and its consequent association with death itself. Yew trees can grow to a very great age and have long been thought to have a range of protective powers. They were frequently planted near homes because they were believed to protect the house and its occupants from witchcraft or evil spirits, and it has been conjectured that some churches were deliberately sited close to existing yews because of their protective qualities. On a more negative note the thick foliage of the yew was said to harbour all manner of elves and goblins (hence the old taboo against thrusting one's arm into its leaves), and it is thought to be inadvisable to bring yew wood indoors because it threatens the death of the occupants. Sorcerers also favoured yew wood for their wands and other spell-making utensils, and yew twigs are supposed to be excellent as dowsing rods. Because of its magical associations, it is considered very unlucky to cut down a yew tree, and anyone who does so will die within a year.

Yggdrasil In Norse mythology, the massive cosmic ash tree that bears the universe. The highest branches of the tree cast their shade over VALHALLA, while the world of mortals rests upon the lower branches. The tree is described as having three main roots, located in springs in Asgard (the home of the gods), in Midgard (where the giants live) and in the underworld Niflheim. Each day the gods gather at the foot of the tree to make decisions concerning the affairs of the mortal world. Nearby the monstrous serpent Nidhagg gnaws patiently at the tree's roots, gradually eating them away. On the tree's highest branches sits Vithofnir, a golden cockerel who sees everything and whose crowing will usher in RAGNAROK, when Yggdrasil is fated to fall. The tree is also the home of an eagle, a falcon, a goat, a squirrel and four stags, from whose antlers dew drops onto the world of men.

Ymir In Norse mythology, the father of all the GIANTS. The oldest of the FROST GIANTS, Ymir is supposed to have emerged from the frost of NIFLHEIM and the fire of MUSPELLSHEIM and was said to have been nourished by the four streams of milk that issued from the cow Audhumla. He met his death at the hands of ODIN and his sons Vili and Ve. They used his body as raw material for the construction of the world, and built the heavens out of his skull.

Ysolde *See* ISOLDE OF BRITTANY; ISOLDE OF IRELAND.

Yspaddaden *See* CULHWCH; OLWEN.

yuki onna In Japanese mythology, a female demon who leads travellers to their deaths. These 'snow women' haunt snowy regions, taking the opportunity to lead travellers astray during snowstorms.

Yule candle A large candle that in former times was often burnt at Christmas in many English-speaking and Scandinavian countries. Decorated with holly and other evergreen leaves, the candle was lit on Christmas Eve and left to burn through the night, or else lit on Christmas morning and left to burn all day before being ceremonially extinguished. It might be relit on successive nights through the Christmas period.

The candle was supposed to protect the luck of the household, and it was widely considered a bad omen if it went out prematurely. When the time came to extinguish the candle, the flame was never blown out, as this again was believed to be unlucky. The remains of the candle would then be kept inside the house to safeguard its inhabitants in the coming year, and in some parts of Scandinavia its tallow might be smeared on ploughs to make the spring ploughing easier. Local grocers and chandlers continued to present their customers with free Yule candles until at least the middle of the 19th century.

Candles still play a significant role during the Christmas festivities and may sometimes be seen in windows, where they are supposed to provide light to guide the homeless Christ to shelter.

See also YULE LOG.

Yule log A large log that was ceremonially burnt in hearths throughout Britain and Europe on Christmas Eve. The log might have been taken from an ash, beech, oak or fruit tree, and was dragged into the house on Christmas Eve, sometimes decorated with greenery or sprinkled with ale or cider. It could never be bought for money, as this was very unlucky. The log was always lit with a brand kept over from the previous Christmas Yule log, and the whole ritual was usually celebrated with drinking and merrymaking. It was believed to be unlucky to stir the log while it was burning, and very unlucky if it went out prematurely. It was also a bad omen if the log was burnt in the presence of a cross-eyed, barefooted or flat-footed woman. In some places it had to be kept burning for 12 hours; elsewhere it was kept going through the 12 days of Christmas.

When the fire was out the remains of the log were kept under one of the beds, where it would preserve the good luck of the household and prevent the house being struck by lightning. The ashes might be sprinkled over the fields to promote future crops or (in France) thrown down the well to keep the water pure. Occasionally the remains of the log were rekindled at Candlemas.

The word Yule itself comes from the Old English *geol*, itself from the Icelandic *jol*, the name of a pagan festival celebrated at the time of the winter solstice. The custom probably harked back to the huge bonfires that were once lit to celebrate midwinter and midsummer festivals, and which were associated with fertility and the preservation of the life cycle.

Yvain *See* OWAIN.

Z

zodiac In ASTROLOGY, the 12 'houses' into which the calendar is divided, each corresponding to a constellation or division of the heavens. Each house or sign has its own characteristics, and people born between certain dates are supposed to share certain basic traits (and also share the same birthstone). There is also believed to be a direct connection between the position of the stars at a particular moment and the events then taking place on earth.

The exact psychological make-up of an individual is further influenced by the time of day at which they were born and the position of the stars at the time of birth, among other circumstances. The 12 houses are:

Aries (21 March to 19 April).
Taurus (21 April to 20 May).
Gemini (21 May to 20 June).
Cancer (21 June to 21 July).
Leo (21 July to 20 August).
Virgo (21 August to 20 September).
Libra (21 September to 20 October).
Scorpio (21 October to 20 November).
Sagittarius (21 November to 21 December).
Capricorn (21 December to 21 January).
Aquarius (21 January to 19 February).
Pisces (21 February to 21 March).

It is argued by some astrologers that the system would operate more accurately with the addition of a 13th house.

Different zodiacal systems are in use in different parts of the world. The houses of the Chinese zodiac are named after animals (the rat, the ox, the tiger, the hare, the dragon, the snake, the horse, the goat, the monkey, the cock, the dog and the boar), while both the Arabic and Western zodiacs balance the constellations between north and south, wet and dry and refer them to the elements of air, fire, earth and water. In the Arabic zodiac, the houses are represented by the 12 branches of a tree, from which the constellations hang fruit.

zombie One of the 'living dead', who figure prominently in the VOODOO folk religion of Haiti. The legend goes that they are humans who have died after their souls have been robbed through the use of black magic. Raised from their graves by various rituals and sacrifices, the zombies are usually described as walking with a shambling gait, with downcast eyes, and speaking in an unknown language. If allowed to eat salt, they suddenly become aware of their condition and try to return to their graves. According to tradition they are usually obliged to work as slaves by those who know how to raise them up; if they escape this wretched bondage they are liable to wreak bloody vengeance upon their erstwhile masters. It has been speculated that the idea of the zombie may have resulted from misunderstanding of various mental conditions, or else as a result of coma-inducing poisons secretly administered by voodoo priests.